# Instructional Technology Theory in the Post-Pandemic Era

David D. Carbonara
*Duquesne University, USA*

Lawrence A. Tomei
*Robert Morris University, USA*

A volume in the Advances in Educational Technologies and Instructional Design (AETID) Book Series

Published in the United States of America by
IGI Global
Information Science Reference (an imprint of IGI Global)
701 E. Chocolate Avenue
Hershey PA, USA 17033
Tel: 717-533-8845
Fax: 717-533-8661
E-mail: cust@igi-global.com
Web site: http://www.igi-global.com



Library of Congress Cataloging-in-Publication Data

CIP DATA PROCESSING

2024 Information Science Reference
ISBN(hc): 9798369376454
ISBN(sc): 9798369376461
eISBN: 9798369376478

British Cataloguing in Publication Data
A Cataloguing in Publication record for this book is available from the British Library.

# Advances in Educational Technologies and Instructional Design (AETID) Book Series

Lawrence A. Tomei
Robert Morris University, USA

ISSN:2326-8905
EISSN:2326-8913

**MISSION**

Education has undergone, and continues to undergo, immense changes in the way it is enacted and distributed to both child and adult learners. In modern education, the traditional classroom learning experience has evolved to include technological resources and to provide online classroom opportunities to students of all ages regardless of their geographical locations. From distance education, Massive-Open-Online-Courses (MOOCs), and electronic tablets in the classroom, technology is now an integral part of learning and is also affecting the way educators communicate information to students.

The **Advances in Educational Technologies & Instructional Design (AETID) Book Series** explores new research and theories for facilitating learning and improving educational performance utilizing technological processes and resources. The series examines technologies that can be integrated into K-12 classrooms to improve skills and learning abilities in all subjects including STEM education and language learning. Additionally, it studies the emergence of fully online classrooms for young and adult learners alike, and the communication and accountability challenges that can arise. Trending topics that are covered include adaptive learning, game-based learning, virtual school environments, and social media effects. School administrators, educators, academicians, researchers, and students will find this series to be an excellent resource for the effective design and implementation of learning technologies in their classes.

## Coverage

- Classroom Response Systems
- Educational Telecommunications
- E-Learning
- Game-Based Learning
- Higher Education Technologies
- Online Media in Classrooms
- Social Media Effects on Education
- Virtual School Environments

IGI Global is currently accepting manuscripts for publication within this series. To submit a proposal for a volume in this series, please contact our Acquisition Editors at Acquisitions@igi-global.com or visit: http://www.igi-global.com/publish/.

The (ISSN ) is published by IGI Global, 701 E. Chocolate Avenue, Hershey, PA 17033-1240, USA, www.igi-global.com. This series is composed of titles available for purchase individually; each title is edited to be contextually exclusive from any other title within the series. For pricing and ordering information please visit http://www.igi-global.com/book-series/advances-educational-technologies-instructional-design/73678. Postmaster: Send all address changes to above address. 

## Titles in this Series

For a list of additional titles in this series, please visit: http://www.igi-global.com/book-series/advances-educational-technologies-instructional-design/73678

*Augmented Reality and the Future of Education Technology*
Rashmi Aggarwal (Chitkara Business School, Chitkara University, India) Prachi Gupta (Chitkara Business School, Chitkara University, India) Satinder Singh (Chitkara Business School, Chitkara University, India) and Rajni Bala (Chitkara Business School, Chitkara University, India)
Information Science Reference • copyright 2024 • 297pp • H/C (ISBN: 9798369330159) • US $175.00 (our price)

*Integrating Generative AI in Education to Achieve Sustainable Development Goals*
Ruchi Doshi (Universidad Azteca, Mexico) Manish Dadhich (Sir Padampat Singhania University, India) Sandeep Poddar (Lincoln University College, Malaysia) and Kamal Kant Hiran (Sir Padampat Singhania University, India & Lincoln University College, Malaysia)
Information Science Reference • copyright 2024 • 532pp • H/C (ISBN: 9798369324400) • US $295.00 (our price)

*Considerations and Techniques for Applied Linguistics and Language Education Research*
Hung Phu Bui (University of Economics, Ho Chi Minh City, Vietnam)
Information Science Reference • copyright 2024 • 241pp • H/C (ISBN: 9798369364826) • US $245.00 (our price)

*Comprehensive Sexuality Education for Gender-Based Violence Prevention*
Mariana Buenestado-Fernández (University of Cantabria, Spain) Azahara Jiménez-Millán (University of Córdoba, Spain) and Francisco Javier Palacios-Hidalgo (University of Córdoba, Spain)
Information Science Reference • copyright 2024 • 342pp • H/C (ISBN: 9798369320532) • US $245.00 (our price)

IGI Global
PUBLISHER of TIMELY KNOWLEDGE

701 East Chocolate Avenue, Hershey, PA 17033, USA
Tel: 717-533-8845 x100 • Fax: 717-533-8661
E-Mail: cust@igi-global.com • www.igi-global.com

# Table of Contents

# Detailed Table of Contents



The post-pandemic 21st century has witnessed a significant transformation in the teaching-learning environment due to the widespread adoption of digital learning. The COVID-19 pandemic accelerated the adoption of digital learning, transforming education globally. It led to increased reliance on online platforms, highlighting the importance of technology in education. While it provided flexibility, challenges like the digital divide and the potential loss of hands-on experiences emerged. This chapter explores the themes and gaps in the research to understand the scholarly conversation around digital learning. It also examines previous studies about digital learning published mainly in peer-reviewed journals. This chapter is a literature review with both methodological and theoretical approaches. These findings enabled us to discuss, compare, and contrast other theories, models, and definitions of key concepts. The chapter also covers the impact of digital learning on education, emphasizing its role in fostering flexibility, accessibility, and collaborative approaches.

By examining the historical milestones, pedagogical theories, and technological advancements that have shaped distance learning, we can gain insights into its effectiveness, scalability, and adaptability in times of crisis. Furthermore, this historical review offers a unique perspective to evaluate current practices and envision future uses for educational technology and methodology innovations. This research synthesizes findings from a review of literature consisting of 105 articles, offering insights into the challenges and triumphs of the rapid transition to remote learning. The lessons learned from the COVID-19 pandemic influence the ongoing integration of distance learning in education and help to ensure resilience, accessibility, and quality in schooling across diverse contexts and challenges. Combining the lessons learned and best practices realized during this extreme experience can shape the new normal in education.



The pandemic spanning from 2020 to 2022 has brought about various impacts on society. Post this Covid era,, significant transformations have been witnessed in multiple sectors, including business and education. Throughout the COVID pandemic from 2020 to 2022, an observable shift occurred in the education system, moving away from its conventional distribution to embracing modern technologies. Grasping and applying these innovative technologies presented a challenge for both educators and students alike. For a software engineer, adapting the understanding of traditional educational distribution to a computerized format was indeed a formidable task. This period saw the introduction of numerous software technologies in the market. In this section, we will delve into these technologies and endeavor to discern whether they have demonstrated their effectiveness in the classroom. This chapter is also find out the answer of a pivotal question to explore is whether these technologies can be seamlessly incorporated into traditional classroom settings.

This chapter examines the sudden transition to emergency remote teaching (ERT) necessitated by the COVID-19 pandemic, underscoring the challenges, assumptions, and misconceptions surrounding digital education. The piece critically examines the pedagogical shifts that occurred, highlighting the imperative for educators and institutions to unlearn outdated notions of online learning and adapt evidence-based practices. By drawing upon various studies and expert opinions, the chapter addresses the pedagogical, technological, and organizational hurdles faced during the rapid pivot to ERT, while advocating for a strategic approach to online education that emphasizes pedagogical integrity, accessibility, equity, and institutional support. It proposes a reevaluation of digital learning strategies to leverage the full potential of online education, ensuring it is inclusive, effective, and tailored to meet the diverse needs of the student population, positing a future where higher education can transcend emergency measures to embrace a holistic and enriched digital learning environment.



This study investigates how rural teachers in the Eastern Cape province of South Africa harness their experiences during the pandemic to integrate technology into post-pandemic pedagogical practices. Adopt TPACK theoretical framework, purposively selected 18 teachers in the Eastern Cape province's rural schools in South Africa. Data was collected through interviews and two sharing circles through a phenomenological approach and analyzed thematically. Findings reveal that rural teachers, initially intimidated by technology, adapted to its use out of necessity during the pandemic and came to view it as an essential teaching tool. Teachers embraced digital tools to overcome infrastructural challenges and maintain educational continuity, showing resilience and innovation, prompting teachers to acquire new competencies and reconsider their approach to integrating technology. These experiences continue to shape educational practices and promote sustained technological integration, indicating a marked shift in rural teachers' perspectives towards the role of technology in teaching.

In the wake of the global COVID-19 pandemic, educational institutions worldwide experienced unprecedented challenges, leading to a paradigm shift in the education system. To deal with the need for more flexible learning, educational research and development aimed at providing a richer, more engaging remote learning experience by the creation of virtual classrooms. Within this digital learning environment, the challenge is to create an engaging learning environment to ensure optimal learning outcomes. This chapter addresses the imperative need to foster greater student engagement in virtual classrooms to maximize learning effectiveness. Drawing on established literature which underscores the link between student engagement and positive learning outcomes, the chapter emphasizes the pivotal role of engagement in enhancing student satisfaction and retention in online teaching contexts. By increasing the level of student engagement, instructors can increase the students' satisfaction level and retention, improving the efficiency of online teaching. Moreover, the chapter delves into the evolution of virtual classrooms and elucidates innovative strategies and practical techniques designed to augment student engagement. By synthesizing empirical evidence and best practices, the chapter offers insights into effective pedagogical approaches that educators can employ to create vibrant and interactive virtual learning environments. Through a rigorous examination of research findings and experiential knowledge, this chapter contributes to advancing our understanding of how to optimize student engagement in virtual classrooms, thereby enriching the landscape of online education.

STEM professionals are at the forefront of integrating emerging technologies into manufacturing processes. This includes the development and implementation of technologies like advanced robotics, augmented reality, and virtual reality, which are central to Industry 5.0's human-machine collaboration. IoT devices generate massive amounts of data in Industry 5.0. STEM experts are needed to design and maintain these devices and develop data analytics solutions to extract actionable insights from this data. This data-driven decision-making is critical for optimizing processes. AI and machine learning are central to Industry 5.0, enabling machines to learn from human interaction and adapt accordingly. Data scientists and AI experts develop the algorithms and models that make this possible. As Industry 5.0 evolves, there's a growing emphasis on sustainable manufacturing and reducing environmental impact. STEM professionals contribute to designing eco-friendly manufacturing processes and materials. Protecting the interconnected systems and data in Industry 5.0 is critical.



This chapter outlines the findings of national focus group discussions, as part of a European Erasmus Plus project. It examines the evolution of STEAM education, shaped by online teaching methods during the COVID-19 pandemic. The chapter includes a literature review, research methodology, and an in-depth data analysis. Key themes include the impact of online teaching on STEAM subjects, adaptive teaching, and the skills and requirements necessary in this educational field. The chapter captures the perspectives of students, teachers and technical staff. It summarizes the challenges and potential of online STEAM education.

# Preface

Our book, Exploring *Technology-Infused Education in the Post-Pandemic Era,* was created because of the COVID-19 Pandemic that started in late 2019 and wreaked havoc on the world starting in the Spring of 2020. People from China, throughout the East, through Europe and Africa and finally through North and South America experienced widespread symptoms of difficult breathing, hospitalizations, and death. A cure or a vaccine was not evident in early 2020. Governments sent workers home, businesses closed their doors and schools and universities locked down. All local and long-distance travel was non-existent. Our local police were stationed in major intersections to block all traffic. Eventually, single drivers were permitted to visit pharmacies and local food stores for essential products.

The editors of this book were teaching and conducting research via online tools since early 2000. We were familiar with the tools and the techniques to teach at a distance and wanted to share our expertise and those of our colleagues to assist others to design and deliver technology-rich instruction should face-to-face learning environments could not take place.

Professor Tomei conceived of the *International Journal of Information and Communication Technology Education* (IJICTE) published by IGI-Global, Inc. in 2005. I joined him as a member of the Editorial Review Board and moved to an Associate Editor a few years later. Dr. Tomei edited and authored many publications, including, *Teaching Digitally: Integrating Technology Into the Classroom* (2001), *Technology Facade* (2002), *Taxonomy for the Technology Domain* (2005), *Integrating Pedagogy and Technology: Improving Teaching and Learning in Higher Education Faculty* (2015), *Developing a Center for Teaching Excellence: A Higher Education Case Study Using the Integrated Readiness Matrix* (2016), and *Diverse Teaching Strategies for the Technology-Rich Classroom* (2019). Together, we edited *Handbook of Research on Diverse Teaching Strategies for the Technology-Rich Classroom.* It seemed only natural that we collaborate on this work, namely, *Exploring Technology-Infused Education in the Post-Pandemic Era.*

Professor Carbonara edited *Technology Literacy Applications in Learning Environments (2002),* and presented and published papers, namely, *Technology Literacy Issues for Freshmen Education Majors in a Leading Teacher Program (2002), Technological Pedagogical Content Knowledge (TPCK) as a Curriculum Model for Middle Level Education (2009), Creating Engaging Group Activities in a FlexTech Room: Designing a Student-Centered Environment for Collaborative Research Literacy for First Year Students (2016),* and K-20 Learning Along a Novice to Expert Continuum in Online Learning Environments in Victor Wang (Ed.). *Handbook of Research on Teaching and Learning in K-20 Education.* Hershey, PA: Idea Group Publishing, Dr. Carbonara also authored Video use in teacher education: Transition from a teaching tool to an assessment tool in Prince Nwachukwu Ololube, & Peter James Kpolovie (Eds.*). Enhancing teacher education with advanced instructional technologies*. Hershey, PA: Idea Group Publishing.

During the 2020-2021 academic year, vaccines were developed and distributed, and incidences of COVID-19 sickness were less frequent. Some businesses re-opened while others permanently closed. Travel grew slowly, and schools resumed with teleconferencing technologies. The term social distancing became a well-known practice. Face masks were used but limited the view of facial expressions. We learned the meaning of 'joining a colleague on a Zoom call' to conducting our meetings with physicians via a 'telehealth visit'. Some technologies continued through the pandemic and others were created. We all developed methods to design curriculum, deliver it and assess the learning of our students at a distance.

Thus, when Prof Tomei contacted me to discuss this book, I was excited. We collaborated on many projects, worked in adjoining offices, and created many manuscripts. It was decided to contact the authors from the International Journal of Information and Communication Technology Education (IJICTE) to ask them if they carried technologies and/or procedures through the COVID-19 Pandemic or perhaps abandoned them. The response was over-whelming. The publishers and staff at IGI Global were welcoming and supportive of the project. The proposals arrived and we quickly saw that they fell into two categories. One was the technologies, and the other was the processes about the technologies. It seemed evident to us that two volumes could be employed to organize this book.

The chapters in Vol 2 appear to follow an historical progression. Learning and teaching always started our processes and it is no wonder that *Digital Learning and the Learning Environment* start this section. Prof. Blessing F. Adeoye discusses the transformation in the teaching-learning environment. "This chapter explores the themes and gaps in the research to understand the scholarly conversation around digital learning."

Our second chapter provided us with an historical view in "From Correspondence to Connectivism: Tracing the Evolution of Distance Learning from its Inception to Post-Pandemic Realities. " Prof Christine Boring discussed the "effectiveness, scalability and adaptability" of the tools and processes that "shaped our time of crisis". She wrote, "Combining the lessons learned and best practices realized during this extreme experience can shape the new normal in education."

We've all discussed the paradigm shift many times to indicate how technology influenced our lives and learning and teaching practices, but the COVID-19 Pandemic changed our educational world. Professors Pant, Lohani and Prande discussed this monumental shift in "Educational Paradigm Shift: Embracing Modern Technologies in the Post-COVID Era. " Rather than fear the changes spawned by the COVID-19 Pandemic, we should embrace them and "explore [is] whether these technologies can be seamlessly incorporated into traditional classroom settings."

Another chapter about the post-pandemic era was written by Prof. Steven D'Agustino in the manuscript, titled, "Post-Pandemic Pedagogy: Adapting, Unlearning, and Designing for Online Success. " He wrote in the Abstract, "The piece critically examines the pedagogical shifts that occurred, highlighting the imperative for educators and institutions to unlearn outdated notions of online learning and adapt evidence-based practices." I often felt obstacles to my thinking about the positive changes that could be found from some technologies and their practices. Isn't it better when we physically see that Ah-Ha moment in our students' eyes. Perhaps it was the moment when Archimedes found the explanation of water displacement due to the content of the gold in the crown or the Gestalt moment described by Wolfgang Kohler. In any of these cases we, as teachers, welcomed that moment when our students 'saw the light'. I would sometimes change my teaching to promote these moments. It is no wonder that Prof. D'Agustino discussed the adapting, unlearning, and designing for online success.

These changes occurred around the globe, and I welcomed the next chapter, titled, "Rural School Teachers Leveraging Pandemic Teaching Experiences for Technology Integration in Post-Pandemic Classrooms." Profs. Simulja and Shambare discussed the pandemic-related changes in rural schools in South Africa. They relied on the TPACK theoretical framework to observe and document the changes in digital tools to overcome infrastructural challenges. While we can shape the tools, we can also be shaped by them. The COVID-19 Pandemic provided the opportunity to acquire new teaching and learning competencies and for us to "reconsider [our] approach to integrating technology.

Success in teaching and learning can be affected by time-on-task and engagement with the curriculum, fellow students and interaction between students and teachers. The COVID-19 Pandemic forced us to continue our teaching and learning in virtual environments. Some of our colleagues never taught an online course before.

We knew that the online environment needed to be built from the initial design and goal-setting stages to the presentation, and engagement stages with and of our students. The 'watch a video and answer a few questions' strategy on a worksheet did not work in the classroom before the Pandemic in face-to-face classrooms so I wondered why some faculty thought it would work in a virtual environment. Zahra Pourabedin and Vahid Bigari provided a chapter, titled "Student Engagement in the Post-Pandemic Virtual Classroom."

As we continue through the chapters, the next one discussed The Pandemic Influence of Educational Technology, Student Teacher Attachment and Language Instruction on Value of Education: A Quantitative Approach." Profs. Rugutt, Chemosit and Kaloki " used ANOVA and standard multiple linear regression statistical strategies to address the study research question responses from a sample of 450 elementary and secondary school students". Their analysis found significant predictors of student value in education. "The study concluded with a discussion of the importance of ETU, STALE, ELA, and school level have on SVE."

Some of the chapters discussed specific content areas. The next one discussed engineering education and how education was enhanced with blended learning. Profs. Sidhu, Low and Kang explored the challenges and opportunities in engineering classrooms in the chapter titled "Navigating Engineering Education amidst the Post-Pandemic Era: Enhancing Engineering Education through Blended Learning with a Flipped Classroom Approach." This chapter also explored the classroom strategy of flipped classroom. We may be familiar with flipped classrooms as a strategy where the students read about a concept at home and then the classroom time is devoted to problems and discussion of the content. Their abstract states, "Preliminary findings suggest that the adoption of blended learning with a flipped classroom approach positively influences student learning outcomes, fosters a more dynamic and participatory learning environment, and addresses the challenges posed by the post-pandemic educational landscape." The chapter is a welcome read about this phenomenon.

I remember many study sessions with my classmates and how we learned and discussed a topic together. The next chapter is titled, "Enhancing Learning Through Companionship in Distance Education." Remember that we were shut down in some form from March 2020 until December 2020. Face-to-face classrooms did not exist during the COVID-19 Pandemic. Profs Coşkunserçe and Becit discussed the problems that the pandemic caused and how we must overcome the technical issues and promote companionship.

Authors Nawi, Ibrahim, Sawai, et. al. presented an analysis in the chapter, titled, "Linking Social Support, Self-Support, and Emotional Regulation of Students Learning Online at Home During the Covid-19 Pandemic." It presented findings from 300 public higher-education students that showed the linkages of social support and self-support on the emotional regulation of students during online learning during the COVID-19 pandemic. The results empirically showed the impact of self-support and social support on the learning process. Students who were perceived as open and flexible showed a greater flexibility to use creative ideas. They wrote, "This empirical study can serve as a basis for developing a comprehensive action plan to improve training methods and strengthen existing support systems."

We sought help and support of colleagues and professionals when the COVID-19 Pandemic hit. Prof. Tomei and I discussed our progress of our teaching-learning practices and procedures and discovered others. Our next chapter discussed how we supported each other. "Concept of Instructional Coaching for Professional Teacher Development in Post-Pandemic Epoch" explores "the essential concept of instructional coaching as a dynamic approach to enhance student learning outcomes by promoting teacher competence and efficiency in the classroom". Profs Makinde and Ganiyu wrote about the importance of professional help and support during the pandemic but also that this help and support should continue beyond the pandemic.

One of our roles was to prepare students to become teachers. These pre-service teachers had difficult times while visiting K-12 classrooms, but the COVID-19 Pandemic created impossible situations to visit schools. Another set of authors discussed the views of these pre-service teachers while using an online flipped learning model. Profs. Kadıoğlu and Oskay found positive and negative themes from the pre-service teachers as reported in "Investigation of Pre-Service Teachers' Views on the Impact of the COVID-19 on Online Flipped Learning Model Based General Chemistry Laboratory."

During that fateful spring semester of 2020, I planned a STEM unit with my undergraduate pre-service teachers. It was designed to be many group projects in the university classroom. When the COVID-19 Pandemic hit I realized that I could not have the students work in groups on the robotic units in the university classroom. Fortunately, the Dean was receptive with my request to drop-ship many supplies to groups of students rooming together. I merely restructured the groups. The newly formed groups built their STEM robots and videoed the process. The uploaded videos could be shared by other groups of students. The next chapter was written by Prof. Prasad and discussed *Investigation of STEM in Industry 5.0.*

The next chapter, titled "Adaptive Online STEAM Education. Insights from Stakeholders' Perspectives," outlined a group of discussions from the European Erasmus Plus project. This chapter discusses how the COVID-19 Pandemic forced us to change our mode of teaching and learning. While we had some challenges with this change, we also had great potential opportunities to provide a better teaching-learning environment for all of us.

The potential for changing and adapting our teaching/learning strategies presented us with design opportunities also. "Designing A Flipped Learning Model Based Laboratory Safety Course for Undergraduates" was our next chapter to discuss the flipped model considering laboratory safety courses. One of my doctoral students wrote his dissertation about how science laboratories changed with the advent of technology, especially in terms of safety concerns. The authors of this chapter discussed the themes of pre-class and post-class activities that took place during and after the COVID-19 Pandemic. I think you'll enjoy the chapter by Profs Oskay, Yilmaz, and Kadıoğlu and how they and their students discussed the "use of the model in their future professional life".

The next chapter saw the opportunity to adapt laboratories in the chapter, titled, "Adapting Virtual Laboratories in Post COVID-19 Pandemic Learning Landscapes: An Exploration of Science Teacher Perceptions and Adoption in Rural Schools." Profs Shambare and Simuja discuss the innovative tools similar to Virtual Labs (VL). This chapter applied the principles of the Unified Theory of Acceptance and Use of Technology (UTAUT) and discussed how the technology was used during and after the COVID-19 Pandemic.

The final chapter is from a group of scholars that examine the resilience of online learning in English as a Foreign Language instruction during and after the COVID-19 pandemic. They discuss adaptive strategies and resources in Saudi Universities. This empirical study of quantitative and qualitative data reviewed strategies among 84 EFL teachers. It was encouraging to read that they found significant increases in teachers' and students' digital skills during the pandemic and more importantly that the increase in skills continued after the pandemic. They recommended that research be expanded to include different academic disciplines in near and remote locations during online learning. Perhaps the readers of this publication will contribute to the exploration of instructional methods used in asynchronous learning.

**David D. Carbonara**
*Duquesne University, USA*

**Lawrence A. Tomei**
*Robert Morris University, USA*

# Acknowledgment

The co-editors would like to acknowledge the heroic efforts of the 37-member Editorial Review Board as well as those of 79 contributing author-editors who took the time to evaluate over fifty chapter submissions from November 2023 through May 2024. This team of professionals offered their skilled observations that included, but not limited to, practical managerial significance; appropriateness for this book; adequacy of literature review, topic background, and analysis of key issues; clarity of presentation; and, organization of the chapter. Together, they aided the editors in culling the field of 52 proposed chapters to the final two-volume digest that you see here, comprising 34 scholarly works for your consideration. We would also like to acknowledge the efforts of the IGI Global team, especially Melissa Wagner, Vice President of Editorial, and Elizabeth Barrantes, Senior Development Editor.

# Chapter 1
# Digital Learning and the Teaching-Learning Environment in the Post-Pandemic 21st Century

**Blessing Foluso Adeoye**
https://orcid.org/0000-0002-9142-0048
*Dilla University, USA*

**Adesoji A. Oni**
https://orcid.org/0000-0001-6774-2672
*University of Lagos, Nigeria*

## ABSTRACT

*The post-pandemic 21st century has witnessed a significant transformation in the teaching-learning environment due to the widespread adoption of digital learning. The COVID-19 pandemic accelerated the adoption of digital learning, transforming education globally. It led to increased reliance on online platforms, highlighting the importance of technology in education. While it provided flexibility, challenges like the digital divide and the potential loss of hands-on experiences emerged. This chapter explores the themes and gaps in the research to understand the scholarly conversation around digital learning. It also examines previous studies about digital learning published mainly in peer-reviewed journals. This chapter is a literature review with both methodological and theoretical approaches. These findings enabled us to discuss, compare, and contrast other theories, models, and definitions of key concepts. The chapter also covers the impact of digital learning on education, emphasizing its role in fostering flexibility, accessibility, and collaborative approaches.*

DOI: 10.4018/979-8-3693-7645-4.ch001

# INTRODUCTION

## Overview of Digital Learning

Digital learning is a comprehensive phenomenon. Innovations in teaching are often synonymous with digital learning; therefore, its polysemous nature made it difficult to have a commonly agreed definition and classification (Audrin, & Audrina, 2022). Audrin and Audrina provide an overview of the research field of digital literacy in learning and education using text mining; it reviews 1037 research articles published on the topic between 2000 and 2020. This review reveals a plurality of terms associated with digital literacy. Audrin and Audrina identified six key factors that define the literature: information literacy, developing digital literacy, digital learning, ICT, social media, and twenty-first-century digital skills. According to Audrin and Audrina, these factors can be further grouped into three main streams, which are 1) digital literacy, 2) digital learning, and 3) twenty-first-century digital skills. Informational and technological foundations support these three streams. These results provide research avenues and a framework for digital literacy in education.

Digital learning can revolutionize education by fundamentally changing the nature of teaching and learning. It offers enhanced and interactive educational experiences, greater customization and personalization, and, perhaps most importantly, greater access to educational resources and opportunities. The extensive use of technology in the classroom also provides unprecedented chances for collaboration and communication between students, teachers, and other groups, opening up a world of possibilities for instruction, assessment, and research. Through digital learning, students can receive tailored instruction and feedback, engage in a wide range of activities that develop cognitive and affective skills, and encourage the development of creativity and problem-solving skills. Furthermore, digital learning can improve teaching practices, deepen student engagement, and support critical learning objectives.

Every Student Succeeds Act of 2015 [ESSA] refers to the term "digital learning" as "any instructional practice that effectively uses technology to strengthen a student's learning experience and encompasses a wide spectrum of tools and practices." This definition includes using online resources with the impact of the COVID-19 experiences. Our goal in this chapter is to identify the themes and gaps in the research to understand the scholarly conversation around digital learning. This chapter examined previous studies about digital learning published mainly in peer-reviewed journals. The databases used are Education Source, Google Scholar, ScienceDirect, SAGE Journals, Taylor & Francis Online, and ProQuest Central. The keywords and phrases used include information and communication technology, digital media, and the impact of the COVID-19 experiences. Only articles that followed rigorous measures for research quality were considered for this review.

## The Importance of Digital Learning and the Teaching-Learning Environment in the Post-Pandemic 21st Century

Several researchers, e.g., Rakitskaya, (2023) and Haleem et al. (2022), reported that in the post-pandemic 21st century, digital learning and the teaching-learning environment hold immense importance due to several key factors:

**Resilience and Adaptability:** The pandemic necessitated a rapid shift to remote and hybrid learning, highlighting the need for educational systems to be flexible and adaptable. Digital learning provides the means to continue education during crises and adapt to changing circumstances, ensuring continuity in learning.

**Equity and Access**: Digital learning can bridge geographical and socioeconomic gaps, providing access to education for learners who may face barriers to traditional schooling. In the post-pandemic era, ensuring equitable access to digital learning resources and technologies becomes crucial for addressing disparities in education.

**Personalized and Flexible Learning:** Digital learning platforms offer personalized and self-paced learning opportunities catering to individual learning styles and preferences. In the post-pandemic 21st century, where diverse learner needs must be accommodated, digital tools enable educators to tailor instruction to meet each student's unique requirements.

**Integration of Emerging Technologies**: The post-pandemic era presents opportunities to leverage emerging technologies such as artificial intelligence, virtual reality, and augmented reality to enhance the teaching-learning experience. Integrating these technologies into digital learning environments can create immersive and engaging educational experiences that prepare learners for the demands of the 21st-century workforce.

**Lifelong Learning and Professional Development**: Digital learning extends beyond traditional classroom settings, offering lifelong learning and professional development opportunities. In the post-pandemic 21st century, where rapid technological advancements require continuous upskilling and reskilling, digital learning platforms play a crucial role in supporting individuals' pursuit of knowledge and skill development.

Overall, digital learning and the teaching-learning environment are essential pillars of education in the post-pandemic 21st century, enabling resilience, equity, personalized learning, collaboration, integration of emerging technologies, and lifelong learning opportunities.

# THE EVOLUTION OF DIGITAL LEARNING

## Historical Background

The historical background of digital learning can be traced back to the early developments in computing and telecommunications. Here are some key milestones as documented by Decuypere, Grimaldi, & Landri (2021) and Anglin, (1995):

**Early Experiments (1950s-1970s):** The roots of digital learning can be found in early experiments with computer-based instruction. In the 1950s and 1960s, researchers began exploring the potential of computers to deliver educational content. One notable example is the PLATO system developed at the University of Illinois, which allowed students to access educational materials and interact with computer-based lessons.

**Mainframe Computers and Time-sharing Systems (1960s-1970s):** Mainframe computers and time-sharing systems in the 1960s and 1970s enabled greater access to computing resources. Educational institutions and research centers started using these systems to develop computer-assisted instruction (CAI) programs and courseware.

**Microcomputers and Personal Computers (1970s-1980s):** The proliferation of microcomputers and personal computers in the 1970s and 1980s revolutionized digital learning. With the introduction of affordable computing devices, educators and learners gained access to powerful tools for creating and delivering educational content. This period saw the development of early educational software and multimedia applications.

**Distance Learning and Online Education (1990s-2000s):** The rise of the internet in the 1990s paved the way for the expansion of distance learning and online education. Institutions began offering courses and degree programs entirely online, enabling students to learn remotely from anywhere with internet access. Learning management systems (LMS) emerged as platforms for delivering online courses and managing educational resources.

**The emergence of Open Educational Resources (OER) and Massive Open Online Courses (MOOCs) (2000s-present):** The 21st century witnessed the emergence of open educational resources (OER) and massive open online courses (MOOCs), democratizing access to education on a global scale. OER platforms provide free and openly licensed educational materials, while MOOCs offer large-scale online courses taught by expert instructors from renowned institutions.

**Advancements in Technology and Learning Analytics (2010s-present):** Recent advancements in technology, such as artificial intelligence, virtual reality, and learning analytics, further shape the landscape of digital learning. These technologies enable personalized learning experiences, immersive simulations, and data-driven insights into learner performance and engagement.

Overall, the historical background of digital learning reflects a trajectory of innovation and evolution driven by advancements in computing technology, telecommunications, and the internet. From early experiments with computer-based instruction to the widespread adoption of online education and emerging technologies, digital learning continues transforming how education is delivered and accessed worldwide (Decuypere, Grimaldi, & Landri, 2021).

## Technological Advancements Shaping Digital Learning

Technological advancements have been instrumental in shaping digital learning and revolutionizing education by offering new tools, methods, and platforms to enhance learning experiences. Here are some key advancements and their impacts:

1. **Online Learning Platforms**: Platforms like Coursera, Udemy, and Khan Academy offer vast courses and resources accessible to learners worldwide. These platforms provide flexibility, allowing learners to study at their own pace and convenience.
2. **Mobile Learning**: The proliferation of smartphones and tablets has enabled learning anytime, anywhere. Mobile apps and responsive websites provide access to educational content on the go, making learning more accessible and convenient.
3. **Artificial Intelligence (AI) and Adaptive Learning**: AI-powered tools can analyze students' learning patterns and adapt content to their needs. This personalization enhances engagement and effectiveness by providing tailored learning experiences.
4. **Virtual and Augmented Reality (VR/AR)**: VR and AR technologies create immersive learning environments, allowing students to interact with virtual objects and scenarios. These technologies are particularly useful for hands-on training in medicine, engineering, and architecture.
5. **Gamification**: Integrating game elements into educational content makes learning more engaging and enjoyable. Gamified platforms motivate students through rewards, progress tracking, and competitive elements, fostering deeper engagement and retention.
6. **Big Data and Learning Analytics**: Educational institutions can collect and analyze vast amounts of student performance and behavior data. This data-driven approach enables personalized interventions, early identification of struggling students, and continuous improvement of teaching methods.
7. **Cloud Computing**: Cloud-based platforms facilitate collaboration, storage, and access to educational resources from anywhere with an internet connection. This technology enables seamless sharing of materials among students and instructors, fostering collaboration and productivity.

8. **Blockchain Credentials**: Blockchain technology offers secure and verifiable credentials, ensuring the integrity of certificates and qualifications earned through digital learning platforms. This innovation enhances the credibility and recognition of online education.
9. **Natural Language Processing (NLP)**: NLP tools enable interactive and conversational learning experiences through chatbots, virtual tutors, and language processing applications. These tools provide instant feedback, answer queries, and facilitate language learning.
10. **Social Media Integration**: Social media platforms serve as hubs for educational communities, facilitating collaboration, discussion, and knowledge sharing among students and educators. Integrating social media into digital learning environments enhances engagement and fosters a sense of community.

These technological advancements continue to evolve, offering new opportunities and challenges for digital learning. As educators and institutions embrace these innovations, they can create more dynamic, personalized, and effective learning experiences for learners worldwide.

## REVIEW OF LITERATURE RELATED TO DIGITAL LEARNING

### Sociological Perspectives of the Use of Digital Technology in Education

One of the functions of education is social integration. For a society to work, functionalists say, people must subscribe to shared beliefs and values (Schildkraut, 2005). In today's society, accessing, adapting, and creating knowledge using information and communication technologies is critical to social inclusion. This focus on social inclusion shifts the discussion of the "digital divide" from gaps to be overcome by providing equipment to social development challenges to be addressed through the effective integration of technology into communities, institutions, and societies. Most important is the physical availability of computers and the Internet and people's ability to use those technologies to engage in meaningful social practices.

Information technology can be an essential facilitator of social inclusion for people with disabilities in society. However, the goals specified in this area by organizations such as the European Commission have not yet been achieved in their totality (Manzoor & Vimarlund, 2018). Manzoor and Vimarlund explored which information communication technology-based applications and digital services have been suggested to facilitate the social integration of people with different types of disabilities. They performed a literature review that included studies published for six years (2010-2016). The results show that no concrete patterns can be identified regarding the technology or technological trends supporting the social integration/interaction of individuals with disabilities. The literature review is relevant to identifying other research areas and issues that must be considered in developing and implementing technological innovations to promote or facilitate the social inclusion of individuals with disabilities.

## Implementation of Digital Learning in Education

Research suggesting the advantages of digital learning over face-to-face learning remains problematic. Some studies conclude that students achieve marginally better learning and feel slightly more supported with online and distance learning (Atchley et al., 2013; Sachar & Neumann, 2010; Department of Education, 2010). Many others suggest little to no difference (Holmes & Reid, 2017; Means et al., 2013), while many still point to the benefits of face-to-face learning (Saghafian & O'Neill, 2018; Bandara & Wijekularathna, 2018). While digital benefits may seem obvious (for instance, reviewable lectures, after-hours learning, new visualizations), they are counterbalanced with problems, including technological distractions and accessibility with socioeconomic concerns.

Cole et al. (2013) presented the results of a pilot study in which researchers sought to discover how students and instructors at two universities used selected digital technologies in their coursework. To what extent were digital technologies being used, and did students find their use helpful in learning course material? Researchers surveyed undergraduate students at the University of Lagos, Nigeria, and undergraduate, master, and doctoral students at Robert Morris University in Western Pennsylvania. Comparing responses from both universities demonstrated similarities in how and what digital technologies were used in the coursework. However, significant differences were found when examining the uses of specific technologies at each institution and how helpful they were to students' learning. A significant difference was found in determining how soon new digital technologies would be adopted.

Adeoye (2020) reported that the influence of digital technology in society has made it crucial for all students in the 21st century to become literate using digital tools. One way to understand the evolving role of digital technologies in education in Nigeria is to review the literature and examine how the use of digital technologies in the classroom is documented. The development and proliferation of the internet have contributed to a revolution in teaching and learning; they have also provided new opportunities for delivering instruction through various media.

Despite the numerous opportunities for learning through digital technology and improving access to education in the country at all levels, there are some setbacks. This chapter presented some success stories with both benefits and drawbacks.

Although many educational institutions, from elementary to university levels, use digital devices and applications for teaching and learning purposes, these tools may fail in many places due to the dominance of traditional pedagogical approaches and methods (Adeoye, 2020).

In digital and traditional learning environments, collaboration and social learning are at the heart of the learning process. However, like traditional learning, digital learning can reinforce various modes of engagement that do not always prioritize collaboration, primarily student-content interaction (Martin & Bolliger, 2018).

Student engagement, however, among themselves and with the instructor has been found to correlate positively in digital environments with student perception of learning and student satisfaction (Richardson et al., 2017). Unfortunately, research into the level of sociability in digital learning and its effects on student learning outcomes is limited, mainly because digital pedagogy studies focus on content and design rather than student learning outcomes (Sjølie & van Petegem, 2022). A major meta-study of digital learning assessments (Esfijani, 2018) revealed that most "quality of online learning" measures focus more on "Open Educational resources, input, and processes" and far less on "output- and outcome-oriented approaches." Measures focused more on inputs that heighten institutional visibility and student perceptions cannot effectively measure actual learning outcomes. Performance data is often missing in digital learning environments: the National Education Policy Center found that only 15 of 38 surveyed states maintained overall performance rating data for K-12 virtual schools (Molnar, 2017).

Yale Poorvu Center for Teaching and Learning (2021) presented the following examples and recommendations for contextualizing digital resources and approaches in broader learning frameworks that address known learning processes, effective teaching strategies, and inclusivity concerns.

- An instructor makes various open educational resources available to his students, including an open-source textbook, to reduce textbook costs and invite students to annotate and build the course textbook. themselves.
- An instructor uses a soundscape and visual representation of early modern London to immerse students in the sensory context of Shakespeare's plays in performance and help them answer complex questions about the experience of his plays.
- An instructor integrates virtual reality technology into her class, allowing students to stand in an ancient temple and reflect on the experiences of historical populations.

- An instructor records their lectures, using small increments and rich visual displays to explain complex concepts in physics for students to watch, review, and respond to via the course's canvas discussion (link is external) and class discussion.
- A university's online certificate program provides learning objectives, assessments, and regular writing prompts alongside video content to clarify learning goals and help learners target areas of weakness or misunderstanding.

## Characteristics of the Post-Pandemic 21st Century Teaching-Learning Environment

The post-pandemic 21st-century teaching-learning environment will likely exhibit several key characteristics influenced by the lessons learned during the pandemic and ongoing technological advancements. Here are some of these characteristics:

**Hybrid Learning Models:** The pandemic accelerated the adoption of hybrid learning models, combining in-person and online instruction. In the post-pandemic era, hybrid learning will continue to be prevalent, offering flexibility and accessibility while allowing valuable face-to-face interactions. Enhanced Collaboration and Communication: Digital learning environments facilitate collaboration and communication among students, teachers, and peers regardless of physical location. As remote and hybrid learning models become more prevalent, fostering effective collaboration and communication skills through digital platforms becomes essential for success in education and beyond.

**Personalized Learning:** Personalized learning is a multifaced approach that involves distinct changes in the roles of students and teachers and a significant shift in the learning environment. According to Bernacki et al. (2021), it involves empowering students to take more responsibility for their learning, as opposed to more traditional models of instruction wherein the teachers make all the critical decisions about what and how the students will engage with new content and skills. Teachers, schools, districts, states, and technology developers endeavor to personalize student learning experiences, but definitions of personalized learning (PL) vary, and designs often span multiple components. Variability in definition and implementation complicates the study of PL and how designs can leverage student characteristics to achieve targeted learning outcomes reliably (Bernacki et al.).

Personalized learning (PL) has been promoted as a primary aim and reform effort across the modern educational system (Zhang et al., 2020). Based on these premises, Zhang et al. systematically identified and synthesized 71 empirical studies conducted between 2006 and 2019 and discovered that many studies explored the role of technology in supporting PL implementation. In contrast, a few studies examined the effectiveness of PL as a whole-school initiative. They also presented issues around PL conceptualization, and empirical evidence was discussed. This synthesis examined the current research efforts on PL implementation, focusing on the identified studies' primary purposes, overall methodological characteristics, and associated student learning outcomes. Using the method of critical interpretive synthesis, they identified two overarching themes about PL across various disciplines of study. The two themes included investigating (a) the role of varying technologies and (b) contextual factors that impacted the implementation of PL. However, only some studies have examined the effects of PL as a whole-school initiative on student educational outcomes. They ended by discussing the issues with the conceptualization and empirical evidence of PL and providing implications for the future advancement of the field.

**Blended Learning Strategies:** Blending traditional classroom instruction with online resources and activities enhances the learning experience by offering a variety of learning modalities. In the post-pandemic era, educators will continue to utilize blended learning strategies to optimize learning outcomes and adapt to changing circumstances.

**Emphasis on Social-Emotional Learning (SEL):** The pandemic highlighted the importance of supporting students' social and emotional well-being. In the post-pandemic teaching-learning environment, there will be a greater emphasis on integrating social-emotional learning (SEL) into curriculum and instruction to foster resilience, empathy, and emotional intelligence.

**Collaborative and Project-Based Learning:** Collaborative and project-based learning experiences promote critical thinking, problem-solving, and teamwork skills. Educators will increasingly incorporate collaborative and project-based learning activities in the post-pandemic era to engage students and prepare them for success in a rapidly changing world.

**Flexibility and Adaptability**: The pandemic underscored the need for educators to be flexible and adaptable in response to unforeseen challenges and disruptions. In the post-pandemic teaching-learning environment, educators' flexibility and adaptability will be valued as they navigate evolving educational landscapes and student needs.

**Global Perspective and Cultural Competence**: Technology has connected students across geographical boundaries, fostering a global perspective and cultural competence. Educators will emphasize global citizenship and intercultural understanding in the post-pandemic era, preparing students to thrive in an interconnected world.

**Data-Informed Decision Making**: Data analytics tools provide valuable insights into student performance, engagement, and learning outcomes. In the post-pandemic teaching-learning environment, educators will increasingly use data to inform instructional decisions, identify areas for improvement, and personalize learning experiences.

**Lifelong Learning Mindset**: The rapid pace of technological change requires a commitment to lifelong learning and skill development. Educators and students will embrace a lifelong learning mindset in the post-pandemic era, continuously seeking new knowledge and skills to adapt to an ever-evolving world.

Overall, the post-pandemic 21st-century teaching-learning environment will be characterized by a blend of in-person and online instruction, a focus on digital literacy and personalized learning, an emphasis on social-emotional learning and collaboration, and a commitment to flexibility, adaptability, and lifelong learning.

## Digital Learning Resources

Wang et al. framework divides digital learning resources into six categories: basic knowledge classes, auxiliary extension classes, tool software classes, network platform classes, virtual reality classes, and generative learning resources, and proposes a digital learning resource compass from three dimensions: discipline, acquisition mode of digital learning resources and types of digital learning resources. Also, following the purpose, hierarchical and faceted classifications of digital learning resources are analyzed, and their advantages and disadvantages are highlighted (Balalaieva, 2021). Balalaieva stated that the positive aspects of the hierarchical classification are traditionalism and the relative simplicity of structure, and the negative aspects, such as its inexhaustibility, ambiguity, and rigidity of the scheme, so the hierarchy method is better applied to objects with relatively stable features. The main advantage of faceted classification is the flexibility of its structure, which causes good adaptability to the changing nature of the issues and is especially relevant for the classification of digital learning resources, which, due to relative novelty and rapid development, have no stable features, the very concept of which is constantly clarified and concretized in content and scope (Balalaieva, 2021).

Many other online digital education resources fit any subject or grade level. Many resources are free to use, although schools may decide to purchase essential resources like digital textbooks. Several types of digital learning resources are available for educators, as listed by Bixler (2021).

- Simulations and interactive models can deepen learning and are especially helpful in math and science.
- Graphics such as public-domain images (illustrations and photographs), charts, and graphs can help learners better comprehend concepts.

- Videos and animations from websites like YouTube help explain topics. When school districts use a tool like Hāpara's Web Filter, YouTube can be safer for learners.
- Digital textbooks can be used anywhere across devices and are more quickly updated than traditional textbooks.
- Online assessments, including formative and summative assessments, give teachers and administrators instant data. They are also interactive and engaging for learners.
- Podcasts and audio, such as music, boost participation and reach students with different learning styles.
- Online educational games make learning concepts fun for students.
- Literature and online news articles are examples of digital learning materials that are quick to access and share.
- Primary source documents that have been digitized help teachers supplement curriculum without needing physical copies.
- Interactive maps give students a hands-on digital experience.
- Tools like graphing calculators help students learn math without purchasing a physical calculator.
- Full online courses can provide review or enrichment, allowing students to work on their learning goals.

The summary of the digital learning resource classification framework provided by Wang et al. is related to the digital learning classification provided by the ESSA. Every Student Succeeds Act of 2015 [ESSA] enumerated digital learning as (a) interactive learning resources, digital learning content (which may include openly licensed content), software, or simulations that engage students in academic content; (b) access to online databases and other primary source documents; (c) the use of data and information to personalize learning and provide targeted supplementary instruction; (d) online and computer-based assessments; (e) learning environments that allow for rich collaboration and communication, which may include student collaboration with content experts and peers; (f) hybrid or blended learning, which occurs under direct instructor supervision at a school or other location away from home and, at least in part, through online delivery of instruction with some element of student control over time, place, path, or pace; and (g) access to online course opportunities for students in rural or remote areas (p. 1969). As described by ESSA, various technological tools and practices can fall under "digital learning resources, and this paper presents a review of these seven areas mentioned above. Also, this paper reviewed existing and previous studies about the theoretical and conceptual frameworks related to digital learning. Finally, a summary of the review and the conclusions was presented, highlighting the implications for teaching and learning.

## Practical Uses of Digital Resources

Yale Poorvu Center for Teaching and Learning (2021) enumerated some practical uses of digital resources.

1. **Clarify Your Own Goals**: Instructors should first consider authoring their course learning objectives and considering what kinds of practice and content students should experience to attain course learning goals. Digital strategies, like any strategy, should be explicitly used in the service of student learning.
2. **Consider Active Learning**: While digital learning often provides students with interactive opportunities, it also introduces new distractions, complexity, and equipment. Instructors may consider ways that various active learning exercises provide the same or greater interactivity and visualization approaches than digital resources without the additional layer of equipment and access needs. Activities like jigsaw discussions, role play, and debate keep students engaged and reduce the opportunity for distraction while presenting ideas and concepts in imaginative, multimodal ways. At the same time, digital tools contextualized within broader active learning approaches can ensure that students are not left behind in a struggle with equipment or prevented from participating entirely due to socioeconomic status or digital literacy. Digital learning can also help enhance active learning strategies through technology like polling and active learning spaces.
3. **Clarify Digital Procedures**: Because students will most likely have varying degrees of familiarity with tools like learning management systems (Canvas et al.), polling software, video content, and even basic technological literacy, instructors can provide detailed help guides and/or additional help sessions hosted by the instructor, or a TA. Additionally, instructors can ensure their syllabus clarifies expectations like online submission protocols, participation measures in digital opportunities, and reasoning for including major digital resources in course design.
4. **Be Sensitive to Inclusion and Accessibility**: Students will arrive at class with varying levels of technological literacy 3and sensory ability, which will limit some and privilege others in using digital tools or environments. By being sensitive to inclusivity concerns in class, instructors can drastically improve the learning experience for students. While respecting privacy, instructors must seek out the needs of each student in their class and provide additional support or alternative pathways to crucial digital scenarios in class.
5. **Clarify Technology Policies**: Because digital pedagogy increases the likelihood of devices in class, instructors should develop clear classroom policies regarding laptops and mobile devices. Students can see digital pedagogy as an

advertisement for lax classroom technology policies, and instructors must ensure they maintain control over such policies early in the semester.

6. **Be Present for Students:** More than the depth and breadth of content or sophistication of digital interface, effective learning emerges from an instructor's ability to express care and intentionality for students and to create an environment of social belonging (Freeman et al., 2007). This practice can be difficult in a fully digital environment. Even blended environments or environments with a significant technological focus can introduce distractions that remove students' focus from collaboration and classroom togetherness (both vital components of student satisfaction, according to Freeman et al.). Presence and focus can be equally problematic in traditional classrooms. Both start with the personality and commitment of instructors who can make efforts to connect with students (the link is external).

Source: Yale Poorvu Center for Teaching and Learning (2021). Digital Learning, https://poorvucenter.yale.edu/DigitalLearning

## Pre-Pandemic Applications of Digital Learning Resources and the Teaching-Learning Environment

Digital learning has been used for teaching and learning before COVID-19 period; it continues to expand at educational institutions around the globe. In a quantitative research method with a quasi-experimental design, Sinaga, et al. (2022) examined the impact of electronic interactive teaching materials (EITMs) distributed and operated on students' mobile phones. Sinaga et al. conducted a study using the purposive sampling technique that consisted of junior high school students divided into experimental and control classes of 23 students each. The instruments included a critical thinking ability test and a four-rating scale questionnaire. The data were analyzed by determining the average normalized gain, t-test means, and effect size and descriptively analyzing the questionnaire. Sinaga, et.al. found that (1) The critical thinking skills of the experimental group increased with high criteria, and the control group increased with medium criteria. (2) The increase in the critical thinking skills of students who used the EITMs, both in the overall and per-item mean scores, was higher than that of students who used electronic textbooks; (3) There was a significant difference in the increased critical thinking skills between the experimental class and control class, and (4) Students responded positively to the EITMs stored and operated on their mobile phones.

Technology advancements amplified the imperative to gain further insights into how the delivery of course materials can enhance and support the learning process (Murray et al. 2012). Murray et al. investigated student patterns of access to instructional resources in an asynchronous online digital literacy course offered at a regional university in the United States. Frequency counts and access rates collected from a learning management system were used to assess patterns of students' retrieval of course materials in core materials, direct support, indirect support, and ancillary materials. Results were consistent with student survey responses and indicated that students selectively access course content based on the degree to which they perceive it and how it will positively influence performance and outcomes on assignments and assessments.

## Learning Outcomes in Digital Learning Settings

Sailer et al. (2021) investigated how often teachers apply digital technology and which student learning activities teachers initiated. Further, they analyzed the factors relating to technology use. Four hundred and ten teachers reported spending substantial time using digital technologies in a typical lesson and that teachers' basic digital and technology-related teaching skills with digital technology resources are crucial. The analysis further revealed that teachers frequently employ digital technologies in their teaching. When using technology for a significant amount of time, students are passive. The availability of technology does not relate to the type of technology teachers use. Teachers' skills are positively associated with the frequency and types of technology use. Even though a certain threshold level of digital technology is necessary for schools, their results suggest shifting the focus from equipping schools to teachers' skills using technologies effectively.

Lohr et al. (2021) also investigated the initiation of digitally supported learning activities and personal and institutional factors associated with them in different higher education courses based on the C♭-model. The C♭-model is a theoretical framework that systematizes contextual factors, which influence student learning activities as the most important facilitator of students' learning success. Using a self-assessment instrument with anchored scenarios in a sample of 1625 higher education teachers, Lohr et al. was able to identify three levels at which higher education teachers initiated digital learning activities: a low-level use (PowerPoints), a moderate level use (clickers), and a high-level use (digital pros). The findings support the relevance of the contextual factors specified in the C♭-model for initiating a high level of digital learning activities, namely digitalization policy and commitment of university administration, institutional equipment, technical and educational support, self-assessed basic digital skills, and technology-related teaching skills. These factors explain a substantial variance in the level of initiated digital learning activities. Lohr et al. concluded that a comprehensive approach rather than isolated measures might contribute to successful teaching and learning in higher education.

## Individual and Social Perspectives on Learning

Understanding the importance of individual and social perspectives on learning is critical. This section summarizes the key ideas, methods of the individual and social perspectives on digital learning environments, and relevant studies about approaches to operationalized learning settings. The impact of digital tools in educational development in many educational institutions is increasing. It is, therefore, imperative for all educational institutions at all levels to embrace the use of digital tools in learning. An article to uncover what makes learning enjoyable for Generation Z college students (born 1995-2010) in the United States (U.S.) and Brazil was published by Seemiller et al., (2021). Qualitative data was collected from 1,282 participants in the U.S. and 775 participants in Brazil. The data were analyzed independently and for comparison using content analysis and thematic coding. The study's results show similarities and differences between these two populations. Both groups enjoy interesting, inspiring, relevant, and engaging learning. United States students enjoy knowledge acquisition, learning for societal impact, and having competent and relatable instructors. Brazil students, on the other hand, enjoy peer learning. While these results align with previous research findings on preferences for learning and cultural nuances, it is essential to note that studies on Generation Z college students and learning are sparse (Seemiller et al., 2021). According to Seemiller et al., understanding this generational cohort in higher education is paramount for informing and supporting individual pedagogical practices and shaping training initiatives on teaching and learning in higher education. In addition, given the impact of globalization on technology, commerce, entertainment, and information, uncovering the similarities in how young people from different cultures perceive learning may have global implications on research, training, and individual instruction in a more macro and universal way (Seemiller et al., 2021). While teachers may share digital education resources with the entire class, resources can also help individual learners. As listed below, Bixler (2021) enumerated some strategies for ensuring online resources are adequate for each learner.

## Data Gathering and Feedback

Data gathering and feedback is an effective way to understand which digital resources individual learners need. Online assessments help teachers collect data quickly and spot where learners are struggling or excelling. From there, teachers can share resources to re-teach concepts or differentiate instruction for gifted learners. By gathering data consistently, teachers can guarantee each learner gets the instruction they need.

*Data*: For many educators, "data" conjures up images of cumbersome spreadsheets, stacks of student reports, and lists of cold, complex numbers. When conceived in this way, data can seem at odds with the holistic and nuanced way teachers think about their students, but the truth is that data is just information. Teachers collect and use information about their students nearly every day, whether or not they call it "data". Data sources include attendance, behavior, quizzes, observations, comments, grades, and test scores. Data collected and organized systematically can be used to make classroom, district, or system decisions. It should provide an accurate measurement of student progress or lack of progress of content knowledge on tasks, activities, or behaviors. Data can be quantitative or qualitative. When improving instruction and learning, it is not the quantity of the data that counts but how the information is used (Madison-Harris et al., 2012).

*Baseline Data*: Baseline data is information about students' level of performance at the "start" of the instruction interval. It is generally the most recent data available. It can include the prior year's assessment scores or grades, results from a beginning-of-the-year benchmark assessment, a pre-test, or other evidence of students' learning, such as portfolio work samples that measure the pre-requisite knowledge and skills necessary for the course. The baseline is a "line in the sand" that can be used to measure student change toward important academic indicators during a course or academic year. The key to measuring student learning is to select the appropriate assessments or sources of evidence. Baseline data are used to establish students learning targets (the expected outcome at the end of the instructional period). Consider teachers' rationale for identifying and using baseline data to establish groups and targets. There is no value in assessing students if it does not impact learning and instruction (Fullan et al., 2006); (Sharratt & Fullan, 2013).

## Empower Learners

The COVID-19 pandemic has transformed the educational system, causing a fundamental shift in how students learn and teachers teach. Post-pandemic education through digital technologies has improved accessibility, inclusivity, and future readiness. Students can explore a teacher's selection of resources or search for resources themselves. Self-directed learning at a student's own pace makes education more meaningful. Teachers can also offer different pathways for learning with resources along the way. Then, students can choose which pathway they would like to take.

Digital technology has allowed asynchronous learning, transcended geographic limitations, and enabled students to access resources conveniently. Learners can also set goals for themselves and dig deeper into concepts or explore other topics. One way to encourage this is by teaching them how to find appropriate digital resources. Language arts teachers can create lessons on this topic, but teachers in any subject should reinforce these skills. With digital literacy skills, learners can use online materials responsibly and find appropriate content.

Digital learning environments are online learning platforms with various interactive digital technology tools and resources that provide students with an engaging and collaborative learning experience. They allow students and educators to access digital course materials and resources, participate in virtual classrooms, collaborate on projects, and connect with peers online. Examples of digital learning environments include online educational portals, virtual learning platforms, and virtual classrooms.

## Digital Learning and the Teaching-Learning Environment During the Pandemic

The COVID-19 pandemic has caused massive changes globally among educational institutions. All educational activities have shifted digitally. Due to the effect of the COVID-19 pandemic, digital learning has experienced significant change. For example, Gopika and Rekha (2023) analyzed the pre-COVID-19 and post-COVID-19 perceptions and usage of digital learning among school children. They also investigated how COVID-19 impacted the students' digital learning knowledge. Two surveys were conducted, one before the COVID-19 outbreak and after the outbreak. Gopika and Rekha's findings show that students' digital learning usage increased significantly after the outbreak of COVID-19, and they are more satisfied with the digital learning facilities. The study revealed that students' knowledge about digital learning has also increased. However, after COVID-19, the students' motivation dropped. The majority of respondents had never used digital learning before COVID-19. The widespread usage of digital learning has also raised barriers. The barriers outweighed the benefits of digital learning (Gopika & Rekha, 2023).

Yan et al., (2021) explored how students at different stages of their K-12 education reacted to the mandatory full-time online learning during the COVID-19 pandemic. They conducted a province-wide survey study in which the online learning experiences of 1,170,769 Chinese students were collected from the Guangdong Province of China. They performed cross-tabulation and Chi-square analysis to compare students' online learning conditions, experiences, and expectations. Results from this survey study provide evidence that students' online learning experiences are significantly different across school years (Yan et al., 2021).

## Learning Environments Aligned to Social Perspectives

The learning environments and activities that align with social learning perspectives include authentic, collaborative activities, project-based learning, flipped learning environments, and online collaborative spaces.

Based on a literature review, Kümmel et. Al. (2020) examined to what extent individual or social perspectives determined the learning outcome variables researchers have used as measurements in existing studies. They analyzed prototypical approaches to operationalize learning settings (individual vs. social) published in peer-reviewed journals and identified their relation to several measures of learning outcomes. They targeted 356 articles, but 246 were used in their final analysis. One hundred fifty-nine studies (64.6%) used an individual learning setting, while 87 (35.4%) used a social learning setting. We observed self-reports, observable behavior, learning skills, elaboration, personal initiatives, digital activity, and social interactions as learning outcome measures. The two types of learning settings differed regarding the measurement of elaboration and social interactions. Kümmel, et. al. discussed the implications of their findings for future research and concluded that researchers should investigate further measures of learning outcomes in digital learning settings.

There are various ways in which digital technologies can support the use of social learning theories in the classroom. Through emerging technologies such as Augmented Reality, Virtual Reality, Robotics, Adaptive Learning Algorithms, Asynchronous Learning and Microlearning (and associated micro-credentials), Live Streaming (school to school, school to expert, remote teaching and learning, etc. via Zoom, for example), Artificial Intelligence, Social Learning (obviously closely related to synchronous and asynchronous learning), and Learning Games and Simulations, as well as hands-on, collaborative technology in the classroom, such as; SMART Tables and iPads, Peergrade, quizlet, Yo!Teach, Flipgrid, etc.; students have robust opportunities to experience meaningful collaborative learning in physical and virtual settings that embody tenets of sociocultural learning.

All these technology tools and other online tools can assist with more extraordinary communication strategies, more realistic simulations of real-world problem scenarios, and even greater flexibility when seeking to scaffold instruction within students' ZPD. Embracing technology within collaborative learning can also foster an equal distribution of voices and an opportunity for active participation among all students.

## CHALLENGES AND OPPORTUNITIES IN DIGITAL LEARNING

### Integrating Digital Tools into Non-Traditional Learning Environments

Integrating digital tools into non-traditional learning environments such as vocational training requires careful consideration of vocational education's unique characteristics and requirements. By leveraging the opportunities offered by digital technologies while addressing the associated challenges, vocational training programs can enhance student learning outcomes and better prepare students for success in their chosen careers. Some of the digital tools that can be incorporated into non-traditional learning environments are:

**Simulation Software**: Vocational training often involves hands-on skills that can be effectively simulated using software. For example, automotive repair students can use virtual car repair simulations to practice diagnostics and repair techniques. However, developing high-fidelity simulations that accurately replicate real-world scenarios can be resource-intensive. Additionally, ensuring access to appropriate hardware and software infrastructure may be challenging for some training programs.

**Mobile Applications:** Mobile applications can provide on-the-go access to training materials, instructional videos, and interactive learning modules. Vocational students can use mobile apps to review content and practice skills outside the classroom. However, designing mobile apps that are user-friendly and accessible to a diverse range of learners is essential. Moreover, ensuring that mobile learning activities align with the hands-on nature of vocational training can be a challenge.

Virtual Reality (VR) and Augmented Reality (AR): VR and AR technologies can immerse vocational students in realistic training environments without needing physical equipment or materials. For example, construction apprentices can use VR simulations to practice safety protocols on virtual construction sites. However, implementing VR and AR technologies requires investment in hardware such as headsets and controllers. Designing effective VR and AR experiences that align with specific vocational training objectives can also be complex.

**Online Learning Platforms:** Online learning platforms offer flexibility for vocational students to access training materials, participate in discussions, and complete assessments remotely. These platforms can accommodate diverse learning styles and schedules. However, ensuring that online learning activities are interactive and engaging can be challenging in vocational training, where hands-on practice is often crucial. Moreover, providing adequate support and guidance for students who may have limited experience with online learning is important.

**Simulated Work Environments**: Simulated work environments, such as virtual laboratories or virtual workshops, can provide vocational students with realistic practice opportunities in a safe and controlled setting. These environments can help students develop confidence and competence before transitioning to real-world work settings. However, creating and maintaining simulated work environments requires careful attention to detail to ensure authenticity and effectiveness. Additionally, integrating feedback mechanisms and assessment tools into simulated environments can enhance the learning experience but may require technical expertise.

**Digital Credentialing and Portfolios**: Digital credentialing platforms enable vocational students to showcase their skills and accomplishments through digital badges, certificates, and portfolios. These credentials can be easily shared with employers and industry partners, enhancing students' employability. However, ensuring the credibility and integrity of digital credentials is essential for their acceptance by employers and industry stakeholders. Moreover, it is important to provide guidance and support for students to curate and present their digital portfolios effectively.

## Digital Equity and Access Challenges, Especially in Under-Resourced Regions

Digital equity and access challenges are particularly acute in under-resourced regions due to various socio-economic and infrastructural factors. Addressing these digital equity and access challenges in under-resourced regions requires a multi-faceted approach involving collaboration between governments, non-profit organizations, private sector entities, and local communities. Strategies may include investing in infrastructure development, providing subsidies for digital devices and internet access, offering digital literacy training programs, developing culturally relevant educational content, and advocating for digital inclusion policies. By addressing these challenges, stakeholders can work towards ensuring that all individuals, regardless of their socio-economic background or geographic location, have equitable access to digital resources and educational opportunities. These challenges can significantly hinder individuals' ability to benefit from digital resources and educational opportunities. Here's a closer look at some of these challenges:

## Limited Infrastructure

**Internet Connectivity**: One of the primary challenges in under-resourced regions is the lack of reliable internet connectivity. Many rural areas and marginalized communities have limited or no access to high-speed internet, making it difficult for residents to access online learning materials, educational platforms, and digital resources.

**Power Supply**: In some regions, unreliable electricity supply exacerbates digital access issues. Without consistent power, individuals may struggle to use digital devices or access online resources effectively.

## Socioeconomic Disparities

**Affordability:** The cost of digital devices such as computers, tablets, or smartphones, as well as internet access, can be prohibitive for individuals in under-resourced regions. Low-income families may prioritize basic needs over-investing in digital technology, leading to a lack of access to educational resources.

**Digital Literacy:** Even when digital devices are available, there may be disparities in digital literacy skills. Individuals from underprivileged backgrounds may lack the skills to navigate online platforms, effectively utilize digital tools, or critically evaluate online information.

## Geographic Isolation:

**Remote Communities**: In remote or isolated areas, access to educational facilities, libraries, and other traditional learning resources may be limited. Digital technologies have the potential to bridge this gap, but without adequate infrastructure and support, residents of these regions may remain disconnected from digital learning opportunities.

**Transportation:** Even if digital resources are available, transportation challenges in remote areas may prevent individuals from accessing centralized locations where they can use digital facilities, such as community centers or internet cafes.

## Language and Cultural Barriers

**Language Accessibility:** Digital resources may not be available in local languages, hindering comprehension and accessibility for individuals who do not speak the dominant language used online.

Cultural Relevance: Educational content and digital resources may not always reflect the cultural contexts and needs of under-resourced communities, making them less engaging and relevant for learners.

## Policy and Regulatory Issues

**Government Support**: Inadequate government investment in digital infrastructure and educational initiatives can perpetuate disparities in access to digital resources and learning opportunities.

**Regulatory Barriers**: Regulatory barriers, such as restrictions on internet access or censorship of online content, can further limit digital access in under-resourced regions.

## Digital learning's Limitations and Potential Negative Impacts

While digital learning offers numerous benefits, it also has limitations and potential negative impacts that warrant critical examination. Acknowledging these limitations and potential negative impacts of digital learning is essential for developing effective strategies to mitigate risks and maximize benefits. Educators, policymakers, and technology developers must take a balanced approach, integrating digital tools judiciously while recognizing the importance of offline interactions and traditional pedagogical methods in fostering holistic learning experiences. By addressing these challenges thoughtfully, stakeholders can work towards harnessing the full potential of digital learning while minimizing its drawbacks. Here's a more nuanced perspective on some of these challenges:

### Digital Distraction

The ubiquitous presence of digital devices and online platforms can lead to distractions during learning activities. Students may be tempted to multitask, check social media, or browse unrelated websites, which can impede concentration and hinder learning outcomes.

Constant digital distractions can lead to reduced attention spans and cognitive overload, making it challenging for students to focus on complex learning tasks. Moreover, excessive screen time has been linked to issues such as eye strain, sleep disturbances, and decreased productivity.

### Technological Dependence

Over-reliance on digital technologies for learning can create dependence, where students struggle to engage with traditional learning methods or offline activities.

Impact: In the event of technological failures or disruptions, such as internet outages or device malfunctions, students may encounter significant obstacles in accessing learning materials and completing assignments. This dependence can also exacerbate inequalities, as students without access to digital resources may be left behind.

### Social Isolation

Digital learning environments, especially fully online ones, may lack the social interactions and interpersonal connections inherent in traditional classroom settings.

Prolonged isolation from peers and instructors can lead to feelings of loneliness and disconnection, impacting students' mental health and overall well-being. Moreover, the absence of face-to-face interactions may hinder collaborative learning experiences and interpersonal skills development.

## Inequities in Access

Despite efforts to promote digital inclusion, inequities in access to technology and internet connectivity persist, particularly in under-resourced communities. Students from disadvantaged backgrounds may face barriers to accessing digital learning resources, exacerbating existing disparities in educational outcomes. This digital divide can widen inequalities, limiting opportunities for socio-economic mobility and perpetuating cycles of poverty.

## Quality of Online Content

Not all online educational content is created equal, and the quality and accuracy of digital resources may vary widely. Students may encounter misinformation or low-quality educational materials, leading to misconceptions and misunderstandings. Additionally, the lack of curation and oversight in digital learning environments can make it challenging for students to discern credible sources from unreliable ones.

## Privacy and Security Concerns

Digital learning platforms often collect and store sensitive student data, raising concerns about privacy and security. Inadequate safeguards against data breaches or unauthorized access can compromise the confidentiality of student information. Moreover, the commercialization of educational technology may lead to the exploitation of student data for targeted advertising or other purposes, undermining trust in digital learning platforms.

## Successful Digital Learning Implementations Across Various Educational Contexts

There are numerous examples of successful digital learning implementations across various educational contexts. These examples highlight the diverse ways in which digital learning technologies have been successfully implemented to enhance educational experiences and outcomes for learners worldwide. Whether through personalized learning platforms, interactive language apps, or online course marketplaces, digital learning has proven to be a powerful tool for expanding access to education, improving learning outcomes, and fostering lifelong learning. Here are a few notable examples:

## Khan Academy

Khan Academy is a non-profit organization that offers a wide range of educational resources, including instructional videos, practice exercises, and personalized learning dashboards. It has been widely praised for its effectiveness in providing free, high-quality education to learners worldwide. Its adaptive learning platform tailors content to individual student needs and has been shown to improve academic performance in subjects such as mathematics and science.

## Duolingo

Duolingo is a popular language-learning platform that uses gamification and adaptive learning techniques to teach over 30 languages. Duolingo's engaging and interactive approach to language learning has attracted millions of users globally. Research studies have demonstrated its effectiveness in helping learners achieve proficiency in target languages, with outcomes comparable to traditional classroom instruction.

## Coursera

Coursera is an online learning platform that offers courses, specializations, and degrees from leading universities and institutions worldwide. Coursera has democratized access to higher education by making university-level courses accessible to learners worldwide. Its flexible learning format allows individuals to pursue education at their own pace and on their own schedule, leading to improved career prospects and skill development.

## Codecademy

Codecademy is an interactive platform that offers coding courses in programming languages such as Python, JavaScript, and HTML/CSS. Codecademy has empowered millions of individuals to learn coding skills and pursue careers in technology. Its hands-on, project-based approach to learning has been praised for its effectiveness in helping beginners build practical coding skills quickly.

## SMART Learning Suite

SMART Learning Suite is an integrated set of digital learning tools designed for interactive and collaborative classroom experiences. It includes interactive whiteboard software, lesson delivery tools, and formative assessment features. SMART Learning Suite has transformed traditional classrooms into dynamic learning environments, allowing educators to create engaging and interactive lessons that cater to diverse learning styles. Research studies have shown improvements in student engagement, participation, and academic achievement by integrating SMART technologies.

## edX

edX is a massive open online course (MOOC) platform founded by Harvard University and MIT, offering a wide range of courses from universities and institutions worldwide. edX has expanded access to high-quality education for millions of learners globally. Its diverse course offerings cover various subjects, from computer science and engineering to humanities and social sciences, empowering individuals to pursue lifelong learning and professional development.

## Implications of Digital Learning and the Teaching-Learning Environment in the Post-Pandemic 21st Century

Digital learning has profoundly impacted the teaching-learning environment in the post-pandemic 21st century, fostering flexibility, accessibility, and collaborative approaches. It has transformed traditional classrooms into dynamic, tech-integrated spaces, enhancing engagement and providing diverse learning resources. However, challenges such as the digital divide and the need for adequate teacher training persist. Other implications are listed below.

1. Increased Accessibility: Digital learning allows for anytime, anywhere access to material, meaning that those who may not otherwise have access to educational material can now do so.
2. Improved Learning Outcomes: With digital learning, teachers can adjust the learning experience to an individual student's needs and create a more personalized approach to learning. This can lead to improved learning outcomes.
3. Increased Engagement: Digital learning can be more interactive and engaging for students, helping to keep them interested and focused on the material and leading to better learning outcomes.
4. Cost Savings: Digital learning can be a more cost-effective option than traditional education in terms of materials and resources. It can also reduce operating costs, such as utilities.

5. Higher Standards: Digital learning opens up possibilities to teach advanced topics and subjects, which can lead to higher education standards.

## THEORETICAL FRAMEWORKS AND PRACTICAL APPLICATIONS IN DIGITAL LEARNING

Operationalizing educational theories in digital learning technologies involves translating theoretical principles into practical applications that guide the design, development, and implementation of educational tools and platforms. By operationalizing educational theories in digital learning technologies, developers and educators can create more effective and pedagogically sound educational interventions. Integrating theoretical frameworks into practical applications strengthens the alignment between research-based principles and real-world educational practices, ultimately enhancing learning outcomes for students in digital environments. Here are some concrete examples of how theories are operationalized in educational technologies:

### Constructivism

Constructivism posits that learners actively construct knowledge through their experiences and interactions with the environment. Learning is viewed as a process of meaning-making and sense-building. In digital learning, constructivist principles can be operationalized through interactive simulations, problem-based learning activities, and collaborative projects. For example, virtual labs allow students to explore scientific concepts through hands-on experimentation, while online discussion forums facilitate peer interaction and knowledge construction.

### Cognitive Load Theory

Cognitive Load Theory emphasizes the limitations of working memory and the importance of managing cognitive load to optimize learning. It distinguishes between intrinsic, extraneous, and germane cognitive load. Educational technologies can apply cognitive load theory by presenting information in a structured and organized manner, minimizing extraneous cognitive load. For instance, multimedia presentations may incorporate visual aids and narration to reduce cognitive overload. Adaptive learning systems can also adjust the level of difficulty to match individual students' cognitive abilities, optimizing learning efficiency.

## Social Learning Theory

Social Learning Theory emphasizes the role of social interactions and observational learning in shaping behavior and cognition. Learning is viewed as a social process that occurs through observation, modeling, and imitation of others. Digital learning platforms can operationalize social learning theory by incorporating features that facilitate collaboration, peer feedback, and knowledge sharing. For example, wikis enable students to collaboratively create and edit content, while video conferencing tools support synchronous discussions and group projects. Social media integration can also foster informal learning communities and peer support networks.

## Connectivism

Connectivism asserts that learning is distributed across networks of people, resources, and technologies. Knowledge continually evolves, and learners must develop skills to navigate and make sense of this distributed information landscape. Educational technologies grounded in connectivism leverage networked learning environments, open educational resources (OER), and social media platforms to facilitate knowledge acquisition and sense-making. For instance, personalized learning platforms use algorithms to recommend relevant resources and connect learners with communities of practice. Online courses that utilize OER enable learners to access diverse perspectives and engage with up-to-date content worldwide.

## Behaviorism

Behaviorism emphasizes the role of reinforcement and conditioning in shaping observable behaviors. Learning is viewed as a process of stimulus-response associations, emphasizing external rewards and punishments. While behaviorist principles have been critiqued in contemporary educational psychology, they are still relevant in specific contexts, such as skill acquisition and mastery learning. Educational technologies can operationalize behaviorism through adaptive learning algorithms that provide immediate feedback and rewards for correct responses. Gamified learning platforms also incorporate elements of behaviorist reinforcement, such as badges, points, and leaderboard rankings, to motivate learners and track progress.

## Theory Snapshot

Playground perspectives on education fall nicely into the functional, conflict, and symbolic interaction approaches (Ballantine & Hammack, 2009). The "Theory Snapshot" summarizes what these approaches say.

*Table 1. Theory snapshot*

| Theoretical perspective | Major assumptions |
|---|---|
| Functionalism | Education serves several functions for society. These include (a) socialization, (b) social integration, (c) social placement, and (d) social and cultural innovation. Latent functions include child care, establishing peer relationships, and lowering unemployment by keeping high school students out of the full-time labor force. |
| Conflict theory | Education promotes social inequality through the tracking and standardized testing and the impact of its "hidden curriculum." Schools differ widely in funding and learning conditions, and this type of inequality leads to learning disparities that reinforce social inequality. |
| Symbolic interactionism | This perspective focuses on social interaction in the classroom, playground, and other school venues. Specific research finds that social interaction in schools affects the development of gender roles and that teachers' expectations of pupils' intellectual abilities affect how much pupils learn. |

## FUTURE DIRECTIONS AND IMPLICATIONS

### Emerging Digital Learning Technologies Post-2020, Focusing on Their Impact and Effectiveness in Modern Educational Settings

The landscape of digital learning technologies has seen significant evolution post-2020, with several emerging trends reshaping modern educational settings. Here's a detailed analysis of some key technologies and their impact:

*Table 2. Emerging digital learning technologies post-2020, focusing on their impact and effectiveness in modern educational settings*

| | Impact | Effectiveness |
|---|---|---|
| Virtual Reality (VR) and Augmented Reality (AR): | VR and AR technologies have revolutionized experiential learning by creating immersive environments. These environments offer students the opportunity to explore concepts hands-on, such as historical sites or conducting science experiments. | VR and AR can improve knowledge retention and engagement levels. For instance, medical students who practice surgeries in virtual environments perform better in real-life scenarios. |
| Artificial Intelligence (AI): | AI is being integrated into educational platforms to provide personalized learning experiences. AI-powered tutors can adapt content to individual student needs, track progress, and offer targeted feedback. | Personalized learning through AI has shown promising results in improving student outcomes. Adaptive learning platforms can identify gaps in understanding and provide additional support, leading to more efficient learning. |

continued on following page

*Table 2. Continued*

| | Impact | Effectiveness |
|---|---|---|
| Gamification: | Gamification elements, such as badges, leaderboards, and leveling up, are incorporated into educational platforms to enhance engagement and motivation. They can make learning more interactive and enjoyable. | Gamification has been found to increase student participation and motivation. Educators can create a more dynamic learning environment that encourages active participation and rewards progress by introducing game-like elements. |
| Mobile Learning: | Mobile learning has become increasingly popular with the widespread availability of smartphones and tablets. It offers flexibility and accessibility, allowing students to learn anytime, anywhere. | Mobile learning can accommodate diverse learning styles and preferences, catering to modern learners accustomed to accessing information on their mobile devices. However, ensuring the quality of content and user experience on mobile platforms is essential for effectiveness. |
| Adaptive Learning Systems: | Adaptive learning systems use data analytics and AI to personalize learning pathways for individual students. They assess students' strengths and weaknesses and dynamically adjust content delivery accordingly. | By providing tailored instruction, adaptive learning systems can address the unique needs of each student, leading to improved learning outcomes. They can also help educators identify struggling students early on and intervene proactively. |
| Blockchain in Education: | Blockchain technology is being explored for credentialing and verification purposes in education. It offers a secure and tamper-proof way to store and share academic records and certifications. | Blockchain can streamline administrative processes such as credential verification and transcript management, reducing fraud and ensuring the integrity of academic credentials. It also empowers learners to have greater control over their educational records. |

## Post-Pandemic Sustained Use of Digital Learning and the Teaching-Learning Environment

Several Emerging Technologies tools that support teaching and learning during and after COVID-19 are enumerated below.

The technologies used in the environment should be evaluated to ensure they are up-to-date, secure, and appropriate for their data types. Potential technologies evaluated for this chapter include standard emerging technologies that are presently or close to being developed but have yet to be widely used or implemented in education. Examples of such emerging technologies include hybrid and blended learning, artificial intelligence (AI), robotics and simulators, blockchain, the Internet of Things (IoT), augmented reality (AR), virtual reality (VR), quantum computing, nanotechnology, and autonomous vehicles.

## Hybrid and Blended Learning

In this digital age, many students are learning from home. Therefore, they embraced home-schooling as their best option, which runs entirely online. However, those students and parents who have experienced blended learning prefer blended learning to online education.

Pappas (2015) claims that there were different learning approaches before the blended learning model in the 21st century. According to Pappas, the first "Distance Course" started in the 1840s, followed by "Mainframe Computer-Based Training" in the 1960s and 1970s and then "TV-Based Technology to Support Live Training" in the 1970s and 1980s with "CD-ROM Training and Rise of LMS (Learning Management System)" in the 1980s and 1990s. Ghimire's "blended learning has a proven track record of bringing traditional classrooms into the tech-friendly 21st century" (Pappas, 2015). Regarding the use of blended learning in English language teaching, Hockly (2018) states that "the term blended learning" has been widely used in English language teaching since at least 2007, when Sharma and Barrett published their eponymous teachers" resource book."

## Artificial Intelligence (AI)

Given the rapid growth of AI, there is an urgent need to understand how educators can best utilize AI techniques for students' academic success (Zhai, et al. 2021). The emergence of big data, cloud computing, artificial neural networks, and machine learning have enabled engineers to create a machine that can simulate human intelligence. Building on these technologies refers to machines that can perceive, recognize, learn, react, and solve problems as artificial intelligence (AI) (Kumar & Thakur, 2012). Such innovative technologies will eventually revolutionize future workplaces (Horakova et al., 2017). Thus, while AI can interact and help humans perform at higher levels, it is emerging as the next disruptive innovation (Lawler & Rushby, 2013).

Zhai, et al. (2021) conducted a content analysis of studies aiming to disclose how artificial intelligence (AI) has been applied to the education sector and explore the potential research trends and challenges of AI in education. One hundred papers, including 63 empirical papers (74 studies) and 37 analytic papers, were selected from the Social Sciences Citation Index database's education and educational research category from 2010 to 2020. The content analysis showed that the research questions could be classified into a development layer (classification, matching, recommendation, and deep learning), an application layer (feedback, reasoning, and adaptive learning), and an integration layer (affection computing, role-playing, immersive learning, and gamification). Moreover, four research trends were suggested for further investigation, including the Internet of Things, swarm intelligence, deep learning, neuroscience, and an assessment of AI in education. However, Zhai, et al. (2021) also proposed that the challenges in education may be caused by AI, such as inappropriate use of AI techniques, changing roles of teachers and students, and social and ethical issues. The results provide insights into an overview of the AI used for education, which helps strengthen the theoretical foundation of AI in education and provides a promising channel for educators and AI engineers to carry out further collaborative research.

## Robotics and Simulators in Education

Robotics has allowed complicated medical procedures to be simplified, the work of dangerous construction projects to be safer, and the discovery of our universe to be possible. When applied to education, robotics, and simulators can change how students learn and ultimately create a more knowledgeable and well-adjusted student. Robots can be used to bring students into the classroom that otherwise might not be able to attend. In New York, a second grader with severe, life-threatening allergies could not attend school due to his condition. A four-foot-tall robot provided the boy with a 'real school' experience, 'attending' school and bringing the boy with him via an internal video conferencing system (Wright, 2008). Robots like the one mentioned can 'bring school' to students who cannot physically be present. Many careers require specialized knowledge in delicate practices, specifically in healthcare. When receiving a medical education, many students find benefits in using robotics. A human subject is not feasible when learning to perform complicated medical procedures, so educators use robots as stand-ins. Robots can be created and programmed to give off all indications of human life, including breath and heartbeat. Their use can also be seen in such procedures as injections, surgeries and even delivering children. Students with special requirements are reaching new levels of learning through the use of robotics in the classroom. With these technologies, children with autism learn communication and social skills, and students with developmental issues and attention disorders are learning focus (Valencia et al., 2019).

## Assistive Technology

Assistive technology is growing, and the abilities it provides to special education students are limitless. Simulation and robotics technologies offer a range of possibilities within education, with a helpful solution for every student's learning needs. As the technological world unveils innovations daily, the educational world will continue to benefit from the opportunities offered by these groundbreaking tools.

## The Use of Blockchain in Education

Blockchain is most commonly associated with cryptocurrencies such as Bitcoin. Data entered on a blockchain is stored in blocks linked together in chronological order, making tracing the data's origins and verifying its authenticity relatively easy (Maryville University, 2021). Blockchain is just beginning to make a mark in education; however, its use in education is still in its infancy, with only a handful of institutions adopting the technology.

A student takes an exam on a laptop using blockchain technology. The institutions that have adopted blockchain primarily use it to store and share academic records and credentials. However, researchers believe that the technology could revolutionize education in many ways: enhancing opportunities for lifelong learning, creating greater efficiencies for educators through smart contracts, and offering students ownership of their academic records, among other benefits. While the possibilities are promising, issues such as data security, scalability, and cost all present challenges to the widespread adoption of blockchain in the education sector.

## The Internet of Things (IoT)

One of the buzzwords in Information Technology is the Internet of Things (IoT). The future is the Internet of Things, which will transform real-world objects into intelligent virtual objects. The IoT aims to unify everything in our world under a shared infrastructure, giving us control of things around us and keeping us informed of the state of things (Madakam, 2015). It comprises millions of private, public, academic, business, and government networks of local to global scope linked by a broad array of electronic, wireless, and optical networking technologies.

## Augmented Reality (AR)

Augmented Reality (AR) is an emerging form of experience in which the Real World (RW) is enhanced by computer-generated content tied to specific locations and/or activities (Yuen, et. al., 2011). AR applications have become portable and widely available on mobile devices. It also becoming visible in audio-visual media (e.g., news, entertainment, sports) and is beginning to enter other aspects of lives (e.g., e-commerce, travel, marketing) in tangible and exciting ways. Facilitating ubiquitous learning, AR will give learners instant access to location-specific information compiled and provided by numerous sources. In addition to the 2D and 3D objects which many may expect, digital assets such as audio and video files, textual information, and even olfactory or tactile information can be incorporated into users' perceptions of the real world (Yuen, et. al., 2011).

According to Yuen, et. al., (2011), researchers believe that AR has vast potential implications and numerous benefits for the augmentation of teaching and learning environments; e.g., AR has the potential to (a) engage, stimulate, and motivate students to explore class materials from different angles, (b) help teach subjects where students could not feasibly gain real-world first-hand experience (e.g., astronomy and geography), (c) enhance collaboration between students and instructors and among students, (d) foster student creativity and imagination, (e) help students take control of their learning at their own pace and on their path, and (f) create an authentic learning environment suitable to various learning styles.

## Virtual Reality (VR)

Immersive VR can offer significant advantages for learning: it allows a natural feeling of objects and events that are physically out of our reach, it supports training in a safe environment, avoiding real potential dangers, and, with the game approach, it increases the learner's involvement and motivation while widening the range of learning styles supported (Freina, & Ott, 2015). Freina and Ott reviewed the literature on the use of Immersive VR and HMD in education; they found that most papers report experiments in high education or adult training, but very little was reported on younger children and in the field of disability. They recommended that since immersive VR can interfere with children's cognitive and physical development, its use with this audience has to be limited. They also reported that they could not find any paper reporting experiments with children under 10 and only a few between 10 and 17. Starting from middle school, VR could give some advantages by allowing a physical exploration of objects that are not accessible in reality, helping the learners to understand and memorize them better. Nevertheless, the constant presence of a teacher to mediate and regulate the use of the VR tools is needed, and the VR system should be used only for a limited period. Disabled people represent a population where immersive VR can make a difference; intellectually impaired people can take advantage of such an approach. Learning in a virtual environment that reproduces the real one can minimize the problems related to learning transfer (Freina, & Ott, 2015).

## Data Security

Data security should be evaluated to ensure maximum protection. This should include access controls, audit trails, anti-malware and antivirus protection, and penetration testing. Proper logins and monitoring should also be in place to detect suspicious activity or data breaches.

Data security is essential in today's digital world. It is defined as the ability to protect data from unauthorized access, use, and modification. This includes protecting digital information from malicious activities like cyber-attacks, malware, and other threats. Educational institutions must proactively ensure their data and networks are safe from unauthorized access. These steps include encryption, access control, data backups, disaster recovery plans, and regular system audits. They should also implement user authentication solutions to protect their data. Ultimately, data security is essential for protecting confidential information and ensuring the privacy of individuals.

### Open Access

It is critical to ensure that the environment resides on an open-access platform. If so, appropriate security measures should be taken, such as authentication methods, encryption, and other measures to ensure the environment is secure from external threats. Open access platforms are online publishing systems that allow anyone with an internet connection free and immediate access to research articles and other academic literature. These platforms allow people to access free research and other academic information, enabling greater engagement between readers, researchers, and institutions, regardless of location or economic status. Examples of open-access platforms include the Public Library of Science (PLOS), arXiv, PubMed Central, and OpenDOAR.

## CONCLUSION

In conclusion, the COVID-19 pandemic has accelerated the shift toward digital learning, forcing educators to adapt and innovate in response to the unprecedented disruption. As we look to the future, it is clear that digital learning will continue to play a critical role in shaping the teaching-learning environment. While there are many challenges to overcome, including issues of equity, access, and pedagogical design, the benefits of digital learning are undeniable. By embracing digital learning, educators can create more inclusive, personalized, and flexible learning environments that cater to the diverse needs of students in the post-pandemic 21st century.

The pandemic has also highlighted the importance of human connection and community in the teaching-learning environment. As we move forward, we must prioritize the technical infrastructure of digital learning and the social and emotional dimensions that underpin effective teaching and learning. This includes fostering a sense of community and belonging among students and providing teachers with the support and resources they need to navigate the complexities of digital pedagogy.

Ultimately, the future of digital learning is not just about technology but about creating a more equitable, accessible, and effective education system that prepares students for success in an increasingly complex and interconnected world. By embracing the opportunities and challenges presented by digital learning, we can build a brighter future for education and create a more just and equitable society for all.

## REFERENCES

Adeoye, B. F. (2020). The era of digital technology in teaching and learning in Nigerian educational institutions. In Adeoye, B., & Arome, G. (Eds.), *The Roles of Technology and Globalization in Educational Transformation* (pp. 43–51). IGI Global. 10.4018/978-1-5225-9746-9.ch004

Anglin, G. J. (Ed.). (1995). *Instructional technology: Past, present, & future* (2nd ed.). Libraries Unlimited. 10.5040/9798216974697

Atchley, W., Wingenbach, G., & Akers, C. (2013). Comparison of course completion and student performance through online and traditional courses. *International Review of Research in Open and Distance Learning*, 14(4), 4. 10.19173/irrodl.v14i4.1461

Audrin, C., & Audrina, B. (2022). Key factors in digital literacy in learning and education: A systematic literature review using text mining. *Education and Information Technologies*, 27(6), 7395–7419. 10.1007/s10639-021-10832-5

Balalaieva, O., (2021). The problem of classification of digital learning resources. *Euromentor Journal, 12*(2), 65-78.

Ballantine, J. H., & Hammack, F. M. (2009). *The sociology of education: A systematic analysis* (6th ed.). Prentice Hall.

Bandara, D., & Wijekularathna, D. K. (2018). Comparison of student performance under two teaching methods: Face to face and online. *International Journal of Education Research, 12.*

Bernacki, M., Greene, M., & Lobczowski, N. (2021). A Systematic review of research on personalized learning: Personalized by whom, to what, how, and for what purpose(s)? *Educational Psychology Review*, 33(4), 1–41. 10.1007/s10648-021-09615-8

Bernacki, M. L., Greene, M. J., & Lobczowski, N. G. (2021). A systematic review of research on personalized learning: Personalized by whom, to what, how, and for what purpose(s)? *Educational Psychology Review*, 33(4), 1675–1715. 10.1007/s10648-021-09615-8

Bixler, N. (2021). *How to use digital education resources effectively*. Hapara. https://hapara.com/blog/how-to-use-digital-education-resources-effectively

Cole, M., Shelley, D., Swartz, L., & Adeoye, B. F. (2014). Using digital technologies to aid e- learning: A pilot study. In Adeoye, B. F., & Tomei, L. (Eds.), *In Effects of information capitalism and globalization on teaching and learning* (pp. 22–35). IGI Global. 10.4018/978-1-4666-6162-2.ch002

Decuypere, M., Grimaldi, E., & Landri, P. (2021). Introduction: Critical studies of digital education platforms. *Critical Studies in Education*, 62(1), 1–16. 10.1080/17508487.2020.1866050

Esfijani, A. (2018). Measuring quality in online education: A Meta-synthesis. *American Journal of Distance Education* 31.1 (57-73).

Freeman, T., Anderman, L., & Jensen, J. (2007). Sense of belonging in college freshmen at the classroom and campus levels. *Journal of Experimental Education, 75*.

Freina, L., & Ott, M. (2015). A literature review on immersive virtual reality in education: state of the art and perspectives. In *The International Scientific Conference eLearning and Software for Education, 1*(133). 10-1007. 10.12753/2066-026X-15-020

Fullan, M., Hill, P., & Crévola, C. (2006). *Breakthrough*. Corwin Press.

Gopika, J. S., & Rekha, R. V. (2023). Awareness and use of digital learning before and during COVID-19. *International Journal of Educational Reform*, 0(0). 10.1177/10567879231173389

Haleem, A., Javaid, M., Qadri, M., & Suman, R. (2022). Understanding the role of digital technologies in education: A review. *Sustainable Operations and Computers*, 3, 275–285. 10.1016/j.susoc.2022.05.004

Hockly, N. (2018). Blended learning. *ELT Journal*, 72(1), 97–101. https://academic.oup.com/eltj/article-International Journal of Technology in Education (IJTE) abstract/72/1/97/4812363. 10.1093/elt/ccx058

Holmes, C., & Reid, C. (2017). A comparison study of on-campus and online learning outcomes for a research methods course. *The Journal of Counselor Preparation and Supervisor*, 9, 2. 10.7729/92.1182

Horakova, T., Houska, M., & Domeova, L. (2017). Classification of the educational texts styles with artificial intelligence methods. *Journal of Baltic Science Education*, 16(3), 324–336. 10.33225/jbse/17.16.324

Kumar, K., & Thakur, G. S. M. (2012). Advanced applications of neural networks and artificial intelligence: A review. *International Journal of Information Technology and Computer Science*, 4(6), 57–68. 10.5815/ijitcs.2012.06.08

Kümmel, E., Moskaliuk, J., Cress, U., & Kimmerle, J. (2020). Digital learning environments in higher education: A literature review of the role of individual vs. social settings for measuring learning outcomes. *Education Sciences*, 10(3), 78. 10.3390/educsci10030078

Lawler, R. W., & Rushby, N. (2013). An interview with Robert Lawler. *British Journal of Educational Technology*, 44(1), 20–30. 10.1111/j.1467-8535.2012.01372.x

Lohr, N., Stadler, M., Schultz-Pernice, F., Chernikova, O., Sailer, M., Fischer, F., & Sailer, M. (2021). On powerpointers, clickerers, and digital pros: Investigating the initiation of digital learning activities by teachers in higher education. *Computers in Human Behavior*, 119, 106715. 10.1016/j.chb.2021.106715

Madakam, S., Ramaswamy, R., & Tripathi, S. (2015). Internet of things (IoT): A literature review. *Journal of Computer and Communications*, 3(5), 164–173. 10.4236/jcc.2015.35021

Madison-Harris, R. D., Muoneke, A., & Times, C. (2012). *Using formative assessment to improve student achievement in the core content areas*. Briefing Paper.

Manzoor, M., & Vimarlund, V. (2018). Digital technologies for the social inclusion of individuals with disabilities. *Health and Technology*, 8(5), 377–390. 10.1007/s12553-018-0239-130416930

Martin, F. & Bolliger, D. (2018). Engagement matters: Student perceptions on the importance of engagement strategies in the online learning environment. *Online Learning Journal*.

Maryville University. (2021). *How blockchain is used in education*. Maryville University. https://online.maryville.edu/blog/blockchain-in-education/

Means, B., Toyama, Y., Murphy, R., & Bakia, M. (2013). The effectiveness of online and blended learning: A meta-analysis of the empirical literature. *Teachers College Record*, 115(3), 3. 10.1177/016146811311500307

Molnar, A. (2017). *Virtual schools in the U.S. University of Colorado*. National Education Policy Center.

Murray, M. C., Pérez, J., Geist, D., & Hedrick, A. (2012). Student interaction with online course content: Build it, and they might come. *Journal of Information Technology Education: Research*, *11*(1), 125-140. Informing Science Institute. https://www.learntechlib.org/p/111496/

Pappas, C. (2015, October 8). *The history of blended learning*. eLearning Industry. https://elearningindustry.com/history-of-blcndcd-lcarning

Rakitskaya, E. (2023). Collaborative learning in the online environment. *Handbook of Research on Facilitating Collaborative Learning Through Digital Content and Learning Technologies*. 10.4018/978-1-6684-5709-2.ch011

Richardson, J., Lv, J., & Caskurlu, S. (2017). Social presence in relation to students' satisfaction and learning in the online environment. *Computers in Human Behavior*, 71, 402–417. 10.1016/j.chb.2017.02.001

Sachar, M., & Neumann, Y., (2010). Twenty years of research of the academic performance differences between traditional and distance learning: Summative meta-analysis and trend examination. *MERLOT Journal of Online Learning and Teaching*.

Saghafian, M., & O'Neill, D. (2018). A phenomenological study of teamwork in online and face- to-face student teams. *Higher Education*.

Sailer, M., Murböck, J., & Fischer, F. (2021). Digital learning in schools: What does it take beyond digital technology? *Teaching and Teacher Education*, 103, 103346. Advance online publication. 10.1016/j.tate.2021.103346

Schildkraut, D. J. (2005). *Press "one" for English: Language policy, public opinion, and American identity*. Princeton University Press.

Seemiller, C., Grace, M., Dal Bo Campagnolo, P., Mara Da Rosa Alves, I., & Severo De Borba, G. (2021). What makes learning enjoyable? Perspectives of today's college students in the U.S. and Brazil. *Journal of Pedagogical Research*, 5(1), 1–17. 10.33902/JPR.2020065267

Sharratt, L., & Fullan, M. (2013). *Putting Faces on the Data*. Corwin Press.

Sinaga, P., Setiawan, W., & Liana, M. (2022). The impact of electronic interactive teaching materials (EITMs) in e-learning on junior high school students' critical thinking skills. *Thinking Skills and Creativity*, 46, 101066. 10.1016/j.tsc.2022.101066

Sjølie, E., & van Petegem, P. (2022). Measuring the sociability of virtual learning environments for interdisciplinary student teams – a validation study. *Scandinavian Journal of Educational Research*. Advance online publication. 10.1080/00313831.2022.2148279

Tayebinik, M., & Puteh, M. (2012). Blended learning or E-learning? *International Magazine on Advances in Computer Science and Telecommunications*, *3*(1), 103-110. https://papers.ssrn.com/sol3/papers.cfm?abstract_id=2282881 Ghimire.

Valencia, K., Rusu, C., Quiñones, D., & Jamet, E. (2019). The Impact of technology on people with autism spectrum disorder: A Systematic Literature Review. *Sensors (Basel)*, 19(20), 4485. Advance online publication. 10.3390/s1920448531623200

Wang, J., Han, M., & Wang, W. (2020). Research on the evolution and classification of digital learning resources. *Proceedings of the International Conference on Education, Economics and Information Management*. Research Gate. 10.2991/assehr.k.200401.025

Wright, P. (2008). *When a school refuses to protect a child with life-threatening allergies*. PrintFriendly. http://www. printfriendly.com/p/g/GYdHrx

Yan, L., Whitelock-Wainwright, A., Guan, Q., Wen, G., Gašević, D., & Chen, G. (2021). Students' experience of online learning during the COVID-19 pandemic: A province-wide survey study. *British Journal of Educational Technology*, 52(5), 2038–2057. 10.1111/bjet.1310234219755

Yuen, S. C., Yaoyuneyong, G., & Johnson, E. (2011). Augmented reality: An overview and five directions for AR in Education [JETDE]. *Journal of Educational Technology Development and Exchange*, 4(1). https://aquila.usm.edu/jetde/vol4/iss1/11. 10.18785/jetde.0401.10

Zhai, X., Chu, X., Chai, C. S., Jong, M.S., Istenic, A., Spector, M., Liu, J., Yuan, J., & Li, Y. (2021). *A review of artificial intelligence (AI) in education from 2010 to 2020*. Wiley. .10.1155/2021/8812542

Zhang, L., Basham, J. D., & Yang, S. (2020). *Understanding the implementation of personalized learning: A research synthesis*. Educational Research Review. 10.1016/j.edurev.2020.100339

# Chapter 2
# From Correspondence to Connectivism:
## Tracing the Evolution of Distance Learning From Its Inception to Post-Pandemic Realities

**Christine Boring**
http://orcid.org/0009-0006-4545-1325
*PPG, USA*

## ABSTRACT

*By examining the historical milestones, pedagogical theories, and technological advancements that have shaped distance learning, we can gain insights into its effectiveness, scalability, and adaptability in times of crisis. Furthermore, this historical review offers a unique perspective to evaluate current practices and envision future uses for educational technology and methodology innovations. This research synthesizes findings from a review of literature consisting of 105 articles, offering insights into the challenges and triumphs of the rapid transition to remote learning. The lessons learned from the COVID-19 pandemic influence the ongoing integration of distance learning in education and help to ensure resilience, accessibility, and quality in schooling across diverse contexts and challenges. Combining the lessons learned and best practices realized during this extreme experience can shape the new normal in education.*

DOI: 10.4018/979-8-3693-7645-4.ch002

## INTRODUCTION

The global events of the early 21st century, marked by the COVID-19 pandemic, have underscored the importance of distance learning in ensuring educational continuity. The rapid pivot from brick-and-mortar sessions to remote education facilitated the immediate need for online platforms and spotlighted both the good and the bad in the evolving landscape of digital learning environments.

To fully understand the rapid expansion and implementation of distance learning in schools amidst the pandemic and its aftermath, it is important to understand its development and the pedagogical theories associated with that development. This involves tracing the origins and progression of distance learning, from its early days as correspondence courses in the 19th century to today's online learning systems and methodologies. This representation can be extrapolated to inform the current state of online learning and eLearning and how the current state will shape the future.

## METHODOLOGY

Narrative analysis was developed from the work of Jerome Bruner (1991) and is concerned with the array of information communicated through speech and text (Bamberg, 2012; Crossley, 2000). This study explores the evolution of distance learning by analyzing its history, theory, and use by applying a narrative analysis methodology. It utilizes a traditional review method to link studies on various topics to provide a current-day literature review. The synthesized knowledge from this analysis can be used to identify knowledge gaps or areas for possible research and best practices for continued use.

This study uses a case study methodology to discuss the background informing the development of eLearning and the impact the pandemic had on eLearning by studying primary and secondary school responses to the pandemic in the United States. The research included 105 articles from scholarly publications, conference proceedings, magazine articles, and blog posts describing different facets of teaching in the United States during the COVID-19 crisis. All articles were in English and referenced learning effects on primary and secondary students. After review, the research was limited to the evolution of distance learning; educator, parent, student, and technological issues during the pandemic; and future learning trends.

## The Evolution of Distance Learning

Throughout history, methods of learning have constantly evolved to meet the changing needs of society. From the days of correspondence courses and radio broadcasts to the digital age of online learning and micro-lessons, the evolution of learning has brought about a wealth of new opportunities for people of all ages and backgrounds to expand their knowledge and skills. These advancements have revolutionized the education sector and have made learning more convenient and flexible than ever before.

The United States saw the emergence of four generations of learning, starting in the early 18th century, and these have paved the way for modern knowledge acquisition. Nipper's (1989) classification began by highlighting three generations: correspondence courses, multimedia courses, and computer-mediated courses. Six years later, Taylor (1995) introduced a fourth generation, known as "flexible learning," which could be associated with the development of the eLearning and microlearning methods used today.

## Correspondence Courses

Distance learning involves a physical or time-based separation between the teacher and the student. As defined by the American Association for Distance Learning (USDLA), distance learning is "the process of acquiring knowledge and skills through a variety of media for the transfer of education and information, including all types of technology and various forms of education level for distance learning" (USDLA, 2004).

The United States has a long-standing tradition of distance learning, dating back to 1728 when Caleb Phillips provided shorthand lessons via the U.S. Postal Service (Holmberg, 1995). Almost 150 years later, this practice evolved into the first distance-learning organization, the "Society to Encourage Studies at Home." By the late 1800s, universities had begun offering correspondence courses (Dawson, 2017) and soon incorporated media such as radio, television, and film to enrich the experience of distance education.

## Multimedia Courses

In 1913, Thomas Edison foresaw a future where learning would rely more on visual aids than books. He predicted that multimedia would transform the learning experience within ten years (Smith, 1913). Though visual broadcast learning progressed slowly, multimedia learning, in general, took off in 1921 with the introduction of radio broadcasts.

Latter Day Saints' University in Salt Lake City, Utah, was issued the first educational radio license, making it the first university to broadcast distance learning courses through radio broadcast. The Universities of Wisconsin and Minnesota (Saettler, 2004) and Pennsylvania State University (Dawson, 2017) soon followed. By 1946, the Federal Communications Commission (FCC) had issued more than 200 educational radio broadcast licenses (Casey, 2008).

Iowa State University made history in 1950 by securing the first educational television license and becoming the first educational broadcaster worldwide (Saettler, 2004), a remarkable feat that partially realized the prophecy Edison made in 1913. As the decade ended, a total of 17 programs harnessed the power of broadcast television to disseminate their educational materials to a broader audience (Harting & Erthal, 2005). This marked the dawn of a new era where technology would play an instrumental role in expanding educational opportunities for students worldwide.

## Computer-Mediated Courses

During the 1960s, there was a belief that programmed learning would revolutionize education (Hameed & Macintyre, 2007). However, it took more than two decades for the necessary infrastructure to be developed, which included the introduction of the Internet by the Department of Defense. It was not until the mid-1990s that the National Science Foundation made the Internet available to colleges and universities (Saba, 2011), enabling institutions to harness the power of programmed learning.

Advancements in personal computer power, network capacities, digital video, and the release of the World Wide Web laid the foundation for online learning throughout the 90s. While the first computer-mediated learning programs used command prompts (Harting & Erthal, 2005), browsers were soon developed for graphics and interaction (Hubackova, 2015). This advancement made online learning accessible to the general population.

## ELearning

The proliferation of technology played a significant role in the widespread adoption of flexible learning approaches, including online learning and eLearning (Hameed & Macintyre, 2007). The technological shift made online education, learning via an Internet connection, increasingly mainstream and features multimedia as an everyday staple in academic learning environments (Pastore, 2016).

Though definitions of eLearning vary, some consistencies exist. Collectively, eLearning is viewed as a method of learning that utilizes electronic media and devices to enhance access to education, communication, and interaction (Sangrà et al., 2012) and does not necessarily require an Internet connection. However, because of the varying definitions found, for the purposes of this study, eLearning will broadly represent "electronic learning" and include terms such as remote learning, online learning, and virtual learning.

ELearning emerged as a convenient and flexible learning method with two distinct approaches, asynchronous and synchronous, each offering distinct benefits. Asynchronous eLearning allows learners to learn at their own pace and convenience. In contrast, synchronous eLearning offers real-time virtual classes where learners can interact with instructors and peers in a collaborative environment. While asynchronous online learning began in 1989 through the University of Phoenix, it was not until years later that technology had advanced enough to support synchronous online learning. Moreover, when synchronous online learning became available in 1994, there was still a significant gap between passive and active learning.

Passive learning mainly involves teacher-centric activities, such as lectures, while active learning is more student-centered. The active learning virtual space allowed participants to gather and share the same experience, allowing learners to engage in the learning process more effectively and take ownership of their education. Active learning progressed with the integration of interactive tools and collaborative features. Using these tools and features, synchronous online learning could provide a more active and engaging, student-centric learning experience, enhancing cognitive skills, critical thinking abilities, and overall academic performance (Jaiswal & Al-Hattami, 2020; Soubra et al., 2022).

## Microlearning

A subset of eLearning, known as microlearning, evolved in 2002 to address the rising demand for on-demand knowledge (Hug, 2007). Microlearning involves providing small, self-contained packets of information that can be accessed and consumed quickly (ATD, 2017; Cole, 2017). Though microlearning is mainly passive, the smaller bites of information enable learners to understand complex topics quickly, improving academic performance (Boring, 2020).

Today, learning is often accessed through mobile devices, making mobile learning (mLearning) the norm. Because microlearning can be delivered through various formats, such as videos, podcasts, and quizzes, it provides learners with multiple learning methods. It also enables easy access to information via smartphones and tablets, satisfying on-demand mLearning requirements.

## Evolving Pedagogical Theories

### Behaviorist Theory

In the early 1900s, psychology was just in its infancy. However, in the second half of the 20th century, distinguished figures in this theoretical paradigm, including John Watson, Edward Thorndike, B.F. Skinner, and Jerome Bruner aimed to bring measurable outcomes to the learning process, enabling learners to enhance their skills and knowledge.

John Watson's "Behaviorist Manifesto," published in 1913, marked the beginning of a new era in psychology. Watson believed psychology should be a science that studies observable and measurable phenomena, much like the physical sciences. He proposed studying Behavioralism through observable behaviors that could be measured and quantified (Watson, 1913).

However, it was Jerome Bruner (1991) who expanded the Behavioralist movement by incorporating the study of how the mind processes information. Bruner's theory included learner attitude and ability, proper sequencing of material, and carefully considered rewards for effective learning. Bruner's contributions have been instrumental in shaping our understanding of how people learn and process information.

Despite not being intentionally designed as such, the original correspondence courses employed a Behavioralist approach to facilitate learning. This approach placed considerable emphasis on the observable outcomes of learning processes, and as the courses provided feedback on these outcomes, the feedback, although delayed, could be viewed as the stimulus to repeat specific behaviors and actions (Osnes & Adelinis, 2005).

### Cognitivism and Constructivism

Over the years, the field of psychology has undergone significant changes alongside advancements in learning. The theory of Cognitivism, which focuses on how information is received, remembered, and recalled (Schunk, 2012), evolved to include the emergence of multimedia technologies. This paved the way for the emergence of a subdivision of cognitivism, Multimedia Learning Theory (MLT), the principle that integrating diverse learning modalities can significantly improve information retention and comprehension (Mayer, 2002).

As learning technologies advanced, learning methodologies shifted; Cognitivism theory was no longer as relevant as it once was. Instead, Constructivism theory, which emphasizes integrating prior knowledge to build new understanding (Schunk, 2012; Kimmons & Caskurlu, 2020), became crucial in connecting eLearning with educational practices. However, despite this linkage and its apparent connection to online learning, a newer model is better suited to the specific demands of online learning and eLearning, including its subsets such as microlearning and mLearning.

## Connectivism

Connectivism suggests that learning occurs through creating networks of information that can be applied to real-world problems (Downes, 2006; Siemens, 2004). Connectivism relies on communication, which has been made possible by the increasing development of technology and Internet connectivity.

Siemens (2004) states that Connectivism is a successor to Behaviorism, Cognitivism, and Constructivism because the previous theories failed to address the role of technology in learning. Connectivism posits that technology can now support processes previously addressed by learning theories. However, unlike traditional learning theories, Connectivism is not concerned with how a person learns or what is gained through learning. The principles of Connectivism solely indicate that knowledge is created by cultivating and connecting sources from various opinions to learn the latest information (Siemens, 2004).

While the study of Connectivism may have drawbacks, researchers agree that Connectivism will help develop new learning theories (Mackness et al., 2010; Bell, 2011) and inform new learning practices. With the rapid advancement of technology, the adoption of Connectivism has become more critical than ever before. This approach to learning can help students navigate the vast amount of information available and leverage technology to enhance their learning experiences, which means that knowing where to find knowledge may be just as important as retention.

## The Pandemic as a Catalyst

Because the norm for primary and secondary instruction is face-to-face education, elementary schools and high schools are not featured in the discussion of the historical development of distance learning. In fact, in the 2017-2018 school year, only 21 percent of public high schools and 13 percent of private high schools offered completely remote courses (NCES, 2022b).

During the COVID-19 pandemic, schools were forced to transition from traditional brick-and-mortar classrooms to virtual environments, sending over 55 million children into remote learning by April 2020 (Education Week, 2020). It is important to remember throughout this discussion that this transition represented an emergency remote teaching (ERT) model, which differs from purposefully planned online education. When using ERT, teachers and districts are focused on providing access to content and support quickly and not on providing everything that a remote environment can offer (Hodges et al., 2020).

This quick shift in learning methodology produced disparities in terms of accessibility and equity. In addition, making such a transition so quickly did not enable teachers inexperienced in online learning to take full advantage of all the possibilities of teaching in such a format (Hodges et al., 2020). These concerns had long been present in traditional classroom settings (Mossberger, 2023), but the massive shift to remote learning during the pandemic shed new light on the inadequacies experienced by diverse populations.

## The Shift to Online Learning

When remote learning became the new norm for education, Connectivism played an even more significant role in ensuring that students received quality instruction despite the problems posed by the pandemic. However, this presented challenges with the technological infrastructure and support of many schools. The sudden shift highlighted primary and secondary schools' inadequate use of learning management systems (LMSs), lack of teacher preparation, devices for the student population, and remote access to online education.

Driven by the need to continue educational activities amid widespread lockdowns and social distancing measures, online platforms and digital tools became essential for delivering classroom activities, assignments, and assessments, fundamentally changing the traditional classroom dynamic. LMSs became increasingly important to the remote learning experience. Before the pandemic, many high schools had yet to establish an LMS, and high schools that did have an LMS used a fraction of their capability (Langreo, 2022). During the pandemic, LMSs were purchased rapidly and, in some instances, set up within months. What started as a method to assign and collect completed work turned into pivotal hubs for managing all facets of the online environment. Integrating this technology into the classroom so fully resulted in permanent technological changes that signified a structural shift in primary and secondary education (Prothero, 2021).

## Teacher Preparation

The closure of brick-and-mortar schools not only prompted educators to develop new pedagogical approaches compatible with digital platforms (Ahmed & Opoku, 2022; Cramarenco et al., 2023), but the rapid integration of technology into the classroom also exposed the need for teachers to address technological deficiencies when adapting their teaching methods to remote learning.

Despite the lack of in-person interaction, teachers were still expected to maintain high educational standards. This presented a significant challenge and an opportunity for innovative solutions in educational delivery. Teachers had to quickly acquire new skills and adjust their teaching methods accordingly to ensure that the quality of education remained uncompromised.

Equally pressing was the need for teachers to redesign their curricula for online delivery. Teachers found themselves spending extra hours recording lectures, learning online assessment tools, and finding ways to interact with students virtually (An et al., 2021). As the pandemic progressed, educators and institutions began to create interactive online content, virtual simulations, and stimulating virtual in-person sessions to engage students of all ages. This redesign required a deep understanding of the principles of online education, which many educators were unfamiliar with (Garbe et al., 2020).

Although incorporating technology into teaching can "accelerate, amplify, and expand the impact of effective teaching practices" (NETP, 2017, p. 5), a recent study showed that while nearly half of the educators surveyed expressed interest in effectively implementing technology into their classrooms, only 18 percent felt confident in doing so (Grey & Lewis, 2021). In addition, the study showed that nearly a third of teachers expressed concerns about utilizing technology due to a lack of support and guidance. Moreover, a mere 50 percent of school districts reported providing their educators with training on technology integration for teaching and learning before the pandemic (NCES, 2022a).

## Parents as Teachers

Parents also faced significant challenges supporting their children's online learning. Many were thrust into navigating new educational platforms without sufficient guidance from school districts (Ancho, 2023; Garbe et al., 2020). The situation was worsened for parents balancing other responsibilities, such as being essential workers, and for those with limited educational backgrounds or language barriers (NCES, 2023, Michelson, et al., 2021).

Parents with children who had special educational needs also encountered unique challenges. The lack of tailored support services typically offered in traditional school environments placed the onus on parents to satisfy these needs (Goldberg, 2021). This often resulted in parents feeling inundated and ill-equipped, potentially impacting the caliber of their children's education (Tokatly Latzer et al., 2021; Shaw & Shaw, 2023; Garbe et al., 2020).

While navigating the parent-as-teacher role was challenging, it was exasperated by a lack of technological knowledge. More than a quarter of Americans do not have the necessary skills to set up new electronic devices like computers and smartphones (Pew Research Center, 2021). Because this low digital self-efficacy is common (Povey et al., 2016), it should have been expected that many parents and guardians found it difficult to assist their children with technological issues (McClain et al., 2021).

For parents who did not struggle with low digital self-efficacy, digital access devices were still not ubiquitous. Unfortunately, according to the National Center for Education Statistics (2022a), only 59 percent of parents reported that their child's school district had provided computers by the end of the pandemic, leaving many students without the technology they needed to be successful during ERT.

## The Digital Divide

The Digital Divide, a term established in the 1990s, describes unequal access to technology based on socioeconomic status, race, gender, or age (Mossberger, 2003). This gap became much more apparent during the pandemic. As virtual platforms, such as Zoom, Google Classroom, and Microsoft Teams, became the new norm for learning, participation was limited for families without the necessary devices or reliable Internet access (Irwin, 2021; McClain et al., 2021; NCES, 2021).

Before the pandemic, 15 to 16 million students in the United States lacked proper access to high-speed Internet connectivity and/or a device to use at home (Bielski, 2020; Braff, 2020). Throughout the pandemic, the Internet access gap for students in K – 12 shrunk by 20 to 40 percent, and the device access gap by up to 60 percent (Lieberman, 2021). However, by the end of the pandemic, approximately 30 percent of K-12 public school students still lacked the tools to access the online learning environment, including millions of completely disconnected students (Common Sense Media, 2021).

To address the challenges posed by ERT, institutions and governments took steps to ensure continued learning for all students. The Affordable Connectivity Program (ACP), introduced by the U.S. government, is one such measure that has helped bridge the digital divide. However, as the ACP ends in April 2024, around one in six American households may lose funding for high-speed Internet, significantly impacting their ability to access online education and other resources (Federal Communications Commission, n.d.).

## Access to Technology

By April 2020, nearly all adults reported that their children's classes were affected by the pandemic (99.6 percent), and by 2021, the number of parents reporting that their children have had some online instruction since the beginning of the pandemic rose to 93 percent (McClain et al., 2021). However, because high-income districts were more likely to distribute technology (Lake & Makori, 2020), educational access often did not reach the population that needed it most.

Remote schooling requires Internet access for academic success, which poses a challenge for some school districts (Irwin, 2021). In 2019, 11 percent of households identified in the lowest quarter of income did not have Internet access and those who did reported problems 60 percent of the time (McClain et al., 2021). Fourteen percent of those who did have Internet connectivity solely accessed it through a smartphone (Irwin, 2021). The statistics drop further when evaluating parental education levels in households. According to the 2023 Children's Internet Access at Home report, households with parents who had not completed high school had the lowest Internet access rate at 78 percent (NCES, 2023).

To solve this, schools took varying approaches, such as offering stipends or vouchers for Internet access or installing mobile hotspots (Grey & Lewis, 2021; Garbe et al., 2020; Lockee, 2021). However, despite these efforts, the Census Bureau reported that in 2020, access to the Internet from the lowest quartile income group had decreased to 83 percent (U.S. Census Bureau, 2020), raising important considerations regarding the role of the Internet as an educational tool (Irwin, 2021).

## The Human Element

### Teacher Preparation

Students' varying access to reliable Internet and appropriate devices created a barrier that hindered some learners' ability to engage with online content. However, even with access, students need high-quality resources and support systems to remain engaged and motivated. Therefore, the significant challenge of training teachers in effective online instructional techniques remained.

To address this, teachers were quickly briefed on online teaching methods, providing the ability to properly incorporate some of the tools and resources available (DeCoito & Estaiteyeh, 2022). However, depending on their pedagogical beliefs, some educators are more inclined to incorporate technology in student-centered activities than others (Palak & Walls, 2009). Therefore, despite efforts to integrate digital technologies into classroom activities, a tendency toward teacher-centric education often prevailed (Johnson et al., 2016; Muniandy & Abdullah, 2023).

## Transactional Distance Theory

Transactional Distance Theory (TDT) is an essential pedagogical concept that has been widely applied to online learning environments. This theory was initially developed by Michael Moore in the 1970s to describe technology-based training. Since then, TDT has become one of the most relevant theories in distance learning, with some believing that it is the only applicable pedagogical theory associated with distance learning (Abuhassna & Yahaya, 2018; Benson & Samarawickrema, 2009).

TDT is composed of three key components: the content that needs to be learned, the interaction between the instructor and the learner, and the unique characteristics of the learner (Moore, 1989). In the context of online learning, the human element is most evident in the second component of TDT. Effective online learning heavily depends on human interaction, and the distance between teacher and student can significantly impact its efficacy (Moore, 1989). Therefore, it is necessary to establish an environment that encourages interaction and fosters engagement between learners and educators while providing resources to support their success. This proved to be difficult for instructors who were not accustomed to online teaching. Sadly, many teachers were ill-equipped to transition to a fully online environment, and as a result, the human element suffered.

## Psychological Impacts

The pandemic forced many professions to adopt remote work, and teachers found themselves in unfamiliar territory. The abrupt shift to online teaching came with a steep learning curve, requiring educators to quickly familiarize themselves with various digital tools and platforms (Scherer et al., 2021). This impacted their confidence and well-being as they navigated the challenges of delivering quality education in a virtual environment.

While remote learning allowed us to continue educating in the face of crisis, it also brought about various psychological challenges, causing emotional stress for all involved (Baltà-Salvador et al., 2021). Moreover, teachers found it difficult to draw the line between work and home, constantly feeling like they were under the spotlight. The blurred boundaries made it even more challenging to maintain a healthy work-life balance (Klusmann et al., 2022). In addition, educators also faced the added challenge of managing their own stress while being compassionate, accommodating, and readily available to support their students' well-being.

The pandemic forced students to adapt to a new classroom environment, vastly different than the in-person education that provided a steady state for their social, emotional, and physical well-being (NASEM, 2019). With limited social interaction, many students experienced feelings of loneliness and isolation, making it challenging for them to adjust (Hoffman & Miller, 2020).

Parents had to juggle work responsibilities with their children's learning needs, this was even more difficult for those who were less familiar with or lacked access to technology (Ancho, 2023). Like teachers, parents dealt with their stress and anxiety while providing emotional support to their children (Harth & Mitte, 2020).

To counteract the adverse effects of pandemic-induced isolation and unease, educators and institutions worked to foster a sense of community and connection in the online learning environment by implementing strategies such as collaborative and interactive activities in their curricula, virtual social gatherings, and increasing communication with their students (Turnbull et al., 2021).

## Lessons Learned and Best Practices Post-Pandemic

The rapid shift to online learning during the COVID-19 pandemic underlined a crucial lesson for education. In an age of technology, schools need to be ready with infrastructure and pedagogical flexibility to accommodate sudden changes and push education forward (Rapanta, 2021). The pandemic highlighted the need for technological capability in education, including teacher training, access devices and Internet for all, parental guidance, and resources to support the emotional well-being of teachers, students, and parents (Donohue & Miller, 2020).

### Connectivism

Connectivism resonates with the realities of the digital age. It emphasizes the importance of finding, filtering, connecting, and applying information in ways that were not emphasized in traditional learning theories (Pappas, 2023; Siemens, 2006). This approach recognizes that learning can occur from non-traditional sources and diverse perspectives, which is essential given the constant flux of information in our modern world.

However, it is critical to note that not all educators and learners have equal access to the technological resources required to employ the Connectivist approach. For this approach to be practical, there must be equitable access to these resources, making bridging the digital divide essential.

### Instructional Technology

The pivot to online classes highlighted gaps in digital literacy and access among educators who had previously integrated little technology into their pedagogy (Hodges et al., 2020). Therefore, teachers accustomed to the interpersonal dynamics of in-person classroom instruction found themselves navigating an unfamiliar digital landscape.

While the world saw high growth and adoption of educational technology during the COVID-19 pandemic, at the onset, technology was still an afterthought for many educators. Many who did incorporate technology into their daily classes still lacked the pedagogical knowledge to operate in a completely remote model. As a result, at the onset of ERT, many online learning environments lacked direct social interaction and hands-on experiences, which negatively affected student engagement and learning outcomes.

To provide effective online education, it is necessary to design courses that are engaging and accessible. To achieve this, teachers should receive education and training in the components of a well-designed online learning course through teacher training programs and professional development. This training will enable educators to create virtual learning spaces that are easy to navigate, intuitive, and accessible, while simultaneously promoting self-directed learning, collaboration, and academic rigor. Teachers should also be trained on how to incorporate multimedia resources, synchronous and asynchronous learning opportunities, and clear learning objectives. This will ensure that online courses are of high quality and meet the needs of all learners.

## The Digital Divide

While the quick adoption of online platforms demonstrated the resilience and innovation of educators and institutions, it also revealed the need to cultivate digital literacy. Moreover, the immediate change reintroduced the inequalities among families in disadvantaged circumstances and those with special needs students.

Despite being identified as a problem as early as 1980, the country has made minimal progress in reducing the gap in access to technology and Internet connectivity, and the pandemic further highlighted the inadequacies in our efforts to bridge this divide (NETP, 2024). Disparities in technological readiness among households often mirrored broader socioeconomic and demographic lines, revealing the crucial need for equitable access to educational technology. To learn to perform in online education, students need reliable Internet access and adequate devices; simply put, not everyone has equal access to the necessary technology to succeed.

In the year following the pandemic, the 2021 EdWeek Research Center Survey (Lieberman,2021) indicated notable progress in both device and Internet access. The survey denoted that 95 percent of students have the devices required to participate in online learning consistently. While the number seems remarkable, it is essential to note that even a 5 percent lack of access among the K-12 population translates into a staggering count of over 2 million students.

In 2021, President Joe Biden signed a 2 trillion-dollar stimulus package introducing a federal infrastructure investment to provide nationwide broadband access, including $7 billion for school districts and families' home Internet access (Lieberman, 2021). While the program showed commitment to closing the digital divide across the nation, it is set to expire in April 2024 (Federal Communications Commission, n.d.), with the access gap still present. With the connected nature of education in the digital age, the country has much more work to do to ensure that digital access devices and Internet access are available to all to close the widening learning gap.

## Technological Shift

ERT, while forced, highlighted the potential for online education to become a more integral part of the educational landscape, suggesting ongoing shifts in how learning is approached post-pandemic and changing future expectations of students and educators regarding the flexibility of education with the possibilities of virtual learning. This ongoing process involves not just the use of digital tools for teaching and learning but also the incorporation of digital competence as a core component of the curriculum. As such, the integration of digital tools and traditional learning into a blended learning model has become much more widely used in post-pandemic education.

ERT may very well influence future primary and secondary school educational practices, making online and blended learning a central component of educational systems. This shows that the rapid adoption of digital platforms for learning during COVID-19 paved the way for new paradigms in education, highlighting the need for balanced educational approaches that use technology to aid in flexibility. It also spotlights the significant role of teachers' beliefs in the effective use of technology.

Prior to the onset of the pandemic, schools used, on average, 895 educational technology tools (Statistica, n.d.). During the 2022 - 2023 school year, the average number of these tools used in the classroom increased to 2591, almost a 3-fold increase. In addition, in the 2022 - 2023 school year, about 58 percent of educational technology tools were identified as learner-centric. This finding suggests not only a growing trend toward digitizing, modernizing, and innovating in the academic landscape, but it also highlights a change in pedagogical strategy from a teacher-centric to a learner-centric methodology.

Throughout the pandemic, virtual education improved and expanded, including changes to video conferencing platforms and LMSs and the development and adoption of interactive and adaptive learning technologies. Zoom, Google Meet, and Microsoft Teams saw massive adoption rates and became essential for live virtual classes. LMS systems, such as Google Classroom and Canvas, provided spaces for assignments, communication, and organization of resources. Educational apps were developed or grew in popularity, including Kahoot, Seesaw, DuoLingo, and Remind, and some apps began to address inclusivity issues, offering new possibilities for accommodation. Multimedia resources such as videos, podcasts, infographics, and collaborative tools, including virtual laboratories, were quickly expanded to keep students engaged. As emerging technologies like Artificial Intelligence (AI), Virtual Reality, and Augmented Reality continue to mature, they will likely play a more significant role in creating immersive and interactive learning experiences in the future.

## Parents as Teachers

While ERT has stopped for the time being, districts need to anticipate a future where some of the methods from ERT remain in current-day practices. Many parents struggled to take a more active role in their children's education due to their lack of technological skills. While it is acknowledged that most parents are not trained as educators, in order for parents to actively participate in this digital era of education, school districts need to provide more support. This includes access to technology, training, and flexible learning options tailored to each family's situation. Resources and guidance on facilitating home learning are vital for parents to support their children through expanding transitions in learning modalities to include online education as part of the learning environment. Underscoring this idea, researchers are strongly encouraging schools and policymakers to provide more robust support systems for parents (Garbe et al., 2020; Lewin & Luckin, 2010).

## Teacher Training

In the context of the digital divide, there were instances where teachers themselves lacked the necessary devices and Internet connectivity to implement ERT effectively. School districts must give top priority to this issue. In addition to proper training, it is imperative that each teacher is provided with a computer, reliable high-speed Internet, and adequate resources. Even if in-person instruction has resumed, access to the plethora of online information and activities remains crucial for teachers to continue delivering impactful and engaging lessons in the modern era.

Leveraging technology in teaching has transformed educational approaches, enabling innovative pedagogies that extend beyond the physical confines of the classroom. Technology integration empowers educators to enhance their lessons with digital tools, such as interactive simulations, virtual labs, and multimedia presentations. This integration fosters an active learning environment and aligns with MLT.

Technology provides avenues for real-time feedback, facilitates collaboration through online discussion forums and group projects, and supports diverse instructional strategies, such as flipped classrooms and blended learning models. It also allows for personalized learning experiences, where students can learn at their own pace and access a wealth of available resources. By embracing the array of technologies available, teachers can create a dynamic and inclusive educational experience that meets the needs of the 21st-century learner.

Moving forward, the irreversible shift towards digital education, whether used as a primary method or for secondary resources, necessitates thoroughly examining teacher training and preparation methods to ensure educators are equipped to meet the demands of the modern age. Research shows that systemic support and training are imperative for educators navigating the challenges of online teaching (NETP, 2024; USDOE, 2017; Whalen, 2020), including when preparing for careers in teaching. "The ultimate goal for teacher preparation programs should be a technology-infused program that provides a more concerted effort to address teaching with technology throughout the curriculum (Foulger, et al., 2017, p. 4). Further, investing in professional development programs for existing teachers that focus on digital literacy, online pedagogy, and curriculum development is essential to better prepare for future remote instruction needs. Though not currently employing ERT, it is still imperative to make a deliberate effort to provide educators with access to training and resources that will enable them to deliver high-quality online education.

## Technology Integration in the Digital Age

As we continue to explore the possibilities of technology and pedagogy in education, we can envision a future where learning is more engaging, personalized, and accessible than ever before. Thanks to remote learning platforms, geographical barriers are slowly breaking down, providing students worldwide with access to quality education, assuming they have an Internet connection. Technology is also helping to make education more engaging and interactive. Personalized learning has become more accessible, enabling educators to tailor the curriculum to meet the unique needs of each student.

### Blended Learning

Although educational technology can be a viable alternative to certain aspects of traditional learning, a well-rounded approach incorporating electronic devices and traditional materials may be the ideal way to keep students engaged and alleviate social isolation. Innovatively combining educational technology with more traditional forms of learning can significantly enhance the effectiveness of remote instruction.

Extensive studies on the implementation of educational technology have highlighted the importance of exercising prudence when considering online learning in primary and secondary schools as a complete replacement for conventional teaching methods (Topping et al., 2022; Vallée et al., 2020; Kumar et al., 2021; Means et al., 2013; Nagel, 2009). Therefore, combining the flexibility of online learning and the social learning of in-person education can offer the best of both worlds.

In the post-pandemic education era, integrating newly realized approaches and a Connectivist mindset has become increasingly important in creating a hybrid learning environment that optimizes learning outcomes and enhances the student experience. Preliminary studies conducted post-pandemic showed that those participating in a connected, blended classroom had better academic results than those who did not (Pressley & Ha, 2021).

Emphasizing the importance of connections and networks in this new teaching paradigm has enabled educators to create a more dynamic and engaging learning experience for their students. As such, a hybrid learning environment combining traditional and modern approaches has become a popular choice in the academic community.

## Collaborative learning

Collaborative learning is a fundamental aspect of the Constructivist approach. This pedagogical method leverages the collective intelligence of groups to enhance learning outcomes by encouraging students to engage in dialogue, exchange perspectives, and discuss meanings.

**Flipped Classroom.** While the implementation of flipped classrooms, or the idea that direct instruction should happen asynchronously outside of the classroom, has been prevalent for many years, it has recently re-emerged as a promising pedagogical approach that integrates social interaction with online learning. The modern-day flipped classroom model is a powerful tool that enables collaborative learning, combining Constructivism and Connectivism. By flipping the traditional classroom dynamic, students can take charge of their learning, interact more frequently with their peers, and develop a deeper understanding of the subject matter.

As we navigate the new normal in education, more studies are expected to be conducted to better understand the efficacy of collaborative learning through the flipped classroom. However, repeated empirical studies dating back multiple decades have consistently shown that collaborative learning led to improved critical thinking skills, increased retention, and higher overall achievement (Johnson & Johnson, 1999a; Johnson & Johnson, 1999b; Gokhale, 1995).

**Problem-based Learning (PBL).** An effective way to enhance the learning experience is by integrating classroom discussions with practical applications of theoretical concepts to solve real-world problems. This approach can help students to better understand and retain the information they learn in class while also equipping them with the skills necessary to apply these concepts in everyday life.

PBL encourages students to engage in discussions and apply their knowledge to real scenarios. This approach is directly linked to Connectivism, which suggests that learning happens by connecting networks of information to solve real-world problems. By integrating the flipped classroom with Connectivism and PBL, students can leverage online connectivity to access a vast number of resources, develop a deeper understanding of the material, and apply it to real-life situations.

PBL actively involves students in the learning process, making education more engaging and applicable to real-world scenarios. By focusing on complex, real-world issues, PBL encourages students to research, collaborate, and employ critical thinking skills to devise solutions, mirroring the type of problem-solving they will encounter outside the academic setting. In addition, the interactive and participatory nature of PBL fosters greater cognitive retention and equips students with the skills necessary for lifelong learning in a digital world (Trullàs et al., 2022; NETP, 2024).

## Microlearning

Microlearning has emerged as a crucial strategy in online education, catering to the modern learner's need for concise, targeted, and flexible learning options. This approach breaks down complex information into bite-sized, manageable segments, making learning more digestible and less overwhelming for students navigating the vast information landscape online.

Microlearning modules can quickly address specific learning goals, fitting conveniently into students' increasingly fragmented schedules. They are particularly effective in maintaining engagement and improving retention (Kossen & Ooi, 2021; Shatte & Teague, 2020), as the brevity of content allows for rapid comprehension and frequent reinforcement. Additionally, microlearning is ideally suited for mobile learning, supporting the trend toward on-the-go education and just-in-time knowledge that is accessible across various devices.

Microlearning is a flexible and efficient way to incrementally build knowledge and skills, which can also be used as the background knowledge fueling the flipped classroom. This form of learning is expected to integrate increasingly with the blended learning methodology as mLearning becomes progressively more popular (Lee et al., 2021; Kohnke, 2021). This can only enhance its effectiveness and usefulness for learners across various domains.

## Adaptive Learning Technology

Adaptive learning is a modern approach to differentiated instruction that focuses on providing personalized learning journeys to students based on their interests, needs, and skills. The idea of personal learning journeys is not new. However, adaptive learning technology uses AI to generate a dynamic and customized learning environment utilizing technology to simplify the process.

Adaptive learning systems can identify each student's strengths and weaknesses and adjust the content and pace of their learning accordingly (Yang & Wen, 2023; Tatineni, 2020). Adaptive assessments can customize the learning experience to cater to the learner's unique needs, including the level and complexity of learning modules and practice activities given. This ensures that every student receives a tailored education rather than a one-size-fits-all approach.

To support personalized learning journeys, many LMSs incorporate a learning experience platform (LXP). Where LMSs are used to house and advertise content and then record content completion, the LXP ensures that the right level of content goes to the learner at the right time. Currently, LXPs are more common in the corporate learning environment; however, this platform for adaptive learning can easily be incorporated into primary and secondary schools to provide a system that responds to the learner's needs rather than solely pushing content in a one-size-fits-all model.

While studies are still underway to examine the impact of adaptive learning technologies on student success, currently, they have been found to help maintain student engagement and motivation (Xiaoyu & Tobias, 2023; Yakin & Linden, 2021; Liu et al., 2022).

## CONCLUSION

The COVID-19 pandemic has had a significant impact on education, forcing institutions to embrace technology at an unprecedented level. As a result, the intersection of technology and pedagogy in education is rapidly evolving and holds great promise for transforming how we approach and deliver learning. The pandemic catalyzed the development of newer educational models that favor flexible, student-centric approaches, and this shift has opened new opportunities to prepare students for the digital age, focusing on skills like digital literacy, critical thinking, and adaptability.

The closure of educational institutions, industries, and offices compelled individuals to confine themselves to their homes for prolonged periods, permanently altering how we learn, work, and connect. In learning, the pandemic forced parents to be teachers and teachers to upskill. While this abrupt shift to ERT was successful for some, it threw a spotlight on the need to advance teaching paradigms for others. Moreover, because the transition was rocky for some, studies persist on the learning lost during the pandemic.

Adopting a Connectivist mindset changes how we learn in today's interconnected world. With information readily available at our fingertips, a technology-driven approach to learning becomes essential, particularly considering the impact of the COVID-19 pandemic on students. As the world emerged from the pandemic, the educational system had undergone a significant and irreversible transformation.

New learning methodologies emphasizing flexibility and personalized learning show the potential for a more blended approach to education post-pandemic. While the pandemic showed resilience and adaptability in the educational community, it also informed a new era of learning in which the lessons learned from the past will inform future innovations.

## REFERENCES

Abuhassna, H., & Yahaya, N. (2018). Students' utilization of distance learning through an interventional online module based on Moore transactional distance theory. *Eurasia Journal of Mathematics, Science and Technology Education*, 14(7), 3043–3052. 10.29333/ejmste/91606

Ahmed, V., & Opoku, A. (2022). Technology supported learning and pedagogy in times of crisis: The case of COVID-19 pandemic. *Education and Information Technologies*, 27(1), 365–405. 10.1007/s10639-021-10706-w34462626

An, Y., Kaplan-Rakowski, R., Yang, J., Conan, J., Kinard, W., & Daughrity, L. (2021). Examining K-12 teachers' feelings, experiences, and perspectives regarding online teaching during the early stage of the COVID-19 pandemic. *Educational Technology Research and Development*, 69(5), 2589–2613. 10.1007/s11423-021-10008-534220171

Ancho, I. (2023). Parents as teachers as students: Managing multiple roles during the covid-19 pandemic. *International Journal of Instruction*, 16(3), 205–220. 10.29333/iji.2023.16312a

Association for Talent Development (ATD). (2017, April). *Microlearning: Delivering bite-sized knowledge*. ATD.

Baltà-Salvador, R., Olmedo-Torre, N., Peña, M., & Renta-Davids, A. I. (2021). Academic and emotional effects of online learning during the COVID-19 pandemic on engineering students. *Education and Information Technologies*, 26(6), 7407–7434. 10.1007/s10639-021-10593-134108843

Bamberg, M. (2012). Narrative analysis. In H. Cooper, P. M. Camic, D. L. Long, A. T. Panter, D. Rindskopf, & K. J. Sher (Eds.), *APA handbook of research methods in psychology, Vol. 2. Research designs: Quantitative, qualitative, neuropsychological, and biological* (pp. 85–102). American Psychological Association. 10.1037/13620-006

Bell, F. (2011). Connectivism: Its place in theory-informed research and innovation in technology-enabled learning. *International Review of Research in Open and Distance Learning*, 12(3), 98–118. 10.19173/irrodl.v12i3.902

Bennett, A. (2024). *For the first time, all states will have a plan to address digital equity*. National Telecommunications and Information Administration.

Benson, R., & Samarawickrema, G. (2009). Addressing the context of e-learning: Using transactional distance theory to inform design. *Distance Education*, 30(1), 5–21. 10.1080/01587910902845972

Bielski, Z. (2020). Social media awash with bragging about pandemic productivity. *The Globe and Mail.*

Bond, M. (2020). Facilitating student engagement through the flipped learning approach in K-12: A systematic review. *Computers & Education*, 151, 103819. 10.1016/j.compedu.2020.103819

Braff, D. (2020). The new helicopter parents are on Zoom. *New York Times.*

Bruner, J. (1991). The narrative construction of reality. *Critical Inquiry*, 18(1), 1–21. 10.1086/448619

Casey, D. M. (2008). A journey to legitimacy: The historical development of distance education through technology. *TechTrends*, 52(2), 45–51. 10.1007/s11528-008-0135-z

Cheng, L., Ritzhaupt, A. D., & Antonenko, P. (2019). Effects of the flipped classroom instructional strategy on students' learning outcomes: A meta-analysis. *Educational Technology Research and Development*, 67(4), 793–824. 10.1007/s11423-018-9633-7

Cohen, J., & Kupferschmidt, K. (2020). Countries test tactics in 'war' against COVID-19. *Science*, 367(6484), 1287–1288. 10.1126/science.367.6484.128732193299

Cole, M. (2017, March 23). *Just how micro is microlearning?* [blog post].

Cramarenco, R. E., Burcă-Voicu, M. I., & Dabija, D. C. (2023). Student perceptions of online education and digital technologies during the COVID-19 pandemic: A systematic review. *Electronics (Basel)*, 12(2), 319. 10.3390/electronics12020319

Crossley, M. (2000). *Introducing narrative psychology*. McGraw-Hill Education.

DeCoito, I., & Estaiteyeh, M. (2022). Transitioning to online teaching during the COVID-19 pandemic: An exploration of STEM teachers' views, successes, and challenges. *Journal of Science Education and Technology*, 31(3), 340–356. 10.1007/s10956-022-09958-z35369535

Donohue, J., & Miller, E. (2020). Covid-19 and school closures. *Journal of the American Medical Association*, 324(9), 845. 10.1001/jama.2020.1309232745182

Downes, S. (2006). E-learning 2.0. eLearning magazine: education and technology in perspective. *20*(2007), 29–1.

Edison, T. (n.d.). An exclusive interview with the master inventor. *The New York Dramatic Mirror.*

Education Week. (2020, April 6). Map: Coronavirus and School Closures. [blog post]. *Education Week.*

Foulger, T. S., Graziano, K. J., Schmidt-Crawford, D., & Slykhuis, D. A. (2017). Teacher educator technology competencies. *Journal of Technology and Teacher Education*, 25(4), 413–448.

Garbe, A., Ogurlu, U., Logan, N., & Cook, P. (2020). COVID-19 and remote learning: Experiences of parents with children during the pandemic. *American Journal of Qualitative Research*, 4(3), 45–65. 10.29333/ajqr/8471

Gokhale, A. A. (1995). Collaborative learning enhances critical thinking. *Journal of Technology Education*, 7(1), 22–30. 10.21061/jte.v7i1.a.2

Goldberg, S. B. (2021). *Education in a pandemic: The disparate impacts of COVID-19 on America's students*. Department of Education.

Gray, C., & Lewis, L. (2021, November 26). *Use of Educational Technology for Instruction in Public Schools: 2019–20*. U.S. Department of Education, NCES.

Hameed, S. & Macintyre, T. (2007). The effective use of multimedia tools in e-learning and computer aided learning environments within traditional university education. *International The Journal of Education (Knowledge),3*(1).

Harth, N. S., & Mitte, K. (2020). Managing multiple roles during the covid-19 lockdown: Not men or women, but parents as the emotional "loser in the crisis.". *Social Psychological Bulletin*, 15(4), 1–17. 10.32872/spb.4347

Harting, K., & Erthal, M. J. (2005). History of distance learning. *Information Technology, Learning and Performance Journal*, 23(1), 35.

Hodges, C. B., Moore, S., Lockee, B. B., Trust, T., & Bond, M. A. (2020). *The difference between emergency remote teaching and online learning.*

Hoffman, J., & Miller, E. (2020). Addressing the consequences of school closure due to covid-19 on children's physical and mental well-being. *World Medical & Health Policy*, 12(3), 300–310. *Advance online publication*. 10.1002/wmh3.36532904951

Holmberg, B. (1995). The evolution of the character and practice of distance education. *Open Learning*, 10(2), 47–53. 10.1080/0268051950100207

Hubackova, S. (2015). History and Perspectives of eLearning. *Procedia: Social and Behavioral Sciences*, 191, 1187–1190. 10.1016/j.sbspro.2015.04.594

Hug, T. (2007). *Didactics of microlearning*. Waxmann Publishing Company.

Irwin, V. (2021). *Students' internet access before and during the coronavirus pandemic by household socioeconomic status*. NCES.

Jaiswal, P., & Al-Hattami, A. (2020). Enhancing learners' academic performances using student centered approaches. [iJET]. *International Journal of Emerging Technologies in Learning*, 15(16), 4–16. 10.3991/ijet.v15i16.14875

Johnson, A. M., Jacovina, M. E., Russell, D. E., & Soto, C. M. (2016). Challenges and solutions when using technologies in the classroom. In Crossley, S. A., & McNamara, D. S. (2017). *Adaptive Educational Technologies for Literacy Instruction* (pp. 13 -29). Routledge. 10.4324/9781315647500-2

Johnson, D. W., & Johnson, R. T. (1999a). *What Makes Cooperative Learning Work*. Cooperative Learning.

Johnson, D. W., & Johnson, R. T. (1999b). Making cooperative learning work. *Theory into Practice*, 38(2), 67–73. 10.1080/00405849909543834

Kimmons, R., & Casjurlu, S. (Eds.). (2020). *The Students' Guide to Learning Design and Research*. EdTech Books. 10.59668/10

Klusmann, B., Trippenzee, M., Fokkens-Bruinsma, M., Sanderman, R., & Schroevers, M. J. (2022). Providing emergency remote teaching: What are teachers' needs and what could have helped them to deal with the impact of the COVID-19 pandemic? *Teaching and Teacher Education*, 118, 103815. 10.1016/j.tate.2022.10381535874644

Kohnke, L. (2021). Optimizing microlearning materials for mobile learning. In *Microlearning in the digital age* (pp. 80–94). Routledge. 10.4324/9780367821623-7

Kossen, C., & Ooi, C. Y. (2021). Trialing micro-learning design to increase engagement in online courses. *Asian Association of Open Universities Journal*, 16(3), 299–310. 10.1108/AAOUJ-09-2021-0107

Kumar, A., Krishnamurthi, R., Bhatia, S., Kaushik, K., Ahuja, N. J., Nayyar, A., & Masud, M. (2021). Blended learning tools and practices: A comprehensive analysis. *IEEE Access : Practical Innovations, Open Solutions*, 9, 85151–85197. 10.1109/ACCESS.2021.3085844

Lake, R., & Makori, A. (2020). *The digital divide among students during COVID-19: Who has access? Who doesn't?* Langreo, L. (2022). What Teachers Really Think about Their Learning Management Systems. *Education Week*.

Lee, Y. M., Jahnke, I., & Austin, L. (2021). Mobile microlearning design and effects on learning efficacy and learner experience. *Educational Technology Research and Development*, 69(2), 885–915. 10.1007/s11423-020-09931-w33584077

Lewin, C., & Luckin, R. (2010). Technology to support parental engagement: Lessons learned and future directions. *Computers & Education*, 54(3), 749–758. 10.1016/j.compedu.2009.08.010

Liberman, M. (2021, April 20). Most students now have home internet access. But what about the ones who don't? [blog post]. *Education Week*.

Liu, H. L., Wang, T. H., Lin, H. C. K., Lai, C. F., & Huang, Y. M. (2022). The influence of affective feedback adaptive learning system on learning engagement and self-directed learning. *Frontiers in Psychology*, 13, 858411. 10.3389/fpsyg.2022.85841135572271

Lockee, B. B. (2021). Online education in the post-COVID era. *Nature Electronics*, 4(1), 5–6. 10.1038/s41928-020-00534-0

Mackness, J., Mak, S., & Williams, R. (2010). The ideals and reality of participating in a MOOC. In *Proceedings of the 7th international conference on networked learning 2010*. University of Lancaster.

Mayer, R. E. (2002). Multimedia learning. In *Psychology of learning and motivation* (Vol. 41, pp. 85–139). Academic Press. 10.1016/S0079-7421(02)80005-6

McClain, C., Vogels, E., Perrin. A., Sechopoulos, S., & Rainie, Lee (2021, September 1). *The internet and the pandemic*. Pew Research Center: Internet & Technology.

Means, B., Toyama, Y., Murphy, R., & Baki, M. (2013). The effectiveness of online and blended learning: A meta-analysis of the empirical literature. *Teachers College Record*, 115(3), 1–47. https://psycnet.apa.org/doi/10.1177/016146811311500307. 10.1177/016146811311500307

Michelson, R., DeWitt, A., Nagar, R., Hiniker, A., Yip, J., Munson, S. A., & Kientz, J. A. (2021). Parenting in a pandemic: juggling multiple roles and managing technology use in family life during COVID-19 in the United States. *Proceedings of the ACM on Human-Computer Interaction, 5*(CSCW2), (pp. 1-39). ACM. 10.1145/3479546

Moore, M. G. (1989). Editorial: Three types of interaction. *The American Journal of Distance Learning*, 3(2), 1–7.

Mossberger, K., Tolbert, C. J., & Stansbury, M. (2003). *Virtual inequality: Beyond the digital divide*. Georgetown University Press.

Muniandy, T., & Abdullah, N. (2023). A comprehensive review: An innovative pedagogy for future education. [IJOPCD]. *International Journal of Online Pedagogy and Course Design*, 13(1), 1–15. 10.4018/IJOPCD.315816

Nagel, D. (2009). *Meta-analysis: Is blended learning most effective?* The Journal.

National Academies of Sciences, Engineering, and Medicine (NASEM). (2019). *Monitoring Educational Equity*. Washington, DC: The National Academies Press.

National Center for Education Statistics (NCES). (2021). *Summary report: Students' internet access before and during the coronavirus pandemic by household socioeconomic status*. U.S. Department of Education.

National Center for Education Statistics (NCES). (2022a). *Impact of the coronavirus pandemic on the elementary and secondary education system. Condition of Education*. U.S. Department of Education, Institute of Education Sciences.

National Center for Education Statistics (NCES). (2022b). *Impact of the coronavirus (COVID-19) pandemic on public and private elementary and secondary education in the United States (Preliminary Data): Results from the 2020-21 National Teacher and Principal Survey*. NTPS.

National Center for Education Statistics (NCES). (2023). *Children's internet access at home. Condition of Education*. U.S. Department of Education, Institute of Education Sciences.

National Education Technology Plan (NETP). (2017). *Reimagining the role of technology in education*. U.S. Department of Education, Office of Educational Technology.

Nipper, S. (1989). Third generation distance learning and computer conferencing. *Mindweave: Communication, Computers and Distance Education*, 63-73.

Osnes, P. G., & Adelinis, J. (2005). Correspondence training, rule governance, generalization, and stimulus control: Connections or disconnections? *Behavioral Development Bulletin*, 12(1), 48–54. 10.1037/h0100560

Palak, D., & Walls, R. (2009). Teachers' beliefs and technology practices: A mixed-methods approach. *Journal of Research on Technology in Education*, 41(4), 417–441. 10.1080/15391523.2009.10782537

Pappas, Christopher. (2023, May 1). *Everything you need to know about connectivism learning theory*. eLearning Industry. [blog post]

Pastore, R. (2016, March). Multimedia: Learner preferences for multimedia learning. In *Society for Information Technology & Teacher Education International Conference* (pp. 3015–3022).

Pew Charitable Trusts. (2020). *How states Are expanding broadband access*. Pew Research.

Pew Research Center. (2021, September 1). *The internet and the pandemic*. Pew Research.

Povey, J., Campbell, A. K., Willis, L. D., Haynes, M., Western, M., Bennett, S., Antrobus, E., & Pedde, C. (2016). Engaging parents in schools and building parent-school partnerships: The role of school and parent organisation leadership. *International Journal of Educational Research*, 79, 128–141. 10.1016/j.ijer.2016.07.005

Pressley, T., & Ha, C. (2021). Teaching during a pandemic: United States teachers' self-efficacy during COVID-19. *Teaching and Teacher Education*, 106, 103465. 10.1016/j.tate.2021.10346534754135

Prothero, A. (2021). Pandemic fuels tech advances in schools – Here's what that looks like. *Education Week*.

Rapanta, C., Botturi, L., Goodyear, P., Guàrdia, L., & Koole, M. (2021). Balancing technology, pedagogy and the new normal: Post-pandemic challenges for higher education. *Postdigital Science and Education*, 3(3), 715–742. 10.1007/s42438-021-00249-1

Saba, F. (2011). Distance education in the United States: Past, present, future. *Educational Technology*, 11–18.

Saettler, P. (2004). *The evolution of American educational technology*. IAP.

Sangrà, A., Vlachopoulos, D., & Cabrera, N. (2012). Building an inclusive definition of e-learning: An approach to the conceptual framework. *International Review of Research in Open and Distance Learning*, 13(2), 145–159. 10.19173/irrodl.v13i2.1161

Scherer, R., Howard, S. K., Tondeur, J., & Siddiq, F. (2021). Profiling teachers' readiness for online teaching and learning in higher education: Who's ready? *Computers in Human Behavior*, 118, 106675. 10.1016/j.chb.2020.106675

Schunk, D. H. (2012). *Learning theories an educational perspective*. Pearson Education, Inc.

Common Sense. (2021). 2021 Annual Report. *Common Sense Media Report*.

Shatte, A. B. R., & Teague, S. (2020, July 14). Microlearning for improved student outcomes in higher education: A scoping review. 10.31219/osf.io/fhu8n

Shaw, P. A., & Shaw, A. (2023). COVID-19 and remote learning: Experiences of parents supporting children with special needs and disability during the pandemic. *Education 3-13, 51*(3), 371–385. 10.1080/03004279.2021.1960579

Siemens, G. (2004). Connectivism: A learning theory for the digital age.

Siemens, G. (2006) *Knowing knowledge.*

Smith, F. J. (1913). The evolution of the motion picture. *The New York Dramatic Mirror, 9.*

Soubra, L., Al-Ghouti, M. A., Abu-Dieyeh, M., Crovella, S., & Abou-Saleh, H. (2022). Impacts on student learning and skills and implementation challenges of two student-centered learning methods applied in online education. *Sustainability (Basel)*, 14(15), 9625. 10.3390/su14159625

Statista. (n.d.). Average number of EDTech tools used per K-12 district in the U.S. in the 2022 – 23 school year.

Tatineni, S. (2020). Recommendation Systems for Personalized Learning: A Data-Driven Approach in Education. [JCET]. *Journal of Computer Engineering and Technology*, 4(2).

Taylor, J. C. (1995). Distance education technologies: The fourth generation. *Australasian Journal of Educational Technology*, 11(2). Advance online publication. 10.14742/ajet.2072

Tokatly Latzer, I., Leitner, Y., & Karnieli-Miller, O. (2021). Core experiences of parents of children with autism during the COVID-19 pandemic lockdown. *Autism*, 25(4), 1047–1059. 10.1177/136236132098431733435701

Topping, K. J., Douglas, W., Robertson, D., & Ferguson, N. (2022). Effectiveness of online and blended learning from schools: A systematic review. *Review of Education*, 10(2), e3353. 10.1002/rev3.3353

Trullàs, J. C., Blay, C., Sarri, E., & Pujol, R. (2022). Effectiveness of problem-based learning methodology in undergraduate medical education: A scoping review. *BMC Medical Education*, 22(1), 104. 10.1186/s12909-022-03154-835177063

Turnbull, D., Chugh, R., & Luck, J. (2021). Transitioning to E-Learning during the COVID-19 pandemic: How have Higher Education Institutions responded to the challenge? *Education and Information Technologies*, 26(5), 6401–6419. 10.1007/s10639-021-10633-w34177349

U.S. Census Bureau. (2020). *Household Pulse Survey*. U.S. Census Bureau.

U.S. Department of Education [USDOE]. (2017). *Reimagining the role of technology in education: 2017 National Educational Technology Plan update*. U.S. Department of Education, Office of Educational Technology.

Vallée, A., Blacher, J., Cariou, A., & Sorbets, E. (2020). Blended learning compared to traditional learning in medical education: Systematic review and meta-analysis. *Journal of Medical Internet Research*, 22(8), e16504. 10.2196/1650432773378

Van Alten, D. C., Phielix, C., Janssen, J., & Kester, L. (2019). Effects of flipping the classroom on learning outcomes and satisfaction: A meta-analysis. *Educational Research Review*, 28, 100281. 10.1016/j.edurev.2019.05.003

Watson, J. B. (1913). Psychology as the behaviorist views it. *Psychological Review*, 20(2), 158–177. 10.1037/h0074428

Whalen, J. (2020). Should teachers be trained in emergency remote teaching? Lessons learned from the COVID-19 pandemic. *Journal of Technology and Teacher Education*, 28(2), 189–199.

Xiaoyu, Z., & Tobias, T. (2023). Exploring the Efficacy of Adaptive Learning Technologies in Online Education: A Longitudinal Analysis of Student Engagement and Performance. [IJSEA]. *International Journal of Software Engineering and Its Applications*, 12(12), 28–31. 10.7753/IJSEA1212.1007

Yakin, M., & Linden, K. (2021). Adaptive e-learning platforms can improve student performance and engagement in dental education. *Journal of Dental Education*, 85(7), 1309–1315. 10.1002/jdd.1260933825184

Yang, M., & Wen, F. (2023). AI-Powered Personalized Learning Journeys: Revolutionizing Information Management for College Students in Online Platforms. *Journal of Information Systems Engineering & Management*, 8(1), 23196. 10.55267/iadt.07.14079

# Chapter 3 Educational Paradigm Shift: Embracing Modern Technologies in the Post-COVID-19 Era

**Harsh Vardhan Pant**
https://orcid.org/0000-0003-1295-5966
*COER University, Roorkee, India*

**Manoj Chandra Lohani**
https://orcid.org/0000-0002-3017-164X
*Graphic Era University, India*

**Jeetendra Pande**
https://orcid.org/0000-0003-1750-0231
*Uttarakhand Open University, India*

## ABSTRACT

*The pandemic spanning from 2020 to 2022 has brought about various impacts on society. Post this Covid era,, significant transformations have been witnessed in multiple sectors, including business and education. Throughout the COVID pandemic from 2020 to 2022, an observable shift occurred in the education system, moving away from its conventional distribution to embracing modern technologies. Grasping and applying these innovative technologies presented a challenge for both educators and students alike. For a software engineer, adapting the understanding of traditional educational distribution to a computerized format was indeed a formidable task. This period saw the introduction of numerous software technologies in the market. In this section, we will delve into these technologies and endeavor to discern whether they have demonstrated their effectiveness in the classroom. This*

DOI: 10.4018/979-8-3693-7645-4.ch003

*chapter is also find out the answer of a pivotal question to explore is whether these technologies can be seamlessly incorporated into traditional classroom settings.*

## INTRODUCTION

The COVID-19 pandemic has reshaped virtually every aspect of our lives, and education is no exception. As schools and universities grappled with lockdowns and social distancing measures, a rapid shift towards digital learning became imperative. This transition not only highlighted the resilience of educational systems but also underscored the potential of modern technologies in shaping the future of learning.

Reflecting on my personal experience during the pandemic, I witnessed first-hand the challenges and opportunities presented by this educational paradigm shift. As classrooms migrated to virtual platforms and online resources became indispensable, it became evident that embracing modern technologies was no longer a choice but a necessity.

This introduction seeks to delve into the rapid shift observed within the education industry towards digital platforms during and post the pandemic. Furthermore, it aims to explore the anticipated evolution of the online education sector, specifically focusing on the adoption of hybrid learning models in the aftermath of the pandemic.

Through this exploration, we will endeavor to uncover innovative strategies, address existing challenges, and pave the way for a more inclusive, adaptive, and technologically-driven approach to education in the post-COVID era.

Ultimately the objectives of this chapter in this unit are as follows:

a) To grasp the sudden move of the education industry toward digital platforms during and after the pandemic.
b) To explore the prospective future evolution of the online education sector after the pandemic regarding the adoption of hybrid learning.

## LITERATURE REVIEW

The educational landscape has undergone a transformative shift post the COVID-19 era, with a significant focus on integrating modern technologies into pedagogical practices. This shift represents a fundamental change, altering traditional classroom dynamics and embracing innovative digital tools and platforms. The literature review delves into various aspects of this educational transformation, examining its theoretical underpinnings and practical implications.

## Key Themes

i. **Virtual Learning Environments**: Institutions worldwide, including Harvard in Boston, Massachusetts, have embraced Massive Open Online Courses (MOOCs) as a means to extend education digitally. This shift has been facilitated by top-tier schools and companies like Apple offering free course creation tools through platforms like iTunesU (Siemens, 2012).
ii. **Indian Education Landscape**: India, with a population exceeding 1.3 billion, is witnessing a surge in demand for higher education. The New Education Policy (NEP) 2020 recognizes the potential of MOOCs and online learning in revolutionizing the Indian education system (Selwyn, Hillman, Eynon, & Gisell, 2020).
iii. **Challenges and Opportunities**: Despite the benefits, MOOC platforms face challenges such as low retention rates among learners. However, unexplored factors like content localization, credit mobility, and course impact present opportunities for enhancing the effectiveness of MOOC systems (Khan, 2017).
iv. **Technological Integration**: The integration of innovative technologies like Artificial Intelligence (AI) and digital platforms into education is a focal point. Studies highlight the significance of AI in addressing educational challenges and creating new learning opportunities (Mishra & Gupta, 2021).
v. **Global Perspectives**: The digital divide, post-COVID recovery strategies, and challenges in teaching during the pandemic are discussed globally. UNESCO's initiatives and scholarly discussions shed light on the transition from educational disruption to recovery (UNESCO, 2020).

## RESEARCH METHODOLOGY

Online learning has played a crucial role in addressing the skills gap prevalent in education sectors (Pant, Lohani, & Pande, 2021). Given the swift pace of technological advancements, employers are facing growing challenges in locating adequately skilled workers capable of fulfilling the requirements of the job market (siddique, 2023). Can these technologies effectively continue to be utilized in conjunction with traditional classroom settings? To get the answer for this question authors have done the following procedure and methodology:

*Figure 1. Illustrates the flowchart of current research methods and steps*

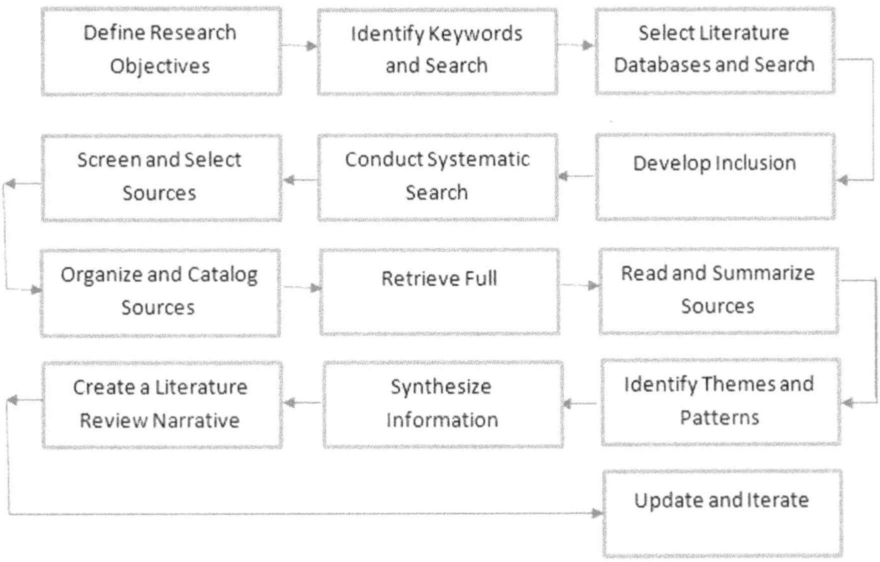


Content analysis is a research method used to systematically analyze and interpret the content of textual, visual, or audio material. This method is widely employed in various disciplines, including communication studies, sociology, psychology, and marketing (Mariette, 2016). Hence research has used the content analysis and choose the data as secondary data from various journals of literatures and business magazines. The whole steps can be understanding from the above flow chart (Figure 1).

a. **Define the Research Objectives:** Understanding the swift transition of the education sector to digital platforms during and post-pandemic. Investigating the potential future developments in online education post-pandemic, particularly regarding the integration of hybrid learning methods. These are the specific goals or purposes of a research study.
b. **Identify Keywords:** Keywords are terms or phrases that are used to conduct searches in literature databases to find relevant sources. After following the strategy suggested by (Kitchenham, 2005), the following search keywords were identified:

- *The Impact of Virtual Learning Environments on Education Post-COVID.*
- *Digital Transformation in Education: Leveraging Technology for Enhanced Learning.*

- *Adapting Curriculum Design for Online and Hybrid Learning Models in the Post-COVID Era.*
- *The Role of Artificial Intelligence and Machine Learning in Revolutionizing Education.*
- *Augmented Reality and Virtual Reality Applications in Modern Education.*
- *Online Assessment Tools and Strategies for Effective Evaluation in Remote Learning.*

c. **Select Literature Database:** The current research has find out a collection of scholarly articles, books, journals related to the current research from the academic database like IEEE xplore, Elsevier's Science Direct, Wiley Online Library, Springer Link and Scopus.

d. **Develop Inclusion Criteria:** Online Academic performance, Parental consent, course type, satisfaction level are the inclusion criteria in the current research.

e. **Conduct Systematic Search:** This involves using selected keywords and inclusion criteria to systematically search literature databases for relevant sources. The current researcher use Elicit, the AI research assistant and use search operators, filters, and advanced search techniques to refine their search results.

f. **Screen and Select Sources:** After conducting the search, researchers screen the search results to identify potentially relevant sources.

g. **Organize and Catalog Sources:** Once sources are selected, the researchers organize and catalog them for easy reference and retrieval.

h. **Retrieve Full Text:** Researchers retrieve the full text of selected sources to thoroughly review and analyze the content.

i. **Read and Summarize Sources:** Researchers read and summarize the key findings, methodologies, and arguments of each selected source.

j. **Identify Themes and Patterns:** Through careful analysis of the summarized sources, the researchers identify common themes, patterns, trends, or gaps in the literature related to their research objectives. This step finds the following themes like: Virtual Learning Environments, Indian Education Landscape, Challenges and Opportunities, Technological Integration, Global Perspectives

k. **Synthesize Information:** Researchers synthesize the information gathered from the literature review to develop a coherent narrative or discussion.

l. **Create Literature Review Narrative:** The literature review narrative is a structured and organized presentation of the synthesized information.

m. **Update and Iterate:** Literature reviews are dynamic and iterative processes. Researchers continuously update and refine their literature review based on new findings, feedback, and insights gained during the research process.

Overall, it has enabled the current researchers to uncover meaningful patterns, gain new perspectives, and generate valuable insights relevant to their research objectives. These valuable insights are described in the data analysis part.

## DATA ANALYSIS

Researchers have effectively analysed the educational paradigm shift and the integration of modern technologies in the post-COVID educational landscape by following the aforementioned steps and employing suitable data analysis tools and techniques. The analysis revealed several significant aspects, which can be categorized into three main categories as explained in sections 4.1, 4.2, and 4.3.

### The Education Industry Toward Digital Platforms During and After the Pandemic

During the pandemic, the sudden shift to remote learning compelled many teachers to adopt and adapt to new technologies that they might not have used extensively before (Kyungmee, Mik, Brett, & Xuefei, 2022). Here's a closer look at these technologies:

- **Virtual Classroom Platforms:** Facilitated real-time interaction between teachers and students, offering a virtual space for lectures, discussions, and collaboration.
- **Video Conferencing Tools:** Enabled synchronous communication, allowing teachers to conduct live classes, engage with students, and promote interactive learning.
- **Learning Management Systems (LMS):** Managed and organized educational content, assignments, assessments, and provided a centralized platform for students and teachers to access resources.
- **Online Collaboration Tools:** Supported group projects and collaborative learning experiences, fostering student engagement and teamwork in a virtual environment.
- **Adaptive Learning Technologies:** Personalized learning experiences by adjusting the difficulty level of content based on individual student performance, enhancing the effectiveness of learning.
- **Educational Apps:** Offered supplementary resources, interactive content, and gamified learning experiences, making education more engaging and accessible.

- **Cloud-Based Platforms:** Facilitated easy storage, sharing, and access to educational materials, ensuring seamless collaboration and content availability from any location.

This sudden adoption of new technologies, driven by the necessity of remote learning, challenged educators to quickly learn and integrate these tools into their teaching methods (Li, 2022). While it presented initial challenges, it also opened up new possibilities for more flexible and innovative approaches to education. Teachers found creative ways to use these technologies to enhance student engagement, collaboration, and overall learning experiences.

## Unveiling the Significance of Technologies Embraced During the Pandemic

The value of the technologies adopted during the pandemic, including virtual classrooms, videoconferencing, and social media, can be demonstrated through several key aspects:

- **Continuity of Education:** These technologies allowed for the seamless continuation of education during challenging times. Virtual classrooms and videoconferencing enabled educators to deliver lectures, conduct discussions, and engage with students, ensuring minimal disruption to the learning process.
- **Accessibility:** Remote learning technologies increased accessibility to education. Students could participate in classes from the safety of their homes, overcoming geographical barriers. Virtual classrooms made education accessible to those who might face challenges attending in-person classes.
- **Flexibility:** The adoption of these technologies introduced a more flexible learning environment. Recorded virtual classes allowed students to review lectures at their own pace, catering to diverse learning styles. This flexibility accommodated students with varied schedules and time zones.
- **Interactive Learning:** Videoconferencing and virtual classrooms facilitated interactive learning experiences. Features like live chats, polls, and breakout sessions encouraged student participation, making the learning process more engaging and collaborative (Mark Anthony & Adriana Caterina, 2022).
- **Community Building:** Social media platforms played a crucial role in community building. Teachers and students could connect beyond formal class hours, fostering a sense of community and support. Social media also provided a space for sharing additional resources and facilitating peer-to-peer communication.

- **Professional Development:** The adoption of new technologies necessitated educators to upskill and adapt to changing teaching methodologies. This unintentional professional development equipped teachers with valuable digital skills that can continue to benefit education in the long run.
- **Innovation in Teaching:** The shift to virtual environments encouraged innovation in teaching methods. Educators explored creative ways to use technology for assessments, collaborative projects, and engaging activities, enhancing the overall educational experience.

While the initial adoption might have been prompted by necessity, the lasting value lies in the transformation of education methodologies, increased accessibility, and the development of a more adaptable and technology-integrated educational landscape. The significance of online education and the enumerated benefits were scrutinized and acknowledged by learners and governments across numerous countries during the pandemic. Subsequently, the education sector witnessed a sudden transformation towards digital platforms, leading to a rapid surge in the online education market, particularly in countries like India and China.

## Data Analysis and Interpretation to Explore the Prospective Future Evolution of the Online Education Sector

Exploring the prospective future evolution of the online education sector the current researchers has analysed the current trends, technologies, and practices to anticipate how the field may develop in the coming years. There are following valuable results after analysing prospective future of the online education sector:

*Table 1. Popular website centric ed-tech platforms statistics (Data as per Oct. 2023)*

| Indian Platform | | United States | | Chinese Platform | |
|---|---|---|---|---|---|
| **Major Traffic Country** | **Traffic in Million** | **Major Traffic Country** | **Traffic in Million** | **Major Traffic Country** | **Traffic in Million** |
| BYJU's | 60-70 M | KhanAcademy | 45-55 M | iCourse | 60-70 M |
| Vedantu | 5-3 M | Study | 25-30 M | xuetangx | 12-20 M |
| Udemy | 10-18 M | Duolingo | 12-18 M | Zhihuishu | 10-28 M |
| Unacademy | 0.5 M | Coursera | 8-12 M | UOOC | 8-13 M |
| Adda247 | 2-3 M | Instructables | 8-12 M | CNMOOC | 2-5 M |

India, the United States, and China play crucial roles in the realm of online education. China and India are also the most populous and the youngest nations in the world where all the benefits of online education can be availed. Applications of online education platforms like BYJU's, Duolingo, and Icourse have been downloaded and utilized by millions of people, as confirmed by the figures presented in Tables 1 and 2 above. When researchers analysed the web traffic of some popular online education platforms of these countries between November and December 2023, certain facts came to light. These figures are enough to prove that even after COVID, millions of learners are taking help to online education and these technologies have proven themselves in the classroom. Although traditional regular classes have already started after COVID, but it has been observing that still Online learning technologies are helping continue to be used effectively in combination with the traditional classroom. Understanding the significance of online education, the University Grants Commission (UGC) has permitted universities and colleges to offer a maximum of 40 percent of the syllabus of a program in a semester online through the government's e-learning platform "Study Webs of Active-Learning for Young Aspiring Minds (SWAYAM)".

*Table 2. Popular app centric ed-tech platforms eLearning*

| Indian Platform | | United States | | Chinese Platform | |
|---|---|---|---|---|---|
| **Major Traffic Country** | **No. Of Users** | **Major Traffic Country** | **No. Of Users** | **Major Traffic Country** | **No. Of Users** |
| BYJU's | 100M | KhanAcademy | 10 M | iCourse | 500 M |
| Vedantu | 10 M | Study | 5 M | xuetangx | 100 M |
| Udemy | 10 M | Duolingo | 500 M | Zhihuishu | 3M |
| Unacademy | 1 M | Coursera | 10 M | UOOC | 1M |
| Adda247 | 10 M | Instructables | - | Chinese University MOOC | 10M |

*Figure 2. Illustrates the trend of students towards online education from 2017 to 2023*

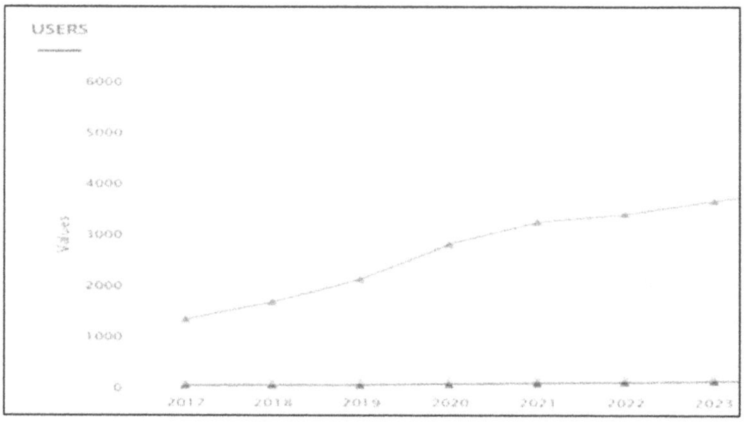

## Results After Analysis to Explore the Prospective Future Evolution of the Online Education Sector

- The United States, India, and China are the leading country in the Global eLearning Industry. The eLearning market is anticipated to experience a Compound Annual Growth Rate (CAGR) of 14.22% from 2022 to 2027 (Mritunjay, Sreedhar, Akhilesh, Narayanan, & Nitin, 2017).
- The popularity of online education has risen steadily because it provides learners with the flexibility to access courses and programs from any location and at any time.
- Online learning has made a substantial impact on the job market by offering individuals new opportunities to enhance their skills and knowledge. This, in turn, makes them more competitive and appealing to employers. The global online education market is projected to reach a value of USD 247.46 billion by 2024, with the Asia-Pacific (APAC) region expected to offer the most significant opportunities for revenue generation (Morris, Ivancheva, & Coop, 2020).
- Approximately 70% of the global e-learning services market users are anticipated to see a 200% surge in the market between 2020 and 2025, as per (Steve, 2023).
- Distance learning uses 90% less energy and 85% fewer CO2 emissions per student compared to campus-based learning (Dr. Sally, 2023)
- The corporate e-learning sector is projected to reach an estimated value of nearly $50 billion by 2026, as reported by Business Wire.
- "According to the National Curriculum Framework for School Education 2023," students can be encouraged to access relevant digital content and connect with it, complementing their textbook materials (NCERT, 2023).
- As Tao, the Vice President of Tencent Cloud and Vice President of Tencent Education, posited, "the integration of information technology in education will be further accelerated and that online education will eventually become an integral component of school education." (Li & Lalani, 2020).
- Despite the advantages of online learning, including flexibility and accessibility, there is a concern that it may not be as successful in keeping students engaged compared to traditional classroom settings. One of the primary challenges faced in online learning is the retention of student engagement.

## CONCLUSION

Online education has traditionally been viewed as an alternative pathway, one that is particularly well suited to adult learners seeking higher education opportunities. The advent of new learning platforms and delivery methods has ushered in fresh competition and opportunities for educational institutions. Traditional learning institutions, in response, have had to navigate the evolving digital educational landscape by investing in new technologies, infrastructure, and fostering innovation to stay relevant. Despite introducing challenges related to quality control and accreditation, online education has presented institutions with novel avenues to broaden their reach and impact. In essence, online education has left a profound mark on traditional learning institutions, and its influence is expected to continue growing in the years ahead. Nevertheless, there is no entirely equivalent alternative to in-person (classroom) teaching and learning. This has led us to the era of hybrid teaching and learning, where a combination of online and offline systems is incorporated to augment outcomes. This integration might be envisioned as a result of the implementation of Education 4.0.

## REFERENCES


Khan, B. (2017). Massive open online course (MOOC) evaluation methods: An overview. *Educational Technology Research and Development*, 65(5), 263–1287.

Kitchenham, B. (2005). *Procedures for Performing Systematic Reviews*. Keele University.

Kyungmee, L., Mik, F., Brett, B., & Xuefei, S. L. (2022). Adoption of online teaching during the COVID-19 Pandemic: A systematic analysis of changes in university teaching activity. *Educational Review*, 74(3), 460–483. 10.1080/00131911.2021.1978401

Li, D. (2022). *The Shift to Online Classes During the Covid-19 Pandemic: Benefits, Challenges, and Required Improvements from the Students' Perspective*. The Electronic Journal of e-Learning Volume.

Mariette, B. (2016). How to plan and perform a qualitative study using content analysis. *NursingPlus Open*, 2, 8–16. 10.1016/j.npls.2016.01.001

Mark Anthony, C., & Adriana Caterina, C. (2022). Remote learning via video conferencing technologies: Implications for research and practice. *Technology in Society*, 68, 101881. 10.1016/j.techsoc.2022.10188135034998

Mishra, L., & Gupta, T. (2021). Artificial Intelligence in Education: Challenges and Opportunities. *International Journal of Emerging Technologies in Learning*, 16(2), 64–78.

Morris, N., Ivancheva, M., Coop, T., Mogliacci, R., & Swinnerton, B. (2020). Negotiating growth of online education in higher education. *International Journal of Educational Technology in Higher Education*, 17(48), 48. 10.1186/s41239-020-00227-w

Mritunjay, K., Sreedhar, P., Akhilesh, T., Narayanan, R., & Nitin, B. (2017). *Online Education in India 2021, A Market Analysis of Online Education*. KGMPG International.

NCERT. (2023). *National Curriculum Framework for School Education*. NCERT. https://www.education.gov.in/sites/upload_files/mhrd/files/infocus_slider/NCF-School-Education-Pre-Draft.pdf

Pant, H., Lohani, M., & Pande, J. (2021). MOOCs in Higher Education: Current Trends in India and Developed Countries. In Rahman, H. (Ed.), *Ubiquitous Technologies for Human Development and Knowledge Management*. IGI Global., 10.4018/978-1-7998-7844-5.ch004

Sally, C. (2023, 12 15). *The environmental impact of teaching and learning*. Retrieved from www.open.edu: https://www.open.edu/openlearn/mod/oucontent/view.php?id=13707&printable=1

Selwyn, N., Hillman, T., Eynon, R., Ferreira, G., Knox, J., Macgilchrist, F., & Sancho-Gil, J. M. (2020). What's next for Ed-Tech? Critical hopes and concerns for the 2020s. *Learning, Media and Technology*, 45(1), 1–6. 10.1080/17439884.2020.1694945

Siddique, a. (2023). The rise of online education and its impact on traditional learning institutions. *The times of Inda*. https://timesofindia.indiatimes.com/readersblog/ecommercetrends/the-rise-of-online-education-and-its-impact-on-traditional-learning-institutions-52621/

Siemens, G. (2012). MOOCs: The tsunami of educational innovation. *elearnspace*.

Steve, B. (2023, 12 07). *Digital Learning Platforms Statistics 2023 – Everything You Need to Know*. Webinarcare. https://webinarcare.com/best-digital-learning-platforms/digital-learning-platforms-statistics/

UNESCO. (2020). *Education: From Disruption to Recovery*. UNESCO Institute for Statistics. https://en.unesco.org/covid19/educationresponse

# Chapter 4
# Post-Pandemic Pedagogy:
## Adapting, Unlearning, and Designing for Online Success

**Steven D'Agustino**
http://orcid.org/0009-0008-4735-9922
*Fordham University, USA*

## ABSTRACT

*This chapter examines the sudden transition to emergency remote teaching (ERT) necessitated by the COVID-19 pandemic, underscoring the challenges, assumptions, and misconceptions surrounding digital education. The piece critically examines the pedagogical shifts that occurred, highlighting the imperative for educators and institutions to unlearn outdated notions of online learning and adapt evidence-based practices. By drawing upon various studies and expert opinions, the chapter addresses the pedagogical, technological, and organizational hurdles faced during the rapid pivot to ERT, while advocating for a strategic approach to online education that emphasizes pedagogical integrity, accessibility, equity, and institutional support. It proposes a reevaluation of digital learning strategies to leverage the full potential of online education, ensuring it is inclusive, effective, and tailored to meet the diverse needs of the student population, positing a future where higher education can transcend emergency measures to embrace a holistic and enriched digital learning environment.*

DOI: 10.4018/979-8-3693-7645-4.ch004

## INTRODUCTION

In the transformative wake of the COVID-19 pandemic, the academic landscape has undergone a seismic shift, propelling higher education institutions into a largely unanticipated and, in many cases, unprepared era of digital transformation. Digital transformation in higher education has accelerated significantly due to the COVID-19 pandemic, presenting both challenges and opportunities for institutions worldwide (García-Morales et al., 2021; Nurhas et al., 2021; Weerawardane, 2021). The need for resilience and adaptability in higher education institutions to manage post-pandemic uncertainties has been emphasized, advocating for robust frameworks that support continuous improvement and flexibility (Rasli et al., 2022). Moreover, the complexities and challenges of rapid digital transformation highlight the necessity of a solid technological infrastructure and the readiness of faculty to adapt to new digital tools and methodologies (Arnold et al., 2021; Coral & Bernuy, 2022; Mospan, 2022; Rogozin et al., 2022).

The sudden and essential pivot to Emergency Remote Teaching (ERT) not only highlighted the crucial role of online education but also exposed an array of assumptions, challenges, and misconceptions about digital learning methodologies. This article aims to dissect and analyze the multifaceted impact of this abrupt transition to ERT on higher education, focusing particularly on pedagogical approaches, equity issues and faculty development needs.

Moore and Hodges (2023) define ERT as "a temporary shift of instructional delivery to an alternate delivery mode due to crisis circumstances," distinguishing it from online learning and education in emergencies. This definition sets the stage for understanding the unique nature and context of ERT, separate from premeditated, effectively designed online courses. The pandemic-induced shift to ERT, while crucial for maintaining educational continuity, unveiled significant gaps in the online learning ecosystem, spanning from pedagogical inadequacies to technological barriers. Moreover, Al Shlowiy et al.,(2021) highlight the unanticipated shift to virtual learning environments due to emergencies, emphasizing the challenges of teacher-student miscommunication in ERT. This underscores the importance of understanding and addressing the discrepancies between the concerns of teachers and those of students to enhance the effectiveness of ERT. Ng (2021) discusses the challenges posed by ERT and recommends strategies for engaging students despite the abrupt transition. The focus on promoting student engagement, despite the rapid move to online platforms, is pivotal in overcoming the pedagogical challenges highlighted by the emergency response to COVID-19. Erdem-Aydin (2021) uses the socio-ecological model to understand instructors' perspectives towards ERT, suggesting it as a temporary measure expected to revert back to face-to-face classrooms. This perspective provides insight into the pedagogical adjustments and expectations of educators during the pandemic.

Maldonado and Dzul Maldonado (2022) evaluate the implementation of ERT in medical education during COVID-19, discussing satisfaction with digital resources and educational inter-modality. This evaluation contributes to understanding the specific impacts of ERT on medical education and the broader implications for pedagogical strategies in emergency situations.

As we begin this comprehensive examination of the post-pandemic pedagogical landscape, it becomes essential to acknowledge the broader implications of these insights for higher education. The lessons learned from this period of unprecedented disruption offer a unique opportunity to reimagine and reshape the future of education. By addressing the pedagogical shortcomings of ERT, overcoming the inertia of satisficing solutions, and harnessing the full potential of online learning, institutions can enrich the educational experience for all stakeholders in the digital age. This critical examination offers a pathway to not only address the immediate exigencies brought about by the pandemic but also to lay the groundwork for sustainable, inclusive, and pedagogically sound digital learning environments.

## Post-Pandemic Teaching and Learning in Higher Education

The COVID-19 pandemic has profoundly reshaped the landscape of higher education, prompting a significant shift towards online and hybrid learning models. This transformation, initially driven by necessity, has catalyzed persistent changes that are likely to define the future of higher education. One of the most notable changes is the adoption of hybrid or blended learning models. The shift towards online and distance learning during the pandemic has been both a challenge and an opportunity for higher education institutions globally. Chan et al. (2021) reflect on the novel initiatives and unexpected challenges posed by the pandemic, suggesting that investigating best practices can guide the future development of online teaching and learning in post-pandemic higher education. Furthermore, the pandemic has emphasized the need for a robust framework to support blended learning and online pedagogy. Kara (2021) envisions a wide-scale uptake of blended delivery of academic programs, capacity building for staff and students on online pedagogy, and a holistic quality assurance framework. This framework should integrate strategic planning for disasters and focus on entrepreneurial university models (Kara, 2021).

The transition to emergency remote teaching during the pandemic created numerous challenges but also opportunities for curriculum enhancement. Hughes et al. (2020) argue that this rapid transition has prompted educators to consider situational factors affecting teaching and learning, encouraging them to reflect on real-life contexts to improve course delivery. According to Kuforiji and Kuforiji (2022), hybrid or blended learning instruction will effectively compete with the traditional brick-and-mortar classroom settings in the future physical campus of higher education. This shift was facilitated by the development of more efficient online learning and teaching software and devices, which enhanced and improved student learning outcomes during the Covid-19 lockdowns (Kuforiji & Kuforiji, 2022).

The acceleration of changes in higher education, long emergent but amplified by the pandemic, has necessitated a reevaluation of pedagogical models and institutional structures. Deshmukh (2021) notes that this watershed moment has "amplified specific deficiencies and strengths in pedagogical models," urging institutions to rethink their vision and purpose. The evolution of campuses is now on an uneven path, risking the loss of beneficial elements without comprehensive rethinking and responsive planning (Deshmukh, 2021). Blended or hybrid learning models are widely seen as the future of higher education post-pandemic. A significant majority of respondents in a study by Guppy et al. (2022) foresee the most growth in these forms of digital learning. However, student opinion remains skeptical about future changes, with most envisioning only modest increases in fully online courses (Guppy et al., 2022). The pandemic highlighted the importance of understanding varying student preferences and satisfaction levels with different online modalities. Research by Chen et al. (2022) demonstrates that curriculum rigor and field of study significantly influence student satisfaction with online courses. Additionally, the effectiveness of online learning is closely linked to instructor competency and technology effectiveness across different modalities (Chen et al., 2022).

Teacher satisfaction with online teaching during the pandemic is influenced by several factors, including online interaction, institutional support, and technology-related issues. Pham and Nghiem (2022) found that these factors are crucial in affecting lecturer satisfaction and suggest practical implications for long-term investments in online education in developing countries. Finally, Dumulescu et al. (2021) emphasize the importance of creating new learning environments with digital technologies. The effectiveness of university teaching in the post-digital era depends on the ability to foster cognitive-transferable learning experiences and emotionally safe learning environments, promoting self-regulated learning (Dumulescu et al., 2021). International collaboration in higher education has also seen new possibilities due to the pandemic. Poirier et al. (2023) highlight that the COVID-19 pandemic has made transnational inter-university teaching-learning feasible and beneficial, enriching the learning experience through diverse perspectives and debates (Poirier et al., 2023).

The COVID-19 pandemic has prompted a profound transformation in higher education, leading to the widespread adoption of hybrid and online learning models. These changes, driven by necessity, are likely to persist and shape the future of teaching and learning in higher education.

## Assumptions about Online Learning Before the COVID-19 Pandemic

Prior to the COVID-19 pandemic, higher education institutions largely underestimated the potential and effectiveness of online learning, influenced by longstanding assumptions and limited exposure to digital pedagogies. Many faculty members and institutions were unprepared for the sudden shift to online education, lacking the necessary infrastructure and training to deliver high-quality online courses (Lederman, 2020; Aristovnik et al, 2023). This lack of preparation contributed to a perception that online education was inferior to traditional face-to-face instruction, an assumption that was only exacerbated by the emergency remote teaching methods hastily adopted during the pandemic (Blignaut & Renaud, 2021). Research highlighted that many of the challenges associated with online learning, such as student engagement and equitable access to technology, were not new but were brought to the forefront by the pandemic. Addressing these misconceptions is essential for higher education institutions to develop more effective and inclusive digital learning strategies (Aristovnik et al., 2023). One prevalent assumption was that online learning was inherently easier and less rigorous than traditional, in-person instruction. This belief stemmed from a misunderstanding of the flexibility characteristic of online courses, which was often conflated with a diminished academic challenge. Sieber (2005) addresses this misconception, emphasizing that effective online learning requires a high level of responsibility on the part of students and a shift in the power dynamic between teachers and students. This necessitates a focus on learning processes rather than outcomes, highlighting the rigor and self-discipline required in online environments (Sieber, 2005).

Furthermore, there existed a widespread belief that online courses were inherently isolating, lacking the dynamic interaction and exchange of ideas that animate traditional classroom settings. This assumption underestimated the capacity of digital platforms to facilitate rich, interactive learning communities through forums, collaborative projects, and real-time discussions. Compton, Davis, and Correia (2010) identified misconceptions surrounding virtual schooling (VS), including concerns about reduced interaction and feedback, which they found to be unfounded as VS can support diverse modes of interaction, fostering a sense of community and engagement among students and between students and instructors (Compton et al., 2010).

The perception of online learning as predominantly involving passive consumption of video-based lectures also prevailed. This narrow view overlooked the broad array of instructional methods employed in well-designed online courses, including interactive simulations, engaging multimedia content, and active learning projects. Bennett and Green (2001) discuss the importance of constructivism as a theoretical framework for enhancing student learning in the online environment, proposing diverse methodologies that cater to different learning styles and preferences, thus challenging the notion of passive learning in online education (Bennett & Green, 2001).

Another common misconception was that in online education, technology supplants pedagogy. This belief failed to acknowledge that effective online learning is grounded in solid pedagogical principles, with technology serving as an enabler rather than the foundation of educational experiences. The role of technology in online learning is to augment and enhance teaching strategies, not to replace the pedagogical intent and design of courses. Sieber (2005) addresses this misconception, emphasizing that successful online education relies on the integration of technology to support, not replace, pedagogical strategies. This perspective underscores the importance of viewing technology as a tool to enhance the learning experience, guided by solid instructional design and pedagogical principles (Sieber, 2005).

Concerns about assessment integrity also contributed to hesitations about online learning, with some assuming that cheating was more prevalent and that online assessments could not effectively gauge learning. However, this assumption did not take into account the innovative assessment strategies developed for online contexts, designed to ensure academic integrity and accurately measure student outcomes. Gaytan and McEwen (2007) discuss several strategies for maintaining instructional quality and assessment integrity in online learning environments, including the importance of using a variety of instructional methods and providing meaningful and timely feedback to support the integrity of online assessments. Similarly, Kaisara and Bwalya (2023) focus on strategies that universities could use to improve assessment information integrity in mobile learning, highlighting the importance of assessments in evaluating knowledge and maintaining academic integrity in online contexts. These efforts demonstrate a commitment to upholding academic integrity while ensuring that online assessments are both fair and capable of accurately measuring student learning outcomes.

The assumption that online learning environments are impersonal and lack community overlooked the potential for creating meaningful connections and support networks online. Digital platforms can foster a sense of belonging and community among students, facilitated by interactive tools and deliberate community-building efforts by instructors. Thurston (2000) explores the development of an online learning community among postgraduate students, demonstrating that active engagement with a virtual learning environment (VLE) can enhance students' sense of connectedness and lead to higher academic completion rates. Similarly, Nye (2015) examines the creation of an online space that promotes interdisciplinary dialogue among a broad cohort of students, highlighting how digital platforms can facilitate a sense of belonging and community engagement in higher education. These efforts illustrate that through interactive tools and deliberate community-building efforts by instructors, digital platforms can indeed foster a sense of belonging and engagement among students, enabling meaningful connections and support networks to flourish online.

Moreover, the belief that online education was unsuitable for certain subjects, particularly those requiring hands-on or experiential learning, neglected the creative and technological solutions that have been developed to address these challenges. Makransky et al. (2019) demonstrate that virtual reality science simulations can achieve learning outcomes equivalent to those conducted in traditional settings, underscoring the effectiveness of virtual laboratories in delivering complex scientific concepts online. Similarly, Márquez et al., (2011) introduce the concept of augmented remote laboratories (ARL), showing how augmented reality can enhance the teaching of science and engineering subjects by offering experiences that may even surpass those in traditional lab classes. Furthermore, Rojas-Contreras and Ruiz-Bautista (2020) discuss the use of virtual reality to develop online laboratories, providing an immersive experience that effectively simulates physical laboratory practices for higher education. These innovations, including virtual laboratories, simulations, and augmented reality experiences, are enabling the effective online delivery of a wide range of disciplines, challenging previous assumptions about the limitations of online education in delivering hands-on and experiential learning.

Another assumption was that online education primarily served non-traditional students, such as adult learners or working professionals. This perspective underestimated the appeal and applicability of online learning for traditional college-age students, overlooking the benefits of flexibility, accessibility, and personalized learning pathways that online education can offer to learners across the lifespan. Tanner et al., (2009) explore the perceptions of online learning among both business faculty and undergraduate students, revealing the growing acceptance of online education among traditional college-age students, thus challenging the notion that online learning is only suitable for non-traditional students. Similarly, Cooper (2001) compares student perceptions and performance in online and traditional classes, indicating that the convenience and flexibility offered by online classes have broad appeal, including to traditional college-age students. Furthermore, Langan (1997) provides insight from a student's perspective on the effectiveness and benefits of online education, emphasizing its potential to cater to a wide range of learners, including those seeking personalized learning pathways and flexibility in their education. These studies underscore the broad appeal of online education and its capacity to serve not just non-traditional students but traditional college-age students as well, offering flexibility, accessibility, and personalized learning experiences to all learners.

Lastly, there was an underestimation of the importance of faculty development for online teaching. Some believed that instructors could seamlessly transition from in-person to online teaching without the need for specialized training or support. This assumption disregarded the distinct skills and competencies required for effective online pedagogy, highlighting the need for comprehensive professional development programs for educators transitioning to online environments. Johnson et al., (2019) discuss the critical role of faculty in ensuring the quality of online education and the necessity of comprehensive training and support to prepare faculty for the online learning environment. Similarly, Cook and Steinert (2013) emphasize the advantages and challenges of online faculty development, suggesting next steps for practice and future research to enhance the effectiveness of such programs. Scott (2019) proposes a competency-based professional development course that guides faculty through an application- and task-based series of activities to create or enhance an online course, underscoring the importance of preparing and supporting faculty to teach effectively online. These sources illustrate the necessity of recognizing and addressing the unique challenges of online pedagogy through targeted professional development initiatives.

These assumptions, widely held before the COVID-19 pandemic forced a global reevaluation of online learning, underscore the necessity of challenging misconceptions and promoting a nuanced understanding of digital education. By critically examining and addressing these beliefs, higher education can leverage the full potential of online learning methodologies to enhance educational quality, accessibility, and student engagement in an increasingly digital world.

## ERT During the COVID-19 Pandemic

In the wake of the COVID-19 pandemic, educational institutions worldwide were compelled to transition rapidly from traditional in-person teaching methods to online formats. This transition, termed Emergency Remote Teaching (ERT), was a crisis response measure, distinct in both intent and execution from premeditated, effectively designed online courses (Shim & Lee, 2020; Trust & Whalen, 2020). The distinction between ERT and these online offerings is crucial, not only for understanding the challenges faced during the pandemic but also for informing future approaches to online education.

ERT was characterized by its foundational necessity; it was an immediate solution to an unprecedented problem. Lacking a solid pedagogical foundation, decisions in ERT were made quickly, prioritizing the continuity of instruction over the optimization of online learning environments. This often led to a direct, ill-adapted transposition of in-person materials to digital platforms, sidelining the potential for innovative teaching and learning strategies that are emblematic of well-designed online courses (Iglesías-Pradas et al., 2021). These courses, in contrast, are built upon educational theories and instructional design principles, ensuring that their pedagogical strategies are tailor-made for digital consumption.

The design and development phase under ERT constraints inherently lacked the depth of planning that effectively designed online courses benefit from. The latter involves the integration of multimedia elements, interactive activities, and digital resources tailored specifically to the online learning context, enhancing engagement and facilitating a richer educational experience.

Moreover, the role of technology in ERT was primarily utilitarian, serving as a means to continue instruction and assessment with minimal adaptation to the new medium. This stands in stark contrast to effectively designed online offerings, where technology is leveraged not just for content delivery but as a pivotal component in creating interactive, engaging learning experiences. Using collaborative tools, simulations, and personalized feedback mechanisms, these courses utilize technology to its fullest potential, enhancing the learning process and outcomes (Schlesselman, 2020).

Assessment strategies further delineate ERT from its intentionally designed counterparts. ERT often replicated traditional, in-person assessment methods in an online format, which may not effectively measure student learning in a digital environment. Conversely, effectively designed online courses employ diverse, innovative assessment methods that align with the courses' learning outcomes and the unique affordances of the online environment.

Support and resources—a critical component of the online learning ecosystem—were also limited under ERT, impacting both instructors' teaching quality and students' learning experiences. Effective online courses, however, are complemented by comprehensive support systems, including technical assistance, online tutoring, and accessible instructor office hours, ensuring a conducive learning environment for all participants (Misirli & Ergulec, 2021).

Communication and feedback, essential for student engagement and learning, were challenged under ERT due to the adaptation period and increased instructor workloads. Effectively designed online courses, on the other hand, prioritize timely and constructive feedback, maintaining open and continuous communication channels between instructors and students (Yang et al., 2021).

Flexibility and accessibility sharply differentiate ERT from thoughtfully designed online education. ERT's rapid deployment often overlooked the diverse needs of the student body, potentially compromising accessibility. In contrast, effectively designed online courses are inherently flexible and accessible, accommodating a wide range of learning preferences and needs, ensuring educational materials are available to all students.

While ERT served as a necessary interim solution during the height of the COVID-19 pandemic, its limitations highlight the importance of moving towards well-planned, pedagogically sound online courses. These courses not only cater to the immediate educational needs during crises but also pave the way for sustainable, inclusive, and effective long-term online learning strategies. As the educational landscape continues to evolve, distinguishing between the exigencies of ERT and the opportunities offered by effectively designed online courses will be crucial for harnessing the full potential of digital education.

## Online Learning, ERT, and Equity

The COVID-19 pandemic precipitated a global shift to emergency remote teaching (ERT), revealing significant diversity, equity, and inclusion (DEI) issues within higher education. This unprecedented transition has underscored existing disparities and created new challenges for students and faculty, particularly those from disadvantaged backgrounds.

One of the most prominent DEI issues exacerbated by ERT is the digital divide, which disproportionately affects students from lower socioeconomic backgrounds. According to Jili et al., (2021), "some staff and students experience challenges related to the lack of resources and exposure to remotely use information and communication technology." The transition to ERT has intensified the need for adequate technological infrastructure, which is often lacking in disadvantaged communities. As a result, institutions must "acquire suitable information and communication technology equipment and develop the requisite facilities to provide easy access to teaching and learning by both students and academic staff at an affordable and fixed (secure) cost" (Jili et al., 2021). Bond et al., (2021) also emphasize the digital divide, noting that research during the pandemic "discussed the digital divide and vast educational/socioeconomic inequalities that became more pronounced with the shift to emergency remote teaching." These findings highlight the need for targeted interventions to ensure equitable access to digital resources.

Banerjee (2022) highlights significant technological access challenges faced by disadvantaged students, particularly those who are first-generation, low-income, and nonwhite. According to Banerjee, "a critical subset of the sample who were first generation, low income, and nonwhite had significantly lower levels of Technological Access with respect to access to devices and Internet access, when compared to the larger sample." The implications of smartphone dependence among disadvantaged students further exacerbate this divide, as reliance on less capable devices hinders effective participation in online learning environments. Building on Banerjee's findings, Mathrani et al. (2021) extend the discussion to developing countries, where large sections of the population have limited access to basic digital services. They note that "large sections of the population in developing economies have limited access to basic digital services; this restricts how digital media are being used in everyday lives." This structural issue, including the lack of digital media access and supporting services, disproportionately affects female students, placing them lower on the digital divide access scale. Pashkov et al. (2022) examine the impact of the digital divide on students in transnational online education, noting that "the digital divide can impact students and their learning in transnational online education which has been in greater demand since the onset of the pandemic." They contribute to the literature by "articulating the levels and aspects of digital inequalities in the context of online learning and offering a practical model of pedagogical design" to mitigate these effects, suggesting that tailored instructional methods can help bridge the gap created by unequal access to technology.

In contrast, Laufer et al. (2021) emphasize the role of higher education leaders in addressing digital inequalities. They found "multiple and overlapping factors that contribute to an institution's ability to realize the potential of digital education, highlighting deeply rooted inequalities." Their study suggests that institutional policies and leadership decisions are crucial in realizing the potential of digital education. This perspective complements Pashkov et al.'s focus on pedagogical design by highlighting the importance of leadership in fostering an inclusive digital learning environment.

Mathrani et al. (2021) provide a comprehensive framework for understanding digital inequalities in developing countries during the COVID-19 lockdown. They find that limited access to digital services significantly restricts how digital media is used in everyday lives, impacting educational access and quality. Najab and Amrani (2022) analyze digital accessibility in Moroccan higher education, revealing that "the digital divide and unequal access to technological tools in higher education raise questions of social justice and equal opportunity." Both studies underscore the urgent need for infrastructural investments and policy interventions to address digital disparities in developing regions.

Azionya and Nhedzi (2021) explore the digital divide in South African universities, comparing historically marginalized and privileged institutions. Their findings indicate that "online learning did not increase the accessibility of university education during the pandemic for students attending marginalized universities," reinforcing the notion that digital inequalities are deeply rooted in historical and socioeconomic contexts. Werfhorst et al., (2020) investigate inequalities in digital preparedness before the pandemic, stating that "the COVID-19 pandemic has disordered the educational process globally, raising concerns about the potential effects of forced digitalization on learning inequalities." They find that ICT skills, strongly related to socioeconomic background, are important drivers of the digital divide. Together, these studies illustrate how pre-existing inequalities in digital preparedness can exacerbate educational disparities during crises.

Makumane et al. (2023) discuss blended learning as a potential solution to neutralize the digital divide. They argue that "blended learning has the capacity to neutralize the digital divide as it affords students flexibility to design and engage in individualized learning experiences." However, they caution that "the installation of internet infrastructure in communities should not be considered as the sole facility to access; disparities in resources still exist," indicating that blended learning alone cannot completely bridge the digital divide.

Sydorenko et al. (2021) emphasize the need for digital transformation in higher education to bridge the digital divide. They describe the digital divide as "a component of information inequality, which characterizes unequal opportunities in terms of access, use, and production of information." They advocate for the creation of modern digital universities with advanced management systems and educational activities. This perspective aligns with Laufer et al.'s call for leadership in digital education, suggesting that systemic modernization is necessary for equitable access. Deng and Yi (2022) focus on the digital divide among underserved college students during the COVID-19 pandemic. They highlight that "access to technology is essential to educational success, but disparities in access can handicap students." Their study suggests that "individual background should be considered in designing policies to mitigate the digital divide and enhance student learning in online education," reinforcing the need for policies that consider individual backgrounds in mitigating the digital divide. Karakose (2021) suggests that "integrating the digital and online learning approach into the higher education system correctly and effectively may help to eliminate digital inequality in the higher education student population." Similarly, Stewart (2021) recommends that future research should "focus on long-term impacts of ERT and strategies to mitigate these inequalities," emphasizing the need for sustained efforts to address equity issues in remote education.

ERT has also highlighted gendered challenges, with women often facing greater difficulties in adapting to remote learning environments. Gelles et al., (2020) discuss the importance of flexible and compassionate teaching approaches to support diverse student needs, particularly for women. They note that "faculty members showed compassion and flexibility by adjusting the curriculum and assessment, which was especially important for supporting students' well-being" (Gelles et al., 2020). Shin and Hickey (2020) further illustrate this point, stating that "issues in terms of accessibility, digital divide, inequity, and mental/emotional/physical health that the participants, more likely females, experienced during emergency remote learning were especially concerning." This underscores the need for inclusive pedagogies that consider the unique challenges faced by different demographic groups.

The abrupt shift to ERT has also had significant implications for students' mental health and well-being. According to Shin and Hickey (2020), "the pre-existing educational and social inequities seemed exacerbated and amplified during ERT and the COVID-19 crisis." These inequities have led to increased stress and anxiety among students, necessitating a focus on socio-emotional support. Faculty members have played a crucial role in providing this support. Gelles et al. (2020) highlight the importance of "faculty members communicating care and incorporating flexibility into their courses" to support students during this challenging period. This approach not only addresses immediate needs but also promotes long-term resilience and adaptability in the face of ongoing uncertainties.

The shift to emergency remote teaching during the COVID-19 pandemic has exposed and amplified significant DEI issues within higher education. Addressing these challenges requires a multifaceted approach that includes improving access to digital resources, integrating inclusive pedagogies, and providing robust socio-emotional support. By focusing on these areas, institutions can work towards creating a more equitable and inclusive educational environment for all students.

## Understanding Engagement in Online Learning in Higher Education

The concept of engagement in online learning within higher education has garnered significant attention due to its critical role in influencing learning outcomes and overall student success and emerged as a central concern during the transition to ERT. Engagement, broadly defined, is a multi-dimensional construct that encompasses behavioral, cognitive, emotional, and agentic dimensions (Azevedo, 2015). Despite its recognized importance, the term remains complex and multifaceted, often requiring nuanced interpretations depending on the context and the specific educational environment. Moreover, Duke et al. (2017) highlight that engagement varies across different online learning models, and a qualitative study can provide insights into effective engagement strategies. This is echoed by Wang (2021), who points out that while engagement is a significant gauge of student skill and quality, "the term engagement remains vague and is construed in different ways in the literature."

Kahu (2013) outlines that "engagement is widely recognized as an important influence on achievement and learning in higher education" and can be understood from multiple perspectives, including behavioral, psychological, socio-cultural, and holistic viewpoints. This multi-perspective approach highlights the necessity of a comprehensive framework to fully capture the diverse elements that constitute student engagement. Ashwin and Mcvitty (2015) argue that "student engagement has increasingly been positioned as a defining characteristic of high-quality teaching and learning in higher education." They emphasize that analyzing both the focus and degree of student engagement can address the vagueness often associated with the term. This analysis is crucial for developing effective policies and practices that enhance educational outcomes. Foley and Marr (2019) discuss the importance of extracurricular activities in supporting student engagement, asserting that "engagement is seen as a major factor for success in higher education." They argue that learning from peers and applying academic skills more broadly are essential components of effective engagement.

In the realm of online education, engagement requires distinct strategies to ensure effective learning. Sarder (2014) notes that "teaching methods from traditional courses may not directly translate to the online learning model," necessitating innovative approaches to foster student interaction and critical thinking. This is supported by Boulton et al. (2019), who identify that engagement in higher education includes various forms such as "lecture attendance, self-study, and usage of online/digital systems," all of which contribute to the overall learning experience. Harris et al. (2020) explore the specific challenges in engaging students in compulsory online learning, stating that engagement encompasses "behavioral, emotional, cognitive, and sometimes agentic aspects." They suggest that teachers can effectively engage students by building relationships, creating safe environments, and utilizing inclusive technologies. Chen et al. (2008) emphasize the critical nature of quality engagement in distance learning, noting that "quality engagement in distance learning is critical for achieving similar outcomes to face-to-face learning." This underscores the importance of adapting teaching strategies to the unique demands of online education to ensure student success. Kahu et al. (2013) provide insights into the engagement of mature online students, noting that while their engagement may differ from traditional students, it is equally significant in terms of student satisfaction and learning outcomes. They suggest that mature students often integrate learning with work experience, highlighting a unique aspect of engagement in this demographic.

In exploring strategies to maximize engagement in online learning, Sandid et al. (2023) emphasize the need for active participation, stating that "maintaining active participation throughout the learning process is essential" for skill development and enriching learning experiences. Similarly, Bai et al. (2023) highlight that improving engagement in online learning involves addressing cognitive, emotional, and behavioral dimensions to enhance the overall educational experience. Pittaway (2012) proposes an engagement framework that includes personal, academic, intellectual, social, and professional dimensions, arguing that "engagement is increasingly understood as a prerequisite for effective learning." This framework aims to enhance unit design, teaching practices, and student support systems.

The varied interpretations and approaches to engagement in online learning illustrate its complexity and the necessity for tailored strategies to foster meaningful student participation. By recognizing and addressing the different dimensions of engagement, educators can enhance the learning experiences and outcomes for students in higher education.

## Challenges with Learning Engagement During the Transition to ERT

The global shift to ERT revealed numerous immediate challenges related to student engagement. Anthony and Noel (2021) explored the broader adoption of ERT and identified significant challenges in maintaining student engagement. They noted that "The rapid transition to ERT led to significant challenges in maintaining student engagement" and "Students struggled with disengagement due to the lack of preparation and support for ERT" (Anthony & Noel, 2021). According to Stewart (2021), "Findings are indicative of the immediate aftermath of transitions to ERT, highlighting the lack of interaction as a significant issue for student engagement." This lack of interaction has been a common theme, as students struggled with the absence of face-to-face communication, which is vital for maintaining engagement in the learning process. In Ireland, part-time learners faced significant disengagement due to the sudden shift to ERT. Flynn, et al, (2022) found that "Many learners reported feelings of isolation and disengagement due to the abrupt transition to ERT." This isolation was compounded by the challenges of balancing work, family, and study, particularly without the structured environment of in-person classes. The authors further noted that "The lack of face-to-face interaction and the challenges of online learning have led to significant disengagement among part-time learners" (Flynn et al., 2022).

In Latin America, the transition to ERT also resulted in decreased student engagement. Lobos et al. (2023) observed that "Students experienced disengagement due to the sudden shift from face-to-face to ERT, lacking interactive learning strategies." This transition not only affected educational performance but also impacted students' emotional and mental health. The study concluded that "The transition to ERT has negatively impacted student engagement and educational performance" (Lobos et al., 2023). Exchange students in Korea also faced engagement issues during ERT. Stewart et al., (2022) found that "Exchange students reported significant disengagement during ERT due to the lack of institutional support and interaction." This lack of support and interaction was particularly detrimental during the initial phase of ERT, leading to a decline in student engagement (Stewart et al., 2022).

First-year students at Macao Polytechnic University exhibited lower engagement levels during ERT compared to pre-pandemic learning. Lei and Cheong (2022) reported that "First-year students showed lower engagement levels during ERT compared to pre-pandemic face-to-face learning." This decline in engagement was attributed to the sudden change in the learning environment, which disrupted students' academic experiences (Lei & Cheong, 2022). In the Philippines, Alvarez (2020) highlighted that "Disengagement was prevalent due to poor internet access and lack of technological devices, impacting students' ability to participate fully in

ERT." Financial constraints and lack of emotional support further contributed to significant disengagement among students (Alvarez, 2020). In the UAE, El-Sakran et al., (2022) noted high levels of disengagement among college students due to the rapid shift to ERT. They observed that "Students reported high levels of disengagement due to the sudden shift to ERT and lack of preparation." The transition also significantly affected students' mental health and engagement levels (El-Sakran et al., 2022). In Northeastern Thailand, Fuchs (2022) found that "Students had low expectations and negative experiences with peer relationships and engagement during ERT." This disengagement was primarily due to the lack of social interactions and academic support (Fuchs, 2022). The study emphasized the need for improved support systems to enhance student engagement during remote learning periods. Newly arrived migrant students in Belgium experienced similar challenges. Seynhaeve et al. (2022) reported that "Participants indicated a lack of learner–teacher interaction, which led to disengagement during ERT." The limited opportunities for learner-learner interaction further compounded these issues, contributing to overall disengagement (Seynhaeve et al., 2022).

The transition to ERT during the COVID-19 pandemic highlighted critical issues related to student engagement. Addressing these challenges requires comprehensive strategies that include enhancing digital infrastructure, providing adequate support and training for both students and educators, and developing interactive and engaging online learning environments.

## Risks of Conflating ERT With Online Learning

Prior to the transition to ERT, regular and meaningful online learning experiences for both learners and instructors in higher education were outside the norm. As result of the now global experience of ERT, it's possible that there has been a conflation of ERT with online learning in general. The conflation of ERT with intentionally designed online learning embodies significant risks that can critically impact the perception, efficacy, and development of digital education within higher education landscapes. Such a conflation, born out of the rapid and necessary pivot to online modalities during crises, obscures the nuanced distinctions between emergency measures and the rich potential of fully realized online education. This misalignment carries implications for institutional policies, pedagogical approaches, and the overall quality of education delivered digitally.

Firstly, equating ERT with the broader spectrum of online learning risks fostering a misunderstanding of the nature and capabilities of digital education. Moore and Hodges (2023) emphasize that ERT, a crisis response measure, lacks the robust design of intentionally crafted online courses. This misperception can lead to underestimations of the pedagogical diversity, interactive possibilities, and educational richness that intentionally designed online courses can offer. Consequently, there's a danger of institutionalizing lower academic standards if the improvised and sometimes under-resourced approaches characteristic of ERT are mistaken for the norm in online education, potentially diluting the quality of learning outcomes and academic rigor.

Moreover, innovation in pedagogy may be stifled. The emergency nature of ERT might not fully represent the engaging, interactive, and pedagogically sound experiences that can be achieved through careful design and implementation of online learning. By conflating the two, institutions risk overlooking the need for continuous pedagogical innovation that can enhance the effectiveness of digital teaching strategies.

This conflation also poses a risk to student engagement and the overall learning experience. Al Shlowiy et al., (2021) discuss the potential for teacher-student miscommunication in ERT settings, suggesting the need for explicit guidelines and clearer expectations. If the compromises made during ERT—such as reduced student-instructor interaction and limited collaborative opportunities—are perceived as inherent to online learning, there may be less emphasis on creating dynamic, interactive learning environments. This perception could significantly diminish student engagement and satisfaction with their educational experiences.

The distinction between ERT and intentionally designed online learning is critical for faculty development as well. Misinterpreting ERT as the standard for online education may lead to an underestimation of the need for comprehensive training in online pedagogy. This oversight hinders instructors' ability to effectively engage students and deliver high-quality digital learning experiences, ultimately affecting educational outcomes.

Additionally, the conflation may influence student enrollment and retention negatively. Potential learners, drawing on experiences or perceptions of ERT, might seek alternative educational opportunities that promise higher quality and more engaging experiences, thus impacting the institutions' ability to attract and retain students. There's also the matter of effectively leveraging technology in education. Treating ERT as synonymous with online learning overlooks the opportunities to utilize educational technologies to their fullest extent. Innovations such as simulations, interactive tools, and adaptive learning platforms can significantly enhance the learning experience, a potential that might not be fully realized under the constraints of ERT.

The diverse needs for accessibility and flexibility, paramount to the ethos of online learning, might be overlooked. ERT, while effective as an emergency measure, may not adequately address the broad spectrum of student needs that intentionally designed online courses can cater to, potentially excluding or disadvantaging students who rely on these considerations. The approach to assessment within the context of conflating ERT with online learning risks undervaluing the potential for diverse and innovative assessment methods. Well-designed online courses employ a variety of assessment strategies that align with learning objectives and the digital environment, ensuring the validity and reliability of assessments. This nuanced approach to assessment might be compromised if ERT practices are viewed as representative of online learning as a whole.

The conflation of ERT with intentionally designed online learning presents a myriad of risks that challenge the development, perception, and quality of digital education. Recognizing and addressing these distinctions is essential for advancing the field of online education, ensuring that it remains a vibrant, effective, and inclusive component of higher education.

## Pedagogical Shortcomings of ERT

The Emergency Remote Teaching (ERT) phase prompted by the COVID-19 pandemic necessitated an unprecedented and rapid shift to digital learning modalities across the educational landscape. This abrupt transition, while critical for maintaining educational continuity, inadvertently sidelined the integration of several pedagogical approaches foundational to creating inclusive, equitable, and effective learning environments. The complexity of implementing these methodologies, each requiring intentional design and a nuanced understanding of student needs, presented significant challenges under the time constraints and pressures of ERT.

Among these approaches, trauma-informed pedagogy stands out for its focus on recognizing and addressing the psychological and emotional impacts of trauma among students. Sherwood et al. (2021) and Bennett et al. (2021) discuss how the swift pivot to ERT often lacked the depth and consideration necessary to embed trauma-informed principles into the online curriculum, missing crucial opportunities to support students' well-being during a period of global crisis.

Similarly, culturally-responsive teaching, which tailors educational experiences to the cultural backgrounds of students to foster an inclusive and affirming learning environment, was not broadly implemented. Henshaw (2022) and Carrillo and Flores (2020) highlight the rapid transition to ERT posed significant obstacles to integrating culturally-responsive practices, potentially overlooking the rich diversity of student backgrounds in the haste to continue instructional delivery.

The principles of Universal Design for Learning (UDL), aimed at optimizing teaching and learning for all individuals, also saw limited application. The hurried development of online courses may not have fully considered UDL guidelines, thus impacting the accessibility and engagement of diverse learners. Likewise, differentiated instruction, which adapts teaching methods to meet the varied needs of students, faced challenges in remote learning contexts, where personalization and adaptability are paramount.

The implementation of anti-racist education and inquiry-based learning similarly suffered. The urgency with which ERT was deployed may have marginalized the integration of anti-racist principles and the promotion of inquiry as a central learning strategy. These omissions highlight a missed opportunity to engage students in critical reflection and exploration at a time when societal issues of inequity and injustice were increasingly prominent.

Asset-based pedagogies and social-emotional learning (SEL), which recognize the strengths students bring to their learning environments and integrate emotional intelligence development, respectively, were not adequately emphasized. The nature of ERT, focused predominantly on content delivery, likely limited the application of these approaches, which are vital for recognizing student assets and supporting their emotional and social development.

Community-based learning, which connects academic content with community needs and issues, was constrained by the remote nature of ERT, reducing opportunities for students to engage with their communities meaningfully. Critical pedagogy, with its emphasis on empowering students to challenge dominant narratives and structures, also saw diminished implementation, as the rapid move online may not have provided sufficient space for the critical discourse and reflection essential to this approach.

The ERT phase of the COVID-19 pandemic, while necessary, illuminated the challenges of rapidly integrating comprehensive pedagogical approaches into online learning. As educational institutions navigate the post-pandemic era, there exists an imperative to revisit these methodologies, ensuring that digital and hybrid learning environments are designed to be not only inclusive and equitable but also responsive to the complex needs of all students. This reflection and subsequent action are crucial for leveraging the full potential of education as a transformative force in an increasingly digital world.

In the evolution of higher education from the exigencies of ERT towards the realization of fully-fledged, high-quality online learning environments, three overarching challenges emerge as central to this transformative process. These challenges encapsulate the multifaceted obstacles identified across various dimensions of online education, offering a holistic view of the critical areas requiring focused attention and concerted action. Ferri et al. (2020) explore the technological, pedagogical, and social challenges of ERT, suggesting actions to face these challenges in future crises. This encompasses not only the refinement of digital pedagogies but also a significant cultural shift within educational communities towards valuing and embracing online modes of learning. The essence of this challenge lies in creating and implementing effective online teaching strategies, adapting curriculum content for digital delivery, and fostering a supportive environment for faculty through targeted professional development opportunities. It necessitates a paradigm shift that integrates digital pedagogy at the core of educational practices, aligning with the broader cultural transformation needed to fully embrace the potentials of online education. The issue of comprehensive access and equity highlights the critical need for ensuring equitable access to online learning opportunities across the student body. Al Shlowiy et al. (2021) investigate teacher-student miscommunication in ERT, emphasizing the need for clear guidelines and expectations, which plays into the broader challenge of ensuring access and equity. This challenge merges considerations of technological infrastructure, support systems, and the need to create inclusive and accessible learning environments for all students. It addresses the imperative to bridge the digital divide and ensure that students, regardless of their socioeconomic status, geographic location, or individual learning needs, can access and succeed in online education. Achieving comprehensive access and equity requires a concerted effort to provide the necessary resources, support, and accommodations to meet the diverse needs of the student population, thereby fostering an online learning environment where every student has the opportunity to thrive.

Lastly, the challenge of sustainable institutional adaptation encapsulates the organizational, financial, and regulatory dimensions of transitioning to effective online learning. This challenge underscores the need for institutions to undergo strategic and structural adaptations to support the sustainable implementation and growth of online programs. It involves navigating the complex landscape of financial constraints, regulatory requirements, and accreditation standards, requiring strategic resource allocation, policy development, and a commitment to continuous quality assurance and improvement, as discussed by Colclasure et al. (2021). Sustainable institutional adaptation demands visionary leadership and a strategic approach to cultivating an organizational culture that is agile, innovative, and aligned with the evolving demands of higher education in a digital era.

Together, these challenges—integrative pedagogical development, comprehensive access and equity, and sustainable institutional adaptation—define the critical path forward for higher education institutions aspiring to harness the full potential of online learning. Addressing these core challenges through a coordinated and strategic approach is essential for realizing the vision of creating equitable, effective, and high-quality online learning environments that meet the needs of a diverse and global student population.

## Satisficing Solutions in Online Learning

In the aftermath of the COVID-19 pandemic, the landscape of online learning within higher education institutions has been significantly shaped by the rapid deployment of satisficing solutions. These solutions, adopted out of necessity during the emergency transition to remote teaching, have exhibited a notable persistence in the post-pandemic era. This phenomenon can be attributed to a confluence of factors that underscore the complexities and pragmatic considerations facing educational institutions as they navigate the evolving terrain of digital learning, as highlighted by studies from Aguilera-Hermida (2020), Hussein et al. (2020), and Anthony & Noel (2021). This shift highlighted significant challenges in maintaining the quality of education (García-Morales et al. 2021; Hodges et al. 2020). Many students and faculty expressed concerns about the effectiveness of these hastily designed online courses, which has led to a lasting perception of their inadequacy (Chan et al., 2021; Broadbent et al., 2022).

Institutional inertia plays a critical role in the continued reliance on satisficing solutions. The momentum gathered by the adoption of certain technologies and pedagogical strategies during the pandemic creates a path dependency, making deviations from established practices a challenge. The inertia is compounded by the resource-intensive nature of overhauling online learning environments, which necessitates navigating the intricacies of institutional change management, a challenge discussed by Kovacevic et al. (2021) and Shin & Hickey (2020). Cost considerations further cement the place of satisficing solutions in the post-pandemic educational landscape. The financial implications of upgrading or replacing these interim solutions with more sophisticated alternatives pose a significant barrier, especially against the backdrop of budgetary constraints exacerbated by the pandemic. This economic calculus often favors the maintenance of existing practices over the uncertain returns of investment in new technologies or methodologies. Technological constraints also contribute to the persistence of satisficing solutions. The compatibility issues and infrastructural limitations associated with rapidly adopted technologies during the pandemic can deter institutions from undertaking the complex process of transitioning to more optimal solutions, despite their potential advantages for enhancing online learning. Risk aversion, heightened by the disruptions and uncertainties brought about by the pandemic, further influences the decision-making processes within institutions. The cautious approach to making substantial changes in the online learning environment reflects a desire to avoid potential failures or disruptions, prioritizing stability over optimal effectiveness.

The familiarity and comfort that faculty and staff have developed with satisficing solutions represent another dimension of this phenomenon. The human aspect of change resistance, where individuals prefer the known to the unfamiliar, can slow the pace of innovation and adoption of more effective online learning practices. Student adaptation to the online learning modalities established during the pandemic similarly acts as a deterrent to significant changes. The potential impact on the student experience, coupled with the challenges of managing transition-related disruptions, underscores the importance of considering student adaptation in the evolution of online learning environments.

Ongoing uncertainties, including the potential for future disruptions, reinforce the reliance on satisficing solutions. The known quantities provided by these solutions offer a semblance of reliability and continuity in the face of unpredictable challenges, underscoring their utility as a strategic response to uncertainty. The challenges associated with evaluating the effectiveness of emergency online learning solutions and the delayed feedback loop from students and faculty further contribute to the inertia. Without clear, timely, and actionable insights into the impact of these solutions on learning outcomes and satisfaction, institutions may default to maintaining the status quo.

The broad acceptance of satisficing solutions among stakeholders within the educational ecosystem can diminish the perceived urgency to seek out and implement more optimal solutions. This acceptance, born out of necessity and adaptation during the pandemic, lends a sense of stability and continuity to online learning programs, even as it potentially constrains the pursuit of pedagogical excellence and innovation.

The persistence of satisficing solutions in the post-pandemic online learning landscape is shaped by a multifaceted array of institutional, economic, technological, and human factors. While these solutions played a critical role in ensuring educational continuity during the pandemic, their continued use highlights the need for a strategic, nuanced approach to advancing the quality and effectiveness of online education in the long term. Addressing the underlying challenges and leveraging the lessons learned from the pandemic experience will be essential for institutions aiming to fully realize the potential of digital learning in higher education.

## Post-Pandemic Research About Online Learning

The sudden change to ERT prompted extensive research to understand the implications and future directions of online education. Zhang et al. (2022) conducted a comprehensive bibliometric analysis to examine how the global academic community responded to this crisis and identified key themes and trends in the literature.

The study revealed a substantial increase in research output related to online learning, highlighting the academic community's proactive response to the pandemic. Zhang et al. (2022) noted that “the significant surge in research output reveals the academic community’s response to the pandemic. Various themes have emerged in online learning research, encompassing online teaching, flipped classrooms, mental health, and blended learning." This indicates a broad interest in understanding how different pedagogical approaches and learning environments can be optimized for online platforms.

Moreover, the study identified a shift in research focus over time. Initially, studies concentrated on immediate responses to the pandemic, but they gradually evolved to explore more refined strategies and interdisciplinary perspectives. According to Zhang et al. (2022), "the evolution trajectory of research has traversed three stages, reflecting a shift in research focus from immediate pandemic responses to more refined strategies and interdisciplinary perspectives." This progression underscores the need for a long-term, strategic approach to online education that integrates insights from various disciplines.

A notable finding of the study was the application of technology acceptance theories and structural equation modeling to investigate the factors influencing the adoption and impacts of online learning. Zhang et al. (2022) reported that "many researchers applied technology acceptance theories and structural equation modeling to investigate factors associated with adoption and impacts of the pandemic-imposed online learning." These theoretical frameworks help in understanding the complexities involved in transitioning to online learning environments and in identifying the factors that can enhance or hinder this process.

The research also highlighted the most investigated disciplines and instructional approaches during the pandemic. Zhang et al. (2022) found that "medical education and chemical education were the most investigated disciplines, with inquiry-based learning, discovery learning, hands-on learning, and collaborative learning emerging as instructional approaches frequently discussed or utilized across the target studies." These findings suggest that certain fields and pedagogical methods have received more attention due to their specific challenges and opportunities in an online context.

Furthermore, the study emphasized the importance of global scholarly engagement and collaborative networks in shaping the field of online learning. Zhang et al. (2022) noted that "the study underscores the global scholarly engagement, collaborative networks, and principal themes that have shaped the field. As medical education adapts to the shifting landscape, the trajectory of online learning research points toward increased learner autonomy, integration of advanced technologies, and interdisciplinary collaboration." This global perspective is crucial for developing comprehensive and effective online education strategies that can be adapted to different contexts and needs.

Koh et al. (2022) conducted a systematic literature review of 36 peer-reviewed empirical articles and their findings described "failure for students to gain an enhanced learning experience, problems encountered in designing and implementing robust assessment and online examinations, cases of academic misconduct, inequitable access to digital technologies, and increased faculty workload." Zhang et al. (2022)

emphasized the need for "adequate professional training, improved internet connectivity, and emotional support to ensure quality online learning post-pandemic." Similarly, Demuyakor (2020) assessed the perceptions of Ghanaian international students in China regarding online learning. He reported that "the study also revealed that students have adequate knowledge of the COVID-19 pandemic and that the implementation of online learning programs was a very great idea as the majority of the sampled students supported the initiative" (Demuyakor, 2020). However, the study also highlighted that "students outside China due to the COVID-19 spend so much money to buy internet data for online learning" (Demuyakor, 2020), underscoring the need for affordable internet access. Tsantopoulos et al. (2022) investigated the experiences of undergraduate students during and after the pandemic. They found that "satisfaction with in-person learning was higher than online learning pointing to a preference for face-to-face modes of education" (Tsantopoulos et al., 2022). Despite this preference, students "acknowledged the importance of protecting the environment and biodiversity in order to prevent pandemic outbreaks in the future" (Tsantopoulos et al., 2022), indicating a potential openness to sustainable online learning solutions.

Khalili (2020) focused on interprofessional education and the challenges of creating engaging online learning environments. He noted that "teachers of interprofessional education are expected to employ online education, but some may lack the knowledge and expertise to create and facilitate an engaging, positive, and supportive online environment for their students" (Khalili, 2020). Khalili advocated for the application of "Meaningful Discourse and the Community of Inquiry principles to help in developing online learning communities" (Khalili, 2020). Djidu et al. (2021) identified two main challenges for lecturers and students during the pandemic: "limited resources such as electronic devices and internet connections, and lack of knowledge/skills on how to use online learning media" (Djidu et al., 2021). They emphasized that "most students from low economic families and those living in areas with limited access to learning facilities lost learning opportunities because of these limitations" (Djidu et al., 2021).

Al-Kumaim et al. (2021) developed a conceptual model to address the challenges faced by university students during online learning. They reported that "students disclosed various obstacles they encountered when using IT platform applications for online learning, including work and information overload, inadaptability, and personal health challenges related to stress and anxiety" (Al-Kumaim et al., 2021). The study proposed "a set of motivational factors and a conceptual model for sustainable and healthy online learning" (Al-Kumaim et al., 2021). Nugroho (2023) emphasized the importance of systematic evaluation and continuous improvement in online learning. He stated that "post-pandemic learning should be strengthened by an evaluation process and a level of satisfaction involving students, lecturers, and admin staff to ensure the mechanism meets standards" (Nugroho, 2023). He also highlighted that "the quality assurance mechanism should systematically evaluate online learning and take continuous improvement actions" (Nugroho, 2023).

Chen et al. (2022) assessed online learning preferences and satisfaction among business education students. They found that "graduate and undergraduate learners exhibit different preferences for online modalities, influenced by curriculum rigor and field of study" (Chen et al., 2022). The study also noted that "the evidence suggests varying dependence on instructor competency and technology effectiveness across asynchronous, hybrid, and synchronous modalities" (Chen et al., 2022).

Sim, Sim, and Quah (2021) explored the acceptance and challenges of online learning among Malaysian university students. Their study revealed that "results showed a moderate high level of acceptance of online learning among university students, with enhancement of English language skills ranking highest as a facilitating factor" (Sim et al., 2021). However, they also found that "challenges encountered by the majority of students include delivery speed of teaching and learning, students' attitudes, and stress of online learning mode" (Sim et al., 2021).

The COVID-19 pandemic has exposed significant challenges in online learning in higher education, including the need for better digital infrastructure, comprehensive professional development, and sustainable online learning models. Addressing these challenges requires a multifaceted approach that involves continuous evaluation, targeted training, and the incorporation of innovative pedagogical strategies. By learning from the experiences during the pandemic, higher education institutions can develop more resilient and effective online learning environments that can support diverse student needs and adapt to future crises.

## Faculty Development Needs in Higher Education Post-Pandemic

The transformation in higher education during the pandemic, as discussed by García-Morales et al. (2021), highlights the need for ongoing faculty development to enhance digital teaching competencies. To maintain high standards of education, institutions must provide continuous professional development opportunities focused on digital tools and online teaching methodologies (García-Morales et al., 2021). Higher education institutions must invest in training educators to effectively use digital tools and adapt to new educational environments to mitigate psychological and pedagogical challenges (Babelyuk et al., 2021). The COVID-19 pandemic underscored the urgent need for comprehensive professional development programs to enhance educators' digital literacy and teaching strategies (Babelyuk et al., 2021). This sentiment is echoed in the work of Vijayan (2021), who notes that the transition to online teaching highlighted significant gaps in digital literacy among faculty, necessitating ongoing professional development and support. There is a critical need for training programs focused on the effective use of online teaching tools to ensure the continuity and quality of education during and after the pandemic (Vijayan, 2021).

The experience in Serbia, as discussed by Vasiljević et al. (2021), further illustrates that the pandemic revealed many educators lacked the necessary digital skills, emphasizing the need for targeted training and support to improve online teaching capabilities. To adapt to the new educational landscape, institutions must prioritize professional development that equips faculty with the skills to integrate digital technologies into their teaching (Vasiljević et al., 2021). This need is not unique to Serbia; educators worldwide need ongoing training in digital tools and social media to enhance their teaching effectiveness in a post-pandemic world (Sosniuk & Ostapenko, 2021). The shift to online learning has made it clear that professional development in digital literacy is crucial for both educators and students to succeed in the new learning environment (Sosniuk & Ostapenko, 2021).

Schalk et al. (2022) explored the identity of the digital educator, emphasizing that developing digital competencies among faculty is essential for adapting to the changing educational landscape and ensuring effective online instruction. The pandemic has shown that continuous professional development in digital education is necessary for faculty to stay current with technological advancements and pedagogical practices (Schalk et al., 2022). Sultanova et al. (2021) also identify the pressing need for professional development programs that prepare educators for the challenges of online teaching and enhance their digital literacy. Institutions must invest in training their faculty to ensure they are equipped with the necessary skills and knowledge to deliver quality education in a post-pandemic world (Sultanova et al., 2021).

The Online and Campus (OaC) model proposed by Petronzi and Petronzi (2020) suggests that professional development in blended learning models is essential for faculty to effectively combine online and face-to-face teaching methods post-pandemic. Institutions should prioritize training programs that equip educators with the skills to navigate and integrate digital technologies into their teaching practices (Petronzi & Petronzi, 2020). The success of professional upskilling programs in enhancing teachers' digital competence demonstrates the importance of continuous training and support (Elsayary, 2023). Investing in professional development that focuses on digital literacy and technological integration is crucial for the future of education in a post-pandemic world (Elsayary, 2023).

The COVID-19 pandemic has brought to light the critical need for ongoing professional development in digital literacy and the use of educational technologies among faculty. To ensure the quality and effectiveness of education in a post-pandemic era, higher education institutions must invest in comprehensive training programs that address these needs. Continuous professional development will enable educators to adapt to the evolving educational landscape, integrate digital technologies into their teaching, and maintain high standards of education.

## CONCLUSION

As we reflect upon the expansive terrain navigated in this discourse, it becomes evident that the journey through the challenges and transformations induced by the COVID-19 pandemic within the sphere of higher education is both intricate and multifaceted. The pandemic's unprecedented impact catalyzed a swift and necessary pivot to Emergency Remote Teaching (ERT), unveiling a plethora of pedagogical, technological, and organizational challenges. Simultaneously, it spotlighted the resilience and adaptability of institutions, educators, and students alike, as they navigated the uncharted waters of online education under crisis conditions. This reflection has not only dissected the pre-existing assumptions about online learning but also illuminated the potential pathways for redefining pedagogical strategies in the digital age.

The examination of the pedagogical shortcomings inherent in the ERT model, alongside the persistence of satisficing solutions post-pandemic, underscores a pressing imperative: the need for a strategic reevaluation and enhancement of online learning frameworks. As highlighted throughout this discourse, the conflation of ERT with intentionally designed online education presents significant risks to the quality, efficacy, and perception of digital learning within higher education landscapes. Therefore, distinguishing between the exigencies of ERT and the opportunities offered by well-crafted online courses is crucial for advancing the field of online education.

Moving forward, the imperative for higher education institutions lies in embracing a holistic approach to addressing the multifaceted challenges delineated herein. This encompasses fostering integrative pedagogical development, ensuring comprehensive access and equity, and facilitating sustainable institutional adaptation. By prioritizing these core areas, institutions can transcend the limitations exposed by the pandemic, leveraging the lessons learned to cultivate dynamic, inclusive, and pedagogically sound online learning environments.

In conclusion, the post-pandemic era presents a unique opportunity to reimagine the contours of digital education. The reflections and analyses presented in this article advocate for a concerted effort to unlearn outdated assumptions, critically address the pedagogical challenges unveiled by ERT, and confront the inertia sustaining satisficing solutions. As higher education institutions navigate this transformative journey, the goal should not merely be to adapt to the new normal but to envision and realize an elevated standard of online education that is equitable, effective, and resonant with the needs of a diverse and global student population. Through strategic innovation, collaborative endeavor, and a commitment to continuous improvement, the potential to redefine online learning for the betterment of all stakeholders in the educational ecosystem is within reach.

## REFERENCES

Aguilera-Hermida, P. (2020). College students' use and acceptance of emergency online learning due to COVID-19. *International Journal of Educational Research Open*, 1, 100011. 10.1016/j.ijedro.2020.10001135059662

Al-Kumaim, N. H., Alhazmi, A. K., Mohammed, F., Gazem, N. A., Shabbir, M. S., & Fazea, Y. (2021). Exploring the impact of the COVID-19 pandemic on university students' learning life: An integrated conceptual motivational model for sustainable and healthy online learning. *Sustainability (Basel)*, 13(5), 2546. 10.3390/su13052546

Al Shlowiy, A., Al-Hoorie, A. H., & Alharbi, M. (2021). Discrepancy between language learners and teachers concerns about emergency remote teaching. *Journal of Computer Assisted Learning*, 37(4), 1528–1538. 10.1111/jcal.12543

Alvarez, A. (2020). The phenomenon of learning at a distance through emergency remote teaching amidst the pandemic crisis. *Asian Journal of Distance Education*, 15(2), 127–143. 10.5281/zenodo.4299933

Anthony, B. J., & Noel, S. (2021). Examining the adoption of emergency remote teaching and virtual learning during and after COVID-19 pandemic. *International Journal of Educational Management*, 35(6), 1136–1150. 10.1108/IJEM-08-2020-0370

Aristovnik, A., Karampelas, K., Umek, L., & Ravšelj, D. (2023). Impact of the COVID-19 pandemic on online learning in higher education: A bibliometric analysis. *Frontiers in Education*, 8, 1225834.. 10.3389/feduc.2023.1225834

Arnold, M., Vogel, A., & Ulber, M. (2021). Digitalizing higher education in light of sustainability and rebound effects—Surveys in times of the COVID-19 pandemic. *Sustainability (Basel)*, 13(22), 12912. 10.3390/su132212912

Ashwin, P., & Mcvitty, D. (2015). The meanings of student engagement: Implications for policies and practices. *Higher Education Policy*, 28(1), 1–14. 10.1057/hep.2014.17

Azevedo, R. (2015). Defining and measuring engagement and learning in science: Conceptual, theoretical, methodological, and analytical issues. *Educational Psychologist*, 50(1), 84–94. 10.1080/00461520.2015.1004069

Azionya, C., & Nhedzi, A. (2021). The digital divide and higher education challenge with emergency online learning: Analysis of tweets in the wake of the COVID-19 lockdown. *Turkish Online Journal of Distance Education*, 22(4), 164–182. 10.17718/tojde.1002822

Babelyuk, O., Koliasa, O., Lopushanskyy, V., Smaglii, V., & Yukhymets, S. (2021). Psychological difficulties during the Covid lockdown: Video in blended digital teaching language, literature, and culture. *Arab World English Journal (AWEJ) Special Issue on Covid 19 Challenges,* (1), 172-182. 10.24093/awej/covid.13

Bai, X., Shao, Y., Liu, Y., Cai, M., Ma, M., & Yang, H. (2023). Current status of college students' learning engagement level in online learning and strategies to improve it: Take a university in Western China as an example. *Proceedings of the 2023 4th International Conference on Education Development and Studies*. Research Gate./10.1145/3591139.3591152

Banerjee, M. (2022). The digital divide and smartphone reliance for disadvantaged students in higher education. *Journal of Systemics, Cybernetics and Informatics*, 20(3), 31–39. 10.54808/JSCI.20.03.31

Bennett, B., Ross, D., & Gates, T. G. (2021). Creating spatial, relational, and cultural safety in online social work education during COVID-19. *Social Work Education*, 41(7), 1660–1668. 10.1080/02615479.2021.1924664

Bennett, G., & Green, F. (2001). Student learning in the online environment: No significant difference? *Quest*, 53(1), 1–13. 10.1080/00336297.2001.10491727

Blignaut, R. J., & Renaud, K. (2021). Higher education students' perceptions of online learning during COVID-19—A comparative study. *Education Sciences*, 11(8), 403. 10.3390/educsci11080403

Bond, M., Bedenlier, S., Marín, V. I., & Händel, M. (2021). Emergency remote teaching in higher education: Mapping the first global online semester. *International Journal of Educational Technology in Higher Education*, 18(50), 50. 10.1186/s41239-021-00282-x34778537

Boulton, C., Hughes, E., Kent, C., Smith, J. R., & Williams, H. T. P. (2019). Student engagement and wellbeing over time at a higher education institution. *PLoS One*, 14(11), e0227057. 10.1371/journal.pone.022577031774878

Broadbent, J., Ajjawi, R., Bearman, M., Boud, D., & Dawson, P. (2023). Beyond emergency remote teaching: Did the pandemic lead to lasting change in university courses? *International Journal of Educational Technology in Higher Education*, 20(1), 58. 10.1186/s41239-023-00428-z

Carrillo, C., & Flores, M. (2020). COVID-19 and teacher education: A literature review of online teaching and learning practices. *European Journal of Teacher Education*, 43(4), 466–487. 10.1080/02619768.2020.1821184

Chan, R., Bista, K., & Allen, R. (2021). Is online and distance learning the future in global higher education? The faculty perspective. In Chan, , (Eds.), *Online Teaching and Learning in Higher Education during COVID-19* (pp. 5–14). Routledge. 10.4324/9781003125921-2

Chen, C., Landa, S., Padilla, A., & Yur-Austin, J. (2022). Post-pandemic assessment of online teaching and learning in higher business education. *International Journal of Educational Management*, 36(6), 1065–1079. 10.1108/IJEM-11-2021-0430

Chen, P., Gonyea, R. M., & Kuh, G. D. (2008). Learning at a distance: Engaged or not? *Innovate: Journal of Online Education, 4*(3). https://hdl.handle.net/2022/24106

Colclasure, B. C., Marlier, A., Durham, M. F., Brooks, T. D., & Kerr, M. (2021). Identified challenges from faculty teaching at predominantly undergraduate institutions after abrupt transition to emergency remote teaching during the COVID-19 pandemic. *Education Sciences*, 11(9), 556. 10.3390/educsci11090556

Compton, L., Davis, N., & Correia, A. (2010). Pre-service teachers' preconceptions, misconceptions, and concerns about virtual schooling. *Distance Education*, 31(1), 37–54. 10.1080/01587911003725006

Cook, D. A., & Steinert, Y. (2013). Online learning for faculty development: A review of the literature. *Medical Teacher*, 35(11), 930–937. 10.3109/0142159X.2013.82732824006931

Cooper, L. (2001). A comparison of online and traditional computer applications classes. *T.H.E. Journal, 28*(8). https://thejournal.com/Articles/2001/03/01/Online-and Traditional-Computer-Applications-Classes.aspx?m=1

Coral, M. A., & Bermuy, A. E. (2022). Challenges in the Digital Transformation Processes in Higher Education Institutions and Universities. *International Journal of Information Technologies and Systems Approach*, 15(1), 1–14. 10.4018/IJITSA.290002

Demuyakor, J. (2020). Coronavirus (COVID-19) and online learning in higher institutions of education: A survey of the perceptions of Ghanaian international students in China. *Online Journal of Communication and Media Technologies*, 10(3), e202018. 10.29333/ojcmt/8286

Deng, X., & Yi, S. (2022). The digital divide in online education: a study of underserved college students. *Proceedings of the 55th Hawaii International Conference on System Sciences*. IEEE. 10.24251/HICSS.2022.624

Deshmukh, J. (2021). Speculations on the post-pandemic university campus – a global inquiry. *Archnet-IJAR: International Journal of Architectural Research,* 15(1), 10–23. 10.1108/ARCH-10-2020-0245

Djidu, H., Mashuri, S., Nasruddin, N., Sejati, A., Rasmuin, R., La Eru Ugi, L., & La Arua, A. (2021). Online learning in the post-Covid-19 pandemic era: Is our higher education ready for it? *Journal of Research and Education Studies: e-Saintika, 5*(1), 15-29. 10.36312/esaintika.v5i2.479

Duke, J., Francis, G., & Nagro, S. (2017). Student Engagement Across Distance Learning Models. *Learning in a Digital World, 9*. 10.13021/G8ITLCP.9.2017.1849

Dumulescu, D., Pop-Păcurar, I., & Necula, C. V. (2021). Learning design for future higher education – Insights from the time of COVID-19. *Frontiers in Psychology,* 12, 647948. http://doi.ord/10.3389/fpsyg.2021.647948. 10.3389/fpsyg.2021.647948

El-Sakran, A., Salman, R., & Alzaatreh, A. (2022). Impacts of emergency remote teaching on college students amid COVID-19 in the UAE. *International Journal of Environmental Research and Public Health*, 19(5), 2979. 10.3390/ijerph1905297935270670

Elsayary, A. (2023). The impact of a professional upskilling training programme on developing teachers' digital competence. *Journal of Computer Assisted Learning*, 39(4), 1154–1166. 10.1111/jcal.12788

Erdem-Aydin, I. (2021). Investigation of higher education instructors' perspectives towards emergency remote teaching. *Educational Media International*, 58(1), 78–98. 10.1080/09523987.2021.1908501

Ferri, F., Grifoni, P., & Guzzo, T. (2020). Online learning and emergency remote teaching: Opportunities and challenges in emergency situations. *Societies (Basel, Switzerland)*, 10(4), 86. 10.3390/soc10040086

Flynn, S., Collins, J., & Malone, L. (2022). Pandemic pedagogies: The impact of ERT on part time learners in Ireland. *International Journal of Lifelong Education, 41*(2), 182. https://doi.org/10.1080/02601370.2021.2022792

Foley, K., & Marr, L. (2019). Scaffolding extracurricular online events to support distance learning university students. *Journal of Interactive Media in Education*, 2019(1), 1–9. https://jime.open.ac.uk/articles/10.5334/jime.525. 10.5334/jime.525

Fuchs, K. (2022). Online learning and emergency remote teaching in higher education during COVID-19: Student perspectives. *International Journal of Information and Education Technology (IJIET)*, 12(9), 741–748. 10.18178/ijiet.2022.12.9.1704

García-Morales, V. J., Garrido-Moreno, A., & Martín-Rojas, R. (2021). The transformation of higher education after the COVID disruption: Emerging challenges in an online learning scenario. *Frontiers in Psychology*, 12, 616059. 10.3389/fpsyg.2021.61605933643144

Gaytan, J., & McEwen, B. (2007). Effective online instructional and assessment strategies. *American Journal of Distance Education*, 21(3), 117–132. 10.1080/08923640701341653

Gelles, L., Lord, S., Hoople, G., Chen, D. A., & Mejia, J. (2020). Compassionate flexibility and self-discipline: Student adaptation to emergency remote teaching in an integrated engineering energy course during COVID-19. *Education Sciences*, 10(11), 304. 10.3390/educsci10110304

Guppy, N., Verpoorten, D., Boud, D., Lin, L., Tai, J., & Bartolic, S. K. (2022). The post-COVID 19 future of digital learning in higher education: Views from educators, students, and other professionals in six countries. *British Journal of Educational Technology*, 6(53), 1750–1765. 10.1111/bjet.13212

Harris, L., Dargusch, J., Ames, K., & Bloomfield, C. (2020). Catering for 'very different kids': Distance education teachers' understandings of and strategies for student engagement. *International Journal of Inclusive Education*, 26(8), 848–864. 10.1080/13603116.2020.1735543

Henshaw, L. A. (2022). Building trauma-informed approaches in higher education. *Behavioral Sciences (Basel, Switzerland)*, 12(10), 368. 10.3390/bs1210036836285937

Hodges, C., Moore, S., Lockee, B., Trust, T., & Bond, A. (2020). The difference between emergency remote teaching and online learning. *EDUCAUSE Review*. https://er.educause.edu/articles/2020/3/the-difference-between-emergency remote -teaching-and-online-learning

Hughes, M. C., Henry, B. W., & Kushnick, M. R. (2020). Teaching during the pandemic? An opportunity to enhance curriculum. *Pedagogy in Health Promotion*, 6(4), 235–238. 10.1177/2373379920950179

Hussein, E., Daoud, S., Alrabaiah, H., & Badawi, R. (2020). Exploring undergraduate students' attitudes towards emergency online learning during COVID-19: A case from the UAE. *Children and Youth Services Review*, 119, 105699. 10.1016/j.childyouth.2020.105699

Iglesías-Pradas, S., Hernández-García, Á., Chaparro-Peláez, J., & Prieto, J. (2021). Emergency remote teaching and students' academic performance in higher education during the COVID-19 pandemic: A case study. *Computers in Human Behavior*, 119, 106713. 10.1016/j.chb.2021.10671334866769

Jili, N., Ede, C. I., & Masuku, M. (2021). Emergency remote teaching in higher education during Covid-19: Challenges and opportunities. *International Journal of Higher Education*, 10(5), 1. 10.5430/ijhe.v10n5p1

Johnson, K. R., Hewapathirana, G. I., & Bowen, M. M. (2019). Faculty development for online teaching. In Keengwe, J. (Ed.), *Handbook of Research on Virtual Training and Mentoring of Online Instructors* (pp. 40–55). IGI Global. 10.4018/978-1-5225-6322-8.ch003

Kahu, E. R. (2013). Framing student engagement in higher education. *Studies in Higher Education*, 38(5), 758–773. 10.1080/03075079.2011.598505

Kahu, E. R., Stephens, C., Leach, L., & Zepke, N. (2013). The engagement of mature distance students. *Higher Education Research & Development*, 32(5), 791–804. 10.1080/07294360.2013.777036

Kaisara, G., & Bwalya, K. (2023). Strategies for enhancing assessment information integrity in mobile learning. *Informatics (MDPI)*, 10(1), 29. 10.3390/informatics10010029

Kara, A. (2021). COVID-19 pandemic and possible trends into the future of higher education: a review. *Journal of Education and Educational Development, 8*(1), 09 26. 10.22555/joeed.v8i1.183

Karakose, T. (2021). Emergency remote teaching due to COVID-19 pandemic and potential risks for socioeconomically disadvantaged students in higher education. *Educational Process: International Journal*, 10(3), 53–61. 10.22521/edupij.2021.103.4

Khalili, H. (2020). Online interprofessional education during and post the COVID-19 pandemic: A commentary. *Journal of Interprofessional Care*, 34(5), 687–692. 10.1080/13561820.2020.179242432674721

Koh, J. H. L., & Daniel, B. K. (2022). Shifting online during COVID-19: A systematic review of teaching and learning strategies and their outcomes. *International Journal of Educational Technology in Higher Education*, 19(56), 56. 10.1186/s41239-022-00361-736404984

Kovacevic, I., Labrović, J., Petrović, N., & Kužet, I. (2021). Recognizing Predictors of Students' Emergency Remote Online Learning Satisfaction during COVID-19. *Education Sciences*, 11(11), 693. 10.3390/educsci11110693

Kuforiji, P., & Kuforiji, J. (2022). The transition from Covid-19 pandemic induced online learning to the future physical campus: is the higher education ready? In Salman Nazir (eds) *Training, Education, and Learning Sciences.* AHFE International, USA. 10.54941/ahfe1002380

Langan, T. (1997). Online education: A student's perspective. *Campus-Wide Information Systems*, 14(4), 128–132. 10.1108/10650749710194565

Laufer, M., Leiser, A., Deacon, B., Perrin de Brichambaut, P., Fecher, B., Kobsda, C., & Hesse, F. (2021). Digital higher education: A divider or bridge builder? Leadership perspectives on edtech in a COVID-19 reality. *International Journal of Educational Technology in Higher Education*, 18(1), 51. 10.1186/s41239-021-00287-634778538

Lederman, D. (2020, April 8). Survey gauges the state of the online education landscape pre-coronavirus. *Inside Higher Ed.* https://www.insidehighered.com/news/2020/03/25/survey-gauges-state-online education-landscape-pre-coronavirus

Lei, V., & Cheong, C. (2022). Emergency remote teaching and first-year student engagement during the COVID-19 pandemic: Emergency remote teaching and student engagement during COVID-19. *Proceedings of the 8th International Conference on Education and Training Technologies*, (pp. 60-65). IEEE. 10.1145/3535756.3535766

Lobos, K., Cobo-Rendón, R., García-Álvarez, D., Maldonado-Mahauad, J., & Bruna, C. (2023). Lessons learned from the educational experience during COVID-19 from the perspective of Latin American university students. *Sustainability (Basel)*, 15(3), 2341. 10.3390/su15032341

Makransky, G., Mayer, R., Veitch, N., Hood, M., Christensen, K., & Gadegaard, H. (2019). Equivalence of using a desktop virtual reality science simulation at home and in class. *PLoS One*, 14(4), e0214944. Advance online publication. 10.1371/journal.pone.021494430973900

Makumane, M., Mataka, T. W., Sengai, W., & Ngcobo, S. (2023). Neutralising the digital divide: Is blended learning a viable solution? *International Journal of Research in Business and Social Science*, 12(1), 1–10. 10.20525/ijrbs.v12i7.2740

Maldonado, K., & Maldonado, L. (2022). Emergency remote teaching and the medical student. *Technium Social Sciences Journal*, 36, 157–162. 10.47577/tssj.v36i1.7424

Márquez, J., Mejías, A., & Marquez, M. (2011). Augmented reality for the improvement of remote laboratories: An augmented remote laboratory. *IEEE Transactions on Education*, 54(3), 492–500. 10.1109/TE.2010.2085047

Mathrani, A., Sarvesh, T., & Umer, R. (2021). Digital divide framework: Online learning in developing countries during the COVID-19 lockdown. *Globalisation, Societies and Education*, 19(4), 513–528. 10.1080/14767724.2021.1981253

Misirli, O., & Ergulec, F. (2021). Emergency remote teaching during the COVID-19 pandemic: Parents experiences and perspectives. *Education and Information Technologies*, 26(6), 6699–6718. 10.1007/s10639-021-10520-433814956

Moore, S., & Hodges, C. B. (2023). *Emergency Remote Teaching*. EdTechnica., 10.59668/371.11681

Mospan, N. (2022). Trends in emergency higher education digital transformation during the COVID-19 pandemic. *Journal of University Teaching and Learning Practice, 20*(1). 10.53761/1.20.01.04

Najab, A., & Amrani, O. (2022). Digital accessibility and distance higher education in the context of COVID-19: lessons from the experience of FSJES-Souissi and future perspectives. In Haoucha, M. (Ed.), *Policies and Procedures for the Implementation of Safe and Healthy Educational Environments: Post-COVID-19 Perspectives* (pp. 88–105). IGI Global. 10.4018/978-1-7998-9297-7.ch006

Ng, B. (2021). Engaging students in emergency remote teaching: strategies for the instructor. In Ktoridou, D., Doukanari, E., & Eteokleous, N. (Eds.), *Fostering Meaningful Learning Experiences Through Student Engagement* (pp. 74–91). IGI Global. 10.4018/978-1-7998-4658-1.ch004

Nugroho, I. (2023). The puzzle of how higher education learning does in post-COVID-19 pandemic. *Journal of Socioeconomics and Development*, 6(2), 145–156. 10.31328/jsed.v6i1.3285

Nurhas, I., Aditya, B., Witarsyah, D. J., & Pawlowski, J. (2021). Understanding the challenges of rapid digital transformation: The case of COVID-19 pandemic in higher education. *Behaviour & Information Technology*, 41(2), 2924–2940. 10.1080/0144929X.2021.1962977

Nye, A. (2015). Building an online academic learning community among undergraduate students. *Distance Education*, 36(1), 115–128. 10.1080/01587919.2015.1019969

Pashkov, M., Pashkova, V. M., & Starostenko, V. A. (2022). Transnational online education and digital inequality: Issues of pedagogical design. *Vestnik of Saint Petersburg University. Sociology, 15*(3), 368-387. https://typeset.io/papers/transnational online-education-and-digital-inequality-issues-mref2rf2

Petronzi, R., & Petronzi, D. (2020). The Online and Campus (OaC) model as a sustainable blended approach to teaching and learning in higher education: A response to COVID-19. *Journal of Pedagogical Research*, 4(4), 498–507. 10.33902/JPR.2020064475

Pham, N., & Nghiem, H. V. (2022). Online teaching satisfaction amid the Covid-19 pandemic: Evidence from a Vietnamese higher education context. *International Journal of TESOL & Education*, 2(4), 45–57. 10.54855/ijte.222119

Pittaway, S. (2012). Student and staff engagement: Developing an engagement framework in a Faculty of Education. *The Australian Journal of Teacher Education*, 37(4), 37–45. 10.14221/ajte.2012v37n4.8

Poirier, M. J. P., Hard, J., & Holst, J. (2023). COVID-19 pandemic providing a window of opportunity for higher education: Case study of a three-country teaching-learning experience. *South Eastern European Journal of Public Health*, 9(1), 45–60. 10.56801/seejph.vi.223

Rasli, A., Tee, M., Lai, Y. L., Tiu, Z. C., & Soon, E. H. (2022). Post-COVID-19 strategies for higher education institutions in dealing with unknown and uncertainties. *Frontiers in Education*, 7, 992063. Advance online publication. 10.3389/feduc.2022.992063

Rogozin, D., Solodovnikova, O., & Ipatova, A. (2022). How University Teachers View the Digital Transformation of Higher Education. *Studies of E-Learning*. 10.17323/1814-9545-2022-1-271-300

Rojas-Contreras, M., & Ruiz-Bautista, L. (2020). Online laboratories supported with virtual reality for higher education. *Journal of Physics: Conference Series*, 1708(1), 012036. Advance online publication. 10.1088/1742-6596/1708/1/012036

Salas-Pilco, S. Z., Yang, Y., & Zhang, Z. (2022). Student engagement in online learning in Latin American higher education during the COVID-19 pandemic: A systematic review. *British Journal of Educational Technology*, 53(3), 593–619. 10.1111/bjet.1319035600418

Sandid, B., Belhaj, L., & Elmadani, O. (2023). Strategies for student engagement in distance learning. *International Journal For Multidisciplinary Research*, 5(6), 9473. Advance online publication. 10.36948/ijfmr.2023.v05i06.9473

Sarder, M. B. (2014). Improving student engagement in online courses. *ASEE Annual Conference and Exposition, Conference Proceedings*. ASEE. 10.18260/1-2--20611

Schalk, A., McAvinia, C., & Rooney, P. (2022). Exploring the concept of the digital educator during COVID-19. *Australasian Journal of Educational Technology*, 38(2), 129–141. 10.14742/ajet.7316

Schlesselman, L. S. (2020). Perspective from a teaching and learning center during emergency remote teaching. *American Journal of Pharmaceutical Education*, 84(6), 8142. 10.5688/ajpe814232934391

Scott, J. (2019). Professional development for online post-secondary faculty. *Eighth International Conference on Educational Innovation through Technology (EITT)*. IEEE. 10.1109/EITT.2019.00017

Seynhaeve, S., Deygers, B., Simon, E., & Delarue, S. (2022). Interaction in online classes during Covid-19: The experiences of newly-arrived migrant students. *Educational Research*, 64(3), 334–352. 10.1080/00131881.2022.2090981

Sherwood, D., Vandeusen, K. M., Weller, B., & Gladden, J. (2021). Teaching trauma content online during COVID-19: A trauma-informed and culturally responsive pedagogy. *Journal of Social Work Education, 57*(sup1), 99-110. 10.1080/10437797.2021.1916665

Shim, T., & Lee, S. (2020). College students' experience of emergency remote teaching due to COVID-19. *Children and Youth Services Review*, 119, 105578. 10.1016/j.childyouth.2020.10557833071405

Shin, M., & Hickey, K. (2020). Needs a little TLC: Examining college students' emergency remote teaching and learning experiences during COVID-19. *Journal of Further and Higher Education*, 45(7), 973–986. 10.1080/0309877X.2020.1847261

Sieber, J. (2005). Misconceptions and realities about teaching online. *Science and Engineering Ethics*, 11(3), 329–340. 10.1007/s11948-005-0002-716190274

Sim, S., Sim, H. P., & Quah, C. (2021). Online learning: A post COVID-19 alternative pedagogy for university students. *Asian Journal of University Education, 17*(4), 137 149. https://doi.org/10.24191/ajue.v16i4.11963

Sosniuk, O., & Ostapenko, I. (2021). Usage of digital tools and social media for learning: Ukrainian experience in the context of the COVID-19 pandemic. In *Proceedings of the 2021 International Conference on Education and New Learning Technologies*. Research Gate. /10.30525/978-9934-26-076-6-23

Stewart, W. (2021). A global crash-course in teaching and learning online: A thematic review of empirical emergency remote teaching (ERT) studies in higher education during year 1 of COVID-19. *Open Praxis*, 13(1), 89–102. 10.5944/openpraxis.13.1.1177

Stewart, W., Baek, Y., & Lowenthal, P. R. (2022). From emergency remote teaching (ERT) to sustained remote teaching (SRT): A comparative semester analysis of exchange students' experiences and perceptions of learning online during COVID-19. *Online Learning : the Official Journal of the Online Learning Consortium*, 26(1), 22–40. 10.24059/olj.v26i2.2661

Sultanova, L., Milto, L., & Zheludenko, M. (2021). The impact of the COVID-19 pandemic on the development of higher education. *Acta Paedagogica Vilnensia*, 46, 132–147. 10.15388/ActPaed.46.2021.9

Sydorenko, V., Akhnovska, I., Smirnov, S. V., Verbovskyi, I., & Melnychuk, O. V. (2021). Bridging the digital divide as a basic imperative in higher education. *Estudios de Economía Aplicada*, 39(9). 10.25115/eea.v39i9.5798

Tanner, J. R., Noser, T. C., & Totaro, M. W. (2009). Business faculty and undergraduate students' perceptions of online learning: A comparative study. *Journal of Information Systems Education*, 20(1), 29–40. https://www.learntechlib.org/p/105718/

Thurston, A. (2000). Building online learning communities. *Technology, Pedagogy and Education*, 14(3), 353–369. 10.1080/14759390500200216

Trust, T., & Whalen, J. (2020). Should teachers be trained in emergency remote teaching? Lessons learned from the COVID-19 pandemic. *Journal of Technology and Teacher Education*, 28(2), 189–199. https://www.learntechlib.org/primary/p/215995/

Tsantopoulos, G., Karasmanaki, E., Ioannou, K., & Kapnia, M. (2022). Higher education in a post-pandemic world. *Education Sciences*, 12(12), 856. 10.3390/educsci12120856

van de Werfhorst, H. G., Kessenich, E., & Geven, S. (2020). The digital divide in online education: Inequality in digital preparedness of students and schools before the start of the COVID-19 pandemic. *Computers and Education Open*, 3, 100100. 10.1016/j.caeo.2022.100100

Vasilijević, D., Bojović, Ž., Semiz, M., & Sudzilovski, D. (2023). Personal predictors of online teaching - Experiences of the teachers in Serbia in the COVID regime. *International Journal of Cognitive Research in Science. Engineering and Education*, 11(1), 63–75. 10.23947/2334-8496-2023-11-1-63-75

Vijayan, R. (2021). Teaching and learning during the COVID-19 pandemic: A topic modeling study. *Education Sciences*, 11(7), 1–15. 10.3390/educsci11070347

Wang, A. L. (2021). Models of student engagement in music education classroom in higher education. *Frontiers in Psychology*, 12, 668981. 10.3389/fpsyg.2021.73820734484089

Weerawardane, D. (2021). Digital transformation of Higher Education: What's next? *New Vistas.*, 7(2), 3–7. 10.36828/newvistas.147

Yang, Y., Liu, K., Li, M., & Li, S. (2021). Students' affective engagement, parental involvement, and teacher support in emergency remote teaching during the COVID 19 pandemic: Evidence from a cross-sectional survey in China. *Journal of Research on Technology in Education*, 54(sup1, S1), S148–S164. 10.1080/15391523.2021.1922104

Zhang, L., Carter, R., Qian, X., Yang, S., Rujimora, J., & Wen, S.-L. (2022). Academia's responses to crisis: A bibliometric analysis of literature on online learning in higher education during COVID-19. *British Journal of Educational Technology, 53*(6), 1161 1177. 10.1111/bjet.13191

# Chapter 5 Rural School Teachers Leveraging Pandemic Teaching Experiences for Technology Integration in Post-Pandemic Classrooms

**Clement Simuja**
https://orcid.org/0000-0002-0105-0013
*Rhodes University, South Africa*

**Brian Shambare**
https://orcid.org/0000-0002-4869-8407
*Rhodes University, South Africa*

## ABSTRACT

*This study investigates how rural teachers in the Eastern Cape province of South Africa harness their experiences during the pandemic to integrate technology into post-pandemic pedagogical practices. Adopt TPACK theoretical framework, purposively selected 18 teachers in the Eastern Cape province's rural schools in South Africa. Data was collected through interviews and two sharing circles through a phenomenological approach and analyzed thematically. Findings reveal that rural teachers, initially intimidated by technology, adapted to its use out of necessity during the pandemic and came to view it as an essential teaching tool. Teachers embraced digital tools to overcome infrastructural challenges and maintain educational continuity, showing resilience and innovation, prompting teachers to*

DOI: 10.4018/979-8-3693-7645-4.ch005

*acquire new competencies and reconsider their approach to integrating technology. These experiences continue to shape educational practices and promote sustained technological integration, indicating a marked shift in rural teachers' perspectives towards the role of technology in teaching.*

## INTRODUCTION

The global emergence of the COVID-19 pandemic has significantly transformed nearly every facet of life, including the realm of education (Dhawan, 2020). This shift posed a formidable challenge to the education sector, disrupting the learning experiences of over 1.7 billion students, as reported by UNESCO's COVID-19 Educational Disruption and Response guidelines for 2020 (UNESCO, 2020). Faced with this unprecedented situation undoubtedly occasioned an unprecedented disruption in the global education system(Takona,2023), forcing a rapid andin many cases, unprepared shift from traditional in-person instruction to technology-mediated education(Shambare & Simuja,2022). This significant shift also set and expanded the role of digital methodologies in educational settings, crucially shaping the dynamics of teaching and learning (Child & Song,2023). This transition necessitated teachers to rapidly acquire and hone digital competencies, with some educators adapting the forced digital immersion to innovate their pedagogical practices.

Prior to the pandemic, educational technologies were already being integrated in education in some developed and developing countries with an emphasis on improving the quality of education (Linnes, Ronzoni, Agrusa & Lema,2022). However, the school closures stemming from the pandemic swiftly turned this growing interest into an imperative need. The abrupt transition to online education was facilitated by digital platforms, e-learning, and other technologies (Dhawan,2020), presenting a spectrum of challenges, particularly in developing countries such as South Africa, hindered by resource scarcity and limited access to the Internet (Mare, Woyo & Amadhila,2022).

Moreover, in the context of rural education in South Africa, teachers were faced with unique challenges due to the lack of infrastructure, digital divide, and professional development opportunities to effectively incorporate technology in their pedagogical practices (Azionya & Nhedzi,2021). Similarly, rural areas, like those in the Eastern Cape Province in South Africa are often characterized by inadequate access to technological resources (Fanteso & Yessoufou,2022), making the sudden demand for online teaching during the pandemic a discouraging practice (Shambare & Simuja,2022). Despite these challenges, some rural educators were able to make remarkable resilience and adaptability. Studies indicate that even with limited resources, many educators managed to integrate technology into their methodologies throughout the pandemic (Azionya & Nhedzi,2021; Takona,2023; Mapisa & Makena,2024). The experiences during this period could offer an outline for the sustained incorporation of technology in teaching, highlighting rural teachers' innovative solutions to technology integration under constrained circumstances.

The schools in South Africa, and particularly in the Eastern Cape province have been significantly altered by the pandemic (Shambare and Simuja,2022). The shift to online learning presented an array of challenges that went beyond adapting to new teaching platforms. These included inadequate electricity, limited or no internet connectivity, and a scarcity of technological devices among both teachers and students. However, the push towards embracing technological pedagogies during pre and post covid has unveiled some opportunities to reconsider longstanding educational practices and explore new approaches in technology integration, particularly for educators in rural school settings. Despite a lack of prior training or experience with digital tools, many teachers in rural schools in the Eastern Cape province, demonstrated a commendable commitment to maintaining educational continuity during school closures (Mdoda & Mdiya,2022), improvising with available resources and often relying on community support to facilitate learning (Pillay & Shipalana, 2023). The pandemic, therefore, inadvertently became a catalyst for digital transformation in rural classrooms, challenging educators to develop new competencies and re-evaluate their attitudes towards the role of technology in education.

While studies have explored the general impact of COVID-19 on teaching methods (Peimani & Kamalipour,2021) and the effectiveness of digital education (Batd, Doğan & Talan,2023), the specific experiences of rural teachers navigating the abrupt change and their continued use of technology in the post-pandemic period remain underexamined. Therefore, this study, to bridge this gap, explores how rural teachers in Eastern Cape province in South Africa have used their pandemic driven experiences teaching with technology to enrich post-pandemic pedagogical practices.

The central problem addressed is the dearth of research centred on the narratives of rural school teachers, whose experiences during the pandemic are crucial for informing the future trajectory of educational technology in similar contexts. The study was guided by the research question: How do rural school teachers leverage their pandemic teaching experiences for technology integration in post-pandemic classrooms? To respond to the research question, the chapter starts by reviewing the existing literature to establish the central theme and introduces a theoretical framework to guide the research. Next, the research methods, including how data was collected and analyzed, are explained in detail. Then, the findings are detailed, and the chapter presents conclusions of the results and suggests future directions for further research.

## LITERATURE REVIEW

The worldwide outbreak of Covid-19 prompted a departure from in-person instructional methods (Dutta,2020; Estrella, 2023; Mare et al.,2021). To preserve the continuity of education throughout this global health crisis, instructional practices in most schools in developed and developing countries predominantly transitioned to online remote education (Shambare & Simuja, 2022; Xue & Crompton,2024). Moreover, COVID-19 pandemic accelerated the integration of educational technology in African schools, as highlighted by UNESCO's policy reports of 2021, which emphasized that the urgent transition to online learning platforms became a necessary response to maintain educational continuity during school closures (Meinck, Fraillon & Strietholt,2022). This adaptation included not only the usage of digital tools such as videoconferencing platforms and learning management systems, which are generally dependent on Internet connectivity but it was also maintained in certain areas through the provision of tangible study aids, including books and printed materials (Ayega,2020; Matete, Ennam, 2024; Kimario & Behera,2023).

Starting in 2020, the pandemic necessitated a sudden alteration in the traditional teaching methodologies employed by educators who were pressed to incorporate innovative technologies to meet educational objectives, and the readiness for this pedagogic shift varied among teaching professionals. In the context of South Africa, the Department of Basic Education (DBE) in 2020 released guidelines that focused on adapting and adopting both high-technology and low-technology solutions to mitigate the challenges of remote learning, particularly in under-resourced rural areas (DBE,2020). Such a jump into the realms of technology enhanced teaching and learning conditions required adaptability within educational frameworks. In the study by Adov and Maeots (2021) titled 'What can we learn about science teachers' technology use during the Covid-19 pandemic?' presented findings that teachers who had a more positive attitude towards using technology during the pandemic period were better equipped to navigate the challenges and adapt to the imposed remote learning settings. The same study outlined common deterrents such as lack of internet connection, a deficit in digital proficiency among students and teachers, and the teachers' perceptions of employing technology within their pedagogical strategies. The study recommended the need for support for teachers to overcome the diverse barriers which arise when integrating technology into education during the pandemic.

Similarly, Li, Yang, Chen and Li (2022) observed that school closures during the COVID-19 pandemic interrupted traditional education delivery mechanisms and imposed significant economic burdens on families. This was particularly pertinent in economically disadvantaged communities and developing countries where the scarcity of resources pronounced educational inequities (Matete et al.,2023).

Nonetheless, some schools in these countries demonstrated resilience by employing alternative instructional methods. For instance, an exploratory study conducted by Gore, Twine, Botha and Naidoo (2023) revealed the diverse ways in which schools reacted to the crisis in Africa. Schools in different countries in Africa displayed variable levels of adherence to government guidelines on distance learning. Their study underscored that while each school attempted to adopt and adapt governmental directives, there was a considerable disparity influenced by local realities and infrastructural capabilities. Much like their Western countries' counterparts, educators in some African countries meticulously modified their curricula to better align with the exigencies posed by the pandemic and the heterogeneity of student needs (Shambare & Simuja,2022). However, similar to other researchers' findings, one salient challenge encountered was the design of pedagogically sound digital content and equitable assessment strategies, exacerbated by a deficiency in technical competencies among teachers (Ayega,2020).

Furthermore, research by Mpungose (2020) highlighted South Africa's educators' efforts to integrate technology within the learning environment as a direct result of pandemic constraints. The study revealed efforts to strengthen the technological infrastructure in schools to facilitate continued educational activities. One such endeavour involved the introduction of free and open learning management systems such as Google Classroom in some schools, which served as a digital platform for conducting evaluations and supporting remote instruction. Fanteso and Yessoufou (2022) highlighted the substantial difficulties teachers faced during the shift to the use of technologies amid school closures in developing countries. These challenges included ambiguous guidelines for the transition, deficiency in both technological pedagogy and content knowledge and issues surrounding equity and learners' accessibility to online lessons and technologies. Moreover, most teachers grappled with the absence of infrastructural support for online teaching, limited technical assistance, and a lack of familiarity with digital teaching methods, as noted by Azionya and Nhedzi (2021). These adversities further led to inconsistent teaching outcomes influenced by the varying levels of teachers' experience, inadequate skills in distance teaching, informational deficiencies, and the intricacies inherent in the social contexts of learners.

In most rural school settings in Africa, the shift to technological integration in education during the pandemic posed distinct challenges, as underscored by Badaru and Adu (2022), who found that rural teachers grappled with limited internet connectivity and inadequate access to digital technologies. According to the study by Muhuro and Kang'ethe (2021), many rural schools in Africa lacked the basic ICT infrastructure, which severely hindered the adoption of online teaching methods. Furthermore, these educators often lacked the requisite training to effectively utilize digital tools for instructional purposes, impeding their ability to deliver quality education (Kang'ethe,2022). The study by Kusuma (2022) revealed that rural teachers were not just faced with technological hindrances but also experienced significant challenges in accessing professional development opportunities which are crucial for developing digital literacy and pedagogical skills. This finding aligns with Dzansi and Amedzo's (2014) insights on the slower ICT adoption in rural versus urban schools in South Africa.

Despite the obstacles, some rural educators displayed commendable resourcefulness as noted by many scholars. According to Shava (2022), many rural teachers harnessed basic mobile technologies to facilitate learning, repurpose widespread mobile phone use among learners for educational purposes. They adapted teaching content to be accessible via SMS, Whatsapp groups and used community radio broadcasts to reach learners, a hybrid approach that proved exceptionally relevant in technology-poor contexts. Moreover, community involvement emerged as a critical factor in the successful integration of technologies in some rural areas particularly in South Africa. The study of Bryson and Andres (2020), for example, illustrates how community volunteers assisted in setting up temporary digital learning centres using local resources. These centres, often set up in community halls or churches, provided learners with access to pre-recorded lessons and digital content, thereby fostering a collective approach to education.

Post-pandemic, Mmakola and Maphalala (2023) highlight the emergent blended learning models that incorporate local knowledge and digital tools, setting a precedent for culturally relevant pedagogies in rural African school contexts. Moreover, a study by Sahoo and Rana (2023) demonstrated a continual upsurge in the use of open-source platforms like Google Classroom in rural schools, promoting interactive digital learning environments. The sustainability of these approaches and technologies, as argued by Ochieng,Asego and Gyasi (2023) relies on ongoing policy support and investment in rural educational technology infrastructure. Simuja and Shikesho (2024) suggest a pivotal role for government intervention in normalizing these improvisations into sustained policies that foster long-term educational technology integration in rural areas.

Reflecting on these experiences, the body of literature indicates that the COVID-19 pandemic has accelerated the potential for ongoing integration of technology in teaching practices in rural South African schools post-pandemic. Maja (2023) suggests that the creative use of available technology during the pandemic has laid a foundation for informal blended learning environments, which could be formalized and expanded with post-pandemic recovery efforts. However, for this potential to be realized, policy interventions are necessary. A case study by Monyai (2024) posits that the governments in developing countries such as South Africa prioritize equipping rural schools with the necessary technological infrastructure. This includes stable internet access and training for teachers in the use of educational technology.

## Theoretical Framework

The study draws on the Technological Pedagogical Content Knowledge(TPACK) framework, which is central to understanding the integration of technology in teaching practices. TPACK suggests that effective technology integration in education requires an understanding of the interplay between three primary forms of knowledge: Content, Pedagogy, and Technology (Mishra & Koehler, 2006). These interwoven knowledge bases are necessary for teachers to facilitate learning with the aid of technology (Mishra and Koehler,2008). In this study, TPACK served as the foundational framework to investigate how rural school teachers in Eastern Cape Province have used their experiences during the pandemic to integrate technology in their post-COVID teaching practices. The study explicitly examines the confluence of teachers' content knowledge, pedagogical knowledge, and technological knowledge that they have developed or enhanced as a response to the challenges posed by the pandemic.

Moreover, the relevance of TPACK to this study lies in the way it acknowledges the complex, multifaceted nature of teaching with technology, which extends beyond simply knowing how to use digital tools (Niess & Gillow-Wiles,2021). It involves an understanding of how to select, adapt, and use these tools to provide instruction that is both pedagogically sound and content specific (Nepembe & Simuja,2023). TPACK in this study is particularly pertinent in the context of rural education, where resources are limited and teachers often have to adapt and innovate with the technology available to them.

Connecting TPACK to phenomenology in this study was critical as phenomenology centres on the lived experiences of individuals (Gill & Dalgarno,2017). The phenomenological approach in this study aims to deeply understand the shared experiences of the 18 rural teachers who participated in the study. The phenomenological analysis provides rich, contextual insights into how these educators internalized and reflected upon their learning and teaching during pre and post pandemic, thus acting as a lens to discern the transformation in their TPACK competencies(Clark & Boyer,2016). This perspective not only enhances the study's understanding of technology's role in rural education during the transition to post-pandemic teaching but also underscores the resilience and innovation of rural teachers. It illustrates how they have reconceptualized their instructional strategies by integrating their newly acquired or improved technology knowledge and skills with their existing pedagogical and content knowledge, consequently enriching the educational experiences of their learners.

## METHODOLOGY

To explore how rural school teachers have integrated technology in their classrooms following the pandemic, the study adopted a qualitative research approach (Merriam,2002) featuring phenomenological methods (Finlay,2012). Phenomenology is well-suited for this study as it seeks to understand the lived experiences of individual's (Neubauer, Witkop & Varpio,2019), in this case, teachers' perspectives. The focus is on their subjective experiences and the meanings they attach to those experiences with technology during and post pandemic of COVID-19. To ensure a comprehensive understanding of these experiences, the study adopted a purposeful sampling method (Yin, 2003) suited to phenomenological research. The study targeted the Eastern Cape Province, an area characterized by its rural attributes and frequently overlooked in the realm of educational technology discourse and closer to us authors. A total of 18 rural school teachers participated in the study.

The sample size was in alignment with phenomenological study standards, which typically range from 5 to 25 participants (Neubauer et al.,2019). The inclusion criteria were as follows: current employed as a teacher in a rural school in Eastern Cape Province, involvement in teaching during the COVID-19 pandemic, and engagement in technology use for educational purposes during and after the pandemic. This criterion ensured that only those with relevant experiences were included in the study. The educators had a diversity of teaching experiences and educational backgrounds. The participating educators were involved in teaching different subjects, including Mathematics, English, and Science. Their experience ranged broadly, with an average of six years in teaching in rural schools. The qualifications among the participants varied from diplomas to bachelor degrees in education, reflecting a wide spectrum of academic training within the group.

Data were collected through in-depth interviews and the facilitation of two sharing circles, through which the teachers narrated their transition on a personal and professional level. The sharing circle, in particular, is a traditional way of facilitating discussion and storytelling, allowing participants to feel at ease and respected within a familiar cultural practice (Hunt & Young,2021). We received ethical approval for the study from our affiliated university's Ethics Committee, which was also supported by the regional education department and the schools taking part in the research. Adhering to ethical standards, we ensured confidentiality and anonymity for all participants. Informed consent was obtained, and participants were given the right to withdraw at any stage of the research. Respect for their privacy and thoughtful handling of sensitive information was upheld throughout the study process.

## Data Analysis

The data analysis for this study was methodically carried out using thematic analysis, an approach that is particularly adept at identifying, analyzing, and reporting patterns within qualitative data (Nowell et al.,2017). The process started with transcribing the recorded interviews and sharing circle discussions, followed by a careful reading and re-reading of the transcripts to gain an initial familiarity with the depth of the data. The initial codes were generated by systematically highlighting and annotating meaningful portions of the text that related to the research question. These codes were then sorted into potential themes, with attention paid to both the prevalence of ideas and their significance within the context of rural education (Castleberry & Nolen,2018).

The emergent themes were reviewed and refined to ensure they accurately represented the data set as a whole. This involved a recursive process of moving back and forth between the dataset, the coded extracts, and developing themes, hence producing a thematic map of the analysis. The themes were further refined and named, with a clear definition for each to ensure clarity and coherence. To enhance the reliability of the analysis, the themes were crosschecked against the raw data to ensure they reliably represented the collected interviews and sharing circles discussions. Throughout the analysis, reflections on the literature were integrated, drawing parallels and noting divergences between our findings and existing research. The first author distilled the essence of the teachers' experiences into a narrative account, rich in context and anchored in the participants' perspectives. The findings present this narrative by selecting verbatim quotes from participants chosen for their illustrative power and relevance to the research questions.

The reliability and validity of our findings are rooted in transparently reporting the methodology and utilizing pseudonyms derived from indigenous clan names for participant anonymity, thereby honouring their cultural significance while maintaining the integrity and ethical considerations of the research. This use of clan names as pseudonyms provided a culturally sensitive approach to data representation, ensuring participants' identities were protected while allowing them to be recognized and respected within the context of their community values and traditions.

## Research Findings

In this section, we present the research findings which elucidate how rural school teachers in the Eastern Cape province have navigated the integration of technology in their classrooms post-pandemic. The data was analyzed to uncover trends and patterns in educators' approaches to technology use, reflecting adaptations made during the pandemic. This study data offers an in-depth look at rural school teachers' integration of technology into their classrooms, particularly highlighting the shift in their practices post-pandemic.

## Technology Integration in Rural Schools

It is notable that the selected educators, once wary of technological incorporation due to its perceived inaccessibility, gradually embraced these tools, viewing them as indispensable to their teaching methods. It became evident that resourcefulness in the face of limited infrastructure played a crucial role in this shift, with teachers improvising solutions and adapting available community resources. The findings reveal an initial resistance to technology, narrated by a Mandlovu and Mthembu:

*It felt like a mountain too high to climb; the technologies, the Internet, everything was just out of our reach. (Mandlovu)*

*At first, the thought of using technology in my lessons was daunting, resources were scarce and my own skills very limited. But over time, the pandemic forced us to adapt, and now I see these digital tools as good in educating our learners. (Mthembu)*

This sentiment captures the overarching intimidation that many rural teachers initially felt towards technology, compounded by their limited exposure and access to these resources before the advent of the pandemic. However, as the pandemic unfolded, these initial perceptions underwent a profound shift. Teachers began to see technology as a necessary part of their teaching tools. Cirnha shared:

*I realized that if I did not adapt, my learners would be left behind. It became a challenge I was willing to take on...*

The quote above marked an acknowledgement of technology's utility in reaching and engaging learners, especially at a time of physical distancing. During the pandemic, the absence of traditional classroom settings forced most teachers to explore and integrate technology into their pedagogy. With limited resources, teachers exhibited resourcefulness, using mobile phones, radio, and television broadcasts to deliver lessons. Zondo expressed:

*...we had to use what was available to us, sometimes that meant teaching over WhatsApp Groups...*

Mathambo commented, showcasing the innovative use of commonly available technology to maintain educational continuity:

*It was a steep learning curve, but we leaned on each other and the community. We organized WhatsApp study groups, managing to keep the learning process alive even from a distance.*

The transformation in attitudes was particularly evident when technology went from being perceived as a foreign addition to becoming an integral element within the classroom. This shift from apprehension to acceptance illustrates a broader example of change in education, where necessity drove innovation in pedagogical strategies. Teachers, initially overwhelmed by the prospect of employing technology, gradually recognized its potential to facilitate learner engagement and continuity of education amidst disruptions. During the sharing circle, Kathumba narrated their experience, emphasizing the broadened perspective that came with technological familiarity:

*It is like we discovered a hidden world where the possibilities for teaching are endless,*

The study revealed that rural school teachers in the Eastern Cape province faced considerable challenges while integrating technology during the COVID-19 pandemic. During the Sharing circle Lwazi stated:

*Even when we had access to devices, constant power outages made it nearly impossible to maintain a consistent teaching schedule.*

Kwekwe shared similar concerns:

*Our reliance on mobile data due to the lack of stable internet connectivity was financially unsustainable for both teachers and students.*

Ma'bele emphasized the improvisation required:

*We often had to resort to using community centres with generators to charge devices and download materials during brief windows of electricity.*

The collective experiences of these educators highlight a wider systemic issue, the lack of infrastructural support severely impeded the effectiveness of technology-based education in most rural schools. This persistent struggle with access and resources not only affected the continuity of education but also added a significant emotional and financial strain on both teachers and learners. It is clear that addressing these core infrastructural deficiencies is not just about improving education, but also about alleviating the broader socio-economic pressures faced by rural communities.

Post-pandemic, these technologies have not only remained present but have become a cornerstone of teaching practices, leading to an evolved educational environment that is more inclusive and adaptive. The teachers' journey from intimidation to embracing technology was fraught with challenges, but the experiential learning from the pandemic period served as a catalyst for development. A lack of resources and training was overcome through community support, self-driven learning, and peer collaboration. The educators' tenacity seems to have led to a more confident use of digital tools, as Moyo expressed:

*We learned by doing, and now I feel more confident to integrate technology in ways I never thought I could.*

These narratives illustrate the resilience and adaptability of rural teachers. They painted a picture of educators who were undaunted by the digital divide, willing to employ whatever means available to ensure that their learners received an education. This determination often translated into innovative approaches, like creating makeshift digital classroom setups or harnessing community radio for lesson dissemination. Such strategies painted a picture of an educational community ripe with ingenuity. These teachers found themselves in the dual role of learners and educators, navigating the new terrain of digital education together with their learners. This period of mutual learning fostered a community spirit and a shared resolve to make the most of technology for education.

As these rural educators continued to integrate technology into their teaching post-pandemic, their stories of improvisation and creativity provide an outline for others in similar contexts. One compelling example comes from Makoni, who continues to turn the lack of Internet access in schools into an opportunity for collaborative learning:

*I download lesson materials during my infrequent trips to places with Internet, then we work through the materials in class, sometimes with the learners teaching each other.*

This level of flexibility and collaborative problem solving emphasizes the evolving role of technology in rural classrooms as more than just tools for instruction. They have become vehicles for community building and learner empowerment, with technology fostering an interactive and participatory classroom environment.

## Post Pandemic Technology Integration in rural classroom

The integration of technology in post-pandemic rural classrooms in Eastern Cape, South Africa, reflects a significant transformation in educational practices. Notably, the pandemic's compelling circumstances have catalyzed a continued and innovative use of technology in these rural schools. Despite the resource constraints, teachers have brought the resilience and ingenuity shown during the crisis into their current pedagogical practices.

Sibanda emotionally recounted, *"What seemed unreachable before has now become our daily bread."* This statement encapsulates the shift from seeing technology as intimidating to recognizing it as indispensable. The pandemic has acted as an accelerator for technology use, pushing some teachers beyond their comfort zones. They have learned to make do with limited resources, as Cirnha mentioned, *"We learned to do more with less now it is just how we teach."*

Resourcefulness is evident in how some schools have repurposed everyday technology for educational use. For example, mobile phones, previously seen as distractions and barred in the classroom have become tools for learning and communication. The use of such available and easily accessible technology not only seems to facilitate learning but also fosters a culture of innovation among teachers and learners. Educational technologies and online resources, once a rarity in these rural schools, are now being integrated into daily lessons, encouraging interactive and student-centred learning.

Teachers' adaptability has facilitated the evolution of teaching methods pushing technology for enhanced student engagement and individualized instruction. Interactive and game-based technologies such as Kahoot! once a novelty, are now commonplace, enriching teaching practices with dynamic content and immediate feedback mechanisms. A particularly evocative narrative came from Phiri, who said:

> *Now my lessons are alive…the students do not just listen they interact, they lead, and we are all learning together...*

Moreover, technology has enabled a shift towards more student-centred learning, with Mbite noticing:

> *It is no longer just about passing exams; it is about equipping our learners for a world where technology is everywhere.*

Profoundly, the post-pandemic period has seen these teachers integrate their pandemic acquired skills into a more thoughtful and deliberate use of technology in education. The necessity of the pandemic has given way to a balanced and selective integration of technology, as Mthembu stated during the sharing circle:

*We have learned not just to use technology but when and how to use it to actually make a difference*

In the post-pandemic education period, there has been a noticeable trend where the previously enforced use of technology has transcended into a voluntary and essential aspect of teaching practices. Mambele expressed that:

*Technology was a daunting endeavor, but now, it is hard to imagine teaching without it...*

This indicates not just a shift in attitude, but an alignment of pedagogy with technology means. The integration of technology, which started as a response to a global crisis, has evidently influenced current pedagogical practices in some of these rural schools in the Eastern Cape province. Educators have harnessed their pandemic experiences to develop blended learning environments that prioritize accessibility and adaptability. Bengo shared:

*We have moved beyond chalk and talk; now, our lessons are a mix of technologies and hands-on learning*

Challenges remain, including infrastructure issues, lack of electricity and the need for ongoing professional development. However, the narratives of these rural teachers echo a determination to overcome these barriers. "I take every chance to learn something new," claimed Phiri, emphasizing the proactive attitude toward personal growth and learner benefit. The teachers' ability to innovate within their means has turned their schools into hubs of community drive, problem solving and technology enabled education. The experience of teaching through the pandemic has not only enriched teachers' pedagogical approaches but has also instilled a culture of innovation, resourcefulness, and learner engagement that continues to shape rural education. This shift has also prompted collaboration between schools, as teachers share resources and strategies that have proven effective in their local contexts.

## DISCUSSION OF FINDINGS

The study presents enlightening findings on the integration of technology in rural South African schools during and after the COVID-19 pandemic. It reveals the profound adaptability and ingenuity of teachers who harnessed technology under constrained circumstances, an evolution rooted in the urgent necessity brought about by the pandemic. This section ventures to interpret and discuss these findings, providing connections to previous research and their implications in education.

Initially, the sentiment amongst rural teachers towards technology ranged from scepticism to outright apprehension. As reported, teachers like Mandlovu and Mthembu felt overwhelmed by the prospects of incorporating digital tools into their pedagogy, citing limited resources, technological knowledge and skills. However, as the pandemic progressed, these initial fears were supplanted by a realization of technology's essential role, as shared by another educator, Cirnha. The necessity to continue education during school closures became a motivational force, driving educators to navigate the digital tools. This shift echoes a study by Mpungose(2020) stressed the significance of technology in overcoming barriers created by the pandemic, particularly the absence of face-to-face instruction. Similarly, Fanteso and Yessoufou (2022) pointed out the massive hurdles teachers faced during the transition, which ranged from inadequate technological proficiency to a lack of clear guidelines for the new modes of teaching. This resonances the study of Muhuro and Kangethe(2021), highlighted the dire lack of ICT infrastructure as a barrier to technology integration.

Despite inadequate technical competencies and infrastructure, some rural South African teachers demonstrated remarkable agility by integrating free and easily accessible technologies such as mobile phones, Whatsapp groups,SMS etc. This confirms Shava's (2022) study that highlights the innovative use of mobile technologies, such as basic mobile phones becoming conduits for educational content, bridging the gap in technology poor settings. Community radio broadcasts and WhatsApp groups also became unconventional platforms for learning, as expressed by the teachers in this study and as noted by scholars like Bryson and Andres (2020). These adaptive strategies are a shred of evidence of the resilient nature of educational practices in rural school environments.

As rural teachers transitioned to online learning management platforms such as Google Classroom, they contended with designing pedagogical materials suitable for digital mediums and fair assessment techniques, which were complicated by their deficiency in technological knowledge and technological pedagogical knowledge, a concern also expressed by Azionya and Nhedzi(2021). With most rural schools in Eastern Cape province in South Africa lacking basic ICT infrastructure, the pandemic undeniably pressured teachers to overcome not only technological hindrances but also to seek professional development. Moreover, these teachers now view technology as enhancing the inclusivity of education by affording learners in rural areas opportunities that were previously available only to urban counterparts. In their narratives, educators expressed the belief that technological aptitude could level the playing field and access to quality education for their learners.

The study also uncovers an intrinsic motivation among teachers to continue learning and growing professionally, using technology as a vehicle for pedagogical innovation. Teachers have started to explore blended learning models, combining traditional teaching with virtual methods, to cater to diverse learning needs and to better prepare learners for a rapidly digitizing world. Importantly, the findings reveal a change in mindset from viewing technology solely as a teaching tool to acknowledging it as a facilitator for broader educational reform. This implies a fundamental shift in educational paradigms, recognizing the transformative potential of technology to reimagine rural education.

The experiences of the teachers in this study, while they seem to be innovative, should not overshadow the systemic challenges that still exist in rural schools. The successful incorporation of digital tools into teaching practice depends not only on the resourcefulness of teachers but also on the broader infrastructural environment. In South African rural schools, issues like inadequate Internet connectivity and a dearth of digital educational technologies remain significant obstacles. These findings are consistent with those by Muhuro and Kangethe (2021), who found that the lack of basic ICT infrastructure was a formidable barrier. The need for bolstering infrastructural support, as suggested by Monyai (2024) is reinforced, stressing that government initiatives are crucial for sustaining technology-enhanced learning.

Furthermore, the findings in this study suggest that the pandemic has set a precedent for an unprecedented level of technology integration in rural educational contexts. Maja (2023) recommends that in such a context, the creative use of technology when supported by appropriate policy interventions, could lead to the development of robust blended learning environments. As the world moves into the post-pandemic era, the groundwork laid by necessity during the pandemic provides an outline for future educational technology practices, provided that governments prioritize the equitable distribution of resources and infrastructure required for sustained technological implementation in education.

In integrating technology into post-pandemic pedagogical practices, rural teachers in the Eastern Cape Province have demonstrated how the convergence of their content knowledge, pedagogical knowledge, and technological knowledge encapsulated in the TPACK framework can enrich educational outcomes. This framework underlies the importance of simultaneously developing these interrelated domains for effective teaching with technology, which is a cornerstone for contemporary and future educational endeavours. As teachers continue to use their acquired knowledge, experiences, and skills to foster student-centered learning environments, there is potential for greater equity and quality in education, impacting both current and future generations.

## SOLUTIONS AND CONCLUSION OF FINDINGS

The study offers evidence that the COVID-19 pandemic has played a crucial role in catalyzing rural school educators' adoption of digital tools despite the multitude of challenges faced. To capitalize on the progress made, it is imperative that long term policies be put in place to support the ongoing integration of technology into rural schools education. This would include the provision of necessary infrastructure and the professional development of teachers to bolster their technological pedagogical content knowledge. Further, there should be an equitable distribution of resources to ensure all schools, particularly those in rural areas can benefit from technology-integrated education. Simultaneously, it is vital to acknowledge and address the infrastructural challenges that remain, to avoid widening the digital divide.

The innovative solutions crafted by rural teachers, illustrated in adopting and adapting available and easily accessible technologies and community resources, signify a significant shift towards informal blended learning environments. These adaptations have not only addressed immediate educational disruptions but have also set a precedent for continual technological integration in rural education. The significance of these emergent practices lies in their potential to overcome historical inequities and access constraints. This study reaffirms the findings of others in the field, resonating the imperative need for policies aimed at equipping rural schools with the necessary technological infrastructure and professional development of teachers to enhance their technological pedagogical content knowledge. The implications of the findings in this study for the educational field are multifaceted. The creative and resilient responses of rural teachers during and post the pandemic indicate a pathway towards more equitable education through technology. However, without sustained support and infrastructure development, the possibility of fully realizing the benefits of technology-integrated education remains precarious.

This study concludes by recommending that education policymakers should prioritize the development of robust technological infrastructure in rural schools, including stable internet connectivity, to facilitate effective access to online educational technologies and content. In addition, professional development programs should be established to equip educators with the necessary digital literacy and pedagogical skills to creatively utilize technology in their instruction. Moreover, initiatives should be put in place to foster community participation in supporting technological integration in education, using local resources and knowledge to build resilient, context-appropriate educational environments. Future studies include longitudinal research to assess the sustainability and long-term impact of these emergent teaching practices, investigations into the psychological effects of this digital shift on teachers and learners, and comparative studies between urban and rural settings to better tailor support mechanisms.

## LIMITATIONS

The study provides valuable insights into the adaptation of educational technology in rural settings; however, its scope is limited to the Eastern Cape Province, which may affect the broader applicability of its findings. The reliance on participants' self-reported data could introduce subjective biases, and a relatively small sample size might not fully represent the diverse experiences of all rural educators.

## REFERENCES

Adov, L., & Mäeots, M. (2021). What can we learn about science teachers' technology use during the COVID-19 pandemic? *Education Sciences*, 11(6), 255. 10.3390/educsci11060255

Ayega, D. (2020). Pandemics and education in Sub-Saharan Africa: Invest in education technology. *American Journal of Educational Research*, 8(8), 581–586. 10.12691/education-8-8-10

Azionya, C. M., & Nhedzi, A. (2021). The digital divide and higher education challenge with emergency online learning: Analysis of tweets in the wake of the COVID-19 lockdown. *Turkish Online Journal of Distance Education*, 22(4), 164–182. 10.17718/tojde.1002822

Badaru, K. A., & Adu, E. (2022). Prospects of Blended Learning for the Post-COVID-19 Higher Education: The Instructors' Perspectives at a University in South Africa. *E-Journal of Humanities. Arts and Social Sciences*, 3(11), 126–139. 10.38159/ehass.2022SP31111

Batdı, V., Doğan, Y., & Talan, T. (2023). Effectiveness of online learning: A multi-complementary approach research with responses from the COVID-19 pandemic period. *Interactive Learning Environments*, 31(7), 4113–4146. 10.1080/10494820.2021.1954035

Bryson, J. R., & Andres, L. (2020). Covid-19 and rapid adoption and improvisation of online teaching: Curating resources for extensive versus intensive online learning experiences. *Journal of Geography in Higher Education*, 44(4), 608–623. 10.1080/03098265.2020.1807478

Castleberry, A., & Nolen, A. (2018). Thematic analysis of qualitative research data: Is it as easy as it sounds? *Currents in Pharmacy Teaching & Learning*, 10(6), 807–815. 10.1016/j.cptl.2018.03.01930025784

Child, G. S., & Song, K. (2023). Digital Inequities: Promoting Digital Justice during the COVID-19 Pandemic. *Sustainability (Basel)*, 15(17), 12862. 10.3390/su151712862

Clark, C., & Boyer, D. D. (2016). Twenty-first-century technology integration staff development: A phenomenology. *Journal of Computers in Education*, 3(1), 1–20. 10.1007/s40692-015-0053-y

Department of Basic Education. (2020). *Standard operating procedure for the prevention, containment and management of covid-19 in schools and school communities*. DBE. 10.1017/CBO9781107415324.004

Dhawan, S. (2020). Online learning: A panacea in the time of COVID-19 crisis. *Journal of Educational Technology Systems*, 49(1), 5–22. 10.1177/0047239520934018

Dutta, A. (2020). Impact of digital social media on Indian higher education: alternative approaches of online learning during COVID-19 pandemic crisis. *International journal of scientific and research publications, 10*(5), 604-611. 10.29322/IJSRP.10.05.2020.p10169

Dzansi, D. Y., & Amedzo, K. (2014). Integrating ICT into rural South African schools: Possible solutions for challenges. *International Journal of Educational Sciences*, 6(2), 341–348. 10.1080/09751122.2014.11890145

Ennam, A. (2024). Assessing Covid-19 pandemic-forced transitioning to distance e-learning in Moroccan universities: An empirical, analytical critical study of implementality and achievability. *Journal of North African Studies*, 29(1), 153–177. 10.1080/13629387.2021.1937138

Estrella, F. (2023). The effectiveness of using digital platforms to practice English during the COVID-19 crisis as perceived by Ecuadorian students. *Journal of Applied Research in Higher Education*, 15(1), 66–82. 10.1108/JARHE-05-2021-0194

Fanteso, B., & Yessoufou, K. (2022). Diversity and determinants of traditional water conservation technologies in the Eastern Cape Province, South Africa. *Environmental Monitoring and Assessment*, 194(3), 161. 10.1007/s10661-022-09848-235137295

Finlay, L. (2012). Debating phenomenological methods. In *Hermeneutic phenomenology in education* (pp. 15–37). Brill. 10.1007/978-94-6091-834-6_2

Gill, L., & Dalgarno, B. (2017). A qualitative analysis of pre-service primary school teachers' TPACK development over the four years of their teacher preparation programme. *Technology, Pedagogy and Education*, 26(4), 439–456. 10.1080/1475939X.2017.1287124

Gore, O., Twine, C., Botha, J., & Naidoo, S. (2023). Teachers' perceptions of the psycho-social effects of COVID-19 on learners' well-being in South African schools. *Perspectives in Education*, 41(4). 10.38140/pie.v41i4.7042

Hunt, S. C., & Young, N. L. (2021). Blending Indigenous sharing circle and Western focus group methodologies for the study of Indigenous children's health: A systematic review. *International Journal of Qualitative Methods*, 20, 16094069211015112. 10.1177/16094069211015112

Kang'ethe, S. M. (2022). Unpacking South African Institutions of Higher Learning Efforts and Hurdles to Respond to COVID-19: Social Service Professionals' Lenses. *Perspectives on Global Development and Technology*, 21(1), 84–99. 10.1163/15691497-12341618

Kuhfeld, M., Soland, J., Lewis, K., Ruzek, E., & Johnson, A. (2022). The COVID-19 school year: Learning and recovery across 2020-2021. *AERA Open*, 8, 23328584221099306. 10.1177/23328584221099306

Kusuma, I. P. I. (2022). EFL teachers' online teaching in rural schools during the COVID-19 pandemic: Stories from Indonesia. *Studies in English Language and Education*, 9(1), 203–221. 10.24815/siele.v9i1.21239

Li, J., Yang, S., Chen, C., & Li, H. (2022). The Impacts of COVID-19 on distance education with the application of traditional and digital appliances: Evidence from 60 developing countries. *International Journal of Environmental Research and Public Health*, 19(11), 6384. 10.3390/ijerph1911638435681971

Linnes, C., Ronzoni, G., Agrusa, J., & Lema, J. (2022). Emergency Remote Education and Its Impact on Higher Education: A Temporary or Permanent Shift in Instruction? *Education Sciences*, 12(10), 721. 10.3390/educsci12100721

Maja, M. M. (2023). Teachers' perceptions of integrating technology in rural primary schools to enhance the teaching of English first additional language. *Journal of Curriculum Studies Research*, 5(1), 95–112. 10.46303/jcsr.2023.8

Mapisa, B. Z., & Makena, B. (2024). The Impact of ICT Adoption in Enhancing Teaching and Learning in Primary Schools of Amathole East District, Eastern Cape. *Research in Social Sciences and Technology*, 9(1), 213–231. 10.46303/ressat.2024.12

Mare, A., Woyo, E., & Amadhila, E. M. (2022). Harnessing the technological dividends in African higher education institutions during and post-COVID-19 pandemic. In *teaching and learning with digital technologies in higher education institutions in Africa* (pp. 1-24). Routledge. 10.4324/9781003264026-1

Matete, R. E., Kimario, A. E., & Behera, N. P. (2023). Review on the use of eLearning in teacher education during the coronavirus disease (COVID-19) pandemic in Africa. *Heliyon*, 9(2), e13308. 10.1016/j.heliyon.2023.e1330836743851

Mdoda, L., & Mdiya, L. (2022). Factors affecting the using information and communication technologies (ICTs) by livestock farmers in the Eastern Cape province. *Cogent Social Sciences*, 8(1), 2026017. 10.1080/23311886.2022.2026017

Meinck, S., Fraillon, J., & Strietholt, R. (2022). *The Impact of the COVID-19 Pandemic on Education: International Evidence from the Responses to Educational Disruption Survey (REDS)*. International Association for the Evaluation of Educational Achievement.

Merriam, S. B. (2002). Introduction to qualitative research. *Qualitative research in practice: Examples for discussion and analysis, 1*(1), 1-17.

Mishra, P., & Koehler, M. J. (2006). Technological pedagogical content knowledge: A framework for teacher knowledge. *Teachers College Record*, 108(6), 1017–1054. 10.1111/j.1467-9620.2006.00684.x

Mmakola, S., & Maphalala, M. C. (2023). Blended teaching and learning in south african secondary schools in the post-covid-19 pandemic era. *International Journal of Innovative Technologies in Social Science*, 4(40). 10.31435/rsglobal_ijitss/30122023/8081

Monyai, R. B. (2024). Exploring the Role of Technology in Enhancing Adult Education and Skills Development in Urban Areas of South Africa. In *Adjunct Faculty in Online Higher Education: Best Practices for Teaching Adult Learners* (pp. 105-131). IGI Global. 10.4018/978-1-6684-9855-2.ch006

Mpungose, C. B. (2020). Emergent transition from face-to-face to online learning in a South African University in the context of the Coronavirus pandemic. *Humanities & Social Sciences Communications*, 7(1), 1–9. 10.1057/s41599-020-00603-x

Muhuro, P., Kangethe, S. M., & Muhuro, P. (2021). Prospects and pitfalls associated with implementing blended learning in rural-based higher education institutions in Southern Africa. *Perspectives in Education*, 39(1), 427–441. 10.18820/2519593X/pie.v39.i1.26

Nepembe, V., & Simuja, C. (2023). Instructors' perspectives of TPACK in a vocational training classroom in Namibia. *Journal of Vocational. Adult and Continuing Education and Training*, 6(1), 90–107. 10.14426/jovacet.v6i1.315

Neubauer, B. E., Witkop, C. T., & Varpio, L. (2019). How phenomenology can help us learn from the experiences of others. *Perspectives on Medical Education*, 8(2), 90–97. 10.1007/S40037-019-0509-230953335

Niess, M. L., & Gillow-Wiles, H. (2021). Online instructional strategies for enhancing teachers' TPACK: Experiences, discourse, and critical reflection. In *Research anthology on developing effective online learning courses* (pp. 326–348). IGI Global. 10.4018/978-1-7998-8047-9.ch019

Nowell, L. S., Norris, J. M., White, D. E., & Moules, N. J. (2017). Thematic analysis: Striving to meet the trustworthiness criteria. *International Journal of Qualitative Methods*, 16(1), 1609406917733847. 10.1177/1609406917733847

Ochieng, V. O., Asego, C. S., & Gyasi, R. M. (2023). The place of academia and industry in the adoption and adaptation of educational technologies for a post-COVID-19 recovery in Africa. *Scientific African*, 20, e01658. 10.1016/j.sciaf.2023.e0165837035634

Peimani, N., & Kamalipour, H. (2021). Online education and the COVID-19 outbreak: A case study of online teaching during lockdown. *Education Sciences*, 11(2), 72. 10.3390/educsci11020072

Pillay, R. M., & Shipalana, M. L. (2023). The Effects of School Infrastructure on Curriculum Policy Implementation. *International Journal of Social Science Research and Review*, 6(8), 167–182.

Sahoo, M., & Rana, K. (2023). Digital Education During COVID-19 in Odisha: Challenges and Prospects. *Changing World Economic Order in the Post-Pandemic Period*, 147-165. 10.4018/978-1-7998-6896-5.ch009

Shambare, B., & Simuja, C. (2022). A critical review of teaching with virtual lab: A panacea to challenges of conducting practical experiments in science subjects beyond the COVID-19 pandemic in rural schools in South Africa. *Journal of Educational Technology Systems*, 50(3), 393–408. 10.1177/00472395211058051

Shava, E. (2022). Reinforcing the role of ICT in enhancing teaching and learning post-COVID-19 in tertiary institutions in South Africa. *Journal of Culture and Values in Education*, 5(1), 78–91. 10.46303/jcve.2022.7

Simuja, C., & Shikesho, H. (2024). Investigating the Experiences of Mathematics Teacher Technology Integration in the Selected Rural Primary Schools in Namibia. [IJTEE]. *International Journal of Technology-Enhanced Education*, 3(1), 1–15. 10.4018/IJTEE.340028

Takona, J. P. (2023). Flipping the Script: Post-COVID-19 Opportunities, Challenges, and Threats amidst the Digital Revolution in Higher Education. *International Journal on Social and Education Sciences*, 5(4), 847–863. 10.46328/ijonses.569

Xue, S., & Crompton, H. (2024). Educational technology research during the COVID-19 pandemic. *Interactive Technology and Smart Education*, 21(1), 83–107. 10.1108/ITSE-05-2022-0067

Yin, R. K. (2003). Designing case studies. *Qualitative research methods, 5*(14), 359-386.

# Chapter 6
# Student Engagement in the Post-Pandemic Virtual Classroom

**Zahra Pourabedin**
*Shepherd University, USA*

**Vahid Biglari**
*Shepherd University, USA*

## ABSTRACT

*In the wake of the global COVID-19 pandemic, educational institutions worldwide experienced unprecedented challenges, leading to a paradigm shift in the education system. To deal with the need for more flexible learning, educational research and development aimed at providing a richer, more engaging remote learning experience by the creation of virtual classrooms. Within this digital learning environment, the challenge is to create an engaging learning environment to ensure optimal learning outcomes. This chapter addresses the imperative need to foster greater student engagement in virtual classrooms to maximize learning effectiveness. Drawing on established literature which underscores the link between student engagement and positive learning outcomes, the chapter emphasizes the pivotal role of engagement in enhancing student satisfaction and retention in online teaching contexts. By increasing the level of student engagement, instructors can increase the students' satisfaction level and retention, improving the efficiency of online teaching. Moreover, the chapter delves into the evolution of virtual classrooms and elucidates innovative strategies and practical techniques designed to augment student engagement. By synthesizing empirical evidence and best practices, the chapter offers insights into effective pedagogical approaches that educators can employ to create vibrant and interactive virtual learning environments. Through a rigorous examination of*

DOI: 10.4018/979-8-3693-7645-4.ch006

*research findings and experiential knowledge, this chapter contributes to advancing our understanding of how to optimize student engagement in virtual classrooms, thereby enriching the landscape of online education.*

## INTRODUCTION

This chapter starts with exploring the evolution, application, and implications of virtual classrooms, particularly examining their pre-pandemic utilization, responses during the COVID-19 outbreak, and sustained post-pandemic integration. The chapter adopts a multidimensional theoretical framework. This framework draws upon Thornburg et al. (2021) which explores the impact of the COVID-19 pandemic on student readiness and engagement in virtual classrooms.

The literature review critically examines the pre-pandemic landscape of virtual education, shedding light on the challenges and opportunities inherent in online teaching methodologies. While acknowledging the historical utilization of virtual classrooms for distance education and professional development purposes, the review highlights the shortcomings of early approaches characterized by simplistic lecture-based formats. Through an analysis of seminal works by Dykman & Davis (2008), Gaytan & McEwen (2007), and Palmer & Holt (2008), among others, the review underscores the imperative for active student engagement and pedagogical innovation in virtual learning environments.

The study addresses a significant gap in existing literature by offering a comprehensive exploration of virtual classrooms' evolution, challenges, and potentials across pre-pandemic, pandemic, and post-pandemic contexts. By synthesizing historical insights with contemporary empirical findings, the research contributes to a nuanced understanding of virtual education's role in facilitating educational continuity, fostering student engagement, and promoting pedagogical innovation amidst unprecedented disruptions. Moreover, by delineating practical recommendations for educators based on insights gleaned from Dias et al. (2020), Redinger et al. (2020), and Akhtar et al. (2020), the study offers actionable strategies to enhance the efficacy and inclusivity of virtual teaching practices.

The research illuminates the dynamic evolution of virtual classrooms and underscores their enduring relevance in shaping the future of education. By elucidating the historical antecedents, contemporary challenges, and emerging trends in virtual education, the study provides valuable insights for educators, policymakers, and researchers navigating the complexities of online teaching and learning. Moreover, by highlighting the need for ongoing professional development initiatives and pedagogical innovation in virtual education, the research underscores the importance of adapting instructional practices to meet the evolving needs of digital learners in a post-pandemic world.

## METHODOLOGY

This study used a systematic literature review methodology. This systematic literature review aimed to identify, evaluate, and synthesize existing research on hybrid classrooms and students' engagement strategies. A comprehensive search strategy was employed to identify relevant studies published between January 2002 and December 2023. The following electronic databases were searched: Scopus, Web of Science, ERIC, and Google Scholar.

The search terms used were hybrid classroom, education and pandemic, theories of online learning, educational technology, student engagement. The inclusion criteria encompassed studies within higher education that delved into hybrid classrooms, examining their impact on student learning, teacher development, or instructional design. Eligible studies were required to be published in English and employ quantitative, qualitative, or mixed-methods research designs.

Two reviewers independently extracted data from each included study, using a standardized data extraction form. The extracted data included study characteristics, research design, participants, interventions, outcomes, and findings. Disagreements were resolved through discussion and consensus. The extracted data were synthesized using narrative and thematic analysis.

This systematic literature review aimed to provide a comprehensive overview of the existing research on hybrid classrooms, highlighting the benefits, challenges, and best practices for effective implementation.

## PRE-PANDEMIC APPLICATIONS OF VIRTUAL CLASSROOMS

In 1840, Sir Isaac Pitman pioneered modern virtual education by mailing transcribed texts on postcards and receiving responses from students. Although short-lived, Pitman's method gained recognition, leading to the establishment of the Phonological Correspondence Society to oversee these courses and subsequently the founding of Pitman Colleges nationwide. The University of London was the first to offer a degree in virtual education, commencing its program in 1858. In the United States, the inaugural correspondence school, established in 1873, aimed to promote home study. William Rainey Harper, founder of the first virtual university in the United States, the University of Chicago, championed the concept of virtual education.

Online teaching environment can refer to both fully virtual lessons where physical interaction is not involved, and it can include mixed courses that combine face-to-face and virtual meetings, such as face-to-face courses with complementary virtual activities outside the classroom on the Internet, which are popular today, hence, "making time and space more flexible, extending the teaching and learning spaces that were until now practically confined to the classroom" (Tschannen-Moran, Parish, & Dipaola, 2006).

Sangrà, González Sanmamed, and Anderson (2015) found four general categories of definitions of online learning which are as follows:

(1) Technology-driven: Use of technology to deliver learning and training programs; (2) delivery-system-oriented: The delivery of a learning, training, or education program by electronic means; (3) communication-oriented: Learning facilitated using digital tools and content that involves some form of interactivity, which may include online interaction between the learner and their teacher or peers; and (4) educational-paradigm-oriented: Information and communication technologies used to support students to improve their learning (Valverde-Berrocoso, Garrido-Arroyo, Burgos-Videla, & Morales-Cevallos, 2020).

In general, online learning is defined as an innovative web-based system rooted in digital technology and other types of educational materials, whose primary objective is to provide students with a personalized, accessible, enjoyable, and interactive learning environment that supports and enhances learning processes (Rodrigues, Almeida, Figueiredo, & Lopes, 2019).

Before the COVID-19 pandemic, virtual classrooms were already being utilized in various contexts, albeit not as extensively as during and after the pandemic. Virtual classrooms have been the main element of distance education for many years. This form of education could benefit students who couldn't attend physical classes in traditional institutions due to geographical constraints, work commitments, or other reasons. Many organizations and institutions offered virtual classrooms for continuing education and professional development purposes. These virtual classrooms provided professionals with opportunities to enhance their skills, earn certifications, and stay updated with industry trends without needing to attend physical workshops or seminars. In addition, Virtual classrooms were utilized to complement traditional classroom instruction by providing supplementary materials, resources, and tutorials. Students could access online lectures, interactive modules, and practice exercises to reinforce their learning outside of regular classroom hours. Classes initially began by sharing PowerPoint presentations and progressively expanded to incorporate audio, video, and hyperlinks to relevant YouTube videos. This transition occurred as faculty members became more acquainted and at ease with online tools and technology. However, uninterrupted high-speed internet connectivity is essential for effective online education, which may not be universally accessible. With this in consideration, rather than live streaming, didactic lectures were uploaded to provide students with the flexibility to download and review lectures at their convenience. Finally, universities started to use virtual classrooms to facilitate international education programs, allowing students from different countries to participate in joint classes, collaborative projects, and cultural exchanges. These programs promoted cross-cultural understanding, language proficiency, and global citizenship among students. The study by Andrew and Ewens (2015) investigated the role of virtual interactive classrooms in enhancing the online learning environment. The results emphasized the importance of a user-friendly environment and computer literacy.

Prior to the COVID-19 outbreak, educators often failed to recognize the distinctions between teaching methods in online versus traditional classroom settings (Kentnor, 2015). Many instructors simply shared lecture materials from in-person classes with online students, assuming it would suffice. Nonetheless, research indicates that a well-structured online course that fosters active student engagement is crucial for achieving success (Dykman & Davis, 2008; Palmer, Holt, & Bray, 2008). Carlson and Carnevale (2001) argue that the initial shortcomings were not solely attributable to online teaching methods but were also exacerbated by inadequate institutional support for faculty and a dearth of leadership with a grasp of online education.

While the adoption of virtual classrooms was not as widespread before the pandemic, these applications demonstrate the versatility and potential of virtual learning environments in various educational, professional, and social contexts. The pandemic accelerated the mainstream adoption of virtual classrooms and highlighted their importance in ensuring continuity of education during times of crisis. The COVID-19 pandemic has significantly accelerated the evolution of virtual classrooms, pushing educational institutions to develop adaptative strategies to meet the emerging demand for remote learning.

## VIRTUAL CLASSROOM DURING THE PANDEMIC

As schools and universities around the world were forced to close their doors to prevent the spread of the virus, educators were compelled to explore alternative methods to ensure continuity in learning. This led to the rapid adoption of virtual classrooms, which emerged as a crucial tool in navigating the challenges posed by the pandemic. Virtual classrooms have played a pivotal role in maintaining educational continuity during the pandemic. With the help of digital technologies, educators were able to conduct classes remotely, ensuring that students could continue their studies without interruption. This shift to virtual learning platforms allowed schools and universities to adapt to the new normal swiftly and efficiently. Additionally, virtual classrooms provided flexibility in scheduling, enabling students to access educational resources from the safety of their homes.

Despite its significance, the transition to virtual classrooms presented numerous challenges for both educators and students. Technical issues such as poor internet connectivity, software compatibility issues, and lack of access to digital devices posed significant barriers to effective online learning. Moreover, educators had to redesign their teaching methodologies to suit the online environment, which required additional training and resources. Additionally, maintaining student engagement and motivation in a virtual setting proved to be a daunting task for many educators. According to Thornburg, Ceglie, and Abernathy (2021) students preferred to use mobile devices because they perceive them as more convenient due to their ease of use, offering greater mobility and flexibility, and notably being more affordable compared to other hardware options.

Zoom classes were one of the popular virtual classes during the pandemic. de Oliveira Dias et al. (2020) investigated the challenges faced by teachers, and executive education professors in Brazil, through live online classes via the Zoom platform. Key findings pointed out (i) the lack of stable online connection; (ii) security issues; (iii) limited pedagogical resources; (iv) background noises; (v) shortage of equipment supply due to the lockdowns, as barriers to online live classes dispensed with the Zoom platform.

Thornburg et al. (2021) developed a conceptual framework (figure 1) to explore how the sudden shift to virtual classrooms, caused by the COVID-19 pandemic, has impacted university students and their learning outcomes.

*Figure 1. Conceptual framework*

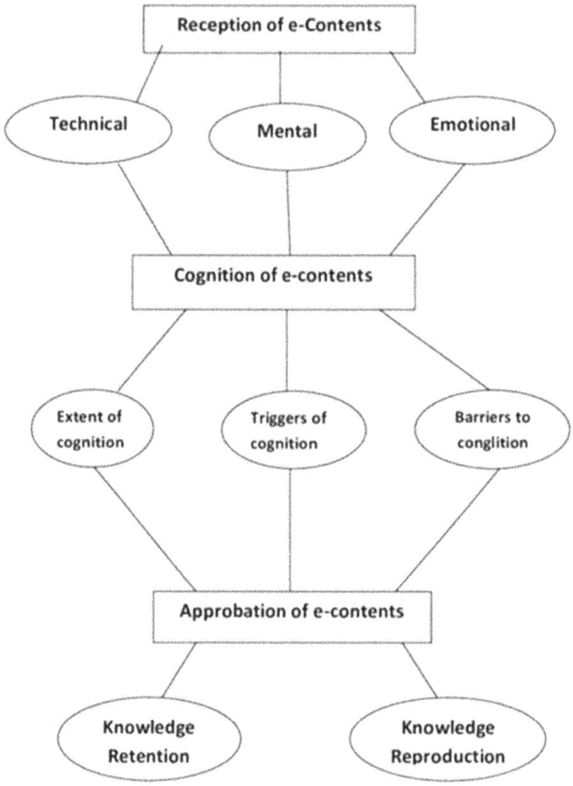


The results showed that students lacked technical and emotional readiness to engage with e-content during the COVID-19 pandemic. Additionally, they acknowledged feeling emotionally unprepared to absorb any knowledge during the lockdown period enforced by the pandemic. These factors led to a lack of mental readiness and focus to receive online content in virtual classes.

Redinger et al. (2020) after conducting virtual classes during the pandemic suggested practices when implementing a virtual approach to classroom-based learning:

Practice: Beforehand, conduct a trial run to familiarize yourself with the virtual classroom and identify any potential issues. It is suggested to conduct this trial session exclusively with faculty members and enable live chat to receive immediate feedback.

Establish Expectations: Clearly outline expectations at the start of each session to avoid misunderstandings. Describe the virtual learning tools to be utilized, specify whether the session will be interactive, and indicate whether verbal or typed communication via chat is preferred.

Engage Students: Simply delivering a slide-based lecture via live video conference resembles having students watch a pre-recorded instructional video. Additionally, a student who keeps their microphone muted and camera off may become easily distracted. It is recommended to encourage camera usage and employ features such as virtual small group breakouts, screen sharing, or virtual chalkboards to replicate the active learning atmosphere of an in-person classroom.

Conducting virtual classrooms during the pandemic revealed that there is a growing need to prioritize the creation of teacher training initiatives focused on digital literacy (Sánchez-Cruzado, Santiago Campión, & Sánchez-Compaña, 2021). These programs should not only facilitate proficiency in digital resources but also encourage a reevaluation of their significance within evolving educational environments. The aim is to transition towards student-centered teaching, where information and communication technology (ICT) plays a pivotal intermediary role. Along the same line the study by R. N. Akhtar (2020) revealed the majority of students expressed a desire for increased interactivity during virtual class sessions and recommended incorporating student presentations. They highlighted the lack of genuine student-teacher interaction in online classes, leading to monotony.

The pandemic, along with the associated changes it has brought, presents an opportunity to identify the essential skills required for a successful transition to online platforms, thereby maximizing outcomes.

# POST-PANDEMIC SUSTAINED USE OF VIRTUAL CLASSROOM

## Online Teaching Methods

Virtual education employs diverse methods and objectives, broadly categorized into two types based on their instructional approach:

1. Instructor-centered method: These courses are structured around instructor-led presentations, with learners playing a more passive role. The teacher typically shares their desktop, webcam, and microphone, while learners primarily listen. This format mirrors traditional classroom settings.
2. Dialogue-oriented method: In contrast, these courses foster active learner participation, encouraging interaction and engagement in online discussions. Both the teacher and students can share their desktops, webcams, and microphones, facilitating collaborative learning experiences. This approach is particularly suitable for language courses, where conversational practice is essential. Platforms like Skype exemplify this model.

Technological advancements have broadened the scope of online education, offering various formats such as e-learning and Massive Open Online Courses (MOOCs), leveraging open educational resources. Virtual education encompasses synchronous, asynchronous, hybrid, and correspondence formats, catering to diverse learning preferences and needs.

## Synchronous Learning

Synchronous learning, also known as concurrent education or conferencing, is a distance learning approach where all participants convene on a common online platform simultaneously, despite being geographically dispersed. This method closely resembles traditional classroom instruction, wherein individuals engage in audio or video classes via phone or group chat applications like Skype. Synchronous learning necessitates careful scheduling and coordination, utilizing technologies such as web conferencing, video streaming, and television broadcasts. Additionally, tools like text chat and polls are integrated into web conferencing software to enhance interaction among participants. Immersive environments and robot proxies have emerged as innovative means to further enrich synchronous learning experiences, with some institutions incorporating telerobotics devices for remote instruction.

## Asynchronous Learning

In asynchronous learning, participants enjoy flexible access to educational materials, allowing them to engage with course content at their convenience without the need for simultaneous attendance. This method employs various correspondence mediums, including emails, audio and video recordings, voice mail, and fax, enabling learners to access tutorials and assignments at their own pace.

## Hybrid Courses

Hybrid courses blend online education with traditional classroom methods, requiring students to attend periodic face-to-face sessions on campus. These in-person classes, organized as scheduled meetings within the university, supplement online instruction and vary in duration depending on the course structure.

## Correspondence Courses

Correspondence courses entail the exchange of educational materials and assignments via mail, making it the oldest form of distance education. This asynchronous teaching method allows students to engage in learning activities remotely using mediums such as email, audio and video recordings, voice mail, and fax for communication and submission of coursework.

## LITERATURE REVIEW

### Student Engagement

Teaching goes beyond delivering course material; it entails guiding students to analyze, synthesize, and exercise critical judgment. Developing these skills necessitates substantial interaction between educators and learners.

What may be novel to many is the significant impact of extracurricular relationships on student learning, surpassing that of interactions within the classroom. Wilson and colleagues posit that relationships between students and professors outside the classroom can profoundly influence student outcomes. However, a drawback of e-learning is the diminished face-to-face communication, hindering the conveyance of emotions crucial for effective communication. (Wilson, 1975).

Research demonstrates the importance of facial expressions in conveying emotions such as fear, surprise, joy, and sadness. This poses a challenge in electronic communication, where nuances are often overlooked. (Orange & Hobbs, 2018).

Proper utilization of asynchronous and synchronous electronic communication in electronic education can address these concerns and enhance the quality of education and learning. Asynchronous communication technologies include voicemail, email, and bulletin boards, offering flexibility and reflection time. Simultaneous communication technologies like live online seminars and discussion forums promote real-time interaction, motivation, and quick feedback, thereby enhancing social cohesion and facilitating prompt task completion (Cook-Sather, Bovill, & Felten, 2014).

The key lies in employing communication methods appropriately to the situation. For instance, in email correspondence, timely responses and varied communication modalities beyond text are essential for maintaining engagement and fostering a supportive learning environment.

Conway (2003) explores the benefits of both online and offline communication. Regarding asynchronous communication, its advantages lie in its flexibility, allowing students to access course materials at their convenience, providing ample time for reflection and retention. It is also well-coordinated and adaptable to specific learning approaches, enabling students to relate course content to their professional environments.

Simultaneous technologies offer cost-effectiveness and foster group motivation through real-time interaction, enhancing social cohesion and facilitating prompt feedback exchange. These systems also promote timely completion of tasks, instilling order and discipline in the learning process (Cook-Sather, Bovill, & Felten, 2014).

It is crucial to use synchronous and asynchronous communication methods appropriately according to the context. For instance, in email communication, it is essential to respond promptly to students' queries using varied communication tools beyond text, ensuring effective engagement and support (Conway, 2003).

Efficient communication between professors and students is pivotal in electronic education. Chafee (2013) delineates strategies for enhancing communication effectiveness, including encouraging student engagement, sharing personal experiences, and clearly outlining communication policies. However, it's essential to acknowledge the irreplaceable role of face-to-face interactions alongside electronic communication methods (Kelsey & D'souza, 2004). Face-to-face meetings enable educators to address limitations posed by online communication, contributing to a comprehensive educational experience (Jackson, Jones, & Rodriguez, 2010).

In electronic education, it's imperative for professors to foster collaboration among students. Collaborative learning offers students the chance to assess their comprehension of the subject in comparison to their peers. Through this process, knowledge takes on a social dimension and becomes a collective asset.

However, group learning activities in electronic education present unique challenges. It's essential not to equate the group work method in distance education with that in traditional settings. Students must be equipped with guidelines and strategies for effective group participation in e-learning. Additionally, evaluating group work requires defining standards and responsibilities, akin to traditional classes. This may involve assigning both group and individual scores, alongside outlining ethical considerations such as equitable evaluation practices among group members.

Research on cooperative learning groups highlights five key elements contributing to their efficacy: mutual and constructive dependence, face-to-face interaction, individual responsibility, verbal skills, and group processing (Conway, 2003). Technologies like simulations, games, chat rooms, and group projects can enhance these elements in e-learning, facilitating knowledge transfer to real-world contexts.

Both synchronous and asynchronous communication tools play a crucial role in strengthening collaborative learning experiences. Asynchronous communication, in particular, benefits quieter and reserved students who may struggle to participate in traditional classroom discussions. It provides them with the necessary time to formulate and articulate their thoughts effectively.

Professors facilitating e-learning courses can enhance student cooperation through various strategies:

1. Implementing group cooperation projects that require input from all members and are iterative, demanding diverse collaborations for completion.
2. Ensuring students grasp effective group project dynamics by defining roles at project onset and rotating them as needed.
3. Establishing project milestones to enable students to track personal progress indicators.
4. Offering examples of exemplary, subpar, and average projects to guide student understanding.
5. Familiarizing students with essential electronic tools necessary for project completion.
6. Organizing students into small groups of 3 to 5 members.
7. Limiting each semester to one primary group project to focus collaboration efforts.
8. Emphasizing participation in discussion groups and defining participation criteria.
9. Prioritizing central topics for discussions and conversations.
10. Illustrating examples of exemplary, subpar, and average participation levels.
11. Randomly evaluating some negotiations to uphold quality standards (Conway, 2003).

It's noteworthy that project indicators primarily follow a qualitative approach, although some quantitative metrics may be unavoidable. This qualitative style allows flexibility in assessment, enabling teachers to prioritize certain strengths in project evaluation, ensuring creativity and diversity in project design and completion.

## Active Learning

Active learning can be succinctly defined as any learning method wherein students engage in activities and reflect on their actions. In essence, active learning entails learners' involvement in tasks, leveraging the human mind's inclination to seek information relevant to individual circumstances. Examples include problem analysis, problem-solving, challenging discussions, and other interactive activities commonly found in higher education settings.

In the realm of e-learning, active learning is not just recommended but essential. Student engagement hinges on their active participation. For instance, in online courses, if students fail to contribute articles for discussion, instructors lack a gauge of their presence.

As the fourth generation of distance education methods, online courses necessitate students' active pursuit and discussion of information pertinent to their field of study. In electronic education, students are perceived as creators of meaning who actively construct information by selecting, organizing, and synthesizing existing knowledge with their own experiences.

In the age of knowledge and information networks, where information is dynamic and unstable, rote memorization of specific subjects diminishes in value. Therefore, students must develop the skill of learning how to learn and actively engage in the learning process rather than passively receiving knowledge. Effective learning involves transferring information from existing knowledge to new contexts, thereby forming new internal connections that facilitate the transfer of new knowledge from short-term to long-term memory (Slavin, 2012).

Students who actively absorb, comprehend, and internalize new concepts are more likely to achieve deep and sustained learning. Active engagement serves as a formative assessment wherein learners, faced with challenges, refine their sub-skills and equip themselves with necessary tools for mastery (Jochems, Van Merrienboer, & Koper, 2004).

Employing case study approaches and problem-based learning is a suitable method for fostering active learning among students. These approaches immerse students in real-world examples, facilitating better understanding and integration of concepts. By grounding learning in authentic experiences, e-learning enhances learning growth and its application to real-world scenarios.

Problems and case examples can be presented through various mediums such as video films, software games, articles, and writings. Several techniques can be employed in this regard:

1. Encouraging students to articulate explanations, reasons, and arguments demonstrating deep understanding, while adjusting their messages to reflect their own tone and expression.
2. Utilizing question-answer-discussion cycles to stimulate engagement and critical thinking.
3. Promoting reasoned responses from students.
4. Prompting students to provide answers that require synthesis, integration, and conclusion drawing from disparate pieces of knowledge.
5. Incorporating real-world projects and assignments to enable students to relate course content to practical applications and personal insights (Slavin, 2012).

The presentation of assignments in e-learning courses holds significance in fostering active learning. Bates (2005) advocates for assignment policies that integrate scientific topics with student experiences rather than merely translating written content. In essence, every homework assignment should incorporate an experimental dimension, and internet-based activities should be integrated into assignments, requiring at least one internet search. Additionally, participation in research assignments in each course is recommended (Bates, 2005).

Providing timely feedback is essential for students to gauge their academic progress and align themselves with course expectations. Students must continually assess their understanding and progress by answering questions like "Where was I? Where am I? And where am I going?" Feedback from instructors plays a pivotal role in this process. Without clear feedback, students may feel adrift and disconnected, particularly in e-learning environments, where feelings of isolation are more prevalent (Levine-Sauberman, 2015).

Levine-Sauberman (2015) suggests that while delayed feedback produces superior outcomes compared to immediate feedback, providing prompt feedback during training sessions is advisable to engage students actively in learning and alleviate feelings of alienation to some extent. Besides timeliness, feedback should also be proportional, meaning students should possess awareness of the type, quantity, and quality of their knowledge before receiving feedback from instructors. Lemley, Sudweeks, Howell, Laws, and Sawyer (2007) emphasize the necessity of using evaluation criteria to assess student activities, including the volume of student engagement, the substance of submitted materials, and the clarity of expression.

It's crucial for students to understand how their work will be evaluated from the outset of the course, including the significance of participation, article submissions, engagement in discussions, and other aspects. Utilizing digital portfolios for assessment is recommended, as they encapsulate students' academic endeavors throughout the term. Wiedmer and Kappan (1998) propose three evaluation approaches for portfolios: analytical evaluation, which assesses each section of the portfolio using a rating scale; holistic evaluation, which forms a judgment based on an overall impression of the portfolio; and criterion-referenced evaluation, which measures student achievement against specific criteria.

Several techniques can be employed to provide prompt, effective, and appropriate feedback:

1. Conducting an initial assessment to enhance students' awareness of their knowledge base and preconceptions.
2. Offering study feedback to students, which not only reflects the quality of their performance but also provides practical insights.
3. Delivering valuable feedback by summarizing topics and drawing conclusions over designated periods, such as biweekly intervals.
4. Encouraging peer feedback through structured peer review processes.
5. Implementing random and unanticipated assessments throughout the academic term (Zamani & Madani, 2011).
6. Establishing a leadership system in e-learning that utilizes feedback as a primary tool to enhance learning during critical moments and provide diverse perspectives to students.
7. Emphasizing the importance of allocating sufficient time for completing tasks.

In traditional classroom settings, homework time is typically regulated by established norms dictating the expected duration of class sessions. Conversely, in online courses, the absence of such norms often leads to a tendency to augment course content to ensure students' learning. To address this, it's essential to underscore the importance of adhering to assignment deadlines and implement strategies such as:

1. Setting specific deadlines to promote regular student participation.
2. Establishing clear criteria for project submissions.
3. Encouraging consistent work habits and effective time management.
4. Distributing assignment deadlines evenly across the academic semester rather than concentrating them around a few specific dates (Zamani & Madani, 2011) .
5. Monitoring and addressing any decline in academic performance promptly, as it is a common occurrence in online education.

Some e-learning experts, recognizing the unique characteristics of online learners, advocate for instructors to request personal histories, including details about students' work and family situations, at the beginning of the course. This approach allows instructors to demonstrate flexibility regarding assignment deadlines while also considering individual circumstances.

Understanding the expectations of the course is crucial for student success. Students who approach their studies with diligence and dedication typically achieve higher grades. However, some students may underestimate the rigor of online courses and perceive the standards as lax. To counter this misconception and align students' expectations with course requirements, instructors can:

1. Demonstrate active engagement with students' activities to convey personal investment.
2. Clearly articulate educational expectations on the university's website or course platform.
3. Acknowledge and commend exemplary performance.
4. Provide comprehensive feedback to the entire class.
5. Base performance evaluation primarily on quality rather than quantity.
6. By addressing these points, instructors can foster a conducive learning environment and enhance student engagement and success in online courses (Rosenberg & Koehler, 2015).

In electronic education, particularly in online courses, learners are primarily concerned about their skill level upon completion of the course. They seek to understand the practical implications of their learning for their careers, innovation, and overall success (Gress, Fior, Hadwin, & Winne, 2010). Therefore, it's crucial to elucidate the value of investing time in the program to enhance their motivation to learn. Here are some strategies to achieve this:

Respect for diverse talents and learning styles: Students exhibit varying talents, learning styles, educational backgrounds, and cultural influences, each with unique expectations and attitudes. While creating an ideal learning environment for every student may be impractical, fostering awareness of individual learning styles can empower students to become lifelong learners. Attention to diverse learning styles doesn't necessarily entail presenting each lesson in multiple formats but should encourage students to experience different learning approaches and develop additional skills. In electronic education, where students often control the pace of information consumption, breaking study units into smaller sections offers ample opportunities for reflection (Simonson, Zvacek, & Smaldino, 2019). Consider the following methods to respect and accommodate diverse talents:

1. Allow students to select project topics of their choice.
2. Conduct research on students' areas of interest.
3. Encourage students to voice both positive and negative opinions (Javed, 2023).
4. Incorporate real-life examples into learning experiences.
5. Facilitate collaboration among students from diverse backgrounds on projects.

Identifying learners' preferred learning strategies is essential. These strategies can be categorized into four types:

1. Experiential strategy: Emphasizes personal experiences and emotions in learning situations, fostering adaptability and openness to change.
2. Conceptualization strategy: Involves abstract thinking, logical analysis of ideas, and systematic planning, with individuals preferring to withhold judgment until a clear understanding is attained.
3. Observational strategy: Relies on personal thoughts, feelings, and emotions, while prioritizing impartiality, accurate judgment, and the ability to comprehend ideas from various perspectives.
4. Active testing strategy: Requires substantial time and effort to experiment with problem-solving approaches and adapt learning methods accordingly (Nicholls, 2005).

It's important to recognize that understanding different learning styles necessitates significant interaction between teachers and students. Once the teacher understands students' learning styles, they can tailor their teaching methods, design appropriate assignments, and group students with similar styles together. Additionally, the teacher should clarify their approach to learning concerning the type and nature of assignments. Broadly classified, learning approaches fall into two categories: deep and surface learning. A deep approach to learning is characterized by a strong intention to understand concepts and topics, linking them to existing experiences for maximum comprehension (Vermunt, 1998). Its main characteristics include:

1. Intent to understand.
2. Attention to assignments.

3. Focus on important aspects, such as the author's main claim or concepts applicable to problem-solving.
4. Integration of previous knowledge with new knowledge.
5. Connection of theoretical dimensions to daily experiences.
6. Organization of content into a cohesive framework (Vermunt, 1998).

So, how can a teacher foster a deep approach to learning? Engaging in activities such as the following can be effective (Mupinga, 2005):

1. Choosing teaching and evaluation methods that encourage active and sustained engagement in learning tasks.
2. Demonstrating a teaching style that reflects personal commitment to the subject and its relevance and importance to students.
3. Clearly stating academic expectations.
4. Allowing students the opportunity to choose their study methods and content (Vermunt, 1998).

In contrast, a surface approach to learning is primarily concerned with completing assignments and memorizing information without understanding its relevance or connections. Its main features include:

1. Focus on superficial elements, such as only paying attention to the words and sentences of the text or mechanically using formulas to solve problems.
2. Attention to isolated parts of assignments.
3. Memorization of information for evaluations.
4. Thoughtless association of concepts and facts.
5. Inability to differentiate principles from examples.
6. Viewing assignments as external obligations (Gordon & Debus, 2002).

Here, external expectations play a significant role, with students responding only to evaluation requirements. In general, certain factors contribute to a surface approach to learning, and teachers should strive to minimize them as much as possible.

In conclusion, effective communication, collaborative learning, active engagement, and accommodation of diverse learning styles are imperative in electronic education. By embracing asynchronous and synchronous communication modalities and fostering a deep approach to learning, educators can create inclusive and engaging learning environments conducive to student success in electronic education. However, it's crucial to recognize the complementarity of electronic and face-to-face interactions in fostering comprehensive educational experiences. Thus, further research and pedagogical innovations are warranted to harness the full potential of electronic education while addressing its inherent challenges.

## FINDINGS AND DISCUSSION

The expectancy-value model was developed by Eccles et al in 1983. This model has been used in both traditional and online learning environments to study student engagement. According to Eccles and Wigfield (2002), the expectancy-value model can help us understand the student engagement process. Students seek value in instructional practices and learning activities, and their beliefs about the anticipated outcomes of these factors are positively associated with student engagement. Students are looking for interest value, utility value, and attainment value in a given task (Eccles & Wigfield, 2002, 2020). Firstly, utility value refers to the perceived practical benefit of engaging in an activity or course of action. Secondly, attainment value signifies the significance of performing well in a given task. For example, a student with ambitions of becoming a salesperson may consider a presentation task important because delivering compelling presentations about products is integral to their future profession. Lastly, interest value reflects the enjoyment derived from completing a task. Research within online learning environment showed that when students perceived online learning tasks as enjoyable, beneficial, and significant, aligning with their future objectives and interests they show deeper engagement in the online learning experience.

Teacher support, student connectedness, task relevance, and course clarity are the four important dimensions of student engagement in online learning environments as they influence task value beliefs. These factors shape the student experience in online classrooms influencing the level of student engagement.

Course clarity refers to how easily students can understand and navigate the organization and instructional materials of a course. Students need clear direction on how to succeed and achieve learning goals in the online learning environment (Hoi, 2022). The positive influence of clear communication of expectations and guidance on engagement in online courses has been widely accepted (Chiu, 2021; Martin, Wang, & Sadaf, 2018). In online learning, students expect well-organized courses with explicit guidelines for navigating the course materials to be successful in the online learning environment. students may feel less competent and demotivated in online classes if they encounter unclear instructional videos or find the lesson content overly challenging (Chiu, 2021).

Task relevance pertains to aligning online learning tasks with students' interests and future aspirations, as highlighted (C.-Y. Lee, 2015). For instance, students aspiring to become digital marketers may find tasks requiring them to develop digital marketing campaigns. When students are assigned tasks that resonate with their academic, professional, and personal interests and future goals, they tend to feel a greater sense of autonomy, showing a higher level of engagement in online learning (M. J. Lee & Ko, 2015). Research indicates that students demonstrate higher levels of effort, enthusiasm, and commitment to online learning when presented with tasks and materials directly relevant to their interests and future job goals (Martin et al., 2018). In summary, students expect a clear connection between knowledge presented in an online course and real-world applications.

Relatedness is established within online learning settings when students perceive teachers as displaying supportive behaviors and feel a sense of connection with their peers. Supportive teacher behaviors encompass expressions of concern, care, respect, and understanding towards students, as well as being approachable (E. Kaufmann & Budescu, 2020).

Student connectedness refers to the degree to which students view their peers as supportive, cooperative, and respectful (R. Kaufmann & Vallade, 2022). The strong positive relationship between student connectedness and students' behavioral, cognitive, affective, and social engagement has been widely accepted by previous research. When students receive personal support to deal with learning challenges or personal issues, they are more likely to develop positive relationships with teachers and peers, fostering a sense of belonging within the online learning community (Stone & Springer, 2019).

The findings underscore the importance of leveraging the expectancy-value model to design compelling virtual classrooms. Educators can enhance engagement by designing interactive course materials and activities. Encouraging student participation in discussion forums, where they can comment on their peers' posts, fosters a sense of competition within the classroom. To bolster connectivity, scholars recommend organizing sessions dedicated to addressing questions, offering feedback, and resolving any issues that may arise (Lan & Hew, 2020). Social cognitive theory developed by Bandura (1986) supports the use of discussion boards in virtual classrooms. Online discussion boards "…it is only through active intervention of a teacher that a powerful communications tool such as collaborative computer conferencing, or cooperative learning becomes a useful instructional and learning resource." (Rourke, Anderson, Garrison, & Archer, 2001). Additionally, incorporating videos into the virtual classroom environment is recommended as a valuable tool for engagement.

## CONCLUSION

This chapter summarizes the key findings and insights around virtual engagement strategies, emphasizing their potential impact on student learning outcomes. It emphasizes the importance of anticipating emerging trends and technologies, encouraging educators to embrace a continuous learning mindset and adapt their strategies to the evolving needs of digital learners. How online instructors and professors manage online students' requirements and demands will determine the effectiveness of the instruction and the satisfaction of the students. By using tailored strategies and tools, online education can be as engaging and meaningful as the traditional learning environment. This chapter suggests areas for future research and development to continuously improve virtual engagement strategies and adapt to evolving educational landscapes. By addressing the challenges and providing practical solutions, this chapter aims to contribute to the ongoing dialogue on effective virtual teaching practices, ultimately fostering a more engaging and enriching learning experience for students in virtual classrooms.

In summary, this chapter serves as a comprehensive guide for educators seeking to enhance engagement level in virtual classrooms. The virtual learning environment is still open for improvement regarding connectivity, motivation, and engagement. By exploring the technological, pedagogical, and socio-emotional dimensions of virtual education, educators can equip themselves with the knowledge and tools necessary to create vibrant and effective virtual learning environments. Finally, this chapter is a resource for fostering motivation and engagement in the ever-evolving area of virtual classrooms. It underscores the importance of continued research, innovation, and adaptation to meet the evolving needs of students and educators alike in the digital age.

## REFERENCES

Akhtar, M., & Saeed, M. (2020). Assessing the Effect of Agree/Disagree Circles, Exit Ticket, and Think-Pair-Share on Students' Academic Achievement at Undergraduate Level. *Bulletin of Education and Research*, 42(2), 81–96.

Akhtar, R. N. (2020). Exploring Experiential Learning Models and developing an EL based ERE cycle in teaching at higher education in Pakistan. *International Journal of Experiential Learning & Case Studies*, 5(2). 10.22555/ijelcs.v5i2.44

Bandura, A. (1986). Social foundations of thought and action. *Englewood Cliffs, NJ, 1986*(23-28), 2.

Bates, A. W. Tony. (2005). *Technology, e-learning and distance education*. Routledge.

Carlson, S., & Carnevale, D. (2001). Debating the demise of NYUonline. *The Chronicle of Higher Education*, 48(16).

Chafee, L. D. (2013). Expanded learning opportunities are key to student learning. *Expanding and Opportunities, 5*.

Chiu, T. (2021). Digital support for student engagement in blended learning based on self-determination theory. *Computers in Human Behavior, 124*, 106909.

Conway, E. D. (2003). *Teaching Strategies for Distance Education*.

Cook-Sather, A., Bovill, C., & Felten, P. (2014). *Engaging students as partners in learning and teaching: A guide for faculty*. John Wiley & Sons.

de Oliveira, D., & Murillo, L. (2020). Will virtual replace classroom teaching? Lessons from virtual classes via zoom in the times of COVID-19. *Journal of Advances in Education and Philosophy*, 4(05), 208–213. 10.36348/jaep.2020.v04i05.004

Dykman, C. A., & Davis, C. K. (2008). Part One The Shift Toward Online Education. *Journal of Information Systems Education*, 19(1).

Eccles, J. S., & Wigfield, A. (2002). Motivational beliefs, values, and goals. *Annual Review of Psychology*, 53(1), 109–132. 10.1146/annurev.psych.53.100901.13515311752481

Eccles, J. S., & Wigfield, A. (2020). From expectancy-value theory to situated expectancy-value theory: A developmental, social cognitive, and sociocultural perspective on motivation. *Contemporary Educational Psychology*, 61, 101859. 10.1016/j.cedpsych.2020.101859

Fredricks, J. A., Blumenfeld, P. C., & Paris, A. H. (2004). School Engagement: Potential of the Concept, State of the Evidence. *Review of Educational Research*, 74(1), 59–109. 10.3102/00346543074001059

Gordon, C., & Debus, R. (2002). Developing deep learning approaches and personal teaching efficacy within a preservice teacher education context. *The British Journal of Educational Psychology*, 72(4), 483–511. 10.1348/00070990260377488 12495563

Hoi, V. N. (2022). *Online Learning Environments and Student Engagement: Meeting the Psychological Needs of Learners during the COVID-19 Pandemic Global Perspectives on Educational Innovations for Emergency Situations*. Springer International Publishing Cham.

Jackson, L. C., Jones, S. J., & Rodriguez, R. C. (2010). Faculty actions that result in student satisfaction in online courses. *Online Learning : the Official Journal of the Online Learning Consortium*, 14(4), 78–96. 10.24059/olj.v14i4.129

Javed, F. (2023). *Transformative Learning Strategies for Successful Teaching and Learning in the Transforming Higher Education Active and Transformative Learning in STEAM Disciplines*. Emerald Publishing Limited.

Jeffery, M. (2019). *School Success After Trauma: Examining the Parallels Among Trauma, Bullying, and School Disengagement*. The University of Western Ontario.

Jochems, W., Van Merrienboer, J., & Koper, R. (2004). Integrated e-learning. *Implications for pedagogy, technology & organization*. Londres.

Kaufmann, E., & Budescu, D. V. (2020). Do teachers consider advice? On the acceptance of computerized expert models. *Journal of Educational Measurement*, 57(2), 311–342. 10.1111/jedm.12251

Kaufmann, R., & Vallade, J. I. (2022). Exploring connections in the online learning environment: Student perceptions of rapport, climate, and loneliness. *Interactive Learning Environments*, 30(10), 1794–1808. 10.1080/10494820.2020.1749670

Kelsey, K. D., & D'souza, A. (2004). Student motivation for learning at a distance: Does interaction matter. *Online Journal of Distance Learning Administration*, 7(2), 1–10.

Kentnor, Hope E. (2015). Distance education and the evolution of online learning in the United States. *Curriculum and teaching dialogue, 17*(1), 21-34.

Lan, M., & Hew, K. F. (2020). Examining learning engagement in MOOCs: A self-determination theoretical perspective using mixed method. *International Journal of Educational Technology in Higher Education*, 17(1), 7. 10.1186/s41239-020-0179-5

Lee, C.-Y. (2015). Changes in self-efficacy and task value in online learning. *Distance Education*, 36(1), 59–79. 10.1080/01587919.2015.1019967

Lee, M. J., & Ko, A. J. (2015). Comparing the effectiveness of online learning approaches on CS1 learning outcomes.*Paper presented at the Proceedings of the eleventh annual international conference on international computing education research*. ACM. 10.1145/2787622.2787709

Levine-Sauberman, M. H. (2015). *A case study of faculty development in a community college's teaching and learning center*. Northeastern University.

Martin, F., Wang, C., & Sadaf, A. (2018). Student perception of helpfulness of facilitation strategies that enhance instructor presence, connectedness, engagement and learning in online courses. *The Internet and Higher Education*, 37, 52–65. 10.1016/j.iheduc.2018.01.003

Mupinga, D. M. (2005). Distance education in high schools: Benefits, challenges, and suggestions. *The Clearing House: A Journal of Educational Strategies, Issues and Ideas*, 78(3), 105–109. 10.3200/TCHS.78.3.105-109

Nicholls, G. (2005). New lecturers' constructions of learning, teaching and research in higher education. *Studies in Higher Education*, 30(5), 611–625. 10.1080/03075070500249328

Orange, G., & Hobbs, D. (2018). *International perspectives on tele-education and virtual learning environments*. Routledge. 10.4324/9781315200330

Palmer, S., Holt, D., & Bray, S. (2008). Does the discussion help? The impact of a formally assessed online discussion on final student results. *British Journal of Educational Technology*, 39(5), 847–858. 10.1111/j.1467-8535.2007.00780.x

Redinger, J. W., Cornia, P. B., & Albert, T. J. (2020). Teaching during a pandemic. *Journal of Graduate Medical Education*, 12(4), 403–405. 10.4300/JGME-D-20-00241.132879676

Rodrigues, H., Almeida, F., Figueiredo, V., & Lopes, S. L. (2019). Tracking e-learning through published papers: A systematic review. *Computers & Education*, 136, 87–98. 10.1016/j.compedu.2019.03.007

Rosenberg, J. M., & Koehler, M. J. (2015). Context and technological pedagogical content knowledge (TPACK): A systematic review. *Journal of Research on Technology in Education*, 47(3), 186–210. 10.1080/15391523.2015.1052663

Rourke, L. (2001). Methodological issues in the content analysis of computer conference transcripts. *International Journal of Artificial Intelligence in Education*, 12, 8–22.

Sánchez-Cruzado, C., & Campión, S. (1858). Raúl, & Sánchez-Compaña, Mª Teresa. (2021). Teacher digital literacy: The indisputable challenge after COVID-19. *Sustainability (New Rochelle, N.Y.)*, 13(4).

Sangrà, A. (2015). *Meta-analysis of the research about MOOC during 2013-2014.*

Simonson, M., Zvacek, S. M., & Smaldino, S. (2019). *Teaching and learning at a distance: Foundations of distance education*. Research Gate.

Slavin, R. E. (2012). Cooperative learning and achievement: Theory and research. *Handbook of Psychology, Second Edition, 7.*

Thornburg, A. W., Ceglie, R. J., & Abernathy, D. F. (2021). *Handbook of research on lessons learned from transitioning to virtual classrooms during a pandemic*. IGI Global. 10.4018/978-1-7998-6557-5

Tschannen-Moran, M., Parish, J., & Dipaola, M. (2006). School climate: The interplay between interpersonal relationships and student achievement. *Journal of School Leadership*, 16(4), 386–415. 10.1177/105268460601600402

Valverde-Berrocoso, J., Garrido-Arroyo, M. C., Burgos-Videla, C., & Morales-Cevallos, M. B. (2020). Trends in educational research about e-learning: A systematic literature review (2009–2018). *Sustainability (Basel)*, 12(12), 5153. 10.3390/su12125153

Vermunt, J. D. (1998). The regulation of constructive learning processes. *The British Journal of Educational Psychology*, 68(2), 149–171. 10.1111/j.2044-8279.1998.tb01281.x

Wiedmer, Terry L, & Kappan, Phi Delta. (1998). Digital portfolios: capturing and demonstrating skills and levels of performance. *Phi Delta Kappan, 4*, 01.

Wilson, R. C. (1975). *College professors and their impact on students.*

Zamani, B. B. E., & Madani, S. A. (2011). Guidelines for increasing the efficiency and effectiveness of teachers in virtual: Education. *Interdisciplinary Journal of Virtual Learning in Medical Sciences*, 2(3), 39–50.

# Chapter 7
# The Pandemic Influence of Educational Technology, Student Teacher Attachment, and Language Instruction on Value of Education:
## A Quantitative Approach

**John Rugutt**
*Illinois State University, USA*

**Caroline C. Chemosit**
http://orcid.org/0009-0008-3438-300X
*Illinois State University, USA*

**Philip K. Kaloki**
*Tarrant County College, USA*

## ABSTRACT

*This study used ANOVA and standard multiple linear regression to address the study research questions with a sample of 450 elementary and secondary school students. The measures used in the study assessed school culture elements. Regression results indicate that the overall model significantly predicts student value of education, R2 =.217, R2adj = .206, F (4, 370) = 20.29, p<.001 and the model accounted for 21.7% of variance in student value of education (SVE). Student teacher attachment*

DOI: 10.4018/979-8-3693-7645-4.ch007

*and learning equity (STALE), educational technology usage (ETU), and English language arts (ELA) were significant predictors of SVE while gender and school level were not. STALE, ETU, ELA, and SVE Cronbach alpha reliability coefficients were .70, .80, .73, and .76 respectively. Elementary students had a higher SVE than secondary school students. ANOVA results indicated significant main effect for school level, F (1, 403) = 24.99, p < .001,* $\eta 2$ *= 0.06. The study concluded with a discussion of the importance of ETU, STALE, ELA, and school level have on SVE.*

## INTRODUCTION

With the effects of a pandemic still sweeping throughout the world, school districts across the nation and around the world continue to grapple with various remote learning models leaving many education stakeholders having to choose between synchronous, asynchronous, or a combination of both (blended/hybrid). The underlying questions that call for further research, particularly by education experts under these conditions of learning and more so in the midst of the effects of a pandemic include but not limited to: 1) whether there is a significant difference in overall learning for students who are participating in either synchronous live instruction versus those students receiving asynchronous instruction, or blended instructional format, 2) whether there a significant difference in the types of digital tools used to support learning, and 3) whether there is a significant difference in the types of feedback given (formative, summative, in person, digital) in either of the three instructional delivery formats. The call for further research is needed to identify more effective instructional delivery models that result in greater learning while at the same time preventing students from achieving below proficiency levels.

Whether learning a new skill or reinforcing an existing one, educators across the globe are building their technology skills to be effective in remote learning environments and want to know how to meet the needs of their students through effective approaches that are grounded in sciences and research. Regardless of the developmental stage a student is at, reading instruction and intervention must be explicit, systematic, and evidence based (Hindman, Morrison, Connor, & Connor, 2020). While educational systems have been put to the test during the pandemic, there is a growing need to provide educators with relevant and essential research to ensure high-quality instructional delivery methods, and interventions that are supported by cognitive science and student overall learning.

According to the U.S. Department of Education (2017), American society is growing increasingly technological in both how individuals interact and in how individuals learn. Modern social life is comprised of networks of people that communicate, teach, and learn through the usage of advanced tools such as smartphones and the Internet (United States Department of Education, 2017). Thus, at the most basic level, student learning occurs as an interaction of interpersonal relationships and tool use (Siemens, 2013; Vygotsky, 1978). Student-teacher attachment is one of the underpinning factors of successful social relationships within the school setting that can have dramatic effects on students' self-perceptions of academic proficiency and ability (Baroody, Rimm-Kaufman, Larsen, & Curby, 2014).

## BACKGROUND OF THE STUDY

New evidence reveals that the closing of schools caused by the coronavirus disease (COVID-19) in recent years have and continue to exacerbate existing achievement gaps (Dorn, Hancock, Sarakatsannis, & Viruleg, 2020). According to The National Assessment of Educational Progress, recent statistics reveal that just 35 percent of American 4th graders are proficient readers (Hindman et al., 2020). Hindman et al. (2020) indicate that staggering statistics such as this have been the pattern for quite some time and since the lifetime of the National Assessment of Educational Progress administration. Critical educational and health resources for nearly 60 million students nationwide have been severed as a result of elementary and secondary school closures due to COVID-19 (Masonbrink & Hurley, 2020). As students reach the end of elementary school and are unable to read proficiently, they often face persistent struggles through the rest of their academic career (Fiester, 2013). It is unfortunate that early reading challenges are linked to higher odds of later special education referrals, grade retention, school dropout, and involvement in crime (Hindman et al., 2020). However, research shows that by helping students build and develop foundational literacy skills, any achievement gaps in their early years will drastically minimize before they begin to tackle more complex materials (Shanahan & Lonigan, 2010).

Indeed, the COVID-19 pandemic brought the issue of educational technology to the forefront. Students all over the country and some in most countries worldwide were homebound while the inequities of educational technology became apparent. It became clear that some students had access to reliable Internet at home while others did not (Darling-Hammond et. al, 2024). The global spread of COVID-19, "led to the suspension of classes for more than 850 million students worldwide, disturbing the original teaching plans of schools in all countries and regions," forcing institutions to make some changes (Sahito et al., 2022, p. 2). Darling-Hammond, et al. (2020), noted that rural areas tended to have less access than urban and suburban areas. There were also clear differences among learners since some students had digital literacy skills that allowed them to continue as there were no interruptions to learning while others did not. This continued to widen the digital gap since some students continued to get ahead while others were left behind due to lack of digital access and digital literacy. Given this digital gap, students who seemed to be most affected were students with a low-socioeconomic status and minority students (Darling-Hammond, et al., 2020).

The COVID-19 pandemic highlighted disparities in access to technology devices and the Internet and this was compounded by frequent school closures that further exacerbated academic widening gap. This has had significant impact on families and learning and particularly families of low-income communities and communities of color (Darling-Hammond et.al, 2020).

As institutions of learning continue to build their capacities in educational technology, best practices have moved from basic skills and drill activities to those that work on twenty-first century skills. These include using educational technology for collaborative learning, critical thinking, communication, and problem solving (Vegas et. al., 2019). Research has shown that technology access is not equitable to all learners and there is need for institutions to strive to improve on equity of technology so that all students have a chance to learn and grow. This will help in narrowing the learning gap that continues to be a challenge nationally and around the world.

In response to this devastating causal effect, education today is undergoing major shifts in instructional design and delivery as the science of reading continues to evolve. Schools across the nation and around the world are determining where students need support the most in foundational literacy skills and content knowledge.

## FRAMEWORK

Learning can be viewed as the product of social interaction and tool use (Vygotsky, 1978). When viewed through this lens, individual learning is understood as a bidirectional process between learners and their environment. The flow of knowledge into and out of a learner is mediated by the tools of the learner's society (Vygotsky, 1978). Within the context of this study, tools are electronic devices and software that are used to obtain, operate on, and disseminate knowledge (i.e. computers, e-mail, and internet). These tools allow students to communicate with instructors and obtain knowledge that resides outside of the learner (Siemens, 2013). According to Siemens' (2013) theory of connectivism, educational technology has not only increased the flow of information within a society, but it has also created new avenues of social interaction for the purpose of learning. Within the theory of connectivism, students' learning is affected by both students' attitudes and attachment towards their teachers and their use of educational technology.

## PURPOSE OF THE STUDY

The primary purpose of this study is threefold: 1) to investigate the COVID-19 global health pandemic through summarizing and synthesizing prior research of pre-pandemic applications of digital technology, during the pandemic use of digital technology and post-pandemic sustained use of digital technology; and two use empirical data 2) to investigate whether there is a significant linear relationship between students' perceived attitudes and attachment to their teacher, educational technology usage, English language arts and the value students attach to education; 3) to investigate whether there are significant mean differences in technology, the value students to education, student teacher attachment, and English language arts as a function of school level and gender using factorial ANOVA.

## SIGNIFICANCE OF THE STUDY

The present study is significant for several reasons. First, the study provides a summary and synthesis of prior research on the applications of digital technology while identifying the impact of COVID-19 on E-learning during pandemic and post-pandemic period. Second, this research uses empirical data to assess the impact technology has on learning and equity issues. It considers the importance of student learning through an investigation of the effects of school level and gender on the usage of technological tools and whether technology explains the value student places on education in a K-12 teaching and learning environment. Previous research has generally focused on college age students (Arch & Cummins, 1989; Joiner et al., 2011; Yau & Cheng, 2012). Furthermore, previous research has consistently evidenced that males tend to be more comfortable with educational technology usage (Comber & Colley, 1997; Yau & Cheng, 2012), but there is little in the way of examining the combined effects of school level and gender.

## RESEARCH QUESTIONS

This study is guided by the following research questions.

1. What does prior research indicate about COVID-19 global health pandemic during pre-pandemic applications of digital technology, during the pandemic and during post-pandemic use of digital technology?
2. Is there is a significant linear relationship between educational technology usage, students' perceived attitudes and attachment to their teacher, English language arts and the value students attach to education?

3. a) Are there significant mean differences in educational technology usage as a function of school level and gender?
    a. b) Are there significant mean differences in student value of education based on school level and gender?
    b. c) Are there significant mean differences in student teacher attachment and learning equity as a function of school level and gender?
    c. d) Are there significant mean differences in English language arts for gender and school level?

## PRIOR RESEARCH

### Technology During the Pandemic

The COVID-19 pandemic created significant shifts in the way institutions of learning deliver instruction. The COVID-19 health crisis forced institutions to rush through the acquisition and deployment of digital devices. This quick deployment of technology did not provide enough time for acquiring appropriate digital equipment and associated professional development for students, staff, teachers, and administrators. As a result, institutions started experiencing a high number of technology incidents such as inequities in technology access and technology breakages and damages. The low-income students, those eligible for free and reduced lunches, appear to be most affected. For learning equity to be realized for all learners, it is important to note that all students receive the same access to school issued devices and technology education to give equitable access to educational curriculum. Evans (2019) noted that technology has the promise to level the teaching and learning playing ground for all students. However, this is only possible if all students have access to the same technology and high-quality teaching and learning instructional resources. During the school day, this is possible if all students are provided with the same devices and same access. But when the students go home, they may lack adequate access outside of the school building, due to socioeconomic factors or other factors such as living in a rural area with limited access to the Internet. To help with the digital divide, schools are implementing many different solutions. Some learning institutions are allowing students to come to school early or stay after school (McLaughlin, 2016). Some schools are discouraging homework that is Internet based since not all families have access to digital devices and Internet. Innovative technology strategies schools have adopted include one-to-one with computers or Chromebooks, installing WiFi on buses, providing WiFi hotspots to parents for student use, and working with Internet service providers to secure low-cost Internet for families (McLaughlin, 2016). All these innovative ways have been implemented to try to close the digital divide for students.

The digital divide also includes technological gap based on access, digital literacy, and cultural limitations. National Center for Educational Statistics (2019) indicated that thirty-three percent, or one-third of rural America has little to no Internet coverage and that six out of ten parents say it is likely their homebound children will experience at least one digital obstacle while doing their schoolwork. In addition, students in lower income households also suffer. These lower income families also have lower levels of technology adoption. National Center for Education Statistics (2019) further stated that 56% of families in the lower income bracket have access to Broadband as compared to 94% of families in the higher income bracket. Research has also found cultural barriers to be one of the contributing factors to adoption of technology. Research has shown that twenty-five percent of Black teens are unable to complete their homework due to lack of a reliable computer or Internet connection, while thirty-nine percent of Hispanic teens do their homework on a cell phone (National Center for Educational Statistics, 2019).

## Technology During Post-Pandemic

While technology has the potential to be an equalizer, research has shown that it can also be more divisive. Reich (2019) found that even when digital access gaps are closed, technology usage between white and affluent students is different from students from minority backgrounds and students from low-income households. The white and affluent students are more likely to use technology to create and problem solve. They are also more likely to have greater levels of mentorship from adults. In contrast, the students from minority groups and low-income households use technology more for routine drills and with less support from (Journell, 2007).

Journell (2007) and Picciano (2011) also noted that while some may think that as the cost of technology decreases, and access becomes more readily available, the digital inequities will disappear. This is not actually the case as research has shown that access to technology does not necessarily translate to digital equity (Journell, 2007; Picciano, 1991; Picciano, 2011). Digital literacy must be addressed and that digital literacy and how comfortable one is in using different technologies is based on their life experiences as institutions of learning nationally do not teach the same computer skills, even when access to technology is not an issue. Differences in access to technology instruction also tend to follow geographic, socioeconomic, and racial undertones, and quality of instruction (Journell, 2007; Picciano, 1991).

It is imperative to note that gender has been a factor when assessing the equity of technology. Bravo, Gilbert, and Kearney (2003) noted that technology is often constructed as a male domain, starting as early as middle school. Classes such as computer programming and coding are often filled with male and few female students. Some districts are implementing programs such as "Girls Who Code" to encourage female participation in the computer sciences. "Gender equity in the schools is vital to developing the full potential of both female and male students" (Bravo, Gilbert, & Kearney, 2003, p. 108).

Digital citizenship has become very important as young children and adults are using computer technology more and more. Students are interacting with classmates, as well as people across the world. During the school shutdown during the COVID-19 pandemic, remote learning was the only way students could connect and communicate with their classmates and teachers.

Hollandsworth, Dowdy, and Donovan (2011) explained that digital citizenship can be compared to American citizenship. They state, "All digital citizens have the same basic rights: privacy, free speech, and creative work rights. Teaching everyone how to protect their privacy is critical" (p. 41). They noted that everyone has a right to free speech, but students need to be taught about the far-reaching effects posting online has. They explained that with rights comes responsibility.

Passey et al. (2018) define digital citizenship as "digital competence, digital confidence, and digital accountability, which is the individual's ability to control and adapt to a digital world" (p. 426). They further stated that digital competence is the ability to navigate the digital world safely and effectively and that digital confidence emphasizes having the skills and knowledge base to navigate the digital platform. Passey et al. (2018) further elaborated on three parts to digital competence to be: a) the ability to use a variety of computer applications, software, and the Internet with ease, b) the confidence to handle technology in different contexts, and the exercise of digital autonomy, and c) digital accountability which includes having digital responsibility for yourself and taking digital responsibility for others as well. In addition, digital accountability means the user has knowledge of the digital world and the ethical issues associated with it. Passey et al. (2018) further stressed that digital accountability means understanding concerns about digital privacy and the impact of digital services has others.

Payne (2016), explore how digital citizenship concepts were being taught in 5th grade classrooms. The findings of the study indicated that teachers were unaware of the importance of teaching digital citizenship to their students and that there was little consistency in what was taught. There were significant variations in how teachers provided lessons for students. Inconsistency in delivering instruction was noted to contribute to further widening of the gap in understanding students' appropriate digital technology use.

Martin et al. (2020) emphasized the need for digital citizenship in schools. Their research found that the beginnings of high-risk digital behaviors start with middle school students. To address student technology needs and to better protect and prepare them for life in a digital world, schools have the responsibility to teach students responsible online behavior (Dalinghaus, 2023).

Macgilchrist (2019) said that it is evident that the way digital technology is being used, even though it may be inadvertently, is strengthening existing socio-economic inequalities. Even when the digital divide has been addressed, students must have access to equitable access to technological devices. Many schools and school districts are struggling to keep devices in students' hands due to theft, loss, or damage of student devices. Schools are having to create new policies to address new realities of how technology is being used in their district (Texas Association of School Boards, 2020). Schools have had to implement stringent digital use policies such as having students who cannot afford to pay for damages be left without a device. This further causes an equity issue.

The higher education sector has also been affected. The COVID-19 global health crisis forced higher education institutions to quickly adjust learning environments and without preparation. Some institutions were able to withstand the disruption because of the resilience of their organization and creative business decisions while others were even forced to reinvent themselves (Llopis, 2020). Without a doubt, technology continues to impact almost every aspect of our lives. It has grown into a powerful tool that has transformed how instruction is delivered to the learners. With technology, instructors are introducing collaborative learning environments and encouraging students to learn and work together. Technology, through the Internet makes it possible for educational opportunities to stretch far beyond learning boundaries unlike when it was just confined to the walls of a classroom. Technology is enhancing communication skills, opening opportunities for learners to interact nationally and internationally, and providing immediate access to information.

In higher education institutions, faculty have had to incorporate technology into their instruction to adapt and develop their teaching and to interact with students who increasingly rely on technology and use of social media daily (Kajiwara, 2015). Technology is constantly changing and to be a good digital citizen, students must be taught how to be good stewards of digital technology.

## Educational Technology Usage

Educational technology is nebulously defined, but the areas of focus for this study, e-mail, computers, and internet are typically included within its purview (Al-Ammary, 2013). The implementation of educational technology in the classroom has been previously studied. Its implementation has been related to a host improved student outcomes (Joiner et al., 2011).

For instance, Al-Ammary (2013) examined the impact of the adoption of educational technology on university students' overall academic performance. The author observed that the student sample (72% female) indicated that the usage of educational technology increased their sense of ownership over their academic experience. Furthermore, the students indicated that they felt it improved their ability to communicate with teachers and their general classroom functioning.

Despite the positive outcomes of implementing educational technology in the classroom, the benefits of its use may be differentially obtained. Previous research has indicated that males report feeling more comfortable with using technology (Comber & Colley, 1997; Yau & Cheng, 2012). This increased level of comfort may lead to greater ease and acceptance of the use of educational technology. For example, Yau and Cheng (2012) administered a survey to university students in Hong Kong to determine their levels of comfort with assorted educational technology tools. The results indicated that while members of both genders found educational technology use important, males were more confident in using educational technology for learning.

Li and Kirkup (2007) obtained similar results with college-aged samples from China and the United Kingdom. The researchers found that males reported using e-mail and the Internet more frequently than did females. Further, males from both countries tended to report feeling more confident in their skills using educational technology. Finally, both genders tended to hold favorable attitudes towards the Internet as a source of knowledge.

## Student Teacher Attachment and Learning Equity

Students spend a large portion of their day within the confines of their school buildings. The classroom is a social unit, secondary to the family, in which students develop interpersonal relationships (Madill et al., 2014). The teacher often acts as a surrogate guardian to students in the classroom during the school day. Students who feel a positive attachment towards their teachers have been shown to possess higher rates of intrinsic motivation for learning and improved achievement outcomes (Madill et al., 2014).

For instance, Madill et al. (2014) conduct a study in Illinois and Pennsylvania to examine early elementary school (grades 1, 3, and 5) children's perceptions of attachment to their teachers. The researchers observed both grade and gender effects for students' feelings of closeness to their teachers. Generally, females and students in first and third grade showed higher perceptions of attachment to their teachers.

These results were also observed by Suldo, Thalji-Raitano, Hasemeyer, Gelley, and Hoy (2013) with a sample of middle school students from the Southeastern United States. The researchers found that both male and female students benefited from feelings of a positive attachment to their teachers. Suldo et al. (2013) state that students' attachments to their teachers is facilitated by providing students with multiple opportunities to be active participants in the learning process.

Furthermore, while student teacher attachment is important for a student's well-being, it is also important for adequate academic achievement (Durlak, Weissber, Dymnicki, Taylor, & Schellinger, 2011). Durlak et al. (2011) conducted a meta-analysis examining the varied effects of interventions directly and indirectly targeting student teacher attachment. The investigators observed a positive relationship between academic achievement and feelings of closeness between students and teachers.

## English Language Arts

Since the advent of COVID-19, delivering a balanced literacy instruction has resulted in teachers having to pivot from their previous instructional delivery approaches without a roadmap and are plotting out how to teach students from a distance (Kelly, 2020). Decades of research has shown that explicitly teaching students how letters correspond to spoken sounds and teaching phonics through skill-based instruction is the most effective way to help them learn to decode words but translating this to the remote environment is lacking research (Schwartz, 2020).

According to literacy expert Timothy Shanahan (Schwartz, 2020), little research also exists on what an upheaval of this magnitude could do to learning and literacy development in children, especially when one compares the research about the loss of skills during summer break, which evidence shows that students from under-resourced backgrounds or struggling with trauma suffer more severe losses. Shanahan posits that there is just no question that is harder than what they are used to, for both students and teachers (Schwartz, 2020). The most common reading curriculums assume one key factor: that children are taught in person. Additional variables exist as teachers attempt to rebuild instructional lessons to teach literacy skills while also confronting hurdles related to technology access and enticing students to actively engage and participate remotely online. New reports indicate that teachers have developed various techniques to teach reading remotely and manage their students, however, they are finding it difficult to accurately assess comprehension levels (Schwartz, 2020).

Teachers are being confronted with daunting new challenges in teaching millions of young children how to read without the opportunity to be in person with them. One compelling argument is identifying the most effective approach in supporting the youngest learners in their early literacy skills while meeting end-of-the year reading level benchmarks. Three key models receiving significant attention currently include in-person learning (synchronous), distance learning (asynchronous), and concurrent combination of both (blended learning) that are used in other levels of education.

While this understanding has grown more profuse in education during the last twenty years, there are still many questions to be examined. Of these many questions, it is still unknown as to how school level and gender interact to impact students' usage of educational technology in the eighth and twelfth grade contexts (Yau & Cheng, 2012). Further, there remain unknown impacts of gender and school level on students' attachment to teachers (Madill, Gest, & Rodkin, 2014). Finally, in an increasingly social and technologically based educational environment there remain unknown relationships between student-teacher attachment, technology usage, and internalized student value of education (Siemens, 2013).

Despite its significance, and as stated previously, student-teacher attachment is but one factor in student learning. As Siemens (2013) indicates, the "half-life" of knowledge is growing increasingly truncated. To stay abreast of the rapidly advancing pace of knowledge generation, students must make use of the technological tools (computers, e-mail, current instructional delivery methods of traditional, online, and blended and the internet databases) available to them in their environments. Thus, new learning is mediated by the interaction of social relationships and tool use (Siemens, 2013; Vygotsky, 1978).

# METHODOLOGY

## Research Design

The research design of this study is divided into two broad areas: 1) summarizes and synthesizes prior research on COVID-19 global health pandemic during and after the COVID-19 pandemic, and 2) uses empirical data to investigate; a) whether there are significant mean differences in educational technology, student value on education, student teacher attachment and English language arts as a function of school level and gender using factorial ANOVA, and b) whether there is a significant linear relationship between students' perceived attitudes and attachment to their teacher, educational technology usage, English language arts and the value students attach to education.

The empirical part of the study uses cross-sectional survey design in that it considered variables of a specific elementary and secondary schools' teaching and learning environment at a specific point in time. It also used a survey design to collect information from primary and secondary school students on the key variables related to teaching, learning and use of educational technology. Further, a post hoc correlation design was used as a framework for data analysis in the study. Thus, relationships among the variables were explored (rather than manipulated) to develop a regression model for examining the relative contribution of each of the predictor variables to school leadership.

## Measures

This study used measures developed to assess school culture. Specifically, the study investigated a select number of variables, such as educational technology usage, student teacher attachment and learning equity, the value students place on, gender, and school level. Student teacher attachment and learning equity (STALE) comprised of the sum of scores for ten items. Participants respond using a four-point Likert scale as follows: 1 = strongly disagree, 2 = disagree, 3 = agree, 4 = strongly agree. Educational technology usage (ETU) construct comprised of eight items and participants respond using a four-point scale as follows: 1 = strongly disagree, 2 = disagree, 3 = agree, 4 = strongly agree. The student value of education (SVE) factor comprised of twelve items and participants respond using a four-point scale as follows: 1 = strongly disagree, 2 = disagree, 3 = agree, 4 = strongly agree. English language arts (ELA) is a composite variable comprising the sum of scores for six items. Participants respond using a four-point Likert scale as follows: 1 = strongly disagree, 2 = disagree, 3 = agree, 4 = strongly agree. A complete list of the survey items associated with each of the four constructs is provided in Appendix B.

Exploratory factor analysis was used to assess the factor structure of the Student Learning Environment Survey (SLES) items. This research used the principal components analysis with varimax rotation on the Likert scale items of the survey. The factor analysis generated nine components with eigenvalues greater than 1. The nine-factor solution accounted for 41.02% of the total variance. The pattern of loadings on the factors were then examined using the decision guidelines provided in Chemosit (2004), that is: 1) (a) the minimum value for retaining an item on a factor was 0.40; (b) an item was retained if it loaded primarily on one factor; (c) an item was retained on the factor on which its loading was greatest; and (d) if an item loaded on more than one factor, the item was retained if the difference of the squared loadings was 0.20 or greater. The Cronbach alpha reliability coefficients for the four factors used in this study are reported in Table 1. The examination of the items comprising the first factor reflected student value of education, the second factor reflected student teacher attachment, the third reflected English language arts, and the fourth reflected educational technology usage. The internal consistency coefficients using Cronbach alpha reliability coefficients were then computed and reported in Table 1. Composite scores for each of the four factors were computed and used in the subsequent analyses.

The selected subscales of the instrument, items per scale and their corresponding Cronbach alpha reliabilities are presented in Table 1.

*Table 1. Study variables and corresponding Cronbach alpha reliability coefficients*

| Variable (#)* | Variable Description | Alpha Reliabilities |
|---|---|---|
| STALE (10) | Student Teacher Attachment and Learning Equity | .70 |
| ETU (8) | Educational Technology Usage | .85 |
| SVE (12) | Student Value of Education | .76 |
| ELA (6) | English Language Arts | .73 |

* Number of items comprising measure

## Sample and Sampling Procedures

A sample of 1,000 elementary and secondary school students in Kenya were surveyed. Data were collected for the study using individual instrument packets that were distributed to students within each of the 70 schools in seven regional offices of education (school divisions) in Kericho County, Kenya. The central office personnel (district education office personnel) spread throughout the seven school divisions explained the purpose of the study, assured students of anonymity, encourage participation, and left their classrooms while participants completed the set of measures. All the data was collected voluntarily, and the anonymity of respondents was maintained. All completed packets were sealed in envelopes and collected by designated central office personnel. Complete and usable surveys were received from 450 students, yielding an overall response rate of 45%. Table 2 summarizes the demographic distributions of the study sample for selected study variables.

*Table 2. Demographic distributions of the study sample*

| Variable | N* | Percent (%) |
|---|---|---|
| Gender | | |
| Female | 221 | 49.1 |
| Male | 203 | 45.1 |
| School level | | |
| Elementary School | 399 | 88.7 |
| High School | 51 | 11.3 |
| Regional Office of Education (Division) | | |
| Ainamoi | 64 | 14.2 |
| Belgut | 85 | 18.9 |
| Chilchila | 86 | 19.1 |
| Kipkelion | 24 | 5.3 |

continued on following page

*Table 2. Continued*

| Variable | N* | Percent (%) |
|---|---|---|
| Londiani | 141 | 31.3 |
| Sigowet | 44 | 9.8 |
| Soin | 6 | 1.3 |
| During the school year, how much time (hours per week) did you spend during a typical week playing video or computer games? | | |
| None | 289 | 64.2 |
| <1 hour | 40 | 8.9 |
| 1-2 hours | 32 | 7.1 |
| 3-5 hours | 19 | 4.2 |
| 6-10 hours | 8 | 1.8 |
| 11-15 hours | 5 | 1.1 |
| 6-20 hours | 4 | 0.9 |
| >20 hours | 4 | 0.9 |

Note: * Total for each demographic variable may not add up to 450 due to non-responses

## Data Preparation Procedures and Analysis

The results completed for this study are as follows; (a) descriptive statistical analyses of demographic and related instrument items as well as composite variables; (b) factor analyses, (c) internal consistency (Cronbach Alpha) reliability analyses of instrument subscales; (d) two-factor ANOVA, and (e) multiple regression analyses.

First, data was screened to identify missing data and outliers and to evaluate the fulfillment of test assumptions utilizing guidelines discussed in Meyers, Gamst, and Guarino (2017) and in Mertler and Vannatta (2005). The independent variables were assessed for possible multicollinearity problems through tolerance statistics available under regression feature in SPSS. Tolerance values range from 0 to 1 and multicollinearity is indicated for a particular variable if the tolerance value is .01 or less (Meyers, Gamst, & Guarino, 2017). For this study, the tolerance values ranged from .619 to .780 for all predictor variables.

This study used a two-factor ANOVA and standard multiple linear regression to address the study research questions with a sample of 450 elementary and secondary school students. The measures used in the study assessed elements of school culture among elementary and high school students with focus on four subscales of the instrument (see Table 1 and appendix B). Data screening using mahalanobis distances identified four outliers that did not have any significant impact on the data analysis and were not deleted from the data.

## SUMMARY OF RESULTS

This study was guided by two main research questions and the results are summarized as per the research questions.

**Research Question #1:** Is there a significant linear relationship between students' perceived attitudes and attachment to their teacher, educational technology usage, English language arts and the value student place on their education?

This question was answered using multiple linear regression analysis. The results indicate that the overall model significantly predicts student value of education, $R^2 = .264$, $R^2_{adj} = .256$, F (4, 370) = 33.25, $p < .001$. This model accounts for 26.4% of variance in student value of education (SVE). Student teacher attachment and learning equity (STALE), educational technology usage (ETU), English language arts were statistically significant predictors of SVE while school level and gender were not. Elementary students had a higher SVE mean value than secondary school students.

**Research Question #2 a)**: Are there significant mean differences in educational technology usage as a function of school level and gender?

The ANOVA analysis with educational technology usage (ETU) as the dependent variable and school level and gender as independent variables indicate an overall *F* test as not statistically significant indicating that either gender, school level or the interaction between gender and school level was not significant, $F$ (3, 354) = .51, $p = .679$, $\eta^2 = 0.004$. The ANOVA indicated no significant interaction effect between gender and school level, $F$ (1, 354) = .92, $p = .34$. Both school level and gender main effects were not statistically significant.

**Research Question #2 b):** Are there significant mean differences in student value of education based on school level and gender?

The results indicate school level had a significant main effect on student value of education ($F$[1, 419] = 11.37, $p < .001$, ES = .026) but does not significantly interacts with gender, ($F$[1, 419] = 1.36, $p = .24$, ES = .003). Gender main effect was not statistically significant. The effect sizes for the three tests were very small. The school level main effect indicated that students in elementary school tended to have higher SVE mean score for both male and female students. The means, standard deviations, and sample sizes for the two groups of school level and gender are reported in Table 3.

continued on following page

*Table 3. Continued*

*Table 3. Gender, school level, mean, standard deviation, sample size*

| Gender | School Level | Mean | Std. Deviation | N |
|---|---|---|---|---|
| Female | Elementary School | 27.58 | 3.18 | 193 |
| | High School | 24.93 | 5.70 | 27 |
| | Total | 27.25 | 3.67 | 220 |
| Male | Elementary School | 26.90 | 3.73 | 185 |
| | High School | 25.61 | 3.36 | 18 |
| | Total | 26.78 | 3.71 | 203 |
| Total | Elementary School | 27.24 | 3.47 | 378 |
| | High School | 25.20 | 4.87 | 45 |
| | Total | 27.03 | 3.69 | 423 |

**Research Question #2 c):** Are there significant mean differences in student teacher attachment and learning equity as a function of school level and gender?

To answer the research question, A 2 X 2 ANOVA was conducted to evaluate the effects of gender and school level on student teacher attachment and learning equity. The ANOVA indicated that the overall $F$ test was significant indicating that either gender, school level or the interaction between gender and school level was significant, $F$ (3, 403) = 8.94, $p < .001$, $\eta^2 = 0.062$. The ANOVA indicated no significant interaction between gender and school level, $F$ (1, 403) = .37, $p = .55$, $\eta^2 = .001$, but significant main effect for school level, $F$ (1, 403) = 24.99, $p < .001$, $\eta^2 = 0.06$. The gender main effect was not significant, $F$ (1, 403) = .002, $p = .97$. The school level main effect indicated that elementary students tended to have higher STALE mean score for both male and female students than secondary school students.

**Research Question #2 d):** Are there significant mean differences in English language arts for gender and school level?

The 2 X 2 ANOVA analysis for English language arts as dependent variable and school level and gender as independent variables indicate an overall $F$ test that is not statistically significant, $F$ (3, 402) = 1.55, $p = .200$, $\eta^2 = 0.011$. These results show that no main effects or interaction to be statistically significant.

## DISCUSSION, CONCLUSION, AND IMPLICATIONS

The review and synthesis of research about the COVID-19 pandemic, before, during and post-pandemic highlighted disparities in access to technology devices and the Internet for both K-12 and post-secondary learning institutions. The experiences from the COVID-19 health crisis have forced learning institutions to continue to build their capacities in educational technology, best practices, and provision of professional development and using educational technology for collaborative learning, communication, and enhancing problem solving (Vegas et. al., 2019).

While student teacher attachment and learning equity is widely held as an important factor in their general academic functioning (Durlack, 2011), much of the previous research has focused on elementary or middle school students (Baroody et al., 2014; Madill et al., 2014; Suldo et al., 2013). There has been little in the way of examining students' attachment to their teachers at the junior high or high school levels. This is an important area of investigation as these students often have more than one teacher during the course of a school day, which may impact their perceptions of attachment to their teachers. Furthermore, it remains unknown if differential levels of attachment to teachers as a result of student gender persist into the high school years.

During my years as a high school teacher in East Africa, students were smiling, investigating, and demonstrating a daily hunger for learning that radiated throughout the school. It was clear that each classroom was a tight knit community centered around the idea that the most important thing about school was making deep connections with one another. Today, I carry these experiences with me and strive to create a classroom that puts relationships first. I believe that if students feel wanted, if students feel safe, and if students perceive their teacher as someone who cares about them, then and only then can we begin to look at outcomes that many stakeholders in education prioritize (e.g., assessment scores, student behavior, student engagement).

At heart of survey questions used in the study and listed in Appendix B and summarized as composite variables Table 1, there was one question that stood out, "Teachers in this school really care about me and make me feel important." Every question after went on to describe how this interest was shown by asking if the teacher answered questions, if the teacher addressed them, if the teacher considered their feelings, and if the student felt safe approaching the teacher. All the items listed centered around attitude and attachment to teachers.

Hughes and Kwok (2007) hypothesized that there was a relationship between the quality of teachers' relationships with students and student-rated classroom engagement. Although the study was also aimed at examining reading achievement levels of struggling readers, it revealed so much more. The current study also investigated the impact English Language Arts (ELA) has on the value student place on education. The results of Hughes and Kwok (2007) found that students who did not feel relatable with their teachers self-identified as less engaged. It should be noted that the 1st graders ($N = 443$) in Hughes and Kwok research were ethnically diverse and lower-achieving readers. When looking at ethnicity, African American students' positive perception of teachers was much lower than Hispanic and Caucasian children. The implications are clear – students who do not feel connected to their teacher may experience lower levels of achievement and engagement. Further, Hughes and Kwok's (2007) results align to the decades of research that suggests certain demographics of students may lag in school due to the expectations the teacher sets for the given group due to a self-fulfilling prophecy. However, Rubie-Davies (2006) explored self-fulfilling prophecies class-wide rather than individual. Teachers who had high class-level expectations were found to have statistically significant differences when looking at student outcomes and the teacher-student relationship. This further illustrates the connection between relationships, expectations, and engagement.

Roorda, Koomen, Spilt, and Oort (2011) did a meta-analysis to investigate the associations between teacher-student relationships and students' school engagement and achievement. Using 99 studies, both positive and negative associations with engagement were statistically significant. In other words, students who had a better relationship with their teachers were more engaged in class while the inverse of that remained true as well. Interestingly, for the primary grades, the negative relationships were stronger when looking at level of significance. Meanwhile, the positive relationships were stronger for secondary schools. Given that secondary teacher preparation programs tend to prioritize content over student centered coursework (i.e., child psychology, special education, adolescent development), their findings are important. Their findings of their research support and strengthens the findings of this study.

Regarding educational technology usage, previous research has consistently indicated the existence of gender-based differences in the applied usage and confidence in the use of educational technology (Al-Ammary, 2013; Comber & Colley, 1997; Li & Kirkup, 2007; Yau & Cheng, 2012). Despite these results, the surveyed research has generally been conducted in countries besides the United States. Further, all the reviewed studies utilized samples consisting of individuals recruited from university settings (Al-Ammary, 2013; Comber & Colley, 1997; Li & Kirkup, 2007; Yau & Cheng, 2012). It continues to remain unknown if gender-based differences in the rate of educational technology usage are present within the junior high and high school levels in the United States.

Finally, much research exists indicating that confidence in one's abilities and their feelings of trust in others can promote positive mental health (Durlak et al., 2011). The use of educational technology has been shown to improve student teacher communication (Al-Ammary, 2013). It has also been offered as a means for increasing student ownership in her or his learning (Suldo et al., 2013). Both possible products may improve feelings of attachment towards teachers, which has been shown to improve student's self-perceptions of their abilities (Durlak et al., 2011). Despite this possible pathway, the specific interactional relationship between educational technology usage and student teacher attachment on individual educational perspectives remains inclusive.

## REFERENCES

Al-Ammary, J. (2013). Educational technology: A way to enhance student achievement at the University of Bahrain. *The Online Journal of New Horizons in Education, 3*(3), 54-65. http://tojned.net/?pid=showissue&issueid=102

Arch, E. C., & Cummins, D. E. (1989). Structured and unstructured exposure to computers: Gender differences in attitude and use among college students. *Sex Roles*, 20(5-6), 245–254. 10.1007/BF00287722

Baroody, A. E., Rimm-Kaufman, S. E., Larsen, R. A., & Curby, T. W. (2014). The link between responsive classroom training and student-teacher relationship quality in the fifth grade: A study of fidelity of implementation. *School Psychology Review*, 43(1), 69–85. 10.1080/02796015.2014.12087455

Bravo, M. J., Gilbert, L. A., & Kearney, L. K. (2003). Interventions for promoting gender equitable technology use in classrooms. *Teacher Education Quarterly*, 30(4), 95–109.

Chemosit, C. C. (2004). *Predictors and correlates of student academic achievement: student-faculty interaction, active learning strategies, and academic rigor*. [Unpublished master's Thesis, Illinois State University, Normal].

Comber, C., Colley, A., Hargreaves, D. J., & Dorn, L. (1997). The effects of age, gender and computer experience upon computer attitudes. *Educational Research*, 39(2), 123–133. 10.1080/0013188970390201

Dalinghaus, L. J. (2023). *A qualitative study of digital citizenship practices and the fear of missing out: perceptions of middle school students and principals*. [Doctoral Dissertation, Kansas State University]. ProQuest Dissertations Publishing.

Darling-Hammond, L., Schachner, A., & Edgerton, A. K. (2020). Restarting and reinventing school: Learning in the time of COVID and beyond. In *Learning Policy Institute*. Learning Policy Institute.

Dorn, E., Hancock, B., Sarakatsannis, J., & Viruleg, E. (2020). *COVID-19 and Student Learning in the United States: The Hurt Could Last a Lifetime*. Child Institute. https://www.childrensinstitute.net/sites/default/files/documents/COVID-19-and-student-learning-in-the-United-States_FINAL.pdf

Durlak, J. A., Weissber, R. P., Dymnicki, A. B., Taylor, R. D., & Schellinger, K. B. (2011). The impact of enhancing students' social and emotional learning: A meta-analysis of school-based universal interventions. *Child Development*, 82(1), 405–432. 10.1111/j.1467-8624.2010.01564.x21291449

Evans, J. A. (2019). *Digital learning: Peril or promise for our K-12 students.* Project Tomorrow. https://files.eric.ed.gov/fulltext/ED605281.pdf

Fiester, L. (2013). Early Warning Confirmed: A Research Update on Third-Grade Reading. *The Annie E. Casey Foundation, Baltimore, Maryland.* file:///Users/srhoads/Downloads/AECF-EarlyWarningConfirmed-2013.pdf

Hindman, A., Morrison, F., Connor, C., & Connor, J. (2020). Bringing the Science of Reading to Preservice Elementary Teachers: Tools That Bridge Research and Practice. *International Literacy Association.*https://ila-onlinelibrary-wiley-com.libproxy.lib.ilstu.edu/doi/10.1002/rrq.34

Hollandsworth, R., Dowdy, L., & Donovan, J. (2011). Digital citizenship in K-12: It takes a village. *TechTrends*, 55(4), 37–47. 10.1007/s11528-011-0510-z

Hughes, J., & Kwok, O. (2007). Influence of student-teacher and parent-teacher relationships on lower achieving readers' engagement and achievement in the primary grades. *Journal of Educational Psychology*, 99(1), 39–51. 10.1037/0022-0663.99.1.3918084625

Joiner, R., Iacovides, J., Owen, M., Gavin, C., Clibbery, S., Darling, J., & Drew, B. (2011). Digital games, gender and learning in engineering: Do females benefit as much as males? *Journal of Science Education and Technology*, 20(2), 178–185. 10.1007/s10956-010-9244-5

Journell, W. (2007). The inequities of the digital divide: Is e-learning a solution? *E-Learning and Digital Media*, 4(2), 138–149. 10.2304/elea.2007.4.2.138

Kajiwara, M. (2015, August 12). *5 trends that could change the face of higher education* [Online forum post]. Higher Ed Live. http://higheredlive.com/5-trends-that-could-change-the-face-of-higher-education/

Kelly, K. (2020). *Meaningful Remote Learning and Literacy Practices During COVID-19.* International Literacy Association. https://literacyworldwide.org/blog%2Fliteracy-now%2F2020%2F05%2F29%2Fmeaningful-remote-learning-and-literacy-practices-during-covid-19

Li, N., & Kirkup, G. (2007). Gender and cultural differences in internet use: A study of China and the UK. *Computers & Education*, 48(2), 301–317. 10.1016/j.compedu.2005.01.007

Llopis, G. (2020, October 17). Post pandemic: How must colleges and universities reinvent themselves? *Forbes.*https://www.forbes.com/sites/glennllopis/2020/10/17/post-pandemic-how-must-colleges-and-universities-reinvent-themselves/?sh=14f0a3413e88

Macgilchrist, F. (2019). Cruel optimism in edtech: When the digital data practices of educational technology providers inadvertently hinder educational equity. *Learning, Media and Technology*, 44(1), 77–86. 10.1080/17439884.2018.1556217

Madill, R. A., Gest, S. D., & Rodkin, P. C. (2014). Students' perceptions of relatedness in the classroom: The roles of emotionally supportive teacher-child interactions, children's aggressive-disruptive behaviors, and peer social preference. *School Psychology Review*, 43(1), 86–105. 10.1080/02796015.2014.12087456

Martin, F., Hunt, B., Wang, C., & Brooks, E. (2020). Middle school student perception of technology use and digital citizenship practices. *Computers in the Schools*, 37(3), 196–215. 10.1080/07380569.2020.1795500

Masonbrink, A., & Hurley, E. (2020). Advocating for Children During the COVID-19 School Closures. P*ediatrics - Official Journal of the American Academy of Pediatrics*. https://pediatrics.aappublications.org/content/146/3/e20201440

McLaughlin, C. (2016). *The homework gap: The 'cruelest part of the digital divide'*. NEA Today. https://www.nea.org/nea-today/all-news-articles/homework-gap-cruelest-part-digital-divide

National Center for Educational Statistics. (n.d.). *The condition of education 2019*. Institute of Education Sciences, National Center for Education Sciences. https://nces.ed.gov/pubs2019/2019144.pdf

Passey, D., Shonfeld, M., Appleby, L., Judge, M., Saito, T., & Smits, A. (2018). Digital agency: Empowering equity in and through education. *Tech Know Learn*, 23(3), 425–439. 10.1007/s10758-018-9384-x

Payne, J. L. (2016). *A case study of teaching digital citizenship in fifth grade*. [Doctoral Dissertation, The University of Alabama]. ProQuest Dissertations Publishing.

Picciano, A. G. (1991). Computers, city, and suburb: A study of New York City and Westchester County public schools. *The Urban Review*, 23(3), 93–109. 10.1007/BF01108428

Picciano, A. G. (2011). *Educational Leadership and Planning for Technology* (5th ed.). Pearson Education, Inc.

Reich, J. (2019). Teaching our way to digital equity. *Educational Leadership*, 76(5), 30–35.

Roorda, D. L., Koomen, H., Spilt, J. L., & Oort, F. J. (2011). The influence of affective teacher-student relationships on students' school engagement and achievement: A meta-analytic approach. *Review of Educational Research*, 81(4), 493–529. 10.3102/0034654311421793

Rubie-Davies, C. M. (2006). Teacher expectations and student self-perceptions: Exploring relationship. *Psychology in the Schools*, 43(5), 537–552. 10.1002/pits.20169

Schwartz, S. (2020). How to Use Digital Reading Programs During COVID-19. Teachers Still Matter. *Education Week*. https://www.edweek.org/ew/articles/2020/09/30/how-to-use-digital-reading-programs-during.html

Shanahan, T., & Lonigan, C. J. (2010). The National Early Literacy Panel. *Educational Researcher*, 39(4), 279–285. 10.3102/0013189X1036917222294803

Siemens, G. (2013). Connectivism: A learning theory for the digital age. *International Journal of Instructional Technology and Distance Learning*, 2(1), 3–10. http://www.itdl.org/journal/jan_05/article01.htm

Suldo, S. M., Thalji-Raitano, A., Hasemeyer, M., Gelley, C. D., & Hoy, B. (2013). Understanding middle school students life satisfaction: Does school climate matter? *Applied Research in Quality of Life*, 8(2), 169–182. 10.1007/s11482-012-9185-7

United States Department of Education. (2017). *Reimagining the role of technology in education: 2017 national education technology plan update*. Washington, DC: U.S. Department of Education. http://tech.ed.gov

Vegas, E., Ziegler, L., & Zerbino, N. (2019). *How ed-tech can help leapfrog progress in education*. Center for Universal Education at The Brookings Institution. https://files.eric.ed.gov/fulltext/ED602936.pdf

Vygotsky, L. S. (1978). *Mind in society: The development of higher psychological processes*. Harvard University Press.

Yau, H. K., & Cheng, A. L. F. (2012). Gender differences of confidence in using technology for learning. *The Journal of Technology Studies*, 38(2), 74–79. https://scholar.lib.vt.edu/ejournals/JOTS/v38/v38n2/yau. 10.21061/jots.v38i2.a.2

# APPENDIX

## Definitions of the Study Variables

This study examined six variables derived from the administration of the School Learning Environment Survey (SLES) to students in eighth and twelfth grade. The composite variables included Student Teacher Attachment and Learning Equity (STALE), Educational Technology Usage (ETU), English language arts (ELA) and Student Value of Education (SVE). For a listing of the individual items contained within each variable, see the below table. Two demographic variables, gender and school level were also utilized in the study's analyses.

*Student Teacher Attachment and Learning Equity (STALE)*- STALE is composite variable comprising of 10 Likert-type items. The 10 items consisted of statements related to how study participants view their attachment to their teachers. Attachment is evidenced by a teacher's willingness to provide encouragement, listen to ideas, and maintain positive student-teacher relationships. Participants indicated how strongly they agreed with each statement using a four-point Likert scale with the response options ranging from 1 = strongly disagree to 4 = strongly agree. A student's score on this variable represents the sum of their responses to each item. STA is assumed to be a continuous interval variable for purposes of statistical analysis.

*Educational Technology Usage (ETU)*- ETU is a composite variable comprising of eight items. This composite variable examined how frequently students used electronic tools to complete homework, communicate with teachers and peers, and engage in non-assigned activities. It utilized identical response options as did the STA variable. A student's score on this composite variable represents the sum of their responses to each item. Just like STA, ETU is assumed to be a continuous interval variable for the purposes of data analysis.

*Student Value of Education (SVE)*- SVE is the third composite variable used for analysis in this study. This composite variable consisted of 12 items utilizing the same Likert format as above discussed. The items within the SVE variable tapped into students' perceptions of their personal enjoyment of learning, value of schooling, and desire to be successful in school. And as the other composite variables in the study, it assumed to be an interval-level variable. that is the dependent variable for question three.

*English Language Arts (ELA)*- ELA is the fourth composite variable used for analysis in this study. This composite variable consisted of 6 items utilizing the same Likert format as discussed above. The items within the ELA composite variable tapped into English language arts learning and class activities a teacher required of their students, e.g., explaining one point of view in a discussion, writing a paper or an essay, discussing connections between reading and real-life issues, writing few paragraphs to answer questions about a reading, alongside other class participation activities.

*Grade Level*- Grade level is the self-report grade of enrollment at the time of completing the study survey for each student. The available response options were Elementary (eight grade) and High School (twelfth grade). It is a dichotomous variable. It is used as an independent in the study.

*Gender* - Gender is the self-reported biological gender of each participant. The available response options were male and female. This is dichotomous and is also used as an independent variable in the study.

*Interpersonal interactions*- The communicative exchanges between two or more individuals.

*Self-perception*- The manner in which an individual perceives and values their skills, abilities, and worth.

*Attachment*- The feelings of connectedness, trust, and caring an individual possesses towards another person.

*Educational technology*- The tools that are commonly used both within and outside of the classroom to execute assigned tasks and communicate with others.

*Table 4.*

| Variable (#)* | Variable Description | Alpha Reliabilities |
|---|---|---|
| STALE (10) | **Student Teacher Attachment and Learning Equity**<br>Teachers in this school provide us with encouragement.<br>Teachers in this school really care about me and make me feel important.<br>Teachers in this school always keep their promises.<br>The teachers are willing to listen to our concerns.<br>The teachers work with us.<br>I feel safe and comfortable with teachers at this school.<br>When teachers tell me not to do something, I know they have a good reason.<br>Teachers in this school will always listen to students' ideas. | .70 |

continued on following page

*Table 4. Continued*

| Variable (#)* | Variable Description | Alpha Reliabilities |
|---|---|---|
| ETU (8) | **Educational Technology Usage**<br>This school year, I used computer (at school, at home, at a different place… church, library, internet café, friend's house, etc.) to complete CLASS ASSIGNMENTS.<br>I have used a computer at least once (typing a document, an e-mail, in short courses, etc.)<br>I have communicated via electronic mail (e-mail) with teachers.<br>I have used the internet for research or homework.<br>I have communicated via e-mail with other friends or acquaintances.<br>I have used the internet for nonacademic work.<br>I have communicated via e-mail with students at other schools. | .85 |
| SVE (12) | **Student Value of Education**<br>I feel in control of my own learning.<br>I am comfortable being in classes.<br>I would like to be a well-educated person.<br>I want to be successful as a student.<br>I feel confident about my education.<br>I have a clear view of what I need to learn.<br>School is important for me.<br>I enjoy learning.<br>I gain satisfaction from learning new things.<br>My education is important for me.<br>My future will be improved by what I learn.<br>Attending school will be useful for my future education. | .76 |
| ELA (6) | **English Language Arts**<br>Your teacher required you to explain your point of view or an idea in a class discussion about something you have read.<br>Your teacher required you to write a paper or a brief essay (composition).<br>Your teacher required you to rewrite a paper or an essay in response to comments.<br>Your teacher required you to discuss connections between reading and real-life people or situations.<br>Your teacher required you to write a few paragraphs to answer questions about reading.<br>Your teacher required you to explain how writers use tools like symbolism and metaphor to communicate meaning. | .73 |

# Chapter 8
# Navigating Engineering Education Amidst the Post-Pandemic Era:
## Enhancing Engineering Education Through Blended Learning With a Flipped Classroom Approach

**Manjit Singh Sidhu**
*Universiti Tenaga Nasional, Malaysia*

**Min Chi Low**
*Universiti Tunku Abdul Rahman, Malaysia*

**Lee Chen Kang**
https://orcid.org/0000-0003-4426-9274
*Universiti Tunku Abdul Rahman, Malaysia*

## ABSTRACT

*This study explores the challenges and opportunities in engineering education arising from the post-pandemic landscape. In response to the evolving educational paradigm, the research focuses on the implementation of a blended learning model with a flipped classroom approach to enhance the effectiveness of engineering education. The study employs empirical methods to assess the impact of this pedagogical shift on student engagement, learning outcomes, and overall educational experience. The investigation involves the integration of traditional face-to-face instruction with online resources and interactive digital content. The research mainly evaluated the efficacy of the blended learning approach with flipped classroom approach.*

DOI: 10.4018/979-8-3693-7645-4.ch008

*Preliminary findings suggest that the adoption of blended learning with a flipped classroom approach positively influences student learning outcomes, fosters a more dynamic and participatory learning environment, and addresses the challenges posed by the post-pandemic educational landscape.*

## INTRODUCTION

The COVID-19 pandemic has triggered a transformation in educational practices worldwide. Education extends beyond traditional classroom teaching and encompasses various types and functionalities. In an effort to define education, this chapter emphasizes the importance of efforts aimed at enhancing student's knowledge and principles through blended learning with a flipped classroom approach to help them reach their full potential. This understanding of education resonates with the approaches taken by Universiti Tenaga Nasional UNITEN (Malaysia) in structuring the engineering education system to better serve the students.

In Malaysia, the education framework prioritizes universality, ensuring that all university students have access to the institution system. The Malaysian model follows the 7 semesters + 1 structure, with seven semesters of mandatory on campus education, followed by one semester of practical training.

However, the traditional educational learning method had to be re-structured from physical to virtual learning due to the emergence of the COVID-19 pandemic which marked a significant upheaval globally. The coronavirus, with its diverse symptoms ranging from mild cold-like symptoms to severe respiratory distress or pneumonia, was first reported by the World Health Organization in Wuhan, China, on December 31, 2019. Subsequently, the virus spread worldwide, including Malaysia. Malaysia recorded its first case on January 25, 2020, and subsequently experienced fluctuating trends in COVID-19 cases and associated policies. The pandemic necessitated a paradigm shift in education as higher learning institutions transitioned from physical to virtual modes of learning. In Malaysia, education remains predominantly online, with intermittent attempts to resume in-person learning amid rising cases. However, uncertainties persist regarding future educational protocols and procedures to mitigate virus spread.

The shift to online learning had presented challenges for both students and instructors. Issues such as limited internet access and technological resources hinder effective online learning. Instructors also struggled with adapting to technology and adjusting assessment methods. However, efforts have been made by the government and university management to address these barriers and enhance the effectiveness of online learning amidst the ongoing pandemic.

Therefore, the COVID-19 pandemic has profoundly impacted education systems in Malaysia and prompting a transition to online learning and highlighting the need for innovative solutions to ensure continued access to quality education. This research proposed the use of the blended learning using flipped classroom approach in engineering education. The research makes two contributions (i) investigating the learning difficulties in engineering education and (ii) assessing the engineering students' perceived attitude towards the usage of the blended learning approach in engineering education.

## BACKGROUND

Engineering education, as the place where engineers are produced and nurtured, plays an important role to ensure the quality of engineering graduates. With the advent of Information and Communication Technology (ICT), the educational landscape has witnessed a transformative shift towards student-centered methodologies, departing from the conventional teacher-centric paradigms (Miranda et al., 2021; Wang et al., 2021). Unlike traditional pedagogies, which prioritize instructor-led instruction, a student-centered approach fosters personalized learning through skill-set-oriented strategies, bolstered by blended and remote learning modalities, thus broadening educational horizons (Dada et al., 2023). In this milieu, ICT, leveraging multimedia technologies, enhances interactive learning, elucidating intricate concepts and techniques, thereby augmenting the educational experience (Fu, 2022). Consequently, ICT emerges as an effective facilitator in extending the frontiers of engineering education.

Recognizing this opportunity, this research grounds on Mechanics Dynamics, a foundation of Mechanical Engineering education. Mechanics Dynamics, delving into the study of forces and their impact on motion, necessitates adeptness in mathematics, schematic analysis, and foundational physical principles. Oftentimes, students struggle with the fundamentals of Engineering Mechanics Dynamics, leading to a challenge where they struggle to discern the applicable mathematical frameworks for specific problem-solving scenarios (Lee et al., 2020). Previous research has pinpointed myriad issues contributing to students' underperformance in Mechanics courses, encompassing motivational deficits, pedagogical methodologies, and access to online resources (Sidhu & Kang, 2010). In Malaysia, the introduction of TAPS (Technology Assisted Problem Solving) packages represented a pioneering initiative to streamline engineering problem-solving within the realm of mechanical engineering (Lee & Sidhu, 2016). This research builds upon the groundwork laid by Lee and Sidhu (2016), extending the purview of the TAPS software suite (Sidhu, 2009; Sidhu, 2013). While the TAPS packages have previously been confined to

Desktop Virtual Reality (DVR), thereby restricting accessibility solely to university laboratories equipped with the requisite software infrastructure.

Additionally, the Malaysian university education has traditionally adopted a teacher-centric approach (Tawie et al., 2018). TAPS was used as one of the custom in house-built pre-pandemic application whereby students were given a secured network link to access and use the application to learn engineering mechanics dynamics perform problem solving. The main communication application adopted by the university during this time was the MS Teams for teaching and learning. Additionally other applications that were also used during the same time were Google meet, Webex and Zoom.

However, scholarly discourse underscores a perceptible shift towards student-centered learning paradigms, wherein educators assume a facilitative role while students actively engage in the learning process (Tawie et al., 2018). Moreover, a plethora of studies (Miranda et al., 2021), (Coşkun et al., 2019; Keaveney et al., 2021; Rekh & Chandy, 2020) have elucidated evolving qualification requisites, subject matter domains, educational metamorphoses, and innovative laboratory concepts tailored to equip students for the demands of Industry 4.0. Blended learning emerges as a requirement in augmenting students' educational outcomes within the realm of engineering education. Mechanical engineering, being an exemplary discipline within this domain, stands to benefit immensely from blended learning methodologies. Indeed, studies have evinced enhanced learning outcomes among mechanical engineering students following the implementation of innovative blended learning frameworks (de la Flor López et al., 2016). Furthermore, Ghommem and Gunn (2019) underscored the efficacy of an active learning approach in augmenting students' comprehension and problem-solving prowess within mechanical engineering courses (Ghommem & Gunn, 2019). These studies underscored the salutary impact of blended learning, manifesting in heightened student engagement, favorable attitudes towards the learning process, and commensurate academic advancements.

This research concentrates on discussing the transformation of engineering education towards a blended learning approach. Blended learning, defined as an incorporation of diverse pedagogical approaches, emphasized by ICT integration, holds promise in revolutionizing the educational environment, transcending temporal and spatial constraints (Staker & Horn, 2012; Win & Wynn, 2015; Alkhatib, 2018). As educational frameworks pivot from traditional teacher-centric models towards student-centered paradigms, the imperative of ICT integration in higher education assumes paramount importance, fostering interactive learning modalities (Miranda et al., 2021). Moreover, blended learning promotes the incorporation of conventional and innovative pedagogies to cater to diverse learning tendencies. According to Felder and Spurlin (2005) traditional engineering education predominantly caters to passive learning modalities, which may not resonate with students inclined towards active and visual learning modalities. Although traditional lectures have their merits, research underscores their tendency to engender passive learning experiences and diminished student satisfaction (Ghommem & Gunn, 2019). Conversely, active learner involvement is indicated as conducive to deeper learning engagement and heightened educational efficacy (Ghommem & Gunn, 2019). Moreover, the shift towards student-centered paradigms seeks to optimize students' problem-solving insight, time management skills, research proficiencies, critical reasoning abilities, and vocational aptitudes, all of which are essential in navigating multifaceted professional terrains (Mandal, 2017).

In Malaysia, engineering education has embraced blended learning as a pedagogical modality. Contemporary studies (Low et al., 2021; Aziz et al., 2020; Afsharian et al., 2018; Ariffin, & Ghazali, 2018; Lee et al., 2020) have attested to the efficacy of blended learning paradigms in enhancing students' educational experiences. Nonetheless, further inquiry is warranted to define the impact of blended learning on academic performance and learning outcomes. Research has indicated that while students acknowledge the convenience of blended learning modalities, their utilization of online forums and assessments remains suboptimal, leading to instances of fake participation Lee et al., (2020). Addressing this issue necessitates a holistic approach to designing blended learning environments, cognizant of students' participatory dynamics. This research endeavors to undertake an exploratory inquiry to unravel the requisites and furnish guidance for empowering engineering students to overcome their learning hurdles within flipped classroom settings.

## PROBLEM STATEMENT

In Malaysia, since the COVID-19 pandemic outbreak, the education remained online, with several attempts at reopening schools and universities. However, due to the increase of cases in Malaysia, the future of Malaysian education was yet to be sure. Because of the uncertainty in the number of cases in Malaysia, many students and instructors were left in midpoint as they were still unsure of the types of educational protocol and standard operating procedures required to prevent the spread of the coronavirus. Many students faced online learning issues, such as the lack of Internet access and technological devices during online learning. Instructors faced similar issues in regards to their adaptability in the usage of technology and their methods of conduct, specifically in regards to how students are graded and assessed. Since engineering subject such as mechanics dynamics requires hands on practical, it was crucial to use interactive and simulated software packages that could mimic real problems that are taught during traditional class hours where real machineries are usually used. This work will outline the challenges faced and the initiatives undertaken by universities in integrating applications utilized prior to the pandemic, assess the efficacy of online applications in teaching the engineering mechanics dynamics subject at UNITEN during the COVID-19 pandemic, and examine their sustainability beyond the pandemic. We focused our research question on "what are students' perceptions of the flipped learning format and its impact on their learning".

# LITERATURE REVIEW

## Education 4.0 for Engineering Education

Technological advancements and swift progress have brought advantages to both the industrial and engineering fields. Recently, several authors have emphasized the significance of "Education 4.0" in relation to the renowned periods of the four industrial revolutions. The essence of each industrial revolution paradigm has been outlined in Figure 1.

*Figure 1. Paradigm of industrial revolution*

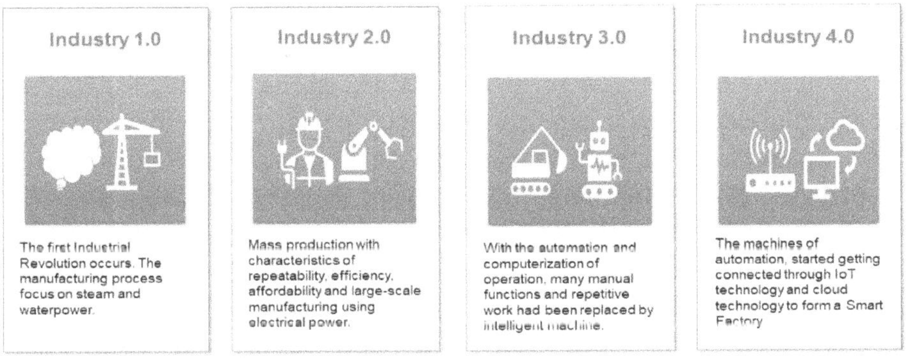


Engineering education originated in France, where the first engineering school was founded in Paris in 1747. This coincided with the advent of the first industrial revolution (Industry 1.0), marked by the emergence of the steam engine in the 1780s. The introduction of the steam engine brought about significant transformations in mobility and the accessibility of energy, benefiting society at large. This era also witnessed a notable increase in population mobility, with a considerable migration from rural to urban areas.

Additionally, historical research indicates that engineering as a major emerged in the 19th century. Civil engineering, initially stemming from military engineering, focused on constructing armaments, fortifications, and infrastructure. During this period, engineering education primarily revolved around practical skills and techniques, typically taught in technical schools.

During the second industrial revolution (Industry 2.0), the focus shifted towards mass production. The groundbreaking idea of the assembly line brought forth characteristics such as repeatability, efficiency, affordability, and large-scale manufacturing. This led to the creation of millions of new job opportunities, resulting in a significant boost to wealth and the economy. Many engineering graduates found employment in government agencies or became involved in establishing public and private enterprises. The emphasis during this period was on developing new infrastructure, including transportation systems, roads, bridges, ports, canals, boats, sewers, water supply networks, and systems for producing and distributing natural gas. Engineering education during this phase prioritized scientific knowledge and technical disciplines, fostering the development of skilled cooperative workers.

Since the 1970s, computerization and automation have driven Industry 3.0 by replacing manual tasks with machines, utilizing software, hardware, and accounting applications. This shift has boosted productivity, efficiency, and economic growth, emphasizing the need for engineering institutions to train adaptable engineers for emerging technologies and challenges.

The fourth industrial revolution, Industry 4.0, emerged in the early 2000s with the aim of enhancing business processes' efficiency and productivity. On the product front, it seeks to derive greater value from data for usage-based design and mass customization, thereby opening up new markets. However, the adoption of Industry 4.0 is expected to lead to the elimination of lower-skilled jobs through automation and digitalization. Industry 4.0 is characterized by the integration of information and communication technology with industrial advancements to develop smart factories that are more efficient, environmentally friendly, and customized. This integration of new technologies, particularly in workplaces where ICT tools are used more frequently, has led to increased productivity, expanded markets, and a new professional image to better meet consumers' needs in this era of innovation (Hernandez-de-Menendez et al., 2020).

An analysis of the Engineering Education paradigm suggests a close relationship between the evolution of engineering education and industrial revolutions (Das et al., 2020). The transition from Industry 1.0 to 2.0 spanned nearly a century and a half, while the shift from Industry 2.0 to 3.0 occurred over a few decades. However, the transition from Industry 3.0 to 4.0 happened much more rapidly, reflecting the accelerated pace of technological change.

Moreover, there has been a significant increase in the number of individuals pursuing education, particularly in engineering, compared to the era of Industry 1.0, resulting in a growth in intellectual capital. Additionally, the role of computer technology, especially in Information and Communication Technology (ICT), has become increasingly vital in both industry and engineering education, bringing about considerable convenience and improvement.

With the advancement of ICT tools, Engineering Education 3.0 has transitioned to a more flexible delivery method, allowing students to access classes online (Rekh & Chandy, 2020; Srivani et al., 2022). Higher education institutions are adopting new learning methods, innovative teaching and management tools, and smart, sustainable infrastructure, largely supported by emerging ICT tools. Importantly, there is a shift towards a more student-centred approach to learning in the engineering education paradigm. This educational paradigm shift is illustrated in Figure 2.

*Figure 2. Paradigm of education shifts*

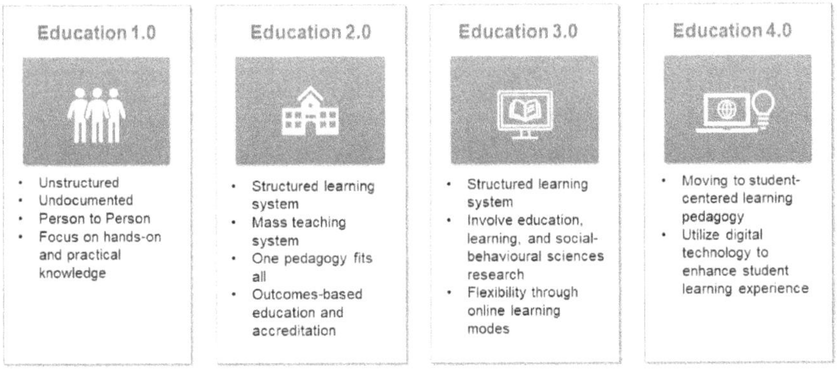


## ENGINEERING EDUCATION IN MALAYSIA

The inception of engineering education in Malaysia dates back to 1956 with the establishment of the Engineering Department at the University of Malaya's Singapore campus (Soon & Quek, 2013). The first bachelor's degree offered by the department was in Civil Engineering. In 1958, with the relocation of the University of Malaya to Kuala Lumpur, the Bachelor of Mechanical Engineering programme commenced. Subsequently, the Engineering Department was elevated to the status of Faculty of Engineering, introducing more engineering courses to cater to the growing demand.

Other public universities in Malaysia also expanded their engineering programmes to meet market demands. Additionally, in response to the increasing prevalence of ICT tools in Malaysia, engineering education underwent various transformations to align with the global marketplace.

Engineering programmes in Malaysia typically span four years and are overseen by the Engineering Accreditation Committee (EAC), established in 2000 under the auspices of the Board of Engineers Malaysia (BEM) (Mohd Said et al., 2011). This committee is tasked with accrediting engineering degree programmes across Malaysia. Research conducted by Soon and Quek (2013) further elaborates on the measures taken to uphold the quality of engineering graduates in the country. This includes the admission and oversight of professional engineers by the Board of Engineers Malaysia, the provision of continuous professional development by the Institution of Engineers Malaysia (IEM), and the certification of engineering courses by the Malaysian Qualifications Agency (MQA) (Mohd Said et al., 2011).

In 2009, a significant milestone in the development of Engineering Education occurred when the Board of Engineers Malaysia (BEM) became a signatory to the Washington Accord. This milestone ensured that degree qualifications in Malaysia are recognized by member countries of the Accord, as well as by countries worldwide (Mohd Said et al., 2011). Consequently, Malaysian engineering graduates gained the advantage of having their qualifications acknowledged in numerous countries, thereby enhancing their employability on a global scale.

Over the years, efforts have been made to maintain the professionalism and quality of Engineering Education in Malaysia. This includes the implementation of Bloom's Taxonomy and Outcome-Based Education (OBE) in the teaching and learning process. Bloom's Taxonomy and OBE serve as standard and crucial criteria used by the Engineering Accreditation Committee (EAC) and BEM to certify engineering programmes in Malaysia (Said et al., 2011; Aziz et al., 2005; Azuma et. al., 2004). Additionally, research indicates that Outcome-Based Education is a prerequisite for full membership of the Washington Accord (Basri et al., 2004).

The Malaysian government has initiated various educational reforms aimed at enhancing educational quality. One such reform involves promoting the use of ICT tools to improve teaching and learning standards. This includes leveraging online resources to facilitate self-paced learning and overcome time and geographical constraints, particularly benefiting individuals in non-urban or rural areas (Ganapathy, 2016; Ministry of Education, Malaysia, 2013).

However, studies have highlighted a significant skill gap between the demands of the industry and the proficiency levels of graduates in Malaysia, particularly in meeting the standards of Industry 4.0 (Jam & Puteh, 2022; Abdullah et al., 2020). As a result, there is a pressing need for greater efforts to deliver high-quality engineering education that not only fosters students' interest in the field but also aligns with the requirements of Industry 4.0.

## Blended Learning

Blended Learning refers to a learning approach that utilizes multiple delivery modes to maximize learning outcomes and minimize the cost of programme delivery. This method integrates various learning activities, encompassing face-to-face teaching, online or e-learning, student-centred learning, and self-paced learning (Halasa et al., 2020).

## Online Learning

Online learning, facilitated by ICT tools, creates a virtual classroom environment that expands the possibilities for educators to disseminate knowledge. MOOCs (Massive Open Online Courses) exemplify this approach by utilizing ICT tools to deliver educational content. Platforms like Google Classroom, Khan Academy, and Coursera are prominent examples of MOOCs. With course materials accessible on the internet in digital multimedia formats, students can easily access vast amounts of relevant information through simple keyword searches, allowing them to stay abreast of the latest developments.

However, experts argue that the transition of the learning process to digital spaces due to COVID-19 cannot be categorized as traditional online learning; instead, it is termed emergency remote teaching. This shift is viewed as temporary and necessitates careful instructional design and planning, as opposed to the deliberate investment in learner support ecosystems required for sustained online learning. Emergency remote teaching is a crisis response, employing remote solutions for instruction, which would otherwise be delivered through face-to-face, blended, or hybrid courses. The development of blended learning aims to address the limitations of both traditional classroom instruction and online learning by offering a combination of various teaching strategies or methods (Tong et al., 2022). Table 1 illustrates the advantages and disadvantages of traditional classroom and online learning.

*Table 1. The comparison between traditional classroom and online learning*

Advantages Disadvantages
Traditional More interaction between lecturer Less feasibility in schedule
Classroom and students Lecture hour is very limited
Can clarify the queries directly Limited knowledge can be delivered
with the lecturer
Receive direct guidance from lecturer
Online Flexible schedule and learning Less interaction with peer and lecturer
Learning environment Difficult to communicate queries.
Easy access to the learning material Require a high self-discipline
Diverse forms to present the
knowledge
Self – paced learning

(Wai Yee & Cheng Ean, 2020; Tong et al., 2022)

Blended learning incorporated into the curriculum offers significant advantages in terms of both quality and cost. In K-12 education, blended learning provides a more consistent and personalized pedagogy, enabling students to learn at their own pace and according to their preferred learning modes (Staker & Horn, 2012). Additionally, the ability to playback or review material grants students' access to more learning resources without being constrained by fixed time and location.

Moreover, blended learning promotes more efficient use of time and space by encouraging educators to utilize ICT tools. This approach involves delivering some content online while engaging students in more interactive activities in the physical classroom, thereby increasing motivation. Overall, blended learning enhances learning outcomes by aligning with how learners prefer to learn and the objectives of the course.

## BLENDED LEARNING USING FLIPPED CLASSROOM APPROACH

Blended learning, a pedagogical approach that integrates various delivery methods, is aimed at enhancing learning outcomes. This study focuses on blended learning through the flipped classroom model during the pandemic to post-pandemic era. The flipped classroom model is a blended learning approach that reverses traditional learning methods. It proposes that teachers deliver content outside the formal class through activities conducted outside class time, assigning pre- or post-class activities to complement in-class work (Lo & Hew, 2017). The classroom designs of both traditional classrooms and flipped classrooms are depicted in Figure 3.

*Figure 3. Comparison between traditional classroom and flipped classroom*

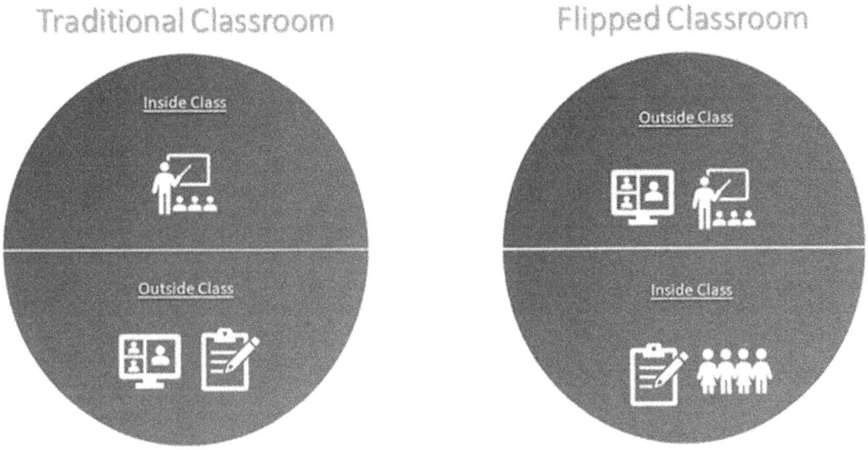


The flipped classroom model may resonate with today's student learners, often referred to as "millennials," "Gen Ys," or the "Net Generation," as it aligns with their preference for instant, portable access to information (See & Conry, 2014). Moreover, the outbreak of COVID-19 has spurred the adoption of flipped classrooms in tertiary education. The flexible nature of the flipped classroom allows for the incorporation of various activities both within and outside the classroom (Divjak et al., 2022). However, research suggests that the transition of educational pedagogy from face-to-face to blended, online, or flipped classrooms due to COVID-19 necessitates careful planning and caution (Daumiller et al., 2021). Despite facing technical challenges such as slow internet connections and interruptions, blended learning approaches help create new opportunities for online delivery to address the ongoing pandemic's needs (Ahmed & Opoku, 2021).

Lecturers often find lecture classes time-consuming due to the challenge of providing diverse teaching methods and personalized experiences. The flipped classroom model addresses this by reversing traditional methods, using pre- or post-class activities and technology, particularly videos, to extend learning beyond formal class time (Alkhatib, 2018). This model allows lecturers to deliver content through pre-recorded videos before class, freeing up class time for interactive, collaborative learning (Cheng et al., 2018). Students review materials beforehand, engage with teachers during face-to-face sessions, and apply knowledge through online platforms or homework assignments after class.

Furthermore, the flipped classroom concept aligns with active learning principles, which advocate for student engagement in teaching activities rather than passive or rote learning (Choi & Lee, 2015). In essence, the flipped classroom is not a novel concept; rather, it represents an enhanced blended learning model driven by technology, particularly multimedia and ICT technologies. These tools assist lecturers in overcoming time constraints and diversifying their methods of delivering knowledge. A few cases that utilized flipped classroom and the finding in the specific courses can be referred to Table 2.

*Table 2. Case studies on the flipped classroom*

| Case Studies | Findings |
|---|---|
| Pharmacy Law (Nazar et al., 2018) | Students were generally satisfied with online teaching materials. Students describe them as more interesting, concise and attractive than traditional lectures. Although they generally respond positively to the presentation of information, students hope to have more guidance on examination requirements, instead of learning to increase their knowledge and understanding. Further study can explore the long-term impact of blended learning curriculum on knowledge retention and application, as to provide the evidence base of this educational approach. |
| Ningbo University of Finance and Econ (Feng, 2020) | The research summarized the current situations of flipped classroom in teaching practice in Colleges and Universities: There is a gap in teachers' comprehensive teaching ability (college teachers lack of in-depth understanding of subject knowledge, the overall system concept is poor and lack of understanding of modern information technology). The roles of teachers and students differ and shifted from "teaching as the center" to "learning as the center". Lack of effective system and sufficient resources to promote flipped classroom and ensure the healthy development of flipped classroom. |
| Bachelor of Science Nursing University of Jordan (Halasa et al., 2020) | The survey results showed that the scores of students in the course experimental group have been significantly improved. Predictability calculation also showed that if they continue to adopt the blended learning of flip classroom design, the learning results will achieve better results in future. |
| Systems programming course in northern Taiwan (Huang et al., 2023) | The research created an AI-powered personalized recommendation system for a flipped classroom and investigated its impact on three aspects of learning success: motivation, engagement, and outcomes. Their findings indicate that the proposed system has the potential to boost students' learning motivation. |

## RESEARCH REFLECTING THE LATEST TRENDS AND CHALLENGES IN DIGITAL LEARNING

One of the key challenges is that administrators often lack adequate time for assessments. Low et al. (2021) proposed that lecturers, acting as administrators in online classes, should consider learners' needs, session or class durations, delivery methods, and internet access before evaluating exams and assignments. Several other studies have emphasized the importance and convenience of using e-learning platforms for submitting assignments and giving feedback to learners.

The following concern revolves around social interactions, which are hindered by the communication barriers between lecturers and students in e-learning settings, as noted by Low et al. (2021). A significant challenge in e-learning lies in overcoming the absence of social interactions. Effective communication between lecturers and students not only enhances students' emotional intelligence but also fosters satisfaction and prevents misunderstandings.

The third issue identified by Low et al. (2023) pertains to technical, connectivity, and data issues. During the shift to online learning amid the 2020 pandemic, numerous challenges emerged, including inadequate data, unstable internet connections, and a shortage of devices. Low et al. (2023) highlighted the importance of addressing technical issues, such as insufficient data, if online learning is to persist, as limited connectivity often leads to problems related to data inadequacy and outdated devices. Their findings align with previous studies in the field, which have identified connectivity as a significant obstacle to the effective implementation of e-learning.

The research also highlighted that students are sacrificing personal time due to their heavy involvement in online learning, struggling to manage their time effectively for participation, thus indicating a need for time management support in adopting online learning (Low et al., 2023). A crucial determinant of whether students continue with online learning is their level of motivation, alongside their preferences for learning methods. Therefore, it falls upon lecturers to boost student motivation. Engaging classroom sessions and discussions are essential to ensure learners grasp the learning material thoroughly. It's imperative to ensure students attain a deep understanding of the subject matter, as the lack of comprehension presents a challenge due to limited interactions and low motivation in e-learning environments (Low et al., 2023).

According to this study, e-learning challenges include internet connectivity, data limits, assessment difficulties, and communication hurdles. Students' preferences and motivation also impact implementation. Tertiary institutions should enhance online assessments, conduct online meetings to boost understanding and motivation, and address accountability issues. Flipped learning, LMS upgrades, and government-provided electronic devices can help overcome these challenges.

## Flipped Classroom in Engineering Education

The flipped classroom approach positively impacts engineering education by increasing lecturer-student engagement and allowing more material coverage (Chua & Islam, 2021; Mason et al., 2013). It restructures content into shorter segments and sets clear expectations, promoting active learning (Mason et al., 2013). This method reduces outside study time for engineering students while improving results (Mason et al., 2013). It also shifts lower cognitive tasks (remembering, understanding) to home and higher cognitive tasks (applying, analyzing, evaluating, creating) to the classroom (see Figure 4) (Divjak et al., 2022; Alvarado et al., 2021).

*Figure 4. Comparison of traditional classroom and flipped classroom in terms of use in revised Bloom's taxonomy*

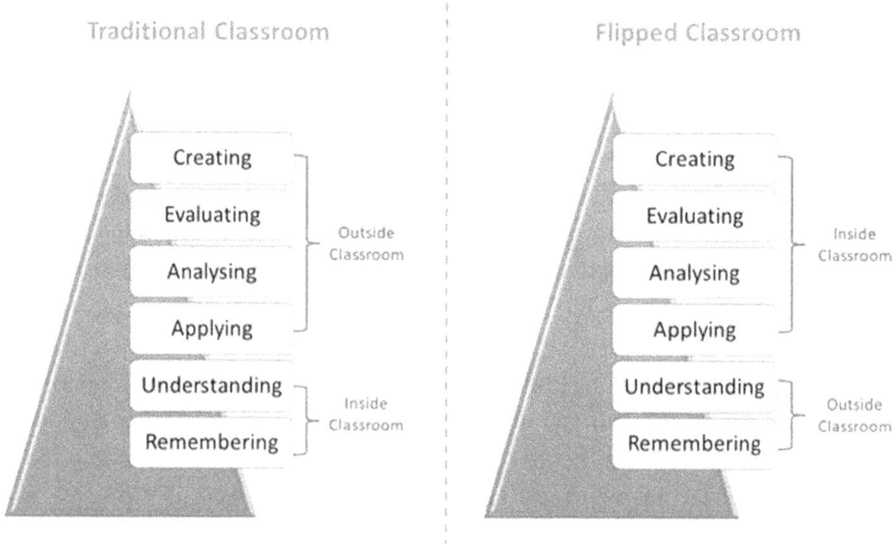


Limited research on flipped classrooms in Malaysian tertiary education suggests the need for improvements, including enhancing student readiness and empowering self-directed learning (Win & Wynn, 2015; Danker, 2015; Zainuddin & Attaran, 2016). Although interest is growing, few studies focus on engineering education, and there is no consensus on the definition or effectiveness of flipped learning (Karabulut-Ilgu et al., 2017). Flipped classrooms can be effective when properly implemented (See & Conry, 2014). More research is needed, particularly in Mechanics Dynamics, to develop practical strategies. Table 3 presents case studies of flipped classrooms in engineering education.

*Table 3. Case studies of the flipped classroom in engineering education*

| Case Studies | Findings |
|---|---|
| The Flipped Classroom Approach to Engineering Electromagnetics (Cohen & Zajic, 2019) | Research reported on the experience and outcomes teaching junior-level engineering electromagnetics at the Georgia Institute of Technology using a flipped classroom strategy. The findings discussed the methods and attempts to compare learning outcomes with a more traditional teacher-centred approach course. |
| Online flipped classroom class for Intro to Systems Engineering (Wu et al., 2021) | This research explored the epidemic characteristics of online teaching, focusing on task-driven online flipped classroom teaching practices. It aimed to develop students' problem-solving skills and evaluate the effectiveness of online learning through diverse evaluations. The study demonstrated that this approach promoted a shift from teacher-centred to student-centred teaching, improving online teaching effectiveness. |
| Flipped Course on Gastronomic Engineering (Aguilera & Moreno, 2021) | The research outlined how an optional flipped classroom course on engineering, science, and gastronomy was implemented for undergraduate students, which included cooking demonstrations in the classroom. The findings showed necessitates a shift from the traditional food engineering education paradigm that emphasises heat, mass, and momentum transfer in individual food processing sector unit operations. |
| Flipped Classrooms in Engineering Labs (Del Río-Gamero, 2022) | This paper examined if the effectiveness of using films in flipped classrooms for lab exercises of the Sustainability and Environment Technologies course in higher education programmes. Overall, the flipped classroom lab practise reported various advantages, such as higher levels of student happiness and engagement as well as advancements in academic performance and skill levels. |
| Online flipped classroom with collaborative learning model in an undergraduate chemical engineering course (Lapitan et al., 2023) | Analytical chemistry was taught online in this project, and the design and implementation of flipped classrooms assisted by collaborative learning were evaluated. There were some potential adverse impacts of online active learning interventions on student attitudes, even if the combination of these active-learning tactics improved the distant learning environment overall. |
| Flipped classroom for master course in Industrial Engineering (Gómez-Coma et al., 2023) | This work's primary objective was to use flipped classroom and problem-based learning approaches to engage students in a Master's programme in Industrial Engineering's study of Chemical Processes by using actual data from nearby businesses. Results showed that the students were satisfied with the course, particularly in the areas of teamwork, analytical ability and self-learning skills. |

## Innovative Assessment Methods for Online and Blended Learning

We identified a few strategies for student feedback collection and analysis on the assessment methods as stated in Table 4 and Table 5. By implementing these innovative assessment methods and feedback collection strategies, educators can enhance the online and blended learning experience, promote student engagement and success, and continuously improve the learning process.

*Table 4. Strategies for student feedback collection on assessment methods*

| Method | Description |
|---|---|
| Peer Assessment and Feedback | Encourage students to evaluate each other's work using structured rubrics or peer review platforms. This fosters collaboration, critical thinking, and provides multiple perspectives on assignments. |
| Self-Assessment Tools | Implement self-assessment quizzes or reflection activities where students can gauge their own understanding and progress. This promotes metacognitive skills and allows learners to take ownership of their learning journey. |
| Interactive Simulations and Virtual Labs | Utilize online simulations or virtual lab environments to assess practical skills and knowledge application. These tools offer hands-on experiences in a digital format, suitable for various subjects like science, engineering, and healthcare. |
| Authentic Projects and Case Studies | Assign real-world projects or case studies relevant to the subject matter. Students can showcase their understanding through practical application, problem-solving, and analysis of authentic scenarios. |
| Gamified Assessments | Integrate gamification elements such as quizzes, challenges, and leaderboards to make assessments more engaging and enjoyable. Gamified assessments can motivate students to participate actively and enhance their learning experience. |

*Table 5. Student feedback collection analysis on assessment methods*

| Method | Description |
|---|---|
| Online Surveys and Polls | Create anonymous surveys or polls using online tools to gather feedback on various aspects of the course, including content, teaching methods, and learning resources. Analyze the responses to identify trends and areas for improvement. |
| Feedback Forums and Discussion Boards | Set up dedicated forums or discussion boards where students can provide feedback openly and engage in constructive discussions with peers and instructors. Monitor these platforms regularly to gather insights and address concerns promptly. |
| One-on-One Feedback Sessions | Offer individual feedback sessions via video conferencing or messaging platforms to provide personalized guidance and support to students. These sessions allow for in-depth discussions and foster a supportive learning environment. |
| Learning Analytics | Use learning analytics platforms to track student engagement, progress, and performance data. Analyze the data to identify patterns, predict student needs, and tailor instruction accordingly. |
| Qualitative Analysis of Feedback | Beyond numerical ratings, conduct qualitative analysis of written feedback to gain deeper insights into students' experiences, perceptions, and suggestions. Look for recurring themes and sentiments to inform instructional decisions. |

## POST-PANDEMIC EDUCATIONAL STRATEGIES, TECHNOLOGY ADOPTION AND LONG-TERM OUTCOMES

The widespread transmission of COVID-19 has generated significant alterations and influences on the digital evolution within numerous higher education establishments. The strategies employed post-pandemic encompass the adoption of technology and anticipated consequences, constituting a method through which educational institutions utilize digital tools and processes to elevate their educational frameworks, environment, student engagement, and overall standing. This encompasses various dimensions, such as educational framework, procedures, technological integration, and attitude, all tailored to enhance effectiveness, creativity, and overall efficacy. In response to changing educational trends, numerous higher learning institutions have embraced digital technologies, resulting in their widespread application and popularization. The outbreak of COVID-19 has brought about substantial changes in the conventional methods of higher education, necessitating a shift for educators and learners from predominantly in-person teaching to virtual formats. This newfound landscape has introduced educators and students to unanticipated hurdles and prospects, as noted by Park et al. (2023). The COVID-19 pandemic has prompted governments to recommend that citizens adopt "*social distancing*" measures, including remote work (de Lucas Ancillo et al., 2023). By thoughtfully addressing and adapting to the difficulties presented by the pandemic, online education has the potential to serve as a viable and efficient method of teaching, especially when integrated with hybrid teaching methods, as highlighted by Adedoyin and Soykan (2020). Findings also support the role played by digital adoption and the role of institutions in promoting innovation through digital tools work (Leal Filho et al., 2023). A study by Haling et al. (2024), showed that digital tools are still being used, indicating long-term acceptability of ICT in higher institution.

## METHODOLOGY

This study employs a descriptive research approach utilizing a literature review methodology. The focus of this observational study is the UNITEN population in Malaysia. It delves into the transformations in education brought about by the COVID-19 pandemic and post-pandemic.

## RESULTS AND DISCUSSION

This section explains briefly on the findings of the students' perception in using flipped classroom approach in engineering education and present the results of the quasi experiment which test the efficacy of proposed flipped classroom as compared to the traditional classroom.

### Perception Towards Blended Learning Using Flipped Classroom Approach

The flipped classroom approach demonstrates promising outcomes in engineering education, fostering increased interaction between lecturers and students. The subsequent section will delve into the descriptive statistics findings regarding students' perceptions of blended learning utilizing the flipped classroom approach in engineering. The descriptive statistics results indicate the students' perceptions of blended learning and the flipped classroom, especially within engineering education. Additionally, this study further examines the students' preferences for an ideal classroom environment in engineering education. The exploration of student perceptions regarding blended learning and flipped classrooms is consolidated in Table 6.

*Table 6. Summary of students' perception on blended learning and flipped classroom*

| | Yes | No |
|---|---|---|
| 1. Have you heard about blended learning before? | 51 (42.1%) | 70(57.9%) |
| 2. Have you heard about flipped classroom before? | 30 (24.8%) | 91 (75.2%) |

Over half of the students (57.9%) were previously unfamiliar with blended learning, while a similar majority (75.2%) had never encountered flipped classrooms. The data in Table 4 illustrates the students' limited exposure to blended learning and flipped classrooms. The synthesis of students' perceptions of Blended Learning and the Flipped Classroom from qualitative data is encapsulated in Table 7.

*Table 7. Students' perception on blended learning and flipped classroom from qualitative data*

| Categories | n | % | Sample Comments |
|---|---|---|---|
| Positive | 46 | 38.0% | "May help us to easy in understanding about the course from light content teaching".<br>"I feel is the best solution. Learn first, discuss in person and attempt the problems."<br>"Better than traditional learning concept. Helps student to prepare early before class started. Prepared brain helps to understand better." |
| Negative | 11 | 9.1% | "Heavier workload."<br>"Pretty sure most student won't prepare if it's not live and if it takes outside class time to prepare".<br>"May help us to easy in understanding about the course from light content teaching". |
| No Idea | 55 | 45.5% | "No Idea".<br>"Never being before." |
| Other | 9 | 7.4% | High involvement of the teaching materials |

The majority of students lack familiarity with the flipped classroom, attributing their lack of exposure to this teaching approach. Nonetheless, 38.0% of students hold a positive perception towards the flipped classroom approach in engineering education. They appreciate its emphasis on delivering lighter content during class time, allowing for better pre-class preparation. Conversely, 9.1% of students hold a negative attitude towards the flipped classroom, citing concerns over increased workload and a perceived lack of student initiative in preparation. Interestingly, 7.4% of students highlight the flipped classroom's heavy reliance on teaching materials. The survey regarding students' preferred learning mode for engineering courses is depicted in Figure 5.

*Figure 5. The learning mode that the students prefer in engineering course*

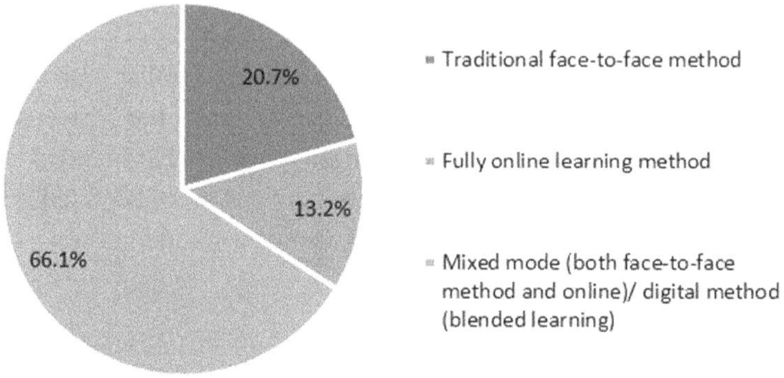


According to Figure 4, 66.1% of students favor a mixed-mode learning approach for their engineering courses. Conversely, only 20.7% of students opt for the traditional face-to-face method, while 13.2% prefer fully online learning. In general, the results from the work provides evidence of the trend that the students encourage the usage of bended learning approach in engineering education.

## EFFICACY OF BLENDED LEARNING USING FLIPPED CLASSROOM APPROACH AS COMPARED TO TRADITIONAL CLASSROOM

The COVID-19 pandemic has shifted tertiary engineering education from traditional to blended, online, or flipped classroom approaches, requiring careful planning (Daumiller et al., 2021). This research assesses the effectiveness of engineering education through blended learning and the flipped classroom approach compared to traditional methods.

The principal findings indicate that the flipped classroom model holds promise for fostering interactive learning among engineering students. Specifically, it aids in enhancing students' ability to visualize engineering models and comprehend given problems. However, the implementation of the flipped classroom approach in engineering education demands a substantial time investment for preparation. Therefore, meticulous planning and strategic considerations are necessary to enhance the usability of flipped learning software.

## Transformations in Education Amidst the COVID-19 Pandemic in Malaysia

In Malaysia's educational framework, behavioral shifts present a multitude of challenges with no immediate solutions owing to the pandemic. The COVID-19's influence on all sectors of education from primary, secondary, tertiary to universities education has led to the adoption of contemporary educational technologies that eliminate the need for physical presence in teaching and learning. Consequently, a paradigm shift towards home-based teaching and learning has emerged, leveraging technological advancements such as internet connectivity.

According to Leow et al. (2020), the impact of online interactions on students varied. Nasir et al. (2018) found that indirect exchanges fostered community participation and eased sharing reluctance, though some students struggled with overwhelming discussions. Online methods often hindered question-asking due to their synchronous nature. Simpson (2018) noted that adept students could marginalize others, reducing their self-confidence. Rovai and Downey (2010) observed that students relied on self-study during the pandemic. Wisneski et al. (2017) recommended that educators outline learning plans and provide materials beforehand to ensure adequate preparation.

In Malaysian educational institutions, there has been a gradual shift from traditional classrooms to virtual ones. Alongside basic computer equipment such as personal computers and laptops, the availability of resources such as fast internet connections and modern IT platforms has become increasingly crucial as educators and students turn to online or distance learning to adhere to social distancing measures implemented on campuses.

The Ministry of Education launched the Digital Educational Learning Initiative Malaysia (Delima) for primary and secondary students, providing digital textbooks, EduwebTV educational videos, and CikgooTube resources (Rahim et al., 2020). Universities have implemented initiatives to help post-secondary students, particularly freshmen, adapt to e-learning using platforms like Zoom. Figure 4 shows students discussing engineering mechanics dynamics via Zoom during the pandemic. Post-pandemic, the education model adopted blended face-to-face and online learning, as shown in Figures 6 and 7.

*Figure 6. Students having a discussion using Zoom*

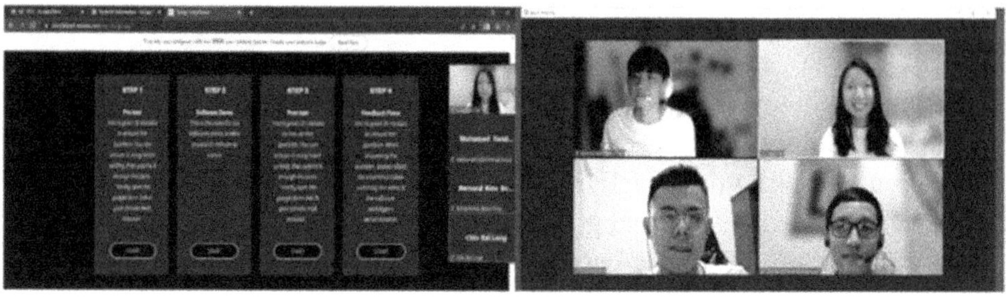

Financial resources play a crucial role in managing and recovering from acute crises. The sudden closure of campuses imposed significant and unforeseen financial burdens on students, who were required to vacate premises at short notice. Consequently, emergency relief funds in the form of soft loans or private contributions could assist students in meeting their day-to-day expenses, enabling them to continue their studies. The government also provided financial aid, known as e-Belia, to selected students.

*Figure 7. Blended face to face and online learning*

During the Movement Control Order (MCO) period, the Malaysia Internet Exchange (MyIX), under the Malaysia Digital Chamber of Commerce (2023), experienced a peak of 588 gigabytes per second (Gbps) in inter-metal traffic, surpassing the previous record of 500 Gbps set in 2019. Consequently, MCMC noted a nationwide increase in internet traffic flow, aligning with predictions made by Rizzato et al., (2020). The average 4G download speed in Malaysia decreased, indicating heightened internet traffic congestion and reduced download speeds due to increased data usage. The Minister of Communications and Multimedia highlighted efforts by telecommunication providers to expand network coverage in areas with poor internet access. Additionally, the Malaysian Prime Minister proposed granting Malaysians 1 gigabyte of free data per day during the MCO period to enhance virtual learning for students and educators.

The repercussions of COVID-19, especially within the Malaysian education system, highlighted the challenges associated with home-based virtual education, access to technical equipment, and internet bandwidth. Despite these hurdles, the local community's sense of solidarity and commitment to continuing the educational process has helped alleviate the strain.

## CONCLUSION

In conclusion, COVID-19 has presented Malaysia with various challenges, particularly within the education sector.

The findings of this study suggest that the flipped classroom approach holds potential for improving interactive learning experiences among engineering students. While students demonstrated improved visualisation of engineering models and problem-solving abilities, the implementation of this approach requires careful planning and investment of time. Despite the challenges associated with preparation and software usability, the benefits of the flipped classroom model in engineering education warrant further exploration and refinement to optimize its effectiveness.

However, these complexities do not necessarily imply significant setbacks for our education systems. Instead, they encourage students to acquire more knowledge through online learning, although there may be some obstacles associated with this new mode of learning. To address these challenges, the government of Malaysia have implemented several solutions, such as online learning platforms and financial assistance, to ensure that no students are left behind. Society has also adapted to using the internet for webinars, extending its utility beyond academia to formal employment. It is imperative to delve further into the effects of the COVID-19 pandemic on education to accurately assess the effectiveness of educational policies for both instructors and students in the future.

## ACKNOWLEDGEMENT

We extend our sincere gratitude to the management of UNITEN for graciously permitting us to conduct this research. Our heartfelt appreciation also goes to the students from the mechanical engineering course who generously contributed their time and insights through the surveys.

## REFERENCES

Abdullah, Q. A., Humaidi, N., & Shahrom, M. (2020). Industry revolution 4.0: The readiness of graduates of higher education institutions for fulfilling job demands. *Romanian Journal of Information Technology and Automatic Control*, 30(2), 15–26. 10.33436/v30i2y202002

Adedoyin, O. B., & Soykan, E. (2020). COVID-19 pandemic and online learning: The challenges and opportunities. *Interactive Learning Environments*, 31(2), 863–875. 10.1080/10494820.2020.1813180

Afsharian, A., Sivapalan, S., & Nordin, S. binti M. (2018). Blended Learning & the Higher Education Classroom: A Critical Review of Developments within Engineering Education. *In 2017 7th World Engineering Education Forum (WEEF), IEEE Xplore*, (pp. 182–187). IEEE. 10.1109/WEEF.2017.8467021

Aguilera, J. M., & Moreno, M. C. (2021). Teaching Engineering and Food: From Traditional Approaches to a Flipped Course on Gastronomic Engineering. *Food Engineering Reviews, 13*, 916–928. Springer. 10.1007/s12393-021-09281-0

Ahmed, V., & Opoku, A. (2021). Technology supported learning and pedagogy in times of crisis: the case of COVID-19 pandemic. *Education and Information Technologies, 27*(1), 365–405. Springer Link. 10.1007/s10639-021-10706-w

Alkhatib, O. J. (2018). An interactive and blended learning model for engineering education. *Journal of Computers in Education*, 5(1), 19–48. 10.1007/s40692-018-0097-x

Alvarado, M., Basinger, K., Lahijanian, B., & Alvarado, D. (2021). Teaching Simulation to Generation Z Engineering Students: Lessons Learned from a Flipped Classroom Pilot Study. *In 2020 Winter Simulation Conference (WSC), IEEE Xplore*. 10.1109/WSC48552.2020.9383950

Ariffin, S. H. S., & Ghazali, N. E. (2018). Structured Techniques in New Academia Learning Innovation (NALI) for Professional Engineering Practices Course. *2017 7th World Engineering Education Forum (WEEF), IEEE Xplore*. IEEE. 10.1109/WEEF.2017.8467118

Aziz, A. A., Megat Mohd Noor, M. J., Abang Ali, A. A., & Jaafar, M. S. (2005). A MALAYSIAN OUTCOME-BASED ENGINEERING EDUCATION MODEL. *IACSIT International Journal of Engineering and Technology*, 2(1), 14–21.

Aziz, A. B. A., Hussin, H. B., & Burham, N. B. (2020). Experiences of Blended Learning using i-LearnV3 Platform in Semiconductor Device Course. *2019 IEEE International Conference on Engineering, Technology and Education (TALE), IEEE Xplore*, (pp. 1–5). IEEE. 10.1109/TALE48000.2019.9225959

Azuma, M., Coallier, F., & Garbajosa, J. (2004). How to apply the Bloom taxonomy to software engineering. *Eleventh Annual International Workshop on Software Technology and Engineering Practice, IEEE Xplore*, 117–122. https://10.0.4.85/STEP.2003.13

Basri, H., Man, A. C., Badaruzzaman, W. W., & Nor, M. M. (2004). Malaysia and the Washington accord: What it takes for full membership. *IACSIT International Journal of Engineering and Technology*, 1(1), 64–73.

Cheng, L., Ritzhaupt, A. D., & Antonenko, P. (2018). Effects of the flipped classroom instructional strategy on students' learning outcomes: a meta-analysis. *Educational Technology Research and Development, 67*(4), 793–824. Springer Link. 10.1007/s11423-018-9633-7

Choi, J., & Lee, Y. (2015). To what extent does "flipping" make lessons effective in a multimedia production class? *Innovations in Education and Teaching International, 55*(1), 3–12. Taylor & Francis Online. 10.1080/14703297.2015.1123105

Chua, K., & Islam, M. (2021). The hybrid Project-Based Learning–Flipped Classroom: A design project module redesigned to foster learning and engagement. *International Journal of Mechanical Engineering Education, 49*(4), 289–315. Sage Journals. 10.1177/0306419019838335

Cohen, M. B., & Zajic, A. (2019). The Flipped Classroom Approach to Engineering Electromagnetics: A Case Study. *2019 IEEE International Symposium on Antennas and Propagation and USNC-URSI Radio Science Meeting, IEEE Xplore*, (pp. 803–804). IEEE. 10.1109/APUSNCURSINRSM.2019.8888789

Coskun, S., Kayıkcı, Y., & Gençay, E. (2019). Adapting Engineering Education to Industry 4.0 Vision. *Technologies, 7*(1), 10. MDPI. 10.3390/technologies7010010

Dada, D., Laseinde, O. T., & Tartibu, L. (2023). Student-Centered Learning Tool for Cognitive Enhancement in the Learning Environment. *Procedia Computer Science, 217*, 507–512. ScienceDirect. 10.1016/j.procs.2022.12.246

Danker, B. (2015). Using Flipped Classroom Approach to Explore Deep Learning in Large Classrooms. *IAFOR Journal of Education, 3*(1), 171–186. ERIC. 10.22492/ije.3.1.10

Das, S., Kleinke, D. K., & Pistrui, D. (2020). Reimagining engineering education: does industry 4.0 need education 4.0? *2020 ASEE Virtual Annual Conference Content Access*, 1–20. https://peer.asee.org/35136

Daumiller, M., Rinas, R., Hein, J., Janke, S., Dickhäuser, O., & Dresel, M. (2021). Shifting from Face-to-Face to Online Teaching During COVID-19: The Role of University Faculty Achievement Goals for Attitudes Towards This Sudden Change, and Their Relevance for Burnout/Engagement and Student Evaluations of Teaching Quality. *Computers in Human Behavior, 118*, 106677. ScienceDirect. 10.1016/j.chb.2020.106677

de la Flor López, S., Ferrando, F., & Fabregat-Sanjuan, A. (2016). Learning/training video clips: an efficient tool for improving learning outcomes in Mechanical Engineering. *International Journal of Educational Technology in Higher Education, 13*(1), 1–13. Springer Link. 10.1186/s41239-016-0011-4

de Lucas Ancillo, A., Gavrila, S. G., & del Val, M. T. (2023). Workplace change within the COVID-19 context: The new (next) normal. *Technological Forecasting and Social Change, 194*, 122673. ScienceDirect. 10.1016/j.techfore.2023.122673

Del Río-Gamero, B., Santiago, D. E., Schallenberg-Rodríguez, J., & Melián-Martel, N. (2022). Does the Use of Videos in Flipped Classrooms in Engineering Labs Improve Student Performance? *Education Sciences, 12*(11), 735. MDPI. 10.3390/educsci12110735

Divjak, B., Rienties, B., Iniesto, F., Vondra, P., & Žižak, M. (2022). Flipped classrooms in higher education during the COVID-19 pandemic: findings and future research recommendations. *International Journal of Educational Technology in Higher Education, 19*(1). Springer Link. 10.1186/s41239-021-00316-4

Felder, R. M., & Spurlin, J. E. (2005). Applications, Reliability and Validity of the Index of Learning Styles*. *International Journal of Engineering Education*, 21(1), 103–112.

Feng, J. (2020). Research on the main problems and countermeasures of Flipped Classroom in college teaching practice. *2020 International Conference on Computer Engineering and Application (ICCEA), IEEE Xplore*, (pp. 166–169). IEEE. 10.1109/ICCEA50009.2020.00043

Ganapathy, M. (2016). Transformation of Malaysia's higher education system: Malaysia Education Blueprint (2015-2025). *Bulletin of Higher Education Research*, 5(1), 10–11.

Ghommem, M., & Gunn, C. (2019). Toward better learning opportunities for undergraduate mechanical engineering students: A case study. *International Journal of Mechanical Engineering Education, 49*(3), 195–213. Sage Journals. 10.1177/0306419019858099

Gómez-Coma, L., Díaz-Sainz, G., Fallanza, M., Ortiz, A., & Ortiz, I. (2023). Integration of chemical engineering skills in the curriculum of a master course in industrial engineering. *Education for Chemical Engineers, 45*, 68–79. ScienceDirect. 10.1016/j.ece.2023.08.002

Halasa, S., Abusalim, N., Rayyan, M., Constantino, R. E., Nassar, O., Amre, H., Sharab, M., & Qadri, I. (2020). Comparing student achievement in traditional learning with a combination of blended and flipped learning. *Nursing Open, 7*(4), 1129–1138. Wiley Online Library. 10.1002/nop2.492

Haling, A., Ilmi, S. N., & Astuty, A. D. (2024). Teaching Practice in a Shifting to Post-COVID 19 Era: A Study from Indonesian Higher Institution. *QWERTY-Interdisciplinary Journal of Technology, Culture and Education*, 1–11. 10.30557/QW000074

Hernandez-de-Menendez, M., Escobar Díaz, C. A., & Morales-Menendez, R. (2020). Engineering education for smart 4.0 technology: a review. *International Journal on Interactive Design and Manufacturing (IJIDeM), 14*(3), 789–803. Springer Link. 10.1007/s12008-020-00672-x

Huang, A. Y. Q., Lu, O. H. T., & Yang, S. J. H. (2023). Effects of artificial Intelligence–Enabled personalized recommendations on learners' learning engagement, motivation, and outcomes in a flipped classroom. *Computers & Education, 194*, 104684. ScienceDirect. 10.1016/j.compedu.2022.104684

Jam, N. A. M., & Puteh, S. (2022). Exploring the Teaching and Learning Indicators towards Education 4.0 in MTUN, Malaysia. *International Journal of Information and Education Technology (IJIET)*, 12(2), 179–184. 10.18178/ijiet.2022.12.2.1602

Karabulut-Ilgu, A., Jaramillo Cherrez, N., & Jahren, C. T. (2017). A systematic review of research on the flipped learning method in engineering education. *British Journal of Educational Technology*, 49(3), 398–411. 10.1111/bjet.12548

Keaveney, S., Athanasopoulou, L., Siatras, V., Stavropoulos, P., Mourtzis, D., & Dowling, D. P. (2021). Development and Implementation of a Digital Manufacturing Demonstrator for Engineering Education. *Procedia CIRP, 104*, 1674–1679. ScienceDirect. Shttps://10.1016/j.procir.2021.11.282

Lapitan, L. DS., Chan, A. L. A., Sabarillo, N. S., Sumalinog, D. A. G., & Diaz, J. M. S. (2023). Design, implementation, and evaluation of an online flipped classroom with collaborative learning model in an undergraduate chemical engineering course. *Education for Chemical Engineers, 43*, 58–72. ScienceDirect. 10.1016/j.ece.2023.01.007

Leal Filho, W., Salvia, A. L., Beynaghi, A., Fritzen, B., Ulisses, A., Ávila, L. V., Shulla, K., Vasconcelos, C. R. P., Moggi, S., Mifsud, M., Anholon, R., Rampasso, I. S., Kozlova, V., Iliško, D., Skouloudis, A., & Nikolaou, I. E. (2023). Digital transformation and sustainable development in higher education in a post-pandemic world. *International Journal of Sustainable Development and World Ecology, 31*(1), 108–123. Taylor & Francis Online. 10.1080/13504509.2023.2237933

Lee, C. K., & Sidhu, M. S. (2016). The Potential of Technology Assisted Engineering Problem Solving Tool for Engineering Education. *Advanced Science Letters, 22*(10), 3092–3095. ingenta connect. 10.1166/asl.2016.7998

Lee, C. K., Sidhu, M. S., Lim, S. P., Hasan, Z., Lim, S. C., & Saw, S. H. (2020). A Preliminary Study on Student Learning Difficulties in Engineering Mechanics Dynamics. *2020 8th International Conference on Information Technology and Multimedia (ICIMU), IEEE Xplore*, (pp. 256–261). IEEE. 10.1109/ICIMU49871.2020.9243582

Lee, W.-K. Mat Isa, C. M., & Tahir, W. (2020). Civil Engineering Student Perception Towards Blended Learning in A Malaysian Public University. *2019 IEEE 11th International Conference on Engineering Education (ICEED), IEEE Xplore*. IEEE. 10.1109/ICEED47294.2019.8994945

Lo, C. K., & Hew, K. F. (2017). Using "First Principles of Instruction" to Design Secondary School Mathematics Flipped Classroom: The Findings of Two Exploratory Studies. *Journal of Educational Technology & Society*, 20(1), 222–236.

Low, M. C., Lee, C. K., Sidhu, M. S., Lim, S. P., Hasan, Z., & Lim, S. C. (2021). Blended Learning to Enhanced Engineering Education using Flipped Classroom Approach: An Overview. *Electronic Journal of Computer Science and Information Technology*, 7(1), 9–19. 10.52650/ejcsit.v7i1.111

Low, M. C., Lee, C. K., Sidhu, M. S., Lim, S. P., Hasan, Z., & Lim, S. C. (2023). Blended learning for engineering education 4.0: Students' perceptions and their learning difficulties. *Computer Applications in Engineering Education, 31*(6), 1705–1722. Wiley Online Library. 10.1002/cae.22668

Malaysia Digital Chamber of Commerce. (2023, July 5). *MyIX reports record surge In Malaysian internet bandwidth demand | MDCC*. Malaysia Digital Chamber of Commerce. https://mdcc.org.my/myix-reports-record-surge-in-malaysian-internet-bandwidth-demand/

Mandal, N. (2017). Student satisfaction – What it means to teaching and learning of undergraduate engineering units. *International Journal of Mechanical Engineering Education, 46*(3), 210–226. Sage Journals. 10.1177/0306419017741996

Mason, G. S., Shuman, T. R., & Cook, K. E. (2013). Comparing the Effectiveness of an Inverted Classroom to a Traditional Classroom in an Upper-Division Engineering Course. *IEEE Transactions on Education*, 56(4), 430–435. 10.1109/TE.2013.2249066

Ministry of Education, Malaysia. (. (2013). Malaysia Education Blueprint 2013 - 2025. *Education*, 27(1), 1–268. 10.1016/j.tate.2010.08.007

Miranda, J., Navarrete, C., Noguez, J., Molina-Espinosa, J.-M., Ramírez-Montoya, M.-S., Navarro-Tuch, S. A., Bustamante-Bello, M.-R., Rosas-Fernández, J.-B., & Molina, A. (2021). The core components of education 4.0 in higher education: Three case studies in engineering education. *Computers & Electrical Engineering, 93*, 107278. ScienceDirect. 10.1016/j.compeleceng.2021.107278

Mohd Said, S., Chow, C.-O., Mokhtar, N., Ramli, R., Tuan Ya, T. M. Y. S., & Mohd Sabri, M. F. (2011). Accreditation of engineering programs: an evaluation of current practices in Malaysia. *International Journal of Technology and Design Education, 23*(2), 313–328. Springer Link. 10.1007/s10798-011-9180-6

Nasir, M. K. N., Mansor, A. Z., & Rahman, M. J. A. (2018). Measuring Malaysian online university student social presence in online course offered. *Journal of Advanced Research in Dynamical and Control Systems*, 10(12), 1442–1446.

Nazar, H., Omer, U., Nazar, Z., & Husband, A. (2018). *A study to investigate the impact of a blended learning teaching approach to teach pharmacy law. International Journal of Pharmacy Practice, 27(3), 303–310*. Academic., 10.1111/ijpp.12503

Park, C., Fuller, M. M., Echevarria, T. M., Nguyen, K., Perez, D., Masood, H., Alsharif, T., & Worthen, M. (2023). A participatory study of college students' mental health during the first year of the COVID-19 pandemic. *Frontiers in Public Health, 11*, 1116865. *Frontiers*, 11, 1116865. Advance online publication. 10.3389/fpubh.2023.111686537026129

Rahim, R., Tan, T., & Carvalho, M. (2020, November 16). Education Ministry: Country's online learning implementation strategy in final stages of preparation. *The Star*. https://www.thestar.com.my/news/nation/2020/11/16/education-ministry-country039s-online-learning-implementation-strategy-in-final-stages-of-preparation

Rekh, S., & Chandy, A. (2020). Implementation of academia 4.0 for engineering college education. *Procedia Computer Science, 172*, 673–678. ScienceDirect. 10.1016/j.procs.2020.05.088

Rizzato, F., Fenwick, S., & Fogg, I. (2020, April 8). *Mobile Experience during the COVID-19 pandemic: 4G Download Speed*. Opensignal. https://www.opensignal.com/2020/04/08/mobile-experience-during-the-COVID-19-pandemic-4g-download-speed

Rovai, A. P., & Downey, J. R. (2010). Why some distance education programs fail while others succeed in a global environment. *The Internet and Higher Education, 13*(3), 141–147. ScienceDirect. 10.1016/j.iheduc.2009.07.001

See, S., & Conry, J. M. (2014). Flip My Class! A faculty development demonstration of a flipped-classroom. *Currents in Pharmacy Teaching and Learning, 6*(4), 585–588. ScienceDirect. 10.1016/j.cptl.2014.03.003

Sidhu, M. S. (2009). *Technology-Assisted Problem Solving for Engineering Education: Interactive Multimedia Applications*. IGI Global.

Sidhu, M. S. (2013). Technology assisted approach for learning, visualizing and problem solving in engineering. *Technics Technologies Education Management*, 8(1), 277–292.

Sidhu, M. S., & Kang, L. C. (2010). Emerging Trends and Technologies for Enhancing Engineering Education. *International Journal of Information and Communication Technology Education, 6*(4), 38–48. IGI Global. 10.4018/jicte.2010100104

Simpson, O. (2018). *Supporting Students in Online, Open and Distance Learning*. Routledge. 10.4324/9780203417003

Soon, T.-K., & Quek, A.-H. (2013). Engineering education in Malaysia - Meeting the needs of a rapidly emerging economy and globalisation. *2013 International Conference on Interactive Collaborative Learning (ICL), IEEE Xplore*, (pp. 583–587). IEEE. 10.1109/ICL.2013.6644659

Srivani, V., Hariharasudan, A., Nawaz, N., & Ratajczak, S. (2022). Impact of Education 4.0 among engineering students for learning English language. *PLoS One*, 17(2), e0261717. 10.1371/journal.pone.026171735108282

Staker, H., & Horn, M. B. (2012). Classifying K–12 Blended Learning. *Cmb.ac.lk*. http://archive.cmb.ac.lk:8080/xmlui/70130/5105

Tawie, R., Neging, M., & Khan, M. Y. M. A. (2018). Preliminary study on creativity in higher education: Perceptions of engineering instructors. *2017 IEEE 9th International Conference on Engineering Education (ICEED)*. IEEE Xplore. 10.1109/ICEED.2017.8251159

Tong, D. H., Uyen, B. P., & Ngan, L. K. (2022). The effectiveness of blended learning on students' academic achievement, self-study skills and learning attitudes: A quasi-experiment study in teaching the conventions for coordinates in the plane. *Heliyon, 8*(12), e12657. ScienceDirect. 10.1016/j.heliyon.2022.e12657

Wai Yee, S. L., & Cheng Ean, C. L. (2020). Malaysian Private University Students' Perception of Online Discussion Forums: A Qualitative Enquiry. *Sains Humanika*, 12(2), 31–38. 10.11113/sh.v12n2.1610

Wang, X., Wang, Z., Wang, Q., Chen, W., & Pi, Z. (2021). Supporting digitally enhanced learning through measurement in higher education: Development and validation of a university students' digital competence scale. *Journal of Computer Assisted Learning, 37*(4), 1063–1076. Wiley Online Library. 10.1111/jcal.12546

Win, N. L., & Wynn, S. D. (2015). Introducing blended learning practices in our classrooms. *Journal of Institutional Research South East Asia*, 13(2), 17–27. http://eprints.intimal.edu.my/id/eprint/154

Wisneski, J. E., Ozogul, G., & Bichelmeyer, B. A. (2017). Investigating the impact of learning environments on undergraduate students' academic performance in a prerequisite and post-requisite course sequence. *The Internet and Higher Education, 32*, 1–10. ScienceDirect. 10.1016/j.iheduc.2016.08.003

Wu, T., Fu, C., Gao, Y., & Zhang, P. (2021). Online Flipped Classroom Based on Task-Driven Teaching Practice: Take Introduction to Systems Engineering as an example. *2020 International Conference on Information Science and Education (ICISE-IE), IEEE Xplore*, (pp. 655–658). IEEE. 10.1109/ICISE51755.2020.00147

Zainuddin, Z., & Attaran, M. (2016). Malaysian students' perceptions of flipped classroom: A case study. *Innovations in Education and Teaching International, 53*(6), 660–670. Taylor & Francis Online. 10.1080/14703297.2015.1102079

## KEY TERMS AND DEFINITIONS

**Blended Learning:** A learning method that combines traditional face-to-face instruction with online learning methods. It integrates digital media and technology into the learning process, allowing for flexibility, personalization, and accessibility. Students engage in a mix of in-person interactions and virtual activities, enhancing their educational experience through a dynamic approach.

**Flipped Classroom:** A method where traditional teaching methods are inverted. Students first engage with instructional content online, typically through videos or readings, outside of class. Classroom time is then dedicated to interactive activities, discussions, and problem-solving, fostering deeper understanding and collaboration under the guidance of the teacher.

**Industry 4.0:** Industry 4.0 refers to the fourth industrial revolution, characterized by the integration of digital technologies into manufacturing and production processes. It encompasses automation, data exchange, artificial intelligence, and the Internet of Things (IoT), leading to enhanced efficiency, productivity, and connectivity across various industries

**MCO:** MCO stands for Movement Control Order, a governmental measure implemented during emergencies or crises, such as pandemics. It restricts movement and social activities, aiming to curb the spread of disease. Under MCO, individuals may be required to stay at home, with exceptions for essential services and activities.

**MOOCs:** MOOCs, or Massive Open Online Courses, are internet-based educational platforms offering free or low-cost courses to a large number of participants globally. They cover diverse subjects and are accessible to anyone with an internet connection, promoting lifelong learning and skill development through interactive multimedia resources and online assessments.

**Pandemic:** A pandemic is an outbreak of a contagious disease that spreads across multiple countries or continents, affecting a significant portion of the global population. It often results in widespread illness, increased mortality rates, and societal disruption, requiring coordinated international efforts to contain and mitigate its impact.

**TAPS:** A custom in house-built pre-pandemic application that could be accessed by students via secured network link to access and use the application to learn engineering mechanics dynamics perform problem solving.

# Chapter 9
# Enhancing Learning Through Companionship in Distance Education

**Ozan Coşkunserçe**
https://orcid.org/0000-0002-1230-324X
*Nevşehir Hacı Bektaş Veli University, Turkey*

**Gökçe Becit**
*Nevşehir Hacı Bektaş Veli University, Turkey*

## ABSTRACT

*While distance education offers individuals the flexibility to learn at their own pace and location, it can also lead to feelings of isolation during the learning process. In order to get over this sensation of isolation, it is essential to establish a sense of learning companionship in distance education. Through the use of learning companionship, individuals in the group are encouraged to share responsibilities, acquire knowledge from one another, and collaborate on finding answers. Developing interaction among learners is crucial to ensure a sense of learning companionship. This connection not only enhances the learning process by making it more comprehensive, engaging, and purposeful, but also fosters cooperation and collaboration among learners. Although learner-learner contact is crucial in distance education, it is often insufficiently implemented and lacks sufficient focus on its enhancement. Learning companionship and learner-to-learner interaction in distance education have been greatly affected and changed by what happened during the COVID-19 pandemic.*

DOI: 10.4018/979-8-3693-7645-4.ch009

## LEARNING COMPANIONSHIP IN DISTANCE EDUCATION

Distance education is an evolving educational approach where students pursue their studies remotely, without physical presence of the instructor or the educational institution (Keegan, 1986; Holmberg, 1995). Distance education provides an alternative global education approach that overcomes the constraints and accessibility challenges of traditional systems. Therefore, distance education is an important field of education that differs from traditional education methods in various aspects. The unique features of distance education, stemming from the physical separation of students, instructors, and institutions, have highlighted the significance of factors like self-esteem and loneliness in influencing academic performance, dropout rates, and course satisfaction, all of which impact students' successful engagement in a distance learning setting. The unique features of distance education, stemming from the physical separation of students, instructors, and institutions, have highlighted the significance of factors like self-esteem and loneliness in influencing academic performance, dropout rates, and course satisfaction, all of which impact students' successful engagement in a distance learning setting (Workman & Stenard, 1996; Von Prummer, 1990; Kurtz et al., 2009). Due to the nature of distance education, it may cause the student to be isolated from other students, teachers, support materials and resources. This scenario might induce feelings of solitude in the student. Obtaining personalized and intelligent assistance from a teacher or peer learner is challenging in distance learning compared to a traditional classroom setting (Brusilovsky, 1999). Although distance education processes provide individuals with spatial and temporal freedom; it is a process that may cause individuals to feel alone in their learning journey. Feelings of loneliness are a major factor causing individuals to abandon their distance education programs. In order to overcome this feeling of loneliness, it is necessary to create learning companionship in distance education processes. Companionship is the state of spending time with someone or having someone to spend time with (Dictionary, n.d.). Based on this definition, the new phenomenon we encounter in distance education processes is "learning companionship". The term "learning companionship" refers to a group of individuals coming together to strengthen their learning processes by providing support to each other. When two or more people come together and share their knowledge, experience and understanding, it can enrich the learning process. Learning companionship involves interactive learning strategies such as group members questioning each other, exchanging ideas, working together and providing feedback. This approach allows individuals to make their own learning more effective and to benefit from the perspectives of others. Learning companionship encourages the participants in the group to share responsibilities, teach each other and generate solutions collectively. Ensuring adequate interaction among learners is crucial for fostering learning companionship in distance education. Interaction among group members can make the learning process richer, more interesting and meaningful. With this section, it is aimed to reveal the current state of learning companionship in distance education in the post-pandemic period and to identify the actions that need to be taken to improve it. With this aim, the content of the chapter was created within the framework of the following research questions:

- How does learner-learner interaction affect learning companionship in distance education?
- How learner-learner interaction can be used to enhance learning companionship in distance education?
- How collaboration among learners can be used to enhance learning companionship in distance education?
- How has the pandemic affected learning companionship in distance education?

## Conceptual and Theoretical Framework

Social cognitive theories emphasize that teaching and learning are highly social activities and that interaction with teachers, peers and instructional materials affects students' cognitive and emotional development. Interacting with other learners, instructors, tools, and contexts can enhance individuals' learning outcomes (Perkins, 2001). Interaction is widely acknowledged as crucial in distance education processes (Abrami, 2011; Billings et al., 2001; Boyle & Wambach, 2001; Meyen et al., 1997; Muirhead, 2000; Sherry, 1995; Tuovinen, 2000; Yazgan, 2022). Interaction in distance education involves the communication and engagement among students, instructors, and peers in online learning settings. It is a crucial component of student education and the overall achievement and efficiency of distance learning. Moore (1989) identified three main types of interaction in distance education:

- Learner-content interaction: This involves learners interacting with the course material and learning resources provided by the instructor.
- Learner-instructor interaction: It refers to the communication between learners and their instructors, which can be initiated by the instructor or learners.
- Learner-learner interaction: This type of interaction allows learners to communicate and co-operate with each other, sharing ideas, thoughts and experiences.

## Learner-Learner Interaction

Learner-learner interaction is a key aspect of interaction in distance education environments. Learner-learner interaction occurs when multiple students participating in the same course engage with each other. Interpersonal engagement among students significantly impacts the efficacy of distance learning programs. Studies indicate that when there is a sufficient level of learner-learner interaction in distance education courses, learning outcomes improve and students' satisfaction with the course increases (Alqurashi, 2019; Baber, 2022; Kurucay & Inan, 2017; Sher, 2009). The main reason for this situation is that in distance learning environments where learner-learner interaction occurs, students do not feel alone by seeing themselves as a member of a social group and thus feel more motivated towards the course. Strong student motivation is considered a crucial element for achieving success in distance education. Furthermore, in this setting, students can collaborate and resolve their issues more readily. Interactions between learners, such as socializing, students helping each other, sharing and discussing ideas, engaging in group activities, and interacting on content-related topics, positively impact student satisfaction and, therefore, enhance the effectiveness of distance education (Alqurashi, 2019; Cole et al., 2014; Khalid & Quick, 2016).

*Figure 1. Types of purposeful interaction in distance education*

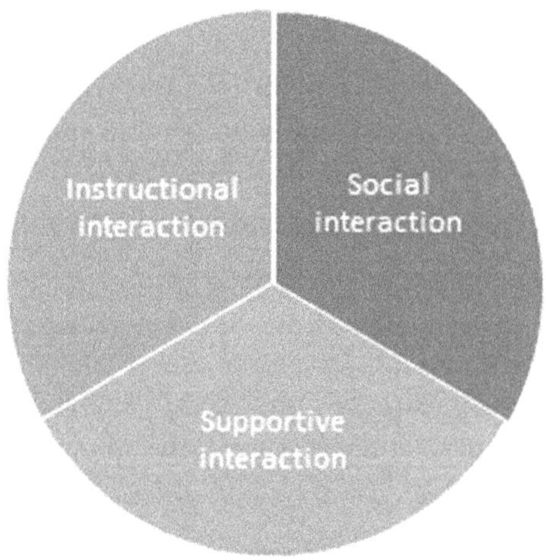


As can be seen in Figure 1, purposeful interactions in distance education can be categorized under three main categories: instructional interaction, social interaction and supportive interaction (Mehall, 2020). When discussing instructional interaction, it is important to not consider the learner-content interaction as defined by Moore (1989). Instructional interaction focuses on the interactions among learners regarding the instructional content. Social interaction refers to interactions that are not directly related to the teaching objectives, but arise from the necessity for socialization and communication among learners. The communication of learners with other learners in order to find solutions to the problems they experience in distance education is included in the support interaction. These three types of interaction occur within the realm of learner-learner interaction. To enhance learner-learner interaction, activities should be designed to target these three types of interaction collectively or individually.

It has been observed that the majority of learner-learner interaction in distance education is realized at a weak level, and that its development is not given sufficient importance (Kaysi & Aydemir, 2017). This is despite the fact that learner-learner interaction is an important aspect of the distance education. Even the students themselves do not want to engage in conversation with other students because they do not want to spend the time and effort to do so (Liu, 2008). In this case, teachers should also encourage learner-learner interaction and student co-operation. In order to develop learner-learner interaction, students have some roles and some responsibilities depending on these roles. İşman (2008) defined 12 learner roles in distance education and in the context of the roles, the duties of the students to ensure learner-learner interaction can be listed as follows:

1. Psychologist: In the role of psychologist, students can support each other's psychological needs and problems by using communication technologies.
2. Tutor: In the role of tutor, students can support each other's learning. A student can communicate with another student and ask for clarification on a subject he/she does not understand or get advice on learning.
3. Technology expert: Students should be able to recognize and actively use the technologies used in distance education environments. Thus, they can communicate effectively with other students and the teacher by using the most appropriate technology.
4. Technician: In distance education, students are expected to produce solutions to the technical problems that they can solve and solve the problem. In addition, students can support other students for the technical problems they encounter.
5. Site instructor: Today, in distance education environments, course contents are mostly shared online. Students need to log in to the system regularly and follow these contents day by day. They are also expected to support other students with the problems they experience in accessing the content.
6. Socialization expert: An important point where distance education is seen as deficient compared to face-to-face education is that students feel isolated due to the limited social communication with other students. In order to overcome

this deficiency, one of the roles of students in OER environments is to socialize by communicating with other students.

7. Researcher: Students need to be able to access accurate and reliable sources in order to conduct research in distance education. In this respect, students can share the resources they have accessed with other students and help them to access resources.
8. Leader: In the role of leader in distance education, the student should increase the motivation of other students and encourage them to learn, distribute responsibilities in group work and generally show leader characteristics.
9. System expert: Within the scope of the system expert role, students should know how to use the learning management system used in distance education. In addition, students are expected to find solutions to the problems encountered while using the system and support other students' problems.
10. Communication expert: In distance education, students need to communicate correctly with their teachers and other students. Within the scope of this role, students are expected to know how to use communication methods, to choose the appropriate communication method for the situation and to use a language in accordance with the rules in communication. In this way, a healthier communication between students can be realized and student-student interaction can be increased.
11. Motivation provider: Motivation is an important component for increasing learning success in distance education environments. For this reason, the student himself/herself also has important duties in terms of increasing student motivation. Students are expected to avoid behaviors and discourses that will decrease their and other students' motivation towards the course.

## Enhancing Learner-Learner Interaction

Learners can engage in collaborative learning activities by utilizing online technologies and participating in mutual dialogue. Dabbagh (2007, p.223) suggested the following guidelines for structuring learning activities according to learners' interaction:

- Asynchronous discussion forums can be utilized to enhance collaboration and interaction among learners by establishing online discussion groups centered on a specific subject, task, project, or objective. Discussion groups can be moderated by a facilitator or left as unstructured open-ended discussions where participants freely share their thoughts.

- An environment can be established for learners to collaboratively share group project documents online. Online sharing can involve sharing the final version of a document or using cloud-based document applications that enable learners to collaborate. Group members can discuss the content of the document via e-mail, video conference or chat.
- Learners can communicate simultaneously using videoconferencing and virtual classroom applications. These cooperative educational activities enable groups of learners to generate ideas and engage in discussions and develop action plans.

Online collaborative learning activities to be organized among learners in distance education can basically be organized in two different structures: teacher-involved activities and activities that take place entirely between learners (McBride & Beers Fägersten, 2008). During learner-only activities, students receive feedback on their ideas from peers and can see how much agreement their ideas receive from others. As a result, learners try to reach a consensus at the end of the activity. Although this process is a component of the collective learning process, in activities that are led by the teacher, the interaction between the learner and the teacher takes place on an individual basis, and the learner is required to participate independently. The learner perceives himself or herself as a member of a group whose contributions are being made when participating in activities between learners. On the other hand, when participating in activities led by the teacher, the learner perceives himself or herself as a student who is being guided and evaluated by the teacher. In this regard, independent study groups that are formed by students and in which the instructor does not play a direct role are more effective in terms of fostering a sense of belonging to a group and fostering an environment that encourages collaborative work.

One more suggestion for enhancing the level of interaction between students is to divide them into smaller groups and then assign them activities to complete together as a group (McBride & Beers Fägersten, 2008). The formation of communities and the strengthening of a sense of belonging to a group are both enhanced by working in small groups, which thereby reduces the likelihood of learners becoming isolated. On the other hand, a leader ought to be chosen from among the members of each group, and this leader ought to be accountable for establishing and sustaining the connection between the members of the group. Group leaders are responsible for facilitating decision-making and making administrative decisions during meetings that are held solely among the students and do not involve the instructor. Additionally, group leaders are responsible for facilitating communication between learners and teachers as well as facilitating communication between group members and the instructor. In general, it is possible to assert that group leaders also take on the responsibility of acting as the spokesperson for the group. The following suggestions were made by Kreijns et al. (2003, p. 339) in order to encourage learners to work together more effectively when they are working in groups:

- Positive interdependence: When working in a group, it is impossible for any individual member of the group to achieve success unless all of the other members of the group achieve success as well. All of the members' efforts are beneficial to the other members of the group. Therefore, each member of the group ought to work in conjunction with the other members of the group.
- Promotive interactions: Promotive interactions suggest that individuals should encourage and support one another in their efforts to accomplish the objectives of the group.
- Individual accountability: All group members should be held responsible for doing their share of the work and for mastering all the material to be learnt.
- Interpersonal and small-group skills: Learners need to have certain skills in order to be able to learn in a group setting. These skills include the ability to work with other people and in small groups. It is important that learners be equipped with the knowledge and skills necessary to collaborate effectively with other people from the beginning.
- Group processing: Members of the group should evaluate how well the group has performed up to this point and determine which behaviors should be maintained or altered in order to achieve the greatest possible level of success.

## Learner's Responsibilities in Learner-Learner Interaction

When compared to the traditional method of instructing students through distance learning, the characteristics that are expected of students participating in distance education today are quite different. The learner model that adapts to collaborative learning activities that emphasize social interaction and cooperation in the online environment is now coming to the forefront (Dabbagh, 2007). This is in contrast to the traditional approach to distance learning, which requires the learner to possess characteristics such as independence, place-boundness, adulthood, self-motivation, discipline, and goal-orientedness. Therefore, students who are learning online should be prepared to share their work, interact with one another in virtual environments for both small and large groups, and work together on projects that are completed online. In that case, they run the risk of being isolated within communities of distance learners, which are becoming increasingly dependent on communication and interaction. Isolation, on the other hand, is likely to result in learners becoming estranged from the learning community, experiencing low levels of motivation, and achieving lower levels of learning overall.

Individual differences in learning are typically explained by the fact that each learner participates in distance education environments possessing unique personality characteristics, knowledge and skills, and socio-economic status. These variables are generally referred to as "individual differences in learning." For students who are learning at a distance to be able to participate in learning in a way that is both constructive and active, they need to comprehend, value, and be willing to take part in the learning opportunities that are made available by technologies that facilitate collaboration and communication. In spite of this, there are students who are naturally inclined to interact with their peers or work together, while there are others who are reluctant to do so. However, these reluctant learners need to understand the educational value of these pedagogical methods. In distance learning environments, students' differences in terms of being open to learner-learner interaction and willingness to participate in group work can be explained in this context. The following is a list of the characteristics that a learner should possess in order to be successful in distance education (Dabbagh, 2007, p. 221):

1. Be able to use the various technologies that are available for online learning, particularly those that are used for communication and coordination.
2. Have a strong academic self-concept and good communication skills.
3. Develop skills that are relevant to the situation and maintain a positive attitude toward learning through collaboration.
4. Develop effective time management and cognitive learning strategies in order to acquire the ability to engage in self-directed learning.

## The Teacher's Role in Facilitating Learner-Learner Interaction

Despite the fact that learners are the primary stakeholders in learner-learner interaction in distance education, teachers also have certain roles to play in order to bring about the interaction at the level and in the manner that is desired. Increasing the amount of interaction between students is primarily the responsibility of the instructor, as stated by Kearsley and Shneiderman (1998). These tasks can be categorized under the headings of managing, building trust among students, managing conflicts among students, and ensuring cooperation among students.

In order to prevent students from experiencing feelings of isolation while they are engaged in their online classes and, as a result, to boost their level of achievement, Kaufmann and Vallade (2022) suggested three strategies that online instructors should implement with their students.

1. Lesson design: In traditional classroom settings, students interact with one another in a manner that is largely unsupervised. When it comes to distance education, on the other hand, there is a requirement for an appropriate course design that allows students to communicate and collaborate, to create oppor-

tunities for students to interact with one another, and to design the atmosphere of the course in accordance with these requirements. It is for this reason that the environments and activities in which students will interact and collaborate in distance education courses need to be carefully planned out. When it comes to distance education, the instructor is responsible for establishing a unique online environment for communication and discussions, as well as grouping the students into appropriate categories. Then, it is necessary to clearly define what the students should be doing in these groups, what kind of technology and format will be used, how they can demonstrate that they are working together, and the schedule that they will be following.

2. Positive instructor communication: In order to establish healthy communication with learners in distance education and to reduce the feelings of isolation and loneliness that learners experience, teachers should pay attention to the communication style that they use on a regular basis. According to Kaufmann et al. (2016), students who participate in distance education have the expectation that their instructors will adopt a communication style that is approachable, supportive, respectful, engaging, understanding, and responsive. There is a wide range of opinions regarding the manner in which educators should communicate with students and which approach is the most effective. According to Hodges (2006), students find more significance in receiving personalized email messages as opposed to messages that are sent electronically via email lists. According to Kim and Keller (2008) and Hodges and Kim (2010), when the use of e-mail groups and personalized messages in communicating with students was compared, it was discovered that neither method made a significant difference in the students' ability to self-regulate their behavior.
3. Facilitating student interaction: In an online environment, students may be more comfortable showing rude behavior than face-to-face communication (Clark et al, 2012). For this reason, in distance education, teachers need to clearly set the rules regarding communication and follow the communication between students. It is important to have a more civilized communication between students in order to prevent conflicts that may occur between students and thus to maintain communication. In addition, the instructor needs to both model and provide resources to his students on how to respectfully criticize comments from other learners online, to give feedback, to enrich the discussion environment, and how to question the opinions of other learners in order to realize higher-level thinking. Thanks to the new online technology, learners can be enabled to interact with each other even when the teacher is not present. Online communication tools such as discussion forums, e-mail and chat rooms can be used for this purpose. For example, a student-only forum can be created where students can discuss

course topics and interests, or chat room sessions can be scheduled for learners to participate in to discuss a specific topic.

Teachers need to create a sense of learning community in order to increase interaction among learners. This is mainly aimed at facilitating communication between learners (Kear et al., 2014). Social media tools can be used to strengthen connections by making it easier for students to get to know each other, but the participation of teachers in the use of these tools increases academic performance (Al-Dheleai & Tasir, 2016). The teacher can communicate with the students through personal messages and messages sent to the group collectively. It has been observed that messages from online or technology-integrated learning environments to increase students' motivation for the course increase students' self-efficacy levels (Hodges, 2008). Self-efficacy can be defined as one's belief in one's ability to organize and accomplish the task assigned to him (Bandura, 1997). In this respect, it is recommended that teachers prefer personal messages instead of collective messages in their communication with their students.

Another method recommended to be used by teachers to increase interaction between learners is the creation of discussion groups. In discussion groups, learners can share homework-related questions or messages, compare learning strategies, and support each other in performing tasks set by the teacher (Vlachopoulos & Makri, 2019). Students can also share messages that are not directly related to the learning activities for socializing purposes. In discussion groups, online technologies such as discussion forums can be used for communication purposes. In online learning environments, it was observed that the absence of discussion, without teacher participation, and when teacher participation and discussion situations were compared, the most interaction between learners occurred when discussions with teacher participation were used (Cho & Tobias, 2016). Sun and Wu (2016) also stated that teachers' participation in discussion groups improves learning. Through organized online discussion groups, students share and compare their thoughts on concepts with each other, resulting in better learning and course success.

Immediacy behaviors are also seen as an important factor in the development of learner-learner interaction. Immediacy behaviors defined by Mehrabian (1969) as "communication behaviors that enhance closeness to and non-verbal interaction with another" (p. 202). In open and distance learning environments, the significant effect of the teacher's immediacy behaviors on learners' perceptions of social presence and satisfaction was observed (Bozkaya & Erdem Aydın, 2007). Therefore, teachers should learn immediacy behaviors to enhance learner interaction and should frequently include verbal and non-verbal immediacy behaviors in their distance education courses.

As a result, teachers have important tasks in terms of ensuring learner-learner interaction among the students who participate in the course and creating a sense of learning community among the students. The teacher should plan activities in which students can interact with each other, organize communication environments and technologies, and lead the formation of a constructive and mutually respectful communication language among students. In this case, stronger relationships develop among students and learners' performance in learning increases.

## Collaboration Among Learners

In the traditional understanding of distance education, it is not very important for students to interact with each other and the student is allowed to be partially isolated. The student's current interaction with the content and the teacher is largely with the teacher. There is little to no interaction between students beyond email blasts, discussion board posts, and the occasional online chat. However, according to the modern understanding and in well-designed distance education environments, interaction and cooperation between learners is an important issue.

In connection with this situation, it is recommended to include collaborative learning practices in distance education environments. Collaboration among learners contributes significantly to success in the learning process, and learner-learner interaction is essential to achieve success in this regard (Kožuh et al., 2015; Said et al., 2016). Collaborative projects in distance education reduce students' feelings of isolation and contribute to the development of a sense of community (Palloff & Pratt, 2001). In collaborative learning environments, the transition from the teacher-centered paradigm to the student-centered paradigm is aimed, and for this reason, it is emphasized that teachers and students should change their roles from time to time in communication (Vlachopoulos & Makri, 2019). Teachers can help create an atmosphere conducive to collaboration by sharing ideas and resources, while students can take the place of the teacher by acting as coordinators in collaborative activities.

In the traditional distance education approach, interaction among students is not a very important issue and the student is allowed to be partially isolated. The interaction that does exist is largely with the content and the teacher. There is little or no interaction between students beyond e-mails, discussion board posts and occasional online chats. However, in modern and well-designed distance education environments, interaction and cooperation between learners is an important issue.

In connection with this situation, it is recommended to include collaborative learning practices in distance education environments. Collaboration among learners contributes significantly to success in the learning process and learner-learner interaction is essential for success in this regard (Kožuh et al., 2015; Said et al., 2016).

Collaborative projects in distance education reduce students' feelings of isolation and contribute to the development of a sense of community (Palloff & Pratt, 2001). Collaborative learning environments aim to shift from a teacher-centered paradigm to a learner-centered paradigm and therefore, it has been emphasized that teachers and learners should change their roles from time to time in communication (Vlachopoulos & Makri, 2019). Teachers can help create a conducive atmosphere for collaboration by sharing ideas and resources, while students can replace the teacher by acting as coordinators in collaborative activities.

Kennedy and Duffy (2004, p. 209) made some recommendations for collaborative work in distance education:

- Collaboration needs to be managed. The appointment of a coordinator facilitated collaborative practices.
- In conducting collaborative studies in distance education, many people should work together in the form of teamwork instead of only the teacher taking part.
- In order to fully test the functionality of the ICT to be used and the collaborative working relationships between the teacher and the students, a trial collaboration exercise at the beginning of the lesson is necessary.
- Teachers should prepare students to work collaboratively.
- It is important to provide effective technical support to all participants, especially at the beginning of the course but also throughout the course.
- Teachers should be assigned, trained and supported for collaborative work. The dimensions and requirements of collaboration should be formally explained.
- There should be institutional awareness about the necessity and dimensions of cooperation in distance education.

For collaborative online learning to take place successfully, it is crucial for learners to feel part of a learning community where their contributions to collaborative work are added to a common pool of knowledge and the community spirit is strengthened through social interactions (Bernard & Rubalcava, 2000). Slavin (1999) recommends the use of protocols to guide learner interactions in online collaborative learning environments and to minimize both off-task and passive behaviors by providing clear guidance and detailed explanations to all learners regardless of ability level. Bernard and Rubalcava (2000) suggested the following practices to encourage collaboration in collaborative online learning environments:

- Small groups should be formed among learners.
- The teacher should take on the role of facilitator.
- The cooperative behavior required from the student should be explained by modeling.

- Techniques should be used to facilitate cooperation among students.
- Visual social cues should be replaced by verbal cues, and cues should be easy to understand.
- In order to achieve success, students should be dependent on each other. This can be achieved through techniques such as collective rewarding, sharing resources among group members, etc.

## Online Communication and Collaboration Tools for Learners

Since communication in distance education cannot take place face-to-face and naturally, communication tools are needed to ensure interaction. Having communication skills and being able to use collaborative online learning technologies fluently are seen as critical competencies for distance learners (Dabbagh & Bannan-Ritland, 2005). Lack of knowledge and skills in the use of online learning technologies, especially communication and collaborative technologies, can be a barrier to learning in online learning environments (Cheurprakobkit et al., 2002). In this respect, learners are expected to be able to recognize and effectively use the communication and collaboration tools used in the online environment. As can be seen in Figure 2, Chickering and Ehrmann (1996) present seven principles for the implementation of new information and communication technologies (ICT) in distance education.

*Figure 2. Seven principles for implementing new ICTs*

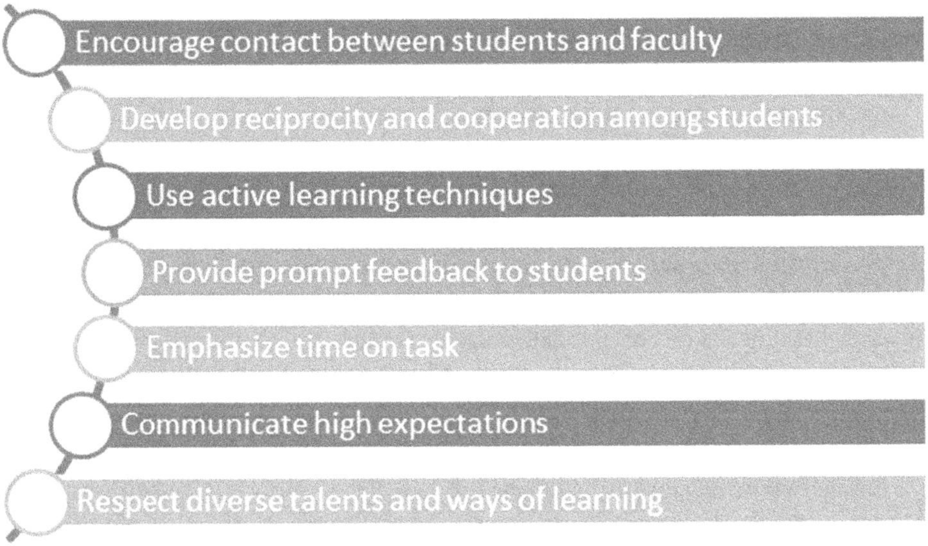


*(Chickering & Ehrmann, 1996)*

With the implementation of the seven principles listed in Figure 2, it will be possible to use synchronous and asynchronous communication tools more effectively in distance education. While synchronous communication in distance education requires the individuals participating in the communication to use the communication tool at the same time, in asynchronous communication tools, messages are stored and can be received by the target person or persons at any time and place. Today, with the developing information and communication technologies, the number and capacity of communication tools that can be used in distance education have increased considerably. Some of these tools work synchronously and some asynchronously. In addition, while some communication tools are suitable for collective communication as a group, some tools are suitable for mutual communication between two individuals. It is very important to choose the appropriate communication tool according to the structure of the communication needed in order to establish a healthy communication. Communication tools can be within the scope of the system used in distance education, but if the system does not meet the needs in terms of communication, other communication tools can be used externally. Karadeniz (2018) lists the communication tools that can be used in distance education as discussion forum, cloud environment online documents, blog, chat room, e-mail, wiki, virtual classroom. Apart from these tools, social media can also be used for communication and collaboration in distance education. These tools are briefly introduced below.

## Discussion Forum

Forums are an information sharing platform that is frequently used in online environments today and offer asynchronous communication. In distance education environments, it is possible for the student and the instructor to open a new topic and respond to an opened topic or comment with discussion forums. In this way, it is possible to discuss a topic collectively or get answers to questions. Kılınç (2022) suggested the use of gamification elements such as assigning ranks to the students' top contributors to the discussions and publishing the list of students who actively participated in order to motivate and increase their participation in the use of discussion forums in distance education. In addition, he emphasized the effective management of the discussion in discussion forums and explained that in order for the discussions to be productive, the lecturer or artificial intelligence algorithms should moderate the discussions (Kılınç, 2020). The following addresses can be given as examples of forum sites:

https://www.bilgisayarbilisim.net/

https://www.okuloncesiforum.com/

## Cloud Environment Online Documents

With the help of Web 2.0 technologies, it is now feasible for a large number of users to collaborate on documents that are stored online in cloud services in both a synchronous and asynchronous manner. One example is that the text on a document created with a word processor can be created by multiple users working together. Additionally, users are able to chat while working on the document. Some examples of services that can be found on Google Drive include Google Docs, Google Sheets, and Google Slides. Here is the link to Google Drive:

https://drive.google.com/

## Blog

Web blogs, which are also a type of Web 2.0 tool, have the potential to serve as an efficient asynchronous communication tool in both face-to-face and distance learning environments. Blogs are a simple and cost-free method of disseminating content across the internet. Other authors can be added to the blog in addition to the person who initially created it, and the content that is shared by the authors is presented in the order that it was originally published. Additionally, there is the ability for users of the blog to comment on and discuss the posts. A student's blog can also serve as an electronic portfolio, allowing them to showcase their work to others. Blogs are an effective tool for facilitating interaction between students who are enrolled in distance education because of these features. Research has shown that students who participate in distance education can benefit from the use of blogs to avoid experiencing feelings of isolation and alienation (Dickey, 2004). Additionally, blogs can be utilized as an effective tool to receive support from their advisors (Wheeler & Lambert-Heggs, 2009). Here are links to two educational web blogs:

https://biyolojikcesitlilik.blogspot.com/

https://karaktervedegerleregitimi.blogspot.com/

## Chat Room

It can be used for learners to communicate in writing and synchronously online. With the developments in communication technologies, documents, audio recordings, photos and videos can be sent in online chat environments in addition to writing. Although software such as Messenger and Skype have been widely used in the past, the use of mobile chat applications has become more prominent with the widespread use of mobile technologies. WhatsApp mobile chat application is seen as a very effective communication tool for socialization and interaction among students in distance education (Misaghi et al., 2021). Students help each other in WhatsApp groups created for each course. Apart from communication and collaboration, WhatsApp is also used as an effective tool for sharing course materials and assignments and reduces the cost of course materials (Mazana, 2018).

## Email

It is a tool used to communicate in writing online and asynchronously. It requires users to create an e-mail account. Within the scope of messaging and announcement applications of the systems used in distance education, messages can be sent to the e-mail accounts of the learners. It is also possible to send the same message to many learners by creating e-mail groups. There are various opinions explaining how teachers should communicate with students and which method is superior when using e-mail. Hodges (2006) states that personalized email messages are more meaningful to students than messages sent via email lists. When the use of e-mail groups and personalized messages in communicating with students was compared, it was seen that neither method made a significant difference in students' self-regulation skills (Kim & Keller, 2008; Hodges & Kim, 2010). In this respect, it would be more effective to communicate with students through personalized e-mail messages instead of group messages when students' motivation towards the course is to be increased.

## Wiki

Wiki is the name given to websites that allow a group of people who come together for a purpose and work in cooperation to create web pages online, to modify the pages already created, and to associate these pages by adding links. It is derived from the Hawaiian word "wiki", which means fast. By using wikis, learners working asynchronously online can collaborate on the same web page and create online content together. Since learners can modify wiki pages without any special editing tools, wikis are an effective tool for sharing knowledge and learning from other learners.

## Virtual Classroom

These are systems that allow learners to gather online by communicating simultaneously in audio, video and written form. Today, virtual classrooms contribute to the enrichment of distance education environments in terms of content and especially visual materials by offering many material sharing opportunities besides rich communication opportunities. In virtual classrooms, the lecture or meeting process is often recorded and can then be watched asynchronously by learners.

## Social Media

These are online systems where people can create accounts using their real names or pseudonyms, communicate with other accounts of their choice and share the content they have prepared. On social media, users can share content consisting of text, images, audio and video, as well as comment on the content shared by others. The purposes of using social media for educational purposes can be summarized as sharing information, requesting support from other learners and supporting learners, creating groups for learning, establishing new connections for collaboration, collaborative work and personal content development (Yükseltürk & Top, 2013). In groups created for educational purposes on social media, only the members of a learning community can participate and learners can work in collaboration within this group. Bozkurt et al. (2017) determined the most commonly used social media tools among distance education students as Facebook, YouTube and Instagram, and found that a significant portion of students think that the use of social media in distance education increases interaction. Greenhow and Chapman (2020) stated that the use of social media from distance education applications in the pandemic period has significant contributions in three areas: supporting students' active learning, improving students' connections with communities inside and outside the classroom, and participation in civil society activities. Due to these features, it is thought that social media in distance education is a communication tool that can be used to increase interaction among students.

### Web 2.0 Tools

Today, there are many online Web 2.0 tools that learners can use to create content and prepare assignments and projects in distance education in a variety of ways. Some of them are even made available to students free of charge. Moreover, some of these Web 2.0 tools allow students to interactively communicate, collaborate and even work together on the same project. Some of these tools can be listed as follows: Canva (graphic design), Google Documents (document editor), Google Drive (file sharing), Asana (project management), Zoom (online meeting), Miro (online white-board), Class Dojo (school communication), Kahoot (online games and quizzes).

The COVID-19 pandemic has brought about substantial shifts in attitudes towards distance education and significant alterations in the dynamics of learning companionship. This process can be examined within three distinct timeframes: pre-pandemic, pandemic-era, and post-pandemic.

## PRE-PANDEMIC APPLICATIONS OF LEARNING COMPANIONSHIP IN DISTANCE EDUCATION

The presence of learning companionship in distance education is crucial for enhancing students' academic achievements, boosting their drive, and fortifying their interpersonal connections. Prior to the pandemic, distance education methods that fostered a sense of companionship among students had the potential to enhance the effectiveness and efficiency of the learning process. In the realm of distance education, students may encounter a decline in motivation as a result of the absence of a tangible classroom setting. Learning companionship facilitates mutual motivation among students through the provision of supportive services. The interaction between students can be constrained by distance and time. Learning companionship fosters social cohesion by promoting intercommunication among students and facilitating the exchange of their experiences. Distance education frequently engenders feelings of solitude among students. Learning companionship can alleviate stress by establishing a support network for students and fostering a sense of solidarity among them. Likewise, fostering a sense of camaraderie among students can enhance their sense of belonging and promote active engagement in the educational endeavor. Engaging in distance education with learning companions can enhance the feeling of community. The integration of students with diverse backgrounds and experiences can enhance the educational process. Learning companionship enables students to leverage this diversity and acquire knowledge from one another. With this section, it is aimed to reveal the current state of learning companionship in the post-pandemic period and to identify the actions that need to be taken to improve it.

## Learning Companionship in Distance Education During the Pandemic

During the pandemic, distance education has necessitated students to completely abstain from traditional classroom settings, resulting in feelings of isolation. At this juncture, the significance of acquiring companionship skills in distance education becomes even more pronounced. Distance education, mandated during the pandemic, restricts the ability of students to gather in person. A study comparing the period before and after the pandemic revealed that students' emotional engagement levels were significantly lower in the online learning environment compared to the traditional learning environment (Salta et al., 2022). This decline was primarily attributed to the reduction in human interaction, whether it was between students or between students and instructors. Developing companionship among students helps to alleviate social isolation by fostering communication and preserving social connections. Distance education poses the potential danger of students losing their dedication to the educational endeavor. Developing a sense of companionship can enhance this dedication by empowering students to provide mutual support and actively engage in the educational process. Furthermore, the pandemic circumstances may have an adverse impact on students' inclination and enthusiasm for learning and educational activities. Furthermore, it was noted that the interaction between learners in the online education process during the pandemic period had a beneficial impact on both student satisfaction and learning outcomes (Su & Guo, 2021). Through the provision of assistance and a sense of unity among students, fostering companionship can contribute to mutual motivation among students. Amidst the pandemic, students engaged in remote learning frequently had to independently complete their academic tasks. Acquiring companionship allows students to cultivate their abilities in teamwork and collaboration. Amidst the pandemic, students may encounter an increased number of education-related challenges. Acquiring companionship can assist students in dealing with these issues and allows them to establish a network of support among their peers.

The study on emergency remote teaching that was conducted during the COVID-19 pandemic period came to the conclusion that there were very few opportunities for learners to interact with one another, that there was a lack of interaction between teachers and students due to the fact that students were able to communicate with their teachers very little, and that the interaction was more of a learner-content interaction (Seynhaeve et al., 2022). The primary factor contributing to the high level of learner-content interaction in this process is that students primarily engage with the course through course materials. During the pandemic, efforts were made to find alternative communication methods to enhance the learner's engagement with others. Amidst the pandemic, social media has been extensively utilized as a means of communication between students and even between students and teachers. This has resulted in enhanced interaction among learners and increased engagement in student learning within a technology-driven educational setting (Rautela et al., 2022).

## Learning Companionship in Distance Education in the Post-Pandemic Period

Although educational institutions switched to face-to-face education after the COVID-19 pandemic process was completed, the experiences experienced during the pandemic process have enabled distance education practices to continue to implement some innovations after the pandemic process. From a pedagogical viewpoint, the shift to distance education during the pandemic period has necessitated the adoption of new instructional strategies and tools to facilitate interaction and collaboration among learners. The strategies that were developed during the pandemic also had an impact on distance education environments after the pandemic. Asynchronous and synchronous learning platforms have become pivotal in supporting these interactions, offering forums, chat rooms, and video conferencing tools as mediums for communication. This shift has led to a reevaluation of teaching methodologies, with a greater emphasis on collaborative and student-centered learning approaches to engage learners and foster a sense of community in virtual environments.

The psychological impact of transitioning to distance education on learner-learner interaction is profound. The absence of physical presence can lead to feelings of isolation and disconnection among students. However, this challenge has also prompted educators and learners to explore innovative ways of building rapport and fostering emotional connections through digital means. The development of online social presence and the cultivation of an inclusive online community have become critical components in mitigating the psychological barriers to effective learner-learner interaction.

Technologically, the pandemic has accelerated the adoption of advanced educational technologies and digital platforms designed to enhance learning companionship. Tools such as virtual breakout rooms, collaborative online whiteboards, and peer feedback systems have been integrated into learning management systems to facilitate interaction and collaboration. Moreover, the rise of adaptive learning technologies and AI-driven educational tools has provided personalized learning experiences, further enriching learner-learner interactions by allowing students to engage based on their individual learning paths and preferences. The hybrid-distance education approach has gained credibility in the post-pandemic era. The use of platforms like Moodle and Zoom, which incorporate electronic mail, blogs, forums, chats, video, and mobile services, is crucial for collaborative purposes in implementing this approach (Masalimova et al., 2021).

In conclusion, the post-pandemic era has witnessed a paradigm shift in the dynamics of learning companionship in distance education. The forced transition to online learning environments has not only presented challenges but also opportunities to reimagine and enrich the way learners interact with each other. As the educational landscape continues to evolve, the lessons learned from this period will undoubtedly shape the future of learning companionship in distance education, emphasizing the importance of adaptability, community-building, and the integration of innovative technologies in fostering engaging and effective learning experiences.

## CONCLUSION

Although distance education processes provide individuals with spatial and temporal freedom; it is a process that may cause individuals to feel lonely in their learning journey. One of the biggest reasons why individuals drop out of distance education processes is the feeling of loneliness they experience in the process. In order to overcome this feeling of loneliness, it is necessary to create learning companionship in distance education processes. The key issue in creating learning camaraderie among learners in distance education is to provide sufficient interaction among learners. Interaction between group members can make the learning process richer, more engaging and meaningful. One of the dimensions of interaction in distance education environments is learner-learner interaction. Learner-learner interaction takes place between two or more students attending the same course. The interaction between students is an important factor affecting the success of distance education courses. In order to ensure learner-learner interaction, the tasks of students can be listed as psychologist, instructor, technologist, technician, site instructor, socialization expert, researcher, leader, system expert, communication expert and motivator. In group studies, in order to increase cooperation among learners, recommendations such as establishing positive interdependence, providing supportive interaction, fulfilling individual responsibilities, developing skills to work with other people and small groups, and making in-group evaluations are made. Since communication in distance education cannot be realized face-to-face and naturally, communication tools are needed to ensure interaction. In this respect, learners are expected to recognize and effectively use the communication and collaboration tools used in the online environment. The communication tools that can be used in distance education are listed as discussion forum, cloud environment online documents, blog, chat room, e-mail, wiki, virtual classroom. Apart from these tools, social media can also be used for communication and collaboration in distance education.

## REFERENCES

Abrami, P. C., Bernard, R. M., Bures, E. M., Borokhovski, E., & Tamim, R. M. (2011). Interaction in distance education and online learning: Using evidence and theory to improve practice. *Journal of Computing in Higher Education*, 23(2-3), 82–103. 10.1007/s12528-011-9043-x

Al-Dheleai, Y. M., & Tasir, Z. (2016). Facebook to facilitate instructor roles in course-related online interaction: A pilot study. *Journal of Theoretical and Applied Information Technology*, 89(2), 343–351.

Alqurashi, E. (2019). Predicting student satisfaction and perceived learning within online learning environments. *Distance Education*, 40(1), 133–148. 10.1080/01587919.2018.1553562

Baber, H. (2022). Social interaction and effectiveness of the online learning–A moderating role of maintaining social distance during the pandemic COVID-19. *Asian Education and Development Studies*, 11(1), 159–171. 10.1108/AEDS-09-2020-0209

Bandura, A. (1997). *Self-efficacy: The exercise of control.* W. H. Freeman and Company.

Bernard, R. M., & Rubalcava, B. R. D. (2000). Collaborative online distance learning: Issues for future practice and research. *Distance Education*, 21(2), 260–277. 10.1080/0158791000210205

Billings, D. M., Skiba, D. J., & Connors, H. R. (2005). Best practices in web-based courses: Generational differences across undergraduate and graduate nursing students. *Journal of Professional Nursing*, 21(2), 126–133. 10.1016/j.profnurs.2005.01.00215806511

Boyle, D. K., & Wambach, K. A. (2001). Interaction in graduate nursing web-based instruction. *Journal of Professional Nursing*, 17(3), 128–134. 10.1053/jpnu.2001.2337611391558

Bozkaya, M., & Erdem Aydin, I. (2007). The Relationship between Teacher Immediacy Behaviors and Learners' Perceptions of Social Presence and Satisfaction in Open and Distance Education: The Case of Anadolu University Open Education Faculty. *The Turkish Online Journal of Educational Technology*, 6(4), 7.

Bozkurt, A., Karadeniz, A., & Kocdar, S. (2017). Social networking sites as communication, interaction, and learning environments: Perceptions and preferences of distance education students. *Journal of Learning for Development*, 4(3), 348–365. 10.56059/jl4d.v4i3.215

Brusilovsky, P. (1999). Adaptive and Intelligent Technologies for Web-based Education. In Rollinger, C., & Peylo, C. (Eds.), *Künstliche Intelligenz, Special Issue on Intelligent Systems and Teleteaching, 4, 19-25.*

Cheurprakobkit, S., Hale, D. F., & Olson, J. N. (2002). Technicians' perceptions about Web-based courses: The University of Texas system experience. *American Journal of Distance Education*, 16(4), 245–258. 10.1207/S15389286AJDE1604_4

Chickering, A. W., & Ehrmann, S. C. (1996). Implementing the seven principles: Technology as lever. *AAHE Bulletin*, 49, 3–6.

Cho, M. H., & Tobias, S. (2016). Should instructors require discussion in online courses? Effects of online discussion on community of inquiry, learner time, satisfaction, and achievement. *International Review of Research in Open and Distance Learning*, 17(2), 605–632. 10.19173/irrodl.v17i2.2342

Clark, C. M., Werth, L., & Ahten, S. (2012). Cyber-bullying and incivility in the online learning environment, part 1: Addressing faculty and student perceptions. *Nurse Educator*, 37(4), 150–156. 10.1097/NNE.0b013e31825a87e522688872

Cole, M. T., Shelley, D. J., & Swartz, L. B. (2014). Online instruction, e-learning, and student satisfaction: A three year study. *International Review of Research in Open and Distance Learning*, 15(6), 111–131. 10.19173/irrodl.v15i6.1748

Dabbagh, N. (2007). The online learner: Characteristics and pedagogical implications. *Contemporary Issues in Technology & Teacher Education*, 7(3), 217–226.

Dabbagh, N., & Bannan-Ritland, B. (2005). *Online learning: Concepts, strategies, and application*. Prentice Hall.

Dickey, M. (2004). The impact of web-logs (blogs) on student perceptions of isolation and alienation in a web-based distance-learning environment. *Open Learning*, 19(3), 279–291. 10.1080/0268051042000280138

Dictionary. (n.d.). *Companionship*. Dictionary. https://www.dictionary.com/browse/companionship

Greenhow, C., & Chapman, A. (2020). Social distancing meet social media: Digital tools for connecting students, teachers, and citizens in an emergency. *Information and Learning Science*, 121(5/6), 341–352. 10.1108/ILS-04-2020-0134

Hodges, C. B. (2006). Skills necessary for learner success in an emporium-designed mathematics course. *Journal of Research in Education*, 16, 69–80.

Hodges, C. B. (2008). Self-efficacy, motivational email, and achievement in an asynchronous math course. *Journal of Computers in Mathematics and Science Teaching*, 27(3), 265–285.

Hodges, C. B., & Kim, C. (2010). Email, self-regulation, self-efficacy, and achievement in a college online mathematics course. *Journal of Educational Computing Research*, 43(2), 207–223. 10.2190/EC.43.2.d

Holmberg, B. (1995). *Theory and practice of distance education*. Routledge.

İşman, A. (2008). *Uzaktan eğitim*. Pegem Akademi.

Karadeniz, A. (2018). *Açık ve uzaktan öğrenmede ders tasarımı*. Gece Kitaplığı.

Kaufmann, R., Sellnow, D. D., & Frisby, B. N. (2016). The development and validation of the online learning climate scale (OLCS). *Communication Education*, 65(3), 307–321. 10.1080/03634523.2015.1101778

Kaufmann, R., & Vallade, J. I. (2022). Exploring connections in the online learning environment: Student perceptions of rapport, climate, and loneliness. *Interactive Learning Environments*, 30(10), 1794–1808. 10.1080/10494820.2020.1749670

Kaysi, F., & Aydemir, E. (2023). Uzaktan eğitim süreçlerindeki etkileşim boyutlarının değerlendirilmesi. *Journal of Social Sciences*, 11(11), 778–790. 10.16990/SOBIDER.3442

Kear, K., Chetwynd, F., & Jefferis, H. (2014). Social presence in online learning communities: The role of personal profiles. *Research in Learning Technology*, 22, 1–15. 10.3402/rlt.v22.19710

Kearsley, G., & Shneiderman, B. (1998). Engagement theory: A framework for technology-based teaching and learning. *Educational Technology*, 38(5), 20–23.

Keegan, D. (1986). *The foundations of distance education*. Routledge.

Kennedy, D., & Duffy, T. (2004). Collaboration—A key principle in distance education. *Open Learning*, 19(2), 203–211. 10.1080/0268051042000224798

Khalid, M. N. M., & Quick, D. (2016). Teaching presence influencing online students' course satisfaction at institution of higher education. *International Education Studies*, 9(3), 62–70. 10.5539/ies.v9n3p62

Kılınç, H. (2020). *Çevrimiçi Grup Tartışmalarının Öğrenenler Üzerindeki Etkisinin Çeşitli Değişkenler Açısından İncelenmesi: Anadolu Üniversitesi Açıköğretim Fakültesi Örneği* [Unpublished doctoral thesis, Anadolu Üniversitesi, Sosyal Bilimler Enstitüsü, Eskişehir].

Kılınç, H. (2022). Tartışma forumlarının açık ve uzaktan öğrenme ortamlarında kullanılabilirliği ve bir ölçme-değerlendirme kriteri olarak değerlendirilmesi. *Açıköğretim Uygulamaları ve Araştırmaları Dergisi*, 8(1), 1–31. 10.51948/auad.1028872

Kim, C., & Keller, J. M. (2008). Effects of motivational and volitional email messages (MVEM) with personal messages on undergraduate students' motivation, study habits and achievement. *British Journal of Educational Technology*, 39(1), 36–51. 10.1111/j.1467-8535.2007.00701.x

Kožuh, I., Jeremić, Z., Sarjaš, A., Bele, J. L., Devedžić, V., & Debevc, M. (2015). Social presence and interaction in learning environments: The effect on student success. *Journal of Educational Technology & Society*, 18(1), 223–236.

Kreijns, K., Kirschner, P. A., & Jochems, W. (2003). Identifying the pitfalls for social interaction in computer-supported collaborative learning environments: A review of the research. *Computers in Human Behavior*, 19(3), 335–353. 10.1016/S0747-5632(02)00057-2

Kurtz, G., Amichai-Hamburger, Y., & Kantor, J. (2009). Psychosocial well-being of Israeli students and attitudes toward open and distance learning. *International Review of Research in Open and Distance Learning*, 10(2), 1–11. 10.19173/irrodl.v10i2.593

Kurucay, M., & Inan, F. A. (2017). Examining the effects of learner-learner interactions on satisfaction and learning in an online undergraduate course. *Computers & Education*, 115, 20–37. 10.1016/j.compedu.2017.06.010

Liu, S. (2008). Student interaction experience in distance learning courses: A phenomenological study. *Online Journal of Distance Learning Administration*, 11(1). https://www.westga.edu/~distance/ojdla/spring111/Liu111.html

Masalimova, A. R., Ryazanova, E. L., Tararina, L. I., Sokolova, E. G., Ikrennikova, Y. B., Efimushkina, S. V., & Shulga, T. I. (2021). Distance Learning Hybrid Format for University Students in Post-Pandemic Perspective: Collaborative Technologies Aspect. *Cypriot Journal of Educational Sciences*, 16(1), 389–395. 10.18844/cjes.v16i1.5536

Mazana, M. Y. (2018). Social media in the classroom: WhatsApp a new communication tool for enhanced class interactions. *Business Education Journal, 4*(1).

Mehall, S. (2020). Purposeful interpersonal interaction in online learning: What is it and how is it measured? *Online Learning : the Official Journal of the Online Learning Consortium*, 24(1), 182–204. 10.24059/olj.v24i1.2002

Mehrabian, A. (1969). Significance of posture and position in the communication of attitude and status relationships. *Psychological Bulletin*, 71(5), 359–372. 10.1037/h00273494892572

Meyen, E. L., Lian, C. H., & Tangen, P. (1997). Teaching online courses. *Focus on Autism and Other Developmental Disabilities*, 12(3), 166–174. 10.1177/108835769701200305

Misaghi, M., Tonioti, E., Batiz, E. C., & Dos Santos, A. J. (2021). WhatsApp as a tool for ıntegration and motivation in distance education. *Social Networking*, 10(3), 29–43. 10.4236/sn.2021.103003

Moore, M. G. (1989). Three types of interaction. *American Journal of Distance Education*, 3(2), 1–6. 10.1080/08923648909526659

Muirhead, B. (2000). Enhancing social interaction in computer-mediated distance education. *Journal of Educational Technology & Society*, 3(4), 1–11.

Palloff, R. M., & Pratt, K. (2001). *Lessons from the cyberspace classroom: The realities of online teaching*. Jossey-Bass.

Parker, A. (2020). Interaction in distance education: The critical conversation. *AACE Review (Formerly AACE Journal)*, 13-17.

Perkins, D. N. (2001). Person-plus: A distributed view of thinking and learning. G. Salomon (Ed.). *Distributed cognition: Psychological and educational considerations* (pp. 88–110). Cambridge University Press.

Rautela, S., Sharma, S., & Virani, S. (2022). Learner-learner interactions in online classes during COVID-19 pandemic: The mediating role of social media in the higher education context. *Interactive Learning Environments*, 1–16. 10.1080/10494820.2022.2093917

Said, M. N. H. M., Tahir, L., & Ali, M. F. (2016). Online collaborative learning interactions in a tertiary ICT education course. *International Information Institute (Tokyo).Information (Basel)*, 19(1).

Salta, K., Paschalidou, K., Tsetseri, M., & Koulougliotis, D. (2022). Shift from a traditional to a distance learning environment during the COVID-19 pandemic: University students' engagement and interactions. *Science & Education*, 31(1), 93–122. 10.1007/s11191-021-00234-x34121814

Seynhaeve, S., Deygers, B., Simon, E., & Delarue, S. (2022). Interaction in online classes during Covid-19: The experiences of newly-arrived migrant students. *Educational Research*, 64(3), 334–352. 10.1080/00131881.2022.2090981

Sher, A. (2009). Assessing the relationship of student-instructor and student-student interaction to student learning and satisfaction in web-based online learning environment. *Journal of Interactive Online Learning*, 8(2), 102–120.

Sherry, L. (1995). Issues in distance learning. *International Journal of Educational Telecommunications*, 1(4), 337–365. https://www.learntechlib.org/primary/p/8937/

Slavin, R. E. (1999). Comprehensive approaches to cooperative learning. *Theory into Practice*, 38(2), 74–79. 10.1080/00405849909543835

Su, C. Y., & Guo, Y. (2021). Factors impacting university students' online learning experiences during the COVID-19 epidemic. *Journal of Computer Assisted Learning*, 37(6), 1578–1590. 10.1111/jcal.1255534908643

Sun, J. C. Y., & Wu, Y. T. (2016). Analysis of learning achievement and teacher–student interactions in flipped and conventional classrooms. *International Review of Research in Open and Distance Learning*, 17(1), 79–99. 10.19173/irrodl.v17i1.2116

Tuovinen, J. E. (2000). Multimedia distance education interactions. *Educational Media International*, 37(1), 16–24. 10.1080/095239800361473

Vassileva, J. (2001). *"Distributed and United"*. ICCE'2001, Seoul. https://julita.usask.ca/homepage/Agents.html

Vlachopoulos, D., & Makri, A. (2019). Online communication and interaction in distance higher education: A framework study of good practice. *International Review of Education*, 65(4), 605–632. 10.1007/s11159-019-09792-3

Von Prummer, C. (1990). Study motivation of distance students: A report on some results from a survey done at the FernUniversitat in 1897/88. *In Research in Distance. Education*, 2(2), 2–6.

Wheeler, S., & Lambert-Heggs, W. (2009). Connecting distance learners and their mentors using blogs: The MentorBlog Project. *Quarterly Review of Distance Education*, 10(4), 323–331.

Workman, J. J., & Stenard, R. A. (1996). Student support services for distance learners. *DEOSNEWS, 6*(3). http://learningdesign.psu.edu/deos/deosnews6_3.pdf

Yazgan, Ç. Ü. (2022). Attitudes and interaction practices towards distance education during the pandemic. *Education and Information Technologies*, 27(4), 5349–5364. 10.1007/s10639-021-10843-235079227

Yükseltürk, E., & Top, E. (2013). Web 2.0 teknolojilerinin öğretmen eğitiminde kullanımı. *In K. Çağıltay ve Y. Göktaş (Eds.), Öğretim teknolojilerinin temelleri: Teoriler, araştırmalar, eğilimler*, 665-680. Pegem Akademi.

# Chapter 10
# Linking Social Support, Self-Support, and Emotional Regulation of Students Learning Online at Home During the COVID-19 Pandemic

**Nurul Hudani Md Nawi**
*Universiti Malaysia Sabah, Malaysia*

**Habibie Ibrahim**
*Universiti Malaysia Sabah, Malaysia*

**Joki Perdani Sawai**
*Universiti Malaysia Sabah, Malaysia*

**Tuan Norbalkish Tuan Abdullah**
http://orcid.org/0000-0002-5557-5173
*Universiti Malaysia Sabah, Malaysia*

**Norazah Mohd Suki**
http://orcid.org/0000-0002-8422-2449
*Universiti Utara Malaysia, Malaysia & Universiti Teknologi MARA, Malaysia*

## ABSTRACT

*This study investigates the linkages of social support and self-support on the emotional*

DOI: 10.4018/979-8-3693-7645-4.ch010

*regulation of students learning online at home during the COVID-19 pandemic. Data collected from 300 public higher-education students were analysed using partial least squares-structural equation modelling (PLS-SEM) via SmartPLS3.0. The results revealed that the emotional regulation of students learning online at home during the COVID-19 pandemic was heavily influenced by self-support, followed by social support. During the COVID-19 pandemic, online learning was perceived as a novel experience, with individuals who were open and flexible being able to access and utilize various creative ideas. This empirical study can serve as a basis for developing a comprehensive action plan to improve training methods and strengthen existing support systems. These efforts are crucial for the successful implementation of educational activities for future generations.*

## INTRODUCTION

The COVID-19 pandemic has emerged as a significant threat to the socio-economic system, with the education sector, including higher education, being particularly hard hit (Abdeahad et al., 2023; Behzadnia et al., 2023; Mao et al., 2023; Salimi et al., 2023). The "new normal" required the adoption of virtual learning facilitated by technology platforms such as Microsoft Teams, Google Meet, Zoom, Google Classroom, Telegram, and WhatsApp (Endrawati & Suwartono, 2023; Ohei, 2023; Windhiyana, 2020). Teachers had to change their approach to maintain continuity of teaching, leading to a rapid transition to virtual learning and the sudden change was challenging for some children and led to psychological anxiety (Masry-Herzallah, 2023; Mohan et al., 2020; Sidi et al., 2023). Online learning brings challenges such as difficulty concentrating due to unfavorable learning conditions and internet problems (Ayusi et al., 2021).

Scholarly works by Noriyani (2017) and Zhooriyati (2021) highlight various barriers to online teaching and learning, including a lack of equipment, poor learning environments and internet connectivity issues, thus placing a psychological burden on some students. They face numerous challenges, such as learning in isolation without the guidance of teachers or the presence of familiar classmates. The long periods of studying in a single room and being confined to a computer screen also contribute to stress. This sudden change and the resulting restrictions make adjustment difficult and contribute to psychological pressure among students (Shazarina et al., 2020). In addition, students from less privileged families have limited or no access to modern devices, forcing them to share a single device with their siblings to participate in online learning. This places an emotional burden on students as they strive to participate in class and not miss out on anything.

The new norm causes discomfort and anxiety for both teachers and students, affecting their psychological well-being, emotions, and attitudes (Fairuz et al., 2020; Shazarina et al., 2020). In the face of these challenges, strong support from the family and immediate environment becomes crucial to students' academic performance (Dennis et al., 2005; Muniroh et al., 2020). Individuals with strong emotional skills tend to have more positive social relationships (Lopes et al., 2004). Students who receive solid emotional support and have effective emotional regulation skills also experience higher life satisfaction. Positive emotions improve concentration, mental clarity, and academic engagement, which ultimately leads to better academic performance. More empirical research to assess the linkages between social support and self-support on emotional students' regulation when studying online and staying at home with their families during the pandemic COVID-19 is deemed necessary. Accordingly, this study aims to investigate the linkages of social support and self-support on the emotional regulation of students learning online at home during the COVID-19 pandemic.

The second section presents the relevant literature review with a proposed research framework and hypotheses development; the third section explains the research methodology. The subsequent section details the findings, followed by a discussion of the findings in section five. Finally, the study presents research future research directions.

## EMOTIONAL REGULATION

Emotional regulation refers to an individual's ability to assess, manage, and maintain emotional balance in their lives (Astuti et al., 2019). Maintaining psychological well-being is highly dependent on adaptability as emotion regulation has a positive influence on a person's thoughts, feelings, and actions (James, 1998; Tiwari, 2017; Winnaiseh, 2017). Efficient emotional regulation promotes optimistic cognition, inner calm, and prudent decision-making. Ayuningtiyas (2020) outlines essential characteristics for successful emotional regulation in the context of online learning, namely self-discipline, constructive interpersonal relationships, prudent emotional expression in reflection, flexibility in adapting to the environment, and a remarkable level of tolerance. Students who have a positive self-perception and optimistic thoughts regarding their current environment are more likely to show positive emotions and manage their emotions well during online learning (Ayuningtiyas, 2020). People with impaired emotion regulation skills are more prone to stress and anxiety when confronted with life events (Fergusson & Horwood, 1987). The COVID-19 epidemic and the accompanying MCO measures have reinforced the importance of capable emotional regulation. This ability is critical for maintaining psychological well-being, mitigating the effects of negative emotions, and promoting enjoyable emotional encounters. In the online classroom, students who have good emotion regulation skills demonstrate self-discipline, maintain constructive relationships, adapt to their environment, and show remarkable levels of tolerance. On the other hand, those who lack emotion regulation skills are more susceptible to the negative consequences of stress and discomfort. The next section discusses the linkages of social support and self-support on emotional regulation.

## SOCIAL SUPPORT

Social support, the perception that others care about one and are responsive to the individual's needs, is an important factor in maintaining well-being when confronted with life's challenges and psychological stressors (Kafetsios & Sideridis, 2006). People need empathy, acknowledgment of their emotional reactions, and social support or resources to cope with stressful situations (Jordan et al., 2002). In the context of students' academic development, which encompasses physical, emotional, mental, and social aspects (Baria & Gomez, 2022), their cognitive and emotional development has a significant impact on academic performance and personal development, both in the present and in the future.

Students need social support from parents, teachers, and peers to effectively manage their academic emotions, and need to have emotional awareness and emotion regulation skills to adapt to the challenges of the COVID-19 situation. Bethell et al. (2017) asserted that the relationships, experiences, and environments that students encounter are crucial to their long-term learning and development. People with strong social networks and adequate social support have fewer mental health problems and higher levels of subjective well-being (Gallagher & Vella-Brodrick, 2008; Kong & You, 2011; Montes-Berges & Augusto, 2007). Conversely, students who lack sufficient support from family members often have problems at school and face challenges in their health development (Blažević, 2016). In addition, students who rate the value of support low are more prone to learning and developmental problems (Karen & Dan, 2022). Therefore, the role and support of family members and peers have a significant impact on student satisfaction, with family serving as a crucial source of life support (Basson & Rothmann, 2018). Family support plays a central role in fostering positive character traits by nurturing loving relationships, modeling desirable skills, and providing guidance (Basson & Rothmann, 2018). Regular interaction with classmates has also been shown to improve students' ability to cope with the emotional demands of others, as it promotes understanding of emotions (Basson & Rothmann, 2018).

Hermawan (2020) asserts that a variety of factors, including the acceptance of social support, influence teens' ability to regulate their emotions. The social support teens receive can promote the development of positive and effective emotion regulation and enable them to adapt their behavior and problem-solving strategies to the situation at hand. Putri, as mentioned in Hermawan (2020), also emphasizes that teenagers' emotional development occurs through interactions with people around them, such as peers. Other studies have also found that social support has an impact on stress, burnout, and depression, all of which are closely linked to emotion regulation. Rohmah (2017) conducted a study that found a significant correlation between social support and stress levels in college students. Insufficient emotion regulation is an indication that a person is suffering from stress (Kadi et al., 2020). Argyle, cited by Veiel et al. (1992), also points out that the presence and support of family members can be effective in coping with stress. Adawiyah (2013) cited Taylor (1999) as saying that people who have high levels of social support not only experience less stress but also can deal with stressors effectively (Zahara et al., 2022). Moreover, Pramono and Prabawati (2021) adds that stress and emotion regulation are closely linked, with higher levels of emotion regulation being associated with lower levels of stress. This highlights that students with inadequate emotion regulation are more vulnerable to stress as they have difficulty adjusting their emotions when faced with challenges.

In a study conducted by Andi (2020), Gold et al. (1993) and Purba et al. (2007), a significant impact was found between social support and burnout, which is closely related to emotion regulation. This is evident during a pandemic when limited social interactions with close people, such as family and friends, result in those affected feeling less supported by their social environment. Similarly, Rahayu and Fauziah (2019) support the notion that burnout is closely linked to emotion regulation. When people have difficulty controlling their emotions, it becomes difficult to turn negative emotions into positive ones, leading to burnout (Rahayu et al., 2019). Low levels of social support are known to contribute to depression. Previous studies have consistently shown that people suffering from depression receive less social support (Lakey et al., 2008). Consequently, people suffering from depression often have problems with emotion regulation. Joormann and Gotlib (2010) emphasized the close relationship between depression and emotion regulation. Depression debilitates sufferers, making it difficult for them to manage their emotions effectively and becoming a source of considerable distress. Subsequently, the following hypotheses have emerged as a result of this discussion:

H1: Social support has a positive effect on the emotional regulation of students learning online at home during the COVID-19 pandemic.

## SELF-SUPPORT

Self-support plays a crucial role in promoting individual well-being and effective emotional regulation in everyday life (Neff, 2003). Self-support dimensions such as flexibility and open-mindedness affect the emotion regulation strategies of individuals (Xia et al., 2014a,b). During the pandemic, flexible students are better able to adapt to new ways of learning to seamlessly navigate through virtual classes to graduation, while individuals with high levels of open-mindedness demonstrate effective emotion regulation by developing new ideas. These individuals can control their emotions, which enables them to behave creatively (Ivcevic & Hoffmann, 2019; Xia et al., 2014a,b). Emotion regulation play an important role as a personal strength that enables individuals to assess, overcome, and achieve their emotional balance (Astuti et al., 2019). In the current pandemic situation, individuals who lack effective emotional regulation may experience heightened emotional stress due to the challenges associated with adapting to the various changes. The inability to regulate emotions can lead to increased anxiety. Winnaiseh (2017) points out that emotion regulation allows individuals to cultivate positive thinking, composure, and wise action. In the context of online learning, students' ability to regulate their emotions is reflected in various indicators of good emotion regulation, such as displaying appropriate behaviors and emotions, maintaining positive interpersonal relationships, considering appropriate emotional responses in various situations, adapting to environmental conditions, and demonstrating high tolerance (Ayuningtiyas, 2020). Consequently, this study asserts that:

H2: Self-support has a positive effect on the emotional regulation of students learning online at home during the COVID-19 pandemic.

Considering the previously presented information, Figure 1 visually depicts the theoretical framework proposed in this study.

*Figure 1. Proposed theoretical framework*

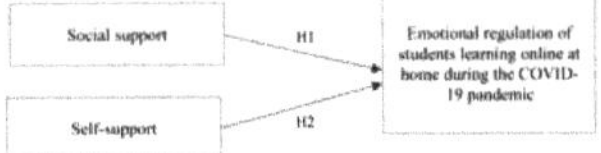

## METHODOLOGY

This cross-sectional study used an online-based approach for data collection, which was conducted during the first year of the mandatory Covid-19 lockdown. The online surveys were distributed to participants through various online learning platforms (Microsoft Teams, Google Meet, Zoom, Google Classroom, Telegram, WhatsApp, etc.) as well as through the university's email systems to ensure accessibility and convenience for participants. Data were collected from 300 students in public higher learning institutions in Sabah Malaysia between April and June 2022. Of this, 263 students provided complete responses, yielding 87.7% response rate. The sample size was appropriate given the generally accepted response rate for social science research, which typically falls between 5% and 35% (Sekaran & Bougie, 2016). All subjects are currently enrolled at the university during the COVID-19 pandemic and are participating in online learning due to the pandemic.

## MEASUREMENT OF INSTRUMENTS

The questionnaire was divided into four parts. Part A collects respondents' demographic data such as gender, place of residence, age, education, race, religion, and health status. Part B consists of instruments to measure social support. Part C measures self-support, while Part D measures emotion regulation. Social support was assessed using a 19-item scale from the Medical Outcome Study Social Support Survey (MOS-SSS) by Zimet et al. (1988). Self-support was assessed using a 20-item scale adapted from the Self-Supporting Personality Scale for Adolescent Students (SSPS-AS) developed by Xia et al. (2014b). Emotion regulation was assessed using a 10-item scale from the ERQ instrument by Gross and John (2003).

### Statistical Technique Used

Partial Least Squares-Structural Equation Modelling (PLS-SEM) via Smart-PLS3.0 was employed to assess the hypothesized relationships. This method is useful for small sample sizes or non-normal data distributions (Hair et al., 2022). This approach provides a flexible and robust method for understanding the structure and dynamics of the research model.

## RESULTS

The demographic profile presented in Table 1 shows that of the 263 respondents, women made up the majority (83%), while men accounted for 17%. In terms of place of residence, approximately 53% of respondents lived predominantly in urban areas, while the remaining 47% lived in rural areas. In addition, the data shows that a large proportion of respondents were in good health—97% of the sample. However, a small percentage of participants reported having diseases or health conditions.

*Table 1. Socio-demographic profile of respondents (n = 263)*

| Characteristics | Frequency | Percentage (%) |
|---|---|---|
| **Gender**<br>Male<br>Female | 44<br>219 | 16.7<br>83.3 |
| **Place of Residence**<br>City areas<br>Rural areas | 139<br>124 | 52.9<br>47.1 |
| **Health status**<br>Have Illness<br>Healthy | 8<br>255 | 3.0<br>97.0 |

## MEASUREMENT MODEL

In the measurement model, the factor loadings, composite reliability, and average variance extracted (AVE) values of the three factors were used to evaluate convergent validity (see Table 2). The Cronbach's alpha coefficient was used to measure scale reliability (Henseler, 2010), requiring a value above 0.70 (Nunnally, 1970). The alpha coefficients of all variables in this study surpassed the cut-off value, indicating high reliability. Besides, all factor loadings more than 0.600 (ranging from 0.809 to 0.905), composite reliability greater than 0.600 (ranging from 0.809 to 0.905), and average variance extracted larger than 0.600 (AVE) (ranging from 0.809 to 0.905) (Hair et al., 2022). Table 3 shows no cross-loading issue. Thus, the criteria for convergent validity were met.

*Table 2. Convergent validity*

| Variables | Items | Loadings | Cronbach's Alpha | CR (> 0.70) | AVE (> 0.50) |
|---|---|---|---|---|---|
| Social Support | SS10 | 0.765 | 0.947 | 0.952 | 0.572 |

continued on following page

*Table 2. Continued*

| Variables | Items | Loadings | Cronbach's Alpha | CR (> 0.70) | AVE (> 0.50) |
|---|---|---|---|---|---|
| | SS11 | 0.707 | | | |
| | SS12 | 0.750 | | | |
| | SS13 | 0.748 | | | |
| | SS14 | 0.717 | | | |
| | SS15 | 0.776 | | | |
| | SS16 | 0.788 | | | |
| | SS17 | 0.785 | | | |
| | SS18 | 0.778 | | | |
| | SS19 | 0.764 | | | |
| | SS2 | 0.706 | | | |
| | SS5 | 0.791 | | | |
| | SS6 | 0.794 | | | |
| | SS7 | 0.722 | | | |
| | SS8 | 0.739 | | | |
| Self-Support | SK14 | 0.703 | 0.799 | 0.789 | 0.555 |
| | SK19 | 0.814 | | | |
| | SK9 | 0.715 | | | |
| Emotional Regulations | EMOS13 | 0.738 | 0.873 | 0.908 | 0.664 |
| | EMOS15 | 0.792 | | | |
| | EMOSI10 | 0.841 | | | |
| | EMOSI7 | 0.831 | | | |
| | EMOSI8 | 0.865 | | | |

Note: CR= Composite reliability; AVE = Average Variance Extracted

*Table 3. Cross loadings*

| Items | Emotion Regulations | Self-Support | Social Support |
|---|---|---|---|
| EMOS13 | **0.738** | 0.307 | 0.142 |
| EMOS15 | **0.792** | 0.430 | 0.219 |
| EMOSI10 | **0.841** | 0.397 | 0.186 |
| EMOSI7 | **0.831** | 0.388 | 0.187 |
| EMOSI8 | **0.865** | 0.394 | 0.208 |
| SK14 | 0.326 | **0.703** | 0.199 |
| SK19 | 0.401 | **0.814** | 0.249 |

continued on following page

*Table 3. Continued*

| Items | Emotion Regulations | Self-Support | Social Support |
|---|---|---|---|
| SK9 | 0.329 | **0.715** | 0.198 |
| SS10 | 0.161 | 0.269 | **0.765** |
| SS11 | 0.146 | 0.250 | **0.707** |
| SS12 | 0.160 | 0.142 | **0.750** |
| SS13 | 0.137 | 0.158 | **0.748** |
| SS14 | 0.094 | 0.210 | **0.717** |
| SS15 | 0.132 | 0.212 | **0.776** |
| SS16 | 0.161 | 0.258 | **0.788** |
| SS17 | 0.193 | 0.278 | **0.785** |
| SS18 | 0.155 | 0.281 | **0.778** |
| SS19 | 0.179 | 0.260 | **0.764** |
| SS2 | 0.224 | 0.179 | **0.706** |
| SS5 | 0.248 | 0.228 | **0.791** |
| SS6 | 0.194 | 0.213 | **0.794** |
| SS7 | 0.218 | 0.171 | **0.722** |
| SS8 | 0.100 | 0.182 | **0.739** |

Subsequently, discriminant validity is assessed through heterotrait-monotrait ratio (HTMT). It is established when all HTMT values obtained are lesser than the threshold of HTMT.85, as suggested by Gold et al. (2001). Table 4 shows that all HTMT values are beneath HTMT.85, which means that discriminant validity is ascertained. Accordingly, when using Fornell-Larcker criterion for checking discriminant validity, all correlations had coefficients lesser than 0.85, thus discriminant validity is satisfactory (see Table 5).

*Table 4. Discriminant validity using HTMT ratio*

| Variable | 1 | 2 | 3 |
|---|---|---|---|
| (1) Emotional Regulations | | | |
| (2) Self Support | 0.647 | | |
| (3) Social Support | 0.240 | 0.383 | |

*Table 5. Discriminant validity using Fornell-Larcker criterion*

| Variable | 1 | 2 | 3 |
|---|---|---|---|
| (1) Emotional Regulations | 0.815 | | |

continued on following page

*Table 5. Continued*

| Variable | 1 | 2 | 3 |
|---|---|---|---|
| (2) Self Support | 0.475 | 0.745 | |
| (3) Social Support | 0.234 | 0.291 | 0.756 |

## STRUCTURAL MODEL

In the structural model stage, bootstrapping procedures with a resample of 5,000 were used to assess the relationships between the constructs and their corresponding beta coefficients, t-values, and p-values (Hair et al., 2022). H1 and H2 of the study aimed to investigate the direct influence of social support and self-support on the emotional regulation of students learning online at home during the COVID-19 pandemic, respectively. Table 6 and Figure 2 show that social support ($\beta_1 = 0.105$, t-value = 2.362, p = 0.018) positively influenced the emotional regulation of students learning online at home during the COVID-19 pandemic. In addition, self-support ($\beta_2 = 0.444$, t-value = 10.277, p = 0.000) was found to have a positive significant relationship with the emotional regulation of students learning online at home during the COVID-19 pandemic.

*Table 6. Direct effects*

| Relationship | Std. Beta | Std. Error | | | LLCI (5%) | ULCI (95%) | | $R^2$ |
|---|---|---|---|---|---|---|---|---|
| H1: Social Support ---> Emotion Regulations | 0.105* | 0.045 | 2.362 | 0.018 | 0.018 | 0.188 | S | |
| H2: Self Support ---> Emotion Regulations | 0.444* | 0.043 | 10.277 | 0.000 | 0.350 | 0.522 | S | |

Note: *$p<0.05$; ULCI = Upper Level Confidence Interval, LLCI = Lower Level Confidence Interval; D = Decision; S = Supported; 1-tailed test

*Figure 2. Results of hypothesized relationships*

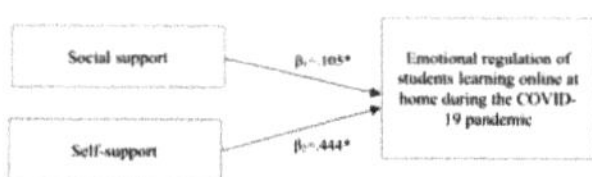

## DISCUSSION

This study investigated the linkages of social support and self-support on the emotional regulation of students learning online at home during the COVID-19 pandemic. The results showed a significant positive relationship between social support and the emotional regulation of students learning online at home during the COVID-19 pandemic (see Table 6 and Figure 2). Thus, H1 was supported. This signifies that social support from the environment plays an important role in influencing emotion regulation. This support can manifest itself in various forms, such as seeking advice and guidance in coping with emotions and promoting a harmonious family atmosphere through mutual love. Sari and Hayati (2015) noted that individuals who receive support from those around them are better able to express appropriate emotions. Effective social support contributes to successful online learning and teaching by giving students the tools to control their emotions and manage difficult situations. It also helps individuals develop a resilient identity that enables them to move forward in life despite pressure and adversity. The findings of Mak et al. (2009) avowed that seeking social support is a common strategy used by respondents when under pressure during a pandemic outbreak. Furthermore, a positive emotional state can serve as a motivating force that empowers individuals to take on challenging tasks and roles. Vienlentia (2021) supports this view, pointing out that social support increases enthusiasm, motivation, and emotional management, facilitating positive change and academic success. In addition, social support can reduce psychological stress (Xia et al., 2014a,b). These findings underscore the critical role of practical and robust social support in health emergencies, as it contributes to effective emotional regulation and helps minimize stress.

Pratisti (2013) emphasizes the crucial role of social support, particularly from family members, especially parents, in the development of children's emotion regulation skills. Parents can influence their children by modeling effective emotion management and guiding them to regulate their own emotions. Vienlentia et al. (2021) also emphasize the importance of social support for students' emotion regulation as it promotes a smooth learning process. They argue that the strength of social support contributes to emotion regulation, which ultimately leads to academic excellence. Furthermore, the combined strength of social support and emotion regulation has been found to reduce academic stress, with lower levels of stress having a positive effect on academic performance (Rahmawati & Indriayu, 2017).

Further examination of the PLS-SEM approach revealed that the emotional regulation of students learning online at home during the COVID-19 pandemic was heavily influenced by self-support (see Table 6 and Figure 2). Therefore, supporting H2. This implies that incorporating flexible aspects of self-support is crucial for individuals to cultivate and maintain positive emotions. During the COVID-19 pandemic, online learning was perceived as a novel experience, with individuals who were open and flexible being able to access and utilize various creative ideas. Rozanki and Kubzansky (2005) asserted that self-support such as flexibility affects the ability to manage emotions and deal with conflict effectively. Individuals with flexible characteristics have an advantage in coping with various life experiences due to their openness and creativity (Bond et al., 2011; Xia et al., 2014a,b). People with greater flexibility tend to experience less anxiety, stress, and pressure when confronted with stressful circumstances (Masuda et al., 2011). These findings are consistent with Koole's (2009) view that emotion regulation plays a role in personality development.

Previous research acknowledged that personality traits influence people's consistent tendencies to respond to adaptations and behaviors (Purnamaningsih, 2017). Therefore, differences in emotion management can be observed for different personality traits. Barańczuk (2019) shows a correlation between neuroticism as a personality trait and people who regulate their emotions to avoid negative situations. On the other hand, extroverted people are often associated with people who regulate their emotions by processing, solving, becoming aware of, and accepting problems. These findings are consistent with those of other studies examining how neuroticism and extroversion affect emotion regulation, especially when it comes to cognitive reappraisal and emotion restraint (Gresham & Gullone, 2012).

## CONCLUSION

In summary, the challenges posed by the COVID-19 pandemic have enhanced individuals' resilience, enabling them to withstand difficulties and adapt to evolving situations. This is particularly true when individuals maintain optimistic thoughts and emotions to achieve a state of well-being. The pandemic has profoundly affected various sectors, including education, necessitating the transition from traditional face-to-face teaching to online platforms for delivering lectures, assigning tasks, conducting tests, and facilitating other educational processes. This decision aims to motivate students to persist in their studies and avoid the need to extend their semesters or drop their courses. These changes require adjusting daily routines to cope with these demanding circumstances. Individuals with an optimistic mindset view the problem as temporary and actively seek solutions. They explore ways to generate income and employ innovative and resourceful problem-solving strategies. However, there may also be more severe consequences, such as despair, emotional distress, and an increased susceptibility to suicidal thoughts.

Future research is recommended to expand the sample size beyond the student context to include the perspectives of teachers from private schools, high-performing schools, sports schools, technical and vocational schools, science schools, missionary and religious schools, as well as teachers from regular and fully-funded public secondary schools. Moreover, future research should consider issues such as students' psychological difficulties, concerns, and reflections during the COVID-19 pandemic as they adjust to an online learning environment, change their behaviour, such as social distancing, and deal with socioeconomic uncertainty. This is because, during the pandemic, self-support and social support significantly impacted the emotional regulation of students learning online from home.

## REFERENCES

Abdeahad, N., & Mock, S. (2023). The role of past campus recreational sports participation in predicting students' stress and competence during the COVID-19 pandemic. *Journal of Leisure Research*, 54(2), 269–285. 10.1080/00222216.2023.2165203

Astuti, D., Wasidi, & Sinthia, R. (2019). Hubungan antara regulasi emosi dengan perilaku memaafkan pada siswa sekolah menengah pertama. *Consilia Jurnal Ilmiah BK, 2*(1), 1-10. https://doi.org/10.33369/consilia.2.1.1-10

Ayuningtiyas, C. (2020). Regulasi emosi siswa dalam pembelajaran daring. *De_Journal (Dharmas Education Journal*), *1*(2), 107–113. https://ejournal.undhari.ac.id/index.php/de_journal/article/view/123

Barańczuk, U. (2019). The five factor model of personality and emotion regulation: A meta-analysis. *Personality and Individual Differences*, 139, 217–227. 10.1016/j.paid.2018.11.025

Baria, K., & Gomez, D. (2022). Influence of social support to student learning and development. *International Journal of Research Studies in Education*, 11(2), 69–97. 10.5861/ijrse.2022.112

Behzadnia, B., Mollaei Zangi, F., Rezaei, F., & Eskandarnejad, M. (2023). Predicting students' basic psychological needs, motivation, and well-being in online physical education: A semester-term longitudinal study. *International Journal of Sport and Exercise Psychology*, 1–19. 10.1080/1612197X.2023.2237051

Dennis, J. M., Phinney, J. S., & Chuateco, L. I. (2005). The role of motivation, parental support, and peer support in the academic success of ethnic minority first-generation college students. *Journal of College Student Development*, 46(3), 223–236. 10.1353/csd.2005.0023

Endrawati, A., & Suwartono, T. (2023). Blended learning through the google classroom in the "new normal" era of the Covid-19 pandemic: EFL teachers' perception and challenges. *Proceedings Series on Social Sciences & Humanities*, 12, 27–37. 10.30595/pssh.v12i.769

Fergusson, D. M., & Horwood, L. J. (1987). Vulnerability to life events exposure. *Psychological Medicine*, 17(3), 739749. 10.1017/S003329170002597636286 34

Gresham, D., & Gullone, E. (2012). Emotion regulation strategy use in children and adolescents: The explanatory roles of personality and attachment. *Personality and Individual Differences*, 52(95), 116–621. 10.1016/j.paid.2011.12.016

Hair, J. F.Jr, Hult, G. T. M., Ringle, C. M., & Sarstedt, M. (2022). *A primer on partial least squares structural equation modeling (PLS-SEM)* (3rd ed.). SAGE.

Ivcevic, Z., & Hoffmann, J. (2019). Emotions and creativity: From process to person and product. In Kaufman, J. C., & Sternberg, R. J. (Eds.), *The Cambridge handbook of creativity* (pp. 273–295). Cambridge University Press. 10.1017/9781316979839.015

Joormann, J., & Gotlib, I. H. (2010). Emotion regulation in depression: Relation to cognitive inhibition. *Cognition and Emotion*, 24(2), 281–298. 10.1080/026999 30903407948203005 38

Jordan, P. J., Ashkanasy, N. M., & Hartel, C. E. J. (2002). Emotional intelligence as a moderator of emotional and behavioral reactions to job insecurity. *Academy of Management Review*, 27(3), 361–372. 10.2307/4134384

Kafetsios, K., & Sideridis, G. D. (2006). Attachment, social support and well-being in young and older adults. *Journal of Health Psychology*, 11(6), 863–875. 10.117 7/1359105306069084 17035259

Koole, S. L. (2009). The psychology of emotion regulation: An integrative review. *Cognition and Emotion*, 23(1), 4–41. 10.1080/02699930802619031

Mak, W. W., Law, R. W., Woo, J., Cheung, F. M., & Lee, D. (2009). Social support and psychological adjustment to SARS: The mediating role of self-care self-efficacy. *Psychology & Health*, 24(2), 161–174. 10.1080/08870440701447649 20186649

Mao, Z., Qin, T., Fan, L., Li, N., & Wang, Y. (2023). Factors associated with psychological distress among college students under COVID-19 pandemic: The moderating role of coping styles and social support. *Current Psychology (New Brunswick, N.J.)*, •••, 1–16.36713621

Masry-Herzallah, A. (2023). Factors promoting and inhibiting teachers' perception of success in online teaching during the Covid-19 crisis. *Technology. Knowledge and Learning*, 28(4), 1635–1659. 10.1007/s10758-023-09690-6

Masuda, A., Anderson, P. L., Wendell, J. W., Chou, Y.-Y., Price, M., & Feinstein, A. B. (2011). Psychological flexibility mediates the relations between self-concealment and negative psychological outcomes. *Personality and Individual Differences*, 50(2), 243–247. 10.1016/j.paid.2010.09.037

Mohan, R., Manvender Kaur, S. S., Arumugam, R., Hisham, D., & Yahya, D. (2021). Covid-19 catastrophe: Internet based learning and safety among foundation students of Universiti Utara Malaysia. *Journal of Language and Linguistic Studies*, 17(4), 2142–2153. 10.52462/jlls.155

Muniroh, H., Siti Balqis, M., Ch'ng, P.E. (2020). Adaptasi pengajaran dan pembelajaran secara maya dalam kebiasaan baharu semasa pandemik COVID-19. *SIG: e-Learning@CS*, 23-30.

Neff, K. D. (2003). Self-compassion: An alternative conceptualization of a healthy attitude toward oneself. *Self and Identity*, 2(2), 85–101. 10.1080/15298860309032

Ohei, K. N. (2023). Using ICT tools and technological applications in this Era of the COVID-19 pandemic to facilitate learning. *HOLISTICA–Journal of Business and Public Administration*, 14(2), 116–136. 10.2478/hjbpa-2023-0019

Pramono, D. N., & Prabawati, C. Y. (2021). *Hubungan regulasi emosi dengan tingkat stres mahasiswa yang melakukan study from home selama pandemi Covid-19 di Indonesia* [Doctoral Dissertation, Universitas Muhammadiyah Surakarta]. https://eprints.ums.ac.id/id/eprint/91599

Pratisti, W. D. (2013). Peran orangtua dalam perkembangan kemampuan regulasi emosi anak: Model. *Seminar Nasional Psikologi,* 322-333.

Purba, J., Yulianto, A., Widyanti, E., Esa, D. F. P. U. I., & Esa, M. F. P. U. I. (2007). Pengaruh dukungan sosial terhadap burnout pada guru. *Jurnal Psikologi*, 5(1), 77–87.

Purnamaningsih, E. H. (2017). Personality and emotion regulation strategies. *International Journal of Psychological Research*, 10(1), 53–60. 10.21500/20112084.2040

Rahayu, D. P., & Fauziah, N. (2019). Hubungan antara regulasi emosi dengan burnout pada Perawat Rawat Inap Rumah Sakit Jiwa Daerah (Rsjd) Dr Amino Gondohutomo Semarang. *Jurnal Empati*, 8(2), 354–360. 10.14710/empati.2019.24398

Rahmawati, S., & Indriayu, M. (2017). Pengaruh tekanan akademik terhadap prestasi akademik mahasiswa pendidikan ekonomi fakultas keguruan dan ilmu pendidikan Universitas Sebelas Maret. *Jurnal Pendidikan Bisnis Dan Ekonomi*, 3(2), 1–15. 10.20961/bise.v3i2.16450

Rozanki, A., & Kubzansky, L. D. (2005). Psychologic functioning and physical health: A paradigm of flexibility. *Psychosomatic Medicine*, 67(1), 47–53. 10.1097/01.psy.0000164253.69550.4915953801

Salimi, N., Gere, B., Talley, W., & Irioogbe, B. (2023). College students mental health challenges: Concerns and considerations in the COVID-19 pandemic. *Journal of College Student Psychotherapy*, 37(1), 39–51. 10.1080/87568225.2021.1890298

Sari, M. D. I., & Hayati, E. N. (2015). Regulasi emosi pada penderita HIV/AIDS. *Empathy*, 3(1), 23–30. 10.12928/empathy.v3i1.3011

Shazarina, Z.A., Suziana Hanini, S., Suhana, M.L., Norshilawani, S., Natasha, A., Mohamad Fuad, I., & Sapie, S. (2020). Tekanan emosi pensyarah dalam melaksanakan pengajaran dan pembelajaran atas talian di era pandemik covid-19. *Seminar Antarabangsa Isu-Isu Pendidikan (ISPEN2020) Kolej Universiti Islam Antarabangsa Selangor (KUIS).* IEEE.l

Sidi, Y., Shamir-Inbal, T., & Eshet-Alkalai, Y. (2023). From face-to-face to online: Teachers' perceived experiences in online distance teaching during the Covid-19 pandemic. *Computers & Education*, 201, 104831. 10.1016/j.compedu.2023.10483137193045

Vienlentia, R. (2021). Peran dukungan sosial keluarga terhadap regulasi emosi anak dalam belajar. *Satya Sastraharing: Jurnal Manajemen*, 5(2), 35–46. 10.33363/satya-sastraharing.v5i2.775

Windhiyana, E. (2020). Dampak COVID-19 terhadap kegiatan pembelajaran online di sebuah perguruan tinggi kristen di Indonesia. *Perspektif Ilmu Pendidikan*, 34(1), 1–8. 10.21009/PIP.341.1

Winnaiseh, L. (2017). *Hubungan regulasi emosi dengan emotional abuse pada remaja akhir yang berpacaran. Doctoral dissertation*. University of Muhammadiyah., http://eprints.umm.ac.id/43797/1/jiptummpp-gdl- leniwinnai- 49754-1-hubungan-n.pdf

Xia, L. X., Gao, X., Wang, Q., & Hollon, S. D. (2014). The relations between interpersonal self-support traits and emotion regulation strategies: A longitudinal study. *Journal of Adolescence*, 37(6), 779–786. 10.1016/j.adolescence.2014.05.00725086455

Xia, L. X., Xu, X. Y., Hollon, S. D., & Zhang, J.-F. (2014). The relation of self-supporting personality, big five personality and depression. *Current Psychology (New Brunswick, N.J.)*, 33(4), 630–643. 10.1007/s12144-014-9233-6

Zahara, M., Martina, M., & Alfandi, R. (2022). Hubungan Regulasi emosi dengan stres akademik pada mahasiswa Universitas Syiah Kuala. *Jurnal Ilmiah Mahasiswa Fakultas Keperawatan, 6*(1), 55-63.

Zhooriyati, S. M. (2021). Memahami tekanan perasaan dalam kalangan pelajar. Berita Harian. https://www.bharian.com.my/berita/pendidikan/2021/08/849398/memahami-tekanan-perasaan-dalam-kalangan-pelajar

Zimet, G. D., Dahlem, N. W., Zimet, S. G., & Farley, G. K. (1988). The multidimensional scale of perceived social support. *Journal of Personality Assessment*, 52(1), 30–41. 10.1207/s15327752jpa5201_22280326

# Chapter 11
# Concept of Instructional Coaching for Professional Teacher Development in Post-Pandemic Epoch

**Semiu Olawale Makinde**
*A-Hikmah University, Ilorin, Nigeria*

**Rasidat Sade Ganiyu**
*Emmanuel Alayande University of Education, Oyo, Nigeria*

## ABSTRACT

*This chapter explores the essential concept of instructional coaching as a dynamic approach to enhance student learning outcomes by promoting teacher competence and efficiency in the classroom. The investigation provides a thorough understanding of instructional coaching, covering its nature, various modes and approaches. Additionally, the chapter highlights key skills associated with instructional coaches in the distinct context of the post-pandemic era. By examining historical perspectives, it traces the evolution of instructional coaching, offering insights into its development over time. Moreover, the chapter critically assesses the impact of instructional coaching during the pandemic and underscores its enduring relevance in the post-pandemic period. In addressing challenges and opportunities in instructional coaching for professional teacher development, the chapter particularly focuses on lessons gleaned from the pandemic experiences. This comprehensive analysis contributes to the ongoing discourse about technology-infused education in the post-pandemic era.*

DOI: 10.4018/979-8-3693-7645-4.ch011

## INTRODUCTION

Over time, there have been significant changes in how schools prepare and support teachers as educational practices evolve (Bamrungsin & Khampirat, 2022). With various crises such as adapting to COVID-19 and coping with educator shortages, schools are compelled to adjust significantly to ensure effective instruction (Carver-Thomas, Kini & Burns, 2020). In 2020, the pandemic led teachers nationwide to modify their instructional approaches, especially with the shift to remote and hybrid learning models (Dos Santos, 2021). Even upon returning to in-person classes, new measures like mask mandates and social distancing require teachers to manage health risks differently (Robinson et al., 2024; Zamarro et al., 2022). Amid these changes, the demand for effective instructional coaching to enhance teacher retention becomes crucial for student and school success during the pandemic. From implementing health protocols to adapting teaching methods for diverse student needs, educators face increasing demands amidst growing teacher shortages (Carver-Thomas, Kini & Burns, 2020).

In the wake of unprecedented challenges, the concept of instructional coaching has emerged as a beacon of hope for professional teacher development in the post-pandemic epoch. Instructional coaching offers a dynamic framework that empowers educators to adapt, innovate, and thrive amidst uncertainty (Barnes, 2023). Hence, due to the changes brought about by the pandemic, instructional coaching stands as a strategic framework, offering support and guidance to educators seeking to refine their teaching practices and adapt to the evolving needs of the educational environment. To facilitate successful teaching and learning experiences, educators need to be furnished with the essential instructional materials and support that can enhance effective lesson delivery within the classroom setting. Achieving this is possible through instructional coaching. Instructional coaching constitutes a form of professional development wherein an instructional coach offers guidance and assistance to teachers, aiming to enhance their instructional methods that usually leads to effective performance of learners in this technological age (Rowe, 2022).

The primary objective of instructional coaching is to enhance student learning results by aiding teachers in enhancing their competence and efficiency within the classroom (Main, 2022). By prioritizing efforts to promote the concept of instructional coaching having observed the influence of it on professional development of teachers, it is essential to cxplorc the significance and application of instructional coaching in shaping resilient and effective teachers in the post-pandemic epoch. This chapter addressed the following crucial aspect of instructional coaching in the context of post pandemic epoch:

i. Meaning and nature of instructional coaching;
ii. Modes, approaches and types of instructional coaching;

iii. Skills associated with instructional coach in post pandemic era;
iv. The historical background of instructional coaching;
v. Influence of instructional coaching during the pandemic and post pandemic era; and
vi. Challenges and prospects of instructional coaching in professional teacher development with Covid-19 pandemic experience

## Conceptual Clarifications

**Instructional Coaching:** Instructional coaching refers to a collaborative, ongoing process between a coach and a teacher aimed at improving teaching practices and student learning outcomes. It involves personalized support, feedback, and guidance provided to teachers to enhance their instructional strategies, classroom management techniques, and overall professional development. The role of an instructional coach can have an impact on instructional practices if utilizing the requisite knowledge, skills, and dispositions of a successful instructional coach (Blaushild et al., 2024).

**Professional Teacher Development:** Professional teacher development encompasses the continuous growth and improvement of educators' knowledge, skills, and practices. It involves various activities such as workshops, seminars, courses, and mentoring programs designed to enhance teachers' effectiveness in delivering instruction, managing classrooms, and meeting the diverse needs of students (Iqbal & Ali, 2024). Exposing teachers to professional development programmes would enhance their capacity to develop new skills, methodologies and best practices in ensuring quality in the teaching and learning processes (Onyekwelu, 2024).

**Post-Pandemic Epoch:** The post-pandemic epoch refers to the period following a significant global health crisis, such as the COVID-19 pandemic (Alirezabeigi, 2023). In this context, it signifies the time after the pandemic when educational institutions are transitioning from emergency remote teaching to more sustainable models of teaching and learning. It involves addressing the challenges and opportunities that emerged during the pandemic and adapting educational practices to a new normal (Pham, 2023).

.**Teacher Support:** Teacher support involves providing educators with the resources, guidance, and assistance they need to effectively fulfill their roles in the classroom (Atobatele, Kpodo, & Eke, 2024). This support can take various forms, including professional development opportunities, access to instructional materials and technology, mentoring, coaching, and collaboration with colleagues (Iqbal & Ali, 2024).

**Professional Growth:** Professional growth refers to the continuous improvement and advancement of teachers' skills, knowledge, and practices throughout their careers (Smith & Gillespie, 2023). It involves reflecting on one's teaching experiences, seeking out learning opportunities, receiving feedback, and engaging in ongoing professional development activities to enhance teaching effectiveness and student learning outcomes (Karlberg & Bezzina, 2022).

## LITERATURE REVIEW

### The Impact of Educational Crises on Teacher Support and Adaptation

Educational crises, such as the COVID-19 pandemic, have significantly disrupted traditional schooling systems worldwide. These crises have imposed unprecedented challenges on educators, requiring rapid adaptation to new teaching modalities and environments. During educational crises, the need for teacher support becomes paramount as educators navigate unfamiliar territory and face increased workloads and stressors. Research by Carver-Thomas, Kini, and Burns (2020) highlighted how educational crises, like the COVID-19 pandemic, have compelled schools to adjust significantly to ensure effective instruction. Teachers have had to rapidly transition to remote and hybrid learning models, requiring extensive support in technology integration, pedagogical strategies, and emotional well-being.

Moreover, the shift to online instruction has magnified existing disparities in access to resources and professional development opportunities among educators. Bamrungsin and Khampirat (2022) emphasized the importance of equitable teacher support systems, particularly for those from marginalized communities or with limited technological proficiency. Without adequate support, educators may struggle to effectively engage students in remote learning environments, exacerbating educational inequalities.

Educational crises necessitate rapid adaptation strategies for educators to maintain instructional quality and student engagement. Miguel et al. (2021) noted that teachers nationwide modified their instructional approaches during the COVID-19 pandemic, utilizing innovative methods to deliver content remotely. However, adapting teaching practices to online platforms requires ongoing professional development and collaboration with peers. Instructional coaching has emerged as a promising approach to support educators in navigating educational crises and refining their teaching practices. Edwards (2023) argues that instructional coaching offers a dynamic framework that empowers educators to adapt, innovate, and thrive amidst uncertainty. By providing personalized guidance and feedback, instructional coaches help teachers enhance their pedagogical skills and confidence in delivering online instruction.

Furthermore, teacher adaptation extends beyond technological proficiency to encompass socio-emotional support for students amidst crisis-related disruptions. Robinson et al. (2023) highlighted the importance of educators managing health risks differently, such as implementing mask mandates and social distancing measures in classrooms. Teachers play a critical role in supporting students' mental health and well-being during periods of uncertainty and upheaval.

## Adapting to the Shift Towards Online Learning in a Post-Pandemic Era

The issue of school scheduling has gained significant attention, particularly due to the widespread transition to fully online and distance learning practices during the pandemic across much of the world (Williamson, Eynon, & Potter, 2020). With the shift to online education, the traditional boundaries of school time and space, typically defined by the physical classroom, have been blurred. This has resulted in a merging of family, leisure, and school time within the home environment. In response to this unprecedented situation, several European, African, and Asian countries have taken steps to accelerate the digital transformation of schools. Initiatives such as Digisprong in Flanders and Digitalpakt in Germany, along with the allocation of COVID recovery funds directly to schools, aim to promote digital innovation within educational settings. These policies place the onus on schools to embrace digital advancements by investing in digital devices, establishing digital infrastructure, and adopting online learning platforms and management systems (Alirezabeigi, 2023).

However, these initiatives not only empower global educational technology (Ed-Tech) companies but also reshape daily classroom practices and the overall organization of school activities (Grek & Landri, 2021). As highlighted by Rapanta et al. (2021), the transition to post-pandemic educational practices will unfold differently from the emergency measures implemented during the pandemic. The challenges schools face in this post-pandemic landscape represent a gradual transition rather than a sudden and temporary shift. Therefore, schools must navigate this ongoing transition and adapt to the evolving educational landscape beyond the immediate crisis. For this to be materialize more effort need to be directed to instructional coaching. Instructional coach has a vital role to play in navigating the transition.

## The Emergence of Instructional Coaching as a Response to Educational Challenges

In recent years, instructional coaching has gained prominence as a strategic response to the evolving landscape of educational challenges. Instructional coaching traces its roots back to the early 20$^{th}$ century, with the emergence of coaching models aimed at enhancing teacher effectiveness and student learning outcomes. Initially developed within the context of sports coaching, the concept gradually transitioned to educational settings, where it gained recognition for its potential to support teacher growth and development (Knight, 2007). Instructional coaching is a form of professional development that involves a collaborative partnership between an instructional coach and a teacher. According to Knight (2019), instructional coaching focuses on improving teaching practices and student learning outcomes through ongoing support, feedback, and reflective dialogue. Unlike traditional professional development models, instructional coaching emphasizes personalized, job-embedded support tailored to individual teacher needs and goals.

Instructional coaching encompasses various modes and approaches tailored to meet the diverse needs of educators and schools. These include one-on-one coaching, small group coaching, peer coaching, and virtual coaching, among others (Hui, Khemanuwong & Ismail, 2020). The choice of coaching approach depends on factors such as school culture, teacher preferences, and available resources.

Research consistently demonstrates the positive impact of instructional coaching on teacher practice and student learning outcomes. A meta-analysis by Kraft, Blazar, and Hogan (2018) found that teachers who participated in coaching programs exhibited significant improvements in instructional practices, student engagement, and academic achievement. Moreover, instructional coaching has been linked to increased teacher job satisfaction, retention rates, and overall school improvement efforts (R Richards, Washburn & Hemphill, 2019).

While instructional coaching holds promise as a powerful professional development tool, several challenges remain, including issues related to sustainability, scalability, and equity (Foltos, 2013). Furthermore, the COVID-19 pandemic has introduced new complexities, such as the need for virtual coaching models and addressing educators' socio-emotional well-being amidst crisis-related stressors (Arrington, 2021). Moving forward, research and practice must continue to explore innovative approaches to instructional coaching that address these challenges while promoting equitable access and outcomes for all educators.

## The Role of Instructional Coaching in Empowering Educators amidst Uncertainty

Educators worldwide are facing unprecedented uncertainty and challenges, particularly in the wake of events such as the COVID-19 pandemic. Hence, educators are confronted with rapidly evolving educational landscapes, including shifts to remote and hybrid learning, changes in teaching modalities, and socio-emotional stressors. This uncertainty can undermine educators' confidence, effectiveness, and job satisfaction (Kutsyuruba & Godden, 2019). Instructional coaching offers a collaborative and personalized approach to support educators in navigating these challenges and achieving their professional goals. According to Knight (2007) coaches work closely with educators to identify areas for growth, set goals, and implement evidence-based instructional practices. Through observation, feedback, and modeling, coaches empower educators to refine their teaching strategies and enhance student engagement and achievement.

Research indicates that instructional coaching can have a profound impact on educator empowerment amidst uncertainty. A study by Kraft, Blazar, and Hogan (2018) found that teachers who participated in coaching programs reported increased confidence, job satisfaction, and instructional effectiveness. Moreover, coaching has been linked to improvements in teacher retention rates, school climate, and student outcomes (Foltos, 2013). By providing ongoing support and encouragement, instructional coaches empower educators to navigate challenges, embrace change, and thrive in their professional roles. In addition to enhancing instructional practices, instructional coaching plays a crucial role in addressing educators' socio-emotional needs amidst uncertainty. Coaches provide a safe and supportive space for educators to express concerns, seek guidance, and develop resilience (Kutsyuruba & Godden, 2019). By fostering a culture of collaboration and trust, instructional coaching promotes educator well-being and contributes to a positive school climate.

## Enhancing Teacher Competence and Student Learning Outcomes Through Instructional Coaching

Instructional coaching encompasses several key concepts that are essential for its effectiveness in supporting teachers' professional growth, competence and improving student learning outcomes. Some of these are:

i. *Trust and rapport:* Building trust and rapport is fundamental to effective instructional coaching, as it fosters a supportive and collaborative relationship between the coach and the teacher (Kraft, Blazar, & Hogan, 2018). Research emphasizes the importance of trust in coaching relationships, highlighting its role in promoting openness, risk-taking, and constructive feedback (Pounder, Carter & Secada, 2020).

ii. *Setting goals:* Setting clear and achievable goals is essential for guiding the coaching process and focusing on areas for teacher improvement (Knight, 2018). According to recent studies, goal-setting in coaching helps align teacher practice with instructional priorities and supports professional growth (Beck et al., 2021).

iii. *Modeling effective teaching practices*: Modeling effective teaching practices allows coaches to demonstrate evidence-based strategies and techniques to teachers (Joyce & Showers, 2021). Recent research underscores the value of modeling as an instructional coaching approach that enhances teacher learning and implementation of new practices (Desimone et al., 2020).

iv. *Observing instruction*: Conducting observations of teachers' instruction provides coaches with valuable data to inform coaching conversations and provide targeted support (Holliday, 2021). Recent studies highlight the importance of observation in coaching for promoting reflective practice and improving instructional effectiveness (Mills & Smith, 2021).

v. *Providing feedback:* Delivering timely and constructive feedback is a critical aspect of instructional coaching that supports teacher growth and development (van Nuland et al., 2020). Recent research emphasizes the role of feedback in coaching for promoting teacher self-awareness, goal attainment, and instructional improvement (Yilmaz, 2021).

vi. *Facilitating professional learning communities (PLCs):* Creating and facilitating PLCs allows teachers to collaborate, share expertise, and engage in ongoing professional learning (Vescio, Ross & Adams, 2021). Recent studies highlight the benefits of PLCs in coaching for promoting collective efficacy, peer support, and collaborative problem-solving (Liu et al., 2020).

By integrating these key concepts into instructional coaching practices, coaches can effectively support teacher growth and enhance instructional quality in schools.

According to various researchers, the role of instructional coaching in enhancing teacher effectiveness and its impact on student achievement cannot be overemphasized. This can be done in various ways such as:

- *Improving Teacher Competence through Coaching:* Instructional coaching focuses on providing personalized support and professional development opportunities tailored to individual teacher needs (Knight, 2007). Coaches collaborate with educators to identify areas for growth, set goals, and implement evidence-based instructional practices Holliday, 2021). By offering ongoing feedback, modeling effective teaching strategies, and facilitating reflective dialogue, instructional coaches empower teachers to refine their instructional practices and enhance their competence in delivering high-quality instruction.
- *Impact on Student Learning Outcomes:* Research consistently demonstrates the positive impact of instructional coaching on student learning outcomes. A mcta-analysis conducted by Kraft, Blazar, and Hogan (2018) found that teachers who participated in coaching programs exhibited significant improvements in student achievement, particularly in literacy and mathematics. Moreover, coaching has been associated with increased student engagement, higher graduation rates, and reduced achievement gaps (Lofthouse, 2019). By

supporting teacher growth and development, instructional coaching contributes to a positive school climate and promotes academic success for all students.

- *Addressing Diverse Student Needs:* Instructional coaching plays a crucial role in supporting educators in meeting the diverse needs of their students. Coaches collaborate with teachers to implement differentiated instruction, develop inclusive practices, and utilize culturally responsive teaching strategies (Holliday, 2021). By fostering a culture of collaboration and continuous improvement, instructional coaching helps educators create learning environments that are equitable, engaging, and supportive of all students' academic and socio-emotional development.
- *Challenges and Future Directions:* While instructional coaching offers significant benefits for teacher competence and student learning outcomes, several challenges remain. These include issues related to sustainability, scalability, and equitable access to coaching resources (Foltos, 2013). Additionally, the COVID-19 pandemic has brought forth new challenges, including the requirement for virtual coaching approaches and the necessity to support educators' emotional wellness in the face of stressors linked to the crisis (Myers & Washburn, 2022). Looking ahead, it is crucial for both research and practice to explore inventive methods in instructional coaching that tackle these hurdles while ensuring fair access and results for every student.

## MAIN CONTENT

### Meaning and Nature of Instructional Coaching

Instructional coaching encompasses a collaborative and personalized approach to professional development aimed at improving teaching practices and enhancing student learning outcomes. In many educational settings, school administrators are opting for or mandated to introduce instructional coaching as a means to enhance student learning experiences especially during pandemic. It's crucial for the school community to recognize that effective instructional coaching is deeply embedded in the job, promotes teachers' reflective practice, and demands dedicated time for implementation. To support instructional coaches adequately, school administrators must ensure significant time allocation for coaches to observe classrooms, provide constructive feedback, and assist teachers in their practice and reflection.

Building trust and rapport with instructional staff, instructional coaches employ best-practice protocols, offer feedback, and collaboratively plan the next steps. For successful implementation, instructional staff should be open to receiving feedback, embracing best practices, and engaging in reflective processes. Introducing instructional coaching in a school necessitates active engagement from school administrators, encouraging collaboration with all stakeholders and acknowledging diverse perspectives throughout the process. It is crucial to underscore the significance of the instructional process and student success when integrating instructional coaching into a school environment (Tanner et al. 2017).

Effective instructional coaching relies on several key components, which include:

1. *Clear Focus:* The coaching process should have a well-defined focus or objective, whether it's enhancing a specific teaching strategy or improving student outcomes.
2. *Building Trusting Connections:* Fostering a constructive and trustworthy bond between the coach and teacher is essential, encouraging clear communication and authentic feedback.
3. *Consistent Collaboration:* Scheduling frequent meetings between the coach and teacher is pivotal for assessing progress, addressing obstacles, and planning forthcoming actions.
4. *Providing Specific Resources*: The coach should supply the teacher with relevant resources, such as instructional materials or chances for professional growth.
5. *Decision Making Based on Data: It* is essential to recognize that instructional coaching does not follow a uniform approach for everyone.

At its core, according to Knight (2019), instructional coaching is guided by several key principles:

- *Collaboration.* Instructional coaching emphasizes collaborative partnerships between coaches and teachers. It fosters mutual respect, trust, and open communication, creating a supportive environment conducive to growth and learning.
- *Reflection.* Central to instructional coaching is the practice of reflective teaching. Coaches encourage teachers to reflect critically on their instructional strategies, classroom practices, and student outcomes. Through guided reflection, educators identify areas for improvement and develop action plans for implementation.
- *Data-Informed Decision Making.* Instructional coaching relies on data to inform decision-making and drive instructional improvement. Coaches help teachers analyze student performance data, classroom observations, and other evidence to identify patterns, trends, and areas of need. Data-driven insights guide the development of targeted interventions and instructional strategies.
- *Differentiation.* Recognizing that teachers have diverse needs and contexts, instructional coaching embraces a differentiated approach. Coaches tailor support and feedback to meet the specific goals, preferences, and professional

growth areas of individual teachers. This personalized approach ensures relevance and effectiveness in the coaching process.

- *Continuous Improvement.* Instructional coaching is characterized by a commitment to continuous improvement. Coaches and teachers engage in ongoing cycles of goal-setting, action planning, implementation, and reflection. This iterative process promotes incremental growth and fosters a culture of lifelong learning within the educational community.

In essence, instructional coaching is defined as a collaborative and reflective process whereby a skilled coach partners with teachers to support their professional growth, enhance instructional practices, and ultimately, improve student achievement. It operates on the principles of collaboration, reflection, data-informed decision making, differentiation, and continuous improvement, with the overarching goal of empowering teachers to achieve excellence in their practice.

In the post-pandemic era, the essence of instructional coaching becomes particularly crucial as educators and schools navigate the complexities and changes brought about by the global health crisis (Reddy et al., 2023). Understanding the key components of this collaborative professional development approach sets a robust foundation for its relevance in the current educational landscape:

- *Adaptability and Flexibility:* Instructional coaching is inherently adaptable, capable of flexing to meet the evolving needs of teachers and students. In the post-pandemic era, where educational norms have shifted, instructional coaching provides a flexible framework to address new challenges, incorporate technology, and adjust teaching strategies.
- *Tailored Support and Differentiation:* The personalized nature of instructional coaching allows for tailored support that considers the unique strengths, weaknesses, and goals of each teacher. Post-pandemic, where teaching experiences may vary widely, instructional coaching ensures that support is tailored to individual contexts, acknowledging the diverse needs arising from varied teaching environments.
- *Technology Integration:* Instructional coaching has the capacity to incorporate technology into professional development strategies. In the post-pandemic era, where technology has become integral to education, instructional coaching can guide teachers in effectively integrating digital tools, fostering digital literacy, and enhancing virtual or hybrid teaching practices.
- *Building Resilience and Addressing Well-Being:* Instructional coaching is not solely focused on pedagogy; it recognizes the importance of teacher well-being and resilience. Post-pandemic, educators may face increased stress and burnout. Instructional coaching can play a vital role in supporting teachers emotionally,

fostering resilience, and promoting strategies for maintaining a healthy work-life balance (Lewis, Popov & Fatima, 2024).

- *Continuous Improvement and Future Readiness:* Instructional coaching is centered on the philosophy of continuous improvement and lifelong learning. In the post-pandemic era, where educational systems are re-evaluating and reforming, instructional coaching becomes a driving force for helping teachers adapt, learn, and remain future-ready in an ever-changing educational landscape (Tharapos et al., 2023).
- *Collaborative Problem-Solving:* Instructional coaching encourages collaborative problem-solving and a culture of shared responsibility. Post-pandemic challenges often require collective efforts. Instructional coaching facilitates collaboration among educators, fostering a supportive community that can collectively address emerging issues.

Understanding these fundamental aspects of instructional coaching establishes its relevance as a dynamic and adaptable tool for professional development in the post-pandemic era. By acknowledging the essence of collaboration, personalization, and continuous improvement, instructional coaching becomes an invaluable resource for educators striving to navigate and excel in the evolving educational landscape.

## Models, Approaches, and Types of Instructional Coaching

There are numerous types of instructional coaching which coaches can adopt for effective coach of the teachers. Literature review reveals various models and approaches that educators and institutions employ to enhance teaching practices and improve student outcomes.

### Models and Approaches of Instructional Coaching

The models and approaches of instructional coaching are as listed below:

- *Traditional Instructional Coaching Models:* Traditional models typically involve one-on-one coaching sessions between a coach and a teacher. These sessions focus on setting goals, implementing instructional strategies, and reflecting on teaching practice. Research suggests that traditional instructional coaching models are effective in promoting teacher growth and improving instructional quality (Kraft, Blazar & Hogan, 2018).
- *Peer Coaching:* Peer coaching involves teachers collaborating with colleagues to provide feedback, share resources, and support each other's professional development. Studies indicate that peer coaching can foster a collaborative

culture, promote teacher autonomy, and facilitate the exchange of best practices (Kretlow & Bartholomew, 2010).

- *Content-Specific Coaching:* Content-specific coaching focuses on improving teaching practices in specific subject areas or content areas. Research shows that content-specific coaching can lead to significant improvements in content knowledge, pedagogical skills, and student achievement in targeted subject areas (Yoon et al., 2007).
- *Technology-Integrated Coaching:* Technology-integrated coaching leverages digital tools and platforms to support teacher development and enhance instructional practices. Literature suggests that technology-integrated coaching can increase teacher engagement, facilitate virtual collaboration, and provide access to resources and professional learning communities (Desimone et al., 2019).
- *Instructional Leadership Coaching:* Instructional leadership coaching focuses on developing leadership skills among teachers and administrators to promote instructional improvement at the school or district level. Studies indicate that instructional leadership coaching can lead to positive changes in school culture, instructional leadership practices, and student achievement outcomes (Knight, 2011a).
- *Data-Driven Coaching:* Data-driven coaching involves using student data, assessment results, and other evidence to inform coaching interactions and instructional decision-making. Research suggests that data-driven coaching can help teachers identify areas for improvement, set measurable goals, and track progress over time (Bambrick-Santoyo, 2010).
- *Hybrid Coaching Models:* Hybrid coaching models blend components from various coaching approaches to accommodate the diverse requirements of educators and schools. Research emphasizes the significance of adaptability and tailoring in coaching frameworks to cater to different contexts, preferences, and objectives (Denton & Hasbrouck, 2009).

Overall, the literature underscores the importance of selecting and adapting instructional coaching models based on specific contexts, goals, and needs. Effective coaching requires ongoing support, collaboration, and a commitment to continuous improvement to maximize its impact on teaching and learning outcomes.

For effective communication in instructional coaching, three component parts must involve that form the learning triangle. The Learning Triangle in instructional coaching represents a collaborative model that integrates the efforts of coaches, teachers, and students to enhance teaching practices and student learning outcomes.

- Coaches: Instructional coaching literature emphasizes the role of coaches as facilitators of professional growth and reflective practice among teachers. Authors like Jim Knight, in works such as Instructional Coaching: A Partnership Approach to Improving Instruction (2007), underscore the importance of coaches in providing support, feedback, and resources to empower teachers.
- Teachers: Teachers are central to the instructional coaching process, actively engaging in collaborative dialogue, goal-setting, and reflective practices. Research by Diane Yendol-Hoppey and Nancy Fichtman Dana, as presented in "The Reflective Educator's Guide to Classroom Research: Learning to Teach and Teaching to Learn through Practitioner Inquiry" (2009), emphasizes the significance of teachers' reflective practices and their role in driving instructional improvement.
- Students: The ultimate goal of instructional coaching is to improve student learning outcomes. Works by Charlotte Danielson, such as "Enhancing Professional Practice: A Framework for Teaching" (2007), highlight the importance of student-centered teaching practices and the impact they have on student achievement.

The Learning Triangle principles resonate throughout the educational research on instructional coaching, collaborative learning, and student-centered instruction. The concept emphasizes the interconnectedness of coaches, teachers, and students in a dynamic process of professional growth and instructional improvement.

## Types of Instructional Coaching

Instructional coaching is of different types that are very essential for teachers and educators. Each type has specific role to play in professional teacher development.

These are: (a) cognitive coaching;
(b) content-focused coaching;
(c) technology integration coaching;
(d) peer coaching;
(e) literacy coaching;
(f) instructional leadership coaching;
(g) data coaching;
(h) peer observation and feedback coaching;
(i) transformational coaching; and
(j) reflective coaching.

- *Cognitive Coaching.* Cognitive coaching focuses on enhancing teachers' thinking and problem-solving skills. It aims to promote self-directed learning and reflective practices, helping educators refine their instructional strategies through dialogue and questioning techniques.
- *Content-focused Coaching:* This type of coaching centers on specific subject matter or academic content. Content-focused coaches work closely with teachers to deepen their understanding of the curriculum, implement effective instructional methods, and integrate subject-specific pedagogy.
- *Technology Integration Coaching:* With the increasing importance of technology in education, technology integration coaching supports educators in effectively using digital tools, applications, and online resources. Coaches help teachers integrate technology seamlessly into their lessons, enhancing engagement and learning outcomes.
- *Peer Coaching:* Peer coaching involves teachers collaborating with their peers to provide feedback, share insights, and improve instructional practices collectively. This collaborative approach fosters a supportive environment for professional growth.
- *Literacy Coaching:* Focused on improving literacy skills, literacy coaching assists teachers in developing effective reading and writing instruction. Coaches may work on strategies for differentiated instruction, literacy assessments, and fostering a literacy-rich classroom environment.
- *Instructional Leadership Coaching:* This coaching type extends beyond individual teacher development to support school leaders in their role as instructional leaders. Instructional leadership coaches assist principals and administrators in creating a school culture that prioritizes effective teaching and learning.
- *Data Coaching:* Data coaching revolves around using data-driven insights to inform teaching practices. Coach help educators analyze assessment data, identify trends, and adjust instructional strategies accordingly to improve student achievement.
- *Peer Observation and Feedback Coaching:* This coaching model involves peer observation of classroom practices, followed by constructive feedback. It promotes a culture of openness and collaboration, encouraging teachers to learn from one another.
- *Transformational Coaching:* Transformational coaching goes beyond specific teaching practices and focuses on empowering teachers to become leaders, change agents, and reflective practitioners. It aims to inspire a mindset shift and transformative change in teaching approaches.

- *Reflective Coaching:* Reflective coaching emphasizes self-reflection and introspection. Coaches guide teachers in analyzing their teaching methods, identifying strengths and weaknesses, and developing strategies for continuous improvement.

## The Skills Associated With Instructional Coaching in Post Pandemic Era

In the post-pandemic era, instructional coaches need a specific set of skills to navigate the evolving educational landscape and effectively support teachers in adapting to new challenges. The followings are key skills associated with instructional coaches in the post-pandemic era:

- *Technology Integration:* Proficiency in integrating technology tools and platforms into teaching practices encourages effective support needed by the teacher. Instructional coaches need to be proficient in various educational technologies and digital tools used for virtual teaching, learning management, and communication. They should be able to guide teachers in effectively integrating technology into their instructional practices.
- *Digital Literacy:* The ability to assess and enhance teachers' digital literacy skills give the needed support to educators in developing the necessary digital literacy competencies to navigate online resources, engage with digital content, and foster digital citizenship in the classroom.
- *Remote Teaching Support:* Expertise in assisting teachers with effective strategies for remote or hybrid teaching. With the ongoing integration of remote learning, coaches should guide teachers in designing engaging virtual lessons, utilizing online resources, and maintaining student engagement in various learning environments.
- *Social-Emotional Support and Leadership Skills:* Capacity to provide social-emotional support to teachers dealing with increased stress and challenges is very essential for instructional coaches. The post-pandemic era has heightened the importance of supporting teachers' well-being. Given the emotional toll of the pandemic on educators and students, instructional coaches should possess strong social-emotional support skills. They should provide empathetic listening, foster resilience, and promote well-being among teachers and students. Coaches should possess strong interpersonal skills to address the emotional needs of educators. Instructional coaches often serve as informal leaders within their schools or districts. They should demonstrate leadership qualities such as vision, initiative, and the ability to inspire and motivate others.

They should also be skilled in influencing change and promoting a growth mindset among teachers and colleagues.

- *Adaptability and Flexibility:* This is the ability of the instructional coaches to adapt coaching strategies to changing educational contexts. The educational landscape is continually evolving. The ability to adapt to changing circumstances and navigate uncertainty is essential for instructional coaches in the post-pandemic era. They must be flexible in adjusting coaching approaches, strategies, and priorities to meet the evolving needs of teachers and students.
- *Cultural Competence and Equity Awareness:* Instructional coaches should possess cultural competence and awareness to support diverse teaching environments. The pandemic has highlighted the importance of understanding and respecting diverse cultural contexts. Coaches should be culturally competent to provide relevant and inclusive support. Instructional coaches must demonstrate cultural competence and sensitivity to diverse backgrounds, experiences, and perspectives. They should be mindful of educational equity concerns and champion inclusive strategies that cater to the needs of all students, especially those belonging to marginalized communities.
- *Analyzing Data and Decision-Making:* Competence in examining student data and employing it to guide instructional choices is crucial for instructional coaches in supporting teachers for successful teaching and learning. Data-driven decision-making is critical for identifying learning gaps, tracking student progress, and tailoring instructional strategies. Instructional coaches should be skilled in analyzing and interpreting student data, assessment results, and other evidence to inform instructional decision-making. They should help teachers use data effectively to identify student learning needs, set goals, and monitor progress.
- *Collaboration and Communication*: Strong collaboration and communication skills are essential skills needed by instructional coaches. Coaches should cultivate cooperative connections with educators, administrators, and other involved parties. Given the increasing prevalence of remote and hybrid learning, instructional coaches must demonstrate proficient virtual collaboration abilities. Effective communication and collaboration skills are essential for instructional coaches to establish trustful relationships with teachers, administrators, and other stakeholders. They should communicate clearly, listen actively, and collaborate effectively to promote a culture of continuous learning and improvement. They need to facilitate productive online meetings, provide virtual support and feedback, and foster a sense of community among teachers in digital environments. Clear communication is essential for conveying information, providing feedback, and building a supportive professional community.

- *Continuous Learning and Professional Development:* Commitment to continuous learning and staying updated on educational trends are part of the skills instructional coaches should exhibit for effective teaching practice. The educational landscape is dynamic, and coaches must stay informed about emerging practices, pedagogies, and technologies to provide relevant and effective support to teachers. Instructional coaches should model reflective practice and encourage teachers to engage in self-reflection and continuous improvement. They should provide structured opportunities for reflection, feedback, and goal-setting to support teacher growth and development.
- *Lastly, Resilience and Problem-Solving:* instructional coaches should have the ability of resilience and adept problem-solving skills. The post-pandemic era may present unforeseen challenges. Coaches need to be resilient and capable of collaboratively solving problems, adapting strategies, and navigating uncertainties. Instructional coaches should be adept at problem-solving and critical thinking. They should help teachers identify challenges (Fairman et al., 2023), brainstorm solutions, and implement innovative strategies to address instructional needs and improve student outcomes in the post-pandemic era of new normal.

In summary, instructional coaches in the post-pandemic era require a blend of technical, interpersonal, and leadership skills to effectively support teachers and promote student success in rapidly changing educational contexts.

## THE HISTORICAL BACKGROUND OF INSTRUCTIONAL COACHING

The evolution of instructional coaching is a dynamic narrative, tracing the development of educational practices and professional development strategies. Originating from diverse fields such as sports and business, its integration into education has seen significant milestones. Grounded in educational theories like constructivism and cognitive coaching, Donald Schön's (1983) introduction of reflective practice laid the foundation for coaching methods emphasizing self-reflection and inquiry. In the 1980s and 1990s, researchers such as Bruce Joyce and Beverly Showers (1980) explored coaching as a professional development tool, underlining the value of ongoing support and collaboration for teachers.

Art Costa and Robert Garmston's Cognitive Coaching model, introduced in the 1980s, significantly influenced the development of early coaching concepts. Art Costa and Robert Garmston (1994) further refined the model, concentrating on enhancing teachers' cognitive and metacognitive abilities through reflective conversations and questioning techniques. Jim Knight's influential work, particularly his book "Instructional Coaching: A Partnership Approach to Improving Instruction" (2007), emphasized collaborative partnerships, data-driven decision-making, and practice-based professional development. Research studies, including Holliday's (2021) and Knight and Cornett's (2009) impact study, provided empirical evidence supporting the positive effects of instructional coaching on teacher practice and student outcomes.

The historical background reveals the evolving nature of instructional coaching, guided by research, practice, and educators' changing needs. Knight's emphasis on collaboration, reflective practice, and continuous professional learning has left an indelible mark on instructional coaching practices. Empirical evidence from studies like Kraft, Blazar and Hogan (2018), meta-analysis and Yoon et al.'s (2007) research further underscores the effectiveness of instructional coaching in enhancing teaching practices and student achievement. As educational policies increasingly underscore the importance of effective professional development, instructional coaching has gained recognition as a promising strategy. Highlighted by the "What Works Clearinghouse" (Borman et al., 2003), coaching has become integral to educational policies and professional development initiatives, contributing to its widespread adoption in schools and districts.

The historical backdrop of instructional coaching is characterized by a gradual acknowledgment of the pivotal role of targeted support and collaboration in improving teaching practices. As instructional coaching continues to evolve, it remains rooted in the principles of collaboration, reflective practice, and ongoing professional learning, all aimed at improving teaching practices and enriching student learning outcomes.

## Influence of Instructional Coaching During the Pandemic and Post Pandemic Era

The role of instructional coaching has been particularly significant during the pandemic period and is poised to continue making substantial contributions beyond. In the face of unprecedented challenges to education, instructional coaching has proven to be a valuable resource, providing crucial support for educators as they navigate remote and hybrid learning environments. The contributions of instructional coaching during this time have been multifaceted and impactful, providing tailored support, fostering resilience, and promoting effective teaching practices. Several relevant references illustrate the significance of instructional coaching in navigating the complexities of education during and after the pandemic as illustrated below:

- *Tailored Support and Professional Development:* Instructional coaching offers personalized support to educators, helping them adapt their teaching strategies to remote, hybrid, or blended learning environments (Kraft, Simon & Lyon, 2020). Coaches collaborate with teachers to develop new skills, integrate technology effectively, and address the diverse needs of students in virtual or socially distanced settings (Dunekack, 2020).

- *Promoting Social-Emotional Well-being:* The pandemic has heightened the importance of supporting educators' social-emotional well-being. Instructional coaches provide a supportive and empathetic space for teachers to process challenges, manage stress, and prioritize self-care (Garvey Berger, 2020). This emphasis on holistic support contributes to teacher resilience and overall well-being.
- *Enhancing Equity and Inclusion:* Instructional coaching plays a crucial role in promoting equity and inclusion during remote learning. Coaches collaborate with educators to design culturally responsive instruction, differentiate learning experiences, and address equity gaps exacerbated by the shift to online learning (Freeman, Zimmer & Allen, 2021).
- *Facilitating Technological Integration:* The rapid transition to online instruction necessitated the integration of technology into teaching practices. Instructional coaches support teachers in navigating digital tools, platforms, and instructional technology resources effectively (Strobel, Johnson & Warrington, 2020). Coaches facilitate professional learning communities focused on sharing best practices and innovative strategies for technology integration.
- *Building Collaborative Learning Communities:* Instructional coaching fosters the development of collaborative learning communities among educators. Coaches facilitate virtual collaboration, peer observation, and reflective dialogue, promoting a culture of continuous improvement and shared expertise (Reynolds et al., 2021).
- *Promoting Student Engagement and Learning Outcomes:* Through targeted support and feedback, instructional coaching enhances student engagement and learning outcomes in remote and hybrid learning environments (Blackburn, 2021). Coaches assist teachers in designing interactive and engaging lessons, implementing effective instructional strategies, and assessing student progress effectively.

In all, instructional coaching has made significant contributions to education during the pandemic period and beyond. By providing tailored support, promoting social-emotional well-being, enhancing equity and inclusion, facilitating technological integration, building collaborative learning communities, and promoting student engagement and learning outcomes, instructional coaching has emerged as a cornerstone of effective teaching and professional development in the post-pandemic era.

## Challenges and Prospects of Instructional Coaching in Professional Teacher Development with Covid-19 Pandemic Experience

In addressing the difficulties presented by the COVID-19 pandemic, instructional coaching can serve as a dynamic force for positive change in professional teacher development. The prospects lie in leveraging technology, fostering collaboration, and embracing innovative strategies to build a resilient and adaptable educational community.

### Challenges of Instructional Coaching in Professional Teacher Development Amidst the COVID-19 Pandemic

During pandemic period, instructional coaching faces a lot of challenges because we have to coach unwilling faculty in the use technology to measure up with the challenges of the pandemic. Hence, the followings are the common challenges encountered during the period:

- *Remote Learning Challenges:* The abrupt shift to remote and hybrid learning models poses challenges for instructional coaches, requiring them to adapt traditional coaching methods to a virtual setting (Foltos, 2013). Remote or hybrid teaching models may contribute to feelings of professional isolation among teachers. Instructional coaches must find ways to foster a sense of community, collaboration, and peer support despite physical distance.
- *Adapting to Changing Educational Landscapes:* Rapid changes in instructional formats, curriculum adjustments, and uncertainties about the educational landscape make it challenging for instructional coaches to provide consistent and targeted support. Flexibility and adaptability become crucial skills.
- *Digital Divide and Technology Integration:* Limited technology proficiency among educators and varying access to digital resources create hurdles in incorporating technology effectively into coaching strategies (Leach, 2020). The shift to remote or hybrid learning has exacerbated the digital divide, with varying levels of access to technology among teachers and students. Instructional coaches must navigate these disparities and support teachers in effectively integrating technology into their instructional practices.
- *Emotional Well-being and Burnout:* The heightened stress and emotional strain experienced by teachers during the pandemic may affect their receptivity to coaching and professional development initiatives (Skaalvik & Skaalvik, 2017). Hence, the pandemic has taken a toll on the emotional well-being of educators, leading to increased stress and burnout. Instructional coaches need to address

the emotional needs of teachers, provide support, and promote strategies for maintaining a healthy work-life balance.

- *Time Constraints:* The demands of adapting to new teaching modalities and increased workload may limit teachers' availability for coaching sessions, affecting the depth and frequency of interactions (Ingersoll & Strong, 2011).
- *Evaluative Pressures:* The integration of instructional coaching with teacher evaluations during the pandemic may create apprehension and resistance, impacting the openness to coaching (Bloom et al., 2014).
- *Data-Driven Decision-Making in Virtual Environments:* The reliance on data for instructional decision-making is crucial, but adapting data-driven practices to virtual environments presents challenges. Instructional coaches need strategies for collecting, analyzing, and interpreting data in online or hybrid teaching settings.

## Prospects of Instructional Coaching in Professional Teacher Development in the Post-Pandemic Era

The role of instructional coaching in professional teacher development has gained significant importance in the post-pandemic era. During the pandemic, instructional coaching became essential for sustaining the educational system, as faculty members were compelled to receive coaching despite any reluctance. Therefore, the followings are the prospects of the instructional coaching recorded:

- *Personalized Professional Development:* Instructional coaching allows for personalized support, addressing individual teacher needs in the aftermath of the pandemic and promoting targeted professional growth (Showers & Joyce, 1996). The flexibility of virtual platforms allows for more personalized professional development opportunities. Instructional coaches can tailor support based on individual teacher needs and provide targeted resources for improvement.
- *Developing Technological Pedagogical Content Knowledge (TPACK):* Assisting teachers in improving their Technological Pedagogical Content Knowledge (TPACK), instructional coaches play a crucial role in integrating technology smoothly into pedagogical methods (Koehler & Mishra, 2009). The incorporation of technology into education has been expedited by the pandemic. Instructional coaches have the opportunity to enhance teachers' digital literacy, support the effective use of educational technology, and promote innovative teaching practices.

- *Building Resilience and Well-being:* Instructional coaching can support teachers' emotional well-being by fostering resilience, providing coping strategies, and creating a supportive professional community (Hargreaves & Fullan, 2012). The challenges posed by the pandemic provide an opportunity for teachers and instructional coaches to develop resilience and adaptability. Through collaborative problem-solving and continuous learning, educators can emerge more resilient and better equipped to face future uncertainties.
- *Data-Driven Decision-Making:* The pandemic underscores the importance of data-informed teaching. Instructional coaching can facilitate the development of teachers' data literacy and the use of evidence to inform instructional decisions (Bambrick-Santoyo, 2010).
- *Promoting a Culture of Collaboration*: Instructional coaching can contribute to building a collaborative school culture, emphasizing shared goals and continuous improvement (Knight, 2011b). Virtual platforms facilitate global collaboration and the creation of online learning communities. Instructional coaches can leverage these opportunities to connect teachers with peers worldwide, fostering a rich exchange of ideas and best practices.
- *Equity and Inclusion Focus*: The pandemic has highlighted disparities in education. Instructional coaches can play a crucial role in advocating for equity and inclusion, providing resources to address diverse needs, and ensuring that professional development initiatives are accessible to all teachers.
- *Innovative Teaching Practices*: The need for alternative instructional approaches has spurred innovation in teaching practices. Instructional coaches can guide teachers in exploring and implementing innovative methods that enhance student engagement and learning outcomes.

Generally, instructional coaching faces challenges in the wake of the COVID-19 pandemic, yet it holds significant prospects for supporting teachers in adapting to new realities, enhancing professional development, and ultimately improving teaching and learning outcomes. The successful integration of instructional coaching in this context requires a thoughtful and adaptive approach that acknowledges and addresses these challenges while leveraging the potential for positive change.

## SUMMARY OF THE CHAPTER

Studies have shown that instructional coaching has been present in education systems for some time, but its significance has become particularly apparent during and after the COVID-19 pandemic. This coaching approach has been found to have positive effects on both teachers' practices and students' learning outcomes. Evidence suggests that teachers who receive instructional coaching are more likely to embrace new teaching strategies, experience greater job satisfaction, and perceive higher levels of professional growth. Additionally, students taught by teachers who undergo instructional coaching tend to achieve higher test scores and greater academic success. Despite these favorable outcomes, it's important to acknowledge certain challenges associated with instructional coaching, including its costs, the need for ongoing training and support for coaches, and the difficulty in measuring its effectiveness.

Instructional coaching comes in various forms, with content-based and process-based coaching being the most common. Content-based coaching focuses on specific subject matter taught in the classroom, such as math or science, while process-based coaching addresses general teaching processes like planning, instruction, and assessment. Other variations include peer coaching, group coaching, and virtual coaching. This coaching is often aimed at improving teachers' overall teaching practices rather than just their knowledge of a particular subject. Coaches may collaborate with teachers to develop more effective teaching styles, enhance classroom management skills, or create more engaging learning environments.

Ultimately, instructional coaching can serve as a valuable tool for supporting teachers' professional development in the post-pandemic era. By providing targeted feedback, support, and growth opportunities, instructional coaching can help educators thrive in the evolving educational landscape and continue to refine their skills and knowledge. It's important to recognize that not all tools and resources are universally applicable, and coaches and teachers must work together to determine which ones are most beneficial for their specific needs. Instructional coaching is a gradual process that requires time and commitment for tangible results. Crucially, it's not just about improving teachers' skills but also enhancing student learning outcomes. Given its positive impact on student achievement, instructional coaching has a crucial role to play in shaping technology-integrated education in the post-pandemic era.

## REFERENCES


Alirezabeigi, S. (2023). What Do We Talk About When We Talk About Post-Pandemic Time in School Education? Reflections on Temporal Plasticity of Post-Pandemic School Education. *Sisyphus: Journal of Education*, 11(1), 107–127.

Arrington, A. (2021). *The use of information and communications technology to continue instruction and professional development in rural Ghana during COVID-19 school lockdowns* [Doctoral dissertation, University of Illinois at Urbana-Champaign].

Atobatele, F. A., Kpodo, P. C., & Eke, I. O. (2024). Faculty engagement in international student success: A review of best practices and strategies. *International Journal of Applied Research in Social Sciences*, 6(3), 440–459. 10.51594/ijarss.v6i3.968

Bambrick-Santoyo, P. (2010). *Driven by Data: A Practical Guide to Improve Instruction.* John Wiley & Son.

Bamrungsin, P., & Khampirat, B. (2022). Improving professional skills of pre-service teachers using online training: Applying work-integrated learning approaches through a quasi-experimental study. *Sustainability (Basel)*, 14(7), 4362. 10.3390/su14074362

Barnes, K. T. (2023). *Integral Instructional Coaching: The Need for Effective Feedback to Develop and Retain Teachers.* University of Dayton. https://etd.ohiolink.edu/acprod/odb_etd/ws/send_file/send?accession=dayton1689354933936445&disposition=inline

Beck, C., Sumowski, E., Dailey-Hebert, A., & Colvin, C. (2021). Instructional Coaching as Professional Development: The Impact of Goal Setting on Teacher Practice. *Journal of Staff Development*, 42(3), 32–40.

Blackburn, D. (2021). Using Instructional Coaching to Improve Online Teaching during COVID-19. *Journal of Faculty Development*, 35(2), 27–34.

Blaushild, N., Blazquez, R., McGee, S., & McGee-Tekula, R. (2024). Balancing teachers' needs in times of crisis: Investigating how computer science instructional coaches and teachers navigated remote professional development during COVID-19. *Computer Science Education*, 1–33. 10.1080/08993408.2024.2313913

Bloom, G., Castagna, C., Moir, E., & Warren, B. (2014). *Blended coaching: Skills and strategies to support principal development*. Corwin Press.

Borman, G. D., Hewes, G. M., Overman, L. T., & Brown, S. (2003). Comprehensive School Reform and Student Achievement: A Meta-Analysis. *Review of Educational Research*, 73(2), 125–230. 10.3102/00346543073002125

Carver-Thomas, D., Kini, T., & Burns, D. (2020). Sharpening the divide: How California's teacher shortages expand inequality. *Learning Policy Institute*. https://eric.ed.gov/?id=ED610882

Costa, A., & Garmston, R. (1994). *Cognitive coaching: A foundation for Renaissance schools*. Christopher-Gordon Publishers.

Dana, N. F., & Yendol-Hoppey, D. (2009). *The reflective educator's guide to classroom research: Learning to teach and teaching to learn through practitioner inquiry*. Corwin Press.

Danielson, C. (2007). *Enhancing professional practice: A framework for teaching*. AsCD.

Denton, C. A., & Hasbrouck, J. E. (2009). *Response to Instruction (RTI) and English Learners: Making It Happen*.

Desimone, L. M., et al. (2019). *Learning in a Digital Age: Instructional Technology in the Learning Sciences*.

Desimone, L. M., Hammerness, K., Keating, B., & Nightingale, K. (2020). The impact of coaching on teacher learning: A review of the research. *Journal of Teaching and Teacher Education*, 92, 103036.

Dos Santos, L. M. (2021). The relationship between workforce sustainability, stress, and career decision: A study of kindergarten teachers during the COVID-19 pandemic. *Sustainability (Basel)*, 13(20), 11521. 10.3390/su132011521

Dunekack, A. (2020). Instructional Coaching in Times of Crisis. *Journal of Staff Development*, 41(3), 30–35

Edwards, C. R. (2023). *Instructional Coaching: A Support for Increasing Engagement in Middle School Mathematics* [Doctoral dissertation, University of South Carolina]. https://scholarcommons.sc.edu/etd/7489

Fairman, J. C., Smith, D. J., Pullen, P. C., & Lebel, S. J. (2023). The challenge of keeping teacher professional development relevant. *Professional Development in Education*, 49(2), 197–209. 10.1080/19415257.2020.1827010

Foltos, L. (2013). *Peer coaching: Unlocking the power of collaboration*. Corwin Press. 10.4135/9781483300252

Freeman, J., Zimmer, K., & Allen, J. (2021). Moving Forward: The Role of Instructional Coaching in Equity. *Journal of Staff Development*, 42(1), 28–35.

Garvey Berger, J. (2020). Coaching for Equity: The Power of Culturally Responsive Coaching. *Phi Delta Kappan*, 102(4), 29–34.

Grek, S., & Landri, P. (2021). Editorial: Education in Europe and the COVID-19 Pandemic. *European Educational Research Journal*, 20(4), 393–402. 10.1177/14749041211024781

Hargreaves, A., & Fullan, M. (2012). *Professional capital: Transforming teaching in every school*. Teachers College Press.

Holliday, C. G. (2021). Culturally Relevant Coaching: Empowering New Teachers. *English in Texas*, 51(1), 33–41.

Hui, K. S., Khemanuwong, T., & Ismail, S. A. M. M. (2020). Keeping teachers afloat with instructional coaching: Coaching structure and implementation. *The Qualitative Report*, 25(7), 1790–1816.

Ingersoll, R. M., & Strong, M. (2011). The impact of induction and mentoring programs for beginning teachers: A critical review of the research. *Review of Educational Research*, 81(2), 201–233. 10.3102/0034654311403323

Iqbal, S., & Ali, A. (2024). Education and professional development: Opportunities and challenges for in-service teachers: A Review. *Gomal University Journal of Research*, 40(1), 117–133. 10.51380/gujr-40-01-10

Joyce, B., & Showers, B. (2021). *Student Achievement through Staff Development* (4th ed.). Association for Supervision and Curriculum Development.

Karlberg, M., & Bezzina, C. (2022). The professional development needs of beginning and experienced teachers in four municipalities in Sweden. *Professional Development in Education*, 48(4), 624–641. 10.1080/19415257.2020.1712451

Knight, J. (2007). *Instructional coaching: A partnership approach to improving instruction*. Corwin Press.

Knight, J. (2011a). *High-Impact Instruction: A Framework for Great Teaching*.

Knight, J. (2011b). *Unmistakable impact: A partnership approach for dramatically improving instruction*. Corwin Press. 10.4135/9781452219721

Knight, J. (2019). Instructional coaching for implementing visible learning: A model for translating research into practice. *Education Sciences*, 9(2), 101. 10.3390/educsci9020101

Knight, J., & Cornett, J. (2009). The Impact of Coaching on Teacher Effectiveness: A District-wide Evaluation. *Educational Policy*, 23(4), 547–576.

Koehler, M. J., & Mishra, P. (2009). What is technological pedagogical content knowledge? *Contemporary Issues in Technology & Teacher Education*, 9(1), 60–70.

Kraft, M. A., Blazar, D., & Hogan, D. (2018). The effect of teacher coaching on instruction and achievement: A meta-analysis of the causal evidence. *Review of Educational Research*, 88(4), 547–588. 10.3102/0034654318759268

Kraft, M. A., Simon, N. S., & Lyon, M. A. (2020). *Sustaining a Sense of Success: The Importance of Teacher Working Conditions during the COVID-19 Pandemic. EdWorking Paper No. 20-279.* Annenberg Institute for School Reform at Brown University.

Kretlow, A. G., & Bartholomew, C. C. (2010). Using coaching to improve the fidelity of evidence-based practices: A review of studies. *Teacher Education and Special Education*, 33(4), 279–299. 10.1177/0888406410371643

Kurz, A., Reddy, L. A., & Glover, T. A. (2017). A multidisciplinary framework of instructional coaching. *Theory into Practice*, 56(1), 66–77. 10.1080/00405841.2016.1260404

Kutsyuruba, B., & Godden, L. (2019). The role of mentoring and coaching as a means of supporting the well-being of educators and students. *International Journal of Mentoring and Coaching in Education*, 8(4), 229–234. 10.1108/IJMCE-12-2019-081

Leach, M. (2020). Effective professional development for teachers during the COVID-19 pandemic. *Journal of Technology and Teacher Education*, 28(2), 189–199.

Lewis, K. O., Popov, V., & Fatima, S. S. (2024). From static web to metaverse: Reinventing medical education in the post-pandemic era. *Annals of Medicine*, 56(1), 2305694. 10.1080/07853890.2024.230569438261592

Liu, S., Yao, J., & Hu, J. (2020). Professional learning communities (PLCs) in coaching: A framework to develop collective teacher efficacy and shared instructional practice. *Teaching and Teacher Education*, 90, 103002.

Lofthouse, R. (2019). Coaching in education: A professional development process in formation. *Professional Development in Education*, 45(1), 33–45. 10.1080/19415257.2018.1529611

Main, P. (2022). *Instructional coaching: A teacher's guide*. Structural Learning. https://www.structural-learning.com/post/instructional-coaching-a-teachers-guide

Miguel, C., Castro, L., Marques dos Santos, J. P., Serrão, C., & Duarte, I. (2021). Impact of COVID-19 on medicine lecturers' mental health and emergency remote teaching challenges. *International Journal of Environmental Research and Public Health*, 18(13), 6792. 10.3390/ijerph1813679234202692

Mills, J., & Smith, A. (2021). The use of instructional coaching and feedback to improve teacher effectiveness. *Improving Schools*, 24(2), 119–133.

Myers, S., & Washburn, J. (2022). Increasing teacher access to instructional coaching through virtual tools: Advantageous before, during, and after the pandemic. *Journal of Technology and Teacher Education*, 30(3), 377–405.

Onyekwelu, R. A. (2024). Enhancing the Quality of Secondary Education through Professional Development of Teachers in Nigeria. *British Journal of Multidisciplinary and Advanced Studies*, 5(1), 194–205. 10.37745/bjmas.2022.0438

Papay, J. P., & Kraft, M. K. (2017). Developing Workplaces Where Teachers Stay, Improve, and Succeed. In *Teaching in Context: How Social Aspects of School and School Systems Shape Teachers' Development & Effectiveness* (pp. 15–35). Harvard Education Press.

Pham, D. H. (2023). Perspectives on Language Teacher Identity in the Context of a Post-Pandemic "New Normal" Epoch. In *Handbook of Research on Language Teacher Identity* (pp. 98-115). IGI Global

Pounder, D., Carter, M. A., & Secada, W. G. (2020). Coaching for instructional improvement: A cross-country comparison of trust, goal setting, and focus. *Teaching and Teacher Education*, 88, 102995.

Rapanta, C., Botturi, L., Goodyear, P., Guàrdia, L., & Koole, M. (2021). Balancing Technology, Pedagogy and the New Normal: Post-pandemic Challenges for Higher Education. *Postdigital Science and Education*, 3(3), 715–742. 10.1007/s42438-021-00249-1

Reddy, L. A., Shernoff, E., & Lekwa, A. (2021). A randomized controlled trial of instructional coaching in high-poverty urban schools: Examining teacher practices and student outcomes. *Journal of School Psychology*, 86, 151–168. 10.1016/j.jsp.2021.04.00134051911

Reddy, L. A., Shernoff, E., Lekwa, A., Matthews, C., Davis, W., & Dudek, C. M. (2019). Coaching to improve teacher instruction and behavior management in a high poverty school: A case study. *School Psychology*, 34(1), 14–21. 10.1037/spq000030230556728

Reddy, M. A., Reddy, B. M., Mukund, C. S., Venneti, K., Preethi, D. M. D., & Boopathi, S. (2023). Social health protection during the COVID-pandemic using IoT. In *The COVID-19 Pandemic and the Digitalization of Diplomacy* (pp. 204–235). IGI Global. 10.4018/978-1-7998-8394-4.ch009

Reynolds, D., Nelsen, J., & Twyman, J. (2021). The Role of Instructional Coaching in a Virtual Teaching World. *The Educational Forum*, 85(3), 325–337.

Richards, R. (2019). Exploring the influence of perceived mattering, role stress, and emotional exhaustion on physical education teacher/coach job satisfaction. *European Physical Education Review*, 25(2), 389–408. 10.1177/1356336X17741402

Robinson, L. E., Valido, A., Drescher, A., Woolweaver, A. B., Espelage, D. L., LoMurray, S., Long, A. C. J., Wright, A. A., & Dailey, M. M. (2023). Teachers, stress, and the COVID-19 pandemic: A qualitative analysis. *School Mental Health*, 15(1), 78–89. 10.1007/s12310-022-09533-235875185

Rowe, F. L. (2022). *A Descriptive Analysis of an Instructional Coaching Process and Its Impact on Student Reading Learning Outcomes* [Doctoral dissertation, University of South Carolina]. https://scholarcommons.sc.edu/etd/ 6917

Schön, D. A. (1983). *The reflective practitioner: How professionals think in action*. Basic Books.

Showers, B., & Joyce, B. (1996). The evolution of peer coaching. *Educational Leadership,* 53(6), 12-16. Sinquefield Center for Applied Economic Research. https://scholarworks.uark.edu/cgi/viewcontent.cgi?article=1128&context=edrepub

Skaalvik, E. M., & Skaalvik, S. (2017). Dimensions of teacher burnout: Relations with potential stressors at school. *Social Psychology of Education*, 20(4), 775–790. 10.1007/s11218-017-9391-0

Smith, C., & Gillespie, M. (2023). Research on professional development and teacher change: Implications for adult basic education. [Routledge.]. *Review of Adult Learning and Literacy*, 7, 205–244. 10.4324/9781003417996-7

Strobel, J., Johnson, B., & Warrington, M. (2020). Supporting Instructional Coaching Through Technology: Reflections on Two Systems. *TechTrends*, 64(2), 254–261.

Tanner, J., Quintis, L., & Gamboa, T.Jr. (2017). Three perspectives of planning, implementation, and consistency in instructional coaching. *Journal of Educational Research and Practice*, 7(1), 30–44. 10.5590/JERAP.2017.07.1.03

Tharapos, M., O'Connell, B., Beatson, N., & De Lange, P. (2023). COVID-19 and accounting, accountability and governance. In *Handbook of Accounting, Accountability and Governance* (pp. 448-472). Edward Elgar Publishing.

Van Nuland, S. E., Schmidt, M. C., Engels, N., & van den Berg, J. (2020). Understanding teacher learning in the context of instructional coaching: A systematic review. *Teaching and Teacher Education*, 96, 103158.

Vescio, V., Ross, D., & Adams, A. (2021). A review of research on the impact of professional learning communities on teaching practice and student learning. *Teaching and Teacher Education*, 107, 103423.

Williamson, B., Eynon, R., & Potter, J. (2020). Pandemic politics, pedagogies and practices: Digital technologies and distance education during the coronavirus emergency. *Learning, Media and Technology*, 45(2), 107–114. 10.1080/17439884.2020.1761641

Yilmaz, K. (2021). The effectiveness of instructional coaching on teachers' professional development: A qualitative study. *Teaching and Teacher Education*, 100, 103346.

Yoon, K. S., Duncan, T., Lee, S. W. Y., Scarloss, B., & Shapley, K. L. (2007). *Reviewing the Evidence on How Teacher Professional Development Affects Student Achievement. Issues & Answers Report, REL 2007-No. 033*. National Center for Education Evaluation and Regional Assistance.

Zamarro, G., Camp, A., Fuchsman, D., & McGee, J. B. (2022). *Understanding how COVID-19 has changed teachers' chances of remaining in the classroom.*

# Chapter 12
# Investigation of Pre-Service Teachers' Views on the Impact of COVID-19 on Online a Flipped Learning Model-Based General Chemistry Laboratory

**Nagihan Kadıoğlu**
*Hacettepe University, Turkey*

**Özge Özyalçın Oskay**
*Hacettepe University, Turkey*

## ABSTRACT

*The aim of this study is to determine the views of pre-service teachers on the online flipped learning based general chemistry laboratory course. 16 pre-service teachers studying in the first year of the department of biology teaching participated in this study, which is based on qualitative research method. In the 11-week study, pre-service teachers participated in a total of nine experiments online. The views of the pre-service teachers were determined with three open-ended questions prepared by the researchers. Content analysis was used to analyze the data. Findings revealed that opinions on the online flipped learning model for this course were divided into positive and negative themes. Although it was observed that pre-service teachers had positive views on subjects such as the time and space flexibility of the flipped*

DOI: 10.4018/979-8-3693-7645-4.ch012

*learning model and conducting experiments online, it was also found that they had difficulties in the process of attending an applied course online, such as technical problems and not finding a suitable environment for attending the course.*

## INTRODUCTION

The COVID-19 pandemic, which has swept the world in a short period of time, has necessitated the immediate migration of all educational environments to online environments. This has made the sustainability of education at all levels difficult. Especially the urgent need to conduct practical courses online brought many problems. It was very difficult to reach students in institutions that did not have the necessary infrastructure for online education. The solutions found to avoid further interruptions in education have generally been to provide students with online materials and to reach students through video conferences.

The rapid transition to online education due to the pandemic and the disruptions caused by this situation caused online education to be perceived as a crisis management rather than a long-term teaching method (Tang et al., 2020). In addition, the concern that conducting practical courses, especially laboratory courses, online may not be effective compared to the traditional method has also come to the fore. Especially in the first period of the pandemic, instructors tried to overcome this problem by incorporating various pedagogical methods into learning environments in order to make laboratory courses that had to be conducted online effective (Anzovino et al., 2020; Elkhatat & Muhtaseb, 2021; Feng et al., 2022; Mojica & Upmacis, 2022; Öztürk & Deniz, 2023; Villanueva & Zimmermann, 2020).

Flipped learning model is one of the teaching methods preferred to increase efficiency during the pandemic period. There are studies showing that the flipped learning model can provide a solution to the difficulties encountered in the transition to online education (Divjak et al., 2022). The flipped learning model, which gained popularity in the pre-pandemic period, especially as an approach that encourages student-centered learning and meets the need to integrate technology into educational processes, was also included in learning processes during the pandemic. The flexible and hybrid learning structure of the flipped learning model has adapted to the flexible working approach brought by the COVID-19 pandemic.

### Flipped Learning Model Based Laboratory Courses

Chemistry is a branch of science in which theoretical and practical knowledge is offered together (Brown et al., 2006), and applied courses are extremely important in understanding the abstract structure specific to chemistry. Laboratory implementations play a key role in the effectiveness of chemistry education (Clough, 2002). Applied courses enable students' upper order learning and thinking skills to develop and they also function as an important bridge between theory and practice (Hofstein & Hugerat, 2021). The general chemistry lab course is also an inseparable and dynamic part of chemistry- an applied branch of science (Qiang et al., 2020) because theoretical knowledge should be offered along with laboratory implementations so that students could understand the abstract aspects of chemistry such as chemical reactions, the structure of atoms and molecular interactions (Atkins & Jones, 2008). While lab implementations contribute to the development of pre-service teachers' psychomotor skills on the one hand, the applications also provide them with appropriate circumstances so that they can deepen their scientific knowledge on the other hand (Hofstein & Lunetta, 2003). Besides, the laboratory setting enables students to attain practical knowledge of course concepts and also allows for exploration of the methodologies employed by scientists in their respective fields (Mojica & Upmacis, 2021).

Even before the COVID-19 process, today's 21st century learning environments were rapidly developing and changing under the influence of technological developments and pedagogical studies (Prensky, 2001). This evolutionary process has forced educators to think about ways to transfer knowledge to students and to revise traditional teaching methods (Bonwell and Eison, 1991; Sanchez et al., 2022). The development of educational technologies has brought about various changes in undergraduate lab courses and made it possible to employ different learning models in the laboratory (Lee et al., 2023). As a result, learning approaches that encourage student engagement and in-depth learning, where students can take active roles in the learning process, have come to the fore in recent years (Abeysekera & Dawson, 2015). Flipped learning model has also become a remarkable learning approach in recent years (Bergmann & Sams, 2012). Flipped learning model is a student-centred learning model which includes educational technologies in this interaction, and which thus enables to design flexible and individualised learning environments. It enables students to learn the class material at their own speed, when they want to and individually outside the classroom and to use the class time actively for learning activities (Strayer, 2012). Materials related to the theoretical part of a lesson are sent to pre-service teachers prior to the class in this model. Thus, learning environments can be organised in a way that pre-service teachers can learn meaningfully in class time.

Flipped learning model makes students think on a subject outside the classroom and enables learning independently of time and place (Herreid & Schiller, 2013, Lage et al., 2000). Several different approaches to be used with pre-class/in-class activities are available in the model and therefore, there are no standardised procedures in implementing the model (Brady & Voronova, 2023). Class material is presented to students in such instruments as class videos or written documents in this learning model and opportunities for more interaction and in-depth discussion with the teacher in the classroom and for designing the material according to students' learning styles and personal characteristics are obtained (Lage et al., 2000; Tucker, 2012; Zappe et al., 2009).

Relevant class material is sent to students prior to the class in the form of written documents or videos to introduce the subject and to prent the prior knowledge to students in lab classes in this model and the stages of knowledge and understanding are actualised. Students are provided with the opportunity to devote more time to experimenting, to discussions about experiments, to going through the stages of analysis, synthesis and evaluation more effectively and to thinking on and discussing about experiments more deeply (Chen et al., 2014).

This learning model can provide students with the time and flexibility necessary for internalising the complicated concepts and equations (Kim et al., 2014). It also secures that teachers spend more one-to-one time with their students – which in turn offers the opportunity for more individualised learning in teaching lab courses (Kim et al., 2014). In this way, teachers can offer students more guidance and support to help them understand the theoretical structure and stages of experiments better. Review of literature demonstrated that studies concerning participants' views on using flipped learning model in laboratory classes were available. To illustrate, Candaş and Altun (2023) investigated the effects of General Chemistry Lab II course designed on the basis of flipped learning model on pre-service science teachers' performance and views. The study concluded that the model supported students in taking on the responsibility of their learning and in studying independently and that it promoted their motivation for learning. Another study conducted by Stieff et al (2018) with the participation of 1089 students divided the first-year students registered in the General Chemistry Lab course into two groups. The findings demonstrated that the students who had participated in two lab activities using videos prior to online lab classes used the lab time more efficiently than the ones who had joined the classes prior to the lab and that they understood the rationale behind the procedures better. On the other hand, no differences were found between the two groups in receiving help from the teacher. Busto et al (2022), in a study conducted with the participation of third year chemistry students, used flipped learning model in teaching molecular biology lab. The students were sent materials such as videos, web pages and laboratory session instructions before the classes. Their views on the teaching method were collected through a 5-pointed Likert type survey, and the rate of their satisfaction was found to be 92.3%. Candaş et al (2022) investigated the effects of analytic chemistry taught in flipped learning model on pre-service science teachers' meaningful understanding and interpretation of knowledge in the context of environment. It was found accordingly that using the model in teaching analytic chemistry had positive effects on the participants' learning and views on the course and that it caused significant improvement in their ability of interpreting chemical environmental problems.

Different applications of the model are available in lab classes. Abdelshafi et al (2017), for instance, designed an iBook supported with classes videos for General chemistry Lab. Thus, students joined the general chemistry lab classes taught partly in flipped learning model for a semester with their iBook. They found that the students had good reactions to the model and that they were excited about using this technology (iBook). The researchers concluded that the students had positive perceptions of learning in this model and of using iBook. They also found that the participants had good reactions to learning in this model and felt excietement in using this technology (iBook).

## Online Flipped Laboratory Courses During the Pandemic

Research initiatives to convert laboratory courses to an online format were underway even before the pandemic. Simulations and virtual laboratory applications are prominent examples of this. Teaching online laboratory courses remotely provides many advantages, such as providing accessibility to students who have difficulty accessing laboratory equipment (Elkhatat & Al-Muhtaseb, 2020). In addition, such online applications are less costly and safer, as there are no unwanted situations such as laboratory accidents. On the other hand, the physical presence of students in the laboratory environment is important for the development of their psychomotor skills. For learning to take place, it is not enough for students to physically participate in the laboratory. In order for this skill to develop, students need to play an active role in laboratory courses. Therefore, time management is also very important in laboratories. Cases in which face-to-face education is obligatorily restricted make the continuity of applied courses difficult. Management of time, which is a limited resource for laboratories even in face-to-face environments, is more difficult in such cases. The effectiveness of lab courses and the issue of how pre-service teachers could improve their lab skills have become a significant problem in the educational process which is obligatorily replaced by online learning. It is important to assure that the pedagogical and educational value of lab courses taught online is equal to the one taught face-to-face in order for students to have beneficial learning experiences (May et al., 2022). Therefore, since students' participation in a course, whether in-class or online, does not necessarily mean that learning has taken place, some practices in online learning, especially the emphasis on utilising live synchronous meetings between instructors and students during live sessions, are believed to enhance online teaching (Tang et al., 2020). Thanks to the flexible and individual-oriented structure of the flipped learning model, it is possible to get positive feedback with its use in online lab environments.

When the literature was examined, it was seen that the flipped learning model was used in online laboratory courses and positive results were obtained (Ahmet & Aşıksoy, 2021; Elkhatat & Al-Muhtaseb, 2021; Feng et al., 2022; Öztürk & Deniz, 2023). For example, Elkhatat and Al-Muhtaseb (2021) investigated how using a hybrid online flipped learning model can make laboratory courses in engineering effective and sustainable during the pandemic. The study showed that the method offers students a more active and effective learning experience.

## Flipped Learning Model and Post-Pandemic

With the end of the pandemic, the face-to-face education process returned. However, in today's digital world, it is impossible to return to the old order completely. Educators, who are now fully aware of the advantages and disadvantages of online education, need to use models that both use online systems, benefit from information and communications technology (ICT), and allow for indispensable face-to-face teaching.

In the post-COVID era, the educational landscape has changed profoundly, with students gaining more autonomy over their learning processes. They now have the freedom to choose their courses, form study groups and dynamically adapt their learning environments, fostering engagement across cultures and geographies. This shift highlights the role of the learner and emphasises pedagogical strategies such as student-centred, exploratory and self-directed learning (Tian, 2023). The pandemic has highlighted the importance of the flipped learning model, making it an essential tool for meeting the demands of distance and hybrid education. By encouraging more effective use of technology and interactive online learning experiences, this model has made educational processes more flexible, accessible and centred on the needs of students. Future educators, having experienced these changes as students, are now ready to embrace and champion these advanced learning models, further enriching the educational experience in a rapidly evolving world. The infrastructure for remote teaching in many institutions, which exists due to the remote education necessitated by the COVID-19 pandemic (Borish et al., 2022), is a facilitating factor for the implementation of the online flipped learning model.

## Research Question

The Covid-19 pandemic has radically changed all levels of education. Especially applied courses have been one of the most affected areas. Initially, urgent solutions were produced only to prevent disruption of education. However, due to the long duration of the pandemic and the possibility of recurrence in the future, a process called "new normal" was entered after the pandemic. In this process, more permanent solutions were tried for reclosures, and different teaching methods and techniques suitable for hybrid teaching were integrated into the lessons.

For example, Pols (2020), in his study conducted during the period when face-to-face lessons were interrupted, developed experiments at home to be used in the first-year physics laboratory course. These designed experiments were used to develop students' inquiry skills. In the same period, Delgado et al. (2021) developed virtual lab protocols for Cell Biology Labs using applications such as Canvas, Zoom and Labster. With these lab protocols, they aimed to keep the learning outcomes of face-to-face labs as close as possible. Chans et al. (2022), in their study on the conduct of Chemistry laboratories during the Covid-19 period, investigated the adaptation of laboratory content to an online format, the evaluation of students' learning outcomes, and students' perceptions of the adapted course format. At the end of the study, it was stated that students generally developed positive attitudes towards the laboratory course conducted in this way and were more likely to recommend it to others.

A review of all the studies shows that even at the beginning of the pandemic response, the only goal was not only to ensure continuity of education. While tackling the challenges of the pandemic, studies have also demonstrated the potential of flexible learning environments that can be used in the future.

As summed up above, studies on using flipped learning model in different ways are available in the literature. Yet, the number of studies on using the model in online general chemistry laboratory course in the process of emergent transition into distant education is limited. Setting out from this fact, the current study seeks answers to the question "what views do pre-service teachers hold in relation to online general chemistry laboratory course which is taught on the basis of flipped learning model in this study?".

## METHOD

This current study uses qualitative research method. Qualitative research methods focus on understanding authentic situations and individual experiences clearly and provide in-depth information in certain contexts instead of reaching generalizable conclusions (Creswell, 2013). The method- which is chosen particularly to understand people's experiences, feelings, thoughts and their interactions in their social context- aims to reveal individuals' worlds, meanings and experiences in an authentic manner (Patton, 2015).

## The Study Group

This study was conducted in the spring semester of 2022-2023 academic year. The participants in the study were 16 pre-service teachers (11 female and 5 male) who enrolled in the General chemistry Laboratory course and who were the first-year students in biology teaching department. The study was conducted with all of the students taking the course.

## Data Collection Process

This study aims to determine students' views on using flipped learning model in general chemistry laboratory course conducted online.

In the study conducted for this purpose; firstly, the online General Chemistry Laboratory sheet was shared with the students on the moodle platform provided by the university. On this platform, it is possible to share various materials such as lecture sessions, lecture videos, lecture notes, homework, exams, quizzes with students. At the same time, students' access information such as when they last logged into the system and when they uploaded assignments can be seen.

Before each experiment, materials containing theoretical information about the relevant experiment were shared with the students, and the experiment videos, in which the experiments were carried out by the researcher in a real laboratory environment, were shared with the students, in which information about the purpose of the experiment, the materials to be used and the experimental setup was also given in addition to the theoretical part of the relevant experiments. In addition to checking whether the students watched the videos before coming to the class through the moodle system, an online quiz was conducted before each lesson and the students' readiness was tested. According to Moodle records, 95% of the students visited the course page once a week and 51% visited the course page the evening before the class.

Before each lesson, quiz questions were first addressed and then the experiments were started. While the experiments were conducted by the researchers in the university laboratory during the lecture, the students participated in the laboratory course online via the zoom platform. During the experiments, question and answer activities were carried out continuously and care was taken to create a suitable discussion environment for students to participate effectively. At the end of each week, students were asked to write reports about the experiments and upload them to the system within the specified time period, and feedback on the reports was given during the next week's class time. The first week of the study was devoted to laboratory safety and laboratory materials. Then, one experiment was conducted each week and the entire content was completed in the 10th week. In the last week, a zoom session was held with each pre-service teacher and the study was finalised by taking their opinions.

## Data Collection Tool

The pre-service teachers' views were collected with three open-ended questions prepared by the researchers. The questions prepared in accordance with the purpose of the study are as in the following:

1. In the online General Chemistry Laboratory course conducted according to the flipped learning model, did learning the theoretical part of the course on your own and then experiencing the laboratory process online help you understand the experiments conducted during the semester? If yes, in which aspects did you find it useful?
2. In the Online General Chemistry Laboratory course conducted according to the flipped learning model, what do you think about the materials sent before the class? Which material was the most useful for you?
3. What difficulties did you face in attending the Online General Chemistry Lab course conducted according to the flipped learning model and accessing the materials sent and how did these difficulties affect you?

## Data Analysis

The interviews were conducted online and individually with each student. Before doing the analyses, the data were examined and efforts were made to determine the ones which were related and associated. Content analysis was preferred for use because the research data were collected through open-ended questions so as to consider the participants' views and experiences multi-dimensionally. Content analysis enables researchers to analyse such data in a structured manner (Mayring, 2000)- which, in turn, helps to obtain consistent and reliable results (Schreier, 2012). After the analyses, the codes for the data were distinguished first, and then, the themes were created. The participants' real names were not used in the study and pre-service teachers were coded as PT1, PT2, etc…

## Trustworthiness of Research

The validity and reliability of qualitative studies are ensured with concepts such as transferability, believability, consistence and confirmability (Denzin & Lincoln, 1994). The participants' consent was received before the online interviews and the interviews were recorded to attain the reliability in this study. The interviews were conducted by the same researcher with each participant separately online. Their identities were kept confidential and the views stated by them were presented without changing and by giving them a code. The pre-service teachers were not guided, no interventions were made to their responses during the interviews and the findings were reported with no comments on them to secure the internal reliability in the study. Their answers were repeated so as to receive their approval, and they were asked to watch the video recordings of the interviews at the end and their confirmation was received. The recordings of the interviews were analysed twice at different times by using a programme and manually. The process was carried out by the researchers separately and the results obtained were compared in terms of similarities and differences. The interrater reliability was found as 90%. The figure is considered adequate (Miles & Huberman, 1994).

## FINDINGS

This section presents the pre-service teachers' views on online General Chemistry Laboratory course taught in flipped learning model in the order of research questions.

### Findings for Research Question One

The categories and themes related to the first question of the study are given in Figure 1. Pre-service teachers' views on laboratory processes were categorized as positive and negative. The most positive aspects frequently emphasized by the pre-service teachers are the flexibility of time and space to learn the course materials and the fact that the experiments are more understandable online. The most negative aspect frequently mentioned by pre-service teachers was the feeling of social isolation.

*Figure 1. Findings for question one*

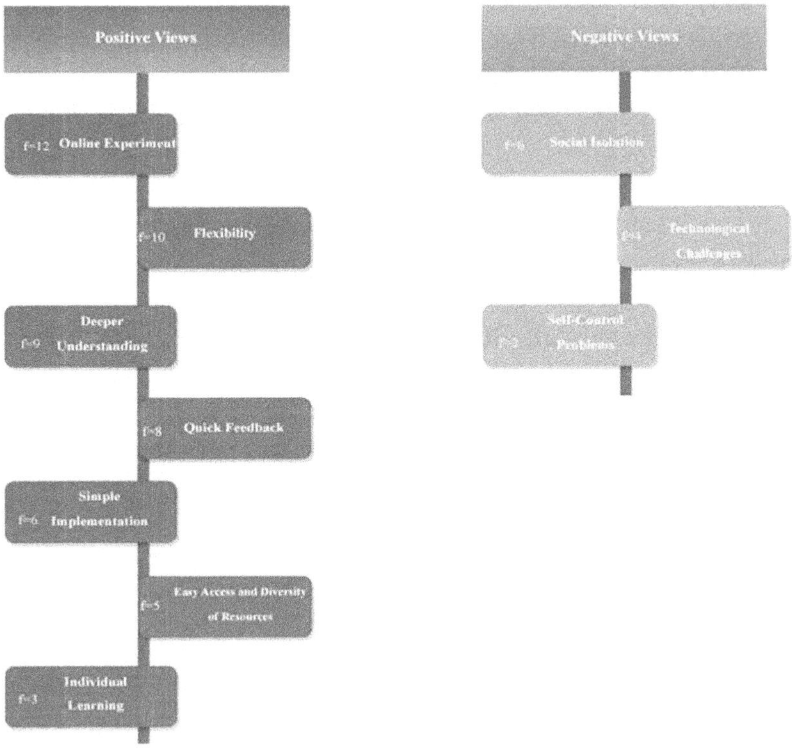


**Frequencies can be bigger than the number of participants because each code was stated by the pre-service teachers.*

On examining Figure 1, it was found that the participants mostly had positive views. Participant PT4, for instance, responded to the question as "*it was both good and bad for me to send the videos before the classes. Because I came to classes with preparation thanks to the videos, but it was difficult for me to learn some of the experiments on my own. I was a bit tense because I could not immediately ask about the things I did not understand.*" PT8, however, responded positively and said, "*sending the videos of subject presentation was beneficial for me. In this way, I had the opportunity to study whenever I wanted. Because I sometimes miss the points that I cannot understand in other courses, but I can pause the video and watch again in this course.*" The pre-service teachers also stated that it would be more useful if the experiments were done in class by the researchers instead of sending the videos of experiments. Thus, PT13 stated that "*It was very good that the experiments were done live in the class by the teachers, I could feel myself a little bit like I was in the laboratory.*"

The word "isolation" was frequently used in answers to the question as the negative aspect. The participants said that being in an environment outside the laboratory for such an applied course had affected them in negative ways. The answer given to the question by PT1 can be an example for negative views. The answer was as in the following: "*I had never joined a class in the laboratory. It was nice to take part in the experiments, but I generally felt as if I had been trapped behind the screen because I could not interact with my friends appropriately. I also had problems with my internet connection. I continuously disconnected and it affected me in negative ways.*" This interpretation of the pre-service teacher may be considered in the framework of social isolation and technical problems.

## Findings for Research Question Two

The categories and themes for research question two are shown in Figure 2. The pre-service teachers' views on the materials sent to them before classes were classified as positive and negative.

*Figure 2. Findings for question two*

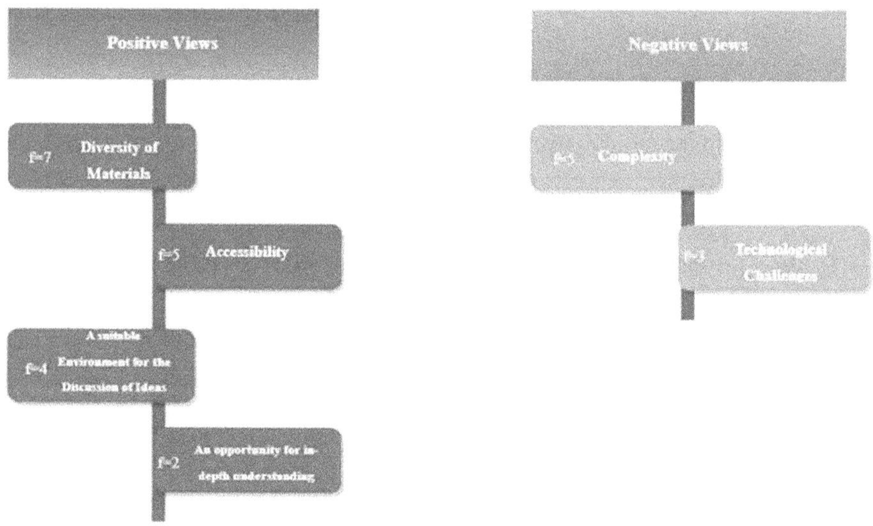


According to Figure 2, it was seen that the views of the pre-service teachers were mainly related to the type of materials sent before the lesson. The majority of the participants thought that the materials such as simulations, animations, study notes, etc. that were sent before the lesson were effective. Additionally, some weeks, discussion questions were also provided to the pre-service teachers. Some of the pre-service teachers considered this as an opportunity both to interact with their friends and to express their opinions.

A positive example may be the answer given by PT11: "*I had a lot of fun answering the discussion questions. They helped me learn better and I also socialised with my classmates in this way.*" Some pre-service teachers, however, thought that the situation caused complexity. The code of complexity was the most frequently emphasised negative aspect. It was remarkable here that the participants' individual differences were reflected into their views. While some of the pre-service teachers considered diversity in materials as a contribution to their learning, some others thought it led to chaos. Still others interpreted the diversity as both positive and negative. Despite the fact that some of them considered diversity of materials as positive, they said that they did not use all the materials. The view stated by PT16 is an example for it: "*In fact, animations were nice but I sometimes didn't have time to work with them. I watched the videos only in that case.*" This answer was both positive and negative. Another participant holding a negative view in this respect was PT4. The participant said, "*in my opinion, some of the additional notes were not consistent with the videos. I sometimes could not decide which one to study.*"

## Findings for Research Question Three

The pre-service teachers' views on difficulties in attending the classes and in reaching the materials sent to them are shown in Figure 3. Their views were classified as positive and negative.

*Figure 3. Findings for question three*

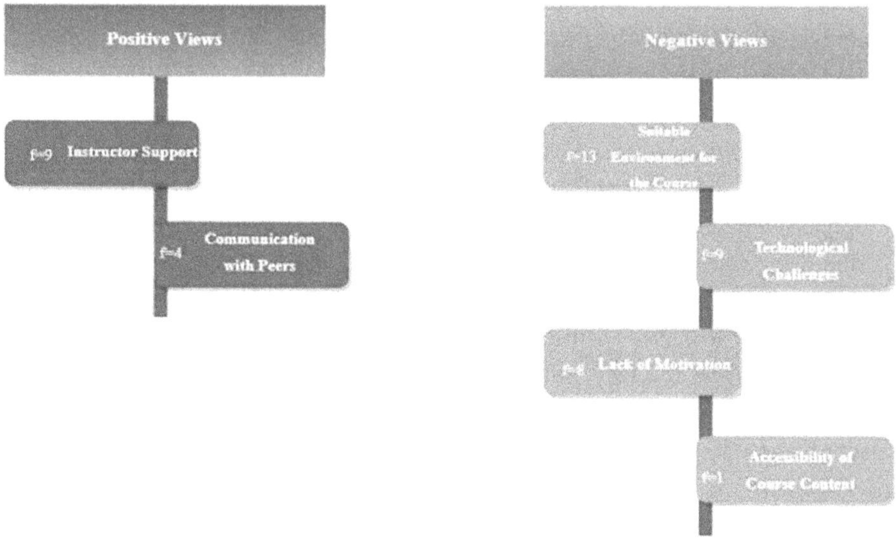


It is evident from Figure 3 that negative views are largely about suitable environments for attending classes and technical problems such as problems with mobile devices and power cut or internet outage. It was found that those difficulties affected pre-service teachers' motivation for the course in negative ways. Another participant mentioned failure to receive the announcement when an announcement was uploaded to the platform as the negative aspect in addition to the above-mentioned problems. Thus, the participant had problems in reaching the content because the message did not reach. The pre-service teachers also stated that suitable places were not sometimes available to them to join the classes. The participants who had brothers or sisters or who were staying in a dormitory in particular mentioned this problem. PT5, who had problems in finding an appropriate device to join the classes said, "*My brother/sister also goes on the internet when the class starts. So we sometimes have problems. I sometimes have to join the classes with my mobile phone.*" Another participants holding negative views in this respect was PT10- who made the statement "*My mother, father and brother are also at home and sometimes we have guests. Then I have difficulty in attending the classes.*"

The pre-service teachers' positive views were considered in the framework of whether or not they could cope with difficulties. A great majority of them said that they could cope with the difficulties by communicating with the lecturer and with their classmates. PT3 described the situation as: "*I had problems in doing the quizzes because I connected to the class with my phone. I told the teacher about it and the teacher helped me to upload the quizzes to the system by scanning them. whenever I had such a problem, I could reach the teacher and the teacher returned to me quickly. So, I feared the quizzes less.*" In a similar way, PT12 mentioned problems in uploading the reports to the system but said that they overcome the problem by communicating with the lecturer and with their classmates. In general, the pre-service teachers said that they could cope with the problems by talking to the lecturer and with peer communication even though they occasionally had technical problems with the system.

## DISCUSSION

This current study identified the views of pre-service teachers who had participated in flipped learning model-based general chemistry laboratory classes taught online concerning the processes of implementation. All the classes were taught in flipped learning model in this 11-week research, and videos of subject presentation and extra materials were sent to the participants prior to the classes. A quiz was given during the classes and then the experiments were done by the researchers. An environment of discussion was created through question-and-answer activities in this process and thus, it was secured that the pre-service teachers participated in the process actively. At the end of the study, it was found that the flipped learning model could be used effectively in teaching the general laboratory course online. The pre-service teachers' views on the implementation process were determined by means of 3 questions developed by the researchers. The participants were found to have positive views on the whole process. The fact that flipped learning model provided individuals with opportunities to learn whenever they wanted and at their own speed was the factor which led to the emergence of those positive views. A great majority of the participants often laid emphasis on this fact and said that they could learn the experiments easily because they come to classes by studying the subject before. However, negative views beside positive ones were also available. Accordingly, the pre-service teachers stated that technological problems caused the most difficulty in the process. In addition to that, another negative side most frequently repeated was the feeling of isolation.

It was found that the participants considered research question one generally in the context of learning experience, communication-interaction, technological experience and motivation. An examination of the answers to the question indicated that the point most frequently emphasised as positive about the model was that the learning model offered opportunities to learn at any time individuals wanted. In addition to that, the participants also stressed that the experiments were done during the classes and that they had the opportunity to participate in classes actively by means of the question and answer activities done during the experiments. It was remarkable on examining the participants' answers that individual differences had influenced participants' views. For example, some of the participants found the supplementary materials sent in addition to the videos effective and beneficial while some others stated that this diversity of materials had caused chaos. In a similar vein, while most of the participants found the process effective because they had the opportunity to learn whenever they wanted at home, two of them did not find the process positive and said that they felt isolated because they did not have the opportunity to interact.

The pre-service teachers considered research question two generally in the context of material effectiveness, student interaction and technological experience. On examining the answers given to the question, it became apparent that the positive views were on such points as accessibility, diversity of materials and being practical. Some of the negative views stated in this respect were also found to stem from individual differences. Beside pre-service teachers who said that they found the diversity of materials effective in learning the subjects in depth, there were also the ones who said that such diversity caused confusion. Additionally, some of the participants also mentioned technical problems they had encountered as the negative side.

A general examination of the participants' views in relation to research question three showed that they had difficulties in having the appropriate environments for joining the classes were the cause of problems they had in participating in the classes. Another most frequently mentioned problem was technical problems of various types. Problems such as situations in which more than one person needed a mobile device in addition to internet outage and power cut was also considered under the heading of technical problems encountered.

## CONCLUSION AND FUTURE DIRECTIONS

In conclusion, the pre-service teachers were found to think that using flipped learning model in the laboratory was effective in such issues as interacting with their classmates and with the lecturer and in getting motivated for the course. Besides, they also emphasised that they could devote more time to in-class activities with this model and that the situation helped them understand the experiments. They said that they had experiences similar to physical laboratory experience in this way. Beside stating these positive views, most of the participants also said that they were anxious about the development of their laboratory skills even though they felt in the laboratory. Review of relevant literature suggested that studies in which flipped learning model was used in teaching the online laboratory course had obtained results similar to the ones obtained in this current study. Teo et al (2014), for instance, used the model in the first- and second-year university students' chemistry laboratory classes. The students watched the videos about how to do the relevant experiments and then answered the questions sent to the mobile device application of the university. The students stated in the interviews held at the end of the study that they had understood the theoretical part of the subject prior to the application part by learning the course in this way. They also added that they had less difficulty in the challenging parts of experimentation. Another study conducted by Feng et al (2022) was concerned with how flipped learning model combined with team-based learning encouraged learning activities in clinical laboratory immunology classes. At the end of the research, it was found that the model increased student participation and learning effect. Öztürk and Deniz (2023) analysed the way flipped learning model contributed to pre-service elementary school teachers' development of efficacies in science laboratory applications during COVID-19 pandemic. The study found that the pre-service teachers made progress in issues such as awareness in terms of the importance of laboratory, being informed of laboratory materials and developing rules and skills in planning and doing a scientific experiment. These results indicate that flipped learning model offers students more individual and more effective laboratory experience.

Online education has become an integral part of our educational life today. Despite the fact that distance education does not fully replace face-to-face education, it is of great importance to teach applied courses such as the laboratory course online effectively. Therefore, it is recommended first of all that internet infrastructure is improved and students are given technical support. Besides, the flexible structure flipped learning model makes it possible to use other teaching methods and techniques. Hence, environments in which flipped learning model and different approaches of teaching are combined can be created in laboratory classes taught at differing grade levels. Using it in STEM laboratories can offer students advantages in displaying their creativity with additional time and prior knowledge that it provides in the laboratory. Such studies could be conducted with larger groups of participants and comparisons between groups could also be made.

It is also recommended to explore the integration of current trending technologies such as artificial intelligence, augmented reality and virtual reality into the flipped learning model. Studying the long-term effects of these integrations on student outcomes in various educational settings could offer valuable insights. Moreover, comparative research on the efficacy of flipped learning across different disciplines and education levels would aid in tailoring pedagogical approaches to specific learning needs and goals.

## REFERENCES

Abeysekera, L., & Dawson, P. (2015). Motivation and cognitive load in the flipped classroom: Definition, rationale and a call for research. *Higher Education Research & Development*, 34(1), 1–14. 10.1080/07294360.2014.934336

Ahmed, H. D., & Asiksoy, G. (2021). The effects of gamified flipped learning method on student's innovation skills, self-efficacy towards virtual physics lab course and perceptions. *Sustainability (Basel)*, 13(18), 10163. 10.3390/su131810163

Anzovino, M. E., Mallia, V. A., Morton, M. S., Barker Paredes, J. E., Pennington, R., Pursell, D. P., Rudd, G. E., Shepler, B., Villanueva, O., & Lee, S. (2020). Insights and initiatives while teaching organic chemistry i and ii with laboratory courses in the time of COVID-19. *Journal of Chemical Education*, 97(9), 3240–3245. 10.1021/acs.jchemed.0c00766

Atkins, P., & Jones, L. (2008). *Chemical principles: The quest for insight*. W. H. Freeman.

Bergmann, J., & Sams, A. (2012). *Flip your classroom: Reach every student in every class every day*. International Society for Technology in Education.

Bonwell, C. C., & Eison, J. A. (1991). ASHE-ERIC Higher Education Report: Vol. 1. *Active learning: Creating excitement in the classroom*. The George Washington University, School of Education and Human Development.

Borish, V., Werth, A., Sulaiman, N., Fox, M. F., Hoehn, J. R., & Lewandowski, H. (2022). Undergraduate student experiences in remote lab courses during the COVID-19 pandemic. *Physical Review. Physics Education Research*, 18(2), 020105. 10.1103/PhysRevPhysEducRes.18.020105

Brady, D., & Voronova, K. (2023). Flipped online active learning environment for large general chemistry courses. *Journal of Chemical Education*, 100(3), 1109–1117. 10.1021/acs.jchemed.2c00602

Brown, T. E., Lemay, H. E., & Bursten, B. R. (2006). *Chemistry: The central science*. Pearson Prentice Hall.

Busto, M. D., Ortega, N., Albillos, S. M., Ramos-Gómez, S., Pilar-Izquierdo, M. C., Velasco, B., & Palacios, D. (2022). Flipped classroom in laboratory practices of molecular biology: perception of the students from chemistry degree. *EDULEARN22 Proceedings*, (pp. 725-732). Research Gate.

Candaş, B., & Altun, T. (2023). Investigating flipped laboratory practices of science student teachers. *Journal of Turkish Science Education*, 20(1), 173–188. 10.36681/tused.2023.010

Candaş, B., Kiryak, Z., & Özmen, H. (2022). Developing prospective science teachers' using of chemical knowledge with flipped learning approach in the context of environmental problems. *Science Education International*, 33(2), 192–202. 10.33828/sei.v33.i2.7

Chans, G. M., Bravo-Gutiérrez, M. E., Orona-Navar, A., & Sánchez-Rodríguez, E. P. (2022). Compilation of chemistry experiments for an online laboratory course: Student's perception and learning outcomes in the context of COVID-19. *Sustainability (Basel)*, 14(5), 2539. 10.3390/su14052539

Chen, Y., Wang, Y., Kinshuk, , & Chen, N.-S. (2014). Is FLIP enough? Or should we use the FLIPPED model instead? *Computers & Education*, 79, 16–27. 10.1016/j.compedu.2014.07.004

Clough, M. P. (2002). Using the laboratory to enhance student learning. In Bybee, R. W. (Ed.), *Learning science and the science of learning, 2002 NSTA yearbook* (pp. 85–97).

Creswell, J. W. (2013). *Qualitative inquiry and research design: Choosing among five approaches*. Sage publications.

Delgado, T., Bhark, S.-J., & Donahue, J. (2021). Pandemic teaching: Creating and teaching cell biology labs online during COVID-19. *Biochemistry and Molecular Biology Education*, 49(1), 32–37. 10.1002/bmb.2148233336883

Denzin, N. K., & Lincoln, Y. S. (1994). *Handbook of qualitative research: California*. Sage Publications.

Divjak, B., Rienties, B., Iniesto, F., Vondra, P., & Žižak, M. (2022). Flipped classrooms in higher education during the COVID-19 pandemic: Findings and future research recommendations. *International Journal of Educational Technology in Higher Education*, 19(1), 9. 10.1186/s41239-021-00316-435252548

Elkhatat, A. M., & Al-Muhtaseb, S. A. (2021). Hybrid online-flipped learning pedagogy for teaching laboratory courses to mitigate the pandemic COVID-19 confinement and enable effective sustainable delivery: Investigation of attaining course learning outcome. *SN Social Sciences*, 1(5), 113. 10.1007/s43545-021-00117-634693317

Feng, Y., Zhao, B., Zheng, J., Fu, Y., & Jiang, Y. (2022). Online flipped classroom with team-based learning promoted learning activity in a clinical laboratory immunology class: Response to the COVID-19 pandemic. *BMC Medical Education*, 22(1), 836. 10.1186/s12909-022-03917-336463210

Herreid, C. F., & Schiller, N. A. (2013). Case studies and the flipped classroom. *Journal of College Science Teaching*, 42, 62–66.

Hofstein, A., & Hugerat, M. (2021). *Teaching and learning in the school chemistry laboratory*. Royal Society of Chemistry., 10.1039/9781839164712

Hofstein, A., & Lunetta, V. N. (2003). The laboratory in science education: Foundations for the twenty-first century. *Science Education*, 88(1), 28–54. 10.1002/sce.10106

Kim, M. K., Kim, S. M., Khera, O., & Getman, J. (2014). The experience of three flipped classrooms in an urban university: An exploration of design principles. *The Internet and Higher Education*, 22, 37–50. 10.1016/j.iheduc.2014.04.003

Lage, M. J., Platt, G. J., & Treglia, M. (2000). Inverting the classroom: A gateway to creating an inclusive learning environment. *The Journal of Economic Education*, 31(1), 30–43. 10.1080/00220480009596759

Lee, G., Kang, D. Y., Kim, M. J., Hong, H., & Martin, S. N. (2023). The emergence of remote laboratory courses in an emergency situation: University instructors' agency during the COVID-19 pandemic. *Cultural Studies of Science Education*, 18(3), 601–629. 10.1007/s11422-023-10169-037360052

May, D., Morkos, B., Jackson, A., Hunsu, N. J., Ingalls, A., & Beyette, F. (2022). Rapid transition of traditionally hands-on labs to online instruction in engineering courses. *European Journal of Engineering Education*, 48(5), 842–860. 10.1080/03043797.2022.2046707

Mayring, P. (2000). *Qualitative content analysis*. Forum qualitative sozialforschung/ forum: qualitative social research.

Miles, B. M., & Huberman, A. M. (1994). *Qualitative data analysis: An expanded source book*. Sage Publications.

Mojica, E. E., & Upmacis, R. K. (2021). Challenges encountered and students' reactions to practices utilized in a general chemistry laboratory course during the COVID-19 pandemic. *Journal of Chemical Education*, 99(2), 1053–1059. 10.1021/acs.jchemed.1c00838

Öztürk, A., & Deniz, İ. D. (2023). Proficiency development in science laboratory practices with the flipped learning model in the distance education process in the COVID-19 pandemic. *Educational Research: Theory and Practice*, 34(1), 17–31.

Patton, M. Q. (2015). *Qualitative research & evaluation methods: Integrating theory and practice*. Sage publications.

Pols, F. (2020). A physics lab course in times of COVID-19. *Electronic Journal for Research in Science & Mathematics Education*, 24(2), 172–178.

Prensky, M. (2001). Digital natives, digital immigrants. *On the Horizon*, 9(5), 1–6. 10.1108/10748120110424816

Qiang, Z., Obando, A. G., Chen, Y., & Ye, C. (2020). Revisiting distance learning resources for undergraduate research and lab activities during COVID-19 pandemic. *Journal of Chemical Education*, 97(9), 3446–3449. 10.1021/acs.jchemed.0c00609

Sanchez, E., Paukovics, E., Cheniti-Belcadhi, L., El Khayat, G., Said, B., & Korbaa, O. (2022). What do you mean by learning lab? *Education and Information Technologies*, 27(4), 4501–4520. 10.1007/s10639-021-10783-x

Schreier, M. (2012). *Qualitative content analysis in practice*. Sage Publications. 10.4135/9781529682571

Stieff, M., Werner, S. M., Fink, B., & Meador, D. (2018). Online Prelaboratory videos improve student performance in the general chemistry laboratory. *Journal of Chemical Education*, 95(8), 1260–1266. 10.1021/acs.jchemed.8b00109

Strayer, J. F. (2012). How learning in an inverted classroom influences cooperation, innovation and task orientation. *Learning Environments Research*, 15(2), 171–193. 10.1007/s10984-012-9108-4

Tang, T., Abuhmaid, A. M., Olaimat, M., Oudat, D. M., Aldhaeebi, M., & Bamanger, E. (2020). Efficiency of flipped classroom with online-based teaching under COVID-19. *Interactive Learning Environments*, 31(2), 1077–1088. 10.1080/10494820.2020.1817761

Teo, T. W., Tan, K. C., Yan, Y. K., Teo, Y. C., & Yeo, L. W. (2014). How flip teaching supports undergraduate chemistry laboratory learning. *Chemistry Education Research and Practice*, 15(4), 550–567. 10.1039/C4RP00003J

Tian, X. (2023). Educational reform and prospects in the post-pandemic era. *Journal of Education. Humanities and Social Sciences*, 19, 262–270. 10.54097/ehss.v19i.11142

Tucker, B. (2012). The flipped classroom. *Education Next*, 12(1), 82–83.

Villanueva, O., & Zimmermann, K. (2020). Transitioning an upper-level, integrated laboratory course to remote and online instruction during the COVID-19 pandemic. *Journal of Chemical Education*, 97(9), 3114–3120. 10.1021/acs.jchemed.0c00740

Zappe, S., Leicht, R., Messner, J., Litzinger, T., & Lee, H. W. (2009). *"Flipping" the classroom to explore active learning in a large undergraduate course.* Paper presented at the American Society for Engineering Education Annual Conference & Exhibition, Nashville. 10.18260/1-2--4545

# Chapter 13
# Investigation of STEM in Industry 5.0

**G. Prasad**
https://orcid.org/0000-0002-5709-9182
*Chandigarh University, Punjab, India*

## ABSTRACT

*STEM professionals are at the forefront of integrating emerging technologies into manufacturing processes. This includes the development and implementation of technologies like advanced robotics, augmented reality, and virtual reality, which are central to Industry 5.0's human-machine collaboration. IoT devices generate massive amounts of data in Industry 5.0. STEM experts are needed to design and maintain these devices and develop data analytics solutions to extract actionable insights from this data. This data-driven decision-making is critical for optimizing processes. AI and machine learning are central to Industry 5.0, enabling machines to learn from human interaction and adapt accordingly. Data scientists and AI experts develop the algorithms and models that make this possible. As Industry 5.0 evolves, there's a growing emphasis on sustainable manufacturing and reducing environmental impact. STEM professionals contribute to designing eco-friendly manufacturing processes and materials. Protecting the interconnected systems and data in Industry 5.0 is critical.*

## INTRODUCTION

STEM (Science, Technology, Engineering, and Mathematics). It is a multidisciplinary approach to education that combines all four disciplines into a unified learning paradigm focused on practical applications in the real world. Science is the methodical examination of the natural and physical world using observation

DOI: 10.4018/979-8-3693-7645-4.ch013

and experiments. It promotes the development of critical thinking skills, the ability to solve problems, and a more profound comprehension of the universe. Scientific education promotes inquisitiveness and provides students with the abilities to formulate hypotheses, conduct experiments, and evaluate evidence. Technology in STEM education encompasses the various tools, methods, and gadgets that are specifically designed to address challenges and enhance the quality of human existence. It encompasses a wide range of items, ranging from basic instruments to intricate computer systems and software. Acquiring knowledge about technology enables students to develop expertise in using and developing technological solutions, which are essential in contemporary society. Engineering is the application of scientific and mathematical concepts to create, construct, and sustain structures, machines, and systems. The focus is on fostering creativity, innovation, and pragmatic problem-solving. Engineering education enables students to acquire the skills and knowledge necessary to develop solutions that effectively address specific requirements, while taking into account several factors such as financial limitations, safety considerations, and environmental consequences. Mathematics serves as the primary means of communication in the fields of science and technology. It encompasses the examination of numerical values, quantities, geometric forms, and regularities. Mathematics education equips pupils with vital proficiencies in deductive reasoning, solution-oriented thinking, and analytical cognition. Comprehending and progressing in the other STEM disciplines is essential.

STEM education focuses on the integration of science, technology, engineering, and mathematics courses into a unified and comprehensive learning experience, rather than teaching them separately. This interdisciplinary approach promotes students' recognition of the interrelations among many disciplines and their collaborative potential in addressing practical challenges. STEM education involves hands-on, project-based learning that allows students to actively participate in meaningful tasks, hence highlighting the practicality and importance of their studies. This technique not only improves their comprehension and memory of information but also fosters a lifetime curiosity in acquiring knowledge and exploring new things.

STEAM (Science, Technology, Engineering, Arts, and Mathematics) signifies a progressive educational approach that incorporates the arts alongside the conventional STEM disciplines. This incorporation acknowledges the significance of originality and advancement in technical disciplines and strives to offer a more comprehensive education. Here is an in-depth examination of STEAM and its importance: STEAM education integrates the arts into the conventional STEM framework, highlighting the significance of creativity and design thinking in addition to scientific and mathematical foundations. The arts component encompasses disciplines such as visual arts, music, drama, and literature. Its primary objective is to cultivate creativity, critical thinking, and problem-solving abilities.

In the last twenty years, there have been major technological changes, brought about by disruptive breakthroughs in both software and hardware. The amalgamation of information, communication, and artificial intelligence is taking place, resulting in the integration of different concepts, generally referred to as the digital transformation. The current discussion over the adoption of sophisticated intelligence systems related to the fourth industrial revolution, often known as Industry 4.0, continues to be a subject of debate. Nevertheless, the dominant characteristics of the fifth industrial revolution, referred to as Industry 5.0, go beyond the simple creation of products and services for monetary benefit. Therefore, it requires a change in both the way people think and the way they behave for everyone involved.

The study conducted by Abichandani et al in 2022 focused on the curriculum, pedagogy, and assessment of Internet-of-Things (IoT) for STEM education. Adel (2022) conducted a study on the prospective impact of Industry 5.0 on society, focusing on human-centered answers, difficulties, and their corresponding remedies. A case study was conducted by Banerjee and Krishnagar in 2023, examining the implementation of the National Education Policy (NEP) 2020 curriculum in India, which was introduced by the University Grant Commission. (Broo et al 2022) conducted a study on the reevaluation of developing engineering education during the era of industry 5.0. (Cui et al 2023) employed Artificial Intelligence's impact on MetaEdu, a novel framework designed for the advancement of education in the future. (Ghobakhloo et al 2022) Identified the contributions of industry 5.0 to sustainable development. The study conducted by Kolade and Owoseni in 2022 examined the concept of Employment 5.0, focusing on the evolving nature of labour and its implications for the future.

(Leng et al 2022) conducted a case study on the potential and historical analysis of Industry 5.0. The study conducted by Nita et al in 2023 examined the difficulties and potential benefits of quantum literacy in the context of future education and problem-solving across many disciplines. Prasad (2022) conducted a study on online education in the context of industry 5.0. The study conducted by Sable and Bhatt in 2023 examined the relationship between emotional intelligence and Bloom's affective domain categories in relation to a new pedagogical and curricular structure. The study conducted by Qu et al. (2022) focused on the role of artificial intelligence in transforming educational approaches. The study conducted by Zizic et al. (2022) examined the transition from Industry 4.0 to Industry 5.0, providing a comprehensive evaluation and analysis of the paradigm change in terms of its impact on people, organisations, and technology.

## PEDAGOGY IN TEACHING

To just a few, the following justifies the need for the application of thought to pedagogy:

- There are several methods that students learn.
- Students have a variety of personality qualities, including introversion and extraversion.
- Theory, skills, and knowledge are lost if they are not applied.
- Knowledge is only enduring when it is useful in day-to-day activities.
- Learning reflections ought to take precedence than grades.
- The best curriculum for transfer is one that incorporates ideas from all subject areas.

(a) Instruction in Context

Similar to service-learning, context enables students to learn via experience and inquiry about concepts, inquiry, and community needs. Furthermore, significant teaching and learning opportunities in the actual world are provided by service learning.

(b) Worldwide Competencies

The focus needs to change from defining 21st-century skills to global competences that all students will require in the future. These capacities won't change. Learners will be able to establish goals for more mastery development by giving them access to learning progressions of these skills and dispositions and the chance to evaluate how well they display them.

(c) Education that is Personalised

Instructors must first understand the significance of adjusting to various learners and learning styles. Understanding each student's position in the competency-based learning path towards mastery and using learner profiles to assist them understand who they are as individuals. Students that understand how to advance in their own learning through learner agency—establishing objectives, benchmarks, self-monitoring, self-evaluation, and global competency development—know when to ask for help and can exercise their right to voice and choice in their education through a variety of learner pathways and adaptable learning settings.

(d) Curriculum Development for Global Citizens

Every institution aims to create citizens who are aware of the world. A closer look at each school's vision and mission statements will reveal a clear link to the formation of globally responsible citizens. As educators, it is our duty to give every student the chance to understand diversity, appreciation, and respect; to understand his or her place in society as an accountable and engaged global citizen.

(e) Diversity that is Interrelated

"Don't Guess My Race" is an online programme created by Interactive Diversity that aims to encourage teenagers to think critically about their race and identity. Its goal is to eradicate bias, assumptions, and preconceptions. The following needs to be taken into account while creating global citizen projects as part of instructional strategies:

- Global themes and issues: education, equity, poverty, and environmental protection.
- The neighbourhood: awareness of its needs and knowledge of them (people learn best when exposed to problems/issues of a community in a practical environment).
- The learner's and the community's objectives and requirements in order to be able to act effectively and think back on making an impact.

(f) Learning via experience

The majority of educators know that when the material is relevant to them personally, kids learn more quickly and remember it better. Additionally, when students take part in the learning process, the learning process becomes even more personalised.

Three things make up experiential learning:

Self-assessment, self-direction, and physical activity

They learn how to cooperate and work well with others, as well as the value that others provide, because they work largely in groups. Students are prepared for future success in the real world by learning critical thinking, adaptability, perseverance, and real-life leadership abilities.

- Learning by doing: an instructional strategy; • Benefits of experiential learning; • Real-world applicationStudents will typically ignore lectures if they believe the material is unrelated to the "real world." Students can better understand a concept when they are assigned hands-on projects. Furthermore, because every student has a different set of experiences, they will all interpret and apply the material differently.The rules for post-COVID era preparation programmes that use action steps towards technology infusion were created by Sprague et al. in 2022. In their study, Pelayo et al. (2023) employed technology to facilitate instruction in general mathematics among marginalised Filipino students through intuitive implications during the post-pandemic period. Technology Use to Improve the Quality of Collaborative Learning Experiences for Engineering Students in the Post-Pandemic Era, Calin & Pislaru (2023). The Post-Covid-19 Pandemic and Library Users' Education: Impact on Examination and Survey was examined by Adetayo (2023). Ojong,

V. (2024) investigated post-pandemic advances and difficulties. In 2023, Sooryamoorthy et al. Exploring the "New Normal" Social World: Post-pandemic Methodological Innovations and Adaptations. Zhai (2023) examined the use of the blended learning model in oral college English courses following the pandemic. In four secondary mathematics classrooms, the views of teachers and students towards blended learning were examined by Attard and Holmes (2022). Imschloss and Schwemmle's (2023) research focused on the conceptual framework and consequences of creation in post-pandemic retailing.

## STEM-DRIVEN INNOVATION

Industry 5.0 might emphasize the importance of STEM skills and knowledge in driving innovation and problem-solving within industrial settings. This could involve using IoT technologies to enhance STEM-related processes and research. STEM disciplines provide the foundation for understanding the natural world, developing technology, solving problems, and advancing society. When applied innovatively, they can lead to significant breakthroughs and improvements.

Here are key aspects of STEM-driven innovation:

(a) **Interdisciplinary Approach:** STEM-driven innovation often involves the collaboration of experts from multiple STEM disciplines. It recognizes that complex problems and opportunities often require a holistic approach that combines knowledge and techniques from different fields.

(b) **Problem Solving:** STEM disciplines provide the analytical and problem-solving skills needed to identify challenges, design experiments, analyze data, and develop evidence-based solutions. This approach is central to innovation.

(c) **Technological Advancements:** Many innovations are rooted in advancements in technology, particularly in fields like engineering and computer science. These innovations can range from new materials and manufacturing processes to software applications and hardware devices.

(d) **Scientific Discovery:** Scientific research, which is a fundamental part of STEM, can lead to ground breaking discoveries that have practical applications. Innovations often emerge from the pursuit of scientific knowledge.

(e) **Education and Workforce Development:** STEM-driven innovation relies on a skilled workforce. Education and training in STEM fields are essential for nurturing innovators and problem solvers who can contribute to advancements in various industries.

(f) **Cross-Industry Impact:** STEM-driven innovation isn't limited to a single industry. It can have a profound impact across diverse sectors, including healthcare, energy, agriculture, transportation, and more.

Examples of STEM-driven innovation include:

- The development of new medical treatments and therapies based on advances in biology and chemistry.
- Breakthroughs in renewable energy technologies that address climate change.
- Improvements in data analytics and artificial intelligence that drive innovation in various sectors, from finance to healthcare.
- Advances in materials science leading to lighter and stronger materials for aerospace and automotive industries.
- Innovations in robotics and automation that enhance manufacturing and logistics.

STEM-driven innovation is a dynamic and ongoing process that continues to shape the modern world. Educational institutions, research organizations, and industries often work together to foster STEM-driven innovation and drive progress in society.

## STEM EDUCATION AND WORKFORCE

Industry 5.0 might require a workforce with strong STEM skills to operate and maintain advanced manufacturing processes. IoT could be used for training and education in these fields. STEM education and the STEM workforce play pivotal roles in driving innovation, economic growth, and technological advancements in today's world. The STEM workforce comprises individuals who have the knowledge and skills in these fields and are actively engaged in STEM-related careers. Here's a closer look at STEM education and its impact on the workforce.

(a) Preparation for the Future: In an increasingly technology-driven world, STEM education prepares students for the jobs and challenges of the future. It equips them with the abilities needed to adapt to rapidly changing industries.

(b) Diversity and Inclusion: Promoting STEM education also aims to increase diversity and inclusion in STEM fields. Efforts are made to encourage underrepresented groups, including women and minorities, to pursue STEM careers.

(c) STEM Career Pathways: STEM education pathways lead to a wide range of career opportunities, including engineering, computer science, healthcare, environmental science, data analysis, and more.

(d) Driving Innovation: The STEM workforce is at the forefront of innovation. Scientists, engineers, programmers, and mathematicians develop new technologies, products, and services that shape industries and improve lives.

(e) Economic Growth: STEM professionals are vital to economic growth. They contribute to the competitiveness of nations by creating high-value jobs and driving industries such as information technology, biotechnology, and clean energy.
(f) Problem Solvers: STEM workers are problem solvers. They tackle complex challenges, from designing sustainable infrastructure to developing new medical treatments, using scientific and technical expertise.
(g) Interdisciplinary Collaboration: Many STEM careers involve collaborating across disciplines. This interdisciplinary approach often leads to breakthroughs and innovative solutions to complex issues.
(h) Lifelong Learning: STEM professionals often engage in lifelong learning and professional development to stay current in their fields. The dynamic nature of STEM disciplines requires ongoing education and skill enhancement.

To support STEM education and the STEM workforce, governments, educational institutions, and industries often collaborate to:

- Provide access to quality STEM education at all levels.
- Encourage STEM career exploration and mentorship.
- Promote diversity and inclusion in STEM fields.
- Invest in research and development.
- Foster a culture of innovation and entrepreneurship.

A strong STEM education system and a skilled STEM workforce are crucial components of a nation's competitiveness and its ability to address the challenges and opportunities of the future.

## IOT FOR STEM RESEARCH

IoT technologies could be applied in STEM research within industrial contexts, such as collecting data from sensors in laboratories or using IoT devices for data analysis in scientific experiments. IoT technologies can provide researchers with valuable data, streamline data collection processes, and enable real-time monitoring and control of experiments and systems. Here are several ways in which IoT can benefit STEM research:
(a) Data Collection and Sensing:

- Environmental Monitoring: IoT sensors can collect data on environmental factors such as temperature, humidity, air quality, and pollution levels. This is crucial in fields like environmental science and ecology.

- Biological and Medical Research: IoT devices can monitor vital signs, track the movement of animals, or measure physiological parameters, aiding biomedical and biological research.
- Agriculture: IoT sensors can monitor soil conditions, crop health, and weather, assisting researchers in optimizing agricultural practices.

(b) Laboratory Automation:

- Smart Lab Equipment: IoT-enabled laboratory equipment can automatically collect and transmit data, reducing manual data entry and minimizing errors.
- Experiment Control: Researchers can remotely control experiments and equipment, making it easier to conduct experiments that require precise timing or control.

(c) Real-Time Data Analysis:

IoT devices can transmit data in real-time, allowing researchers to analyze data as it's collected. This can lead to faster insights and adjustments during experiments. Edge computing, where data is processed locally on IoT devices, can be used to filter and preprocess data before sending it to central servers for further analysis.

(d) Remote Monitoring and Collaboration:

Researchers can remotely monitor experiments and share data with collaborators regardless of geographical location. This facilitates global collaboration and knowledge sharing. IoT enables remote access to equipment and instruments, reducing the need for researchers to be physically present in the lab.

(e) Energy Efficiency:

IoT can help optimize energy consumption in research facilities. Smart energy management systems can reduce energy costs and environmental impact. In renewable energy research, IoT devices can collect data from solar panels, wind turbines, and other sources to improve energy generation efficiency.

(f) Safety and Security:

IoT-based security systems can protect sensitive research data and equipment. Researchers can receive alerts about unauthorized access or potential hazards. Environmental sensors can detect and warn against hazardous conditions, enhancing lab safety.

(g) Field Research:

For field researchers, IoT can provide tools for collecting and transmitting data from remote locations, such as tracking wildlife movements or monitoring geological phenomena. GPS, satellite communication, and IoT devices can aid geospatial research and mapping.

(h) Resource Optimization:

IoT analytics can help optimize resource allocation in research institutions, from managing equipment usage to streamlining procurement based on real-time data. IoT can enable citizen scientists to contribute to research efforts by using accessible, user-friendly IoT devices to collect data, which can then be shared with researchers.

Overall, IoT for STEM research has the potential to accelerate the pace of discovery, improve data quality, increase research efficiency, and enable new types of experiments and studies that were previously challenging or impossible. However, it's essential to address data privacy and security concerns, standardize data formats and protocols, and provide training for researchers to make the most of IoT technologies in their work.

Incorporating STEM into the Internet of Things (IoT) requires a thorough grasp of different protocols and technologies that facilitate smooth communication and interaction between objects. The IoT protocols include MQTT (Message Queuing Telemetry Transport), CoAP (Constrained Application Protocol), HTTP/HTTPS (Hypertext Transfer Protocol / Secure), AMQP (Advanced Message Queuing Protocol), Zigbee, LoRaWAN (Long Range Wide Area Network), Bluetooth Low Energy (BLE), and 6LoWPAN (IPv6 over Low-Power Wireless Personal Area Networks).

## CONCLUSION

This research holds significant importance for a multitude of reasons. Firstly, it introduces a novel approach to overseeing innovation known as "Absolute Innovation Management" with the aim of enhancing the transparency, comprehensiveness, and practicality of adopting innovative ideas. The ultimate innovation management framework not only accelerates the innovation process but also cultivates a culture of accountability across the entire organisation, ensuring that all employees feel invested in its success. Furthermore, it offers a framework for seamlessly incorporating innovation, design thinking, and commercial strategy. An further advantage of absolute innovation management is its seamless integration of innovation into routine company activities, hence facilitating the implementation of novel ideas. Furthermore, through aligning innovation more closely with the overall objectives of the organisation, absolute innovation management effectively reduces the adverse effects of disruptions and limited comprehension. The present analysis proposes a new paradigm, known as "absolute innovation," as the ultimate stage of thinking about innovation. Absolute innovation integrates innovation management as a strategic approach and utilises design thinking to develop economically viable and technically feasible innovations that prioritise the needs of customers and employees. This approach aligns the "innovation ecosystem" with the overall corporate strategy of the organisation. In order to maintain a competitive edge and drive economic expansion in the era of the Internet of Things (IoT) and Industry 5.0, firms need to cultivate an entrepreneurial mindset and prioritise customer feedback by enhancing their commitment to corporate venturing and corporate entrepreneurship.

## REFERENCES


Abichandani, P., Sivakumar, V., Lobo, D., Iaboni, C., & Shekhar, P. (2022). Internet-of-things curriculum, pedagogy, and assessment for stem education: A review of literature. *IEEE Access : Practical Innovations, Open Solutions*, 10, 38351–38369. 10.1109/ACCESS.2022.3164709

Adel, A. (2022). Future of industry 5.0 in society: Human-centric solutions, challenges and prospective research areas. *Journal of Cloud Computing (Heidelberg, Germany)*, 11(1), 1–15. 10.1186/s13677-022-00314-536101900

Adetayo, A. J. (2023). Post Covid-19 pandemic and library users' education: Impact on examination and survey. *Journal of Academic Librarianship*, 49(3), 102695. 10.1016/j.acalib.2023.10269536938152

Attard, C., & Holmes, K. (2022). An exploration of teacher and student perceptions of blended learning in four secondary mathematics classrooms. *Mathematics Education Research Journal*, 34(4), 719–740. 10.1007/s13394-020-00359-2

Banerjee, M., & Krishnagar, N. (2023). *IMPLEMENTATION OF NEP 2020 CURRICULUM: AN OVERVIEW*. NEP 2020: Implementation Phase.

Broo, D. G., Kaynak, O., & Sait, S. M. (2022). Rethinking engineering education at the age of industry 5.0. *Journal of Industrial Information Integration*, 25, 100311. 10.1016/j.jii.2021.100311

Calin, M. D., & Pislaru, C. (2023). Use of Technology to Increase the Quality of Collaborative Learning Experiences for Engineering Students in the Post-Pandemic Period. *Educatia*, 21(25), 73–80. 10.24193/ed21.2023.25.08

Cui, L., Zhu, C., Hare, R., & Tang, Y. (2023). MetaEdu: A new framework for future education. *Discover Artificial Intelligence*, 3(1), 10. 10.1007/s44163-023-00053-9

Ghobakhloo, M., Iranmanesh, M., Mubarak, M. F., Mubarik, M., Rejeb, A., & Nilashi, M. (2022). Identifying industry 5.0 contributions to sustainable development: A strategy roadmap for delivering sustainability values. *Sustainable Production and Consumption*, 33, 716–737. 10.1016/j.spc.2022.08.003

Imschloss, M., & Schwemmle, M. (2023). Value creation in post-pandemic retailing: A conceptual framework and implications. *Journal of Business Economics*, 1–39. 10.1007/s11573-023-01189-x

Kolade, O., & Owoseni, A. (2022). Employment 5.0: The work of the future and the future of work. *Technology in Society*, 71, 102086. 10.1016/j.techsoc.2022.102086

Leng, J., Sha, W., Wang, B., Zheng, P., Zhuang, C., Liu, Q., Wuest, T., Mourtzis, D., & Wang, L. (2022). Industry 5.0: Prospect and retrospect. *Journal of Manufacturing Systems*, 65, 279–295. 10.1016/j.jmsy.2022.09.017

Nita, L., Mazzoli Smith, L., Chancellor, N., & Cramman, H. (2023). The challenge and opportunities of quantum literacy for future education and transdisciplinary problem-solving. *Research in Science & Technological Education*, 41(2), 564–580. 10.1080/02635143.2021.1920905

Ojong, V. (2024). Ethnographic research: Developments and challenges in the post-pandemic era. In *Researching the 'New Normal'Social World* (pp. 50–66). Routledge.

Pelayo-Dacanay, J. A., Pinili, L. C., Etcuban, J. O., Padillo, G. G., Manguilimotan, R. P., & Capuno, R. G. (2023). Technology-Supported Instruction In General Mathematics: Its Intuitive Implications Among Marginalized Filipino Students Amidst The Post-Pandemic Period. *Journal of Positive Psychology and Wellbeing*, 7(3), 86–99.

Prasad, G. (2022). Online education in industry 5.0. In *Pedagogy, Presence, and Motivation in Online Education* (pp. 22-35). IGI Global.

Qu, J., Zhao, Y., & Xie, Y. (2022). Artificial intelligence leads the reform of education models. *Systems Research and Behavioral Science*, 39(3), 581–588. 10.1002/sres.2864

Sable, R. G., & Bhatt, K. D. (2023). NEP 2020: Linking Emotional Intelligence and Bloom's Affective Domain Categories to New Pedagogical and Curricular Structure. International Journal of Professional Business Review: Int. *J. Prof. Bus. Rev.*, 8(7), 119.

Sooryamoorthy, R., & Ojong, V. (Eds.). (2023). *Researching the 'New Normal'Social World: Methodological Adaptations and Innovations Post-Pandemic*. Taylor & Francis. 10.4324/9781003386087

Sprague, D. R., Williamson, J., & Foulger, T. S. (2022). Design guidelines for post-COVID era preparation programs: Action steps toward technology infusion. *Journal of Technology and Teacher Education*, 30(2), 177–187.

Zhai, J. (2023). The Application of Blended Teaching Model in College English Oral Courses in the Post Epidemic Era. *Journal of Theory and Practice of Contemporary Education*, 3(8), 44–50.

Zizic, M. C., Mladineo, M., Gjeldum, N., & Celent, L. (2022). From industry 4.0 towards industry 5.0: A review and analysis of paradigm shift for the people, organization and technology. *Energies*, 15(14), 5221. 10.3390/en15145221

# Chapter 14
# Adaptive Online STEAM Education:
## Insights From Stakeholders' Perspectives

**Teresa Torres-Coronas**
https://orcid.org/0000-0002-9900-4997
*Universitat Rovira i Virgili, Spain*

## ABSTRACT

*This chapter outlines the findings of national focus group discussions, as part of a European Erasmus Plus project. It examines the evolution of STEAM education, shaped by online teaching methods during the COVID-19 pandemic. The chapter includes a literature review, research methodology, and an in-depth data analysis. Key themes include the impact of online teaching on STEAM subjects, adaptive teaching, and the skills and requirements necessary in this educational field. The chapter captures the perspectives of students, teachers and technical staff. It summarizes the challenges and potential of online STEAM education.*

## INTRODUCTION

The global COVID-19 pandemic online education, inspired by the philosophy of connectivism (Rodriguez, 2012), transitioned from an option to a critical necessity. It transformed the educational landscape; compelling institutions to adapt to new teaching methods, when no every university was technologically ready (Mishra, Gupta & Shree, 2020). This shift towards remote learning emphasizes the findings of Bakera, Bujaka, and De Millo (2012), who assert that "effective institutions are those that proactively explore innovative and effective approaches to restructure the

DOI: 10.4018/979-8-3693-7645-4.ch014

delivery of 'content' in conjunction with change" (p. 330), highlighting the critical need for adaptability. These new approaches must include a deep understanding of the benefits and the consequences of implementing technological solutions designed to complement traditional pedagogy. Moreover, innovative change needs to improve current practice, be compatible with existing values and generate observable results (Rogers, 2003), such as students satisfaction.

In online education, student satisfaction is dependent on a well-rounded support network, including institutional, administrative, instructional, and technical support (Butt, Mahmood & Saleem, 2022). However, the shift to online learning during the pandemic frequently led to inadequate support, causing inconsistent student satisfaction and engagement.

In parallel, these educational strategies must effectively ensure that all learners, regardless of their unique needs, learning styles, and experiences, have equitable opportunities for success. In this context, adaptive teaching emerges as an innovative educational approach that uses advanced educational technology, data analytics, and artificial intelligence to personalize learning content, processes, and methods (Wu et al., 2023). This allows teachers to respond more effectively to learners' diversity, creating learning experiences that are more suitable for individual characteristics (Wang et al., 2023). During the pandemic, educational models failed to accommodate the diverse challenges faced by learners with different needs.

This chapter examines the challenges and innovations within online education precipitated by the COVID-19 pandemic, focusing on the STEAM disciplines. Overall, this external crisis accelerated educational transformation to rethink the learning-teaching process, stressing the need for adaptive learning practices and opened opportunities for long-term innovations in STEAM education, including applications of artificial intelligence, machine learning and big data (Anush Kumar, Amudhavan, Arun Kumar & Sasikala, 2021). These changes brought to light challenges such as the rapid need for educators to develop competencies to design and deliver on line and blended courses (Mirriahi et al, 2015), the struggle to maintain student motivation and engagement remotely, and the technological disparities affecting student participation and performance.

Changing the learning environment also means changing the psychosocial and emotional dimensions of a classroom, including relationship, perceptions and attitudes (Fraser, 2012). To explore the perception of the main stakeholders (students, teachers and technical staff) uses focus group discussions. Through the voices of students, teachers and staff, this research analyze the complexities of transitioning to digital platforms, the difficulties of maintaining student engagement in a virtual environment, and the need to develop adaptive teaching methodologies. Results reveal significant transformations in teaching strategies, highlighting the critical necessity for flexible educational practices and the continuous professional development of teachers.

Following this section, a comprehensive literature review relevant to the study topic is presented, exploring existing research and theories that support the research. Subsequently, the research study is described, including the applied methodology and the main findings. A thorough understanding of the research and its implications are provided at the end of this chapter.

## CHALLENGES AND OPPORTUNITIES FOR STEAM EDUCATION

The COVID-19 pandemic has created new challenges and opportunities for education in the STEAM disciplines. According to various studies, online education in STEAM disciplines can promote information retention, flexibility, and innovation. This happens when the curricula and activities are properly designed, and teachers and students are equipped with the necessary digital competencies (Brown et al, 2023). However, several challenges have been highlighted, including lower levels of student motivation and engagement, inadequate technological resources and infrastructure, along with disparities in access to online learning environments.

During the pandemic, students reported that the obstacles to fully online learning were not only technological and instructional challenges but also social and affective challenges of isolation and social distancing (Lemay, Bazelais & Doleck, 2021). The importance of nurturing teacher-student relationships is evident, as an educator's motivational approach can significantly influence student engagement (De Loof et al., 2021). Therefore, it is essential to seek innovative and inclusive solutions that allow exploiting the potential of online education in STEAM disciplines without compromising quality, engagement and equity.

The scholarly literature underscores the need for adaptive instructional methodologies to accommodate the evolving virtual learning environment (Cheung, Kwok, Phusavat & Yan, 2021). It reflects on significant shifts in pedagogical strategies, advocating for the adoption of flexible educational practices and ongoing professional development for educators to navigate these changes with effectivity. According to Margaryan, Bianco and Littlejohn (2015), "the instructional design quality of a course is a critical indicator and prerequisite of the potential of the course for effective learning" (p. 78).

Traditional teaching methods, which typically adopt a uniform approach, often fall short in addressing the diverse needs, learning styles, preferences, and capabilities of individual students. Such educational experiences undermine student self-efficacy, contributing to suboptimal learning outcomes, diminished engagement, and lead to student dropout (Zhu & Wang, 2020). In contrast, the implementation of adaptive learning strategies offers a promising avenue to overcome these limitations inherent in conventional educational approaches (Guerrero-Roldán et al., 2021).

Student acceptance is an important variable for determining the success of any new learning experience. For students to accept online (and hybrid models), the system must be easy to use, applicable and useful, and the teacher must be able to respond in a timely manner (Tselios, Daskalakis & Papadopoulou, 2011; Zhao & Yuan, 2010). In parallel, online students need a teacher who promote positive learning attitudes by continuing to facilitate and guide their learning journey (Zhou, 2016).

A critical issue that emerged during the pandemic was the rapid shift toward remote learning. This transition brought to light the challenges associated with conducting experimental practices online, primarily due to a lack of essential software and interactive platforms. The research conducted by Achuthan et al. (2021) underscores the need for well-designed interactive platforms to support learning experiences in this digital landscape. Managing participation and fostering collaboration presented significant difficulties. It became crucial to prioritize innovative solutions that enhance interactivity and bridge the gap between physical and virtual learning spaces.

Research also examines the challenges in promoting effective teamwork and collaboration online. It explores educators' strategies to overcome these problems by implementing structured virtual sessions and utilizing online collaborative tools to simulate a sense of teamwork. These results align with the community of inquiry framework by Garrison & Anderson (2011), which suggests that a student's educational experience relies on three presences: cognitive (engagement with content), social (interaction with others), and teaching (instructor involvement in the course). Learners must have opportunities to connect with content, with peers, and with teachers. Social presence is required if students are to build trust and be able to comfortably engage into deeper levels of social knowledge construction.

Furthermore, the literature review conducted by Maguraushe, Masimba and Muderedzwa, (2022) addresses issues of equity and access, emphasizing the digital divide that impacted the quality of remote education provided during the COVID-19 crisis. Therefore, there is a need for creative strategies to support all students, particularly those lacking access to technology and stable internet connections. This discussion extends to encouraging student participation through positive reinforcement and adaptive learning strategies to meet individual student needs, as a tool to make adjustments according to the individual characteristics of learners and promote the individualized development of students (Cheung, Kwok, Phusavat & Yan, 2021).

Despite the need for comprehensive teacher training in online education methods and adaptive teaching, current research often ignores the personal characteristics of instructors (Martin, Sun & Westine, 2020). This fact can make it challenging to create effective professional development programs, as understanding each teacher's unique needs is essential for providing appropriate training.

In summary, the COVID-19 pandemic has highlighted the need for adaptive and personalized online education in STEAM disciplines, emphasizing the importance of digital competencies and innovative teaching strategies. Challenges such as technological limitations, student engagement, and equity have underscored the need for comprehensive teacher training and support. Addressing these issues through adaptive methodologies and fostering interactive online environments is crucial for the success of online learning, ensuring quality, equity, and effectiveness in STEAM education during and beyond the pandemic. In the following section, we will explore whether the perspectives of the main stakeholders (teachers, students and technical staff) align with these findings.

## RESEARCH METHODOLOGY AND RESULTS

### Research Methodology

The methodology employed in this study was the focus group technique. This method is particularly valuable in educational research, as it enables researchers to grasp the complexities of teaching and learning processes from the perspectives of the main stakeholders (teachers, students and technical staff). As the study of Fairhurst, Koul and Sheffield (2023) shows, one of the key benefits of using focus groups is their ability to facilitate the expression of thoughts and feelings in a more nuanced and complex manner than other data collection methods. This is due to the dynamic nature of the conversation, where participants can respond to and build upon each other's contributions, leading to a more comprehensive understanding of the subject matter. Additionally, focus groups can reveal not only what participants think but also why they think in certain ways, uncovering underlying motivations, attitudes and behaviors.

In the focus groups, thirty-two participants were divided into students (10), teaching staff (11), and management staff (11). Participants from the teaching group had over fifteen years of experience, covering both traditional and online pedagogical methods. These teachers were particularly engaged in laboratory and simulation activities. The management staff consisted of specialists working on curriculum design, quality control, and the design of professional development programs. All students were from STEAM areas.

Half of the focus groups were conducted in June 2022 as a part of the STEAM project field research, and the other half in October 2023, to validate previous results (see Figure 1). Discussions were recorded for subsequent coding and analysis of the results. During the focus group, participants discussed the shift from traditional in-person teaching to online education, highlighting the challenges faced and adaptations made. Results are presented taking into account the challenges identified and the recommendations for the future.

*Figure 1. Research methodology*

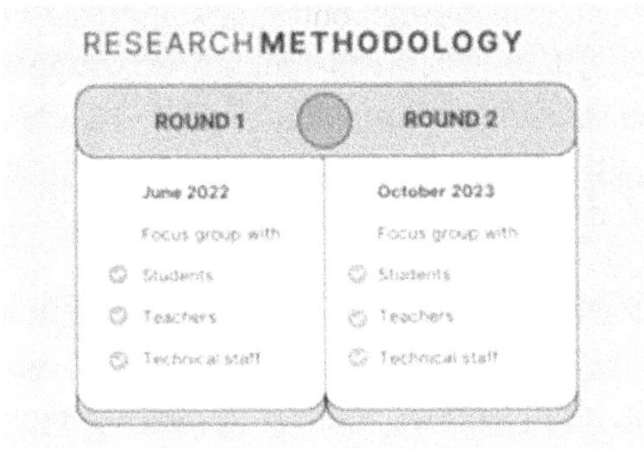


*Source: Own elaboration*

## Analysis From Teachers' Perceptions

The insights from teachers' focus groups stress the challenges STEAM teachers faced during the transition to online education. While acknowledging the potential benefits of personalized learning and advanced technologies, the group emphasized the crucial need for institutional support, training, and a paradigm shift in approaching online education.

### Challenges

1. *Transition to remote learning.* Participants detailed how the shift from traditional in-person classes to online formats was facilitated using virtual campuses and digital tools such as Microsoft Teams and Moodle. This transition showed several challenges, particularly in executing experimental practices and addressing the deficit of essential software for laboratory work. Teachers were forced to employ temporary solutions, such as substituting professional simulators with Microsoft Excel and establishing virtual machines to ensure student could access to necessary resources. One participant stated, "*It was chaotic. Students lacked access to expensive software, leading us to resort to using Excel instead of professional simulators.*"

Another STEAM teacher highlighted the difficulties faced in adapting laboratory practices to an online format, citing issues with technology and student engagement (*"The adaptation of laboratory practices to an online setting presented formidable challenges. It was impossible to conduct practical experiments online due to the lack of access to necessary physical and software resources."*). While the flexibility and interactive nature of online platforms contribute significantly to student engagement (Achuthan et al., 2021), the practical constraints of executing laboratory experiments in a virtual landscape become real problem.

Furthermore, the discussion touched upon the significant challenges faced in executing practical and laboratory work in a remote context, especially for disciplines that necessitate hands-on experimentation. This problem encouraged teachers to use more rudimentary tools or to simplify practical tasks. It was not always easy to translate hands-on learning experiences into an online format.

The lack of physical interaction and the obstacles in monitoring student progress in online laboratory classes were also a problem. One participant noted, "*Classes were predominantly conducted online. I used the virtual campus as a tool for materials, quizzes, and assignments to monitor student progress*."

2. *Student engagement and participation.* A common challenge was the level of student engagement within the online learning environment. A teacher observed that *"the participation is complicated to manage,"* while another noted a marked decline in student participation, highlighting that many students avoid activating their cameras, leading to sessions concluding prematurely due to a lack of interaction. In addition, this problem leads to social isolation.

Focus groups explored the difficulties associated with student participation and collaboration in a digital setting. Teachers reported experiences of students' hesitance to use cameras and a general decline in engagement, particularly noticeable in virtual laboratory sessions. A strategy mentioned by one participant involved the use of post-session questionnaires to assess student progress, which disclosed that only a subset of the student body was actively engaging. Much of the student engagement depends on the teacher's style (De Loof et al., 2021), and the instructor lacked the opportunity to develop skills necessary for facilitating dynamic virtual learning environments. One teacher shared their perspective stating, "*the follow-up on laboratory classes during the pandemic was very negative. We aimed to replicate the traditional in-person model online, but the results were unsatisfactory.*"

3. *Equity and access to resources.* The disparities in student access to technology and stable internet connections were identified as substantial obstacles to achieving equitable education, as highlighted by some teachers. One teacher, for example, expressed concern and noted, "*the digital divide has significantly impacted the quality of education we can deliver remotely. It's not just about*

*having a device but also about having reliable internet access, which many of our students lack.*"

In response to these challenges, another teacher added, "*we have had to think creatively about how we can support all our students, not just those with ready access to technology. This has meant providing offline resources and ensuring that our teaching methods don't disproportionately disadvantage those without high-speed internet or advanced devices.*" This statement underscores the need for adaptive strategies to ensure that education remains accessible and equitable for all students, regardless of their technological circumstances. Adaptive teaching is the solution to the limitations of traditional methods (Guerrero-Roldán et al., 2021) and an effective tool for addressing diversity (Wang et al., 2023).

4. *Teamwork and collaboration.* The challenge of facilitating effective teamwork and collaboration in a remote setting was pointed out by a teacher, who raised concerns about the authenticity of group work in online environments. This teacher remarked, "*It is been tough to replicate the dynamic of in-person group projects online. I often wonder if we are truly achieving meaningful collaboration or if students are just dividing tasks without real interaction.*"

Adding to this observation, another teacher stated "*to address this problem, we have implemented structured virtual breakout sessions and utilized collaborative online tools to foster a sense of teamwork. Despite the obstacles, it's crucial that we find ways to encourage genuine interaction and collective problem-solving among students, even if it's through a screen.*" This shared idea highlights the teachers' commitment to overcoming the inherent limitations of remote learning to preserve the essential components of teamwork and collaboration.

## Recommendations and Future Directions

1. *Integrating hybrid-teaching models.* The pandemic has accentuated the need for adopting a flexible, hybrid teaching model that can integrate in-person and online learning environments. The hybrid model promises to join the advantages of each format while ensuring preparedness for any unpredicted educational disruptions. In reflecting on their experiences beyond the pandemic, teachers emphasized the value of virtual tutorials and the use of communication platforms like Teams to engage with students. Nevertheless, they acknowledged problems while transitioning to this hybrid approach due to the lack of institutional support and targeted training programs.

One teacher shared her view: "*I have continued with virtual tutorials as they offer greater convenience for students. Yet, this flexibility introduces its own set of challenges, necessitating a shift in how we manage attention and engagement. This transition has underscored the pressing need for enhanced support and specialized training to navigate the complexities of hybrid teaching effectively.*" This insight reveals the complex balance teachers must strike in adapting to new teaching paradigms.

2. *Enhancing digital competency*. Focus groups highlighted a critical demand for training in online teaching methodologies; a need also pointed out by Brown et al. (2023). A participant stressed the key lesson learned from the initial transition to online education: "*We need to master the creation of specialized materials for online activities, moving away from merely duplicating methods used in traditional classroom settings.*"

Further emphasizing this point, another teacher said: "*To effectively adapt to online teaching, I require both training and robust support. Merely undergoing training without addressing the need for adequate resources and manageable workloads will not translate into successful implementation.*" This sentiment is related to the idea that teachers need a comprehensive training in the use of digital tools and methodologies suited for the virtual classroom. As suggested by another STEAM teacher, implementing tools designed to track student progress could significantly elevate the efficacy of online instruction, pointing towards a more effective and engaging remote learning environment.

3. *Fostering student participation*. To encouraging active participation, one teacher recommends adopting a positive reinforcement approach by offering rewards instead of imposing penalties to motivate students. This strategy could include incorporating elements of gamification or utilizing interactive platforms to make learning more engaging and interactive. Many of these digital tools are useful for fostering the necessary social interaction and for addressing diversity (Wang et al., 2023).
4. *Personalized and adaptive learning*: The discussions introduced the concept of the adaptive teacher and adaptive learning as strategies to meet the diverse needs and learning styles of students. However, participants raised concerns regarding the practicality of providing personalized attention if there are constraints of resources and training availability. In the same as Wu et al. (2023), participants recognize the potential of adaptive teaching. However, they also agree on the significant gap in readiness for implementing such personalized learning approaches. This draw attention to the critical need for comprehensive training, support, and a transformative change in the mindset at the institutional level.

One participant stated, "*Currently, I lack the skills or resources for adaptive teaching, even with the possibility of training. It necessitates a different methodology, and realistically, additional teaching support would be required to manage personalized student support effectively.*"

The conversation also moved to the potential of integrating artificial intelligence to facilitate adaptive teaching. Participants, as stated in the work of Anush Kumar et al. (2021) agreed that the educational sector is not yet adequately prepared to implement such advanced technologies effectively. This dialogue highlights the need for strategic investment in professional development training courses.

5. *Investment in resources and training.* In relation to this topic, teachers emphasized the importance of improving their virtual communication skills and gaining proficiency in using digital tools to monitor student progress. Additionally, all participants strongly advocated for institutional support and dedicated time for training.
6. *Leveraging technology.* The discussion highlighted optimism for the future of online education, particularly the potential integration of artificial intelligence to provide personalized learning experiences. However, teachers expressed concerns about their current skills to implement such technologies, reflecting sentiments similar to those reported by Brown et al. (2023). The readiness of educators to adopt artificial intelligence technologies emerged as a crucial debate point, with an acknowledgment of the need for strategic investment to exploit the benefits of these innovations.

Additionally, the importance of practical learning was emphasized, particularly in fields requiring direct interaction, such as mechanical engineering, underscoring the need for a blend of online and hands-on experiences. Concerns were also raised about the decreasing effectiveness of video content in engaging students, highlighting a shift towards passive learning and the importance of maintaining active learning and strong teacher-student connections through structured activities, as supported by Garrison & Anderson (2011).

## Analysis From Students' Perceptions

The discussion among students covered various aspects, including difficulties in adapting to online teaching methods, the impact on interaction with professors, and the overall effectiveness of the transition. The students' experiences during the pandemic focused on the importance of flexibility, innovation, and inclusivity in educational practices. As institutions look to the future, there is a clear mandate to enhance the quality and accessibility of education for all students, particularly in adapting to and integrating technology in ways that enrich the learning experience.

## Challenges

1. *Technical and practical limitations.* Students highlighted considerable technical difficulties, including issues with audio quality and camera focus. These problems affected their educational experience. One student remarked, "*There were many problems with the audio. Often, the teacher's microphone battery failed.*" He explained how these interruptions resulted in missing essential parts of the lecture. "
2. *Reduced interaction and engagement.* The absence of direct interaction with instructors and peers was considered as a significant limitation of online learning, intensified by the absence of a physical classroom setting that typically promotes interaction and engagement. One student expressed, "*In my case, it has been similar... I preferred in-person attendance,*" emphasizing the desire for face-to-face classes to overcome these challenges of interaction. Additionally, the virtual format often resulted in a diminished sense of community and collaboration among students, further detracting from the holistic learning experience that in-person education provides.
3. *Difficulty in adapting teaching methods.* The focus group explored the adjustments made by professors during the pandemic. Students recognized the efforts of some instructors to integrate technology into their teaching, with one participant noting, "*They essentially built television studios in some classrooms where there were different cameras.*" This proactive effort by teachers demonstrates their commitment to maintaining educational quality despite the challenges posed by remote instruction.
4. *Innovation in teaching.* Students reported diverse experiences with the innovation in teaching methodologies. Some professors found ways to boost engagement, while others appeared reluctant to embrace change. A student reflected: "*Professors who embraced new tools and methods really transformed our learning experience, making it more engaging*". This statement highlighted the critical role of professors in adopting new tools to energize the learning process.

## Recommendations and Future Directions

1. *Adaptive learning and teacher competence.* The exploration of adaptive learning has shed light on students' expectations regarding teaching approaches. They express a desire for professors to adapt their methods to accommodate both in-person and online learners effectively. Beyond technical proficiency, teachers must demonstrate a willingness to embrace adaptive learning technologies.

A perceptive student remarked, "*Adapting to teach implies considering students' own adaptation to novel learning modalities.*" This student-centered approach to adaptive learning involves customizing teaching techniques and materials to address individual student needs. Such an approach not only fosters innovation but also underscores the importance of implementing diverse strategies to engage remote learners effectively.

2. *Professional development for teachers*: During discussions, a consensus emerged regarding the importance of professional development for teachers. Students recognized that educators require a combination of technical training and pedagogical guidance to elevate student engagement, effectively utilize digital tools, and implement adaptive learning methods.

Recommendations were put forth, emphasizing comprehensive training for teachers. This training should encompass both technical aspects of online teaching, such as troubleshooting hardware issues (e.g., microphone and camera problems), and software proficiency. Additionally, teachers should be adept at navigating diverse online platforms and tools to foster teaching innovation. As one student pointed out, this dual focus on hardware and software proficiency is essential for effective online instruction.

3. *Satisfaction and room for improvement.* Despite recognizing the benefits of collaborative tools, students reported mixed feelings about the overall execution of online learning. Concerns raised about the inconsistent adoption of technology, potentially exacerbating educational inequities tied to students' varying access to digital resources. "*I feel the university is lagging behind,*" one participant expressed, indicating a sense of urgency for modernization.

There was a strong call from students for a more creative application of digital tools to foster interaction and engagement, suggesting the integration of platforms for group projects, like Google Sheets, and the incorporation of other interactive elements to stimulate their learning process.

4. *Hybrid learning.* Students anticipated a shift toward hybrid learning models that combine the best of both worlds: the advantages of remote education and the value of face-to-face interactions. They celebrate the flexibility and accessibility that remote learning offers while also recognizing the importance of preserving physical connections.

Discussions about sustaining positive changes triggered by the pandemic were crucial. Increased infrastructure investment, continuous professor training were among the key factors and interactivity. As highlighted by Achuthan et al. (2021), the role of interactivity cannot be overstated, and this interaction can be facilitated through technology.

5. *Addressing the digital divide*. The digital divide emerged as a significant concern, especially for students from less privileged backgrounds lacking adequate technology access. The imperative for ensuring all students have the necessary online learning tools and resources was highlighted as a critical step towards achieving educational equity.

## Analysis From Staffs' Perceptions

Staff focus group discussions revealed a consensus on evolving STEAM education post-pandemic, highlighting the need for integrating advanced technology, fostering empathy, and utilizing collaborative teaching approaches. These changes aim to foster a more inclusive and engaging learning environment. The dialogue emphasized the importance of continuous collaboration and strategic planning in adapting to the changing higher education landscape.

### Challenges

1. *Paradigm shift in teaching*. Participants called for a fundamental change in the educational paradigm, moving from a focus on individual achievement to embracing collaborative teaching methods that emphasize teamwork and transform the educator's role. The effectiveness of this change relies on thoughtful design, as highlighted by Margaryan, Bianco, and Littlejohn (2015).

There is a clear demand for dynamic and engaging teaching methodologies that go beyond traditional lectures, with a particular focus on enhancing "coaching" and "communication skills" in education. On participant stated, "*There is now a proactive approach in adapting teaching methods. This adaptation underlines the ongoing necessity for teachers to enhance their pedagogical skills, reinforcing that technological proficiency alone is inadequate for effective teaching.*"

2. *Limited resources and virtualization challenges*. The discussions revealed a consensus that certain aspects of STEAM education, particularly those involving hands-on engineering practices, cannot be fully replicated through virtual means. Statements like "*mechanical engineers need to touch things*" and the challenges in virtualizing practical laboratories underscore the intrinsic value of physical interaction with machinery and materials in learning.

A staff member drew attention to the complexities associated with technical support and the limited resources. The role of online system administration support significantly affects user satisfaction with technology usage (Butt, Mahmood, & Saleem, 2022)

1. *Challenges in practical disciplines*: The discussion reached a consensus that certain elements of STEAM education, especially hands-on engineering practices, are not fully replicable in a virtual environment. Expressions such as "mechanical engineering requires hands-on interaction" highlight the essential role of physical engagement with machinery and materials in the learning process.

Some teachers highlighted the complexities linked to the extensive virtualization, pointing out the simultaneous need to virtualize content, provide technical support, and manage the demand on available resources. The conversation critically evaluated the adequacy of emergency virtualization strategies implemented during the pandemic.

2. *Student engagement.* The pandemic emphasized the significance of empathy and comprehension of students' circumstances and their learning journeys. The emergence of empathy through remote teaching experiences indicates a beneficial shift in the dynamics of teacher-student relationships, underlining the necessity for continuous engagement strategies, such as Fraser (2012) and Garrison & Anderson (2011) have demonstrated. The dialogue explored how virtualization led to an increased awareness of the students' learning experiences, addressing the complexities involved in digitizing hands-on disciplines and the essential need to modify teaching approaches.

3. *Collaboration and teamwork in teaching*: Staff members recommended transitioning to collaborative teaching models, emphasizing the need for teachers to operate as a team. This approach suggests that interdisciplinary collaboration could greatly enhance curriculum development and implementation, offering a more unified and comprehensive educational journey for students.

Some participants, who advocated moving from solitary to team teaching methods, mentioned the significance of mentorship. Others pointed out the crucial role of leadership in facilitating the shift in teaching philosophies and roles, highlighting the need for mentorship and the creation of a supportive community for teachers.

## Recommendations and Future Directions

1. *Enhance pedagogical training.* Educators need continuous training that encompasses both technological proficiency and dynamic, empathetic teaching approaches. This training should cover areas such as coaching, effective communication, and the development of engaging, interactive educational experiences.

A participant noted, "*There is a shift towards broader skill sets among teachers, with a focus on coaching, effective communication, and creating dynamic learning environments.*" The group, highlighting the necessity for educators to embrace a wider range of competencies that support more engaging and communicative teaching environments, echoed this sentiment.

2. *Develop hybrid-learning models.* From focus group discussions, it emerged that institutions need to explore and invest in hybrid educational models. These models should combine the flexibility of online learning with the essential hands-on, practical experiences crucial in fields like engineering. Such a strategy would involve integrating in-person laboratory or practical sessions with online theoretical instruction to ensure a balanced and comprehensive educational experience.
3. *Promote interdisciplinary collaboration.* Among participants, institutions are strongly encouraged to promote and support collaborative and interdisciplinary teaching teams. This approach has the potential to provide students with a more integrated and comprehensive understanding of subjects, which is particularly advantageous in multifaceted fields like engineering. One participant expressed this idea: "*The mentality needs to change. The era of the solitary excellent teacher is over. We need teamwork among teachers.*" Furthermore, the role of mentorship in this evolving landscape was also emphasized. Another participant noted, "*We need mentors who can guide other teachers and foster a collaborative environment. It's time to start mentoring new teaching methods.*"
4. *Invest in virtual lab technologies.* While recognizing the constraints of virtual laboratories, there is a clear need for investment in developing and incorporating simulation technologies. These technologies can supplement physical laboratory experiences, particularly for the theoretical and computational components of STEAM subjects.

One participant highlighted, "The challenge lies in resources, as virtualization requires a fully equipped virtual university with necessary technical support." This statement draws attention to the resource-intensive nature of comprehensive virtualization, stressing the importance of providing sufficient technical support to maintain a fully virtualized educational environment.

Moreover, another participant remarked, "Simulations are beneficial, yet it's crucial for students to understand the real-life implications of their engineering decisions." This discussion pointed out the difficulties in virtualizing hands-on experiences in fields like engineering, where understanding the real-world impact of decisions is vital, thereby questioning the total viability of a fully virtualized approach.

5. *Identify and support students' needs.* Institutions are encouraged to develop support mechanisms that recognize students' special needs. Beyond the importance of a tutor guiding learning (Zhou, 2016), such mechanisms should include flexible educational pathways and mental health and well-being support. There is also a consensus among students that during the pandemic, teachers showed more empathy, and that this change in attitude continues to be present.

## Summary of Key Points

Table 1 presents a synthesized comparison of perspectives from teachers, students, and staff on the transition to online teaching. It summarizes the collective experiences and insights on the challenges of adapting to virtual environments, the imperative for adaptive teaching methods, and the evolving educational needs in a digital age.

*Table 1. Comparative perceptions of online STEAM Education: Teachers, students, and staff perspectives*

| Key themes | Teacher's perception | Student's perception | Staff's perception |
|---|---|---|---|
| **Impact of online teaching on STEAM subjects** | Discussed the transition from in-person to online education and challenges in maintaining quality in practical subjects. | Expressed mixed satisfaction with the implementation of online learning, focusing on the challenges of learning mathematical concepts virtually. | Highlighted the focus on virtual methodologies in STEAM education, addressing resource challenges, and maintaining educational quality in a digital context. |
| **Adaptive teaching** | Emphasized the necessity for adaptive teaching skills to maintain quality in practical subjects. | Called for professors to adapt teaching styles for both in-person and online learners, expressing a desire for professors with technical skills and a willingness to embrace adaptive learning technologies. | Stressed the importance of adaptive teaching skills and the introduction of the "adaptive teacher" concept. |
| **Professional development** | Identified a need for teacher training in online teaching methodologies to enhance the quality of education. | Recommended that professors undergo training on both hardware and software aspects to better facilitate online learning. | Focused on developing transversal skills in educators, including coaching and empathy, to support adaptive teaching. |
| **The future** | Anticipated future advancements in online education and expressed concerns about the readiness for integrating advanced technologies. | Suggested sustaining positive changes initiated during the pandemic and envisioning a shift towards hybrid learning models. | Advocated for a fundamental change in educators' mentality, emphasizing the challenges of virtualizing practical disciplines and the importance of mentorship and interdisciplinary collaboration. |

Source: Own elaboration

During the pandemic, the rapid transition to online teaching has been a unifying challenge across teachers, students, and technical staff, despite different perceptions of its effectiveness. The consensus on digitalization's pivotal role in sustaining educational continuity during these times reflects its undeniable impact across the educational landscape.

However, the replication of practical experiences, particularly in STEAM disciplines where laboratory practices and material interactions are essential, presents a shared challenge. The difficulty of fully transitioning these hands-on learning experiences into a virtual format has been acknowledged by all groups, highlighting a common problem in the journey towards effective online education. Alongside these technical barriers, the need for enhanced training and professional development for teachers has been recognized by all participants. There is a clear call for more comprehensive support in navigating digital tools and online methodologies, and to develop soft skills like empathy and coaching to better engage students in new teaching paradigms.

Despite these shared challenges, differences in perspectives emerge, particularly regarding the effectiveness of online learning. Some teachers and technical staff view online education as an opportunity for pedagogical innovation, whereas students express a strong preference for the traditional, in-person learning environment. This divergence shows the complexities of online education, from issues of engagement and participation to the fundamental value of in-person interactions that cannot be replicated virtually.

Students emphasize the critical importance of adaptability and flexibility in teaching methods, urging teachers to be responsive to the evolving circumstances. This contrasts with some teachers and technical staff who note the internal resistance within the teaching community to these rapid changes. Furthermore, while some participants see online learning as an opportunity, others recognize its challenges. With no doubt, the multifaceted nature of this educational shift requires ongoing dialogue and collaboration to navigate successfully.

## CONCLUSION

The learning environment, whether online or face-to-face, involves a complex array of factors that influence learner satisfaction and achievement (Aguilera-Hermida, 2020). The pandemic has highlighted the need for adaptive online STEAM education. It has also acted as a catalyst for the adoption of digital technologies in education, revealing both opportunities and challenges.

Key findings from this research stem from the experiences of teachers, students, and technical staff. These findings emphasize the need for enhanced teacher training in online tools and methodologies, along with a focus on soft skills. Additionally, integrating practical experiences with online learning and addressing students' diversity are crucial. However, the valuation of online experiences varies based on the individual's role. Students, in particular, express a clear preference for face-to-face interaction and practices that mirror real-world job situations, especially in STEAM fields.

The transition toward more flexible and adaptive educational models appears to be the way forward. As we learn from the differences in perceptions and needs of teachers, students, and technical staff, future efforts should concentrate on developing hybrid learning models, enhancing digital competency among educators, and fostering interdisciplinary collaboration. These directions aim to balance traditional and digital learning environments, ensuring both educational equity and effectiveness.

In light of the findings, several future steps are essential to enhance online education, particularly within the STEAM disciplines. Firstly, it's crucial to integrate hybrid teaching models that blend face-to-face and virtual learning, ensuring readiness for any future educational disruptions. Enhancing educators' digital competency through comprehensive training in online teaching methodologies and robust support is essential.

Encouraging student participation with innovative methods like gamification and interactive platforms is recommended to maintain engagement and meet diverse learning needs. Prioritizing personalized and adaptive learning strategies is also key, necessitating significant investment in professional development and resources to provide personalized attention and integrate advanced technologies such as artificial intelligence.

Promoting interdisciplinary collaboration and team teaching models can offer a more integrated educational experience. Lastly, investing in virtual lab technologies is vital to complement physical laboratory experiences, ensuring the practical aspects of STEAM education are effectively delivered online.

## ACKNOWLEDGEMENT

This research was cofounded by the European Commission through the Erasmus Plus project.

## REFERENCES

Achuthan, K., Raghavan, D., Shankar, B., Francis, S. P., & Kolil, V. K. (2021). Impact of remote experimentation, interactivity and platform effectiveness on laboratory learning outcomes. *International Journal of Educational Technology in Higher Education*, 18(38), 38. Advance online publication. 10.1186/s41239-021-00272-z34778531

Aguilera-Hermida, A.P. (2020). College students' use and acceptance of emergency online learning due to covid-19. *International Journal of Educational Research Open, 1*(100), 011.

Anush Kumar, S. Amudhavan, T., Arun Kumar. S., & Sasikala, S. (2021). *Improving effectiveness of STEM Education in Covid-19 Pandemic – A pilot study*. International Conference on Advancements in Electrical, Electronics, Communication, Computing and Automation (ICAECA), Coimbatore, India. 10.1109/ICAECA52838.2021.9675606

Bakera, P. M. A., Bujaka, K. R., & De Millo, R. (2012). The evolving university: Disruptive change and institutional innovation. *Procedia Computer Science*, 14, 330–335. 10.1016/j.procs.2012.10.037

Brown, M., Costello, E., Donlon, E., & Giolla-Mhichíl, M. N. (2023). The rise of online learning during the COVID-19 pandemic. *European Journal of Open. Distance and E-Learning*, 22(2), 1–12. 10.2478/eurodl-2023-0001

Butt, S., Mahmood, A., & Saleem, S. (2022). The role of institutional factors and cognitive absorption on students' satisfaction and performance in online learning during COVID 19. *PLoS One*, 17(6), e02696091. 10.1371/journal.pone.026960935731789

Chen, T., Peng, L., Yin, X., Rong, J., Yang, J., & Cong, G. (2023). Impact of the COVID-19 pandemic on online learning in higher education. *Educational Technology Research and Development*, 69(1), 1–18. 10.1007/s11423-020-09925-637016716

Cheung, S. K. S., Kwok, L. F., Phusavat, K., & Yan, H. H. (2021). Shaping the future learning environments with smart elements: Challenges and opportunities. *International Journal of Educational Technology in Higher Education*, 18(16), 16. Advance online publication. 10.1186/s41239-021-00254-134778521

De Loof, H., Struyf, A., Boeve-de Pauw, J., & Van Petegem, P. (2021). Teachers' motivating style and students' motivation and engagement in STEM: The relationship between three key educational concepts. *Research in Science Education*, 51(4), 109–127. 10.1007/s11165-019-9830-3

Fairhurst, N., Koul, R., & Sheffield, R. (2025). Students' perceptions of their STEM learning environment. *Learning Environments Research*, 12, 1–22. 10.1007/s10984-023-09463-z37360385

Fraser, B. J. (2012). Classroom learning environments: Retrospect, context and prospect. In Fraser, B. J., Tobin, K., & McRobbie, C. (Eds.), *Second international handbook of science education* (pp. 1191–1239). Springer. 10.1007/978-1-4020-9041-7_79

Garrison, D. R., & Anderson, T. (2011). *E-learning in the 21st Century: A framework for research and practice*. London: Routhledge/Falmer.

Garrison, D. R., Cleveland-Innes, M., & Fung, T. S. (2010). Exploring causal relationships among teaching, cognitive and social presence: Student perceptions of the community of inquiry framework. *The Internet and Higher Education*, 13(1–2), 31–36. 10.1016/j.iheduc.2009.10.002

Guerrero-Roldán, A.-E., Rodríguez-González, M. E., Bañeres, D., Elasri-Ejjaberi, A., & Cortadas, P. (2021). Experiences in the use of an adaptive intelligent system to enhance online learners' performance: A case study in Economics and Business courses. *International Journal of Educational Technology in Higher Education*, 18(1), 36. 10.1186/s41239-021-00271-0

Lemay, D. J., Bazelais, P., & Doleck, T. (2021). Transition to online learning during the COVID-19 pandemic. *Computers in Human Behavior Reports*, 4, 100130. 10.1016/j.chbr.2021.10013034568640

Maguraushe, K., Masimba, F., & Muderedzwa, M. (2022). Shrinking the digital divide in online learning beyond the COVID-19 pandemic: A systematic literature review. *1st Zimbabwe Conference of Information and Communication Technologies (ZCICT)*, Harare, Zimbabwe. 10.1109/ZCICT55726.2022.10046024

Margaryan, A., Bianco, M., & Littlejohn, A. (2015). Instructional quality of Massive Open Online Courses (MOOCs). *Computers & Education*, 80, 77–83. 10.1016/j.compedu.2014.08.005

Martin, F., Sun, T., & Westine, C. D. (2020). A systematic review of research on online teaching and learning from 2009 to 2018. *Computers & Education*, 159, 104009. 10.1016/j.compedu.2020.10400932921895

Mirriahi, N., Alonzo, D., McIntyre, S., Kligyte, G., & Fox, B. (2015). Blended learning innovations: Leadership and change in one Australian institution. *International Journal of Education and Development Using Information and Communication Technology*, 11(1), 4–16.

Mishra L, Gupta T, & Shree A. (2020). Online teaching-learning in higher education during lockdown period of COVID-19 pandemic. *International Journal of Educational Research*, 1: 100012. 10.1016/j.ijedro.2020.100012

Rodriguez, C.O. (2012). MOOCs and the AI-Stanford like courses: two successful and distinct course formats for massive open online courses. *The European Journal of Open, Distance and E-Learning*, 15.

Rogers, E. (2003). *Diffusion of innovations* (5th ed.). Free Press.

Tselios, N., Daskalakis, S., & Papadopoulou, M. (2011). Assessing the acceptance of a blended learning university course. *Journal of Educational Technology & Society*, 14(2), 224–235.

Wang, S., Christensen, C., Cui, W., Tong, R., Yarnall, L., Shear, L., & Feng, M. (2023). When adaptive learning is effective learning: Comparison of an adaptive learning system to teacher-led instruction. *Interactive Learning Environments*, 31(2), 793–803. 10.1080/10494820.2020.1808794

Wu, T. T., Lee, H. Y., Wang, W. S., Lin, Ch. J., & Huang, Y. M. (2023). Leveraging computer vision for adaptive learning in STEM education: Effect of engagement and self-efficacy. *International Journal of Educational Technology in Higher Education*, 20(1), 53. 10.1186/s41239-023-00422-5

Zhao, G., & Yuan, S. (2010). Blended learning satisfaction: A study on Peking University students. In *Hybrid Learning* (Vol. 6248, pp. 282–295). LNCS. 10.1007/978-3-642-14657-2_26

Zhou, M. (2016). Chinese university students acceptance of MOOCs: A self-determination perspective. *Computers & Education*, 92-93, 194–203. 10.1016/j.compedu.2015.10.012

Zhu, Q., & Wang, M. (2020). Team-based mobile learning supported by an intelligent system: Case study of STEM students. *Interactive Learning Environments*, 28(5), 543–559. 10.1080/10494820.2019.1696838

# Chapter 15
# Designing a Flipped Learning Model-Based Laboratory Safety Course for Undergraduates

**Özge Özyalçın Oskay**
*Hacettepe University, Turkey*

**Ayhan Yılmaz**
*Hacettepe University, Turkey*

**Nagihan Kadıoğlu**
*Hacettepe University, Turkey*

## ABSTRACT

*The Covid 19 pandemic has brought many changes in the education system as in many systems in the world. The distance education system, which developed and became widespread during the pandemic, continues its impact with hybrid models adopted after the pandemic. Flipped learning model, one of these hybrid models, has been widely used since the pandemic. This study makes an attempt at designing the laboratory safety course offered in chemistry teaching department in flipped learning model. The subjects of laboratory safety course were based on flipped learning model, one of the hybrid learning models, so as to be able to teach them more effectively and to secure retention in learning due to the fact that laboratory work forms the foundation of applied sciences like chemistry; and as a result, a 14-week course was designed. Four themes labelled as the "pre-class and teaching the class," "post-class activities," "general views on the model," and "the use of the model in the future professional life," in the interviews with seven students who*

DOI: 10.4018/979-8-3693-7645-4.ch015

*volunteered to join the application in week 14.*

## INTRODUCTION

Chemistry is an applied science, and laboratory activities are an integral part of chemistry education. Chemical events which are available in classes only theoretically can be concretised through experiments (Hofstein et al., 2001). Students are familiarised with chemicals of different types and characteristics during lab applications and they use them (Walters et al., 2017). They follow such steps of scientific study as making observations, discovering, describing problems, hypothesising, experimenting and collecting data thanks to laboratory applications and thus, they get the opportunity to develop their psychomotor abilities beside enjoying discovery (Palic & Pırasa, 2012). However, laboratory applications should be planned and organised carefully because the chemicals and materials in the lab are risky for people in the environment. Laboratory safety involves using certain methods, the infrastructure and equipment by obeying certain lab rules for the protection of individuals who work in the lab and of the materials worked with. It also means precautions taken to protect the health of people working in the lab and to make them feel safe. Experiments and activities done in the laboratory in chemistry, biology, physics and in other branches of science can have some risks. Therefore, it is of vital importance to be conscious and to take the right precautions in terms of laboratory safety. Providing safety in the lab is possible only through being informed of working in the laboratory beforehand, care, cleanliness, regular work, minimising the errors that can arise and efficient knowledge of the work environment.

Lab environment contains several elements such as chemicals and equipment which can harm the health of people working in the laboratory. Those who work in the laboratory should be informed of laboratory safety so that they can be aware of dangers that can arise and so that they can work duly. The procedures of laboratory safety are important not only for workers' health but also for the accuracy of the research results. The right procedures should be followed, equipment should be calibrated suitably and the right techniques of data recording should be used in order for the data to be accurate and dependable.

The concept of laboratory safety, which was previously applied only on the basis of protecting the person without even being aware of it, and then included many areas, including the environment, due to the increasing industrialization with the developing technology and the variety of chemicals used, is extremely important in the period we are in, both in order to protect the health status of the person and to protect the environment and to minimize the damage caused by chemical wastes to the environment. In addition, it is necessary to determine the minimum requirements to protect the health of workers from the dangers and harmful effects of chemical substances found, used or processed in any way in the workplace and to provide a safe working environment. Due to the size of the area covered by the subject and its sensitivity and importance, the fact that it is a subject that needs to be worked professionally has also revealed the necessity of laboratory safety committees formed by people who will deal with the content and supervise the application conditions. Laboratory Safety Boards 1. To improve the health and safety conditions of employees; to determine a policy for the responsibilities, activities to be carried out and measures to be taken, to make annual work plans, to supervise the operation and to prepare reports. 2. To propose the working groups that will take part in the execution of the practices; to determine the distribution of tasks and to organize meetings with these groups and monitor their work. 3. General safety training periodically review and update the curriculum and training documents to ensure that the government is able to provide the necessary services (Kerimak Öner, 2020).

The principles that students who will work in the laboratory should know and follow about laboratory safety are as follows:

- They should make it a habit to pay attention to safety in the laboratory.
- They should also be concerned about the safety of their fellow students working in the laboratory. - They should have information about the dangers related to the experiments they will do in the laboratory.
- They should know in advance what to do in case of an emergency.
- They should report dangerous situations that may occur in the laboratory to the relevant authorities (Hasenekoğlu, 2003, cited in Aydoğdu, Şener, 2016).

The most important safety precautions to be taken in the laboratory are to have sufficient information about the sources of danger and to apply the procedures to be performed in case of a dangerous situation for any reason. For this reason.

- The properties of the chemicals to be used should be well known and care should be taken during the work.
- The user manuals of the tools should be read carefully and the rules of use should be followed.
- Sufficient information about the dangers that may arise from vehicles must be available.
- First aid to be applied in case of an accident should be done quickly and in accordance with the method detailed in the reference (Bulduk, 2014 cited in Aydoğdu, Şener, 2016).

Research has shown that the great majority of laboratory accidents stem from human errors. Therefore, everything in the laboratory should be thought carefully beforehand. Laboratories as places of work are dangerous locations. Even though people work with fewer chemicals in university laboratories than in laboratories in the industry, serious and fatal accidents can also occur in those laboratories (Abbas et al., 2017; Olewski & Snakard, 2017; Yang et al., 2019). Individuals who work in such places should know of potential dangers and what to do in cases of emergency (Öner, 2020). It is important that people working in those places be trained in chemical safety so as to minimise accidents which happen in laboratories (Walters et al., 2017). Students' knowledge in, skills in and attitudes towards laboratory safety can be formed during university education and in the period prior to it the most efficiently (West et al., 2003). Studies on how to teach the laboratory safety course have been conducted since the 1970s (Kaufman, 1978; Lowry, 1978; Nagel, 1982; Ozaruk, 1976; Pekdağ, 2020; Öner, 2020; Walters et.al, 2017; Zhu et.al, 2018). Differing technologies, methods and techniques have been employed in improving students' knowledge about laboratory safety with the reflection of developed technology into the area of education. Gublo (2003) developed a trivia game which students could easily reach on the web so as to teach them how to work safely in the laboratory. Crockett (2011), having taught all the first year university students two 75-minute courses in laboratory safety in accordance with the laboratory safety programme developed, gave them a quiz on laboratory safety before taking each course available in the curriculum and imposed the condition of passing the quiz to start each course. Carr and Carr (2016) used the activity of analysing short funny videos of the character Mr. Bean in which he violated the rules of laboratory safety as a different and interesting learning activity in relation to laboratory safety in college chemistry classes. Accordingly, each student found and listed the rule violations in the videos according to what they had learnt. It was pointed out that the activity had also contributed to students' higher level cognitive tasks. Pekdağ (2020), in a study conducted with the participation of 61 ninth year students, analysed the effectiveness of video-based instruction in teaching the subjects of laboratory safety. While the rules students were required to obey were explained to the students in the experimental group through video-based instructions, the rules were explained to the students in the control group in traditional approach. Raise was observed in the academic achievement of the students in the experimental group at the end of the 3-week application. Kumasaki et al (2018) investigated the effects of comic strips (Manga) on training students in terms of laboratory safety. Accordingly, the researchers asked students to examine the pictures in comic strips about risks of fire and explosion. The hazards identified were divided into seven categories. Students' answers before and after classes were analysed in order to see the effectiveness of using Manga as an instrument of education in laboratory safety. It was observed that risky behaviours which could be resulted in ignitions, fires and explosions after classes were easily identified by students. A great majority of the students described Manga as a useful instrument in learning chemical safety. Zhu et al (2018) developed an augmented-reality (AR) programme which both students and teachers could use to increase students interest and experience in subjects related to laboratory safety. Efforts were made to create interactive laboratory environments by using various virtual objects, a holographic narrator, images, sounds and other sensations thanks to the programme. The analyses done in a study which was conducted with the participation of 29 university students demonstrated that the students who had used the programme recognised laboratory materials better and that they could tell where the materials should be in the laboratory better than those who had learnt in the traditional approach. It was also found that the students who took the course through the AR programme enjoyed the course more and therefore displayed more interest in the course.

However, news about laboratory accidents has been reported for decades. Accordingly, 34 laboratory accidents were reported in Turkey between 2001 and 2017 (Tekbıyık & Tepe, 2017) and 110 accidents in university laboratories were reported in China between 2000 and 2022 (Bai et al., 2022). Studies have shown that training in working safely in the laboratory offered to young people still has deficiencies and that the deficiencies pose problems (Al-Zyoud et al., 2019; Hill et al., 2019). Innovative approaches and applications are needed in teaching the subject of laboratory safety. Hybrid learning models in which online education and face-to-face education are used in combination are preferred today as a result of developing technology felt in education as in all other areas and due to needs which emerged during pandemic. One of those models is flipped learning model and has become widespread and has been mentioned frequently in recent years because it involves using technology as an inseparable part of education and because it offers a student-centred construct in which students are active.

## Flipped Learning Model

Flipped Learning (FL) emerged in 2007 when two US chemistry teachers, seeking a solution to their students' missing class, sent lecture videos containing theoretical information to their students, and quickly gained popularity (Bergmann and Sams 2012). However, the concept's theoretical foundations were founded on active learning and peer teaching long before it rose to prominence and became a model. These ideas laid the groundwork for FL. When the model first appeared, it was called "flipped classroom"; however, as time passed, the emphasis shifted from the classroom to learning, and the concept became known as "flipped learning"

(Hayırsever & Orhan, 2018). As a result, it was employed as a "flipped learning model" in this study.

One of the important pedagogical approaches that "transforms/reverses" traditional teaching methods is the Flipped Learning Model (FLM). The change in classroom and home roles in traditional learning is the foundation of this model. The operations and processes performed in the classroom environment in traditional learning are transferred to the home environment in this approach, and the processes performed in the home environment are transferred to the classroom environment (Bergmann & Sams, 2012). Students are given learning materials to review before attending the lesson in this model. This frees up face-to-face class time for interactive and collaborative activities.

FLM is a teaching model in which the learner is at the center and individual characteristics are at the forefront. However, the use of this learning model alone is not sufficient for the realization of these objectives and the realization of students' learning goals. The three-phase nature of the model ("pre-class, in-class and post-class") allows for the use of various methods, techniques and technological tools in which the learner can actively participate and realize their learning. The inclusion of educational technologies in the process is of great importance for the design of the environment in accordance with today's understanding of the contemporary learning model. According to Tucker (2012), although FLM has gained an important place today, its use alone is not sufficient for the successful implementation of the model. In order for the FLM to be implemented in the desired way, importance should also be attached to the design of the instructional environment in which students can actively participate, the implementation steps are detailed and pre-planned activities are integrated in a systematic framework. Seery (2015), one of the first researchers to conduct a review study in this field, stated that FLM does not represent a specific teaching method in itself, but a general framework in which learning can take place. It is not a best teaching practice in itself, but a hybrid face-to-face/independent learning model that supports other teaching practices (Eichler, 2022).

Traditional teaching paradigm is reversed- or flipped- in the model. It is described as a two-part model. There is individual teaching which is actualised through technology outside the classroom in part one while there is teaching with interactional group activities inside the classroom in part two. It gives students the opportunity to cope with the stages of knowledge and comprehension during their time at home and to do the more challenging and engaging tasks in the classroom with their teacher and classmates by working together and doing exercises (Bergmann & Sams, 2012).

*Figure 1. Bloom's taxonomy*

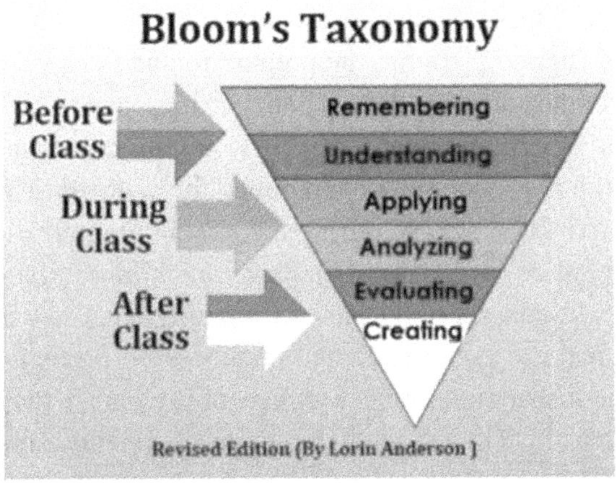


*(Eniola et al.,2020)*

Inverted Learning Network (2014) using the initials "FLIP" determined the four main features of the flipped learning model as follows:

**Flexible environment:** A flexible learning environment allows learners to choose when and where to learn. Learning offers flexibility and the opportunity to learn in different ways and at different speeds . It also allows the teacher to organize the learning environment in different ways. Basic level information is provided to students before the lesson through videos offering teachers the opportunity to make freer and more effective choices in classroom activities. In this way, teachers are able to organize the learning environment in the classroom through a variety of learning activities by planning and can help students individually (Bergmann and Sams, 2014).

**Learning culture:** Learners in flipped learning environments use their valuable time in group space for effective and creative learning processes. Learners actively participate in the construction of knowledge by evaluating their own learning in the classroom. The teacher-centered approach is replaced by a student-centered approach. Since the direct expression of knowledge takes place outside the classroom, the time in the classroom can be used more freely.

**Designed content:** According to Bergmann and Sams (2014), designed content refers to the preparation of content in which classroom activities are organized based on a student-centered approach and interactive learning strategies can be used. Written text, video and materials, such as electronic content, are directly linked to the learning objectives and are of high educational quality. They are also relevant for learners in different locations. Educators, in turn, decide what to teach and what materials to let learners explore on their own.

**Professional trainer:** The trainer has an important role in the flipped learning model. He/she constantly observes, evaluates and gives feedback to the learners. In the realization of flipped learning, the preparation and organization of the content and the creation of the learning environment can be possible with the presence of an educator who can effectively monitor the learning process. Educators are the ones who decide how to plan the time in and out of the classroom and how to incorporate learning materials before and during the lesson (Gündüz & Akkoyunlu, 2016).

According to LaFee (2013), teachers have much more time in flipped learning model than in traditional learning method to apply what has been learnt in home environment by making use of students' readiness, to promote communication in the classroom and to use the strategies which put students in the centre and in which students learn actively. The model also regulates students' study time outside the classroom and makes the time more efficient.

## Flipped Learning Model and Its Applications During Covid-19 Pandemic

As a result of the Coronavirus-2019 (COVID-19) pandemic, which emerged in Wuhan, China in December 2019 and was declared a pandemic by the World Health Organization (WHO) in March 2020, countries all over the world had to change their education systems to distance education. The negative effects of the pandemic have initiated many processes of change and adaptation both at the individual and community level. In this situation, all educators have worked on how to make distance education more efficient and new learning and teaching models have become more popular. In this process, educators have argued that distance education should be structured in a way that puts the student at the center by responding to the student's learning style, interests and needs. This situation has brought up the need to use interactive learning methods in distance education. In the flipped learning approach; although pre-course interactive educational materials meet this requirement, face-to-face in-class activities have created limitations during the pandemic process. In this case, "Online Reverse Face-to-Face Learning", which allows in-class applications to be carried out online instead of face-to-face, has come to the agenda. This situation has been preferred by educators as it increases the interaction between students and educators in the compulsory distance education process. Online flipped learning is a combination of online learning and flipped learning environment. In the online flipped learning process, pre-course activities proceed similarly to flipped learning, while in-class activities that take place face-to-face are moved to the online environment. In flipped learning, active learning methods such as group work and brainstorming are used during in-class activities. (Erden, 2022).

## Advantages and Disadvantages of Flipped Learning Model

Since students can watch the videos or audio recordings of the lesson whenever they want and as often as they want, each student can learn according to his/her own speed of understanding. Advantages of the Flipped Learning Model can be expressed as follows:

- Since students can watch the videos or audio recordings of the lesson whenever they want and as often as they want, each student can learn according to his/her own comprehension speed.
- Students have the opportunity to ask the teacher any questions they may have about the subject since they do the reinforcing practices in the classroom instead of outside the classroom.Öğrencilerin üst düzey becerilerinin gelişmesine olanak sağlamaktadır.
- The teacher can pay more attention to individual students and design activities that cater for individual differences.
- Since students work with their peers in class time, they have the opportunity to construct knowledge.
- It increases the interaction between teacher-student and student-student.
- Students take responsibility for their own learning.

## Disadvantages of the Flipped Learning Model Can Be Expressed as Follows

- Students can use computers and the internet has the necessary technological facilities may not be.
- Videos of students before the lesson it's time to check if you've been watching and requires a concentrated effort.
- Students should attend the lecture without watching the videos to come to class, even if they participate in in-class activities and it causes them to fail to grasp the subject.
- Students can watch lecture videos outside the classroom while they were watching an unrecognisable wrong because they cannot ask questions at this point learning is likely to take place.

- Inadequate in individual learning disadvantaged students, learning knowledge they are left alone in the process.
- Difficulties in creating intrinsic motivation students learn outside the classroom time video or audio recordings can be difficult for them to do so.
- Teachers, students' lessons various lectures so that they can watch them before it takes time to prepare the materials and labour intensive (Hayırsever ve Orhan, 2018)

## Teaching and Learning Models Used in the Post Covid-19 Pandemic Era

The Covid-19 pandemic, which continued for nearly two years all over the world, brought along the need for online education for a long time, access to electronic tools for quality education, the use of different teaching methods and techniques, and the ability to use digital materials effectively in education. In the post-pandemic education system, the place of artificial intelligence applications such as Chat GPT, the use of systems such as Moodle in education, and the use of platforms such as Zoom in education is undeniable. Again, in today's world, hybrid learning models are adopted and used by many educators in the education system that has started face-to-face education again. In this case, the flipped learning model will play an important role in the education system of the future and will continue to be used extensively.

Hill et al (2019) designed a laboratory safety course in which they used the flipped learning model. The researchers employed such active learning approaches as field trips, role-playing, games and group projects beside flipped learning model in their study. They found as a result that the scores obtained in the evaluation survey were higher than the ones obtained in other years and that the active learning approaches they had used provided more concrete experiences for students.

However, review of the literature has shown that there are not many applications of flipped learning model-based laboratory safety course. Therefore, the current study aims to design a laboratory safety course based on flipped learning and to apply it.

Laboratory safety course is taught 2 hours a week in the first semester as an applied course in educational faculties in Turkey. The reason for teaching the course in the first semester is to secure that students learn hazardous chemicals and their properties, their effects on the environment and on humans and the rules for working in the laboratory prior to taking the General Chemistry Laboratory course. The content for the flipped learning model-based laboratory safety course developed accordingly is as in the following:

## COURSE CONTENT

The goal of the Laboratory Safety Course is to raise individuals who are knowledgeable about hazardous chemicals and their properties, who are conscious of such chemicals' effects on humans and on the environment and who have learnt the rules for working in the laboratory safely. The outline for the course content prepared in accordance with this goal is as in the following.

1. Regulation for working safely and for hazardous chemicals, rules to obey in the laboratory,
2. Chemicals the most commonly used in the laboratory and how to classify them,
3. Labelling and storing chemicals,
4. Glass materials, heating and cooling methods, fire and methods for protection from fire,
5. Storing chemical substances and moving them away,
6. Collecting laboratory wastes and disposing of them,
7. First aid

The 14-week content for the flipped learning model-based course prepared in this study is as in the following:

Class 1: The topic of the first class taught after the week when explanations on teaching the course, marking system and examination dates were made: ınformation on the regulation for working safely and hazardous chemicals (general rules, safety equipment, laboratory staff)

Pre-class Assignments:

The students

- were sent and asked to review the regulation for Health and Safety Precautions in working with chemical substances

https://www.mevzuat.gov.tr/mevzuat?MevzuatNo=18709&MevzuatTur=7&MevzuatTertip=5)

- were sent and asked to review the Rules for Protective Equipment and working in the Laboratory

https://institute.acs.org/acs-center/lab-safety/education-training/safety-videos/college-lab-safety-videos.html)

- The materials sent included:

https://www.acs.org/content/dam/acsorg/about/governance/committees/chemicalsafety/publications/safety-in-academic-chemistry-laboratories-students.pdf

During the class:

An introduction was made to the course and general information was given. The lecturer told about an accident which happened in alkali metals' reaction with water while working in the laboratory during the doctoral studies and then pointed out and emphasised that working safely in the laboratory should be the main goal. The regulation for Health and safety precautions in working with chemical substances was reviewed with the students again and their attention was attracted to the importance of the regulation of hazardous chemicals. The rules for protective equipment and for working in the laboratory were taught in direct instruction method (Yılmaz, 2015).

## Class Two: The Classification of Chemicals

### Pre-Class Assignments

The students were asked to research pieces of news about laboratory accidents happening in schools on social media, to read and to bring them into the classroom.

During the class:

The assignments students had done were discussed, then, the videos of accidents were watched in the classroom altogether and information on the causes and on the precautions to be taken against the accidents was presented.

https://www.youtube.com/watch?v=8AVIl_-8kc4
https://www.youtube.com/watch?v=wq344RYQTe0
https://www.youtube.com/watch?v=3ELbwzqyuhs
https://www.youtube.com/watch?v=nsGp4ztkjtk

## Class Three: The Classification of Chemicals

### Pre-Class Assignments

The students were asked to examine the information and pictograms available in CLP (Classification, Labelling, Packaging) and GHS (Globally Harmonized System) in the course book.

During the class:

A discussion was started through pictograms available in the CLP and through the GHS codes- which were assigned to the students as homework.

The classification of chemicals (substances which were explosive, flammable, oxidising, gas cylinder (compressed gases), corrosive, mutagen, carcinogenic, toxic in terms of reproduction, harmful to the environment) was made and 9 pictograms and 28 classes of harmfulness and information on the letters H (representing harmfulness) and P (representing precautions) were taught in direct instruction method (Yılmaz, 2015). For example, news reported in the media that trinitroglycerin and ammonium salts were used in events of explosion and the fact that deodorants and insecticides used in daily life were flammable aerosols, that kerosene, gasoline and acetone were flammable liquids, that flour warehouse was a flammable solid, alkali metals such as Na and K were the substances which released flammable gases when they had contacts with water, that heat was released after reaction and that hydrogen was flammable was mentioned and the importance was stressed.

## Class Four: The Classification of Chemicals

### Pre-Class Assignments

The students were divided into groups so as to examine the "cleaning products", "personal care products" and "pesticides" used in daily life. 6 groups each of which contained 3 students were formed. Each group visited super markets and examined by reading the labels of the chemical substances which were assigned to them.

During the class:

Each group made presentations about the section they were responsible for. All the students were included in the process in the presentations (for instance, the dangers of sodium hypochlorite- which was used as a cleaning substance- were explained in detail). Then, attention was drawn to the pictograms, the GHS codes and the letters H and P. ınformation on symptoms and first aid was also presented and an atmosphere of discussion was created along with the students. Skin corrosion and irritation, eye injury and irritation, pictograms and examples were specially emphasised while working with corrosive substances. Acrylamide was given as the example for the most popular carcinogen substance. The literature about acrylamide and about the formation of other carcinogen substances in heat-processed foods was shared with the students (Gökmen and Şenyuva, 2006).

Discussion on the precautions for reducing the amount of acrylamides formed in fried potatoes at home increased students' motivation for the course. Mercury, methyl alcohol and formaldehyde were given as examples for toxic substances. The pictograms aboutMercury used in thermometers, methyl alcohol used in alcoholic drinks made illegally and formaldehyde which was a product of personal care and which was used in dark coloured nail polish and their dangers were discussed. The dangers of N-nitrosamines available in processed food such as salami and sausage and their harm to human health as carcinogens were also discussed. The students were recommended to read the relevant literature (Sancak et al., 2008). Examples for the assignments done by the students are given in Appendix-1.

## Class Five: Chemical Substances and the Rules to Obey While Working With Them

### Pre-Class Assignments

The students were asked to research in groups certain chemical substances (hydrochloric acid, sulphuric acid, ammonia, alkali metals, mercury and lead) and risks in using them. 6 groups were formed in total. The assignments were discussed in classes 5 and 6.

During the class:

Kahoot application was used and a 5-question quiz was given about the subjects taught (Appendix-2).

Then, the students told about their research, created an atmosphere for discussion and made their presentations. It was emphasised that the vapour coming out of HCI and H2SO4 should not be breathed in, that dilution should be made very carefully and that protective equipment should be used while working with those chemicals. It was also pointed out by them that ammonia had strong odour, that it caused irritation in the eye and in the respiratory tract and that it should not be breathed in and mask should be worn while working with it.

## Class Six: Chemical Substances and the Rules to Obey While Working With Them

Because this class is a continuation of the previous week, pre-assignments were not given.

The subject of risks in using certain chemical substances (hydrochloric acid, sulphuric acid, ammonia, alkali metals, mercury and lead) was continued.

During the class:

The students fulfilled their duty by creating environments of discussion and by making presentations about alkali metals, mercury and lead which had not been completed in the previous week. It was pointed out that alkali metals were very active metals, that they should not be preserved in air, that they created exothermic reactions with water and with watery acids and that care should be taken while working in the laboratory. The knowledge that mercury was a toxic metal, that it evaporated easily and that its vapour was very poisonous was shared. Attention was attracted to the importance of lead poisoning in working with lead.

## Class Seven: Chemical Substances and the Rules to Obey While Working With Them

### Pre-Class Assignments

Various videos on commonly encountered laboratory accidents were sent to the students before they came to the class.

https://www.youtube.com/watch?v=8AVIl_-8kc4

https://www.youtube.com/watch?v=wq344RYQTe0

https://www.youtube.com/watch?v=3ELbwzqyuhs

https://www.youtube.com/watch?v=nsGp4ztkjtk

During the class:

The students were asked to comment on the information they had obtained in the videos at the beginning of the class. A group discussion was conducted about laboratory accidents and safety precautions that should be taken. Then, the videos were watched again and the content of the videos were taught by the lecturer.

## Class Eight: Glass Materials, Heating, Cooling Fire and Methods of Protection From Fire

### Pre-Class Assignments

Videos introducing laboratory materials were sent to the students.

https://www.youtube.com/watch?v=xy1sv6KGjeE

During the class:

The students drew a picture of the 10 glass materials used the most frequently in the laboratory and named them at the beginning of the class. The videos sent prior to the class were watched again and the necessary explanations were made to the students. They were informed of the glass materials, acidic, basic and neutral glass materials.

## Class Nine: Glass Materials, Heating, Cooling Fire and Methods of Protection from Fire

### Pre-Class Assignments

The students were sent an introductive video.

https://isgtedbir.com/acil-durum/yangin/yangin-sondurme-cihazlari/

During the class:

The students were informed of heating, cooling, fire and what should be done for protection from fire.

## Class Ten: Storing Chemical Wastes and Labelling Them

### Pre-Class Assignments

They were asked to do research on the definition and importance of chemical waste.

During the class:

The concept of chemical waste was defined, its importance was mentioned and thus an atmosphere of discussion was created. The significance of the current regulation for the storage, removal and disposal of chemical wastes was explained.

## Class Eleven: Collecting Chemical Wastes and Making Them Harmless

### Pre-Class Assignments

The students' thoughts on collecting the chemical wastes in the laboratories while they were secondary school and high school students and making them harmless were obtained.

During the class:

The great majority of the students said that they had not been sufficiently informed of laboratory safety during their secondary school and high school years. After that, they were instructed in direct method on labelling waste containers, on substance groups of chemical wastes and on the types of waste containers in which they could be collected.

## Class Twelve: First Aid

### Pre-Class Assignments

An activity such as video, course materials or a quiz was not planned in this part.

During the class:

What should be done in case of laboratory accidents was explained to the students on a 50-minute zoom meeting in cooperation with an emergent medicine specialist, and their questions were answered.

As an activity for the final week, the students were divided into groups and were asked to do a role-play activity about examples of laboratory accidents and what to do in such cases in the light of knowledge they acquired throughout the semester.

Class 13: Holiday
Class 14: Interviewing with students
Class 15: Interviewing with students
Class 16: Final exam

## EVALUATION OF THE COURSE

Students' views were obtained for the evaluation laboratory safety course which was designed on the basis of Flipped Learning Model. Online semi-structured interviews were held with 7 volunteering students out of 22 who attended the course in Chemistry Teaching department during the semester. They were asked to make a general evaluation of the activities done in the semester, the advantages and disadvantages of the individual work and of group work was discussed with them and efforts were made to find whether or not the activities helped to learn about and raise awareness in terms of laboratory safety. The findings were considered in four themes labelled as "pre-class and teaching the class", "post-class activities", "views on the model" and "using the model in the future professional life". The themes and sub-themes are shown in Figure 2.

*Figure 2. Themes about students' views on the flipped learning model-based lab safety course*

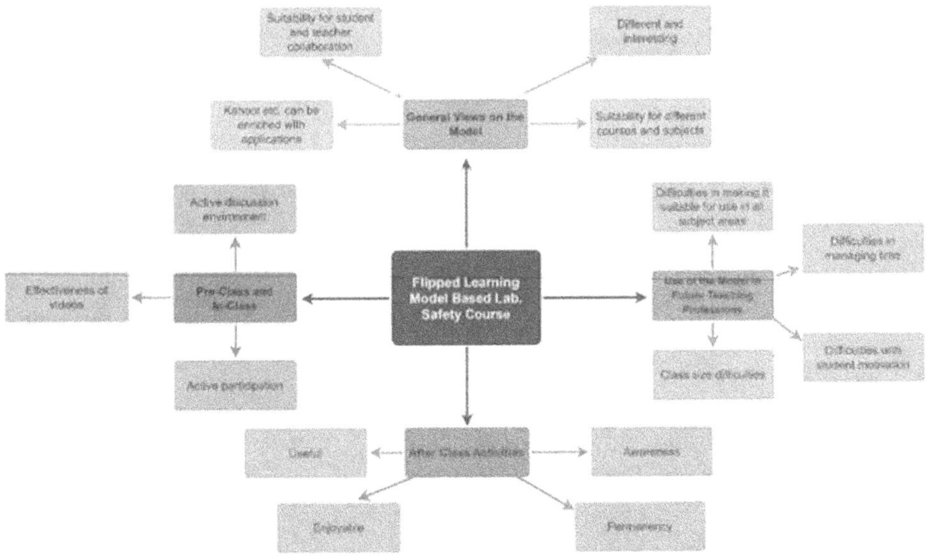

It is clear from Figure 2 that students approached the model from 4 different aspects. The analyses of the interviews demonstrated that the students mostly laid emphasis on the issue of awareness. They stated that the visits to supermarkets, the pre-class activity for the "classification of hazardous substances", was beneficial in recognising the pictograms. The students, having said that sending them videos prior to classes and accessing to theoretical knowledge whenever they wanted had motivated them for the course, also said that they attended classes more and that they had more fun in classes. It was found on examining their views that the Kahoot activity- which was done before teaching the subject of "risks of using certain chemical substances"- was also frequently mentioned. All of the students interviewed stated that they found the activity amusing and beneficial and that it also had contributions in preparing for the mid-term exam. The positive views expressed by the students are shown in Figure 3.

*Figure 3. The students' positive views on the flipped learning model-based lab safety course*

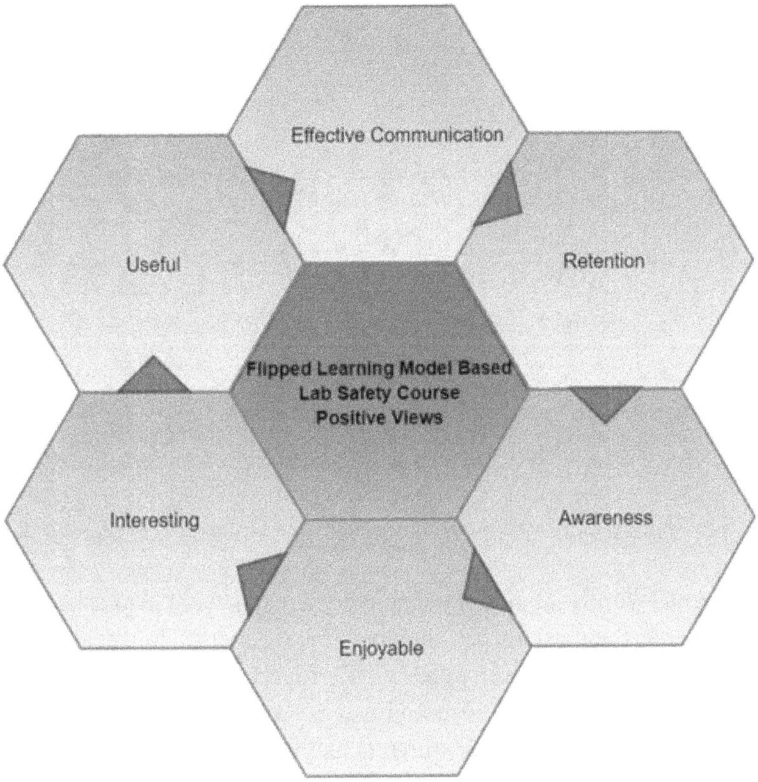


Accordingly, it was found that the students had mostly positive thoughts on the course. Yet, there were also negative views but very few. To exemplify, some of the students said that they would rather do individual activities than group activities. A student, for instance, who stated that awareness of pictograms had been raised attributed the rise in awareness to the general revision offered by the lecturer during the class rather than to the visits to supermarkets. Their negative views on the model are shown in Figure 4.

*Figure 4. The students' negative views on the flipped learning model-based lab safety course*

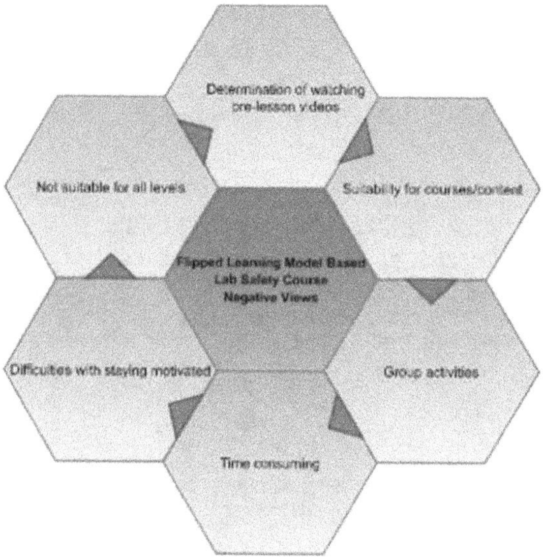


The students- who were also prospective teachers- were also asked whether or not they would use the model when they become teachers. The negative views held by them in relation to the model were heavily found in this theme. They generally said that the model could not be used with every age group. They also argued that it might be difficult to find if their students had watched the videos or not.

The students in general were found to have positive views on Flipped Learning Model Based Lab Safety Course. They stated that they had fun and gained awareness of lab safety through the activities they had done because they had the opportunity to participate actively. They added that they thought the awareness they had would also be influential in lab courses that they would take in the following semesters.

## CONCLUSION

In conclusion, a 14-week Flipped Learning Model-based Laboratory Safety Course- which enabled to use hybrid learning models and digital teaching technologies so as to eliminate the deficiencies in laboratory safety and to create newer, more effective and more permanent educational environments- was designed in this study. Students were made to come to classes by going through the stages of knowledge and comprehension in Bloom's Taxonomy by means of videos sent to them and by means of field research in pre-class activities. More time was devoted to learning environments which would make students more active, which would help them go through the upper order learning stages and which would appeal to their individual differences through group work, Kahoot activities, presentations, role-plays and interviews with experts during classes. Interviews with the students demonstrated that they heavily had positive views and that they were pleased with being taught the laboratory safety course in this design. Activities to be done in the pre-class and in-class time could be diversified in the future studies.

## REFERENCES

Abbas, M., Zakaria, A., & Balkhyour, M. (2017). Implementation of chemical health risk assessment (CHRA) program at chemical laboratories of a university. *J. Saf. Stud.*, 1(1), 53. 10.5296/jss.v3i1.11109

Al-Zyoud, W., Qunies, A. M., Walters, A. U., & Jalsa, N. K. (2019). Perceptions of chemical safety in laboratories. *Safety (Basel, Switzerland)*, 5(2), 21. 10.3390/safety5020021

American Chemical Society. (2017). Safety in Academic Chemistry Laboratories, (8th Ed). ACS, Washington D.C.

Aydoğdu, C., & Şener, F. (2016). Fen eğitiminde laboratuvar kullanım tekniğinin ve güvenliğin önemi ve CLP tüzüğünün getirileri üzerine bir araştırma (A study on the importance of laboratory technique and safety in science education and the implications of the CLP regulation). *Eskişehir Osmangazi Üniversitesi Türk Dünyası Uygulama ve Araştırma Merkezi Eğitim Dergisi*, 1(1), 39–54.

Bai, M., Liu, Y., Qi, M., Roy, N., Shu, C.-M., Khan, F., & Zhao, D. (2022). Current status, challenges, and future directions of university laboratory safety in China. *Journal of Loss Prevention in the Process Industries*, 74, 104671. 10.1016/j.jlp.2021.104671

Bergmann, J., & Sams, A. (2014). *Flipped learning: Gateway to student engagement*. International Society for Technology in Education.

Bergmann, J., & Sams, A. (2012). *Flip your classroom: Reach every student in every class every day*. International Society for Technology in Education.

Carr, J. M., & Carr, J. M. (2016). What can students learn about lab safety from Mr Bean? *Journal of College Science Teaching*, 45(6), 32–35. 10.2505/4/jcst16_045_06_32

Crockett, J. M. (2011). Laboratory safety for undergraduates. *Journal of Chemical Health and Safety*, 18(4), 16–25. 10.1016/j.jchas.2010.08.001

Eichler, J. F. (2022). Future of the Flipped Classroom in Chemistry Education: Recognizing the Value of Independent Preclass Learning and Promoting Deeper Understanding of Chemical Ways of Thinking During In-person Instruction. *Journal of Chemical Education*, 99(3), 1503–1508. 10.1021/acs.jchemed.1c01115

Eniola, I. (2020). Assessment of level of awareness and acceptance of flipped learning strategy among oyo state secondary school teachers. AAUA. *Journal of Science and Technology Education*, 3(1).

Erden, D. (2022). Innovative Learning Approache in Nursing Education: Online Flipped Learning, *Eurasıan. Journal Of Health Scıences*, 5(3), 84–89.

Gökmen, V., & Şenyuva, H. Z. (2006). Study of colour and acrylamide formation in coffee, wheat flour and potato chips during heating. *Food Chemistry*, 99(2), 238–243. 10.1016/j.foodchem.2005.06.054

Gublo, K. I. (2003). A laboratory safety trivia game. *Journal of Chemical Education*, 80(4), 425. 10.1021/ed080p425

Gündüz, A. Y., & Akkoyunlu, B. (2016). From transformed classroom to transformed learning. A. İşman, H. F. Odabaşı, & B. Akkoyunlu (Eds.), *Educational technology readings*.

Hayırsever, F., & Orhan, A. (2018). A Theoretical Analysis of Flipped Learning. *Mersin Üniversitesi Eğitim Fakültesi Dergisi*, 14(2), 572–596. 10.17860/mersinefd.431745

Hill, D. J., Williams, O. F., Mizzy, D. P., Triumph, T. F., Brennan, C. R., Mason, D. C., & Lawrence, D. S. (2019). Introduction to laboratory safety for graduate students: An active-learning endeavor. *Journal of Chemical Education*, 96(4), 652–659. 10.1021/acs.jchemed.8b00774

Hofstein, A., Levy Nahum, T., & Shore, R. (2001). Assessment of the learning environment of ınquiry-type laboratories in high school chemistry. *Learning Environments Research*, 4(2), 193–207. 10.1023/A:1012467417645

Kaufman, J. A. (1978). Safety in the academic laboratory. *Journal of Chemical Education*, 55(9), A337. 10.1021/ed055pA337

Kerimak Öner, M. N. (2020). Kimya Eğitiminde Laboratuvar Güvenliği Kültürünün Yerleştirilmesi (Embedding Laboratory Safety Culture in Chemistry Education). *İSG Akademik*, *2*(1), 15-25.

Kumasaki, M., Shoji, T., Wu, T.-C., Soontarapa, K., Arai, M., Mizutani, T., Okada, K., Shimizu, Y., & Sugano, Y. (2018). Presenting safety topics using a graphic novel, Manga, to effectively teach chemical safety to students in Japan, Taiwan, and Thailand. *Journal of Chemical Education*, 95(4), 584–592. 10.1021/acs.jchemed.7b00451

LaFee, S. (2013, November). Flipped learning. *Education Digest*, 13–18.

Lowry, G. G. (1978). A university-level course in laboratory safety. *Journal of Chemical Education*, 55(6), A263. 10.1021/ed055pA263

Nagel, M. C. (1982). An innovative course in lab safety. *Journal of Chemical Education*, 59(9), 791. 10.1021/ed059p791

Olewski, T., & Snakard, M. (2017). Challenges in applying process safety management at university laboratories. *Journal of Loss Prevention in the Process Industries*, 49, 209–214. 10.1016/j.jlp.2017.06.013

Öner, M. N. K. (2020). Kimya eğitiminde laboratuvar güvenliği kültürünün yerleştirilmesi. [Safety culture placement in chemistry education]. *Ohs Academic*, 2(1), 15–25.

Ozaruk, N. (1976). Lab safety: The case of the errant cylinder. *Journal of Chemical Education*, 53(6), 373. 10.1021/ed053p373

Palic, G., & Pirasa, N. (2012). A study of pre-service teachers' tendency for imprudent behaviour and physics laboratory attitudes. *Procedia: Social and Behavioral Sciences*, 47, 823–828. 10.1016/j.sbspro.2012.06.742

Pekdağ, B. (2020). Video-based instruction on safety rules in the chemistry laboratory: Its effect on student achievement. *Chemistry Education Research and Practice*, 21(3), 953–968. 10.1039/D0RP00088D

Sams, A. ve Bergmann, J. (2013). Flip your students' learning. *Educational Leadership*, 70(6), 16–20.

Sancak, Y. C., Ekici, K., & İşleyici, Ö. (2008). Fermente Türk Sucuğu ve pastırmalarda kalıntı nitrat ve nitrit düzeyleri. [Residual nitrate and nitrite levels in fermented Turkish sausage and pastrami]. *Yüzüncü Yıl Üniversitesi Veteriner Fakültesi Dergisi*, 19(1), 41–45.

Seery, M. K. (2015). Flipped learning in higher education chemistry: Emerging trends and potential directions. *Chemistry Education Research and Practice*, 16(4), 758–768. 10.1039/C5RP00136F

Tekbiyik, A., & Tepe, M. (2017). Türkiye'de 2001-2017 Yılları arasında yaşanan laboratuvar ve deney kazalarının değerlendirilmesi. [Evaluation of laboratory and experimental accidents that occurred in Turkey between 2001 and 2017]. *International Journal of Innovative Approaches in Education*, 1(1), 11–20. 10.29329/ijiape.2017.84.2

Tucker, B. (2012). The flipped classroom. *Education Next*, 12(1).

Walters, A. U., Lawrence, W., & Jalsa, N. K. (2017). Chemical laboratory safety awareness, attitudes and practices of tertiary students. *Safety Science*, 96, 161–171. 10.1016/j.ssci.2017.03.017

West, S. S., Westerlund, J. F., Stephenson, A. L., Nelson, N. C., & Nyland, C. K. (2003). Safety in science classrooms: What research and best practice say. *The Educational Forum*, 67(2), 174–183. 10.1080/00131720308984555

Yang, Y., Reniers, G., Chen, G., & Goerlandt, F. (2019). A bibliometric review of laboratory safety in universities. *Safety Science*, 120, 14–24. 10.1016/j.ssci.2019.06.022

Yılmaz, A. (2015). *Laboratuvarda güvenli çalışma* [*Laboratory safety*]. Hacettepe Üniversitesi Yayınları.

Zhu, B., Feng, M., Lowe, H., Kesselman, J., Harrison, L., & Dempski, R. E. (2018). Increasing enthusiasm and enhancing learning for biochemistry-laboratory safety with an augmented-reality program. *Journal of Chemical Education*, 95(10), 1747–1754. 10.1021/acs.jchemed.8b00116

## APPENDIX ONE: PHOTOS TAKEN BY STUDENTS AT THE MARKET

*Figure 5.*

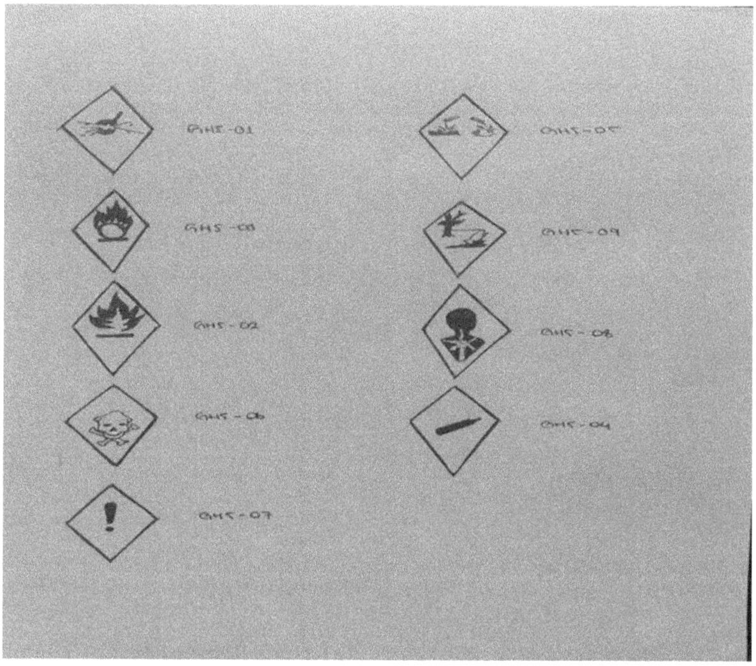

*Figure 6.*

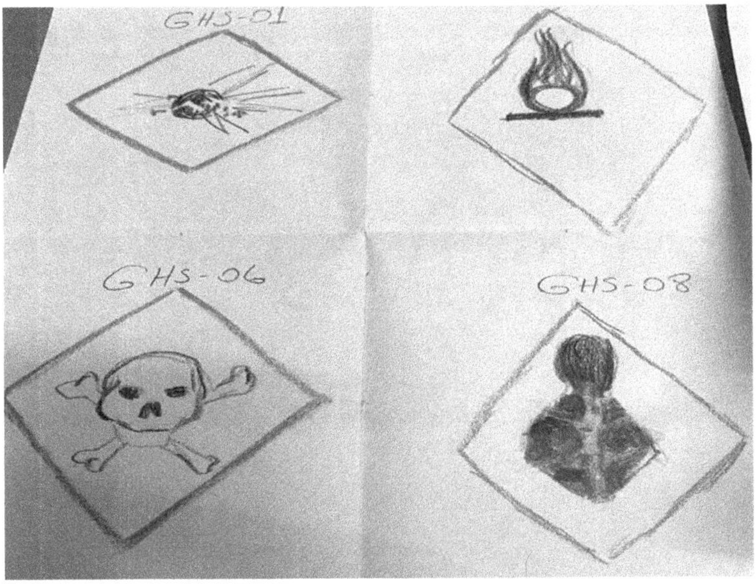


*Figure 7.*

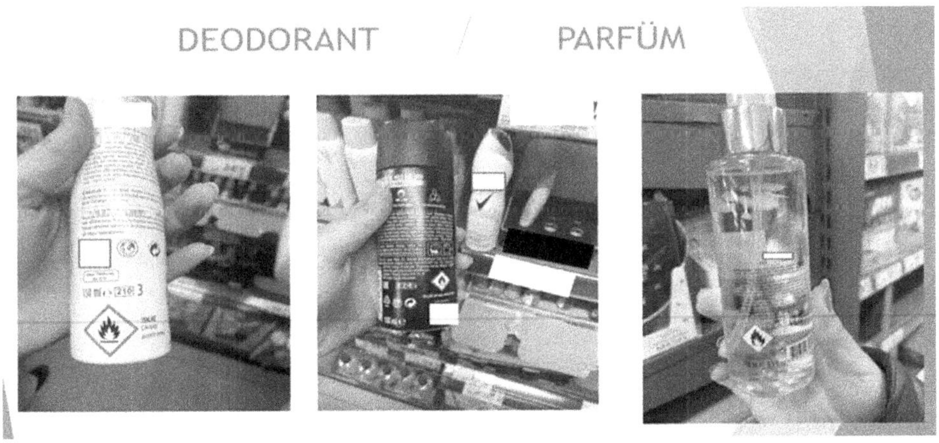

*Figure 8.*

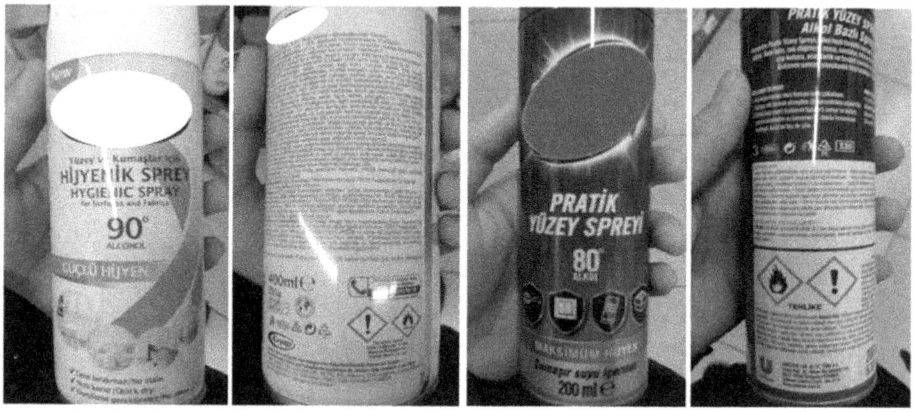


*Figure 9.*

# APPENDIX TWO: KAHOOT QUESTIONS

*Table 1.*

| Chemicals | GHS Code |
|---|---|
| I. Explosive | GHS01 |
| II.Toxic | GHS07 |
| III. Corrosive | GHS05 |
| IV. Oxidizing Agent | GHS04 |

GHS codes of some chemicals are given above. Which of the given GHS Codes is correct?

A. I-III B. III C. II-III-IV D. I-II-III

2. Which of the following information is or are flammable liquids?

I. Ethanol, Toluene

II. Ethylacetate, Ether

III. Sprays, Acetylene

A. I B. II C. I-II D.III

3. I. Corrosive is considered corrosive if its concentration in a mixture is at least ...............

II. Lethal dose for toxic substances. It is symbolized with.

III. Carcinogenic substances............ And it is classified by ..............................

Which of the following is true for the blanks in the sentences given above.

I. I at $\geq 5$

II. II at LD

III. Category 1(1A, 1B and 1C) and Category 2 in III

A. I B. II C. I-II-III D. I-II

4. 4. Which of the following information is correct?

I. In skin abrasion, irreversible damage occurs 4 hours after contact with corrosive substances.

II. In skin irritation, reversible damage occurs 24 hours after contact with the irritant.

Substances that cause abrasion and irritation on the skin are called corrosive substances.

A.I B. I-II C. I-III D. I-II-III

5. I. In acidic solutions, if the pH is 2 and less than 2, the skin is considered corrosive.

II. In basic substances, if the pH is greater than 11 and 11, the skin is considered corrosive.

III. For substances that cause eye damage, the hazard statement is indicated by the P phrase and the precautionary statement by the H phrase.

Which of the above is/are correct?

A.I-II B. II-III C. I D I-II-III

## APPENDIX THREE: URLS USED DURING FLIPPED LEARNING APPLICATIONS

https://www.mevzuat.gov.tr/mevzuat?MevzuatNo=18709&MevzuatTur=7&MevzuatTertip=5)

https://institute.acs.org/acs-center/lab-safety/education-training/safety-videos/college-lab-safety-videos.html)

https://www.acs.org/content/dam/acsorg/about/governance/committees/chemicalsafety/publications/safety-in-academic-chemistry-laboratories-students.pdf

https://www.youtube.com/watch?v=8AVIl_-8kc4

https://www.youtube.com/watch?v=wq344RYQTe0

https://www.youtube.com/watch?v=3ELbwzqyuhs

https://www.youtube.com/watch?v=nsGp4ztkjtk

https://www.youtube.com/watch?v=8AVIl_-8kc4

https://www.youtube.com/watch?v=wq344RYQTe0

https://www.youtube.com/watch?v=3ELbwzqyuhs

https://www.youtube.com/watch?v=nsGp4ztkjtk

https://www.youtube.com/watch?v=xy1sv6KGjeE

https://isgtedbir.com/acil-durum/yangin/yangin-sondurme-cihazlari/

# Chapter 16
# Adapting Virtual Laboratories in Post-COVID-19 Pandemic Learning Landscapes:
## An Exploration of Science Teacher Perceptions and Adoption in Rural Schools

**Brian Shambare**
https://orcid.org/0000-0002-4869-8407
*Rhodes University, South Africa*

**Clement Simuja**
https://orcid.org/0000-0002-0105-0013
*Rhodes University, South Africa*

## ABSTRACT

*The COVID-19 crisis spurred significant advancements in education, leading to the emergence of innovative tools like virtual labs (VL). This chapter presents a qualitative study employing interpretative phenomenological design to explore rural science teachers' perceptions and adoption of VL post-pandemic. Guided by the unified theory of acceptance and use of technology (UTAUT), seven participants from rural schools in South Africa's Eastern Cape province were purposively sampled. Thematic analysis of data from interviews, sharing circle discussions, and document analysis revealed a notable shift in teachers' attitudes towards VL. Perceived initially as daunting, VL evolved into an essential teaching tool in the post-pandemic era,*

DOI: 10.4018/979-8-3693-7645-4.ch016

*representing an unforeseen yet advantageous outcome for rural science education. While the pandemic acted as a catalyst for adoption, persistent challenges such as inadequate internet access and technical support hindered its effective implementation. Addressing these barriers is crucial for meaningful integration of VL into post-COVID-19 education.*

## INTRODUCTION

The COVID-19 outbreak in 2019 significantly impacted various facets of human existence. In response, governments worldwide implemented unprecedented measures such as quarantines and travel restrictions, with 191 nations instituting nationwide closures and five enforcing regional lockdowns (WHO, 2023). These interventions, aimed at curbing the transmission of the disease, necessitated the closure of schools in many countries. According to UNICEF (2022), the pandemic closures affected over 1.6 billion students, constituting approximately 91.3% of the global student population. Particularly vulnerable to the impact of these closures were students in rural regions of the Global South. Amidst this crisis, the utilisation of technology in education garnered significant traction as a means of facilitating virtual learning from home (Thapaliya et al., 2024).

Notably, even prior to the COVID-19 outbreak, several pre-pandemic studies reported a surge in integrating technology into the classrooms, including embracing innovative and cutting-edge immersive technologies. One of these novel technologies is the Virtual Lab (VL), which sparked a global revolution that extended to science education in rural schools in developing countries. This transformative paradigm promised to enrich students' understanding of abstract concepts through experiential learning, effectively replicating real-world laboratory experiences. VL technology has the potential to empower students to immerse themselves in experiments within a fully interactive virtual environment, employing computer-simulated laboratory equipment that remains perpetually functional. This eliminates concerns related to wear and tear, ensuring the enduring utility of chemical reactants (Mohammad Ayasrah et al., 2024). Pioneers in VL adoption have affirmed its efficacy in studying three-dimensional (3D) objects, including minute particles like atomic structures, across varying dimensions, including their interiors (Kapilan et al., 2021).

The literature demonstrates the substantial contribution of VL to improved learning outcomes. Shambare and Simuja's (2022) comprehensive review of 32 pre-pandemic empirical studies across 16 countries unequivocally illustrates the positive impact of VL on students' academic performance. Studies conducted in diverse regions, such as Malaysia (Oloruntegbe & Alam, 2010), Slovenia (Herga et al., 2014), Italy (Pellas, 2014), the USA (Davenport et al., 2018), and Turkey (Kapici et al., 2022), consistently affirm VL's potential to elevate students' educational achievements. Similarly, studies in Africa, including Bhukuvhani et al. (2010) in Zimbabwe, George and Kolobe (2014) in Lesotho, and Aliyu and Talib (2019) in Nigeria, have substantiated the effectiveness of VL in enhancing students' academic achievements.

Research conducted during the COVID-19 era has highlighted the profound influence of the transition from conventional "face-to-face" to virtual teaching. This shift significantly influenced teachers' perceptions of their psychological well-being and their adaptation to virtual modes of teaching (Abumalloh et al., 2021; Kilag et al., 2023; Torres, 2021). Notably, many teachers lacked specific training to effectively integrate VL into their teaching (Ajamu et al., 2024; Gamage et al., 2020). While incorporating technology into teaching became commonplace among teachers before the COVID-19 catastrophe (Mishra et al., 2021; Ratten, 2023), utilising virtual platforms for laboratory experimentation remained relatively uncommon, particularly in rural areas of the Global South. This sluggish adoption has been attributed to the myriad challenges confronting rural science education: inadequate infrastructure, subpar service delivery, and insufficient funding (Assey & Babyegeya, 2022).

The advent of the COVID-19 contagion inadvertently compelled teachers to embrace the untapped potential of educational technologies, including VL, for distance teaching and learning (Shambare & Simuja, 2022). While the COVID-19 crisis might have prompted a positive shift in VL adoption, sustainability necessitates teachers to engage and appreciate this technology more deeply after the pandemic. Hence, it is paramount to delve into the fundamental reasons behind teachers' adoption of VL. This chapter addresses this gap by presenting a qualitative phenomenological study employing an interpretive paradigm and the Unified Theory of Acceptance and Use of Technology (UTAUT) (Venkatesh et al., 2003). The research delved into rural school teachers' perceptions and adoption experiences of VL post-pandemic, leveraging insights gleaned during the COVID-19 crisis. The chapter addresses the question: How has the COVID-19 crisis influenced teachers' perceptions and adoption of VL in rural schools in the aftermath of the pandemic?

Key contributions of this chapter include unpacking the perceptions, opportunities, and challenges in navigating VL adoption post-pandemic from the perspectives of science teachers in rural and marginalised regions. These voices, conspicuously absent in the larger discourse on adopting novel technologies in science education, are crucial for a comprehensive understanding of the landscape. The distinctiveness of this chapter is further accentuated by its provision of insights derived from a longitudinal study conducted throughout the pandemic period in rural schools in the Global South. A notable novelty aspect lies in the chapter's focused exploration of the secondary schooling level, marking a departure from the predominant emphasis on higher education in previous studies. This shift in focus to integrating VL for rural science teaching at the secondary level represents a pioneering research niche in South African science education, both pre- and post-pandemic. By addressing this uncharted territory, the chapter enriches the existing body of knowledge and contributes valuable insights that are directly applicable to the unique challenges and opportunities faced by secondary school science teachers in rural regions post the COVID-19 pandemic.

Specifically, this chapter examines key factors, including Effort Expectancy (EE), Performance Expectancy (PE), Facilitating Conditions (FC), and Social Influence (SI) utilising the UTAUT framework. The chapter is structured as follows: Section 2 synthesises the relevant literature. Then, Section 3 provides the theoretical perspectives. Section 4 outlines the research methods. Next, Section 5 presents the findings, which are discussed in Section 6, culminating in the conclusion. Sections 7 and 8 address limitations and practical implications and suggest future research directions.

## LITERATURE SYNTHESIS

Teaching science in rural schools within developing nations presents numerous challenges unique to the rural context. These difficulties stem from factors such as low socioeconomic status, insufficient school resources and infrastructure, and a shortage of teachers, particularly in science subjects (White & Downey, 2021). For example, Assey and Babyegeya (2022) investigated the impact of various rural factors on the quality of education in the Tabora region of Tanzania, finding that poverty at the family and community levels adversely affected teaching quality. They argued that a combination of poverty and education-related variables can create a cycle of deprivation and poverty, as well as a positive cycle of interaction between education and income.

Similarly, Mtsi and Maphosa (2016) highlighted challenges stemming from the lack of basic science facilities in rural South African schools, particularly the absence of laboratories. Ramnarain and Hlatswayo (2018) noted that inadequate resources hinder meaningful science instruction in most South African rural schools. Additionally, Bantwini (2017) observed poor resourcing in rural schools in the Eastern Cape province of South Africa, based on questionnaire responses and science lesson observations. Similar findings were reported in studies by Tsakeni et al. (2019), and Shambare et al. (2022).

Examining the existing literature on rural teaching contexts reveals several challenges. Firstly, rural areas often face political, social, and economic marginalisation (Cloke, 2006; Sherman & Schafft, 2022), leading to the exclusion of secondary school teachers from national education discussions. Furthermore, rural teachers' needs are often overlooked in policy development and implementation, which predominantly caters to urban settings. Therefore, understanding how teachers' contexts influence their acceptance of VL is crucial, particularly in comprehending Life Sciences teachers' perceptions and experiences of VL in rural teaching.

Secondly, rural areas in developing countries are often geographically dispersed, resulting in schools being far from students' homes (Du Plessis & Mestry, 2019). Consequently, students face challenges such as long commutes, poor infrastructure, and inadequate transportation. Moreover, impassable roads during rainy seasons hinder students' ability to attend classes and participate in experiments. Additionally, the lack of basic amenities like water, sanitation, electricity, and educational materials further impedes students' access to quality science education.

Thirdly, high teacher turnover is a common issue in rural schools, making it difficult to recruit and retain qualified science teachers (Hlalele & Mosia, 2020). Teachers often handle multiple subjects and grades with high teacher-to-learner ratios, contributing to their reluctance to work in rural areas. Even when willing, unfavourable conditions often lead to their departure, leaving behind underqualified or unqualified teachers. Studies have shown that many teachers in rural schools in developing countries lack qualifications in the subjects they teach (White & Downey, 2021). The literature synthesis is structured according to studies conducted before, during and after the COVID-19 pandemic.

## Virtual Laboratories in Science Education pre-COVID-19 Pandemic

The integration of VL technologies in educational settings has been a practice spanning several decades (Berdiyeva, 2024; Ertugrul, 2000). While some studies acknowledge the underutilisation of this technology's potential, numerous authors have extensively explored the educational benefits offered by VLs in academic literature. These advantages encompass:

- Access to sophisticated and costly facilities that may otherwise be inaccessible (Oliveira et al., 2021)
- Cost-effectiveness relative to establishing physical laboratories, with the absence of maintenance expenses, although necessitating periodic updates (Gamage et al., 2020)
- Mitigation of potential hazards inherent in physical labs, such as gas leaks, chemical explosions, and infections, when dealing with micro-organisms (Ganesh et al., 2024).
- Reduction in spatial requirements due to the absence of bulky equipment typically found in traditional laboratories (Shambare & Simuja, 2022).
- Unlimited task repetitions to accommodate individual student preferences (Mohammad Ayasrah et al., 2024).

However, several drawbacks warrant consideration:

- Instructors' extensive experience is pivotal for crafting educational materials that resonate with students (Kolil et al., 2023)
- The rapid pace of technological advancements may lead to the obsolescence of VLs, potentially diminishing student motivation and necessitating periodic redesigns by instructors to maintain relevance and engagement (Falade et al., 2020).

More recently, a mixed methods study conducted by Aljuhani et al. (2018) in Saudi Arabia reviewed the primary advantages of employing VL applications in education. A total of 359 questionnaires were collected, comprising 8.4% parents, 14.2% students, and 68% science teachers. The findings revealed that while traditional laboratory activities are costly and time-intensive, VL activities offer potential savings in terms of money, time, and effort. VL was reported to provide an enjoyable and engaging learning environment engaging, practical, enabling individuals to experiment independently and repeat them as necessary.

In a quantitative study conducted in Turkey, Al Musawi et al. (2015) assessed the efficacy of VL on Omani students' attainment of practical skills and abilities. The study encompassed all students studying science at the first basic education level. Both the control and experimental groups were carefully matched in terms of study factors, with pre-and post-application assessments conducted. The results indicated that VL empowers students to perform experiments more flexibly and interactively using multimedia, aiding in their acquisition of electronic practical training, skills, and inclinations.

Furthermore, Vlachopoulos and Makri (2017) conducted a systematic literature review in the Netherlands that explored the effect of simulations on achieving specific learning objectives. Overall, the findings suggested a positive effect of simulations on learning outcomes. The scholars identified three key outcomes associated with the integration of simulations into the learning process: affective, behavioural, and cognitive. Ultimately, the researchers synthesised evidence to benefit practitioners and scholars in higher education concerned with leveraging simulations for pedagogical purposes, offering potential directions for future research.

## Virtual Laboratories in Science Education During the COVID-19 Pandemic

The devastating effect of COVID-19 prompted the adoption of virtual learning strategies. While theory lessons transitioned smoothly to virtual platforms, educational institutions encountered challenges conducting experiments, which are integral components of science education (Almaiah et al., 2020). VL emerged as a solution to some of these challenges (Shambare & Simuja, 2022), with several studies noting a significant increase in virtual learning traffic as educational institutions grappled with pandemic-related closures.

For instance, Gamage et al.'s (2020) systematic literature review examined the strategies employed by higher learning institutions to offer lab practicals virtually during the COVID-19 pandemic. They found that VL served as a solution, enabling students in the Global North to engage in remote learning. However, internet access remained unequal globally, with only 19% of individuals in the Global South accessing the internet, highlighting existing inequalities.

In another systematic literature review in Australia, Turnbull et al. (2021) explored the role of technology in transitioning from face-to-face to virtual teaching amidst the pandemic. They found five challenges faced by universities in this transition, including privacy and confidentiality, access to technology, synchronous/asynchronous learning tool integration, academic dishonesty, and lecturer and student technology competence.

Additionally, Shyr et al. (2021) conducted quantitative research in Taiwan to assess the integration of 3D Virtual Learning tools during the pandemic. The study confirmed that VL positively influenced attitudes toward learning physical sciences and enhanced learners' understanding of the concepts.

In Saudi Arabia, Abumalloh et al. (2021) investigated the influence of VL in education and its expected benefits during the pandemic. Their findings, based on data from 179 students at Imam Abdulrahman Bin Faisal University, indicated that factors such as social distancing, learning motivation, information sharing, and environmental threats significantly impacted learners' benefits.

Furthermore, Oliveira et al.'s (2021) qualitative exploratory study in Portugal investigated how teachers and students experienced technology-mediated learning during COVID-19. Results revealed mixed outcomes regarding the education process, mostly positive experiences with ICT platform usage and primarily negative experiences with personal adaptation.

Lastly, Torres's (2021) quantitative study in Spain investigated students' views concerning the teaching approach employed in the virtual learning environment during the COVID-19 crisis. The study found widespread dissatisfaction among students, emphasising the need for educational process transitions and teacher training in e-learning.

## Virtual Laboratories in Science Education Post-COVID-19 Pandemic

In the context of suspended face-to-face teaching, Radhamani et al. (2021) conducted a quantitative study titled *'What virtual laboratory usage tells us about laboratory skill education pre-and post-COVID-19: Focus on usage, behaviour, intention and adoption' in India*. This study delved into the role of VLs as Massive Open Online Courses (MOOCs) to ensure continuous teaching and learning beyond the COVID-19 pandemic. By comparing students' use of VL during the years 2019 (pre-COVID) and 2020 (post-COVID), the study aimed to assess the impact of VL on teaching and learning. Initial behavioural analysis conducted before COVID-19 on students (n = 1059) indicated significant acceptance of VLs for instructor dependency and skill training. However, during the pandemic-imposed lockdowns, the adoption of VLs increased, and learners exhibited less dependency on instructors. Notably, 24% of students used VL more than 9 times per week without an instructor. These findings suggest that VL is crucial for promoting self-directed and inquiry-based learning with minimal instructor supervision.

Furthermore, Kolil and Achuthan's (2023) five-year quantitative study in India explored teachers' acceptance of mobile VLs (M-VLs) spanning the pre- and post-pandemic eras. Structural Equation Modeling (SEM) of data from 650 chemistry teachers demonstrated that social influence (SI), habit (HA), and performance expectancy (PE) were significant determinants of behavioural intention (BI) to utilise M-VLs, with HA being the determinant of use behaviour (UB). The results showed that hedonic motivation (HM) influenced teachers' BI and UB pre-COVID-19, whereas facilitating conditions (FC) influenced usage during COVID-19.

Mohammad Ayasrah et al.'s (2024) quantitative investigation compared the effectiveness of using a lab simulation to teach physics in a secondary school versus face-to-face in the United Arab Emirates (UAE) between experimental and control groups. Using 11th-grade students (n =90) from two public schools in Al Ain City, the quasi-experimental design revealed statistically significant differences in students' attitudes toward career interest in science/physics, enjoyment of science lessons and scientific inquiry. This study underscores the significant shift towards technological applications in educational systems worldwide, particularly in the post-COVID-19 era.

In Nepal, Thapaliya's (2024) qualitative study titled '*Opportunity in COVID-19 crisis: Moving away from chalk and talk to technology-integrated teaching in Nepalese higher education institutions*' investigated teachers' utilisation of technology during COVID-19. Data from 11 purposefully selected teachers across three universities in Nepal revealed that while virtual lessons aimed to address learning disruptions due to the pandemic closures, they faced challenges, including teachers' attitudes, lack of trained teachers, and policy inconsistencies. Nevertheless, the study highlighted that teachers perceived the pandemic crisis as a springboard to learn to integrate technologies into their classrooms.

The literature review uncovers several critical gaps in VL research post-COVID-19 pandemic. Firstly, there is an imbalance in geographical representation, with most studies hailing from the Global North, leaving the understanding of VL adoption in the Global South lacking. Secondly, VL research primarily focuses on university lecturers and students, neglecting teachers' perceptions and experiences of VL, particularly in underexplored rural schools. Methodologically, there is a bias towards quantitative and mixed methods, ignoring the depth qualitative approaches can offer. Therefore, this chapter seeks to plug some of these gaps by presenting a qualitative study that focuses on secondary school teachers in rural schools from the Global South.

## THEORETICAL FRAMEWORK – UNIFIED THEORY OF ACCEPTANCE AND USE OF TECHNOLOGY (UTAU)

The UTAUT framework encompasses four primary exogenous factors: Performance Expectancy (PE), Effort Expectancy (EE), Social Influence (SI), and Facilitating Conditions (FCs). Additionally, it includes two endogenous factors, Behavioural Intention (BI) and Use Behaviour (UB) (Venkatesh et al., 2003; Venkatesh, 2022). According to this model, PE, EE, and SI play roles in shaping users' acceptance of technology and subsequent behavioural intentions, thereby influencing adoption. FCs are regarded as direct determinants of actual usage. Intermediate factors, such as voluntariness of use, experience, gender, and age, interact with the main constructs. In this chapter, the UTAUT serves as the theoretical framework for exploring science teachers' perceptions and adoption of VL in the aftermath of the COVID-19 contagion.

*Figure 1. UTAUT*

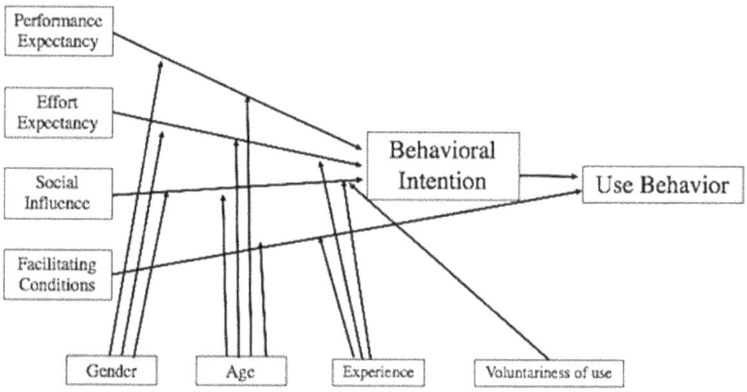


*(Venkatesh et al., 2003, p. 447)*

## Performance Expectations (PE)

PE refers to individuals' perception of their ability to efficiently accomplish tasks using technology (Venkatesh et al., 2003). In this chapter, PE can be viewed as the science teachers' belief that the adoption of VL in their teaching, along with its potential to improve student achievements, leads to improved teaching and learning in rural school settings.

## Effort Expectancy (EE)

EE refers to the level of simplicity with which users can navigate learning a technology (Venkatesh et al., 2003). Previous research consistently indicates that when teachers perceive technology in their teaching as straightforward, requiring minimal effort, and lacking complexity, their intentions toward adoption are more favourable (Rusman et al., 2024; Turnbull et al., 2021; Venkatesh, 2022). In this chapter, EE denotes the level of difficulty encountered in learning to teach with VL in rural school settings post-COVID-19 pandemic.

## Social Influence (SI)

SI is characterised as the degree to which individuals perceive the significance of others' approval or agreement concerning their adoption of a new technology (Venkatesh et al., 2003). Prior works by Aljuhani et al. (2018) and Li and Zhao (2024) show that teachers recognise the significance of others' involvement in their adoption of new technologies. For instance, if stakeholders, school leaders, and colleagues promote technology adoption, teachers become more inclined to adopt the technologies, thereby increasing the perceived value of technologies like VL and further facilitating their adoption. In this chapter, SI can be viewed as the opinions of respected colleagues and friends, support from school leadership, and student preferences in adopting VL into teaching in the post-COVID-19 pandemic.

## Facilitating Conditions (FC)

FC represents the extent to which a user believes that technical and organisational structures are in place to support technology use (Venkatesh et al., 2012). Technical challenges, such as limited mobile technology infrastructure, restricted internet access, and institutional issues like a lack of support staff, could potentially hinder teachers' adoption of VL. Hence, when teachers perceive sufficient support from their schools for the adoption of VL, their willingness to adopt and use it becomes more solid. In this chapter, we view FC as all post-pandemic factors, such as the infrastructure supporting the use of VL, the proficiency in utilising VL, and the accessibility of technical support for addressing any issues encountered during VL usage. We further contend that predicaments such as the COVID-19 pandemic are facilitating conditions themselves, influencing teachers' inclinations toward adopting innovative virtual teaching methods.

## Behavioural Intention (BI)

BI is influenced by individuals' attitudes towards and subjective norms regarding a particular behaviour, and it often predicts their actual behaviour (Pickett et al., 2012). Their behavioural intention can gauge the willingness of users to adopt the technology. Whether it is pre-pandemic or post-pandemic, in this chapter, BI pertains to the degree to which science teachers in rural schools intend to use and persist in VL in their teaching.

## Use Behaviour (UB)

The use behaviour reflects the actual actions taken by individuals in using technology (Venkatesh et al., 2003). BI is considered a reliable predictor of UB. In this chapter, UB refers to the degree to which science teachers in rural schools utilise VL in their teaching post-COVID-19 pandemic.

# METHODOLOGY

We employed a qualitative research methodology, which is particularly suitable for exploring emerging topics with limited existing knowledge, such as the adoption trends of innovative VL technology following the COVID-19 pandemic. We aimed to prioritise the participants' viewpoints on the situation, delving into their thoughts, perceptions, and beliefs about the subject (Corbin & Strauss, 2008; Turner & Hagstrom-Schmidt, 2022). Within this qualitative approach, we chose an interpretative phenomenological design, which is focused on understanding the shared lived experiences of a specific group (Creswell & Poth, 2016; Smith & Fieldsend, 2021). This design enabled us to gain a comprehensive insight into participants' lived experiences (Frechett et al., 2020; Patton, 2022). Employing this approach, we sought to elucidate teachers' perspectives on adopting VL for teaching, aiming to comprehend how they interpreted their experiences. By adopting interpretive phenomenology as our ontology, we aimed to grasp all facets of the phenomenon under study rather than fixating on a singular concept. Initially, we endeavoured to distil individual participants' perspectives and experiences with VL adoption into a depiction of the universal essence, followed by interpreting the significance of these lived experiences. The principal objective of this qualitative interpretive phenomenological inquiry was to investigate science teachers' experiences and perceptions regarding the adoption of VL. To gather the necessary data, we conducted in-depth semi-structured interviews, sharing circles, and document analysis. The research questions articulated at the end of this chapter's introduction guided our efforts to elicit participants' perspectives concerning the adoption of VL for rural teaching in the post-COVID-19 era.

## Research Sites

The research setting for this study is the Eastern Cape province of South Africa, particularly Joe Gqabi. The district's population primarily consists of students from rural households heavily reliant on subsistence farming and government social grants as their main sources of income. These households often face resource scarcity, a circumstance exacerbated by the fact that most schools in the Joe Gqabi district are designated with a quintile one ranking, indicating their rural setting and the resultant lack of resources. In the South African context, a quintile one ranking signifies a school catering to children from the lowest 20% of households in terms of income or expenditure (Department of Basic Education, 2013). Typically, these households are located in rural and remote areas and are at a heightened risk of poverty. Consequently, schools designated as quintile one are entitled to free or subsidised educational services. This contextual backdrop reflects the conditions prevalent in the schools where the current investigation was done.

## Participant Selection

We utilised purposive sampling to select seven participants. This method allowed us to specifically target individuals who could provide insightful perspectives on the investigated issues (Campbell et al., 2020; Patton, 2022). While purposive sampling offers advantages in targeting participants with relevant characteristics aligned with our research objectives, it also introduces limitations, such as potential biases in sampling and researcher perspectives (Creswell & Poth, 2016). To address these limitations, we provided a thorough rationale behind the selection of specific teachers. We aimed to ensure representation from diverse rural schools and science teachers with varying levels of experience and viewpoints on the adoption of VL. However, it is crucial to recognise that this approach may limit the broader applicability of our findings to the entire population of science teachers in rural schools. To mitigate this limitation, we provided detailed descriptions of participant selection criteria and research sites, aiming to enhance the relevance of our findings to similar contexts.

## Sample Size and Sample Size Determination

Boddy (2016) justifies the use of sample sizes as small as 1 to 12 participants in qualitative research. Malterud et al. (2016) similarly advocate for small sample sizes, arguing that when the sample contains highly relevant information for the study, fewer participants are needed. Aligned with these perspectives, we opted for a sample size of seven participants, prioritising in-depth insights over statistical representativeness, given the qualitative nature of our study. We employed purposive sampling to select participants with diverse perspectives on VL adoption among rural science teachers. Additionally, resource constraints, including time and budget limitations, influenced our decision regarding the sample size. Biographical information about the seven selected teachers is presented in Table 1 below.

*Table 1. Biographic information of participants*

| Teacher (Pseudonym) | Age | Gender | Qualifications | Teaching experience (years) |
|---|---|---|---|---|
| E1 | 43 | Female | BEd Physical Sciences | 12 |
| E2 | 27 | Female | BEd Life Sciences | 3 |
| E3 | 58 | Male | BEd Life Sciences | 27 |
| E4 | 39 | Female | BEd in Physical Sciences | 7 |

continued on following page

*Table 1. Continued*

| Teacher (Pseudonym) | Age | Gender | Qualifications | Teaching experience (years) |
|---|---|---|---|---|
| E5 | 47 | Female | BEd Life Sciences | 15 |
| E6 | 29 | Male | BEd Life Sciences | 5 |
| E7 | 33 | Male | BEd Agricultural Sciences | 11 |

## Data Collection

We employed in-depth semi-structured interviews, sharing circle discussions (a form of focus group discussions rooted in indigenous practices), and document analysis. The semi-structured interviews allowed us to extract detailed insights from participants (Patton, 2022). Through skilful question framing, we built rapport with participants, clarified their perspectives, and elicited comprehensive information on the phenomenon under investigation. Drawing from indigenous worldviews, the sharing circles facilitated collaborative meaning-making (Chilisa, 2017; Hanson & Danyluk, 2022; Lavallée, 2009). These circles, prevalent in African and indigenous contexts, provided valuable insights into group perspectives, experiences, and perceptions, enriching our collective understanding. We conducted seven interviews and two sharing circles, each lasting 30 to 45 minutes, between August and October 2021, prioritising participant convenience. Additionally, document analysis supplemented these methods, offering further insights into technology integration guidance within South African education policy documents.

## Data Analysis

We applied a thematic approach to identify, organise, analyse, and summarise themes in the data (Braun & Clarke, 2006). This exercise was characterised by its intricacy, iterative nature, and reflexivity rather than following a linear or systematic path. Analysis and interpretation of the data began during the semi-structured interviews and sharing circles, as emerging themes were recognised. Following this, the audio-recorded files were transcribed into written text using Microsoft Word. Below, we present in Figure 2 a depiction of the six-phase thematic analysis model of Braun and Clarke (2006), which guided our analysis.

*Figure 2. Thematic analysis framework*

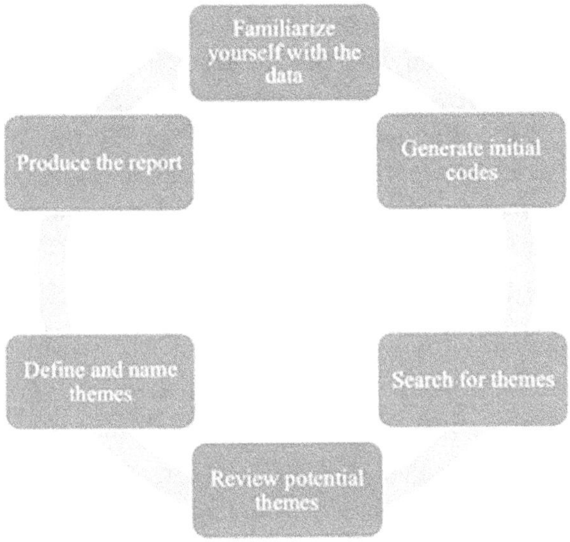


*(adapted from Braun & Clarke, 2006, p.98)*

Despite the structured progression through the six phases, our analysis characteristically involves a recursive approach, moving back and forth between these stages. After completing data collection and transcription, we immersed ourselves in the data by repeatedly reading and re-reading the transcripts to gain familiarity and understanding of the participants' experiences. Open coding was then employed to identify and label meaningful segments of data with descriptive codes, which were subsequently organised into broader categories during axial coding (Braun & Clarke, 2006). This process involved making connections between codes and grouping them into sub-themes or categories based on their similarities and relationships. Through selective coding, we refined and developed the emerging themes by systematically reviewing the data to identify overarching patterns or concepts that captured the central ideas present in the data (Saldana, 2021). Throughout this process, we maintained a reflexive stance, critically reflecting on our interpretations and seeking input from other members of the research team through peer debriefing and discussion. Finally, we conducted a thorough review of the identified themes, refining their definitions and ensuring they accurately reflected the content and context of the data. This approach to theme generation ensured the validity and trustworthiness of our findings. Through this analysis, the themes and subthemes that emerged are presented in Table 2 below.

## Ethics Clearance

We secured ethical clearance from the Education Faculty Ethics Clearance Committee at Rhodes University, with clearance number 2020-1515-3520. This committee reviewed our study to ensure its adherence to ethical standards. Prior to their involvement, we provided all participants with detailed information concerning the study's objectives, processes, potential risks, and gains. We encouraged participants to question any aspect and seek clarification before giving their consent. Consent was documented through signed consent forms, and verbal consent, when obtained, was appropriately recorded. We assured the participants of their voluntary involvement rights, including the option to withdraw at any stage, and were guaranteed privacy and confidentiality.

## RESULTS

We present the results based on the themes, subthemes, and participant responses presented in Table 2.

*Table 2. Themes, subthemes, and participant responses*

| Theme | Subtheme | Participant Responses |
|---|---|---|
| PE | Learning enhancement | *The VL helps students understand complex concepts better through interactive simulations. (E3)* |
| | | *VL allows students to repeat experiments multiple times until they grasp the concept without diminishing lab consumables. (E1)* |
| | | *Students can progress at their own pace, avoiding the fear of making mistakes. (E6)* |
| | Student motivation and enjoyment | *Students find VL engaging, making learning more enjoyable and encouraging active participation in science classes. (E7)* |
| | | *Parents notice an improvement in their children's interest in science subjects after the introduction of VL in the curriculum. (E4)* |
| | Cost-effective | *VL allows students to conduct experiments that are otherwise not feasible in our rural schools' limited laboratory facilities. (E2)* |
| | | *VL provides state-of-the-art science equipment, which is too expensive for my school to purchase and maintain. (E5)* |
| | Safety | *Since there is no moving around as in the physical lab, VL is a safe platform for physically disabled students with limited mobility (E7)* |
| | | *VL eliminates dangers such as gas explosions, toxic chemical leakages, and electrical shocks associated with physical labs (E5)* |

continued on following page

*Table 2. Continued*

| Theme | Subtheme | Participant Responses |
|---|---|---|
| | | *Should infectious pandemics like COVID-19 manifest in the future, VL remains a safe platform for experimentation without being physically present in one space. (E3)* |
| | Cost-effective | *Lab facilities are too expensive for my school, so using VL can really be the way to go. (E1).* |
| | Time-saving | *VL is less time-consuming; experimental results that would take weeks or months in real experiments can be obtained instantly in VL. (E4)* |
| | | *No need for calibration or setting up of apparatus and clean-up after practical in VL, hence saving time. (E6)* |
| EE | User interface | *VL interface is intuitive, making it easy to navigate and perform experiments without much guidance. (E2)* |
| | | *VL is simple to integrate into lesson plans, saving time on lesson preparation. (E5)* |
| | Accessibility across devices | *VL's compatibility with different operating systems minimises technical issues, allowing for a smooth learning experience. (E3)* |
| | | *...VL's accessibility across devices ensures that students can engage with it both at school and home, promoting continuous learning. (E1)* |
| | Easy-to-follow instructions | *I appreciate the clear instructions provided in VL, which reduce confusion and ensure that students focus on learning objectives. (E3)* |
| | | *The setup process is straightforward, requiring minimal technical expertise to get started. (E6)* |
| | | *My challenge is to access the applications, and the instructions are not clear to me. (E4)* |
| | Technological issues | *My students failed to log in to the experiment, they tried for a long time...By the way, I also failed to log in. (E1)* |
| | | *The program was running too slowly, and I suspect there was poor connectivity in our rural area. (E7)* |
| SI | Support from peers | *My colleagues were intrigued by VL the first time they saw me teaching with it. (E4)* |
| | Support from school managers | *My principal has encouraged me to use VL and has pledged to procure all the required facilities. (E2)* |
| FC | Internet connectivity | *Internet infrastructure and reliable connectivity are insufficient in my school. (E6)* |
| | | *My challenge is that my school does not provide data, and I have to buy it from my pocket, so I end up not being able to teach with VL. (E7)* |
| | Technology self-efficacy | *During my initial teacher training, we were not exposed to technology integration, so I always had challenges using these new technologies. (E5)* |
| | | *I had never used technology in my classes before COVID-19, but this pandemic forced me to use it, and it is like a blessing in disguise. (E2)* |
| | Power supply | *The country is currently experiencing power cuts. This disrupts usage of VL...(E2)* |
| | | *A back-up generator is available at my school, but we lack money to buy petrol for the whole day. (E4)* |

continued on following page

*Table 2. Continued*

| Theme | Subtheme | Participant Responses |
|---|---|---|
| BI | Adoption readiness | *VL should have come a long way back; without COVID-19, I would not have known about it. I want to continue using it in my future lessons. (E6)* |
| | | *How I wish my colleagues could also adopt VL. I will be persuading them to use this technology. (E3)* |
| UB | Actual usage | *I cannot say I use VL as I wish to, but hopefully, I will use it more in the future. (E5)* |
| | | *I have used VL a few times. (E4)* |

## Performance Expectancy

### Learning Enhancement

Teachers viewed VL as a beneficial tool for improving students' comprehension of intricate or abstract science concepts. They appreciated its interactive features (E3), noting how it can facilitate deeper engagement with the content. Additionally, VL provided learners with the opportunity to repeat experiments as needed until they fully grasped the underlying concepts (E1), fostering a more thorough understanding. Furthermore, teachers recognised VL's capacity to accommodate individual learning speeds, enabling students to progress at their own pace without feeling intimidated by faster peers (E6). This flexibility in the learning approach can be seen as advantageous in creating a supportive and inclusive learning environment.

### Student Motivation and Enjoyment

Student motivation and enjoyment were highlighted as significant outcomes of incorporating VL into the curriculum. Participants noted that students found VL experiences engaging, which resulted in increased enjoyment of learning and promoted active participation in science classes (E7). Additionally, parents observed a positive change in their children's interest in science subjects following the introduction of VL into the curriculum (E4). This suggests that VL has the potential to enhance learning motivation and enjoyment, as well as garner parental support for such educational initiatives.

### Cost-Effective

Participants noted that VL can allow students to run experiments that may not be feasible due to limitations in laboratory facilities (E2). Additionally, VL provides access to state-of-the-art science equipment, which may be too costly for schools to purchase and maintain independently (E5). This highlights the transformative potential of VL in overcoming resource limitations and ensuring equitable access to high-quality science education, particularly in underserved rural communities. Specifically, schools in rural regions can provide students with opportunities for hands-on experimentation and access to advanced equipment, regardless of their geographical location or financial constraints.

### Safety

Participants emphasised the safety benefits associated with VL. Firstly, VLs were identified as a safe platform for physically disabled students with limited mobility, as they eliminate the need for physical movement typically required in traditional laboratories (E7). Additionally, VL was noted for their ability to mitigate potential dangers present in physical labs, such as gas explosions, toxic chemical leakages, and electrical shocks (E5). Notably, the safety advantages of VL extend beyond typical hazards. They offer a secure platform for experimentation even during infectious pandemics like COVID-19. By enabling experimentation remotely without the need for physical presence in a shared space, VL ensures continuity of learning while prioritising safety (E3). This underscores the resilience and adaptability of VL in ensuring both educational effectiveness and safety in various contexts.

### Time-Saving

VL was praised for its efficiency in saving time compared to traditional laboratory experiments. Participants noted that experimental results, which would typically require weeks or months to obtain in physical experiments, can be obtained instantly in VL (E4). Additionally, VL eliminates the need for calibration or setting up of apparatus, as well as the time-consuming clean-up process after practical sessions, further contributing to time savings (E6). This underscores the significant time-saving advantages of VL, allowing students to engage in more experiments and activities within a shorter timeframe.

## Effort Expectancy

### User Interface

The teachers commended VL for their user-friendly interface, which they described as intuitive and easy to navigate, allowing students to perform experiments with minimal guidance (E2). Additionally, participants noted that VLs are simple to integrate into lesson plans, saving valuable time on lesson preparation (E5). This highlights the accessibility and ease of use of VL, facilitating seamless integration into classroom instruction. By providing an intuitive interface and streamlining lesson planning processes, VL enhances the overall learning experience for both educators and students.

## Accessibility Across Devices

The teachers commended VL for their compatibility with various operating systems, which minimises technical issues and ensures a smooth learning experience (E3). Additionally, participants highlighted VLs' accessibility across devices, emphasising that students can engage with them both at school and at home, thus promoting continuous learning (E1). This highlights the flexibility and versatility of VL in accommodating diverse learning environments and supporting seamless transitions between school and home settings. By enabling access across multiple devices, VL maximise opportunities for student engagement and foster a more inclusive learning experience.

## Easy-to-Follow Instructions

Participants found the instructions and setup process straightforward, requiring minimal technical expertise to get started (E3 and E6). However, some participants faced challenges accessing the applications due to unclear instructions (E4). This highlights the importance of providing comprehensive guidance and support to ensure all users' seamless utilisation of VL. Overall, the positive feedback regarding clear instructions and ease of setup underscores the user-friendly nature of VL while also emphasising the need for improved accessibility and clarity in instruction manuals to address potential challenges.

## Technological Issues

Participants experienced technological issues when attempting to use VL, resulting in difficulties accessing lessons and slow program performance. Some students and educators reported failed login attempts, leading to prolonged waiting times and frustration (E1). Additionally, slow program performance was observed, with participants attributing this to poor connectivity in their rural areas (E7). These challenges underscore the importance of addressing technological barriers to ensure seamless access and functionality of VL. Efforts to improve internet connectivity in rural areas and enhance system reliability are essential for maximising the effectiveness of VL platforms and minimising disruptions to the learning process.

## Social Influence

### Support From Peers and School Managers

Participants received positive feedback and support from both peers and school managers regarding the use of VL. Colleagues expressed intrigue and interest upon observing VL being utilised in teaching, indicating a potential for wider adoption and enthusiasm within the teaching community (E). Furthermore, school managers, including principals, actively encouraged the use of VL and demonstrated commitment by pledging to procure necessary facilities to support their implementation (E). This demonstrates the importance of fostering a supportive environment within educational institutions, where innovative teaching methods such as VL are encouraged and embraced.

## Facilitating Conditions

### Internet Connectivity

The findings revealed significant challenges in internet infrastructure and reliable connectivity within the school environment (E6). Participants noted that the school's inability to provide data packages resulted in educators having to purchase data from personal funds, hindering effective teaching with VL platforms (E7).

### Technology Self-Efficacy

Participants reported challenges with technology integration due to a lack of exposure during their initial teacher training (E5). Many expressed ongoing difficulties in utilising new technologies as a result (E2). However, some participants noted a positive shift in their perspective toward technology use, stating that the COVID-19 pandemic necessitated its adoption in their classes. Despite initial challenges, many viewed this shift as a blessing in disguise, highlighting the opportunity for professional growth and enhanced teaching methods through technology integration (E2). These observations emphasise the need to provide comprehensive training and support to teachers to bolster their technology self-efficacy and facilitate effective utilisation of technology in teaching practices.

### Power Supply

The current state of power cuts in the country has emerged as a significant challenge impacting the usage of VL (E2). Participants noted disruptions in accessing VL platforms due to these power interruptions (E4). While some schools have a back-up generator in place, the availability of petrol to sustain its operation throughout the day remains a challenge (E4). Participants reported financial constraints hindering the purchase of sufficient petrol, thereby limiting the effectiveness of the generator as a solution to power cuts during virtual learning sessions.

## Behavioural Intention

### Adoption Readiness

Teachers expressed a positive outlook towards VL, indicating readiness for its adoption in future lessons (E6). Five acknowledged that without the catalyst of the COVID-19 pandemic, they would not have been introduced to VL, but now see its value and intend to continue its use (E3). Additionally, participants expressed a desire for their colleagues also to adopt VL, recognising its potential benefits for teaching and learning (E3). They expressed intentions to persuade and encourage their peers to embrace this technology in their own teaching practices. These findings highlight a growing readiness and enthusiasm among teachers towards integrating VL into their teaching, suggesting a potential shift towards broader adoption of VL in the future.

## Use Behaviour

### Actual Usage

VL seems to be a new baby whose characteristics many teachers are still trying to understand. Participants indicated varying levels of current usage of VL in their teaching practices (E5). While some expressed dissatisfaction with their current utilisation of VL and hoped to increase usage in the future (E4), others reported having used VL on a few occasions (E). These findings suggest a spectrum of adoption and usage levels among educators, with some experiencing limitations in incorporating VL into their teaching while others have initiated its integration to varying extents. Efforts to address barriers to usage and enhance support for educators may facilitate increased adoption and utilisation of VL in the future.

## DISCUSSION AND CONCLUSION

This chapter stands out as a pioneering effort post-COVID-19 to delve into the perceptions, opportunities, and challenges surrounding VL adoption in rural and marginalised regions of the Global South. These perspectives, often overlooked in the discourse on new technologies in science education, are essential for gaining a holistic understanding of the educational landscape. This chapter sought to address the question: How has the COVID-19 crisis influenced teachers' perceptions and adoption of VL in rural schools in the aftermath of the pandemic?

Our findings reveal a nuanced post-COVID-19 teaching-learning landscape of opportunities and challenges that have profound implications for science education. One of the most striking interpretations is the transformative potential of VL in enhancing teaching experiences in the aftermath of the COVID-19 pandemic, particularly in rural schools. The present study's finding regarding the ability of VL to facilitate deeper engagement with complex concepts, accommodate individual learning speeds, and promote active participation among students signifies a paradigm shift in pedagogical approaches. These observations align with Shyr et al. (2021) and Al Musawi et al. (2015). While other scholars elsewhere have already found that teachers perceive that VL improves learner engagement (Aliyu & Talib, 2019; Aljuhani et al., 2018; Gamage et al., 2020), our chapter's contribution lies in its exploration of rural teachers, a population often neglected in educational research. Moreover, our findings confirm Mohammad Ayasrah et al.'s (2024) observations that VL provides a platform for interactive learning and repeated experimentation, which not only fosters a more thorough understanding of scientific principles but also nurtures intrinsic motivation and enjoyment among students. This suggests that VL can reshape traditional classroom dynamics, empowering educators to create more dynamic and student-centred learning environments.

Additionally, our results indicate that teachers in rural schools perceive VL as cost-effective and accessible, offering promising avenues for addressing equity issues in education. More so, similarly to Mohammad Ayasrah et al. (2024) and Kapilan et al. (2021), the teachers in this study reported that VL can provide access to advanced equipment and experiments, particularly in underserved rural areas, bridging resource gaps for high-quality education). Recognising VL as a cost-effective alternative to traditional labs can alleviate financial burdens on rural schools, allowing funds to be redirected to other educational priorities like teacher development and curriculum enrichment. However, this finding challenges Gamage et al. (2020) and Oliveira et al. (2021), who caution that VL is not cost-effective as the costs of implementing and maintaining VLs, including subscription fees and technical support, may strain resource-constrained schools.

Moreover, the teachers highlighted the safety benefits tied to VL, especially in the context of infectious pandemics like COVID-19, underscoring its resilience and adaptability in ensuring educational continuity while prioritising student safety. Notably, the study found that VL can serve as a valuable tool for promoting inclusive and safe learning environments, particularly for marginalised groups such as physically disabled students. Similar findings were reported by Shambare and Simuja (2022). However, while VLs offer safety and convenience, we contend that they may also exacerbate existing disparities in access to technology and digital resources among students. Rural schools, in particular, may face challenges related to internet connectivity, technological infrastructure, and digital literacy, which could impede equitable access to VLs for all students.

Nevertheless, while acknowledging its potential benefits, our research also brought to light significant challenges that must be tackled to fully leverage VL adoption post-COVID-19. In particular, technological issues like inadequate connectivity and unreliable electricity supply emerged as major obstacles to sustaining VL adoption. These findings underscore the critical need to address such gaps to ensure the successful adoption of VL (Thapaliya, 2024; Turnbull et al., 2021). Additionally, unclear instructions were highlighted as another challenge faced by teachers venturing into VL adoption. We interpret this challenge as indicative of the necessity for customised teacher development training focused on VL utilisation.

In conclusion, this chapter sheds light on the profound impact of the COVID-19 outbreak on teachers, particularly those in rural schools in South Africa. As evidenced by Shambare and Simuja's (2022) study, the crisis significantly disrupted their teaching routines. Additional challenges faced by teachers during this time were highlighted in studies by Kolil and Achuthan (2023), Radhamani et al. (2021), and Thapaliya (2024). Interestingly, despite these formidable challenges, our research reveals a noteworthy trend among the teachers in our study: they viewed the pandemic as an opportunity for transformative change in teaching and learning practices. Rather than succumbing to adversity, they embraced the crisis as a catalyst for shifting their perspectives toward the adoption of VL in education. Moreover, they exhibited a remarkable willingness to influence their colleagues to embrace VL in their teachings. Based on our findings, this chapter anticipates a widespread adoption of VL in the post-COVID-19 era. The resilience and adaptability demonstrated by these teachers suggest a promising trajectory toward a more innovative and technology-driven approach to education in the aftermath of the pandemic.

## LIMITATIONS

One notable limitation of this chapter is the relatively small sample size, comprising seven science teachers from rural secondary schools in South Africa. While we made a concerted effort to choose participants with diverse experiences and backgrounds, the small sample size may limit the generalizability of the results to other contexts or populations. Additionally, the study relied primarily on self-report data obtained through interviews and sharing circle discussions, which could be subject to social desirability bias or recall errors. Furthermore, the study focused solely on science teachers' perspectives, overlooking the viewpoints of other stakeholders such as students, school administrators, or educational policymakers. Notably, we recognised that the limitations such as a small sample size and potential biases in sampling could significantly impact the richness and depth of our data, affecting our interpretation of findings. Biases in our sampling methods, including non-random or purposive sampling, could have introduced distortions by favouring certain voices. To mitigate these limitations, we utilised diverse data collection methods to enhance triangulation. We maximised sample information through saturation and thick description, ensuring depth within the constraints of a small sample. Transparency in our sampling process, coupled with member checking, addressed potential biases and validated our data. Additionally, peer debriefing and maintaining an audit trail strengthened the credibility and validity of our findings, ultimately enhancing the trustworthiness of our research outcomes.

## IMPLICATIONS FOR PRACTICE AND FURTHER RESEARCH

The implications of our findings extend beyond the classroom, with broader implications for educational policies and practices. Addressing the technological, infrastructural, and instructional challenges associated with VL adoption requires coordinated efforts from policymakers, educators, and technology providers. Investments in internet infrastructure, professional development programs, and instructional resources are essential to support educators in effectively integrating VL into their teaching practices. Moreover, efforts to promote a supportive and inclusive learning environment characterised by positive feedback from peers and school managers are crucial for fostering widespread adoption of VL. By addressing these challenges and leveraging the transformative potential of VL, educators can harness the power of technology to enhance learning experiences and promote equitable access to education for all students. Lastly, Future research could address these limitations by including more diverse and larger samples, utilising mixed-methods to triangulate data, and exploring multiple perspectives to provide a comprehensive understanding of VL adoption in rural secondary schools. Moreover, future studies could explore emerging trends. These may include the role of immersive technologies such as virtual reality (VR) and augmented reality (AR). Additionally, researchers could investigate the application of artificial intelligence (AI) to tailor learning experiences on an individualised basis. Furthermore, there's potential to delve into the utilisation of blockchain for securing and verifying lab results and achievements.

**Funding:** There are no sources of funding.

**Conflict of interest:** Authors declare none.

**Consent to participate:** Informed consent was obtained from all study participants.

## REFERENCES

Abumalloh, R. A., Asadi, S., Nilashi, M., Minaei-Bidgoli, B., Nayer, F. K., Samad, S., Mohd, S., & Ibrahim, O. (2021). The impact of coronavirus pandemic (COVID-19) on education: The role of virtual and remote laboratories in education. *Technology in Society*, 67, 101728. https://0-doi.org.wam.seals.ac.za/10.1016/j.techsoc.2021.101728. 10.1016/j.techsoc.2021.10172834538984

Ajamu, G. J., Awotunde, J. B., Jimoh, T. B., Adeniyi, E. A., Abiodun, K. M., Oladipo, I. D., & Abdulraheem, M. (2024). Online Teaching Sustainability and Strategies during the COVID-19 Epidemic. In (Eds) J. Rosak-Szyrocka, J. Żywiołek, A. Nayyar, & M. Naved. *The Role of Sustainability and Artificial Intelligence in Education Improvement* (pp. 106-132). Chapman and Hall/CRC. https://0-doi.org.wam.seals.ac.za/10.1201/9781003425779

Al Musawi, A., Ambusaidi, A., Al-Balushi, S., & Al-Balushi, K. (2015). Effectiveness of E-Lab Use in Science Teaching at the Omani Schools. *Turkish Online Journal of Educational Technology-TOJET, 14*(1), 45-52. https://www.learntechlib.org/p/160569/

Aliyu, F., & Talib, C. A. (2019). Virtual chemistry laboratory: A panacea to problems of conducting chemistry practical at science secondary schools in Nigeria. *International Journal of Engineering and Advanced Technology*, 8(5), 544–549. 10.35940/ijeat.E1079.0585C19

Aljuhani, K., Sonbul, M., Althabiti, M., & Meccawy, M. (2018). Creating a Virtual Science Lab (VSL): the adoption of virtual labs in Saudi schools. *Smart Learning Environments, 5*, 1-13. https://0-doi.org.wam.seals.ac.za/10.1186/s40561-018-0067-9

Alkhattabi, M. (2017). Augmented Reality as E-learning Tool in Primary Schools' Education: Barriers to Teachers' Adoption. *International Journal of Emerging Technologies in Learning*, 12(2), 91. 10.3991/ijet.v12i02.6158

Assey, E. S., & Babyegeya, E. (2022). The Challenges Facing Effective Teaching, Learning and Assessment in Community-Based Secondary Schools in Tabora Region. *American Journal of Education and Practice*, 6(2), 1–17. 10.47672/ajep.1084

Berdiyeva, S. (2024). Exploring Innovative Approaches To Teaching. *Modern Science and Research, 3*(1), 923-927. https://inlibrary.uz/index.php/science-research/article/view/28552

Bhukuvhani, C., Kusure, L., Munodawafa, V., Sana, A., & Gwizangwe, I. (2010). Pre-service Teachers' use of improvised and Virtual Laboratory experimentation in Science teaching. *International Journal of Education and Development using ICT, 6*(4), 27-38. https://www.learntechlib.org/p/42262/

Boddy, C. R. (2016). Sample size for qualitative research. *Qualitative Market Research*, 19(4), 426–432. 10.1108/QMR-06-2016-0053

Braun, V., & Clarke, V. (2006). Using thematic analysis in psychology. *Qualitative Research in Psychology*, 3(2), 77–101. 10.1191/1478088706qp063oa

Campbell, S., Greenwood, M., Prior, S., Shearer, T., Walkem, K., Young, S., Bywaters, D., & Walker, K. (2020). Purposive sampling: Complex or simple? Research case examples. *Journal of Research in Nursing*, 25(8), 652–661. 10.1177/174498712092720634394687

Chilisa, B. (2017). Decolonising transdisciplinary research approaches: An African perspective for enhancing knowledge integration in sustainability science. *Sustainability Science*, 12(5), 813–827. https://0-doi.org.wam.seals.ac.za/10.1007/s11625-017-0461-1. 10.1007/s11625-017-0461-1

Cloke, P. (2006). Conceptualising rurality. *Handbook of rural studies, 18*, 18-28. https://digital.casalini.it/9781446206942

Corbin, J., & Strauss, A. (2008). Qualitative research. *Techniques and procedures for developing grounded theory, 3*.

Creswell, J. W., & Poth, C. N. (2016). *Qualitative inquiry and research design: Choosing among five approaches*. Sage publications. https://docs.edtechhub.org/lib/XAH8M47G

Davenport, J. L., Rafferty, A. N., & Yaron, D. J. (2018). Whether and how authentic contexts using a virtual chemistry lab support learning. *Journal of Chemical Education*, 95(8), 1250–1259. 10.1021/acs.jchemed.8b00048

Department of Basic Education (SA). (2013). *National Policy on Quintile Schools*.

Du Plessis, P., & Mestry, R. (2019). Teachers for rural schools–a challenge for South Africa. *South African Journal of Education*, 39(Supplement 1), S1–S9. 10.15700/saje.v39ns1a1774

Ertmer, P. A. (2005). Teacher pedagogical beliefs: The final frontier in our quest for technology integration? *Educational Technology Research and Development*, 53(4), 25–39. 10.1007/BF02504683

Ertugrul, N. (2000). Towards virtual laboratories: A survey of LabVIEW-based teaching/learning tools and future trends. *International Journal of Engineering Education*, 16(3), 171–180. https://hdl.handle.net/2440/2418

Falade, A. A., Olafare, O. F., & Aladesusi, G. A. (2020). Biology teachers' self-efficacy in the use of Virtual Laboratory for instructional delivery in secondary schools. *Nigerian Online Journal of Educational Sciences and Technology*, 1(1), 54–65. 10.4314/nojest.v1i1.908

Frechette, J., Bitzas, V., Aubry, M., Kilpatrick, K., & Lavoie-Tremblay, M. (2020). Capturing lived experience: Methodological considerations for interpretive phenomenological inquiry. *International Journal of Qualitative Methods*, 19, 1609406920907254. 10.1177/1609406920907254

Gamage, K. A., Wijesuriya, D. I., Ekanayake, S. Y., Rennie, A. E., Lambert, C. G., & Gunawardhana, N. (2020). Online delivery of teaching and laboratory practices: Continuity of university programmes during COVID-19 pandemic. *Education Sciences*, 10(10), 291. 10.3390/educsci10100291

Ganesh, G. V., Harithpriya, K., Umapathy, D., Hoque, M. E., & Ramkumar, K. M. (2024). Laboratory Safety. In (Eds) Ramkumar, R. Senthilkumar, Md Enamul HoqueA, *dvanced Mammalian Cell Culture Techniques* (pp. 11-14). CRC Press. 10.1201/9781003397755

George, M. J., & Kolobe, M. (2014). Exploration of the potential of using a Virtual Laboratory for chemistry teaching at secondary school level in Lesotho. *South African Journal of Chemistry. Suid-Afrikaanse Tydskrif vir Chemie*, 67(1), 113–117. https://hdl.handle.net/10520/EJC157769

Hanson, A., & Danyluk, P. (2022). Talking circles as indigenous pedagogy in online learning. *Teaching and Teacher Education*, 115, 103715. 10.1016/j.tate.2022.103715

Herga Rizman, N., & Dinevski, D. (2012). Virtual Laboratory in chemistry–experimental study of understanding, reproduction and application of acquired knowledge of subject's chemical content. *Organizacija*, 45(3), 108–116. 10.2478/v10051-012-0011-7

Hlalele, D., & Mosia, M. (2020). Teachers' sense of community in rural learning ecologies. *Alternation (Durban)*, 27(2), 101–124. 10.29086/2519-5476/2020/v27n2a6

Kapici, H. O., Akcay, H., & Cakir, H. (2022). Investigating the effects of different levels of guidance in inquiry-based hands-on and virtual science laboratories. *International Journal of Science Education*, 44(2), 324–345. 10.1080/09500693.2022.2028926

Kapilan, N., Vidhya, P., & Gao, X.-Z. (2021). Virtual Laboratory: A Boon to the Mechanical Engineering Education During Covid-19 Pandemic. *Higher Education for the Future, 8*(1), 31-46. https://0-doi.org.wam.seals.ac.za/10.1177/2347631120970757

Kilag, O. K., Miñoza, J., Comighud, E., Amontos, C., Damos, M., & Abendan, C. F. (2023). Empowering Teachers: Integrating Technology into Livelihood Education for a Digital Future. *Excellencia: International Multi-disciplinary Journal of Education (2994-9521), 1*(1), 30-41. https://multijournals.org/index.php/excellencia-imje/article/view/3

Kolil, V. K., & Achuthan, K. (2023). Longitudinal study of teacher acceptance of mobile virtual labs. *Education and Information Technologies*, 28(7), 7763–7796. https://0-doi.org.wam.seals.ac.za/10.1007/s10639-022-11499-2. 10.1007/s10639-022-11499-236532789

Lavallée, L. F. (2009). Practical application of an Indigenous research framework and two qualitative Indigenous research methods: Sharing circles and Anishnaabe symbol-based reflection. *International Journal of Qualitative Methods*, 8(1), 21–40. 10.1177/160940690900800103

Li, Y., & Zhao, M. (2024). The study on the influence factors of intention to continue using MOOCs: Integrating UTAUT model and social presence. *Interactive Learning Environments*, •••, 1–19. 10.1080/10494820.2024.2318562

Malterud, K., Siersma, V. D., & Guassora, A. D. (2016). Sample size in qualitative interview studies: Guided by information power. *Qualitative Health Research*, 26(13), 1753–1760. 10.1177/104973231561744426613970

Mishra, S., Sahoo, S., & Pandey, S. (2021). Research trends in online distance learning during the COVID-19 pandemic. *Distance Education*, 42(4), 494–519. 10.1080/01587919.2021.1986373

Mohammad Ayasrah, F. T., Alarabi, K., Abdel Fattah, H. A., & Al-Said, K. (2024). Enhancing secondary school students' attitudes toward physics by using computer simulations. *International Journal of Data & Network Science*, 8(1), 369–380. 10.5267/j.ijdns.2023.9.017

Mtsi, N., & Maphosa, C. (2016). Challenges encountered in the teaching and learning of the natural sciences in rural schools in South Africa. *Journal of Social Sciences*, 47(1), 58–67. 10.1080/09718923.2016.11893544

Oliveira, G., Grenha Teixeira, J., Torres, A., & Morais, C. (2021). An exploratory study on the emergency remote education experience of higher education students and teachers during the COVID-19 pandemic. *British Journal of Educational Technology*, 52(4), 1357–1376. 10.1111/bjet.1311234219758

Oloruntegbe, K. O., & Alam, G. M. (2010). Evaluation of 3d environments and virtual realities in science teaching and learning: The need to go beyond perception referents. *Scientific Research and Essays,5*(9), 948-954. https://doi.org/10.5897/SRE10.036

Patton, M. Q. (2022). Impact-driven qualitative research and evaluation. *The SAGE handbook of qualitative research design, 2*, 1165-1180. https://digital.casalini.it/9781529766943

Pedretti, E., Mayer-Smith, J., & Woodrow, J. (1998). Technology, text, and talk: Students' perspectives on teaching and learning in a technology-enhanced secondary science classroom. *Science Education*, 82(5), 569–589. 10.1002/(SICI)1098-237X(199809)82:5<569::AID-SCE3>3.0.CO;2-7

Radhamani, R., Kumar, D., Nizar, N., Achuthan, K., Nair, B., & Diwakar, S. (2021). What virtual laboratory usage tells us about laboratory skill education pre-and post-COVID-19: Focus on usage, behaviour, intention and adoption. *Education and Information Technologies*, 26(6), 7477–7495. doi.org.wam.seals.ac.za/10.1007/s10639-021-10583-3. 10.1007/s10639-021-10583-334121909

Raman, R., Vinuesa, R., & Nedungadi, P. (2021). Acquisition and user behaviour in online science laboratories before and during the COVID-19 pandemic. *Multimodal Technologies and Interaction*, 5(8), 46. 10.3390/mti5080046

Ramnarain, U., & Hlatswayo, M. (2018). Teacher beliefs and attitudes about inquiry-based learning in a rural school district in South Africa. *South African Journal of Education*, 38(1), 1–10. 10.15700/saje.v38n1a1431

Ratten, V. (2023). The post COVID-19 pandemic era: Changes in teaching and learning methods for management teachers. *International Journal of Management Education*, 21(2), 100777. 10.1016/j.ijme.2023.100777

Rusman, R., Setiasih, O., Nandi, N., Setiawardani, W., & Yusron, E. (2024). Applying the UTAUT Model to Understand Factors Affecting the Use of Learning Management System for Learning Pedagogical Education. *Pegem Journal of Education and Instruction*, 14(1), 218–255. 10.47750/pegegog.14.01.41

Saldana, J. (2021). *The Coding Manual for Qualitative Researchers*. SAGE. https://eduq.info/xmlui/handle/11515/35868

Shambare, B., & Simuja, C. (2022). A Critical Review of Teaching with Virtual Lab: A Panacea to Challenges of Conducting Practical Experiments in Science Subjects Beyond the COVID-19 Pandemic in Rural Schools in South Africa. *Journal of Educational Technology Systems*, 50(3), 393–408. 10.1177/00472395211058051

Shambare, B., Simuja, C., & Theodorio, A. O. (2022). Understanding rural secondary school teachers' perceptions and attitudes on the use of ICT for teaching and learning. *Journal of African Education*, 3(1), 35–57. https://hdl.handle.net/10520/ejc-aa_jae_v3_n1_a3. 10.31920/2633-2930/2022/v3n1a2

Sherman, J., & Schafft, K. A. (2022). "Turning Their Back on Kids": Inclusions, Exclusions, and the Contradictions of Schooling in Gentrifying Rural Communities. *The Russell Sage Foundation Journal of the Social Sciences : RSF*, 8(3), 150–170. 10.7758/RSF.2022.8.3.06

Shyr, W. J., Liau, H. M., Hsu, C. C., & Chen, C. H. (2021). Assess the engagement with 3D Virtual Learning Tools during the COVID-19 Pandemic. *Sustainability (Basel)*, 13(15), 8632. 10.3390/su13158632

Smith, J. A., & Fieldsend, M. (2021). Interpretative phenomenological analysis. In Camic, P. M. (Ed.), *Qualitative research in psychology: Expanding perspectives in methodology and design* (2nd ed., pp. 147–166). American Psychological Association. 10.1037/0000252-008

Thapaliya, M., Adhikari, S., & Rana, L. (2024). Opportunity in COVID-19 crisis: Moving away from chalk and talk to technology-integrated teaching in Nepalese higher education institutions. *E-Learning and Digital Media*, 21(1), 87–105. https://0-doi.org.wam.seals.ac.za/10.1177/20427530231153944. 10.1177/20427530231153944

Torres Martín, C., Acal, C., El Homrani, M., & Mingorance Estrada, Á. C. (2021). Impact on the virtual learning environment due to COVID-19. *Sustainability (Basel)*, 13(2), 582. 10.3390/su13020582

Tsakeni, M., Vandeyar, S., & Potgieter, M. (2019). Inquiry opportunities presented by practical work in school physical sciences. A South African case study. *Gender & Behaviour*, 17(3), 13722–13733. https://hdl.handle.net/10520/EJC-1975177d59

Turnbull, D., Chugh, R., & Luck, J. (2021). Transitioning to E-Learning during the COVID-19 pandemic: How have Higher Education Institutions responded to the challenge? *Education and Information Technologies*, 26(5), 6401–6419. https://0-doi.org.wam.seals.ac.za/10.1007/s10639-021-10633-w. 10.1007/s10639-021-10633-w34177349

Turner III, D. W., & Hagstrom-Schmidt, N. (2022). Qualitative interview design. *Howdy or Hello? Technical and professional communication*. 10.46743/2160-3715/2010.1178

UNICEF. (2022). *From Learning Recovery to Education Transformation: Insights and Reflections from the Fourth Survey on National Education Responses to COVID-19 School Closures*. UNICEF. https://hdl.handle.net/10986/38112

Venkatesh, V. (2022). Adoption and use of AI tools: A research agenda grounded in UTAUT. *Annals of Operations Research*, 308(1-2), 1–12. 10.1007/s10479-020-03918-9

Venkatesh, V., Morris, M. G., Davis, G. B., & Davis, F. D. (2003). User acceptance of information technology: Toward a unified view. *Management Information Systems Quarterly*, 27(3), 425–478. 10.2307/30036540

Vlachopoulos, D., & Makri, A. (2017). The effect of games and simulations on higher education: A systematic literature review. *International Journal of Educational Technology in Higher Education*, 14(1), 1–33. 10.1186/s41239-017-0062-1

White, S., & Downey, J. (2021). International trends and patterns in innovation in rural education. *Rural education across the world: Models of innovative practice and impact*, 3-21. 10.1007/978-981-33-6116-4_1

World Health Organization. (2023). *COVID-19 monthly update: April 2023* (No. WHO-EM/CSR/658/E). World Health Organization. Regional Office for the Eastern Mediterranean. 10.1136/bmj.p1246

# Chapter 17
# Challenges and Sustainability of E-Learning Adoption Among EFL Teachers in the Post-COVID-19 Era

**Mohammad Mahyoob**
http://orcid.org/0000-0002-6664-1017
*Taibah University, Saudi Arabia & Technical Community College -Taiz, Yemen*

**Jeehaan Algaraady**
http://orcid.org/0000-0003-3901-4648
*Taiz University, Yemen*

**Omer Elsheikh Hago Elmahdi**
http://orcid.org/0009-0009-1335-2607
*Taibah University, Saudi Arabia*

## ABSTRACT

*This study actively examines the resilience of online learning in EFL (English as a foreign language) instruction during the COVID-19 pandemic, focusing on adaptive strategies and resources in Saudi Universities. It shows a significant research gap in how these digital learning strategies have adapted post-pandemic to be sustainable. However, the chapter also provides a qualitative and quantitative analysis of strategies among 84 EFL teachers (81% male, 19% female) used to collect data on online learning experiences during the pandemic. Findings reveal significant increases in teachers' and students' digital skills, facilitating adaptation to online learning*

DOI: 10.4018/979-8-3693-7645-4.ch017

*environments and continuing those practices. These positive outcomes offer hope and optimism for the future of online learning. It concludes by recommending that research be expanded to include different academic disciplines, including students in remote areas, and to explore new instructional methods and support strategies for asynchronous learning to meet the challenges of scheduling and Internet connectivity.*

## INTRODUCTION

Since the onset of the COVID-19 pandemic, online teaching and learning have experienced unprecedented change in the EFL landscape, highlighting the need to evaluate its impact. This study addresses critical gaps in how these changes have affected EFL education, particularly concerning technology adoption, teaching strategies, and the resulting instructional inequalities. It seeks to explain the sustainability, effectiveness, and long-term success of these emerging online learning practices from the EFL perspective.

The impact of the COVID-19 pandemic on various aspects of life is significant. Education is one of the aspects that has positively transmitted to be conducted online and used technology effectively (Papadakis et al. 2023, a). The recent improvement positively impacts EFL learning. This situation has necessitated a closer look at how EFL online learning has adapted and evolved regarding sustainability, resilience, and innovation. Hidalog-Camacho et al. (2021) investigated the difficulties teachers, students, and parents encountered during the pandemic. The study emphasized the necessity for support and resources to ensure equitable access to quality education. The sustainability in EFL e-learning indicates the capacity to overcome these difficulties. To enhance a reliable online platform, it is necessary to have support for the technological infrastructure and internet connectivity (Papadakis et al., 2023a; Rajab et al., 2020; Pellegrini et al., 2020; Byun & Slavin, 2020; Mahyoob, 2021). Teacher training workshops are essential to activate proficient online learning (Tülübaş et al., 2023)

A notable instance is the situation in Saudi Arabia, where the government-imposed curfews and restrictions prompted a swift transition to online education. This transition forced teachers to create alternative assessment methods, positively affecting students' overall skills (Adedoyin & Soykan, 2023; Adeyeye et al., 2022; Chu, 2021; Algaraady & Alrahili, 2022). During the pandemic, innovation in EFL online learning was crucial for maintaining effectiveness and relevance (Al-khresheh,2022).

When the pandemic began, teachers struggled to transition from conventional classroom instruction to online platforms (Betancourt-Odio et al. (2021). Although many teachers initially lacked the necessary digital tools or creativity, they adapted over time (Han and Wang (2021). For example, only about 10% of English language learners spent significant time online before the pandemic, rising to 55% after the pandemic. These changes removed physical barriers, allowing new methods of teaching to overcome traditional barriers (Oraif & Elyas, 2021). Teachers' creativity in online learning environments has been vital to successful educational outcomes. The recent advances in Large Language Models (LLMs) will enhance EFL teachers' and learners' improvements and language skills development (Jeehaan & Mahyoob, 2023; Mahyoob et al., 2023).

Teachers' creativity in teaching style is tailored to specific contexts, further enhancing the language learning process. This creativity is essential in engaging students and increasing their motivation to learn English. A study investigating the impact of the pandemic on teachers' creativity in Saudi EFL contexts revealed a downward trend in creativity regardless of student gender, university level, or teacher's gender Al-khresheh, 2022). A study of EFL teachers and students from three universities in Ecuador focused on teaching practices, learning outcomes, and students' perceptions of the advantages and disadvantages of online learning (Orosz et al., 2021). The impact of the COVID-19 pandemic on EFL online learning has been multifaceted, affecting sustainability, adaptation, and innovation. Understanding these factors is essential to assess the pandemic's overall impact and suggest future actions to support and improve EFL online learning in the face of similar problems.

The need for this study halted from the rapid integration of digital methods and materials in EFL teaching, which made records and wide-ranging accessibility also expose significant inequalities in access to the technical internet, especially in underdeveloped areas. These perceptions emerged online during the pandemic. They seek to determine the sustainability of EFL teaching models, aiming to refine them to be more resilient to future educational upheavals.

This study employs the Technological pedagogical and content knowledge (TPACK) framework, which concerns the activation of technology in teaching and learning, Shulman 1986; Mishra & Koehler (2006). The TRACK framework stipulates a structure for developing and delivering online English language teaching, ensuring a wide-ranging learning experience for students. It encompasses various mechanisms such as curriculum design, instructional strategies, assessment methods, technology integration, and collaborative services tools for engagement.

The contribution of this study is that it clarifies the potential of online EFL instruction to improve student engagement and instructional outcomes through alternative methods. The study enhances the discourse in EFL teaching, especially regarding the rapid transition to online education, which is necessary in emergencies. The emergency to move to online learning forced teachers and institutes to launch and invent new methods and strategies that support EFL learning and teaching. Saudi EFL teachers were among other teachers around the globe who received many workshops and training on using online devices efficiently and effectively.

This paper is organized as follows: The first section discusses the introduction, the study's theoretical background, the objectives, and the research questions. The second section presents the research questions for the study. The third section reviews the literature. The fourth section describes the proposed methodology, including the sample and the instrument used for data collection. Section five discusses the results and their implications and visualizations. Section six introduces the discussion. Section seven discusses the conclusion and future work.

## Online Learning in Saudi Arabia Context

Selecting Saudi Arabia as the focal point for this study, particularly within online and English as a Foreign Language (EFL) education, is grounded in multiple compelling factors. The kingdom has emerged as a leader in integrating technology within its educational sector, a movement propelled by governmental support and substantial investment (Mahyoob, 2021). This dedication is critical to Saudi Arabia's Vision 2030 initiative, which is centring on educational reform and embracing digital advancements.

Saudi Arabia's swift technological progression, particularly its push towards the digitalization of education and other sectors, positions it as an intriguing subject for examining the effectiveness and adaptation of online learning, especially considering unforeseen circumstances such as the COVID-19 pandemic. The country's distinct educational landscape, marked by specific cultural and linguistic nuances, provides insightful perspectives on tailoring online learning for various environments, especially in EFL education (Alammary et al., 2022).

Amid the global health crisis, Saudi Arabia rapidly pivoted to online learning, mirroring a global trend but with its unique trajectory toward educational technology. Analyzing this shift thoroughly explains the hurdles and potential accompanying such a rapid transition. Furthermore, the importance of English language proficiency for academic and professional success in Saudi Arabia underscores the relevance of this study (Oraif & Elyas, 2021). The country's emphasis on enhancing English skills through online modalities underscores its significance in EFL educational advancements. The combination of Saudi Arabia's governmental support, digitalization momentum, distinct educational characteristics, and the impetus for online learning during the pandemic renders it an ideal case for exploring the nuances and impacts of e-learning and EFL education progressions.

## RESEARCH QUESTIONS

What are the main factors that drive online learning to continue post-COVID-19 in teaching and learning English as a foreign language, their effects on the development of EFL learners' performance, and the attitudes of EFL teachers toward using online platforms at Saudi EFL colleges?

To guide this investigation, the following research questions were formulated:

1. What key factors have contributed to the sustainability of online learning at universities after the COVID-19 pandemic?
2. In what ways does online learning enhance the achievement of learning outcomes?
3. What specific challenges do teachers encounter when using online platforms to teach English?
4. Have teachers and learners received adequate training and tutorials to use online learning platforms effectively?

## LITERATURE REVIEW

Through time and the massive spread of the Internet worldwide, online teaching and learning have become much easier, and more people are going to online Education for knowledge. The coronavirus outbreak has put the world in a difficult situation (Abel, 2021; Al-Garaady and Mahyoob, 2022; Bäckman, 2021; Algaraady, 2022). Schools and universities were closed, and studies were suspended in many parts of the world. Here comes the role of online learning as the best alternative. The fast and extensive adoption of online learning has raised questions about the sustainability of this model in the long term Ghanbari and Nowroozi, (2021). In Saudi Arabia, online platforms play a significant role in the educational process at Saudi universities. Now, attention is on what happened after the COVID-19 crisis. Education will not be the same, and people are discussing using online or blended learning. Blended learning is being used more in teaching and learning around the world. The utilization of blended learning in advanced education has expanded during the previous decade and will be used more after the COVID-19 crisis. Regarding sustainability, research suggests that online learning will play an important role in the post-COVID-19 era. This is partially due to the growing availability and affordability of technology and the recognition of the potential benefits of online learning by both students and institutions. Additionally, the pandemic has accelerated the pace of digital transformation in Education, and many institutions are now investing in the infrastructure and resources needed to support online learning in the long term Draxler-Weber et al., 2022.

Hashemi et al. 2024, investigated the pedagogical changes in municipal adult education (MAEd) in Sweden during and after the COVID-19 pandemic. It uses the concept of Fulan educational reform to examine teachers' professional dynamics in the context of evolving issues, changing pedagogies, and changing beliefs about teaching and learning. The study used a multi-information qualitative design. Data were collected through questionnaires, interviews, and question-and-answer sessions with MAEd teachers from the three largest cities in Sweden between 2020 and 2022. Data were analyzed using thematic analysis. The findings suggest that divergent theories of learning have been explicitly explored and are being adopted increasingly in how online and hybrid education is delivered, content is managed, and structured clearly and with a great deal of attention to the quality and organization of the study. Teachers reported a shift from initial skepticism to accepting attitudes toward online education, including increased digital literacy. The study provides empirical evidence on the effectiveness of self-organization and institutional change as necessary for education in response to crises and sudden changes. The results show characteristics of instructional change corresponding to the Fulan triangle, with content revised, instruction changed, and beliefs about teaching and learning changed.

A paper conducted by Jacques et al. 2023, provides an overview of various studies and research in post-COVID education for a sustainable future. It highlights challenges, emerging technologies, and trends in this area. The paper discusses key challenges and developments in post-COVID education, focusing on digital literacy, the importance of inclusive education, and the effective integration of technology into teaching and learning. It emphasizes the importance of innovative approaches and continued adaptation of educational practices in the post-stroke setting. Explores emerging technologies and instructional strategies used to meet these challenges. The paper synthesizes findings and insights from studies presented in the special issue, covering topics related to post-COVID education, including the use of technology, teaching strategies, learning assessment, and student opinion. The paper highlights the important work being done to rethink and adapt university teaching strategies in the post-COVID era, emphasizing the need for innovation and proactive measures to meet challenges and the education department's role. The paper does not explicitly address the limitations of individual studies or all of the research presented in the special issue. Specific recommendations for future work or research directions were also not provided.

Putri et al. 2024 examine how research has progressed in bringing the Sustainable Development Goals (SDGs) into foreign language (EFL) education. It stresses the importance of teaching global issues highlighted by the SDGs to help students gain the understanding, skills, and capacity to tackle today's global challenges. The study uses a systematic literature review guided by the PRISMA (Preferred Reporting Items for Systematic Reviews and Meta-Analyses) methodology. The authors searched through databases like Scopus, Taylor and Francis, and Google Scholar, using keywords related to sustainability, SDGs, and EFL. They selected twenty-five studies based on specific inclusion and exclusion criteria for the final analysis. This review addresses important gaps by examining how SDG research has been incorporated into EFL teaching. The findings highlight the current state of research and the important benefits of integrating global topics into language teaching. Although the authors acknowledge that the studies are limited to analyses of published data, future research could examine other sources, such as unpublished studies.

Delgado (2022) investigated the transition of university physics courses at a Mexican university in the post-COVID-19 era. Employing a case study methodology, he gathered data through interviews with teachers and students. The examination revealed that the shift to online instruction had presented challenges and opportunities in physics education. The results show that some students encountered difficulties due to the lack of physical collaboration and hands-on laboratory experiences; others acknowledged the advantages of flexibility and convenience offered by online learning. Teachers also encountered obstacles in adapting their teaching strategies and materials to the online format; however, many demonstrated resourcefulness by devising innovative approaches to engage students and foster active learning. The study underscored the necessity for ongoing research and developing effective online teaching strategies in physics education. Ghanbari and Nowroozi (2021) examined the practice of online assessment in an EFL context amidst the COVID-19 pandemic, specifically from teachers' perspectives. Their study collected data from a sample of teachers with experience with online assessment in an EFL context during the pandemic. The results displayed that most teachers faced challenges adapting to the online assessment format, particularly regarding technology and the lack of face-to-face interaction with students. However, many teachers also reported finding new opportunities for creativity and flexibility in their assessment methods. The study highlights the importance of delivering suitable support and training for teachers in online assessment practices and the need for further research. Shifat and Khan (2022) explored sustainable e-learning in the context of undergraduate EFL classrooms. This research focuses on the efficiency of online learning as a device for language education and the potential for long-term application. The results show that online learning can increase old classroom instruction, providing learners with flexibility and access to multiple resources. However, they also note that successful implementation requires careful planning and consideration of technological infrastructure, student engagement, and teacher training. The study highlights the potential benefits of e-learning in undergraduate EFL classrooms while emphasizing the need for thoughtful and strategic implementation. A study conducted by Munir (2022) examines the lessons from reshaping sustainable university education in the post-pandemic world. The research exposes that the pandemic has emphasized that institutes must implement more sustainable practices in their procedures and syllabi. The study also highlights the importance of interdisciplinary teamwork and community engagement in promoting sustainability in universities and colleges. The study recommends blended and hybrid learning to undergraduates at the university, requiring digital tools to minimize students' communication barriers. Ionescu et al. (2020) analyzed the sustainability of the e-learning system applied in Romania during the COVID-19 pandemic. In their study, they used a questionnaire to extract the opinions of teachers, students, and parents regarding psychological effects on students because of the corroboration of the online education process and social isolation. The questionnaire involves middle school, high school, and university. They proved that online learning is an operative, sustainable learning resolution in existing and future circumstances. Mohsen (2014) investigates teachers' perceptions of Blackboard in EFL. To collect the data for the study, he interviewed 32 university teachers from Saudi Arabia to know their perceptions of using Blackboard. The study's findings show that EFL teachers positively perceive Blackboard applications to English language teaching. Many teachers think of Blackboard as a structured e-learning online platform that helps to improve the relationship between teachers and students in the course. The study results also revealed that using Blackboard as a blended learning method focuses more on administrative problems than pedagogical significance for language learning. The study also suggests further study of the topic to use other variables like age, gender, experience, etc., with teachers' perceptions. In his study, Yuan (2021) aims to discover university students' attitudes and satisfaction toward e-learning during the pandemic in Malaysia. The survey method was directed at 97 undergraduates from a university in Kuching to understand students' attitudes and satisfaction in four significant aspects: the learning materials, assessments, communications, technological tools, and technical support in their emergency remote learning experience. This study's findings show that most students have a positive attitude and satisfaction with online learning delivery. This study revealed that relevant implications of the instructional pedagogy approach and appropriate integration of technological tools could be beneficial to ensure continuous success in delivering learning content during this COVID-19 pandemic time. Badia (2020) aimed to study teachers' perceptions of Blackboard applications in teaching EFL and its effect on each module in an interrupted method. They collated the data from 80 EFL teachers surveyed and interviewed to investigate their perceptions and experience using Blackboard. The study found that EFL teachers perceive applying the Blackboard to English language teaching positively. Interestingly, the item states that by teaching English via Blackboard, teachers think that Blackboard will increase students' motivation to learn, which means that most teachers have positive pedagogical perceptions toward using technology in language teaching.

Research on online EFL post-COVID highlights several important areas for further investigation. One important approach is the integration of Sustainable Development Goals (SDGs) into online EFL courses, which remain largely unknown. In addition, the long-term effects of online EFL instruction on students' language skills and engagement have not been thoroughly examined. Most studies have focused on immediate outcomes, so more longitudinal studies are needed to gain a fuller understanding. Our study addresses the following important gaps: First, teachers face well-documented challenges in changing online programs. Second, effective training programs and support systems to facilitate their transition to online or hybrid models. Third, student engagement and motivation in online learning environments deserve more attention, especially strategies for fostering engagement in asynchronous environments. Technology infrastructure and differences in access also create differences, and many studies do not adequately address the digital divide that affects equal online education. More research is needed on various methodologies, community engagement, the psychological impact of online learning, and the use of blended learning models. Furthermore, understanding students' perceptions and satisfaction across different populations and developing new research methods for online EFL instruction are important to improve instructional strategies and outcomes.

## METHODOLOGY

### Theoretical/Conceptual Framework

This study is based on a theoretical framework for resilience and sustainability in education Pisano, (2012). It focuses on the integration and long-term viability of post-COVID online learning. The conceptual framework includes challenges and impacts of online methods for teaching English language skills and student learning strategies in virtual environments.

### Participants

The study recruited 84 EFL learners, with a demographic distribution of 81% males and 19% females. These participants came from various fields in EFL learning, including linguistics, English language teaching (ELT), translation, education, and literature, as shown in Figure 1 below. Gender distributions across the experience categories (0-5, 6-15, 16-25, and over 26 years) are shown in Figure 2, which compares the number of male and female teachers in each category.

*Figure 1. Count of participants' subject areas*

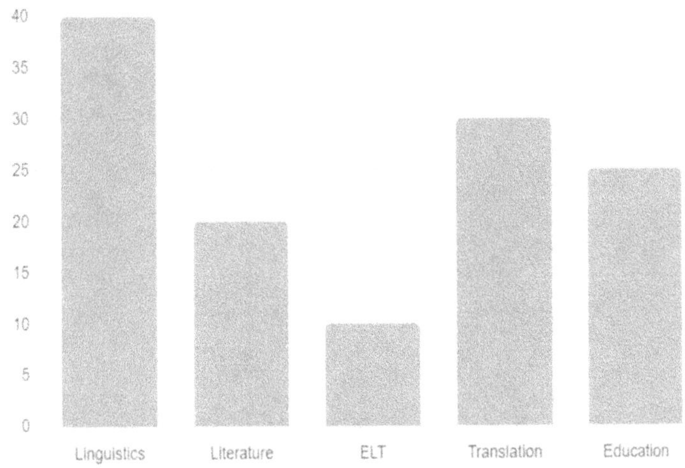


## Reliability and Validity

The survey instrument was developed through a rigorous process, including pilot testing and expert review, to ensure the reliability and validity of the data. Statistical analysis was conducted to verify the consistency and accuracy of the responses.

## Data Collection and Analysis Methods

An online survey-based questionnaire was developed and used as the primary data collection tool to address these research questions. The questionnaire comprises 54 carefully designed questions to probe different aspects of the study objective. The survey was shared through WhatsApp groups in the 2022 second semester. Quantitative survey data were analysed using descriptive and inferential statistics to identify trends and responses. This study gained insights into the factors that contribute to the sustainability of online learning, the effectiveness of online learning strategies, and the challenges faced by instructors' Qualitative data from open-ended survey questions were thematically analysed. They supported quantitative findings to understand teachers' experiences and perspectives better. The perceptions gained from this data collection shed light on the resources available to EFL learners and the main barriers they face in online learning. These findings significantly affect continuous EFL education and development in virtual environments.

*Figure 2. Distribution of teachers by years of experience*

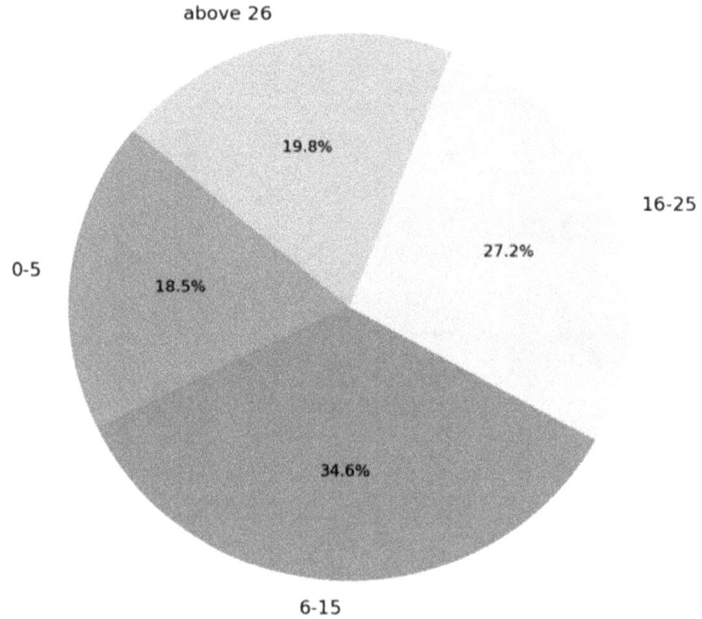


figure 2 visually represents the distribution of male and female teachers across various experience ranges, highlighting gender representation within each category. The pink line represents female teachers, and the blue line represents male teachers. Each point on the lines corresponds to the number of teachers within a specific experience range. By grounding the methodology in an appropriate theoretical framework and explicitly aligning the research questions with the methods of data collection and analysis, this study aims to provide an understanding that follows whole about the long-term resilience and sustainability of post-COVID online EFL teaching.

## RESULTS

This study aimed to understand how online learning during the pandemic positively impacted post-COVID online continuation. Teachers' perspectives on this topic are invaluable because they provide first-hand experience with e-learning during and after the pandemic, shedding light on its enduring reasons. The study aimed to identify the challenges and barriers facing teachers, how to overcome them best, and the specific types of training offered to ensure proficiency in electronic devices and learning methods. In addition, the study explores the satisfaction of teachers who have experienced the overall online learning process.

**Research Question 1:** What key factors have contributed to the sustainability of online learning at universities after the COVID-19 pandemic?

The study showed that most participants preferred using e-learning platforms to enhance learning outcomes. The results showed that 70% of the respondents agreed that e-learning helps to achieve learning objectives, while about 12% disagreed ($p < 0.05$) These findings indicate that services and materials initiatives, such as improved digital literacy, flourished online during the pandemic -Platforms, also play an important role in the sustainability of online learning.

*Figure 3. E-learning enhancement of learning outcomes*

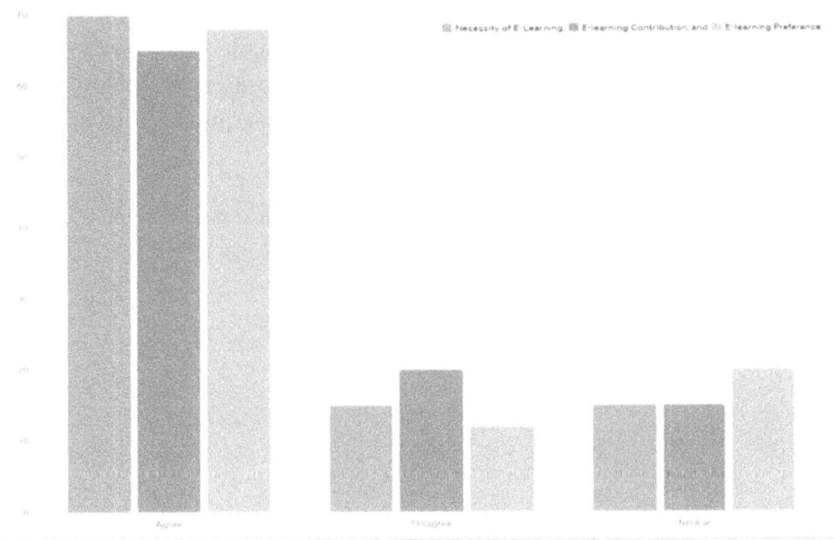


Figure 3 displays the answers to the improvement of learning outcomes through e-learning. It presents participant agreement, disagreement, and neutrality trends regarding the need for, support for, and preference for e-learning in studies.

**Research Question 2**: In what ways does online learning enhance the achievement of learning outcomes?

Research has shown that e-learning platforms significantly improve learning outcomes by providing flexible features that allow students to learn at their own pace and revisit content as needed. These changes were an important factor in developing positive perceptions of e-learning effectiveness.

The line chart above provides an analysis of responses regarding the enhancement of learning outcomes through e-learning. Each line represents a different statement, with markers indicating the percentage of responses in each category (Agree, Disagree, Neutral). The line "Necessity of E-Learning" shows the perceived necessity of e-learning in improving learning outcomes. The "E-learning Contribution" line represents views on how much e-learning contributed to improving course-learning outcomes. The "E-learning Preference" line shows the preference for using e-learning systems in courses. This visualization allows us to compare the response trends across these three aspects of e-learning, highlighting areas of strong agreement, disagreement, or neutrality among the respondents.

**Research Question 3**: What challenges do teachers encounter when using online platforms to teach English?

Teachers reported many challenges, including technical issues, lack of student engagement, and difficulties in assessing language skills online. Technological problems such as Internet instability and unfamiliarity with digital tools were major obstacles. Maintaining student engagement and accurately assessing students' language skills were challenges, even without face-to-face interviews.

*Figure 4. Participants' opinions about e-Learning obstacles*

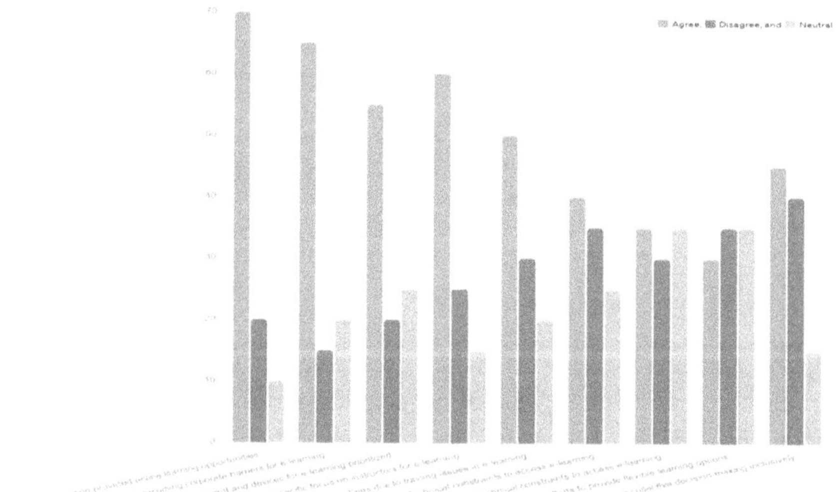


Figure 4 examines the barriers to e-learning applications and teachers during the COVID-19 pandemic. Each line represents the percentage of responses that agree, disagree, or neutral on various statements about e-learning challenges. It compares the participants' experience with e-learning during the pandemic. Different factors have been investigated to determine the main issues related to virtual learning. These factors are related to physical issues, electronic equipment, auxiliary devices, cognitive barriers, manual guidelines for online platforms, tangible financial incentives to activate, the training courses (face-to-face), time effort, and scientific materials. Most of the participants agreed to the difficulties faced by remote learning. The line chart analyses the obstacles to e-learning applications with teachers during the COVID-19 pandemic. Each line represents the percentage of responses that agree, disagree, or are neutral towards various statements about e-learning challenges. The statements range from issues related to physical and cognitive barriers to the availability of equipment, financial incentives, and the effectiveness of training courses. This visualization highlights the perceived challenges and areas of consensus or disagreement among teachers regarding the effectiveness and obstacles of e-learning during the pandemic. Table one summarizes the proportion and dispersion of the dataset, providing a comprehensive view of the distribution of responses across the categories of Agree, Disagree, and Neutral for various statements about e-learning obstacles during COVID-19.

*Table 1. The proportion statistics analysis of the obstacles data*

| Obstacles | Agree (Proportion) | Disagree (Proportion) | Neutral (Proportion |
|---|---|---|---|
| There are physical obstacles to the use of e-learning systems | 0.60 | 0.16 | 0.24 |
| There are cognitive barriers that prevent the use of e-learning systems | 0.53 | 0.14 | 0.33 |
| The equipment and auxiliary devices to use e-learning systems are provided | 0.70 | 0.11 | 0.19 |
| The information about the use of e-learning systems is available | 0.58 | 0.15 | 0.27 |
| The tangible financial incentives to activate e-learning in my courses is provided | 0.78 | 0.03 | 0.19 |
| The training courses (face to face) in e-learning are conducted | 0.66 | 0.16 | 0.18 |
| The training courses (via Blackboard) in e-learning are provided | 0.63 | 0.15 | 0.22 |
| The e-learning training courses are paid for | 0.24 | 0.56 | 0.20 |
| It takes a lot of time to work on e-learning systems | 0.41 | 0.41 | 0.18 |
| Work on e-learning systems requires great effort | 0.55 | 0.21 | 0.24 |
| The scientific material in my courses is | 0.29 | 0.47 | 0.24 |

## Cronbach's Alpha

Cronbach's Alpha measures a set of items' internal consistency or reliability. Higher values indicate better consistency.

$\alpha \approx 0.85$

With a Cronbach's Alpha of approximately 0.85, the internal consistency of the survey items is considered good. This indicates that the items (Agree, Disagree, Neutral) reliably measure the underlying concept of obstacles to e-learning applications with teachers.Top of Form

**Research Question 4:** Have teachers and learners received adequate training and tutorials to use online learning platforms effectively?

The study showed variability in the adequacy and quality of training received by teachers. Effective training programs included hands-on activities and ongoing support, which helped teachers feel more confident and competent in using online forums. Still, some teachers felt the training was insufficient, highlighting the need for access to comprehensive and ongoing professional development opportunities. Figure 5 displays the response to the training workshops attended concerning online learning. This data indicates different types of training for various platforms, tools, and programs.

*Figure 5. Participants' responses to the online learning training and workshops*

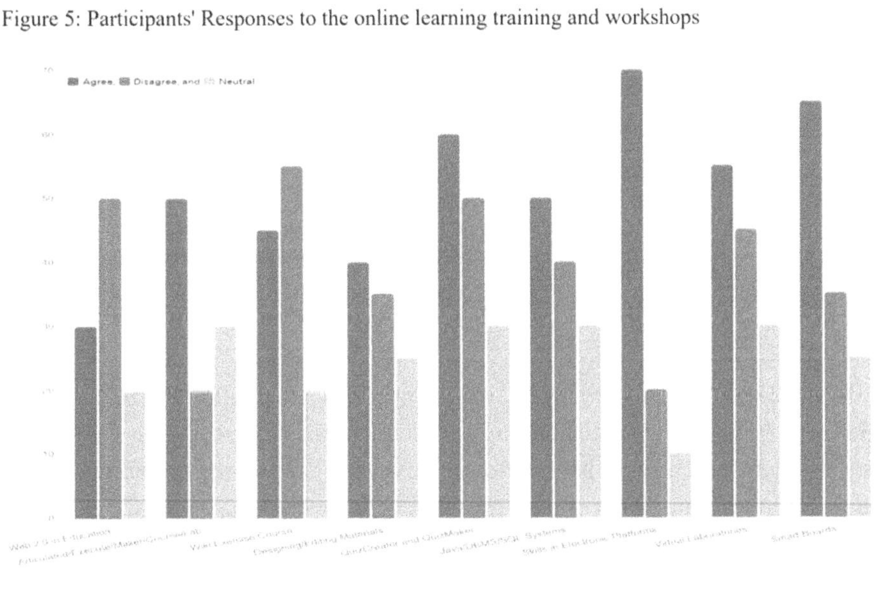


Figure 5 shows the distribution of responses across different training sessions attended. The study reveals under-adopted workplaces, providing insights for improving training programs. The distribution of responses to various training workshops attended, categorized as Agree, Disagree, and Neutral. The Green Line shows the percentage of respondents who agreed that the workshops were practical or relevant. Higher percentages indicate a greater level of agreement or approval for the workshop. For instance, the highest peaks in the green line are for "A training course was attended to develop the skills of using electronic platforms" and "A training course was attended to develop the skills of using smart boards," suggesting that these workshops were well-received and considered beneficial by most of the respondents. Red Line represents the percentage of respondents who disagreed with the effectiveness or relevance of the workshops. Higher values on this line suggest a higher dissatisfaction or disagreement with the workshop. Notably, "Attended Wiki Events Course" and "Workshops attended on designing and editing course materials" have higher percentages in this category, indicating that many respondents found these workshops less effective or relevant. The blue line indicates the respondents who were neutral or undecided about the workshops' effectiveness. Peaks in this line suggest a higher ambivalence or lack of a strong opinion. The chart helps identify which workshops were most and least favourably received and where respondents had no strong opinions. Such insights can be valuable for improving or altering training programs to meet the participants' needs and expectations.

*Table 2. Descriptive statistics of the training workshops*

| Response Type | Mean | Median | Standard Deviation | Minimum | Maximum |
|---|---|---|---|---|---|
| Agree | 37.89% | 34.0% | 17.27 | 20% | 71% |
| Disagree | 49.11% | 50.0% | 14.08 | 22% | 65% |
| Neutral | 13.00% | 15.0% | 3.87 | 7% | 18% |

Table 2 summarizes the central tendency and variability in the dataset. The "Mean" column indicates the average percentage for each response type, the "Median" is the middle value, the "Standard Deviation" shows the amount of variation, and "Minimum" and "Maximum" provide the Range of responses for each category. The data shows a higher average (Mean) of disagreement (49.11%) across the workshops compared to agreement (37.89%) and neutrality (13.00%). This suggests that the respondents generally found the workshops less effective or relevant. The standard Deviation in the 'Agree' category is relatively high (17.27), indicating a wide range of opinions about the effectiveness of the workshops. This variability is less pronounced in the 'Neutral' responses (3.87), suggesting more consistency in neutral opinions. The median values indicate that for at least half of the workshops, the agreement rate is below 34%, the disagreement rate is above 50%, and the neutrality rate is around 15%. The analysis points to a generally negative perception of the training workshops among the respondents, with a significant spread in opinions and a smaller proportion of respondents remaining neutral. This highlights areas for potential improvement in the content or delivery of these training workshops.

## Teacher Satisfaction with Online Learning

The study also examined teachers' satisfaction with various aspects of e-learning. Overall, the average satisfaction level was 54%, with a standard deviation of 10.84, indicating a high degree of variability in satisfaction. Figure 6 displays participants' satisfaction levels across various aspects of e-learning, with each point representing the percentages of agreement, disagreement, and neutrality for different statements. Green bars indicate the percentage of participants who agreed or were satisfied with each aspect. The red bars represent the percentage of participants who disagreed or were unsatisfied. Yellow bars show the percentage of participants who were neutral.

*Figure 6. Responses to the participants' satisfaction*

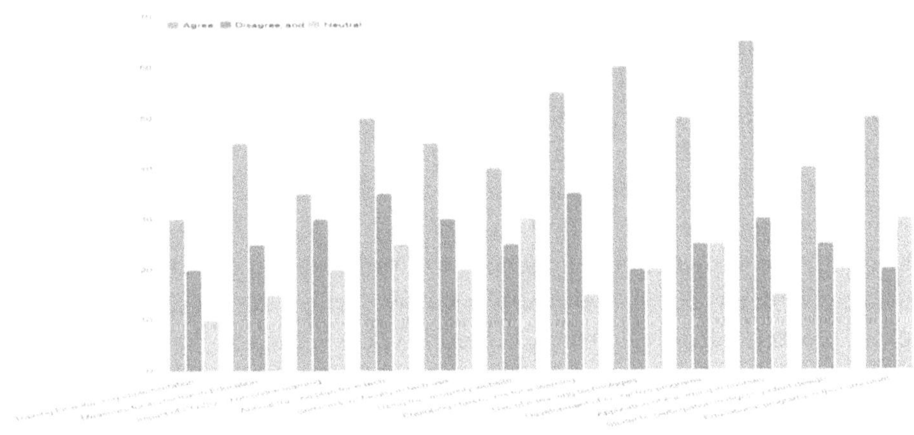


This visualization allows a clear comparison of satisfaction levels across e-learning. By observing the concentration of bars, we can discern which aspects received more agreement, disagreement, or neutrality. For example, high concentrations of green bars in areas like "Using the university website" and "Equipping classrooms for e-learning" suggest higher levels of satisfaction, while areas with higher concentrations of red bars, like "Students' participation in digital content design," might indicate aspects that need improvement.

This study provides important perceptions into the factors contributing to the sustainability of online courses and provides a blueprint for future courses and policy development. For practitioners, it highlights the importance of a robust support system, ongoing training, and addressing technical challenges to improve online education.

## DISCUSSION

This study provides an in-depth analysis of the long-term effects of online learning in a post-COVID EFL environment, highlighting resilience and sustainability. With a unique contribution and in-depth analysis of EFL teachers' experiences and challenges of the epidemic, a rare perspective in the existing literature. In contrast to previous research analyzed, this study focuses on the immediate and ongoing implications of change in EFL education and whether it will be sustainable.

Grounded in a theoretical framework of educational change and sustainability, this research adds new dimensions to our understanding of the evolution of digital literacy and the use of technology in language learning. The findings are consistent with those of Sohil and Sohail (2022) and Bozkurt (2022), who emphasized digital literacy strongly. However, this study extends their work by providing empirical evidence for the continued inclusion of these interventions after the pandemic.

The rapid transition to virtual classrooms and online tools, as highlighted by Alkahtani et al. (2022) and Leal et al. (2021), is supported by our findings. Our research provides new perceptions of how these changes were maintained and contributed to the development of sustainable EFL learning models. In addition, the significant impact of virtual training and workshops on continuous e-learning, as noted by Munir (2022), is also reflected in our study. This highlights the critical role of professional development in fostering resilience in educational practice.

Another important aspect of this research is its focus on targeted teacher training. Results suggest that a comprehensive training program, which included hands-on activities and ongoing support, was necessary for teachers to adapt and retain online learning. This finding highlights the important role of professional development, and emphasis will continue to be placed on ensuring the long-term success of e-learning programs.

The study also highlights teachers' high satisfaction with using technology and interactive activities in virtual learning environments. This satisfaction is important for the continued use of online learning strategies and is consistent with Mahyob (2021). The positive adoption of e-learning tools suggests a successful reform that can persist beyond the epidemic, contributing to the resilience of the education system, which is aligned with Papadakis et al. (2023a).

## CONCLUSION

This study aimed to assess the impact of COVID-19 on the sustainability of online EFL learning. The findings suggest that the epidemic shift to online learning has profoundly affected teachers and students, creating new opportunities for those who previously lacked access to e-learning. These changes emphasize the importance of digital literacy and highlight the sustainability of online and blended learning models. The study extends the theoretical framework of educational resilience and sustainability by providing empirical evidence of how digital literacy and technology inclusion were maintained in the face of epidemics at the back of the box. It highlights the critical role of continuing professional development, aligning and extending previous studies, and demonstrating the impact of ongoing training programs on teacher turnover and competence online. Most participants (70%) agreed that e-learning significantly contributes to achieving learning objectives, showing a consistent positive impact on online learning introduced during the plague. Effective training programs, which included hands-on and ongoing support, were essential for teachers to adapt and sustain online learning. This highlights the need for comprehensive and ongoing professional development, which is so emphasized. Teachers faced technical issues and challenges in maintaining student engagement and assessing language skills online. Addressing these challenges through improved training and support systems is essential for the continued success of eLearning. High teacher satisfaction with technology integration and interactive activities highlights the success and importance of these strategies in future educational strategies. This study contributes to new knowledge by providing detailed insights into the experiences of EFL teachers during the pandemic and highlights the importance of digital literacy and continuous professional development. Findings provide a framework for designing sustainable online and blended learning initiatives and for educators to emphasize the need for robust support programs.

## Limitation and Future Implication

This research highlights the need for actionable, practical interventions in scholarship for scholars. By prioritizing flexible, inclusive policies and investing in professional development, educators and policymakers can take advantage of the opportunities presented by the post-COVID environment. Embracing change and implementing technological advances will be critical to achieving a flexible and equitable future for EFL education.

The study acknowledges limitations in its generalizability due to the participants' unique demographic and geographical characteristics. Future research should collect data from broader industry and educational settings to maximize the applicability of the findings. In addition, further research is recommended on the long-term impact of online learning on student achievement and the effectiveness of training programs.

## REFERENCES

Abel, K. D. (2021, April). Effective online teaching practices during a Covid environment. In *Middle Atlantic ASEE Section Spring 2021 Conference*. ASEE. 10.18260/1-2--36297

Adedoyin, O. B., & Soykan, E. (2023). Covid-19 pandemic and online learning: The challenges and opportunities. *Interactive Learning Environments*, 31(2), 863–875. 10.1080/10494820.2020.1813180

Adeyeye, B., Ojih, S. E., Bello, D., Adesina, E., Yartey, D., Ben-Enukora, C., & Adeyeye, Q. (2022). Online learning platforms and covenant university students' academic performance in practical related courses during COVID-19 pandemic. *Sustainability (Basel)*, 14(2), 878. 10.3390/su14020878

Al-Garaady, J., & Mahyoob, M. (2021). Social network communication: Emojis and EFL learners' writing issues. *TESOL International, 16*(3.1).

Al-Garaady, J., & Mahyoob, M. (2022). Public sentiment analysis in social media on theSARS-CoV-2 vaccination using VADER lexicon polarity. *Humanities and Educational Sciences Journal*, 591-609.

Al-khresheh, M. H. (2022). The impact of COVID-19 pandemic on teachers' creativity ofonline teaching classrooms in the Saudi EFL context. *Frontiers in Education*, 7, 1041446. 10.3389/feduc.2022.1041446

Al-Mashaqba, N.J. (2017). *Use of Blackboard Collaborate at Qassim University: Evaluating Teachers' Perceptions.*

Al-Zumor, A. W. Q., Al-Refaai, I. K., Badereddin, E. A., & Al Rahman, F. H. A. (2013). EFL Students' Perceptions of a Blended Learning Environment: Advantages, Limitations and Suggestions for Improvement. *English Language Teaching*, 6(10), 95–110.

Alammary, A., Alshaikh, M., & Alhogail, A. (2022). The impact of the COVID-19 pandemic on the adoption of e-learning among academics in Saudi Arabia. *Behaviour & Information Technology*, 41(14), 3138–3160. 10.1080/0144929X.2021.1973106

Algaraady, J. (2022). An analysis of Yemenis' responses and sentiments on social media towards the emergence of the COVID-19 pandemic. *Humanities and Educational Sciences Journal*, (27), 589–607. 10.55074/hesj.v0i27.621

Algaraady, J., & Alrahaili, M. (2022). An Investigation of Parental Perspectives on the Efficiency of Online Schooling in Primary Schools During the COVID-19 Outbreak. [IJICTE]. *International Journal of Information and Communication Technology Education*, 18(1), 1–18. 10.4018/IJICTE.309137

Algaraady, J., & Mahyoob, M. (2023). ChatGPT's Capabilities in Spotting and Analyzing Writing Errors Experienced by EFL Learners. Arab World English Journal (AWEJ). *Special Issue on CALL*, (9), 3–17. 10.24093/awej/call9.1

Almekhlafy, S. S. A. (2020). Online learning of English language courses via Blackboard at Saudi universities in the era of COVID-19: perception and use. PSU Research Review. 10.1108/PRR-08-2020-0026

Alqahtani, M. A., Alamri, M. M., Sayaf, A. M., & Al-Rahmi, W. M. (2022). Investigating Students'Perceptions of Online Learning Use as a Digital Tool for Educational Sustainability Duringthe COVID-19 Pandemic. *Frontiers in Psychology*, 13.

Anas, A. (2020). Perceptions of Saudi Students to Blended Learning Environments at the University of Bisha, Saudi Arabia. *Arab World English Journal (AWEJ). Special Issue on CALL*, (6), 261–277. 10.24093/awej/call6.17

Bäckman, G. (2021). The outbreak of coronavirus (COVID-19) plagues the world. *Essays on COVID-19 Research*, 207.

Betancourt-Odio, M. A., Sartor-Harada, A., Ulloa-Guerra, O., & Azevedo-Gomes, J. (2021). Self-perceptions on digital competences for m-learning and education sustainability:A study with teachers from different countries. *Sustainability (Basel)*, 13(1), 343. 10.3390/su13010343

Bozkurt, A. (2022). Resilience, adaptability, and sustainability of higher Education: A systematic mapping study on the impact of the coronavirus (COVID-19) pandemic and the transition to the new normal. *Journal of Learning for Development (JL4D), 9*(1), 1-16.

Byun, S., & Slavin, R. E. (2020). Educational Responses to the COVID-19 Outbreak in South Korea. *Best Evid Chin Edu*, 5(2), 665–680. 10.15354/bece.20.or030

Chu, A. M., Liu, C. K., So, M. K., & Lam, B. S. (2021). Factors for sustainable online learning in higher Education during the COVID-19 pandemic. *Sustainability (Basel)*, 13(9), 5038. 10.3390/su13095038

Delgado, F. (2022). Post-COVID-19 Transition in University Physics Courses: A Case of Study in a Mexican University. *Education Sciences*, 12(9), 627. 10.3390/educsci12090627

Draxler-Weber, N., Packmohr, S., & Brink, H. (2022). Barriers to Digital Higher Education Teaching and How to Overcome Them—Lessons Learned during the COVID-19 Pandemic. *Education Sciences*, 12(12), 870. 10.3390/educsci12120870

El-Sawy, H. E. (2018). Flipping EFL University Classes with Blackboard System. *English Language Teaching*, 11(2), 31. 10.5539/elt.v11n2p31

Fageeh, A.I., & Mekheimer, M.A. (2013). *Effects of Blackboard on EFL Academic Writing and Attitudes.*

Ghanbari, N., & Nowroozi, S. (2021). The practice of online assessment in an EFL context amidst COVID-19 pandemic: Views from teachers. *Language Testing in Asia*, 11(1), 1–18. 10.1186/s40468-021-00143-4

Han, J., Geng, X., & Wang, Q. (2021). Sustainable development of university EFL learners' engagement, satisfaction, and self-efficacy in online learning environments: Chinese experiences. *Sustainability (Basel)*, 13(21), 11655. 10.3390/su132111655

Hidalgo-Camacho, C., Escudero, G. I., Villacís, W., & Varela, K. (2021). The Effects of Online Learning on EFL Students' Academic Achievement during Coronavirus Disease Pandemic. *European Journal of Educational Research*, 10(4), 1867–1879. 10.12973/eu-jer.10.4.1867

Ionescu, C. A., Paschia, L., Nicolau, N. L. G., Stanescu, S. G., Stancescu, V. M. N., Coman, M. D., & Uzlau, M. C. (2020). Sustainability analysis of the e-learning education system during pandemic period—Covid-19 in Romania. *Sustainability (Basel)*, 12(21), 1–22. 10.3390/su12219030

Jacques, S., Ouahabi, A., & Kanetaki, Z. (2023). Post-COVID-19 education for a sustainable future: Challenges, emerging technologies, and trends. *Sustainability (Basel)*, 15(8), 6487. 10.3390/su15086487

Karataş, T. Ö., & Tuncer, H. (2020). Sustaining language skills development of pre-service EFL teachers despite the COVID-19 interruption: A case of emergency distance education. *Sustainability (Basel)*, 12(19), 8188. 10.3390/su12198188

Law, M. Y. (2021). Transformative Learning: A Research Study on Emergency Remote Learning in Tertiary Education. *Creative Education*, 12(3), 494–528. 10.4236/ce.2021.123035

Leal Filho, W., Price, E., Wall, T., Shiel, C., Azeiteiro, U. M., Mifsud, M., Brandli, L., Farinha, C. S., Caeiro, S., Salvia, A. L., Vasconcelos, C. R., de Sousa, L. O., Pace, P., Doni, F., Veiga Avila, L., Fritzen, B., & LeVasseur, T. J. (2021). COVID-19: The impact of a global crisis on sustainable development teaching. *Environment, Development and Sustainability*, 23(8), 11257–11278. 10.1007/s10668-020-01107-z33424430

Ma, X., Jiang, M., & Nong, L. (2023). The effect of teacher support on Chinese university students' sustainable online learning engagement and online academic persistence in the post-epidemic era. *Frontiers in Psychology*, 14, 14. 10.3389/fpsyg.2023.107655236794084

Mahyoob, M. (2020). Challenges of e-Learning during the COVID-19 Pandemic Experienced by EFL Learners. *Arab World English Journal (AWEJ), 11*(4).

Mahyoob, M. (2021). Online Learning Effectiveness During the COVID-19 Pandemic: A Case Study of Saudi Universities. [IJICTE]. *International Journal of Information and Communication Technology Education*, 17(4), 1–14. 10.4018/IJICTE.20211001.oa7

Mahyoob, M., Algaraady, J., & Alblwi, A. (2023). A Proposed Framework for Human-like Language Processing of ChatGPT in Academic Writing. [iJET]. *International Journal of Emerging Technologies in Learning*, 18(14), 282–293. 10.3991/ijet.v18i14.41725

Meajel, T. M., & Sharadgah, T. A. (2018). Barriers to Using the Blackboard System in Teaching and Learning: Faculty Perceptions. *Technology. Knowledge and Learning*, 23(2), 351–366. 10.1007/s10758-017-9323-2

Mei Yuan, L. (2021). Student's attitude and satisfaction towards transformative learning: A research study on emergency remote learning in tertiary Education. *Creative Education*, 12(1), 494–528.

Mishra, P., & Koehler, M. J. (2006). Technological Pedagogical Content Knowledge: A Framework for Teacher Knowledge. *Sage Journals, 108*(6), 1017–1054. 10.1111/j.1467-9620.2006.00684.x

Munir, H. (2022). Reshaping Sustainable University Education in Post-Pandemic World: Lessons Learned from an Empirical Study. *Education Sciences*, 12(8), 524. 10.3390/educsci12080524

Oraif, I., & Elyas, T. (2021). The impact of COVID-19 on learning: Investigating EFL learners' engagement in online courses in Saudi Arabia. *Education Sciences*, 11(3), 99. 10.3390/educsci11030099

Orosz, A., Monzón, M., & Velasco, P. (2021). Ecuadorian Teachers' Perceptions of Teaching English: Challenges in the Public Education Sector. *International Journal of Learning. Teaching and Educational Research*, 20(3), 229–249.

Papadakis, S., Kiv, A. E., Kravtsov, H. M., Osadchyi, V. V., Marienko, M. V., Pinchuk, O. P.,& Striuk, A. M. (2023). Unlocking the power of synergy: the joint force of cloud technologies and augmented reality in education.

Papadakis, S. J., Semerikov, S. O., Yechkalo, Y. V., Velychko, V. Y., Vakaliuk, T. A., Amelina, S. M., & Tkachuk, V. V. (2023). *Advancing lifelong learning and professional development through ICT*. 3L-Person 2023 workshop. Research Gate.

Pellegrini, M., Uskov, V., & Casalino, N. (2020). *Reimagining and Re-Designing the Post COVID-19 Higher Education Organizations to Address New Challenges and Responses.*

Pisano, U. (2012). Resilience and Sustainable Development: Theory of resilience, systems thinking. *European sustainable development network (ESDN), 26*, 50

Pusuluri, S., Mahasneh, A., & Alsayer, B. A. (2017). The Application of Blackboard in the English Courses at Al Jouf University: Perceptions of Students. *Theory and Practice in Language Studies*, 7(2), 106–111. 10.17507/tpls.0702.03

Putri, N. L. P. N. S. (2024). Sustainable Development Goals in EFL Students' Learning: A Systematic Review. *Pegem Journal of Education and Instruction*, 14(2), 1–11.

Rajab, M. H., Gazal, A. M., & Alkattan, K. (2020). Challenges to Online Medical Education During the COVID-19 Pandemi c. *Cureus, 12*(7), e8966. DOI:: 8966.10.7759/cureus

Shifat, N. F., & Khan, M. E. I. (2022). Sustainability of E-Learning in the Undergraduate EFL Classrooms. *FOSTER: Journal of English Language Teaching*, 3(2), 80–89.

Shulman, L. (1986). Those Who Understand. *Knowledge Growth in Teaching*, 15(2), 4–14.

Sofkova Hashemi, S., Berbyuk Lindström, N., & Bergdahl, N. (2024). *Pandemic as Digital Change Accelerator: Sustainable Reshaping of Adult Education Post Covid-19.*

Sohil, F., & Sohail, M. U. (2022). Measuring the impact of COVID-19 on distance learning for educational sustainability. *Cogent Education*, 9(1), 2034248. 10.1080/2331186X.2022.2034248

Tülübaş, T., Karakose, T., & Papadakis, S. (2023). A holistic investigation of the relationship between digital addiction and academic achievement among students. *European Journal of Investigation in Health, Psychology and Education*, 13(10), 2006–2034. 10.3390/ejihpe13100143 37887144

Zawaidy, H. A. (2014). Using Blackboard in Online Learning at Saudi Universities: Faculty Member's Perceptions and Existing Obstacles. *International Interdisciplinary Journal of Education*, 3(7), 45–154. 10.12816/0006902

# Compilation of References


Abbas, M., Zakaria, A., & Balkhyour, M. (2017). Implementation of chemical health risk assessment (CHRA) program at chemical laboratories of a university. *J. Saf. Stud.*, 1(1), 53. 10.5296/jss.v3i1.11109

Abdeahad, N., & Mock, S. (2023). The role of past campus recreational sports participation in predicting students' stress and competence during the COVID-19 pandemic. *Journal of Leisure Research*, 54(2), 269–285. 10.1080/00222216.2023.2165203

Abdullah, Q. A., Humaidi, N., & Shahrom, M. (2020). Industry revolution 4.0: The readiness of graduates of higher education institutions for fulfilling job demands. *Romanian Journal of Information Technology and Automatic Control*, 30(2), 15–26. 10.33436/v30i2y202002

Abel, K. D. (2021, April). Effective online teaching practices during a Covid environment. In *Middle Atlantic ASEE Section Spring 2021 Conference*. ASEE. 10.18260/1-2--36297

Abeysekera, L., & Dawson, P. (2015). Motivation and cognitive load in the flipped classroom: Definition, rationale and a call for research. *Higher Education Research & Development*, 34(1), 1–14. 10.1080/07294360.2014.934336

Abichandani, P., Sivakumar, V., Lobo, D., Iaboni, C., & Shekhar, P. (2022). Internet-of-things curriculum, pedagogy, and assessment for stem education: A review of literature. *IEEE Access : Practical Innovations, Open Solutions*, 10, 38351–38369. 10.1109/ACCESS.2022.3164709

Abrami, P. C., Bernard, R. M., Bures, E. M., Borokhovski, E., & Tamim, R. M. (2011). Interaction in distance education and online learning: Using evidence and theory to improve practice. *Journal of Computing in Higher Education*, 23(2-3), 82–103. 10.1007/s12528-011-9043-x

Abuhassna, H., & Yahaya, N. (2018). Students' utilization of distance learning through an interventional online module based on Moore transactional distance theory. *Eurasia Journal of Mathematics, Science and Technology Education*, 14(7), 3043–3052. 10.29333/ejmste/91606

Abumalloh, R. A., Asadi, S., Nilashi, M., Minaei-Bidgoli, B., Nayer, F. K., Samad, S., Mohd, S., & Ibrahim, O. (2021). The impact of coronavirus pandemic (COVID-19) on education: The role of virtual and remote laboratories in education. *Technology in Society*, 67, 101728. https://0-doi.org.wam.seals.ac.za/10.1016/j.techsoc.2021.101728. 10.1016/j.techsoc.2021.10172834538984

Achuthan, K., Raghavan, D., Shankar, B., Francis, S. P., & Kolil, V. K. (2021). Impact of remote experimentation, interactivity and platform effectiveness on laboratory learning outcomes. *International Journal of Educational Technology in Higher Education*, 18(38), 38. Advance online publication. 10.1186/s41239-021-00272-z34778531

Adedoyin, O. B., & Soykan, E. (2020). COVID-19 pandemic and online learning: The challenges and opportunities. *Interactive Learning Environments*, 31(2), 863–875. 10.1080/10494820.2020.1813180

Adel, A. (2022). Future of industry 5.0 in society: Human-centric solutions, challenges and prospective research areas. *Journal of Cloud Computing (Heidelberg, Germany)*, 11(1), 1–15. 10.1186/s13677-022-00314-536101900

Adeoye, B. F. (2020). The era of digital technology in teaching and learning in Nigerian educational institutions. In Adeoye, B., & Arome, G. (Eds.), *The Roles of Technology and Globalization in Educational Transformation* (pp. 43–51). IGI Global. 10.4018/978-1-5225-9746-9.ch004

Adetayo, A. J. (2023). Post Covid-19 pandemic and library users' education: Impact on examination and survey. *Journal of Academic Librarianship*, 49(3), 102695. 10.1016/j.acalib.2023.10269536938152

Adeyeye, B., Ojih, S. E., Bello, D., Adesina, E., Yartey, D., Ben-Enukora, C., & Adeyeye, Q. (2022). Online learning platforms and covenant university students' academic performance in practical related courses during COVID-19 pandemic. *Sustainability (Basel)*, 14(2), 878. 10.3390/su14020878

Adov, L., & Mäeots, M. (2021). What can we learn about science teachers' technology use during the COVID-19 pandemic? *Education Sciences*, 11(6), 255. 10.3390/educsci11060255

Afsharian, A., Sivapalan, S., & Nordin, S. binti M. (2018). Blended Learning & the Higher Education Classroom: A Critical Review of Developments within Engineering Education. *In 2017 7th World Engineering Education Forum (WEEF), IEEE Xplore*, (pp. 182–187). IEEE. 10.1109/WEEF.2017.8467021

Aguilera, J. M., & Moreno, M. C. (2021). Teaching Engineering and Food: From Traditional Approaches to a Flipped Course on Gastronomic Engineering. *Food Engineering Reviews, 13*, 916–928. Springer. 10.1007/s12393-021-09281-0

Aguilera-Hermida, A.P. (2020). College students' use and acceptance of emergency online learning due to covid-19. *International Journal of Educational Research Open, 1*(100), 011.

Aguilera-Hermida, P. (2020). College students' use and acceptance of emergency online learning due to COVID-19. *International Journal of Educational Research Open*, 1, 100011. 10.1016/j.ijedro.2020.10001135059662

Ahmed, H. D., & Asiksoy, G. (2021). The effects of gamified flipped learning method on student's innovation skills, self-efficacy towards virtual physics lab course and perceptions. *Sustainability (Basel)*, 13(18), 10163. 10.3390/su131810163

Ahmed, V., & Opoku, A. (2022). Technology supported learning and pedagogy in times of crisis: The case of COVID-19 pandemic. *Education and Information Technologies*, 27(1), 365–405. 10.1007/s10639-021-10706-w34462626

Ajamu, G. J., Awotunde, J. B., Jimoh, T. B., Adeniyi, E. A., Abiodun, K. M., Oladipo, I. D., & Abdulraheem, M. (2024). Online Teaching Sustainability and Strategies during the COVID-19 Epidemic. In (Eds) J. Rosak-Szyrocka, J. Żywiołek, A. Nayyar, & M. Naved. *The Role of Sustainability and Artificial Intelligence in Education Improvement* (pp. 106-132). Chapman and Hall/CRC. https://0-doi.org.wam.seals.ac.za/10.1201/9781003425779

Akhtar, M., & Saeed, M. (2020). Assessing the Effect of Agree/Disagree Circles, Exit Ticket, and Think-Pair-Share on Students' Academic Achievement at Undergraduate Level. *Bulletin of Education and Research*, 42(2), 81–96.

Akhtar, R. N. (2020). Exploring Experiential Learning Models and developing an EL based ERE cycle in teaching at higher education in Pakistan. *International Journal of Experiential Learning & Case Studies*, 5(2). 10.22555/ijelcs.v5i2.44

Al Musawi, A., Ambusaidi, A., Al-Balushi, S., & Al-Balushi, K. (2015). Effectiveness of E-Lab Use in Science Teaching at the Omani Schools. *Turkish Online Journal of Educational Technology-TOJET, 14*(1), 45-52. https://www.learntechlib.org/p/160569/

Al Shlowiy, A., Al-Hoorie, A. H., & Alharbi, M. (2021). Discrepancy between language learners and teachers concerns about emergency remote teaching. *Journal of Computer Assisted Learning*, 37(4), 1528–1538. 10.1111/jcal.12543

Al-Ammary, J. (2013). Educational technology: A way to enhance student achievement at the University of Bahrain. *The Online Journal of New Horizons in Education, 3*(3), 54-65. http://tojned.net/?pid=showissue&issueid=102

Alammary, A., Alshaikh, M., & Alhogail, A. (2022). The impact of the COVID-19 pandemic on the adoption of e-learning among academics in Saudi Arabia. *Behaviour & Information Technology*, 41(14), 3138–3160. 10.1080/0144929X.2021.1973106

Al-Dheleai, Y. M., & Tasir, Z. (2016). Facebook to facilitate instructor roles in course-related online interaction: A pilot study. *Journal of Theoretical and Applied Information Technology*, 89(2), 343–351.

Al-Garaady, J., & Mahyoob, M. (2021). Social network communication: Emojis and EFL learners' writing issues. *TESOL International, 16*(3.1).

Al-Garaady, J., & Mahyoob, M. (2022). Public sentiment analysis in social media on theSARS-CoV-2 vaccination using VADER lexicon polarity. *Humanities and Educational Sciences Journal*, 591-609.

Algaraady, J. (2022). An analysis of Yemenis' responses and sentiments on social media towards the emergence of the COVID-19 pandemic. *Humanities and Educational Sciences Journal*, (27), 589–607. 10.55074/hesj.v0i27.621

Algaraady, J., & Alrahaili, M. (2022). An Investigation of Parental Perspectives on the Efficiency of Online Schooling in Primary Schools During the COVID-19 Outbreak. [IJICTE]. *International Journal of Information and Communication Technology Education*, 18(1), 1–18. 10.4018/IJICTE.309137

Algaraady, J., & Mahyoob, M. (2023). ChatGPT's Capabilities in Spotting and Analyzing Writing Errors Experienced by EFL Learners. Arab World English Journal (AWEJ). *Special Issue on CALL*, (9), 3–17. 10.24093/awej/call9.1

Alirezabeigi, S. (2023). What Do We Talk About When We Talk About Post-Pandemic Time in School Education? Reflections on Temporal Plasticity of Post-Pandemic School Education. *Sisyphus: Journal of Education*, 11(1), 107–127.

Aliyu, F., & Talib, C. A. (2019). Virtual chemistry laboratory: A panacea to problems of conducting chemistry practical at science secondary schools in Nigeria. *International Journal of Engineering and Advanced Technology*, 8(5), 544–549. 10.35940/ijeat.E1079.0585C19

Aljuhani, K., Sonbul, M., Althabiti, M., & Meccawy, M. (2018). Creating a Virtual Science Lab (VSL): the adoption of virtual labs in Saudi schools. *Smart Learning Environments, 5*, 1-13. https://0-doi.org.wam.seals.ac.za/10.1186/s40561-018-0067-9

Alkhatib, O. J. (2018). An interactive and blended learning model for engineering education. *Journal of Computers in Education*, 5(1), 19–48. 10.1007/s40692-018-0097-x

Alkhattabi, M. (2017). Augmented Reality as E-learning Tool in Primary Schools' Education: Barriers to Teachers' Adoption. *International Journal of Emerging Technologies in Learning*, 12(2), 91. 10.3991/ijet.v12i02.6158

Al-khresheh, M. H. (2022). The impact of COVID-19 pandemic on teachers' creativity ofonline teaching classrooms in the Saudi EFL context. *Frontiers in Education*, 7, 1041446. 10.3389/feduc.2022.1041446

Al-Kumaim, N. H., Alhazmi, A. K., Mohammed, F., Gazem, N. A., Shabbir, M. S., & Fazea, Y. (2021). Exploring the impact of the COVID-19 pandemic on university students' learning life: An integrated conceptual motivational model for sustainable and healthy online learning. *Sustainability (Basel)*, 13(5), 2546. 10.3390/su13052546

Al-Mashaqba, N.J. (2017). *Use of Blackboard Collaborate at Qassim University: Evaluating Teachers' Perceptions.*

Almekhlafy, S. S. A. (2020). Online learning of English language courses via Blackboard at Saudi universities in the era of COVID-19: perception and use. PSU Research Review. 10.1108/PRR-08-2020-0026

Alqahtani, M. A., Alamri, M. M., Sayaf, A. M., & Al-Rahmi, W. M. (2022). Investigating Students'Perceptions of Online Learning Use as a Digital Tool for Educational Sustainability Duringthe COVID-19 Pandemic. *Frontiers in Psychology*, 13.

Alqurashi, E. (2019). Predicting student satisfaction and perceived learning within online learning environments. *Distance Education*, 40(1), 133–148. 10.1080/01587919.2018.1553562

Alvarado, M., Basinger, K., Lahijanian, B., & Alvarado, D. (2021). Teaching Simulation to Generation Z Engineering Students: Lessons Learned from a Flipped Classroom Pilot Study. *In 2020 Winter Simulation Conference (WSC), IEEE Xplore*. 10.1109/WSC48552.2020.9383950

Alvarez, A. (2020). The phenomenon of learning at a distance through emergency remote teaching amidst the pandemic crisis. *Asian Journal of Distance Education*, 15(2), 127–143. 10.5281/zenodo.4299933

Al-Zumor, A. W. Q., Al-Refaai, I. K., Badereddin, E. A., & Al-Rahman, F. H. A. (2013). EFL Students' Perceptions of a Blended Learning Environment: Advantages, Limitations and Suggestions for Improvement. *English Language Teaching*, 6(10), 95–110.

Al-Zyoud, W., Qunies, A. M., Walters, A. U., & Jalsa, N. K. (2019). Perceptions of chemical safety in laboratories. *Safety (Basel, Switzerland)*, 5(2), 21. 10.3390/safety5020021

American Chemical Society. (2017). Safety in Academic Chemistry Laboratories, (8th Ed). ACS, Washington D.C.

Anas, A. (2020). Perceptions of Saudi Students to Blended Learning Environments at the University of Bisha, Saudi Arabia. *Arab World English Journal (AWEJ). Special Issue on CALL*, (6), 261–277. 10.24093/awej/call6.17

Ancho, I. (2023). Parents as teachers as students: Managing multiple roles during the covid-19 pandemic. *International Journal of Instruction*, 16(3), 205–220. 10.29333/iji.2023.16312a

Anglin, G. J. (Ed.). (1995). *Instructional technology: Past, present, & future* (2nd ed.). Libraries Unlimited. 10.5040/9798216974697

Anthony, B. J., & Noel, S. (2021). Examining the adoption of emergency remote teaching and virtual learning during and after COVID-19 pandemic. *International Journal of Educational Management*, 35(6), 1136–1150. 10.1108/IJEM-08-2020-0370

Anush Kumar, S. Amudhavan, T., Arun Kumar. S., & Sasikala, S. (2021). *Improving effectiveness of STEM Education in Covid-19 Pandemic – A pilot study*. International Conference on Advancements in Electrical, Electronics, Communication, Computing and Automation (ICAECA), Coimbatore, India. 10.1109/ICAECA52838.2021.9675606

An, Y., Kaplan-Rakowski, R., Yang, J., Conan, J., Kinard, W., & Daughrity, L. (2021). Examining K-12 teachers' feelings, experiences, and perspectives regarding online teaching during the early stage of the COVID-19 pandemic. *Educational Technology Research and Development*, 69(5), 2589–2613. 10.1007/s11423-021-10008-534220171

Anzovino, M. E., Mallia, V. A., Morton, M. S., Barker Paredes, J. E., Pennington, R., Pursell, D. P., Rudd, G. E., Shepler, B., Villanueva, O., & Lee, S. (2020). Insights and initiatives while teaching organic chemistry i and ii with laboratory courses in the time of COVID-19. *Journal of Chemical Education*, 97(9), 3240–3245. 10.1021/acs.jchemed.0c00766

Arch, E. C., & Cummins, D. E. (1989). Structured and unstructured exposure to computers: Gender differences in attitude and use among college students. *Sex Roles*, 20(5-6), 245–254. 10.1007/BF00287722

Ariffin, S. H. S., & Ghazali, N. E. (2018). Structured Techniques in New Academia Learning Innovation (NALI) for Professional Engineering Practices Course. *2017 7th World Engineering Education Forum (WEEF), IEEE Xplore*. IEEE. 10.1109/WEEF.2017.8467118

Aristovnik, A., Karampelas, K., Umek, L., & Ravšelj, D. (2023). Impact of the COVID-19 pandemic on online learning in higher education: A bibliometric analysis. *Frontiers in Education*, 8, 1225834.. 10.3389/feduc.2023.1225834

Arnold, M., Vogel, A., & Ulber, M. (2021). Digitalizing higher education in light of sustainability and rebound effects—Surveys in times of the COVID-19 pandemic. *Sustainability (Basel)*, 13(22), 12912. 10.3390/su132212912

Arrington, A. (2021). *The use of information and communications technology to continue instruction and professional development in rural Ghana during COVID-19 school lockdowns* [Doctoral dissertation, University of Illinois at Urbana-Champaign].

Ashwin, P., & Mcvitty, D. (2015). The meanings of student engagement: Implications for policies and practices. *Higher Education Policy*, 28(1), 1–14. 10.1057/hep.2014.17

Assey, E. S., & Babyegeya, E. (2022). The Challenges Facing Effective Teaching, Learning and Assessment in Community-Based Secondary Schools in Tabora Region. *American Journal of Education and Practice*, 6(2), 1–17. 10.47672/ajep.1084

Association for Talent Development (ATD). (2017, April). *Microlearning: Delivering bite-sized knowledge*. ATD.

Astuti, D., Wasidi, & Sinthia, R. (2019). Hubungan antara regulasi emosi dengan perilaku memaafkan pada siswa sekolah menengah pertama. *Consilia Jurnal Ilmiah BK, 2*(1), 1-10. https://doi.org/10.33369/consilia.2.1.1-10

Atchley, W., Wingenbach, G., & Akers, C. (2013). Comparison of course completion and student performance through online and traditional courses. *International Review of Research in Open and Distance Learning*, 14(4), 4. 10.19173/irrodl.v14i4.1461

Atkins, P., & Jones, L. (2008). *Chemical principles: The quest for insight*. W. H. Freeman.

Atobatele, F. A., Kpodo, P. C., & Eke, I. O. (2024). Faculty engagement in international student success: A review of best practices and strategies. *International Journal of Applied Research in Social Sciences*, 6(3), 440–459. 10.51594/ijarss.v6i3.968

Attard, C., & Holmes, K. (2022). An exploration of teacher and student perceptions of blended learning in four secondary mathematics classrooms. *Mathematics Education Research Journal*, 34(4), 719–740. 10.1007/s13394-020-00359-2

Audrin, C., & Audrina, B. (2022). Key factors in digital literacy in learning and education: A systematic literature review using text mining. *Education and Information Technologies*, 27(6), 7395–7419. 10.1007/s10639-021-10832-5

Aydoğdu, C., & Şener, F. (2016). Fen eğitiminde laboratuvar kullanım tekniğinin ve güvenliğin önemi ve CLP tüzüğünün getirileri üzerine bir araştırma (A study on the importance of laboratory technique and safety in science education and the implications of the CLP regulation). *Eskişehir Osmangazi Üniversitesi Türk Dünyası Uygulama ve Araştırma Merkezi Eğitim Dergisi*, 1(1), 39–54.

Ayega, D. (2020). Pandemics and education in Sub-Saharan Africa: Invest in education technology. *American Journal of Educational Research*, 8(8), 581–586. 10.12691/education-8-8-10

Ayuningtiyas, C. (2020). Regulasi emosi siswa dalam pembelajaran daring. *De_Journal (Dharmas Education Journal)*, *1*(2), 107–113. https://ejournal.undhari.ac.id/index.php/de_journal/article/view/123

Azevedo, R. (2015). Defining and measuring engagement and learning in science: Conceptual, theoretical, methodological, and analytical issues. *Educational Psychologist*, 50(1), 84–94. 10.1080/00461520.2015.1004069

Azionya, C., & Nhedzi, A. (2021). The digital divide and higher education challenge with emergency online learning: Analysis of tweets in the wake of the COVID-19 lockdown. *Turkish Online Journal of Distance Education*, 22(4), 164–182. 10.17718/tojde.1002822

Aziz, A. A., Megat Mohd Noor, M. J., Abang Ali, A. A., & Jaafar, M. S. (2005). A MALAYSIAN OUTCOME-BASED ENGINEERING EDUCATION MODEL. *IACSIT International Journal of Engineering and Technology*, 2(1), 14–21.

Aziz, A. B. A., Hussin, H. B., & Burham, N. B. (2020). Experiences of Blended Learning using i-LearnV3 Platform in Semiconductor Device Course. *2019 IEEE International Conference on Engineering, Technology and Education (TALE), IEEE Xplore*, (pp. 1–5). IEEE. 10.1109/TALE48000.2019.9225959

Azuma, M., Coallier, F., & Garbajosa, J. (2004). How to apply the Bloom taxonomy to software engineering. *Eleventh Annual International Workshop on Software Technology and Engineering Practice, IEEE Xplore*, 117–122. https://10.0.4.85/STEP.2003.13

Babelyuk, O., Koliasa, O., Lopushanskyy, V., Smaglii, V., & Yukhymets, S. (2021). Psychological difficulties during the Covid lockdown: Video in blended digital teaching language, literature, and culture. *Arab World English Journal (AWEJ) Special Issue on Covid 19 Challenges,* (1), 172-182. 10.24093/awej/covid.13

Baber, H. (2022). Social interaction and effectiveness of the online learning–A moderating role of maintaining social distance during the pandemic COVID-19. *Asian Education and Development Studies*, 11(1), 159–171. 10.1108/AEDS-09-2020-0209

Bäckman, G. (2021). The outbreak of coronavirus (COVID-19) plagues the world. *Essays on COVID-19 Research*, 207.

Badaru, K. A., & Adu, E. (2022). Prospects of Blended Learning for the Post-COVID-19 Higher Education: The Instructors' Perspectives at a University in South Africa. *E-Journal of Humanities. Arts and Social Sciences*, 3(11), 126–139. 10.38159/ehass.2022SP31111

Bai, X., Shao, Y., Liu, Y., Cai, M., Ma, M., & Yang, H. (2023). Current status of college students' learning engagement level in online learning and strategies to improve it: Take a university in Western China as an example. *Proceedings of the 2023 4th International Conference on Education Development and Studies*. Research Gate./10.1145/3591139.3591152

Bai, M., Liu, Y., Qi, M., Roy, N., Shu, C.-M., Khan, F., & Zhao, D. (2022). Current status, challenges, and future directions of university laboratory safety in China. *Journal of Loss Prevention in the Process Industries*, 74, 104671. 10.1016/j.jlp.2021.104671

Bakera, P. M. A., Bujaka, K. R., & De Millo, R. (2012). The evolving university: Disruptive change and institutional innovation. *Procedia Computer Science*, 14, 330–335. 10.1016/j.procs.2012.10.037

Balalaieva, O., (2021). The problem of classification of digital learning resources. *Euromentor Journal, 12*(2), 65-78.

Ballantine, J. H., & Hammack, F. M. (2009). *The sociology of education: A systematic analysis* (6th ed.). Prentice Hall.

Baltà-Salvador, R., Olmedo-Torre, N., Peña, M., & Renta-Davids, A. I. (2021). Academic and emotional effects of online learning during the COVID-19 pandemic on engineering students. *Education and Information Technologies*, 26(6), 7407–7434. 10.1007/s10639-021-10593-134108843

Bamberg, M. (2012). Narrative analysis. In H. Cooper, P. M. Camic, D. L. Long, A. T. Panter, D. Rindskopf, & K. J. Sher (Eds.), *APA handbook of research methods in psychology, Vol. 2. Research designs: Quantitative, qualitative, neuropsychological, and biological* (pp. 85–102). American Psychological Association. 10.1037/13620-006

Bambrick-Santoyo, P. (2010). *Driven by Data: A Practical Guide to Improve Instruction.* John Wiley & Son.

Bamrungsin, P., & Khampirat, B. (2022). Improving professional skills of pre-service teachers using online training: Applying work-integrated learning approaches through a quasi-experimental study. *Sustainability (Basel)*, 14(7), 4362. 10.3390/su14074362

Bandara, D., & Wijekularathna, D. K. (2018). Comparison of student performance under two teaching methods: Face to face and online. *International Journal of Education Research, 12*.

Bandura, A. (1986). Social foundations of thought and action. *Englewood Cliffs, NJ, 1986*(23-28), 2.

Bandura, A. (1997). *Self-efficacy: The exercise of control.* W. H. Freeman and Company.

Banerjee, M., & Krishnagar, N. (2023). *IMPLEMENTATION OF NEP 2020 CURRICULUM: AN OVERVIEW.* NEP 2020: Implementation Phase.

Banerjee, M. (2022). The digital divide and smartphone reliance for disadvantaged students in higher education. *Journal of Systemics, Cybernetics and Informatics*, 20(3), 31–39. 10.54808/JSCI.20.03.31

Barańczuk, U. (2019). The five factor model of personality and emotion regulation: A meta-analysis. *Personality and Individual Differences*, 139, 217–227. 10.1016/j.paid.2018.11.025

Baria, K., & Gomez, D. (2022). Influence of social support to student learning and development. *International Journal of Research Studies in Education*, 11(2), 69–97. 10.5861/ijrse.2022.112

Barnes, K. T. (2023). *Integral Instructional Coaching: The Need for Effective Feedback to Develop and Retain Teachers*. University of Dayton. https://etd.ohiolink.edu/acprod/odb_etd/ws/send_file/send?accession=dayton1689354933936445&disposition=inline

Baroody, A. E., Rimm-Kaufman, S. E., Larsen, R. A., & Curby, T. W. (2014). The link between responsive classroom training and student-teacher relationship quality in the fifth grade: A study of fidelity of implementation. *School Psychology Review*, 43(1), 69–85. 10.1080/02796015.2014.12087455

Basri, H., Man, A. C., Badaruzzaman, W. W., & Nor, M. M. (2004). Malaysia and the Washington accord: What it takes for full membership. *IACSIT International Journal of Engineering and Technology*, 1(1), 64–73.

Batdı, V., Doğan, Y., & Talan, T. (2023). Effectiveness of online learning: A multi-complementary approach research with responses from the COVID-19 pandemic period. *Interactive Learning Environments*, 31(7), 4113–4146. 10.1080/10494820.2021.1954035

Bates, A. W. Tony. (2005). *Technology, e-learning and distance education*. Routledge.

Beck, C., Sumowski, E., Dailey-Hebert, A., & Colvin, C. (2021). Instructional Coaching as Professional Development: The Impact of Goal Setting on Teacher Practice. *Journal of Staff Development*, 42(3), 32–40.

Behzadnia, B., Mollaei Zangi, F., Rezaei, F., & Eskandarnejad, M. (2023). Predicting students' basic psychological needs, motivation, and well-being in online physical education: A semester-term longitudinal study. *International Journal of Sport and Exercise Psychology*, 1–19. 10.1080/1612197X.2023.2237051

Bell, F. (2011). Connectivism: Its place in theory-informed research and innovation in technology-enabled learning. *International Review of Research in Open and Distance Learning*, 12(3), 98–118. 10.19173/irrodl.v12i3.902

Bennett, A. (2024). *For the first time, all states will have a plan to address digital equity*. National Telecommunications and Information Administration.

Bennett, B., Ross, D., & Gates, T. G. (2021). Creating spatial, relational, and cultural safety in online social work education during COVID-19. *Social Work Education*, 41(7), 1660–1668. 10.1080/02615479.2021.1924664

Bennett, G., & Green, F. (2001). Student learning in the online environment: No significant difference? *Quest*, 53(1), 1–13. 10.1080/00336297.2001.10491727

Benson, R., & Samarawickrema, G. (2009). Addressing the context of e-learning: Using transactional distance theory to inform design. *Distance Education*, 30(1), 5–21. 10.1080/01587910902845972

Berdiyeva, S. (2024). Exploring Innovative Approaches To Teaching. *Modern Science and Research, 3*(1), 923-927. https://inlibrary.uz/index.php/science-research/article/view/28552

Bergmann, J., & Sams, A. (2012). *Flip your classroom: Reach every student in every class every day*. International Society for Technology in Education.

Bergmann, J., & Sams, A. (2014). *Flipped learning: Gateway to student engagement*. International Society for Technology in Education.

Bernacki, M., Greene, M., & Lobczowski, N. (2021). A Systematic review of research on personalized learning: Personalized by whom, to what, how, and for what purpose(s)? *Educational Psychology Review*, 33(4), 1–41. 10.1007/s10648-021-09615-8

Bernard, R. M., & Rubalcava, B. R. D. (2000). Collaborative online distance learning: Issues for future practice and research. *Distance Education*, 21(2), 260–277. 10.1080/0158791000210205

Betancourt-Odio, M. A., Sartor-Harada, A., Ulloa-Guerra, O., & Azevedo-Gomes, J. (2021). Self-perceptions on digital competences for m-learning and education sustainability:A study with teachers from different countries. *Sustainability (Basel)*, 13(1), 343. 10.3390/su13010343

Bhukuvhani, C., Kusure, L., Munodawafa, V., Sana, A., & Gwizangwe, I. (2010). Pre-service Teachers' use of improvised and Virtual Laboratory experimentation in Science teaching. *International Journal of Education and Development using ICT, 6*(4), 27-38. https://www.learntechlib.org/p/42262/

Bielski, Z. (2020). Social media awash with bragging about pandemic productivity. *The Globe and Mail.*

Billings, D. M., Skiba, D. J., & Connors, H. R. (2005). Best practices in web-based courses: Generational differences across undergraduate and graduate nursing students. *Journal of Professional Nursing*, 21(2), 126–133. 10.1016/j.profnurs.2005.01.00215806511

Bixler, N. (2021). *How to use digital education resources effectively*. Hapara. https://hapara.com/blog/how-to-use-digital-education-resources-effectively

Blackburn, D. (2021). Using Instructional Coaching to Improve Online Teaching during COVID-19. *Journal of Faculty Development*, 35(2), 27–34.

Blaushild, N., Blazquez, R., McGee, S., & McGee-Tekula, R. (2024). Balancing teachers' needs in times of crisis: Investigating how computer science instructional coaches and teachers navigated remote professional development during COVID-19. *Computer Science Education*, 1–33. 10.1080/08993408.2024.2313913

Blignaut, R. J., & Renaud, K. (2021). Higher education students' perceptions of online learning during COVID-19—A comparative study. *Education Sciences*, 11(8), 403. 10.3390/educsci11080403

Bloom, G., Castagna, C., Moir, E., & Warren, B. (2014). *Blended coaching: Skills and strategies to support principal development*. Corwin Press.

Boddy, C. R. (2016). Sample size for qualitative research. *Qualitative Market Research*, 19(4), 426–432. 10.1108/QMR-06-2016-0053

Bond, M. (2020). Facilitating student engagement through the flipped learning approach in K-12: A systematic review. *Computers & Education*, 151, 103819. 10.1016/j.compedu.2020.103819

Bond, M., Bedenlier, S., Marín, V. I., & Händel, M. (2021). Emergency remote teaching in higher education: Mapping the first global online semester. *International Journal of Educational Technology in Higher Education*, 18(50), 50. 10.1186/s41239-021-00282-x34778537

Bonwell, C. C., & Eison, J. A. (1991). ASHE-ERIC Higher Education Report: Vol. 1. *Active learning: Creating excitement in the classroom*. The George Washington University, School of Education and Human Development.

Borish, V., Werth, A., Sulaiman, N., Fox, M. F., Hoehn, J. R., & Lewandowski, H. (2022). Undergraduate student experiences in remote lab courses during the COVID-19 pandemic. *Physical Review. Physics Education Research*, 18(2), 020105. 10.1103/PhysRevPhysEducRes.18.020105

Borman, G. D., Hewes, G. M., Overman, L. T., & Brown, S. (2003). Comprehensive School Reform and Student Achievement: A Meta-Analysis. *Review of Educational Research*, 73(2), 125–230. 10.3102/00346543073002125

Boulton, C., Hughes, E., Kent, C., Smith, J. R., & Williams, H. T. P. (2019). Student engagement and wellbeing over time at a higher education institution. *PLoS One*, 14(11), e0227057. 10.1371/journal.pone.022577031774878

Boyle, D. K., & Wambach, K. A. (2001). Interaction in graduate nursing web-based instruction. *Journal of Professional Nursing*, 17(3), 128–134. 10.1053/jpnu.2001.2337611391558

Bozkaya, M., & Erdem Aydin, I. (2007). The Relationship between Teacher Immediacy Behaviors and Learners' Perceptions of Social Presence and Satisfaction in Open and Distance Education: The Case of Anadolu University Open Education Faculty. *The Turkish Online Journal of Educational Technology*, 6(4), 7.

Bozkurt, A. (2022). Resilience, adaptability, and sustainability of higher Education: A systematic mapping study on the impact of the coronavirus (COVID-19) pandemic and the transition to the new normal. *Journal of Learning for Development (JL4D), 9*(1), 1-16.

Bozkurt, A., Karadeniz, A., & Kocdar, S. (2017). Social networking sites as communication, interaction, and learning environments: Perceptions and preferences of distance education students. *Journal of Learning for Development*, 4(3), 348–365. 10.56059/jl4d.v4i3.215

Brady, D., & Voronova, K. (2023). Flipped online active learning environment for large general chemistry courses. *Journal of Chemical Education*, 100(3), 1109–1117. 10.1021/acs.jchemed.2c00602

Braff, D. (2020). The new helicopter parents are on Zoom. *New York Times*.

Braun, V., & Clarke, V. (2006). Using thematic analysis in psychology. *Qualitative Research in Psychology*, 3(2), 77–101. 10.1191/1478088706qp063oa

Bravo, M. J., Gilbert, L. A., & Kearney, L. K. (2003). Interventions for promoting gender equitable technology use in classrooms. *Teacher Education Quarterly*, 30(4), 95–109.

Broadbent, J., Ajjawi, R., Bearman, M., Boud, D., & Dawson, P. (2023). Beyond emergency remote teaching: Did the pandemic lead to lasting change in university courses? *International Journal of Educational Technology in Higher Education*, 20(1), 58. 10.1186/s41239-023-00428-z

Broo, D. G., Kaynak, O., & Sait, S. M. (2022). Rethinking engineering education at the age of industry 5.0. *Journal of Industrial Information Integration*, 25, 100311. 10.1016/j.jii.2021.100311

Brown, M., Costello, E., Donlon, E., & Giolla-Mhichíl, M. N. (2023). The rise of online learning during the COVID-19 pandemic. *European Journal of Open. Distance and E-Learning*, 22(2), 1–12. 10.2478/eurodl-2023-0001

Brown, T. E., Lemay, H. E., & Bursten, B. R. (2006). *Chemistry: The central science*. Pearson Prentice Hall.

Bruner, J. (1991). The narrative construction of reality. *Critical Inquiry*, 18(1), 1–21. 10.1086/448619

Brusilovsky, P. (1999). Adaptive and Intelligent Technologies for Web-based Education. In Rollinger, C., & Peylo, C. (Eds.), *Künstliche Intelligenz, Special Issue on Intelligent Systems and Teleteaching, 4, 19-25.*

Bryson, J. R., & Andres, L. (2020). Covid-19 and rapid adoption and improvisation of online teaching: Curating resources for extensive versus intensive online learning experiences. *Journal of Geography in Higher Education*, 44(4), 608–623. 10.1080/03098265.2020.1807478

Busto, M. D., Ortega, N., Albillos, S. M., Ramos-Gómez, S., Pilar-Izquierdo, M. C., Velasco, B., & Palacios, D. (2022). Flipped classroom in laboratory practices of molecular biology: perception of the students from chemistry degree. *EDULEARN22 Proceedings*, (pp. 725-732). Research Gate.

Butt, S., Mahmood, A., & Saleem, S. (2022). The role of institutional factors and cognitive absorption on students' satisfaction and performance in online learning during COVID 19. *PLoS One*, 17(6), e02696091. 10.1371/journal.pone.026960935731789

Byun, S., & Slavin, R. E. (2020). Educational Responses to the COVID-19 Outbreak in South Korea. *Best Evid Chin Edu*, 5(2), 665–680. 10.15354/bece.20.or030

Calin, M. D., & Pislaru, C. (2023). Use of Technology to Increase the Quality of Collaborative Learning Experiences for Engineering Students in the Post-Pandemic Period. *Educatia*, 21(25), 73–80. 10.24193/ed21.2023.25.08

Campbell, S., Greenwood, M., Prior, S., Shearer, T., Walkem, K., Young, S., Bywaters, D., & Walker, K. (2020). Purposive sampling: Complex or simple? Research case examples. *Journal of Research in Nursing*, 25(8), 652–661. 10.1177/174498712092720634394687

Candaş, B., & Altun, T. (2023). Investigating flipped laboratory practices of science student teachers. *Journal of Turkish Science Education*, 20(1), 173–188. 10.36681/tused.2023.010

Candaş, B., Kiryak, Z., & Özmen, H. (2022). Developing prospective science teachers' using of chemical knowledge with flipped learning approach in the context of environmental problems. *Science Education International*, 33(2), 192–202. 10.33828/sei.v33.i2.7

Carlson, S., & Carnevale, D. (2001). Debating the demise of NYUonline. *The Chronicle of Higher Education*, 48(16).

Carrillo, C., & Flores, M. (2020). COVID-19 and teacher education: A literature review of online teaching and learning practices. *European Journal of Teacher Education*, 43(4), 466–487. 10.1080/02619768.2020.1821184

Carr, J. M., & Carr, J. M. (2016). What can students learn about lab safety from Mr Bean? *Journal of College Science Teaching*, 45(6), 32–35. 10.2505/4/jcst16_045_06_32

Carver-Thomas, D., Kini, T., & Burns, D. (2020). Sharpening the divide: How California's teacher shortages expand inequality. *Learning Policy Institute*. https://eric.ed.gov/?id=ED610882

Casey, D. M. (2008). A journey to legitimacy: The historical development of distance education through technology. *TechTrends*, 52(2), 45–51. 10.1007/s11528-008-0135-z

Castleberry, A., & Nolen, A. (2018). Thematic analysis of qualitative research data: Is it as easy as it sounds? *Currents in Pharmacy Teaching & Learning*, 10(6), 807–815. 10.1016/j.cptl.2018.03.01930025784

Chafee, L. D. (2013). Expanded learning opportunities are key to student learning. *Expanding and Opportunities, 5.*

Chan, R., Bista, K., & Allen, R. (2021). Is online and distance learning the future in global higher education? The faculty perspective. In Chan, , (Eds.), *Online Teaching and Learning in Higher Education during COVID-19* (pp. 5–14). Routledge. 10.4324/9781003125921-2

Chans, G. M., Bravo-Gutiérrez, M. E., Orona-Navar, A., & Sánchez-Rodríguez, E. P. (2022). Compilation of chemistry experiments for an online laboratory course: Student's perception and learning outcomes in the context of COVID-19. *Sustainability (Basel)*, 14(5), 2539. 10.3390/su14052539

Chemosit, C. C. (2004). *Predictors and correlates of student academic achievement: student-faculty interaction, active learning strategies, and academic rigor*. [Unpublished master's Thesis, Illinois State University, Normal].

Chen, P., Gonyea, R. M., & Kuh, G. D. (2008). Learning at a distance: Engaged or not? *Innovate: Journal of Online Education, 4*(3). https://hdl.handle.net/2022/24106

Chen, C., Landa, S., Padilla, A., & Yur-Austin, J. (2022). Post-pandemic assessment of online teaching and learning in higher business education. *International Journal of Educational Management*, 36(6), 1065–1079. 10.1108/IJEM-11-2021-0430

Cheng, L., Ritzhaupt, A. D., & Antonenko, P. (2019). Effects of the flipped classroom instructional strategy on students' learning outcomes: A meta-analysis. *Educational Technology Research and Development*, 67(4), 793–824. 10.1007/s11423-018-9633-7

Chen, T., Peng, L., Yin, X., Rong, J., Yang, J., & Cong, G. (2023). Impact of the COVID-19 pandemic on online learning in higher education. *Educational Technology Research and Development*, 69(1), 1–18. 10.1007/s11423-020-09925-637016716

Chen, Y., Wang, Y., Kinshuk, , & Chen, N.-S. (2014). Is FLIP enough? Or should we use the FLIPPED model instead? *Computers & Education*, 79, 16–27. 10.1016/j.compedu.2014.07.004

Cheung, S. K. S., Kwok, L. F., Phusavat, K., & Yan, H. H. (2021). Shaping the future learning environments with smart elements: Challenges and opportunities. *International Journal of Educational Technology in Higher Education*, 18(16), 16. Advance online publication. 10.1186/s41239-021-00254-134778521

Cheurprakobkit, S., Hale, D. F., & Olson, J. N. (2002). Technicians' perceptions about Web-based courses: The University of Texas system experience. *American Journal of Distance Education*, 16(4), 245–258. 10.1207/S15389286AJDE1604_4

Chickering, A. W., & Ehrmann, S. C. (1996). Implementing the seven principles: Technology as lever. *AAHE Bulletin*, 49, 3–6.

Child, G. S., & Song, K. (2023). Digital Inequities: Promoting Digital Justice during the COVID-19 Pandemic. *Sustainability (Basel)*, 15(17), 12862. 10.3390/su151712862

Chilisa, B. (2017). Decolonising transdisciplinary research approaches: An African perspective for enhancing knowledge integration in sustainability science. *Sustainability Science*, 12(5), 813–827. https://0-doi.org.wam.seals.ac.za/10.1007/s11625-017-0461-1. 10.1007/s11625-017-0461-1

Chiu, T. (2021). Digital support for student engagement in blended learning based on self-determination theory. *Computers in Human Behavior, 124*, 106909.

Choi, J., & Lee, Y. (2015). To what extent does "flipping" make lessons effective in a multimedia production class? *Innovations in Education and Teaching International, 55*(1), 3–12. Taylor & Francis Online. 10.1080/14703297.2015.1123105

Cho, M. H., & Tobias, S. (2016). Should instructors require discussion in online courses? Effects of online discussion on community of inquiry, learner time, satisfaction, and achievement. *International Review of Research in Open and Distance Learning*, 17(2), 605–632. 10.19173/irrodl.v17i2.2342

Chua, K., & Islam, M. (2021). The hybrid Project-Based Learning–Flipped Classroom: A design project module redesigned to foster learning and engagement. *International Journal of Mechanical Engineering Education, 49*(4), 289–315. Sage Journals. 10.1177/0306419019838335

Chu, A. M., Liu, C. K., So, M. K., & Lam, B. S. (2021). Factors for sustainable online learning in higher Education during the COVID-19 pandemic. *Sustainability (Basel)*, 13(9), 5038. 10.3390/su13095038

Clark, C. M., Werth, L., & Ahten, S. (2012). Cyber-bullying and incivility in the online learning environment, part 1: Addressing faculty and student perceptions. *Nurse Educator*, 37(4), 150–156. 10.1097/NNE.0b013e31825a87e522688872

Clark, C., & Boyer, D. D. (2016). Twenty-first-century technology integration staff development: A phenomenology. *Journal of Computers in Education*, 3(1), 1–20. 10.1007/s40692-015-0053-y

Cloke, P. (2006). Conceptualising rurality. *Handbook of rural studies, 18*, 18-28. https://digital.casalini.it/9781446206942

Clough, M. P. (2002). Using the laboratory to enhance student learning. In Bybee, R. W. (Ed.), *Learning science and the science of learning, 2002 NSTA yearbook* (pp. 85–97).

Cohen, J., & Kupferschmidt, K. (2020). Countries test tactics in 'war' against COVID-19. *Science*, 367(6484), 1287–1288. 10.1126/science.367.6484.128732193299

Cohen, M. B., & Zajic, A. (2019). The Flipped Classroom Approach to Engineering Electromagnetics: A Case Study. *2019 IEEE International Symposium on Antennas and Propagation and USNC-URSI Radio Science Meeting, IEEE Xplore*, (pp. 803–804). IEEE. 10.1109/APUSNCURSINRSM.2019.8888789

Colclasure, B. C., Marlier, A., Durham, M. F., Brooks, T. D., & Kerr, M. (2021). Identified challenges from faculty teaching at predominantly undergraduate institutions after abrupt transition to emergency remote teaching during the COVID-19 pandemic. *Education Sciences*, 11(9), 556. 10.3390/educsci11090556

Cole, M. (2017, March 23). *Just how micro is microlearning?* [blog post].

Cole, M. T., Shelley, D. J., & Swartz, L. B. (2014). Online instruction, e-learning, and student satisfaction: A three year study. *International Review of Research in Open and Distance Learning*, 15(6), 111–131. 10.19173/irrodl.v15i6.1748

Cole, M., Shelley, D., Swartz, L., & Adeoye, B. F. (2014). Using digital technologies to aid e-learning: A pilot study. In Adeoye, B. F., & Tomei, L. (Eds.), *In Effects of information capitalism and globalization on teaching and learning* (pp. 22–35). IGI Global. 10.4018/978-1-4666-6162-2.ch002

Comber, C., Colley, A., Hargreaves, D. J., & Dorn, L. (1997). The effects of age, gender and computer experience upon computer attitudes. *Educational Research*, 39(2), 123–133. 10.1080/0013188970390201

Common Sense. (2021). 2021 Annual Report. *Common Sense Media Report.*

Compton, L., Davis, N., & Correia, A. (2010). Pre-service teachers' preconceptions, misconceptions, and concerns about virtual schooling. *Distance Education*, 31(1), 37–54. 10.1080/01587911003725006

Conway, E. D. (2003). *Teaching Strategies for Distance Education.*

Cook, D. A., & Steinert, Y. (2013). Online learning for faculty development: A review of the literature. *Medical Teacher*, 35(11), 930–937. 10.3109/0142159X.2013.82732824006931

Cook-Sather, A., Bovill, C., & Felten, P. (2014). *Engaging students as partners in learning and teaching: A guide for faculty*. John Wiley & Sons.

Cooper, L. (2001). A comparison of online and traditional computer applications classes. *T.H.E. Journal, 28*(8). https://thejournal.com/Articles/2001/03/01/Online-and Traditional-Computer-Applications-Classes.aspx?m=1

Coral, M. A., & Bernuy, A. E. (2022). Challenges in the Digital Transformation Processes in Higher Education Institutions and Universities. *International Journal of Information Technologies and Systems Approach*, 15(1), 1–14. 10.4018/IJITSA.290002

Corbin, J., & Strauss, A. (2008). Qualitative research. *Techniques and procedures for developing grounded theory, 3.*

Coskun, S., Kayıkcı, Y., & Gençay, E. (2019). Adapting Engineering Education to Industry 4.0 Vision. *Technologies, 7*(1), 10. MDPI. 10.3390/technologies7010010

Costa, A., & Garmston, R. (1994). *Cognitive coaching: A foundation for Renaissance schools.* Christopher-Gordon Publishers.

Cramarenco, R. E., Burcă-Voicu, M. I., & Dabija, D. C. (2023). Student perceptions of online education and digital technologies during the COVID-19 pandemic: A systematic review. *Electronics (Basel)*, 12(2), 319. 10.3390/electronics12020319

Creswell, J. W., & Poth, C. N. (2016). *Qualitative inquiry and research design: Choosing among five approaches.* Sage publications. https://docs.edtechhub.org/lib/XAH8M47G

Creswell, J. W. (2013). *Qualitative inquiry and research design: Choosing among five approaches.* Sage publications.

Crockett, J. M. (2011). Laboratory safety for undergraduates. *Journal of Chemical Health and Safety*, 18(4), 16–25. 10.1016/j.jchas.2010.08.001

Crossley, M. (2000). *Introducing narrative psychology*. McGraw-Hill Education.

Cui, L., Zhu, C., Hare, R., & Tang, Y. (2023). MetaEdu: A new framework for future education. *Discover Artificial Intelligence*, 3(1), 10. 10.1007/s44163-023-00053-9

Dabbagh, N. (2007). The online learner: Characteristics and pedagogical implications. *Contemporary Issues in Technology & Teacher Education*, 7(3), 217–226.

Dabbagh, N., & Bannan-Ritland, B. (2005). *Online learning: Concepts, strategies, and application*. Prentice Hall.

Dada, D., Laseinde, O. T., & Tartibu, L. (2023). Student-Centered Learning Tool for Cognitive Enhancement in the Learning Environment. *Procedia Computer Science, 217*, 507–512. ScienceDirect. 10.1016/j.procs.2022.12.246

Dalinghaus, L. J. (2023). *A qualitative study of digital citizenship practices and the fear of missing out: perceptions of middle school students and principals*. [Doctoral Dissertation, Kansas State University]. ProQuest Dissertations Publishing.

Dana, N. F., & Yendol-Hoppey, D. (2009). *The reflective educator's guide to classroom research: Learning to teach and teaching to learn through practitioner inquiry*. Corwin Press.

Danielson, C. (2007). *Enhancing professional practice: A framework for teaching*. AsCD.

Danker, B. (2015). Using Flipped Classroom Approach to Explore Deep Learning in Large Classrooms. *IAFOR Journal of Education, 3*(1), 171–186. ERIC. 10.22492/ije.3.1.10

Darling-Hammond, L., Schachner, A., & Edgerton, A. K. (2020). Restarting and reinventing school: Learning in the time of COVID and beyond. In *Learning Policy Institute*. Learning Policy Institute.

Das, S., Kleinke, D. K., & Pistrui, D. (2020). Reimagining engineering education: does industry 4.0 need education 4.0? *2020 ASEE Virtual Annual Conference Content Access*, 1–20. https://peer.asee.org/35136

Daumiller, M., Rinas, R., Hein, J., Janke, S., Dickhäuser, O., & Dresel, M. (2021). Shifting from Face-to-Face to Online Teaching During COVID 19: The Role of University Faculty Achievement Goals for Attitudes Towards This Sudden Change, and Their Relevance for Burnout/Engagement and Student Evaluations of Teaching Quality. *Computers in Human Behavior, 118*, 106677. ScienceDirect. 10.1016/j.chb.2020.106677

Davenport, J. L., Rafferty, A. N., & Yaron, D. J. (2018). Whether and how authentic contexts using a virtual chemistry lab support learning. *Journal of Chemical Education*, 95(8), 1250–1259. 10.1021/acs.jchemed.8b00048

de la Flor López, S., Ferrando, F., & Fabregat-Sanjuan, A. (2016). Learning/training video clips: an efficient tool for improving learning outcomes in Mechanical Engineering. *International Journal of Educational Technology in Higher Education, 13*(1), 1–13. Springer Link. 10.1186/s41239-016-0011-4

De Loof, H., Struyf, A., Boeve-de Pauw, J., & Van Petegem, P. (2021). Teachers' motivating style and students' motivation and engagement in STEM: The relationship between three key educational concepts. *Research in Science Education*, 51(4), 109–127. 10.1007/s11165-019-9830-3

de Lucas Ancillo, A., Gavrila, S. G., & del Val, M. T. (2023). Workplace change within the COVID-19 context: The new (next) normal. *Technological Forecasting and Social Change, 194*, 122673. ScienceDirect. 10.1016/j.techfore.2023.122673

de Oliveira, D., & Murillo, L. (2020). Will virtual replace classroom teaching? Lessons from virtual classes via zoom in the times of COVID-19. *Journal of Advances in Education and Philosophy*, 4(05), 208–213. 10.36348/jaep.2020.v04i05.004

DeCoito, I., & Estaiteyeh, M. (2022). Transitioning to online teaching during the COVID-19 pandemic: An exploration of STEM teachers' views, successes, and challenges. *Journal of Science Education and Technology*, 31(3), 340–356. 10.1007/s10956-022-09958-z35369535

Decuypere, M., Grimaldi, E., & Landri, P. (2021). Introduction: Critical studies of digital education platforms. *Critical Studies in Education*, 62(1), 1–16. 10.1080/17508487.2020.1866050

Del Río-Gamero, B., Santiago, D. E., Schallenberg-Rodríguez, J., & Melián-Martel, N. (2022). Does the Use of Videos in Flipped Classrooms in Engineering Labs Improve Student Performance? *Education Sciences, 12*(11), 735. MDPI. 10.3390/educsci12110735

Delgado, F. (2022). Post-COVID-19 Transition in University Physics Courses: A Case of Study in a Mexican University. *Education Sciences*, 12(9), 627. 10.3390/educsci12090627

Delgado, T., Bhark, S.-J., & Donahue, J. (2021). Pandemic teaching: Creating and teaching cell biology labs online during COVID-19. *Biochemistry and Molecular Biology Education*, 49(1), 32–37. 10.1002/bmb.2148233336883

Demuyakor, J. (2020). Coronavirus (COVID-19) and online learning in higher institutions of education: A survey of the perceptions of Ghanaian international students in China. *Online Journal of Communication and Media Technologies*, 10(3), e202018. 10.29333/ojcmt/8286

Deng, X., & Yi, S. (2022). The digital divide in online education: a study of underserved college students. *Proceedings of the 55th Hawaii International Conference on System Sciences*. IEEE. 10.24251/HICSS.2022.624

Dennis, J. M., Phinney, J. S., & Chuateco, L. I. (2005). The role of motivation, parental support, and peer support in the academic success of ethnic minority first-generation college students. *Journal of College Student Development*, 46(3), 223–236. 10.1353/csd.2005.0023

Denton, C. A., & Hasbrouck, J. E. (2009). *Response to Instruction (RTI) and English Learners: Making It Happen.*

Denzin, N. K., & Lincoln, Y. S. (1994). *Handbook of qualitative research: California*. Sage Publications.

Department of Basic Education (SA). (2013). *National Policy on Quintile Schools.*

Department of Basic Education. (2020). *Standard operating procedure for the prevention, containment and management of covid-19 in schools and school communities*. DBE. 10.1017/CBO9781107415324.004

Deshmukh, J. (2021). Speculations on the post-pandemic university campus – a global inquiry. *Archnet-IJAR: International Journal of Architectural Research*, 15(1), 10–23. 10.1108/ARCH-10-2020-0245

Desimone, L. M., et al. (2019). *Learning in a Digital Age: Instructional Technology in the Learning Sciences*.

Desimone, L. M., Hammerness, K., Keating, B., & Nightingale, K. (2020). The impact of coaching on teacher learning: A review of the research. *Journal of Teaching and Teacher Education*, 92, 103036.

Dhawan, S. (2020). Online learning: A panacea in the time of COVID-19 crisis. *Journal of Educational Technology Systems*, 49(1), 5–22. 10.1177/0047239520934018

Dickey, M. (2004). The impact of web-logs (blogs) on student perceptions of isolation and alienation in a web-based distance-learning environment. *Open Learning*, 19(3), 279–291. 10.1080/0268051042000280138

Dictionary. (n.d.). *Companionship*. Dictionary. https://www.dictionary.com/browse/companionship

Divjak, B., Rienties, B., Iniesto, F., Vondra, P., & Žižak, M. (2022). Flipped classrooms in higher education during the COVID-19 pandemic: findings and future research recommendations. *International Journal of Educational Technology in Higher Education, 19*(1). Springer Link. 10.1186/s41239-021-00316-4

Djidu, H., Mashuri, S., Nasruddin, N., Sejati, A., Rasmuin, R., La Eru Ugi, L., & La Arua, A. (2021). Online learning in the post-Covid-19 pandemic era: Is our higher education ready for it? *Journal of Research and Education Studies: e-Saintika, 5*(1), 15-29. 10.36312/esaintika.v5i2.479

Donohue, J., & Miller, E. (2020). Covid-19 and school closures. *Journal of the American Medical Association*, 324(9), 845. 10.1001/jama.2020.1309232745182

Dorn, E., Hancock, B., Sarakatsannis, J., & Viruleg, E. (2020). *COVID-19 and Student Learning in the United States: The Hurt Could Last a Lifetime*. Child Institute. https://www.childrensinstitute.net/sites/default/files/documents/COVID-19-and-student-learning-in-the-United-States_FINAL.pdf

Dos Santos, L. M. (2021). The relationship between workforce sustainability, stress, and career decision: A study of kindergarten teachers during the COVID-19 pandemic. *Sustainability (Basel)*, 13(20), 11521. 10.3390/su132011521

Downes, S. (2006). E-learning 2.0. eLearning magazine: education and technology in perspective. *20*(2007), 29–1.

Draxler-Weber, N., Packmohr, S., & Brink, H. (2022). Barriers to Digital Higher Education Teaching and How to Overcome Them—Lessons Learned during the COVID-19 Pandemic. *Education Sciences*, 12(12), 870. 10.3390/educsci12120870

Du Plessis, P., & Mestry, R. (2019). Teachers for rural schools–a challenge for South Africa. *South African Journal of Education*, 39(Supplement 1), S1–S9. 10.15700/saje.v39ns1a1774

Duke, J., Francis, G., & Nagro, S. (2017). Student Engagement Across Distance Learning Models. *Learning in a Digital World, 9*. 10.13021/G8ITLCP.9.2017.1849

Dumulescu, D., Pop-Păcurar, I., & Necula, C. V. (2021). Learning design for future higher education – Insights from the time of COVID-19. *Frontiers in Psychology*, 12, 647948. http://doi.ord/10.3389/fpsyg.2021.647948. 10.3389/fpsyg.2021.647948

Dunekack, A. (2020). Instructional Coaching in Times of Crisis. *Journal of Staff Development*, 41(3), 30–35.

Durlak, J. A., Weissber, R. P., Dymnicki, A. B., Taylor, R. D., & Schellinger, K. B. (2011). The impact of enhancing students' social and emotional learning: A meta-analysis of school-based universal interventions. *Child Development*, 82(1), 405–432. 10.1111/j.1467-8624.2010.01564.x21291449

Dutta, A. (2020). Impact of digital social media on Indian higher education: alternative approaches of online learning during COVID-19 pandemic crisis. *International journal of scientific and research publications, 10*(5), 604-611. 10.29322/IJSRP.10.05.2020.p10169

Dykman, C. A., & Davis, C. K. (2008). Part One The Shift Toward Online Education. *Journal of Information Systems Education*, 19(1).

Dzansi, D. Y., & Amedzo, K. (2014). Integrating ICT into rural South African schools: Possible solutions for challenges. *International Journal of Educational Sciences*, 6(2), 341–348. 10.1080/09751122.2014.11890145

Eccles, J. S., & Wigfield, A. (2002). Motivational beliefs, values, and goals. *Annual Review of Psychology*, 53(1), 109–132. 10.1146/annurev.psych.53.100901.13515311752481

Eccles, J. S., & Wigfield, A. (2020). From expectancy-value theory to situated expectancy-value theory: A developmental, social cognitive, and sociocultural perspective on motivation. *Contemporary Educational Psychology*, 61, 101859. 10.1016/j.cedpsych.2020.101859

Edison, T. (n.d.). An exclusive interview with the master inventor. *The New York Dramatic Mirror*.

Education Week. (2020, April 6). Map: Coronavirus and School Closures. [blog post]. *Education Week*.

Edwards, C. R. (2023). *Instructional Coaching: A Support for Increasing Engagement in Middle School Mathematics* [Doctoral dissertation, University of South Carolina]. https://scholarcommons.sc.edu/etd/7489

Eichler, J. F. (2022). Future of the Flipped Classroom in Chemistry Education: Recognizing the Value of Independent Preclass Learning and Promoting Deeper Understanding of Chemical Ways of Thinking During In-person Instruction. *Journal of Chemical Education*, 99(3), 1503–1508. 10.1021/acs.jchemed.1c01115

Elkhatat, A. M., & Al-Muhtaseb, S. A. (2021). Hybrid online-flipped learning pedagogy for teaching laboratory courses to mitigate the pandemic COVID-19 confinement and enable effective sustainable delivery: Investigation of attaining course learning outcome. *SN Social Sciences*, 1(5), 113. 10.1007/s43545-021-00117-634693317

El-Sakran, A., Salman, R., & Alzaatreh, A. (2022). Impacts of emergency remote teaching on college students amid COVID-19 in the UAE. *International Journal of Environmental Research and Public Health*, 19(5), 2979. 10.3390/ijerph1905297935270670

El-Sawy, H. E. (2018). Flipping EFL University Classes with Blackboard System. *English Language Teaching*, 11(2), 31. 10.5539/elt.v11n2p31

Elsayary, A. (2023). The impact of a professional upskilling training programme on developing teachers' digital competence. *Journal of Computer Assisted Learning*, 39(4), 1154–1166. 10.1111/jcal.12788

Endrawati, A., & Suwartono, T. (2023). Blended learning through the google classroom in the "new normal" era of the Covid-19 pandemic: EFL teachers' perception and challenges. *Proceedings Series on Social Sciences & Humanities*, 12, 27–37. 10.30595/pssh.v12i.769

Eniola, I. (2020). Assessment of level of awareness and acceptance of flipped learning strategy among oyo state secondary school teachers. AAUA. *Journal of Science and Technology Education*, 3(1).

Ennam, A. (2024). Assessing Covid-19 pandemic-forced transitioning to distance e-learning in Moroccan universities: An empirical, analytical critical study of implementality and achievability. *Journal of North African Studies*, 29(1), 153–177. 10.1080/13629387.2021.1937138

Erdem-Aydin, I. (2021). Investigation of higher education instructors' perspectives towards emergency remote teaching. *Educational Media International*, 58(1), 78–98. 10.1080/09523987.2021.1908501

Erden, D. (2022). Innovative Learning Approache in Nursing Education: Online Flipped Learning, *Eurasıan. Journal Of Health Scıences*, 5(3), 84–89.

Ertmer, P. A. (2005). Teacher pedagogical beliefs: The final frontier in our quest for technology integration? *Educational Technology Research and Development*, 53(4), 25–39. 10.1007/BF02504683

Ertugrul, N. (2000). Towards virtual laboratories: A survey of LabVIEW-based teaching/learning tools and future trends. *International Journal of Engineering Education*, 16(3), 171–180. https://hdl.handle.net/2440/2418

Esfijani, A. (2018). Measuring quality in online education: A Meta-synthesis. *American Journal of Distance Education* 31.1 (57-73).

Estrella, F. (2023). The effectiveness of using digital platforms to practice English during the COVID-19 crisis as perceived by Ecuadorian students. *Journal of Applied Research in Higher Education*, 15(1), 66–82. 10.1108/JARHE-05-2021-0194

Evans, J. A. (2019). *Digital learning: Peril or promise for our K-12 students.* Project Tomorrow. https://files.eric.ed.gov/fulltext/ED605281.pdf

Fageeh, A.I., & Mekheimer, M.A. (2013). *Effects of Blackboard on EFL Academic Writing and Attitudes.*

Fairhurst, N., Koul, R., & Sheffield, R. (2025). Students' perceptions of their STEM learning environment. *Learning Environments Research*, 12, 1–22. 10.1007/s10984-023-09463-z37360385

Fairman, J. C., Smith, D. J., Pullen, P. C., & Lebel, S. J. (2023). The challenge of keeping teacher professional development relevant. *Professional Development in Education*, 49(2), 197–209. 10.1080/19415257.2020.1827010

Falade, A. A., Olafare, O. F., & Aladesusi, G. A. (2020). Biology teachers' self-efficacy in the use of Virtual Laboratory for instructional delivery in secondary schools. *Nigerian Online Journal of Educational Sciences and Technology*, 1(1), 54–65. 10.4314/nojest.v1i1.908

Fanteso, B., & Yessoufou, K. (2022). Diversity and determinants of traditional water conservation technologies in the Eastern Cape Province, South Africa. *Environmental Monitoring and Assessment*, 194(3), 161. 10.1007/s10661-022-09848-235137295

Felder, R. M., & Spurlin, J. E. (2005). Applications, Reliability and Validity of the Index of Learning Styles*. *International Journal of Engineering Education*, 21(1), 103–112.

Feng, J. (2020). Research on the main problems and countermeasures of Flipped Classroom in college teaching practice. *2020 International Conference on Computer Engineering and Application (ICCEA), IEEE Xplore*, (pp. 166–169). IEEE. 10.1109/ICCEA50009.2020.00043

Feng, Y., Zhao, B., Zheng, J., Fu, Y., & Jiang, Y. (2022). Online flipped classroom with team-based learning promoted learning activity in a clinical laboratory immunology class: Response to the COVID-19 pandemic. *BMC Medical Education*, 22(1), 836. 10.1186/s12909-022-03917-336463210

Fergusson, D. M., & Horwood, L. J. (1987). Vulnerability to life events exposure. *Psychological Medicine*, 17(3), 739749. 10.1017/S00332917000259763628634

Ferri, F., Grifoni, P., & Guzzo, T. (2020). Online learning and emergency remote teaching: Opportunities and challenges in emergency situations. *Societies (Basel, Switzerland)*, 10(4), 86. 10.3390/soc10040086

Fiester, L. (2013). Early Warning Confirmed: A Research Update on Third-Grade Reading. *The Annie E. Casey Foundation, Baltimore, Maryland.* file:///Users/srhoads/Downloads/AECF-EarlyWarningConfirmed-2013.pdf

Finlay, L. (2012). Debating phenomenological methods. In *Hermeneutic phenomenology in education* (pp. 15–37). Brill. 10.1007/978-94-6091-834-6_2

Flynn, S., Collins, J., & Malone, L. (2022). Pandemic pedagogies: The impact of ERT on part time learners in Ireland. *International Journal of Lifelong Education, 41*(2), 182. https://doi.org/10.1080/02601370.2021.2022792

Foley, K., & Marr, L. (2019). Scaffolding extracurricular online events to support distance learning university students. *Journal of Interactive Media in Education*, 2019(1), 1–9. https://jime.open.ac.uk/articles/10.5334/jime.525. 10.5334/jime.525

Foltos, L. (2013). *Peer coaching: Unlocking the power of collaboration.* Corwin Press. 10.4135/9781483300252

Foulger, T. S., Graziano, K. J., Schmidt-Crawford, D., & Slykhuis, D. A. (2017). Teacher educator technology competencies. *Journal of Technology and Teacher Education*, 25(4), 413–448.

Fraser, B. J. (2012). Classroom learning environments: Retrospect, context and prospect. In Fraser, B. J., Tobin, K., & McRobbie, C. (Eds.), *Second international handbook of science education* (pp. 1191–1239). Springer. 10.1007/978-1-4020-9041-7_79

Frechette, J., Bitzas, V., Aubry, M., Kilpatrick, K., & Lavoie-Tremblay, M. (2020). Capturing lived experience: Methodological considerations for interpretive phenomenological inquiry. *International Journal of Qualitative Methods*, 19, 1609406920907254. 10.1177/1609406920907254

Fredricks, J. A., Blumenfeld, P. C., & Paris, A. H. (2004). School Engagement: Potential of the Concept, State of the Evidence. *Review of Educational Research*, 74(1), 59–109. 10.3102/00346543074001059

Freeman, T., Anderman, L., & Jensen, J. (2007). Sense of belonging in college freshmen at the classroom and campus levels. *Journal of Experimental Education,75.*

Freeman, J., Zimmer, K., & Allen, J. (2021). Moving Forward: The Role of Instructional Coaching in Equity. *Journal of Staff Development*, 42(1), 28–35.

Freina, L., & Ott, M. (2015). A literature review on immersive virtual reality in education: state of the art and perspectives. In *The International Scientific Conference eLearning and Software for Education, 1*(133). 10-1007. 10.12753/2066-026X-15-020

Fuchs, K. (2022). Online learning and emergency remote teaching in higher education during COVID-19: Student perspectives. *International Journal of Information and Education Technology (IJIET)*, 12(9), 741–748. 10.18178/ijiet.2022.12.9.1704

Fullan, M., Hill, P., & Crévola, C. (2006). *Breakthrough.* Corwin Press.

Gamage, K. A., Wijesuriya, D. I., Ekanayake, S. Y., Rennie, A. E., Lambert, C. G., & Gunawardhana, N. (2020). Online delivery of teaching and laboratory practices: Continuity of university programmes during COVID-19 pandemic. *Education Sciences*, 10(10), 291. 10.3390/educsci10100291

Ganapathy, M. (2016). Transformation of Malaysia's higher education system: Malaysia Education Blueprint (2015-2025). *Bulletin of Higher Education Research*, 5(1), 10–11.

Ganesh, G. V., Harithpriya, K., Umapathy, D., Hoque, M. E., & Ramkumar, K. M. (2024). Laboratory Safety. In (Eds) Ramkumar, R. Senthilkumar, Md Enamul HoqueA, *dvanced Mammalian Cell Culture Techniques* (pp. 11-14). CRC Press. 10.1201/9781003397755

Garbe, A., Ogurlu, U., Logan, N., & Cook, P. (2020). COVID-19 and remote learning: Experiences of parents with children during the pandemic. *American Journal of Qualitative Research*, 4(3), 45–65. 10.29333/ajqr/8471

García-Morales, V. J., Garrido-Moreno, A., & Martín-Rojas, R. (2021). The transformation of higher education after the COVID disruption: Emerging challenges in an online learning scenario. *Frontiers in Psychology*, 12, 616059. 10.3389/fpsyg.2021.61605933643144

Garrison, D. R., & Anderson, T. (2011). *E-learning in the 21st Century: A framework for research and practice*. London: Routhledge/Falmer.

Garrison, D. R., Cleveland-Innes, M., & Fung, T. S. (2010). Exploring causal relationships among teaching, cognitive and social presence: Student perceptions of the community of inquiry framework. *The Internet and Higher Education*, 13(1–2), 31–36. 10.1016/j.iheduc.2009.10.002

Garvey Berger, J. (2020). Coaching for Equity: The Power of Culturally Responsive Coaching. *Phi Delta Kappan*, 102(4), 29–34.

Gaytan, J., & McEwen, B. (2007). Effective online instructional and assessment strategies. *American Journal of Distance Education*, 21(3), 117–132. 10.1080/08923640701341653

Gelles, L., Lord, S., Hoople, G., Chen, D. A., & Mejia, J. (2020). Compassionate flexibility and self-discipline: Student adaptation to emergency remote teaching in an integrated engineering energy course during COVID-19. *Education Sciences*, 10(11), 304. 10.3390/educsci10110304

George, M. J., & Kolobe, M. (2014). Exploration of the potential of using a Virtual Laboratory for chemistry teaching at secondary school level in Lesotho. *South African Journal of Chemistry. Suid-Afrikaanse Tydskrif vir Chemie*, 67(1), 113–117. https://hdl.handle.net/10520/EJC157769

Ghanbari, N., & Nowroozi, S. (2021). The practice of online assessment in an EFL context amidst COVID-19 pandemic: Views from teachers. *Language Testing in Asia*, 11(1), 1–18. 10.1186/s40468-021-00143-4

Ghobakhloo, M., Iranmanesh, M., Mubarak, M. F., Mubarik, M., Rejeb, A., & Nilashi, M. (2022). Identifying industry 5.0 contributions to sustainable development: A strategy roadmap for delivering sustainability values. *Sustainable Production and Consumption*, 33, 716–737. 10.1016/j.spc.2022.08.003

Ghommem, M., & Gunn, C. (2019). Toward better learning opportunities for undergraduate mechanical engineering students: A case study. *International Journal of Mechanical Engineering Education, 49*(3), 195–213. Sage Journals. 10.1177/0306419019858099

Gill, L., & Dalgarno, B. (2017). A qualitative analysis of pre-service primary school teachers' TPACK development over the four years of their teacher preparation programme. *Technology, Pedagogy and Education*, 26(4), 439–456. 10.1080/1475939X.2017.1287124

Gokhale, A. A. (1995). Collaborative learning enhances critical thinking. *Journal of Technology Education*, 7(1), 22–30. 10.21061/jte.v7i1.a.2

Gökmen, V., & Şenyuva, H. Z. (2006). Study of colour and acrylamide formation in coffee, wheat flour and potato chips during heating. *Food Chemistry*, 99(2), 238–243. 10.1016/j.foodchem.2005.06.054

Goldberg, S. B. (2021). *Education in a pandemic: The disparate impacts of COVID-19 on America's students*. Department of Education.

Gómez-Coma, L., Díaz-Sainz, G., Fallanza, M., Ortiz, A., & Ortiz, I. (2023). Integration of chemical engineering skills in the curriculum of a master course in industrial engineering. *Education for Chemical Engineers, 45*, 68–79. ScienceDirect. 10.1016/j.ece.2023.08.002

Gopika, J. S., & Rekha, R. V. (2023). Awareness and use of digital learning before and during COVID-19. *International Journal of Educational Reform*, 0(0). 10.1177/10567879231173389

Gordon, C., & Debus, R. (2002). Developing deep learning approaches and personal teaching efficacy within a preservice teacher education context. *The British Journal of Educational Psychology*, 72(4), 483–511. 10.1348/00070990260377488124955563

Gore, O., Twine, C., Botha, J., & Naidoo, S. (2023). Teachers' perceptions of the psycho-social effects of COVID-19 on learners' well-being in South African schools. *Perspectives in Education*, 41(4). 10.38140/pie.v41i4.7042

Gray, C., & Lewis, L. (2021, November 26). *Use of Educational Technology for Instruction in Public Schools: 2019–20*. U.S. Department of Education, NCES.

Greenhow, C., & Chapman, A. (2020). Social distancing meet social media: Digital tools for connecting students, teachers, and citizens in an emergency. *Information and Learning Science*, 121(5/6), 341–352. 10.1108/ILS-04-2020-0134

Grek, S., & Landri, P. (2021). Editorial: Education in Europe and the COVID-19 Pandemic. *European Educational Research Journal*, 20(4), 393–402. 10.1177/14749041211024781

Gresham, D., & Gullone, E. (2012). Emotion regulation strategy use in children and adolescents: The explanatory roles of personality and attachment. *Personality and Individual Differences*, 52(95), 116–621. 10.1016/j.paid.2011.12.016

Gublo, K. I. (2003). A laboratory safety trivia game. *Journal of Chemical Education*, 80(4), 425. 10.1021/ed080p425

Guerrero-Roldán, A.-E., Rodríguez-González, M. E., Bañeres, D., Elasri-Ejjaberi, A., & Cortadas, P. (2021). Experiences in the use of an adaptive intelligent system to enhance online learners' performance: A case study in Economics and Business courses. *International Journal of Educational Technology in Higher Education*, 18(1), 36. 10.1186/s41239-021-00271-0

Gündüz, A. Y., & Akkoyunlu, B. (2016). From transformed classroom to transformed learning. A. İşman, H. F. Odabaşı, & B. Akkoyunlu (Eds.), *Educational technology readings.*

Guppy, N., Verpoorten, D., Boud, D., Lin, L., Tai, J., & Bartolic, S. K. (2022). The post-COVID 19 future of digital learning in higher education: Views from educators, students, and other professionals in six countries. *British Journal of Educational Technology*, 6(53), 1750–1765. 10.1111/bjet.13212

Hair, J. F.Jr, Hult, G. T. M., Ringle, C. M., & Sarstedt, M. (2022). *A primer on partial least squares structural equation modeling (PLS-SEM)* (3rd ed.). SAGE.

Halasa, S., Abusalim, N., Rayyan, M., Constantino, R. E., Nassar, O., Amre, H., Sharab, M., & Qadri, I. (2020). Comparing student achievement in traditional learning with a combination of blended and flipped learning. *Nursing Open, 7*(4), 1129–1138. Wiley Online Library. 10.1002/nop2.492

Haleem, A., Javaid, M., Qadri, M., & Suman, R. (2022). Understanding the role of digital technologies in education: A review. *Sustainable Operations and Computers*, 3, 275–285. 10.1016/j.susoc.2022.05.004

Haling, A., Ilmi, S. N., & Astuty, A. D. (2024). Teaching Practice in a Shifting to Post-COVID 19 Era: A Study from Indonesian Higher Institution. *QWERTY-Interdisciplinary Journal of Technology, Culture and Education*, 1–11. 10.30557/QW000074

Hameed, S. & Macintyre, T. (2007). The effective use of multimedia tools in e-learning and computer aided learning environments within traditional university education. *International The Journal of Education (Knowledge),3*(1).

Han, J., Geng, X., & Wang, Q. (2021). Sustainable development of university EFL learners'engagement, satisfaction, and self-efficacy in online learning environments: Chinese experiences. *Sustainability (Basel)*, 13(21), 11655. 10.3390/su132111655

Hanson, A., & Danyluk, P. (2022). Talking circles as indigenous pedagogy in online learning. *Teaching and Teacher Education*, 115, 103715. 10.1016/j.tate.2022.103715

Hargreaves, A., & Fullan, M. (2012). *Professional capital: Transforming teaching in every school.* Teachers College Press.

Harris, L., Dargusch, J., Ames, K., & Bloomfield, C. (2020). Catering for 'very different kids': Distance education teachers' understandings of and strategies for student engagement. *International Journal of Inclusive Education*, 26(8), 848–864. 10.1080/13603116.2020.1735543

Harth, N. S., & Mitte, K. (2020). Managing multiple roles during the covid-19 lockdown: Not men or women, but parents as the emotional "loser in the crisis.". *Social Psychological Bulletin*, 15(4), 1–17. 10.32872/spb.4347

Harting, K., & Erthal, M. J. (2005). History of distance learning. *Information Technology, Learning and Performance Journal*, 23(1), 35.

Hayırsever, F., & Orhan, A. (2018). A Theoretical Analysis of Flipped Learning. *Mersin Üniversitesi Eğitim Fakültesi Dergisi*, 14(2), 572–596. 10.17860/mersinefd.431745

Henshaw, L. A. (2022). Building trauma-informed approaches in higher education. *Behavioral Sciences (Basel, Switzerland)*, 12(10), 368. 10.3390/bs1210036836285937

Herga Rizman, N., & Dinevski, D. (2012). Virtual Laboratory in chemistry–experimental study of understanding, reproduction and application of acquired knowledge of subject's chemical content. *Organizacija*, 45(3), 108–116. 10.2478/v10051-012-0011-7

Hernandez-de-Menendez, M., Escobar Díaz, C. A., & Morales-Menendez, R. (2020). Engineering education for smart 4.0 technology: a review. *International Journal on Interactive Design and Manufacturing (IJIDeM), 14*(3), 789–803. Springer Link. 10.1007/s12008-020-00672-x

Herreid, C. F., & Schiller, N. A. (2013). Case studies and the flipped classroom. *Journal of College Science Teaching*, 42, 62–66.

Hidalgo-Camacho, C., Escudero, G. I., Villacís, W., & Varela, K. (2021). The Effects of Online Learning on EFL Students' Academic Achievement during Coronavirus Disease Pandemic. *European Journal of Educational Research*, 10(4), 1867–1879. 10.12973/eu-jer.10.4.1867

Hill, D. J., Williams, O. F., Mizzy, D. P., Triumph, T. F., Brennan, C. R., Mason, D. C., & Lawrence, D. S. (2019). Introduction to laboratory safety for graduate students: An active-learning endeavor. *Journal of Chemical Education*, 96(4), 652–659. 10.1021/acs.jchemed.8b00774

Hindman, A., Morrison, F., Connor, C., & Connor, J. (2020). Bringing the Science of Reading to Preservice Elementary Teachers: Tools That Bridge Research and Practice. *International Literacy Association*. https://ila-onlinelibrary-wiley-com.libproxy.lib.ilstu.edu/doi/10.1002/rrq.34

Hlalele, D., & Mosia, M. (2020). Teachers' sense of community in rural learning ecologies. *Alternation (Durban)*, 27(2), 101–124. 10.29086/2519-5476/2020/v27n2a6

Hockly, N. (2018). Blended learning. *ELT Journal*, 72(1), 97–101. https://academic.oup.com/eltj/article-International Journal of Technology in Education (IJTE) abstract/72/1/97/4812363. 10.1093/elt/ccx058

Hodges, C. B., Moore, S., Lockee, B. B., Trust, T., & Bond, M. A. (2020). *The difference between emergency remote teaching and online learning*.

Hodges, C., Moore, S., Lockee, B., Trust, T., & Bond, A. (2020). The difference between emergency remote teaching and online learning. *EDUCAUSE Review*. https://er.educause.edu/articles/2020/3/the-difference-between-emergency remote-teaching-and-online-learning

Hodges, C. B. (2006). Skills necessary for learner success in an emporium-designed mathematics course. *Journal of Research in Education*, 16, 69–80.

Hodges, C. B. (2008). Self-efficacy, motivational email, and achievement in an asynchronous math course. *Journal of Computers in Mathematics and Science Teaching*, 27(3), 265–285.

Hodges, C. B., & Kim, C. (2010). Email, self-regulation, self-efficacy, and achievement in a college online mathematics course. *Journal of Educational Computing Research*, 43(2), 207–223. 10.2190/EC.43.2.d

Hoffman, J., & Miller, E. (2020). Addressing the consequences of school closure due to covid-19 on children's physical and mental well-being. *World Medical & Health Policy*, 12(3), 300–310. *Advance online publication*. 10.1002/wmh3.36532904951

Hofstein, A., & Hugerat, M. (2021). *Teaching and learning in the school chemistry laboratory*. Royal Society of Chemistry., 10.1039/9781839164712

Hofstein, A., Levy Nahum, T., & Shore, R. (2001). Assessment of the learning environment of ınquiry-type laboratories in high school chemistry. *Learning Environments Research*, 4(2), 193–207. 10.1023/A:1012467417645

Hofstein, A., & Lunetta, V. N. (2003). The laboratory in science education: Foundations for the twenty-first century. *Science Education*, 88(1), 28–54. 10.1002/sce.10106

Hoi, V. N. (2022). *Online Learning Environments and Student Engagement: Meeting the Psychological Needs of Learners during the COVID-19 Pandemic Global Perspectives on Educational Innovations for Emergency Situations*. Springer International Publishing Cham.

Hollandsworth, R., Dowdy, L., & Donovan, J. (2011). Digital citizenship in K-12: It takes a village. *TechTrends*, 55(4), 37–47. 10.1007/s11528-011-0510-z

Holliday, C. G. (2021). Culturally Relevant Coaching: Empowering New Teachers. *English in Texas*, 51(1), 33–41.

Holmberg, B. (1995). The evolution of the character and practice of distance education. *Open Learning*, 10(2), 47–53. 10.1080/0268051950100207

Holmberg, B. (1995). *Theory and practice of distance education*. Routledge.

Holmes, C., & Reid, C. (2017). A comparison study of on-campus and online learning outcomes for a research methods course. *The Journal of Counselor Preparation and Supervisor*, 9, 2. 10.7729/92.1182

Horakova, T., Houska, M., & Domeova, L. (2017). Classification of the educational texts styles with artificial intelligence methods. *Journal of Baltic Science Education*, 16(3), 324–336. 10.33225/jbse/17.16.324

Huang, A. Y. Q., Lu, O. H. T., & Yang, S. J. H. (2023). Effects of artificial Intelligence–Enabled personalized recommendations on learners' learning engagement, motivation, and outcomes in a flipped classroom. *Computers & Education, 194*, 104684. ScienceDirect. 10.1016/j.compedu.2022.104684

Hubackova, S. (2015). History and Perspectives of eLearning. *Procedia: Social and Behavioral Sciences*, 191, 1187–1190. 10.1016/j.sbspro.2015.04.594

Hughes, J., & Kwok, O. (2007). Influence of student-teacher and parent-teacher relationships on lower achieving readers' engagement and achievement in the primary grades. *Journal of Educational Psychology*, 99(1), 39–51. 10.1037/0022-0663.99.1.3918084625

Hughes, M. C., Henry, B. W., & Kushnick, M. R. (2020). Teaching during the pandemic? An opportunity to enhance curriculum. *Pedagogy in Health Promotion*, 6(4), 235–238. 10.1177/2373379920950179

Hug, T. (2007). *Didactics of microlearning*. Waxmann Publishing Company.

Hui, K. S., Khemanuwong, T., & Ismail, S. A. M. M. (2020). Keeping teachers afloat with instructional coaching: Coaching structure and implementation. *The Qualitative Report*, 25(7), 1790–1816.

Hunt, S. C., & Young, N. L. (2021). Blending Indigenous sharing circle and Western focus group methodologies for the study of Indigenous children's health: A systematic review. *International Journal of Qualitative Methods*, 20, 16094069211015112. 10.1177/16094069211015112

Hussein, E., Daoud, S., Alrabaiah, H., & Badawi, R. (2020). Exploring undergraduate students' attitudes towards emergency online learning during COVID-19: A case from the UAE. *Children and Youth Services Review*, 119, 105699. 10.1016/j.childyouth.2020.105699

Iglesías-Pradas, S., Hernández-García, Á., Chaparro-Peláez, J., & Prieto, J. (2021). Emergency remote teaching and students' academic performance in higher education during the COVID-19 pandemic: A case study. *Computers in Human Behavior*, 119, 106713. 10.1016/j.chb.2021.10671334866769

Imschloss, M., & Schwemmle, M. (2023). Value creation in post-pandemic retailing: A conceptual framework and implications. *Journal of Business Economics*, 1–39. 10.1007/s11573-023-01189-x

Ingersoll, R. M., & Strong, M. (2011). The impact of induction and mentoring programs for beginning teachers: A critical review of the research. *Review of Educational Research*, 81(2), 201–233. 10.3102/0034654311403323

Ionescu, C. A., Paschia, L., Nicolau, N. L. G., Stanescu, S. G., Stancescu, V. M. N., Coman, M. D., & Uzlau, M. C. (2020). Sustainability analysis of the e-learning education system during pandemic period—Covid-19 in Romania. *Sustainability (Basel)*, 12(21), 1–22. 10.3390/su12219030

Iqbal, S., & Ali, A. (2024). Education and professional development: Opportunities and challenges for in-service teachers: A Review. *Gomal University Journal of Research*, 40(1), 117–133. 10.51380/gujr-40-01-10

Irwin, V. (2021). *Students' internet access before and during the coronavirus pandemic by household socioeconomic status*. NCES.

İşman, A. (2008). *Uzaktan eğitim*. Pegem Akademi.

Ivcevic, Z., & Hoffmann, J. (2019). Emotions and creativity: From process to person and product. In Kaufman, J. C., & Sternberg, R. J. (Eds.), *The Cambridge handbook of creativity* (pp. 273–295). Cambridge University Press. 10.1017/9781316979839.015

Jackson, L. C., Jones, S. J., & Rodriguez, R. C. (2010). Faculty actions that result in student satisfaction in online courses. *Online Learning : the Official Journal of the Online Learning Consortium*, 14(4), 78–96. 10.24059/olj.v14i4.129

Jacques, S., Ouahabi, A., & Kanetaki, Z. (2023). Post-COVID-19 education for a sustainable future: Challenges, emerging technologies, and trends. *Sustainability (Basel)*, 15(8), 6487. 10.3390/su15086487

Jaiswal, P., & Al-Hattami, A. (2020). Enhancing learners' academic performances using student centered approaches. [iJET]. *International Journal of Emerging Technologies in Learning*, 15(16), 4–16. 10.3991/ijet.v15i16.14875

Jam, N. A. M., & Puteh, S. (2022). Exploring the Teaching and Learning Indicators towards Education 4.0 in MTUN, Malaysia. *International Journal of Information and Education Technology (IJIET)*, 12(2), 179–184. 10.18178/ijiet.2022.12.2.1602

Javed, F. (2023). *Transformative Learning Strategies for Successful Teaching and Learning in the Transforming Higher Education Active and Transformative Learning in STEAM Disciplines*. Emerald Publishing Limited.

Jeffery, M. (2019). *School Success After Trauma: Examining the Parallels Among Trauma, Bullying, and School Disengagement*. The University of Western Ontario.

Jili, N., Ede, C. I., & Masuku, M. (2021). Emergency remote teaching in higher education during Covid-19: Challenges and opportunities. *International Journal of Higher Education*, 10(5), 1. 10.5430/ijhe.v10n5p1

Jochems, W., Van Merrienboer, J., & Koper, R. (2004). Integrated e-learning. *Implications for pedagogy, technology & organization*. Londres.

Johnson, A. M., Jacovina, M. E., Russell, D. E., & Soto, C. M. (2016). Challenges and solutions when using technologies in the classroom. In Crossley, S. A., & McNamara, D. S. (2017). *Adaptive Educational Technologies for Literacy Instruction* (pp. 13 -29). Routledge. 10.4324/9781315647500-2

Johnson, D. W., & Johnson, R. T. (1999a). *What Makes Cooperative Learning Work*. Cooperative Learning.

Johnson, D. W., & Johnson, R. T. (1999b). Making cooperative learning work. *Theory into Practice*, 38(2), 67–73. 10.1080/00405849909543834

Johnson, K. R., Hewapathirana, G. I., & Bowen, M. M. (2019). Faculty development for online teaching. In Keengwe, J. (Ed.), *Handbook of Research on Virtual Training and Mentoring of Online Instructors* (pp. 40–55). IGI Global. 10.4018/978-1-5225-6322-8.ch003

Joiner, R., Iacovides, J., Owen, M., Gavin, C., Clibbery, S., Darling, J., & Drew, B. (2011). Digital games, gender and learning in engineering: Do females benefit as much as males? *Journal of Science Education and Technology*, 20(2), 178–185. 10.1007/s10956-010-9244-5

Joormann, J., & Gotlib, I. H. (2010). Emotion regulation in depression: Relation to cognitive inhibition. *Cognition and Emotion*, 24(2), 281–298. 10.1080/0269993090340794820300538

Jordan, P. J., Ashkanasy, N. M., & Hartel, C. E. J. (2002). Emotional intelligence as a moderator of emotional and behavioral reactions to job insecurity. *Academy of Management Review*, 27(3), 361–372. 10.2307/4134384

Journell, W. (2007). The inequities of the digital divide: Is e-learning a solution? *E-Learning and Digital Media*, 4(2), 138–149. 10.2304/elea.2007.4.2.138

Joyce, B., & Showers, B. (2021). *Student Achievement through Staff Development* (4th ed.). Association for Supervision and Curriculum Development.

Kafetsios, K., & Sideridis, G. D. (2006). Attachment, social support and well-being in young and older adults. *Journal of Health Psychology*, 11(6), 863–875. 10.1177/135910530606908417035259

Kahu, E. R. (2013). Framing student engagement in higher education. *Studies in Higher Education*, 38(5), 758–773. 10.1080/03075079.2011.598505

Kahu, E. R., Stephens, C., Leach, L., & Zepke, N. (2013). The engagement of mature distance students. *Higher Education Research & Development*, 32(5), 791–804. 10.1080/07294360.2013.777036

Kaisara, G., & Bwalya, K. (2023). Strategies for enhancing assessment information integrity in mobile learning. *Informatics (MDPI)*, 10(1), 29. 10.3390/informatics10010029

Kajiwara, M. (2015, August 12). *5 trends that could change the face of higher education* [Online forum post]. Higher Ed Live. http://higheredlive.com/5-trends-that-could-change-the-face-of-higher-education/

Kang'ethe, S. M. (2022). Unpacking South African Institutions of Higher Learning Efforts and Hurdles to Respond to COVID-19: Social Service Professionals' Lenses. *Perspectives on Global Development and Technology*, 21(1), 84–99. 10.1163/15691497-12341618

Kapici, H. O., Akcay, H., & Cakir, H. (2022). Investigating the effects of different levels of guidance in inquiry-based hands-on and virtual science laboratories. *International Journal of Science Education*, 44(2), 324–345. 10.1080/09500693.2022.2028926

Kapilan, N., Vidhya, P., & Gao, X.-Z. (2021). Virtual Laboratory: A Boon to the Mechanical Engineering Education During Covid-19 Pandemic. *Higher Education for the Future, 8*(1), 31-46. https://0-doi.org.wam.seals.ac.za/10.1177/2347631120970757

Kara, A. (2021). COVID-19 pandemic and possible trends into the future of higher education: a review. *Journal of Education and Educational Development, 8*(1), 09 26. 10.22555/joeed.v8i1.183

Karabulut-Ilgu, A., Jaramillo Cherrez, N., & Jahren, C. T. (2017). A systematic review of research on the flipped learning method in engineering education. *British Journal of Educational Technology*, 49(3), 398–411. 10.1111/bjet.12548

Karadeniz, A. (2018). *Açık ve uzaktan öğrenmede ders tasarımı*. Gece Kitaplığı.

Karakose, T. (2021). Emergency remote teaching due to COVID-19 pandemic and potential risks for socioeconomically disadvantaged students in higher education. *Educational Process: International Journal*, 10(3), 53–61. 10.22521/edupij.2021.103.4

Karataş, T. Ö., & Tuncer, H. (2020). Sustaining language skills development of pre-service EFL teachers despite the COVID-19 interruption: A case of emergency distance education. *Sustainability (Basel)*, 12(19), 8188. 10.3390/su12198188

Karlberg, M., & Bezzina, C. (2022). The professional development needs of beginning and experienced teachers in four municipalities in Sweden. *Professional Development in Education*, 48(4), 624–641. 10.1080/19415257.2020.1712451

Kaufman, J. A. (1978). Safety in the academic laboratory. *Journal of Chemical Education*, 55(9), A337. 10.1021/ed055pA337

Kaufmann, E., & Budescu, D. V. (2020). Do teachers consider advice? On the acceptance of computerized expert models. *Journal of Educational Measurement*, 57(2), 311–342. 10.1111/jedm.12251

Kaufmann, R., Sellnow, D. D., & Frisby, B. N. (2016). The development and validation of the online learning climate scale (OLCS). *Communication Education*, 65(3), 307–321. 10.1080/03634523.2015.1101778

Kaufmann, R., & Vallade, J. I. (2022). Exploring connections in the online learning environment: Student perceptions of rapport, climate, and loneliness. *Interactive Learning Environments*, 30(10), 1794–1808. 10.1080/10494820.2020.1749670

Kaysi, F., & Aydemir, E. (2023). Uzaktan eğitim süreçlerindeki etkileşim boyutlarının değerlendirilmesi. *Journal of Social Sciences*, 11(11), 778–790. 10.16990/SOBIDER.3442

Kear, K., Chetwynd, F., & Jefferis, H. (2014). Social presence in online learning communities: The role of personal profiles. *Research in Learning Technology*, 22, 1–15. 10.3402/rlt.v22.19710

Kearsley, G., & Shneiderman, B. (1998). Engagement theory: A framework for technology-based teaching and learning. *Educational Technology*, 38(5), 20–23.

Keaveney, S., Athanasopoulou, L., Siatras, V., Stavropoulos, P., Mourtzis, D., & Dowling, D. P. (2021). Development and Implementation of a Digital Manufacturing Demonstrator for Engineering Education. *Procedia CIRP, 104*, 1674–1679. ScienceDirect. Shttps://10.1016/j.procir.2021.11.282

Keegan, D. (1986). *The foundations of distance education.* Routledge.

Kelly, K. (2020). *Meaningful Remote Learning and Literacy Practices During COVID-19.* International Literacy Association. https://literacyworldwide.org/blog%2Fliteracy-now%2F2020%2F05%2F29%2Fmeaningful-remote-learning-and-literacy-practices-during-covid-19

Kelsey, K. D., & D'souza, A. (2004). Student motivation for learning at a distance: Does interaction matter. *Online Journal of Distance Learning Administration*, 7(2), 1–10.

Kennedy, D., & Duffy, T. (2004). Collaboration—A key principle in distance education. *Open Learning*, 19(2), 203–211. 10.1080/0268051042000224798

Kentnor, Hope E. (2015). Distance education and the evolution of online learning in the United States. *Curriculum and teaching dialogue, 17*(1), 21-34.

Kerimak Öner, M. N. (2020). Kimya Eğitiminde Laboratuvar Güvenliği Kültürünün Yerleştirilmesi (Embedding Laboratory Safety Culture in Chemistry Education). *İSG Akademik*, *2*(1), 15-25.

Khalid, M. N. M., & Quick, D. (2016). Teaching presence influencing online students' course satisfaction at institution of higher education. *International Education Studies*, 9(3), 62–70. 10.5539/ies.v9n3p62

Khalili, H. (2020). Online interprofessional education during and post the COVID-19 pandemic: A commentary. *Journal of Interprofessional Care*, 34(5), 687–692. 10.1080/13561820.2020.179242432674721

Khan, B. (2017). Massive open online course (MOOC) evaluation methods: An overview. *Educational Technology Research and Development*, 65(5), 263–1287.

Kilag, O. K., Miñoza, J., Comighud, E., Amontos, C., Damos, M., & Abendan, C. F. (2023). Empowering Teachers: Integrating Technology into Livelihood Education for a Digital Future. *Excellencia: International Multi-disciplinary Journal of Education (2994-9521), 1*(1), 30-41. https://multijournals.org/index.php/excellencia-imje/article/view/3

Kılınç, II. (2020). *Çevrimiçi Grup Tartışmalarının Öğrenenler Üzerindeki Etkisinin Çeşitli Değişkenler Açısından İncelenmesi: Anadolu Üniversitesi Açıköğretim Fakültesi Örneği* [Unpublished doctoral thesis, Anadolu Üniversitesi, Sosyal Bilimler Enstitüsü, Eskişehir].

Kılınç, H. (2022). Tartışma forumlarının açık ve uzaktan öğrenme ortamlarında kullanılabilirliği ve bir ölçme-değerlendirme kriteri olarak değerlendirilmesi. *Açıköğretim Uygulamaları ve Araştırmaları Dergisi*, 8(1), 1–31. 10.51948/auad.1028872

Kim, C., & Keller, J. M. (2008). Effects of motivational and volitional email messages (MVEM) with personal messages on undergraduate students' motivation, study habits and achievement. *British Journal of Educational Technology*, 39(1), 36–51. 10.1111/j.1467-8535.2007.00701.x

Kim, M. K., Kim, S. M., Khera, O., & Getman, J. (2014). The experience of three flipped classrooms in an urban university: An exploration of design principles. *The Internet and Higher Education*, 22, 37–50. 10.1016/j.iheduc.2014.04.003

Kimmons, R., & Casjurlu, S. (Eds.). (2020). *The Students' Guide to Learning Design and Research*. EdTech Books. 10.59668/10

Kitchenham, B. (2005). *Procedures for Performing Systematic Reviews*. Keele University.

Klusmann, B., Trippenzee, M., Fokkens-Bruinsma, M., Sanderman, R., & Schroevers, M. J. (2022). Providing emergency remote teaching: What are teachers' needs and what could have helped them to deal with the impact of the COVID-19 pandemic? *Teaching and Teacher Education*, 118, 103815. 10.1016/j.tate.2022.10381535874644

Knight, J. (2011a). *High-Impact Instruction: A Framework for Great Teaching.*

Knight, J. (2007). *Instructional coaching: A partnership approach to improving instruction.* Corwin Press.

Knight, J. (2011b). *Unmistakable impact: A partnership approach for dramatically improving instruction.* Corwin Press. 10.4135/9781452219721

Knight, J. (2019). Instructional coaching for implementing visible learning: A model for translating research into practice. *Education Sciences*, 9(2), 101. 10.3390/educsci9020101

Knight, J., & Cornett, J. (2009). The Impact of Coaching on Teacher Effectiveness: A District-wide Evaluation. *Educational Policy*, 23(4), 547–576.

Koehler, M. J., & Mishra, P. (2009). What is technological pedagogical content knowledge? *Contemporary Issues in Technology & Teacher Education*, 9(1), 60–70.

Koh, J. H. L., & Daniel, B. K. (2022). Shifting online during COVID-19: A systematic review of teaching and learning strategies and their outcomes. *International Journal of Educational Technology in Higher Education*, 19(56), 56. 10.1186/s41239-022-00361-736404984

Kohnke, L. (2021). Optimizing microlearning materials for mobile learning. In *Microlearning in the digital age* (pp. 80–94). Routledge. 10.4324/9780367821623-7

Kolade, O., & Owoseni, A. (2022). Employment 5.0: The work of the future and the future of work. *Technology in Society*, 71, 102086. 10.1016/j.techsoc.2022.102086

Kolil, V. K., & Achuthan, K. (2023). Longitudinal study of teacher acceptance of mobile virtual labs. *Education and Information Technologies*, 28(7), 7763–7796. https://0-doi.org.wam.seals.ac.za/10.1007/s10639-022-11499-2. 10.1007/s10639-022-11499-236532789

Koole, S. L. (2009). The psychology of emotion regulation: An integrative review. *Cognition and Emotion*, 23(1), 4–41. 10.1080/02699930802619031

Kossen, C., & Ooi, C. Y. (2021). Trialing micro-learning design to increase engagement in online courses. *Asian Association of Open Universities Journal*, 16(3), 299–310. 10.1108/AAOUJ-09-2021-0107

Kovacevic, I., Labrović, J., Petrović, N., & Kužet, I. (2021). Recognizing Predictors of Students' Emergency Remote Online Learning Satisfaction during COVID-19. *Education Sciences*, 11(11), 693. 10.3390/educsci11110693

Kožuh, I., Jeremić, Z., Sarjaš, A., Bele, J. L., Devedžić, V., & Debevc, M. (2015). Social presence and interaction in learning environments: The effect on student success. *Journal of Educational Technology & Society*, 18(1), 223–236.

Kraft, M. A., Blazar, D., & Hogan, D. (2018). The effect of teacher coaching on instruction and achievement: A meta-analysis of the causal evidence. *Review of Educational Research*, 88(4), 547–588. 10.3102/0034654318759268

Kraft, M. A., Simon, N. S., & Lyon, M. A. (2020). *Sustaining a Sense of Success: The Importance of Teacher Working Conditions during the COVID-19 Pandemic. EdWorking Paper No. 20-279.* Annenberg Institute for School Reform at Brown University.

Kreijns, K., Kirschner, P. A., & Jochems, W. (2003). Identifying the pitfalls for social interaction in computer-supported collaborative learning environments: A review of the research. *Computers in Human Behavior*, 19(3), 335–353. 10.1016/S0747-5632(02)00057-2

Kretlow, A. G., & Bartholomew, C. C. (2010). Using coaching to improve the fidelity of evidence-based practices: A review of studies. *Teacher Education and Special Education*, 33(4), 279–299. 10.1177/0888406410371643

Kuforiji, P., & Kuforiji, J. (2022). The transition from Covid-19 pandemic induced online learning to the future physical campus: is the higher education ready? In Salman Nazir (eds) *Training, Education, and Learning Sciences.* AHFE International, USA. 10.54941/ahfe1002380

Kuhfeld, M., Soland, J., Lewis, K., Ruzek, E., & Johnson, A. (2022). The COVID-19 school year: Learning and recovery across 2020-2021. *AERA Open*, 8, 23328584221099306. 10.1177/23328584221099306

Kumar, A., Krishnamurthi, R., Bhatia, S., Kaushik, K., Ahuja, N. J., Nayyar, A., & Masud, M. (2021). Blended learning tools and practices: A comprehensive analysis. *IEEE Access : Practical Innovations, Open Solutions*, 9, 85151–85197. 10.1109/ACCESS.2021.3085844

Kumar, K., & Thakur, G. S. M. (2012). Advanced applications of neural networks and artificial intelligence: A review. *International Journal of Information Technology and Computer Science*, 4(6), 57–68. 10.5815/ijitcs.2012.06.08

Kumasaki, M., Shoji, T., Wu, T.-C., Soontarapa, K., Arai, M., Mizutani, T., Okada, K., Shimizu, Y., & Sugano, Y. (2018). Presenting safety topics using a graphic novel, Manga, to effectively teach chemical safety to students in Japan, Taiwan, and Thailand. *Journal of Chemical Education*, 95(4), 584–592. 10.1021/acs.jchemed.7b00451

Kümmel, E., Moskaliuk, J., Cress, U., & Kimmerle, J. (2020). Digital learning environments in higher education: A literature review of the role of individual vs. social settings for measuring learning outcomes. *Education Sciences*, 10(3), 78. 10.3390/educsci10030078

Kurtz, G., Amichai-Hamburger, Y., & Kantor, J. (2009). Psychosocial well-being of Israeli students and attitudes toward open and distance learning. *International Review of Research in Open and Distance Learning*, 10(2), 1–11. 10.19173/irrodl.v10i2.593

Kurucay, M., & Inan, F. A. (2017). Examining the effects of learner-learner interactions on satisfaction and learning in an online undergraduate course. *Computers & Education*, 115, 20–37. 10.1016/j.compedu.2017.06.010

Kurz, A., Reddy, L. A., & Glover, T. A. (2017). A multidisciplinary framework of instructional coaching. *Theory into Practice*, 56(1), 66–77. 10.1080/00405841.2016.1260404

Kusuma, I. P. I. (2022). EFL teachers' online teaching in rural schools during the COVID-19 pandemic: Stories from Indonesia. *Studies in English Language and Education*, 9(1), 203–221. 10.24815/siele.v9i1.21239

Kutsyuruba, B., & Godden, L. (2019). The role of mentoring and coaching as a means of supporting the well-being of educators and students. *International Journal of Mentoring and Coaching in Education*, 8(4), 229–234. 10.1108/IJMCE-12-2019-081

Kyungmee, L., Mik, F., Brett, B., & Xuefei, S. L. (2022). Adoption of online teaching during the COVID-19 Pandemic: A systematic analysis of changes in university teaching activity. *Educational Review*, 74(3), 460–483. 10.1080/00131911.2021.1978401

LaFee, S. (2013, November). Flipped learning. *Education Digest*, 13–18.

Lage, M. J., Platt, G. J., & Treglia, M. (2000). Inverting the classroom: A gateway to creating an inclusive learning environment. *The Journal of Economic Education*, 31(1), 30–43. 10.1080/00220480009596759

Lake, R., & Makori, A. (2020). *The digital divide among students during COVID-19: Who has access? Who doesn't?* Langreo, L. (2022). What Teachers Really Think about Their Learning Management Systems. *Education Week.*

Langan, T. (1997). Online education: A student's perspective. *Campus-Wide Information Systems*, 14(4), 128–132. 10.1108/10650749710194565

Lan, M., & Hew, K. F. (2020). Examining learning engagement in MOOCs: A self-determination theoretical perspective using mixed method. *International Journal of Educational Technology in Higher Education*, 17(1), 7. 10.1186/s41239-020-0179-5

Lapitan, L. DS., Chan, A. L. A., Sabarillo, N. S., Sumalinog, D. A. G., & Diaz, J. M. S. (2023). Design, implementation, and evaluation of an online flipped classroom with collaborative learning model in an undergraduate chemical engineering course. *Education for Chemical Engineers, 43*, 58–72. ScienceDirect. 10.1016/j.ece.2023.01.007

Laufer, M., Leiser, A., Deacon, B., Perrin de Brichambaut, P., Fecher, B., Kobsda, C., & Hesse, F. (2021). Digital higher education: A divider or bridge builder? Leadership perspectives on edtech in a COVID-19 reality. *International Journal of Educational Technology in Higher Education*, 18(1), 51. 10.1186/s41239-021-00287-634778538

Lavallée, L. F. (2009). Practical application of an Indigenous research framework and two qualitative Indigenous research methods: Sharing circles and Anishnaabe symbol-based reflection. *International Journal of Qualitative Methods*, 8(1), 21–40. 10.1177/160940690900800103

Lawler, R. W., & Rushby, N. (2013). An interview with Robert Lawler. *British Journal of Educational Technology*, 44(1), 20–30. 10.1111/j.1467-8535.2012.01372.x

Law, M. Y. (2021). Transformative Learning: A Research Study on Emergency Remote Learning in Tertiary Education. *Creative Education*, 12(3), 494–528. 10.4236/ce.2021.123035

Leach, M. (2020). Effective professional development for teachers during the COVID-19 pandemic. *Journal of Technology and Teacher Education*, 28(2), 189–199.

Leal Filho, W., Salvia, A. L., Beynaghi, A., Fritzen, B., Ulisses, A., Ávila, L. V., Shulla, K., Vasconcelos, C. R. P., Moggi, S., Mifsud, M., Anholon, R., Rampasso, I. S., Kozlova, V., Iliško, D., Skouloudis, A., & Nikolaou, I. E. (2023). Digital transformation and sustainable development in higher education in a post-pandemic world. *International Journal of Sustainable Development and World Ecology, 31*(1), 108–123. Taylor & Francis Online. 10.1080/13504509.2023.2237933

Leal Filho, W., Price, E., Wall, T., Shiel, C., Azeiteiro, U. M., Mifsud, M., Brandli, L., Farinha, C. S., Caeiro, S., Salvia, A. L., Vasconcelos, C. R., de Sousa, L. O., Pace, P., Doni, F., Veiga Avila, L., Fritzen, B., & LeVasseur, T. J. (2021). COVID-19: The impact of a global crisis on sustainable development teaching. *Environment, Development and Sustainability*, 23(8), 11257–11278. 10.1007/s10668-020-01107-z33424430

Lederman, D. (2020, April 8). Survey gauges the state of the online education landscape pre-coronavirus. *Inside Higher Ed.* https://www.insidehighered.com/news/2020/03/25/survey-gauges-state-online education-landscape-pre-coronavirus

Lee, C. K., & Sidhu, M. S. (2016). The Potential of Technology Assisted Engineering Problem Solving Tool for Engineering Education. *Advanced Science Letters, 22*(10), 3092–3095. ingenta connect. 10.1166/asl.2016.7998

Lee, C. K., Sidhu, M. S., Lim, S. P., Hasan, Z., Lim, S. C., & Saw, S. H. (2020). A Preliminary Study on Student Learning Difficulties in Engineering Mechanics Dynamics. *2020 8th International Conference on Information Technology and Multimedia (ICIMU), IEEE Xplore*, (pp. 256–261). IEEE. 10.1109/ICIMU49871.2020.9243582

Lee, M. J., & Ko, A. J. (2015). Comparing the effectiveness of online learning approaches on CS1 learning outcomes.*Paper presented at the Proceedings of the eleventh annual international conference on international computing education research.* ACM. 10.1145/2787622.2787709

Lee, W.-K. Mat Isa, C. M., & Tahir, W. (2020). Civil Engineering Student Perception Towards Blended Learning in A Malaysian Public University. *2019 IEEE 11th International Conference on Engineering Education (ICEED), IEEE Xplore*. IEEE. 10.1109/ICEED47294.2019.8994945

Lee, C.-Y. (2015). Changes in self-efficacy and task value in online learning. *Distance Education*, 36(1), 59–79. 10.1080/01587919.2015.1019967

Lee, G., Kang, D. Y., Kim, M. J., Hong, H., & Martin, S. N. (2023). The emergence of remote laboratory courses in an emergency situation: University instructors' agency during the COVID-19 pandemic. *Cultural Studies of Science Education*, 18(3), 601–629. 10.1007/s11422-023-10169-037360052

Lee, Y. M., Jahnke, I., & Austin, L. (2021). Mobile microlearning design and effects on learning efficacy and learner experience. *Educational Technology Research and Development*, 69(2), 885–915. 10.1007/s11423-020-09931-w33584077

Lei, V., & Cheong, C. (2022). Emergency remote teaching and first-year student engagement during the COVID-19 pandemic: Emergency remote teaching and student engagement during COVID-19. *Proceedings of the 8th International Conference on Education and Training Technologies*, (pp. 60-65). IEEE. 10.1145/3535756.3535766

Lemay, D. J., Bazelais, P., & Doleck, T. (2021). Transition to online learning during the COVID-19 pandemic. *Computers in Human Behavior Reports*, 4, 100130. 10.1016/j.chbr.2021.10013034568640

Leng, J., Sha, W., Wang, B., Zheng, P., Zhuang, C., Liu, Q., Wuest, T., Mourtzis, D., & Wang, L. (2022). Industry 5.0: Prospect and retrospect. *Journal of Manufacturing Systems*, 65, 279–295. 10.1016/j.jmsy.2022.09.017

Levine-Sauberman, M. H. (2015). *A case study of faculty development in a community college's teaching and learning center*. Northeastern University.

Lewin, C., & Luckin, R. (2010). Technology to support parental engagement: Lessons learned and future directions. *Computers & Education*, 54(3), 749–758. 10.1016/j.compedu.2009.08.010

Lewis, K. O., Popov, V., & Fatima, S. S. (2024). From static web to metaverse: Reinventing medical education in the post-pandemic era. *Annals of Medicine*, 56(1), 2305694. 10.1080/07853890.2024.230569438261592

Liberman, M. (2021, April 20). Most students now have home internet access. But what about the ones who don't? [blog post]. *Education Week*.

Li, D. (2022). *The Shift to Online Classes During the Covid-19 Pandemic: Benefits, Challenges, and Required Improvements from the Students' Perspective*. The Electronic Journal of e-Learning Volume.

Li, J., Yang, S., Chen, C., & Li, H. (2022). The Impacts of COVID-19 on distance education with the application of traditional and digital appliances: Evidence from 60 developing countries. *International Journal of Environmental Research and Public Health*, 19(11), 6384. 10.3390/ijerph1911638435681971

Li, N., & Kirkup, G. (2007). Gender and cultural differences in internet use: A study of China and the UK. *Computers & Education*, 48(2), 301–317. 10.1016/j.compedu.2005.01.007

Linnes, C., Ronzoni, G., Agrusa, J., & Lema, J. (2022). Emergency Remote Education and Its Impact on Higher Education: A Temporary or Permanent Shift in Instruction? *Education Sciences*, 12(10), 721. 10.3390/educsci12100721

Liu, H. L., Wang, T. H., Lin, H. C. K., Lai, C. F., & Huang, Y. M. (2022). The influence of affective feedback adaptive learning system on learning engagement and self-directed learning. *Frontiers in Psychology*, 13, 858411. 10.3389/fpsyg.2022.85841135572271

Liu, S. (2008). Student interaction experience in distance learning courses: A phenomenological study. *Online Journal of Distance Learning Administration*, 11(1). https://www.westga.edu/~distance/ojdla/spring111/Liu111.html

Liu, S., Yao, J., & Hu, J. (2020). Professional learning communities (PLCs) in coaching: A framework to develop collective teacher efficacy and shared instructional practice. *Teaching and Teacher Education*, 90, 103002.

Li, Y., & Zhao, M. (2024). The study on the influence factors of intention to continue using MOOCs: Integrating UTAUT model and social presence. *Interactive Learning Environments*, •••, 1–19. 10.1080/10494820.2024.2318562

Llopis, G. (2020, October 17). Post pandemic: How must colleges and universities reinvent themselves? *Forbes*.https://www.forbes.com/sites/glennllopis/2020/10/17/post-pandemic-how-must-colleges-and-universities-reinvent-themselves/?sh=14f0a3413e88

Lobos, K., Cobo-Rendón, R., García-Álvarez, D., Maldonado-Mahauad, J., & Bruna, C. (2023). Lessons learned from the educational experience during COVID-19 from the perspective of Latin American university students. *Sustainability (Basel)*, 15(3), 2341. 10.3390/su15032341

Lo, C. K., & Hew, K. F. (2017). Using "First Principles of Instruction" to Design Secondary School Mathematics Flipped Classroom: The Findings of Two Exploratory Studies. *Journal of Educational Technology & Society*, 20(1), 222–236.

Lockee, B. B. (2021). Online education in the post-COVID era. *Nature Electronics*, 4(1), 5–6. 10.1038/s41928-020-00534-0

Lofthouse, R. (2019). Coaching in education: A professional development process in formation. *Professional Development in Education*, 45(1), 33–45. 10.1080/19415257.2018.1529611

Lohr, N., Stadler, M., Schultz-Pernice, F., Chernikova, O., Sailer, M., Fischer, F., & Sailer, M. (2021). On powerpointers, clickerers, and digital pros: Investigating the initiation of digital learning activities by teachers in higher education. *Computers in Human Behavior*, 119, 106715. 10.1016/j.chb.2021.106715

Low, M. C., Lee, C. K., Sidhu, M. S., Lim, S. P., Hasan, Z., & Lim, S. C. (2023). Blended learning for engineering education 4.0: Students' perceptions and their learning difficulties. *Computer Applications in Engineering Education, 31*(6), 1705–1722. Wiley Online Library. 10.1002/cae.22668

Low, M. C., Lee, C. K., Sidhu, M. S., Lim, S. P., Hasan, Z., & Lim, S. C. (2021). Blended Learning to Enhanced Engineering Education using Flipped Classroom Approach: An Overview. *Electronic Journal of Computer Science and Information Technology*, 7(1), 9–19. 10.52650/ejcsit.v7i1.111

Lowry, G. G. (1978). A university-level course in laboratory safety. *Journal of Chemical Education*, 55(6), A263. 10.1021/ed055pA263

Macgilchrist, F. (2019). Cruel optimism in edtech: When the digital data practices of educational technology providers inadvertently hinder educational equity. *Learning, Media and Technology*, 44(1), 77–86. 10.1080/17439884.2018.1556217

Mackness, J., Mak, S., & Williams, R. (2010). The ideals and reality of participating in a MOOC. In *Proceedings of the 7th international conference on networked learning 2010*. University of Lancaster.

Madakam, S., Ramaswamy, R., & Tripathi, S. (2015). Internet of things (IoT): A literature review. *Journal of Computer and Communications*, 3(5), 164–173. 10.4236/jcc.2015.35021

Madill, R. A., Gest, S. D., & Rodkin, P. C. (2014). Students' perceptions of relatedness in the classroom: The roles of emotionally supportive teacher-child interactions, children's aggressive-disruptive behaviors, and peer social preference. *School Psychology Review*, 43(1), 86–105. 10.1080/02796015.2014.12087456

Madison-Harris, R. D., Muoneke, A., & Times, C. (2012). *Using formative assessment to improve student achievement in the core content areas*. Briefing Paper.

Maguraushe, K., Masimba, F., & Muderedzwa, M. (2022). Shrinking the digital divide in online learning beyond the COVID-19 pandemic: A systematic literature review. *1st Zimbabwe Conference of Information and Communication Technologies (ZCICT)*, Harare, Zimbabwe. 10.1109/ZCICT55726.2022.10046024

Mahyoob, M. (2020). Challenges of e-Learning during the COVID-19 Pandemic Experienced by EFL Learners. *Arab World English Journal (AWEJ), 11*(4).

Mahyoob, M. (2021). Online Learning Effectiveness During the COVID-19 Pandemic: A Case Study of Saudi Universities. [IJICTE]. *International Journal of Information and Communication Technology Education*, 17(4), 1–14. 10.4018/IJICTE.20211001.oa7

Mahyoob, M., Algaraady, J., & Alblwi, A. (2023). A Proposed Framework for Human-like Language Processing of ChatGPT in Academic Writing. [iJET]. *International Journal of Emerging Technologies in Learning*, 18(14), 282–293. 10.3991/ijet.v18i14.41725

Main, P. (2022). *Instructional coaching: A teacher's guide*. Structural Learning. https://www.structural-learning.com/post/instructional-coaching-a-teachers-guide

Maja, M. M. (2023). Teachers' perceptions of integrating technology in rural primary schools to enhance the teaching of English first additional language. *Journal of Curriculum Studies Research*, 5(1), 95–112. 10.46303/jcsr.2023.8

Makransky, G., Mayer, R., Veitch, N., Hood, M., Christensen, K., & Gadegaard, H. (2019). Equivalence of using a desktop virtual reality science simulation at home and in class. *PLoS One*, 14(4), e0214944. Advance online publication. 10.1371/journal.pone.021494430973900

Makumane, M., Mataka, T. W., Sengai, W., & Ngcobo, S. (2023). Neutralising the digital divide: Is blended learning a viable solution? *International Journal of Research in Business and Social Science*, 12(1), 1–10. 10.20525/ijrbs.v12i7.2740

Mak, W. W., Law, R. W., Woo, J., Cheung, F. M., & Lee, D. (2009). Social support and psychological adjustment to SARS: The mediating role of self-care self-efficacy. *Psychology & Health*, 24(2), 161–174. 10.1080/0887044070144764920186649

Malaysia Digital Chamber of Commerce. (2023, July 5). *MyIX reports record surge In Malaysian internet bandwidth demand | MDCC*. Malaysia Digital Chamber of Commerce. https://mdcc.org.my/myix-reports-record-surge-in-malaysian-internet-bandwidth-demand/

Maldonado, K., & Maldonado, L. (2022). Emergency remote teaching and the medical student. *Technium Social Sciences Journal*, 36, 157–162. 10.47577/tssj.v36i1.7424

Malterud, K., Siersma, V. D., & Guassora, A. D. (2016). Sample size in qualitative interview studies: Guided by information power. *Qualitative Health Research*, 26(13), 1753–1760. 10.1177/104973231561744426613970

Mandal, N. (2017). Student satisfaction – What it means to teaching and learning of undergraduate engineering units. *International Journal of Mechanical Engineering Education, 46*(3), 210–226. Sage Journals. 10.1177/0306419017741996

Manzoor, M., & Vimarlund, V. (2018). Digital technologies for the social inclusion of individuals with disabilities. *Health and Technology*, 8(5), 377–390. 10.1007/s12553-018-0239-130416930

Mao, Z., Qin, T., Fan, L., Li, N., & Wang, Y. (2023). Factors associated with psychological distress among college students under COVID-19 pandemic: The moderating role of coping styles and social support. *Current Psychology (New Brunswick, N.J.)*, •••, 1–16.36713621

Mapisa, B. Z., & Makena, B. (2024). The Impact of ICT Adoption in Enhancing Teaching and Learning in Primary Schools of Amathole East District, Eastern Cape. *Research in Social Sciences and Technology*, 9(1), 213–231. 10.46303/ressat.2024.12

Mare, A., Woyo, E., & Amadhila, E. M. (2022). Harnessing the technological dividends in African higher education institutions during and post-COVID-19 pandemic. In *teaching and learning with digital technologies in higher education institutions in Africa* (pp. 1-24). Routledge. 10.4324/9781003264026-1

Margaryan, A., Bianco, M., & Littlejohn, A. (2015). Instructional quality of Massive Open Online Courses (MOOCs). *Computers & Education*, 80, 77–83. 10.1016/j.compedu.2014.08.005

Mariette, B. (2016). How to plan and perform a qualitative study using content analysis. *NursingPlus Open*, 2, 8–16. 10.1016/j.npls.2016.01.001

Mark Anthony, C., & Adriana Caterina, C. (2022). Remote learning via video conferencing technologies: Implications for research and practice. *Technology in Society*, 68, 101881. 10.1016/j.techsoc.2022.10188135034998

Márquez, J., Mejías, A., & Marquez, M. (2011). Augmented reality for the improvement of remote laboratories: An augmented remote laboratory. *IEEE Transactions on Education*, 54(3), 492–500. 10.1109/TE.2010.2085047

Martin, F. & Bolliger, D. (2018). Engagement matters: Student perceptions on the importance of engagement strategies in the online learning environment. *Online Learning Journal.*

Martin, F., Hunt, B., Wang, C., & Brooks, E. (2020). Middle school student perception of technology use and digital citizenship practices. *Computers in the Schools*, 37(3), 196–215. 10.1080/07380569.2020.1795500

Martin, F., Sun, T., & Westine, C. D. (2020). A systematic review of research on online teaching and learning from 2009 to 2018. *Computers & Education*, 159, 104009. 10.1016/j.compedu.2020.10400932921895

Martin, F., Wang, C., & Sadaf, A. (2018). Student perception of helpfulness of facilitation strategies that enhance instructor presence, connectedness, engagement and learning in online courses. *The Internet and Higher Education*, 37, 52–65. 10.1016/j.iheduc.2018.01.003

Maryville University. (2021). *How blockchain is used in education.* Maryville University. https://online.maryville.edu/blog/blockchain-in-education/

Masalimova, A. R., Ryazanova, E. L., Tararina, L. I., Sokolova, E. G., Ikrennikova, Y. B., Efimushkina, S. V., & Shulga, T. I. (2021). Distance Learning Hybrid Format for University Students in Post-Pandemic Perspective: Collaborative Technologies Aspect. *Cypriot Journal of Educational Sciences*, 16(1), 389–395. 10.18844/cjes.v16i1.5536

Masonbrink, A., & Hurley, E. (2020). Advocating for Children During the COVID-19 School Closures. P*ediatrics - Official Journal of the American Academy of Pediatrics.* https://pediatrics.aappublications.org/content/146/3/e20201440

Mason, G. S., Shuman, T. R., & Cook, K. E. (2013). Comparing the Effectiveness of an Inverted Classroom to a Traditional Classroom in an Upper-Division Engineering Course. *IEEE Transactions on Education*, 56(4), 430–435. 10.1109/TE.2013.2249066

Masry-Herzallah, A. (2023). Factors promoting and inhibiting teachers' perception of success in online teaching during the Covid-19 crisis. *Technology. Knowledge and Learning*, 28(4), 1635–1659. 10.1007/s10758-023-09690-6

Masuda, A., Anderson, P. L., Wendell, J. W., Chou, Y.-Y., Price, M., & Feinstein, A. B. (2011). Psychological flexibility mediates the relations between self-concealment and negative psychological outcomes. *Personality and Individual Differences*, 50(2), 243–247. 10.1016/j.paid.2010.09.037

Matete, R. E., Kimario, A. E., & Behera, N. P. (2023). Review on the use of eLearning in teacher education during the coronavirus disease (COVID-19) pandemic in Africa. *Heliyon*, 9(2), e13308. 10.1016/j.heliyon.2023.e1330836743851

Mathrani, A., Sarvesh, T., & Umer, R. (2021). Digital divide framework: Online learning in developing countries during the COVID-19 lockdown. *Globalisation, Societies and Education*, 19(4), 513–528. 10.1080/14767724.2021.1981253

Ma, X., Jiang, M., & Nong, L. (2023). The effect of teacher support on Chinese university students' sustainable online learning engagement and online academic persistence in the post-epidemic era. *Frontiers in Psychology*, 14, 14. 10.3389/fpsyg.2023.107655236794084

May, D., Morkos, B., Jackson, A., Hunsu, N. J., Ingalls, A., & Beyette, F. (2022). Rapid transition of traditionally hands-on labs to online instruction in engineering courses. *European Journal of Engineering Education*, 48(5), 842–860. 10.1080/03043797.2022.2046707

Mayer, R. E. (2002). Multimedia learning. In *Psychology of learning and motivation* (Vol. 41, pp. 85–139). Academic Press. 10.1016/S0079-7421(02)80005-6

Mayring, P. (2000). *Qualitative content analysis*. Forum qualitative sozialforschung/forum: qualitative social research.

Mazana, M. Y. (2018). Social media in the classroom: WhatsApp a new communication tool for enhanced class interactions. *Business Education Journal, 4*(1).

McClain, C., Vogels, E., Perrin. A., Sechopoulos, S., & Rainie, Lee (2021, September 1). *The internet and the pandemic*. Pew Research Center: Internet & Technology.

McLaughlin, C. (2016). *The homework gap: The 'cruelest part of the digital divide'*. NEA Today. https://www.nea.org/nea-today/all-news-articles/homework-gap-cruelest-part-digital-divide

Mdoda, L., & Mdiya, L. (2022). Factors affecting the using information and communication technologies (ICTs) by livestock farmers in the Eastern Cape province. *Cogent Social Sciences*, 8(1), 2026017. 10.1080/23311886.2022.2026017

Meajel, T. M., & Sharadgah, T. A. (2018). Barriers to Using the Blackboard System in Teaching and Learning: Faculty Perceptions. *Technology. Knowledge and Learning*, 23(2), 351–366. 10.1007/s10758-017-9323-2

Means, B., Toyama, Y., Murphy, R., & Bakia, M. (2013). The effectiveness of online and blended learning: A meta-analysis of the empirical literature. *Teachers College Record*, 115(3), 3. 10.1177/016146811311500307

Mehall, S. (2020). Purposeful interpersonal interaction in online learning: What is it and how is it measured? *Online Learning : the Official Journal of the Online Learning Consortium*, 24(1), 182–204. 10.24059/olj.v24i1.2002

Mehrabian, A. (1969). Significance of posture and position in the communication of attitude and status relationships. *Psychological Bulletin*, 71(5), 359–372. 10.1037/h00273494892572

Mei Yuan, L. (2021). Student's attitude and satisfaction towards transformative learning: A research study on emergency remote learning in tertiary Education. *Creative Education*, 12(1), 494–528.

Meinck, S., Fraillon, J., & Strietholt, R. (2022). *The Impact of the COVID-19 Pandemic on Education: International Evidence from the Responses to Educational Disruption Survey (REDS)*. International Association for the Evaluation of Educational Achievement.

Merriam, S. B. (2002). Introduction to qualitative research. *Qualitative research in practice: Examples for discussion and analysis, 1*(1), 1-17.

Meyen, E. L., Lian, C. H., & Tangen, P. (1997). Teaching online courses. *Focus on Autism and Other Developmental Disabilities*, 12(3), 166–174. 10.1177/108835769701200305

Michelson, R., DeWitt, A., Nagar, R., Hiniker, A., Yip, J., Munson, S. A., & Kientz, J. A. (2021). Parenting in a pandemic: juggling multiple roles and managing technology use in family life during COVID-19 in the United States. *Proceedings of the ACM on Human-Computer Interaction, 5*(CSCW2), (pp. 1-39). ACM. 10.1145/3479546

Miguel, C., Castro, L., Marques dos Santos, J. P., Serrão, C., & Duarte, I. (2021). Impact of COVID-19 on medicine lecturers' mental health and emergency remote teaching challenges. *International Journal of Environmental Research and Public Health*, 18(13), 6792. 10.3390/ijerph1813679234202692

Miles, B. M., & Huberman, A. M. (1994). *Qualitative data analysis: An expanded source book*. Sage Publications.

Mills, J., & Smith, A. (2021). The use of instructional coaching and feedback to improve teacher effectiveness. *Improving Schools*, 24(2), 119–133.

Ministry of Education, Malaysia. (. (2013). Malaysia Education Blueprint 2013 - 2025. *Education*, 27(1), 1–268. 10.1016/j.tate.2010.08.007

Miranda, J., Navarrete, C., Noguez, J., Molina-Espinosa, J.-M., Ramírez-Montoya, M.-S., Navarro-Tuch, S. A., Bustamante-Bello, M.-R., Rosas-Fernández, J.-B., & Molina, A. (2021). The core components of education 4.0 in higher education: Three case studies in engineering education. *Computers & Electrical Engineering, 93*, 107278. ScienceDirect. 10.1016/j.compeleceng.2021.107278

Mirriahi, N., Alonzo, D., McIntyre, S., Kligyte, G., & Fox, B. (2015). Blended learning innovations: Leadership and change in one Australian institution. *International Journal of Education and Development Using Information and Communication Technology*, 11(1), 4–16.

Misaghi, M., Tonioti, E., Batiz, E. C., & Dos Santos, A. J. (2021). WhatsApp as a tool for ıntegration and motivation in distance education. *Social Networking*, 10(3), 29–43. 10.4236/sn.2021.103003

Mishra L, Gupta T, & Shree A. (2020). Online teaching-learning in higher education during lockdown period of COVID-19 pandemic. *International Journal of Educational Research*, 1: 100012. 10.1016/j.ijedro.2020.100012

Mishra, L., & Gupta, T. (2021). Artificial Intelligence in Education: Challenges and Opportunities. *International Journal of Emerging Technologies in Learning*, 16(2), 64–78.

Mishra, P., & Koehler, M. J. (2006). Technological pedagogical content knowledge: A framework for teacher knowledge. *Teachers College Record*, 108(6), 1017–1054. 10.1111/j.1467-9620.2006.00684.x

Mishra, S., Sahoo, S., & Pandey, S. (2021). Research trends in online distance learning during the COVID-19 pandemic. *Distance Education*, 42(4), 494–519. 10.1080/01587919.2021.1986373

Misirli, O., & Ergulec, F. (2021). Emergency remote teaching during the COVID-19 pandemic: Parents experiences and perspectives. *Education and Information Technologies*, 26(6), 6699–6718. 10.1007/s10639-021-10520-433814956

Mmakola, S., & Maphalala, M. C. (2023). Blended teaching and learning in south african secondary schools in the post-covid-19 pandemic era. *International Journal of Innovative Technologies in Social Science*, 4(40). 10.31435/rsglobal_ijitss/30122023/8081

Mohammad Ayasrah, F. T., Alarabi, K., Abdel Fattah, H. A., & Al-Said, K. (2024). Enhancing secondary school students' attitudes toward physics by using computer simulations. *International Journal of Data & Network Science*, 8(1), 369–380. 10.5267/j.ijdns.2023.9.017

Mohan, R., Manvender Kaur, S. S., Arumugam, R., Hisham, D., & Yahya, D. (2021). Covid-19 catastrophe: Internet based learning and safety among foundation students of Universiti Utara Malaysia. *Journal of Language and Linguistic Studies*, 17(4), 2142–2153. 10.52462/jlls.155

Mohd Said, S., Chow, C.-O., Mokhtar, N., Ramli, R., Tuan Ya, T. M. Y. S., & Mohd Sabri, M. F. (2011). Accreditation of engineering programs: an evaluation of current practices in Malaysia. *International Journal of Technology and Design Education, 23*(2), 313–328. Springer Link. 10.1007/s10798-011-9180-6

Mojica, E. E., & Upmacis, R. K. (2021). Challenges encountered and students' reactions to practices utilized in a general chemistry laboratory course during the COVID-19 pandemic. *Journal of Chemical Education*, 99(2), 1053–1059. 10.1021/acs.jchemed.1c00838

Molnar, A. (2017). *Virtual schools in the U.S. University of Colorado*. National Education Policy Center.

Monyai, R. B. (2024). Exploring the Role of Technology in Enhancing Adult Education and Skills Development in Urban Areas of South Africa. In *Adjunct Faculty in Online Higher Education: Best Practices for Teaching Adult Learners* (pp. 105-131). IGI Global. 10.4018/978-1-6684-9855-2.ch006

Moore, M. G. (1989). Editorial: Three types of interaction. *The American Journal of Distance Learning*, 3(2), 1–7.

Moore, M. G. (1989). Three types of interaction. *American Journal of Distance Education*, 3(2), 1–6. 10.1080/08923648909526659

Moore, S., & Hodges, C. B. (2023). *Emergency Remote Teaching*. EdTechnica., 10.59668/371.11681

Morris, N., Ivancheva, M., Coop, T., Mogliacci, R., & Swinnerton, B. (2020). Negotiating growth of online education in higher education. *International Journal of Educational Technology in Higher Education*, 17(48), 48. 10.1186/s41239-020-00227-w

Mospan, N. (2022). Trends in emergency higher education digital transformation during the COVID-19 pandemic. *Journal of University Teaching and Learning Practice, 20*(1). 10.53761/1.20.01.04

Mossberger, K., Tolbert, C. J., & Stansbury, M. (2003). *Virtual inequality: Beyond the digital divide*. Georgetown University Press.

Mpungose, C. B. (2020). Emergent transition from face-to-face to online learning in a South African University in the context of the Coronavirus pandemic. *Humanities & Social Sciences Communications*, 7(1), 1–9. 10.1057/s41599-020-00603-x

Mritunjay, K., Sreedhar, P., Akhilesh, T., Narayanan, R., & Nitin, B. (2017). *Online Education in India 2021, A Market Analysis of Online Education*. KGMPG International.

Mtsi, N., & Maphosa, C. (2016). Challenges encountered in the teaching and learning of the natural sciences in rural schools in South Africa. *Journal of Social Sciences*, 47(1), 58–67. 10.1080/09718923.2016.11893544

Muhuro, P., Kangethe, S. M., & Muhuro, P. (2021). Prospects and pitfalls associated with implementing blended learning in rural-based higher education institutions in Southern Africa. *Perspectives in Education*, 39(1), 427–441. 10.18820/2519593X/pie.v39.i1.26

Muirhead, B. (2000). Enhancing social interaction in computer-mediated distance education. *Journal of Educational Technology & Society*, 3(4), 1–11.

Muniandy, T., & Abdullah, N. (2023). A comprehensive review: An innovative pedagogy for future education. [IJOPCD]. *International Journal of Online Pedagogy and Course Design*, 13(1), 1–15. 10.4018/IJOPCD.315816

Munir, H. (2022). Reshaping Sustainable University Education in Post-Pandemic World: Lessons Learned from an Empirical Study. *Education Sciences*, 12(8), 524. 10.3390/educsci12080524

Muniroh, H., Siti Balqis, M., Ch'ng, P.E. (2020). Adaptasi pengajaran dan pembelajaran secara maya dalam kebiasaan baharu semasa pandemik COVID-19. *SIG: e-Learning@CS*, 23-30.

Mupinga, D. M. (2005). Distance education in high schools: Benefits, challenges, and suggestions. *The Clearing House: A Journal of Educational Strategies, Issues and Ideas*, 78(3), 105–109. 10.3200/TCHS.78.3.105-109

Murray, M. C., Pérez, J., Geist, D., & Hedrick, A. (2012). Student interaction with online course content: Build it, and they might come. *Journal of Information Technology Education: Research, 11*(1), 125-140. Informing Science Institute. https://www.learntechlib.org/p/111496/

Myers, S., & Washburn, J. (2022). Increasing teacher access to instructional coaching through virtual tools: Advantageous before, during, and after the pandemic. *Journal of Technology and Teacher Education*, 30(3), 377–405.

Nagel, D. (2009). *Meta-analysis: Is blended learning most effective?* The Journal.

Nagel, M. C. (1982). An innovative course in lab safety. *Journal of Chemical Education*, 59(9), 791. 10.1021/ed059p791

Najab, A., & Amrani, O. (2022). Digital accessibility and distance higher education in the context of COVID-19: lessons from the experience of FSJES-Souissi and future perspectives. In Haoucha, M. (Ed.), *Policies and Procedures for the Implementation of Safe and Healthy Educational Environments: Post-COVID-19 Perspectives* (pp. 88–105). IGI Global. 10.4018/978-1-7998-9297-7.ch006

Nasir, M. K. N., Mansor, A. Z., & Rahman, M. J. A. (2018). Measuring Malaysian online university student social presence in online course offered. *Journal of Advanced Research in Dynamical and Control Systems*, 10(12), 1442–1446.

National Academies of Sciences, Engineering, and Medicine (NASEM). (2019). *Monitoring Educational Equity*. Washington, DC: The National Academies Press.

National Center for Education Statistics (NCES). (2021). *Summary report: Students' internet access before and during the coronavirus pandemic by household socioeconomic status*. U.S. Department of Education.

National Center for Education Statistics (NCES). (2022a). *Impact of the coronavirus pandemic on the elementary and secondary education system. Condition of Education*. U.S. Department of Education, Institute of Education Sciences.

National Center for Education Statistics (NCES). (2022b). *Impact of the coronavirus (COVID-19) pandemic on public and private elementary and secondary education in the United States (Preliminary Data). Results from the 2020-21 National Teacher and Principal Survey*. NTPS.

National Center for Education Statistics (NCES). (2023). *Children's internet access at home. Condition of Education*. U.S. Department of Education, Institute of Education Sciences.

National Center for Educational Statistics. (n.d.). *The condition of education 2019*. Institute of Education Sciences, National Center for Education Sciences. https://nces.ed.gov/pubs2019/2019144.pdf

National Education Technology Plan (NETP). (2017). *Reimagining the role of technology in education*. U.S. Department of Education, Office of Educational Technology.

Nazar, H., Omer, U., Nazar, Z., & Husband, A. (2018). *A study to investigate the impact of a blended learning teaching approach to teach pharmacy law. International Journal of Pharmacy Practice, 27(3), 303–310*. Academic., 10.1111/ijpp.12503

NCERT. (2023). *National Curriculum Framework for School Education.* NCERT. https://www.education.gov.in/sites/upload_files/mhrd/files/infocus_slider/NCF-School-Education-Pre-Draft.pdf

Neff, K. D. (2003). Self-compassion: An alternative conceptualization of a healthy attitude toward oneself. *Self and Identity*, 2(2), 85–101. 10.1080/15298860309032

Nepembe, V., & Simuja, C. (2023). Instructors' perspectives of TPACK in a vocational training classroom in Namibia. *Journal of Vocational. Adult and Continuing Education and Training*, 6(1), 90–107. 10.14426/jovacet.v6i1.315

Neubauer, B. E., Witkop, C. T., & Varpio, L. (2019). How phenomenology can help us learn from the experiences of others. *Perspectives on Medical Education*, 8(2), 90–97. 10.1007/S40037-019-0509-230953335

Ng, B. (2021). Engaging students in emergency remote teaching: strategies for the instructor. In Ktoridou, D., Doukanari, E., & Eteokleous, N. (Eds.), *Fostering Meaningful Learning Experiences Through Student Engagement* (pp. 74–91). IGI Global. 10.4018/978-1-7998-4658-1.ch004

Nicholls, G. (2005). New lecturers' constructions of learning, teaching and research in higher education. *Studies in Higher Education*, 30(5), 611–625. 10.1080/03075070500249328

Niess, M. L., & Gillow-Wiles, H. (2021). Online instructional strategies for enhancing teachers' TPACK: Experiences, discourse, and critical reflection. In *Research anthology on developing effective online learning courses* (pp. 326–348). IGI Global. 10.4018/978-1-7998-8047-9.ch019

Nipper, S. (1989). Third generation distance learning and computer conferencing. *Mindweave: Communication, Computers and Distance Education*, 63-73.

Nita, L., Mazzoli Smith, L., Chancellor, N., & Cramman, H. (2023). The challenge and opportunities of quantum literacy for future education and transdisciplinary problem-solving. *Research in Science & Technological Education*, 41(2), 564–580. 10.1080/02635143.2021.1920905

Nowell, L. S., Norris, J. M., White, D. E., & Moules, N. J. (2017). Thematic analysis: Striving to meet the trustworthiness criteria. *International Journal of Qualitative Methods*, 16(1), 1609406917733847. 10.1177/1609406917733847

Nugroho, I. (2023). The puzzle of how higher education learning does in post-COVID-19 pandemic. *Journal of Socioeconomics and Development*, 6(2), 145–156. 10.31328/jsed.v6i1.3285

Nurhas, I., Aditya, B., Witarsyah, D. J., & Pawlowski, J. (2021). Understanding the challenges of rapid digital transformation: The case of COVID-19 pandemic in higher education. *Behaviour & Information Technology*, 41(2), 2924–2940. 10.1080/0144929X.2021.1962977

Nye, A. (2015). Building an online academic learning community among undergraduate students. *Distance Education*, 36(1), 115–128. 10.1080/01587919.2015.1019969

Ochieng, V. O., Asego, C. S., & Gyasi, R. M. (2023). The place of academia and industry in the adoption and adaptation of educational technologies for a post-COVID-19 recovery in Africa. *Scientific African*, 20, e01658. 10.1016/j.sciaf.2023.e0165837035634

Ohei, K. N. (2023). Using ICT tools and technological applications in this Era of the COVID-19 pandemic to facilitate learning. *HOLISTICA–Journal of Business and Public Administration*, 14(2), 116–136. 10.2478/hjbpa-2023-0019

Ojong, V. (2024). Ethnographic research: Developments and challenges in the post-pandemic era. In *Researching the 'New Normal'Social World* (pp. 50–66). Routledge.

Olewski, T., & Snakard, M. (2017). Challenges in applying process safety management at university laboratories. *Journal of Loss Prevention in the Process Industries*, 49, 209–214. 10.1016/j.jlp.2017.06.013

Oliveira, G., Grenha Teixeira, J., Torres, A., & Morais, C. (2021). An exploratory study on the emergency remote education experience of higher education students and teachers during the COVID-19 pandemic. *British Journal of Educational Technology*, 52(4), 1357–1376. 10.1111/bjet.1311234219758

Oloruntegbe, K. O., & Alam, G. M. (2010). Evaluation of 3d environments and virtual realities in science teaching and learning: The need to go beyond perception referents. *Scientific Research and Essays,5*(9), 948-954. https://doi.org/10.5897/SRE10.036

Öner, M. N. K. (2020). Kimya eğitiminde laboratuvar güvenliği kültürünün yerleştirilmesi. [Safety culture placement in chemistry education]. *Ohs Academic*, 2(1), 15–25.

Onyekwelu, R. A. (2024). Enhancing the Quality of Secondary Education through Professional Development of Teachers in Nigeria. *British Journal of Multidisciplinary and Advanced Studies*, 5(1), 194–205. 10.37745/bjmas.2022.0438

Oraif, I., & Elyas, T. (2021). The impact of COVID-19 on learning: Investigating EFL learners' engagement in online courses in Saudi Arabia. *Education Sciences*, 11(3), 99. 10.3390/educsci11030099

Orange, G., & Hobbs, D. (2018). *International perspectives on tele-education and virtual learning environments*. Routledge. 10.4324/9781315200330

Orosz, A., Monzón, M., & Velasco, P. (2021). Ecuadorian Teachers' Perceptions of Teaching English: Challenges in the Public Education Sector. *International Journal of Learning. Teaching and Educational Research*, 20(3), 229–249.

Osnes, P. G., & Adelinis, J. (2005). Correspondence training, rule governance, generalization, and stimulus control: Connections or disconnections? *Behavioral Development Bulletin*, 12(1), 48–54. 10.1037/h0100560

Ozaruk, N. (1976). Lab safety: The case of the errant cylinder. *Journal of Chemical Education*, 53(6), 373. 10.1021/ed053p373

Öztürk, A., & Deniz, İ. D. (2023). Proficiency development in science laboratory practices with the flipped learning model in the distance education process in the COVID-19 pandemic. *Educational Research: Theory and Practice*, 34(1), 17–31.

Palak, D., & Walls, R. (2009). Teachers' beliefs and technology practices: A mixed-methods approach. *Journal of Research on Technology in Education*, 41(4), 417–441. 10.1080/15391523.2009.10782537

Palic, G., & Pirasa, N. (2012). A study of pre-service teachers' tendency for imprudent behaviour and physics laboratory attitudes. *Procedia: Social and Behavioral Sciences*, 47, 823–828. 10.1016/j.sbspro.2012.06.742

Palloff, R. M., & Pratt, K. (2001). *Lessons from the cyberspace classroom: The realities of online teaching*. Jossey-Bass.

Palmer, S., Holt, D., & Bray, S. (2008). Does the discussion help? The impact of a formally assessed online discussion on final student results. *British Journal of Educational Technology*, 39(5), 847–858. 10.1111/j.1467-8535.2007.00780.x

Pant, H., Lohani, M., & Pande, J. (2021). MOOCs in Higher Education: Current Trends in India and Developed Countries. In Rahman, H. (Ed.), *Ubiquitous Technologies for Human Development and Knowledge Management*. IGI Global., 10.4018/978-1-7998-7844-5.ch004

Papadakis, S. J., Semerikov, S. O., Yechkalo, Y. V., Velychko, V. Y., Vakaliuk, T. A., Amelina, S. M., & Tkachuk, V. V. (2023). *Advancing lifelong learning and professional development through ICT*. 3L-Person 2023 workshop. Research Gate.

Papadakis, S., Kiv, A. E., Kravtsov, H. M., Osadchyi, V. V., Marienko, M. V., Pinchuk, O. P.,& Striuk, A. M. (2023). Unlocking the power of synergy: the joint force of cloud technologies and augmented reality in education.

Papay, J. P., & Kraft, M. K. (2017). Developing Workplaces Where Teachers Stay, Improve, and Succeed. In *Teaching in Context: How Social Aspects of School and School Systems Shape Teachers' Development & Effectiveness* (pp. 15–35). Harvard Education Press.

Pappas, C. (2015, October 8). *The history of blended learning*. eLearning Industry. https://elearningindustry.com/history-of-blended-learning

Pappas, Christopher. (2023, May 1). *Everything you need to know about connectivism learning theory*. eLearning Industry. [blog post]

Park, C., Fuller, M. M., Echevarria, T. M., Nguyen, K., Perez, D., Masood, H., Alsharif, T., & Worthen, M. (2023). A participatory study of college students' mental health during the first year of the COVID-19 pandemic. *Frontiers in Public Health, 11*, 1116865. *Frontiers*, 11, 1116865. Advance online publication. 10.3389/fpubh.2023.111686537026129

Parker, A. (2020). Interaction in distance education: The critical conversation. *AACE Review (Formerly AACE Journal)*, 13-17.

Pashkov, M., Pashkova, V. M., & Starostenko, V. A. (2022). Transnational online education and digital inequality: Issues of pedagogical design. *Vestnik of Saint Petersburg University. Sociology, 15*(3), 368-387. https://typeset.io/papers/transnational online-education-and-digita l-inequality-issues-mref2rf2

Passey, D., Shonfeld, M., Appleby, L., Judge, M., Saito, T., & Smits, A. (2018). Digital agency: Empowering equity in and through education. *Tech Know Learn*, 23(3), 425–439. 10.1007/s10758-018-9384-x

Pastore, R. (2016, March). Multimedia: Learner preferences for multimedia learning. In *Society for Information Technology & Teacher Education International Conference* (pp. 3015–3022).

Patton, M. Q. (2022). Impact-driven qualitative research and evaluation. *The SAGE handbook of qualitative research design, 2*, 1165-1180. https://digital.casalini.it/9781529766943

Patton, M. Q. (2015). *Qualitative research & evaluation methods: Integrating theory and practice*. Sage publications.

Payne, J. L. (2016). *A case study of teaching digital citizenship in fifth grade*. [Doctoral Dissertation, The University of Alabama]. ProQuest Dissertations Publishing.

Pedretti, E., Mayer-Smith, J., & Woodrow, J. (1998). Technology, text, and talk: Students' perspectives on teaching and learning in a technology-enhanced secondary science classroom. *Science Education*, 82(5), 569–589. 10.1002/(SICI)1098-237X(199809)82:5<569::AID-SCE3>3.0.CO;2-7

Peimani, N., & Kamalipour, H. (2021). Online education and the COVID-19 outbreak: A case study of online teaching during lockdown. *Education Sciences*, 11(2), 72. 10.3390/educsci11020072

Pekdağ, B. (2020). Video-based instruction on safety rules in the chemistry laboratory: Its effect on student achievement. *Chemistry Education Research and Practice*, 21(3), 953–968. 10.1039/D0RP00088D

Pelayo-Dacanay, J. A., Pinili, L. C., Etcuban, J. O., Padillo, G. G., Manguilimotan, R. P., & Capuno, R. G. (2023). Technology-Supported Instruction In General Mathematics: Its Intuitive Implications Among Marginalized Filipino Students Amidst The Post-Pandemic Period. *Journal of Positive Psychology and Wellbeing*, 7(3), 86–99.

Pellegrini, M., Uskov, V., & Casalino, N. (2020). *Reimagining and Re-Designing the Post COVID-19 Higher Education Organizations to Address New Challenges and Responses.*

Perkins, D. N. (2001). Person-plus: A distributed view of thinking and learning. G. Salomon (Ed.). *Distributed cognition: Psychological and educational considerations* (pp. 88–110). Cambridge University Press.

Petronzi, R., & Petronzi, D. (2020). The Online and Campus (OaC) model as a sustainable blended approach to teaching and learning in higher education: A response to COVID-19. *Journal of Pedagogical Research*, 4(4), 498–507. 10.33902/JPR.2020064475

Pew Charitable Trusts. (2020). *How states Are expanding broadband access*. Pew Research.

Pew Research Center. (2021, September 1). *The internet and the pandemic*. Pew Research.

Pham, D. H. (2023). Perspectives on Language Teacher Identity in the Context of a Post-Pandemic "New Normal" Epoch. In *Handbook of Research on Language Teacher Identity* (pp. 98-115). IGI Global

Pham, N., & Nghiem, H. V. (2022). Online teaching satisfaction amid the Covid-19 pandemic: Evidence from a Vietnamese higher education context. *International Journal of TESOL & Education*, 2(4), 45–57. 10.54855/ijte.222119

Picciano, A. G. (1991). Computers, city, and suburb: A study of New York City and Westchester County public schools. *The Urban Review*, 23(3), 93–109. 10.1007/BF01108428

Picciano, A. G. (2011). *Educational Leadership and Planning for Technology* (5th ed.). Pearson Education, Inc.

Pillay, R. M., & Shipalana, M. L. (2023). The Effects of School Infrastructure on Curriculum Policy Implementation. *International Journal of Social Science Research and Review*, 6(8), 167–182.

Pisano, U. (2012). Resilience and Sustainable Development: Theory of resilience, systems thinking. *European sustainable development network (ESDN), 26*, 50

Pittaway, S. (2012). Student and staff engagement: Developing an engagement framework in a Faculty of Education. *The Australian Journal of Teacher Education*, 37(4), 37–45. 10.14221/ajte.2012v37n4.8

Poirier, M. J. P., Hard, J., & Holst, J. (2023). COVID-19 pandemic providing a window of opportunity for higher education: Case study of a three-country teaching-learning experience. *South Eastern European Journal of Public Health*, 9(1), 45–60. 10.56801/seejph.vi.223

Pols, F. (2020). A physics lab course in times of COVID-19. *Electronic Journal for Research in Science & Mathematics Education*, 24(2), 172–178.

Pounder, D., Carter, M. A., & Secada, W. G. (2020). Coaching for instructional improvement: A cross-country comparison of trust, goal setting, and focus. *Teaching and Teacher Education*, 88, 102995.

Povey, J., Campbell, A. K., Willis, L. D., Haynes, M., Western, M., Bennett, S., Antrobus, E., & Pedde, C. (2016). Engaging parents in schools and building parent-school partnerships: The role of school and parent organisation leadership. *International Journal of Educational Research*, 79, 128–141. 10.1016/j.ijer.2016.07.005

Pramono, D. N., & Prabawati, C. Y. (2021). *Hubungan regulasi emosi dengan tingkat stres mahasiswa yang melakukan study from home selama pandemi Covid-19 di Indonesia* [Doctoral Dissertation, Universitas Muhammadiyah Surakarta]. https://eprints.ums.ac.id/id/eprint/91599

Prasad, G. (2022). Online education in industry 5.0. In *Pedagogy, Presence, and Motivation in Online Education* (pp. 22-35). IGI Global.

Pratisti, W. D. (2013). Peran orangtua dalam perkembangan kemampuan regulasi emosi anak: Model. *Seminar Nasional Psikologi,* 322-333.

Prensky, M. (2001). Digital natives, digital immigrants. *On the Horizon*, 9(5), 1–6. 10.1108/10748120110424816

Pressley, T., & Ha, C. (2021). Teaching during a pandemic: United States teachers' self-efficacy during COVID-19. *Teaching and Teacher Education*, 106, 103465. 10.1016/j.tate.2021.10346534754135

Prothero, A. (2021). Pandemic fuels tech advances in schools – Here's what that looks like. *Education Week.*

Purba, J., Yulianto, A., Widyanti, E., Esa, D. F. P. U. I., & Esa, M. F. P. U. I. (2007). Pengaruh dukungan sosial terhadap burnout pada guru. *Jurnal Psikologi*, 5(1), 77–87.

Purnamaningsih, E. H. (2017). Personality and emotion regulation strategies. *International Journal of Psychological Research*, 10(1), 53–60. 10.21500/20112084.2040

Pusuluri, S., Mahasneh, A., & Alsayer, B. A. (2017). The Application of Blackboard in the English Courses at Al Jouf University: Perceptions of Students. *Theory and Practice in Language Studies*, 7(2), 106–111. 10.17507/tpls.0702.03

Putri, N. L. P. N. S. (2024). Sustainable Development Goals in EFL Students' Learning: A Systematic Review. *Pegem Journal of Education and Instruction*, 14(2), 1–11.

Qiang, Z., Obando, A. G., Chen, Y., & Ye, C. (2020). Revisiting distance learning resources for undergraduate research and lab activities during COVID-19 pandemic. *Journal of Chemical Education*, 97(9), 3446–3449. 10.1021/acs.jchemed.0c00609

Qu, J., Zhao, Y., & Xie, Y. (2022). Artificial intelligence leads the reform of education models. *Systems Research and Behavioral Science*, 39(3), 581–588. 10.1002/sres.2864

Radhamani, R., Kumar, D., Nizar, N., Achuthan, K., Nair, B., & Diwakar, S. (2021). What virtual laboratory usage tells us about laboratory skill education pre-and post-COVID-19: Focus on usage, behaviour, intention and adoption. *Education and Information Technologies*, 26(6), 7477–7495. doi.org.wam.seals.ac.za/10.1007/s10639-021-10583-3. 10.1007/s10639-021-10583-334121909

Rahayu, D. P., & Fauziah, N. (2019). Hubungan antara regulasi emosi dengan burnout pada Perawat Rawat Inap Rumah Sakit Jiwa Daerah (Rsjd) Dr Amino Gondohutomo Semarang. *Jurnal Empati*, 8(2), 354–360. 10.14710/empati.2019.24398

Rahim, R., Tan, T., & Carvalho, M. (2020, November 16). Education Ministry: Country's online learning implementation strategy in final stages of preparation. *The Star*. https://www.thestar.com.my/news/nation/2020/11/16/education-ministry-country039s-online-learning-implementation-strategy-in-final-stages-of-preparation

Rahmawati, S., & Indriayu, M. (2017). Pengaruh tekanan akademik terhadap prestasi akademik mahasiswa pendidikan ekonomi fakultas keguruan dan ilmu pendidikan Universitas Sebelas Maret. *Jurnal Pendidikan Bisnis Dan Ekonomi*, 3(2), 1–15. 10.20961/bise.v3i2.16450

Rajab, M. H., Gazal, A. M., & Alkattan, K. (2020). Challenges to Online Medical Education During the COVID-19 Pandemi c. *Cureus, 12*(7), e8966. DOI:: 8966.10.7759/cureus

Rakitskaya, E. (2023). Collaborative learning in the online environment. *Handbook of Research on Facilitating Collaborative Learning Through Digital Content and Learning Technologies.* 10.4018/978-1-6684-5709-2.ch011

Raman, R., Vinuesa, R., & Nedungadi, P. (2021). Acquisition and user behaviour in online science laboratories before and during the COVID-19 pandemic. *Multimodal Technologies and Interaction*, 5(8), 46. 10.3390/mti5080046

Ramnarain, U., & Hlatswayo, M. (2018). Teacher beliefs and attitudes about inquiry-based learning in a rural school district in South Africa. *South African Journal of Education*, 38(1), 1–10. 10.15700/saje.v38n1a1431

Rapanta, C., Botturi, L., Goodyear, P., Guàrdia, L., & Koole, M. (2021). Balancing technology, pedagogy and the new normal: Post-pandemic challenges for higher education. *Postdigital Science and Education*, 3(3), 715–742. 10.1007/s42438-021-00249-1

Rasli, A., Tee, M., Lai, Y. L., Tiu, Z. C., & Soon, E. H. (2022). Post-COVID-19 strategies for higher education institutions in dealing with unknown and uncertainties. *Frontiers in Education*, 7, 992063. Advance online publication. 10.3389/feduc.2022.992063

Ratten, V. (2023). The post COVID-19 pandemic era: Changes in teaching and learning methods for management teachers. *International Journal of Management Education*, 21(2), 100777. 10.1016/j.ijme.2023.100777

Rautela, S., Sharma, S., & Virani, S. (2022). Learner-learner interactions in online classes during COVID-19 pandemic: The mediating role of social media in the higher education context. *Interactive Learning Environments*, 1–16. 10.1080/10494820.2022.2093917

Reddy, L. A., Shernoff, E., & Lekwa, A. (2021). A randomized controlled trial of instructional coaching in high-poverty urban schools: Examining teacher practices and student outcomes. *Journal of School Psychology*, 86, 151–168. 10.1016/j.jsp.2021.04.00134051911

Reddy, L. A., Shernoff, E., Lekwa, A., Matthews, C., Davis, W., & Dudek, C. M. (2019). Coaching to improve teacher instruction and behavior management in a high poverty school: A case study. *School Psychology*, 34(1), 14–21. 10.1037/spq000030230556728

Reddy, M. A., Reddy, B. M., Mukund, C. S., Venneti, K., Preethi, D. M. D., & Boopathi, S. (2023). Social health protection during the COVID-pandemic using IoT. In *The COVID-19 Pandemic and the Digitalization of Diplomacy* (pp. 204–235). IGI Global. 10.4018/978-1-7998-8394-4.ch009

Redinger, J. W., Cornia, P. B., & Albert, T. J. (2020). Teaching during a pandemic. *Journal of Graduate Medical Education*, 12(4), 403–405. 10.4300/JGME-D-20-00241.132879676

Reich, J. (2019). Teaching our way to digital equity. *Educational Leadership*, 76(5), 30–35.

Rekh, S., & Chandy, A. (2020). Implementation of academia 4.0 for engineering college education. *Procedia Computer Science, 172*, 673–678. ScienceDirect. 10.1016/j.procs.2020.05.088

Reynolds, D., Nelsen, J., & Twyman, J. (2021). The Role of Instructional Coaching in a Virtual Teaching World. *The Educational Forum*, 85(3), 325–337.

Richardson, J., Lv, J., & Caskurlu, S. (2017). Social presence in relation to students' satisfaction and learning in the online environment. *Computers in Human Behavior*, 71, 402–417. 10.1016/j.chb.2017.02.001

Richards, R. (2019). Exploring the influence of perceived mattering, role stress, and emotional exhaustion on physical education teacher/coach job satisfaction. *European Physical Education Review*, 25(2), 389–408. 10.1177/1356336X17741402

Rizzato, F., Fenwick, S., & Fogg, I. (2020, April 8). *Mobile Experience during the COVID-19 pandemic: 4G Download Speed*. Opensignal. https://www.opensignal.com/2020/04/08/mobile-experience-during-the-COVID-19-pandemic-4g-download-speed

Robinson, L. E., Valido, A., Drescher, A., Woolweaver, A. B., Espelage, D. L., LoMurray, S., Long, A. C. J., Wright, A. A., & Dailey, M. M. (2023). Teachers, stress, and the COVID-19 pandemic: A qualitative analysis. *School Mental Health*, 15(1), 78–89. 10.1007/s12310-022-09533-235875185

Rodrigues, H., Almeida, F., Figueiredo, V., & Lopes, S. L. (2019). Tracking e-learning through published papers: A systematic review. *Computers & Education*, 136, 87–98. 10.1016/j.compedu.2019.03.007

Rodriguez, C.O. (2012). MOOCs and the AI-Stanford like courses: two successful and distinct course formats for massive open online courses. *The European Journal of Open, Distance and E-Learning*, 15.

Rogers, E. (2003). *Diffusion of innovations* (5th ed.). Free Press.

Rogozin, D., Solodovnikova, O., & Ipatova, A. (2022). How University Teachers View the Digital Transformation of Higher Education. *Studies of E-Learning*. 10.17323/1814-9545-2022-1-271-300

Rojas-Contreras, M., & Ruiz-Bautista, L. (2020). Online laboratories supported with virtual reality for higher education. *Journal of Physics: Conference Series*, 1708(1), 012036. Advance online publication. 10.1088/1742-6596/1708/1/012036

Roorda, D. L., Koomen, H., Spilt, J. L., & Oort, F. J. (2011). The influence of affective teacher-student relationships on students' school engagement and achievement: A meta-analytic approach. *Review of Educational Research*, 81(4), 493–529. 10.3102/0034654311421793

Rosenberg, J. M., & Koehler, M. J. (2015). Context and technological pedagogical content knowledge (TPACK): A systematic review. *Journal of Research on Technology in Education*, 47(3), 186–210. 10.1080/15391523.2015.1052663

Rourke, L. (2001). Methodological issues in the content analysis of computer conference transcripts. *International Journal of Artificial Intelligence in Education*, 12, 8–22.

Rovai, A. P., & Downey, J. R. (2010). Why some distance education programs fail while others succeed in a global environment. *The Internet and Higher Education, 13*(3), 141–147. ScienceDirect. 10.1016/j.iheduc.2009.07.001

Rowe, F. L. (2022). *A Descriptive Analysis of an Instructional Coaching Process and Its Impact on Student Reading Learning Outcomes* [Doctoral dissertation, University of South Carolina]. https://scholarcommons.sc.edu/etd/ 6917

Rozanki, A., & Kubzansky, L. D. (2005). Psychologic functioning and physical health: A paradigm of flexibility. *Psychosomatic Medicine*, 67(1), 47–53. 10.1097/01.psy.0000164253.69550.4915953801

Rubie-Davies, C. M. (2006). Teacher expectations and student self-perceptions: Exploring relationship. *Psychology in the Schools*, 43(5), 537–552. 10.1002/pits.20169

Rusman, R., Setiasih, O., Nandi, N., Setiawardani, W., & Yusron, E. (2024). Applying the UTAUT Model to Understand Factors Affecting the Use of Learning Management System for Learning Pedagogical Education. *Pegem Journal of Education and Instruction*, 14(1), 218–255. 10.47750/pegegog.14.01.41

Saba, F. (2011). Distance education in the United States: Past, present, future. *Educational Technology*, 11–18.

Sable, R. G., & Bhatt, K. D. (2023). NEP 2020: Linking Emotional Intelligence and Bloom's Affective Domain Categories to New Pedagogical and Curricular Structure. International Journal of Professional Business Review: Int. *J. Prof. Bus. Rev.*, 8(7), 119.

Sachar, M., & Neumann, Y., (2010). Twenty years of research of the academic performance differences between traditional and distance learning: Summative meta-analysis and trend examination. *MERLOT Journal of Online Learning and Teaching*.

Saettler, P. (2004). *The evolution of American educational technology*. IAP.

Saghafian, M., & O'Neill, D. (2018). A phenomenological study of teamwork in online and face- to-face student teams. *Higher Education*.

Sahoo, M., & Rana, K. (2023). Digital Education During COVID-19 in Odisha: Challenges and Prospects. *Changing World Economic Order in the Post-Pandemic Period*, 147-165. 10.4018/978-1-7998-6896-5.ch009

Said, M. N. H. M., Tahir, L., & Ali, M. F. (2016). Online collaborative learning interactions in a tertiary ICT education course. *International Information Institute (Tokyo).Information (Basel)*, 19(1).

Sailer, M., Murböck, J., & Fischer, F. (2021). Digital learning in schools: What does it take beyond digital technology? *Teaching and Teacher Education*, 103, 103346. Advance online publication. 10.1016/j.tate.2021.103346

Salas-Pilco, S. Z., Yang, Y., & Zhang, Z. (2022). Student engagement in online learning in Latin American higher education during the COVID-19 pandemic: A systematic review. *British Journal of Educational Technology*, 53(3), 593–619. 10.1111/bjet.1319035600418

Saldana, J. (2021). *The Coding Manual for Qualitative Researchers*. SAGE. https://eduq.info/xmlui/handle/11515/35868

Salimi, N., Gere, B., Talley, W., & Irioogbe, B. (2023). College students mental health challenges: Concerns and considerations in the COVID-19 pandemic. *Journal of College Student Psychotherapy*, 37(1), 39–51. 10.1080/87568225.2021.1890298

Sally, C. (2023, 12 15). *The environmental impact of teaching and learning*. Retrieved from www.open.edu: https://www.open.edu/openlearn/mod/oucontent/view.php?id=13707&printable=1

Salta, K., Paschalidou, K., Tsetseri, M., & Koulougliotis, D. (2022). Shift from a traditional to a distance learning environment during the COVID-19 pandemic: University students' engagement and interactions. *Science & Education*, 31(1), 93–122. 10.1007/s11191-021-00234-x34121814

Sams, A. ve Bergmann, J. (2013). Flip your students' learning. *Educational Leadership*, 70(6), 16–20.

Sancak, Y. C., Ekici, K., & İşleyici, Ö. (2008). Fermente Türk Sucuğu ve pastırmalarda kalıntı nitrat ve nitrit düzeyleri. [Residual nitrate and nitrite levels in fermented Turkish sausage and pastrami]. *Yüzüncü Yıl Üniversitesi Veteriner Fakültesi Dergisi*, 19(1), 41–45.

Sánchez-Cruzado, C., & Campión, S. (1858). Raúl, & Sánchez-Compaña, Mª Teresa. (2021). Teacher digital literacy: The indisputable challenge after COVID-19. *Sustainability (New Rochelle, N.Y.)*, 13(4).

Sanchez, E., Paukovics, E., Cheniti-Belcadhi, L., El Khayat, G., Said, B., & Korbaa, O. (2022). What do you mean by learning lab? *Education and Information Technologies*, 27(4), 4501–4520. 10.1007/s10639-021-10783-x

Sandid, B., Belhaj, L., & Elmadani, O. (2023). Strategies for student engagement in distance learning. *International Journal For Multidisciplinary Research*, 5(6), 9473. Advance online publication. 10.36948/ijfmr.2023.v05i06.9473

Sangrà, A. (2015). *Meta-analysis of the research about MOOC during 2013-2014.*

Sangrà, A., Vlachopoulos, D., & Cabrera, N. (2012). Building an inclusive definition of e-learning: An approach to the conceptual framework. *International Review of Research in Open and Distance Learning*, 13(2), 145–159. 10.19173/irrodl.v13i2.1161

Sarder, M. B. (2014). Improving student engagement in online courses. *ASEE Annual Conference and Exposition, Conference Proceedings*. ASEE. 10.18260/1-2--20611

Sari, M. D. I., & Hayati, E. N. (2015). Regulasi emosi pada penderita HIV/AIDS. *Empathy*, 3(1), 23–30. 10.12928/empathy.v3i1.3011

Schalk, A., McAvinia, C., & Rooney, P. (2022). Exploring the concept of the digital educator during COVID-19. *Australasian Journal of Educational Technology*, 38(2), 129–141. 10.14742/ajet.7316

Scherer, R., Howard, S. K., Tondeur, J., & Siddiq, F. (2021). Profiling teachers' readiness for online teaching and learning in higher education: Who's ready? *Computers in Human Behavior*, 118, 106675. 10.1016/j.chb.2020.106675

Schildkraut, D. J. (2005). *Press "one" for English: Language policy, public opinion, and American identity*. Princeton University Press.

Schlesselman, L. S. (2020). Perspective from a teaching and learning center during emergency remote teaching. *American Journal of Pharmaceutical Education*, 84(6), 8142. 10.5688/ajpe814232934391

Schön, D. A. (1983). *The reflective practitioner: How professionals think in action*. Basic Books.

Schreier, M. (2012). *Qualitative content analysis in practice*. Sage Publications. 10.4135/9781529682571

Schunk, D. H. (2012). *Learning theories an educational perspective*. Pearson Education, Inc.

Schwartz, S. (2020). How to Use Digital Reading Programs During COVID-19. Teachers Still Matter. *Education Week*. https://www.edweek.org/ew/articles/2020/09/30/how-to-use-digital-reading-programs-during.html

Scott, J. (2019). Professional development for online post-secondary faculty. *Eighth International Conference on Educational Innovation through Technology (EITT)*. IEEE. 10.1109/EITT.2019.00017

See, S., & Conry, J. M. (2014). Flip My Class! A faculty development demonstration of a flipped-classroom. *Currents in Pharmacy Teaching and Learning, 6*(4), 585–588. ScienceDirect. 10.1016/j.cptl.2014.03.003

Seemiller, C., Grace, M., Dal Bo Campagnolo, P., Mara Da Rosa Alves, I., & Severo De Borba, G. (2021). What makes learning enjoyable? Perspectives of today's college students in the U.S. and Brazil. *Journal of Pedagogical Research*, 5(1), 1–17. 10.33902/JPR.2020065267

Seery, M. K. (2015). Flipped learning in higher education chemistry: Emerging trends and potential directions. *Chemistry Education Research and Practice*, 16(4), 758–768. 10.1039/C5RP00136F

Selwyn, N., Hillman, T., Eynon, R., Ferreira, G., Knox, J., Macgilchrist, F., & Sancho-Gil, J. M. (2020). What's next for Ed-Tech? Critical hopes and concerns for the 2020s. *Learning, Media and Technology*, 45(1), 1–6. 10.1080/17439884.2020.1694945

Seynhaeve, S., Deygers, B., Simon, E., & Delarue, S. (2022). Interaction in online classes during Covid-19: The experiences of newly-arrived migrant students. *Educational Research*, 64(3), 334–352. 10.1080/00131881.2022.2090981

Shambare, B., & Simuja, C. (2022). A critical review of teaching with virtual lab: A panacea to challenges of conducting practical experiments in science subjects beyond the COVID-19 pandemic in rural schools in South Africa. *Journal of Educational Technology Systems*, 50(3), 393–408. 10.1177/00472395211058051

Shambare, B., Simuja, C., & Theodorio, A. O. (2022). Understanding rural secondary school teachers' perceptions and attitudes on the use of ICT for teaching and learning. *Journal of African Education*, 3(1), 35–57. https://hdl.handle.net/10520/ejc-aa_jae_v3_n1_a3. 10.31920/2633-2930/2022/v3n1a2

Shanahan, T., & Lonigan, C. J. (2010). The National Early Literacy Panel. *Educational Researcher*, 39(4), 279–285. 10.3102/0013189X1036917222294803

Sharratt, L., & Fullan, M. (2013). *Putting Faces on the Data*. Corwin Press.

Shatte, A. B. R., & Teague, S. (2020, July 14). Microlearning for improved student outcomes in higher education: A scoping review. 10.31219/osf.io/fhu8n

Shava, E. (2022). Reinforcing the role of ICT in enhancing teaching and learning post-COVID-19 in tertiary institutions in South Africa. *Journal of Culture and Values in Education*, 5(1), 78–91. 10.46303/jcve.2022.7

Shaw, P. A., & Shaw, A. (2023). COVID-19 and remote learning: Experiences of parents supporting children with special needs and disability during the pandemic. *Education 3-13, 51*(3), 371–385. 10.1080/03004279.2021.1960579

Shazarina, Z.A., Suziana Hanini, S., Suhana, M.L., Norshilawani, S., Natasha, A., Mohamad Fuad, I., & Sapie, S. (2020). Tekanan emosi pensyarah dalam melaksanakan pengajaran dan pembelajaran atas talian di era pandemik covid-19. *Seminar Antarabangsa Isu-Isu Pendidikan (ISPEN 2020) Kolej Universiti Islam Antarabangsa Selangor (KUIS)*. IEEE.|

Sher, A. (2009). Assessing the relationship of student-instructor and student-student interaction to student learning and satisfaction in web-based online learning environment. *Journal of Interactive Online Learning*, 8(2), 102–120.

Sherman, J., & Schafft, K. A. (2022). "Turning Their Back on Kids": Inclusions, Exclusions, and the Contradictions of Schooling in Gentrifying Rural Communities. *The Russell Sage Foundation Journal of the Social Sciences : RSF*, 8(3), 150–170. 10.7758/RSF.2022.8.3.06

Sherry, L. (1995). Issues in distance learning. *International Journal of Educational Telecommunications*, 1(4), 337–365. https://www.learntechlib.org/primary/p/8937/

Sherwood, D., Vandeusen, K. M., Weller, B., & Gladden, J. (2021). Teaching trauma content online during COVID-19: A trauma-informed and culturally responsive pedagogy. *Journal of Social Work Education, 57*(sup1), 99-110. 10.1080/10437797.2021.1916665

Shifat, N. F., & Khan, M. E. I. (2022). Sustainability of E-Learning in the Undergraduate EFL Classrooms. *FOSTER: Journal of English Language Teaching*, 3(2), 80–89.

Shim, T., & Lee, S. (2020). College students' experience of emergency remote teaching due to COVID-19. *Children and Youth Services Review*, 119, 105578. 10.1016/j.childyouth.2020.10557833071405

Shin, M., & Hickey, K. (2020). Needs a little TLC: Examining college students' emergency remote teaching and learning experiences during COVID-19. *Journal of Further and Higher Education*, 45(7), 973–986. 10.1080/0309877X.2020.1847261

Showers, B., & Joyce, B. (1996). The evolution of peer coaching. *Educational Leadership,* 53(6), 12-16. Sinquefield Center for Applied Economic Research.https://scholarworks.uark.edu/cgi/viewcontent.cgi?article=1128&context=edrepub

Shulman, L. (1986). Those Who Understand. *Knowledge Growth in Teaching*, 15(2), 4–14.

Shyr, W. J., Liau, H. M., Hsu, C. C., & Chen, C. H. (2021). Assess the engagement with 3D Virtual Learning Tools during the COVID-19 Pandemic. *Sustainability (Basel)*, 13(15), 8632. 10.3390/su13158632

Siddique, a. (2023). The rise of online education and its impact on traditional learning institutions. *The times of Inda*. https://timesofindia.indiatimes.com/readersblog/ecommercetrends/the-rise-of-online-education-and-its-impact-on-traditional-learning-institutions-52621/

Sidhu, M. S., & Kang, L. C. (2010). Emerging Trends and Technologies for Enhancing Engineering Education. *International Journal of Information and Communication Technology Education, 6*(4), 38–48. IGI Global. 10.4018/jicte.2010100104

Sidhu, M. S. (2009). *Technology-Assisted Problem Solving for Engineering Education: Interactive Multimedia Applications*. IGI Global.

Sidhu, M. S. (2013). Technology assisted approach for learning, visualizing and problem solving in engineering. *Technics Technologies Education Management*, 8(1), 277–292.

Sidi, Y., Shamir-Inbal, T., & Eshet-Alkalai, Y. (2023). From face-to-face to online: Teachers' perceived experiences in online distance teaching during the Covid-19 pandemic. *Computers & Education*, 201, 104831. 10.1016/j.compedu.2023.10483137193045

Sieber, J. (2005). Misconceptions and realities about teaching online. *Science and Engineering Ethics*, 11(3), 329–340. 10.1007/s11948-005-0002-716190274

Siemens, G. (2004). Connectivism: A learning theory for the digital age.

Siemens, G. (2006) *Knowing knowledge.*

Siemens, G. (2012). MOOCs: The tsunami of educational innovation. *elearnspace.*

Siemens, G. (2013). Connectivism: A learning theory for the digital age. *International Journal of Instructional Technology and Distance Learning*, 2(1), 3–10. http://www.itdl.org/journal/jan_05/article01.htm

Sim, S., Sim, H. P., & Quah, C. (2021). Online learning: A post COVID-19 alternative pedagogy for university students. *Asian Journal of University Education, 17*(4), 137 149. https://doi.org/10.24191/ajue.v16i4.11963

Simonson, M., Zvacek, S. M., & Smaldino, S. (2019). *Teaching and learning at a distance: Foundations of distance education.* Research Gate.

Simpson, O. (2018). *Supporting Students in Online, Open and Distance Learning*. Routledge. 10.4324/9780203417003

Simuja, C., & Shikesho, H. (2024). Investigating the Experiences of Mathematics Teacher Technology Integration in the Selected Rural Primary Schools in Namibia. [IJTEE]. *International Journal of Technology-Enhanced Education*, 3(1), 1–15. 10.4018/IJTEE.340028

Sinaga, P., Setiawan, W., & Liana, M. (2022). The impact of electronic interactive teaching materials (EITMs) in e-learning on junior high school students' critical thinking skills. *Thinking Skills and Creativity*, 46, 101066. 10.1016/j.tsc.2022.101066

Sjølie, E., & van Petegem, P. (2022). Measuring the sociability of virtual learning environments for interdisciplinary student teams – a validation study. *Scandinavian Journal of Educational Research*. Advance online publication. 10.1080/00313831.2022.2148279

Skaalvik, E. M., & Skaalvik, S. (2017). Dimensions of teacher burnout: Relations with potential stressors at school. *Social Psychology of Education*, 20(4), 775–790. 10.1007/s11218-017-9391-0

Slavin, R. E. (2012). Cooperative learning and achievement: Theory and research. *Handbook of Psychology, Second Edition, 7.*

Slavin, R. E. (1999). Comprehensive approaches to cooperative learning. *Theory into Practice*, 38(2), 74–79. 10.1080/00405849909543835

Smith, F. J. (1913). The evolution of the motion picture. *The New York Dramatic Mirror, 9.*

Smith, C., & Gillespie, M. (2023). Research on professional development and teacher change: Implications for adult basic education. [Routledge.]. *Review of Adult Learning and Literacy*, 7, 205–244. 10.4324/9781003417996-7

Smith, J. A., & Fieldsend, M. (2021). Interpretative phenomenological analysis. In Camic, P. M. (Ed.), *Qualitative research in psychology: Expanding perspectives in methodology and design* (2nd ed., pp. 147–166). American Psychological Association. 10.1037/0000252-008

Sofkova Hashemi, S., Berbyuk Lindström, N., & Bergdahl, N. (2024). *Pandemic as Digital Change Accelerator: Sustainable Reshaping of Adult Education Post Covid-19.*

Sohil, F., & Sohail, M. U. (2022). Measuring the impact of COVID-19 on distance learning for educational sustainability. *Cogent Education*, 9(1), 2034248. 10.1080/2331186X.2022.2034248

Soon, T.-K., & Quek, A.-H. (2013). Engineering education in Malaysia - Meeting the needs of a rapidly emerging economy and globalisation. *2013 International Conference on Interactive Collaborative Learning (ICL), IEEE Xplore*, (pp. 583–587). IEEE. 10.1109/ICL.2013.6644659

Sooryamoorthy, R., & Ojong, V. (Eds.). (2023). *Researching the 'New Normal' Social World: Methodological Adaptations and Innovations Post-Pandemic*. Taylor & Francis. 10.4324/9781003386087

Sosniuk, O., & Ostapenko, I. (2021). Usage of digital tools and social media for learning: Ukrainian experience in the context of the COVID-19 pandemic. In *Proceedings of the 2021 International Conference on Education and New Learning Technologies*. Research Gate. /10.30525/978-9934-26-076-6-23

Soubra, L., Al-Ghouti, M. A., Abu-Dieyeh, M., Crovella, S., & Abou-Saleh, H. (2022). Impacts on student learning and skills and implementation challenges of two student-centered learning methods applied in online education. *Sustainability (Basel)*, 14(15), 9625. 10.3390/su14159625

Sprague, D. R., Williamson, J., & Foulger, T. S. (2022). Design guidelines for post-COVID era preparation programs: Action steps toward technology infusion. *Journal of Technology and Teacher Education*, 30(2), 177–187.

Srivani, V., Hariharasudan, A., Nawaz, N., & Ratajczak, S. (2022). Impact of Education 4.0 among engineering students for learning English language. *PLoS One*, 17(2), e0261717. 10.1371/journal.pone.026171735108282

Staker, H., & Horn, M. B. (2012). Classifying K–12 Blended Learning. *Cmb.ac.lk*. http://archive.cmb.ac.lk:8080/xmlui/70130/5105

Statista. (n.d.). Average number of EDTech tools used per K-12 district in the U.S. in the 2022 – 23 school year.

Steve, B. (2023, 12 07). *Digital Learning Platforms Statistics 2023 – Everything You Need to Know*. Webinarcare. https://webinarcare.com/best-digital-learning-platforms/digital-learning-platforms-statistics/

Stewart, W. (2021). A global crash-course in teaching and learning online: A thematic review of empirical emergency remote teaching (ERT) studies in higher education during year 1 of COVID-19. *Open Praxis*, 13(1), 89–102. 10.5944/openpraxis.13.1.1177

Stewart, W., Baek, Y., & Lowenthal, P. R. (2022). From emergency remote teaching (ERT) to sustained remote teaching (SRT): A comparative semester analysis of exchange students' experiences and perceptions of learning online during COVID-19. *Online Learning : the Official Journal of the Online Learning Consortium*, 26(1), 22–40. 10.24059/olj.v26i2.2661

Stieff, M., Werner, S. M., Fink, B., & Meador, D. (2018). Online Prelaboratory videos improve student performance in the general chemistry laboratory. *Journal of Chemical Education*, 95(8), 1260–1266. 10.1021/acs.jchemed.8b00109

Strayer, J. F. (2012). How learning in an inverted classroom influences cooperation, innovation and task orientation. *Learning Environments Research*, 15(2), 171–193. 10.1007/s10984-012-9108-4

Strobel, J., Johnson, B., & Warrington, M. (2020). Supporting Instructional Coaching Through Technology: Reflections on Two Systems. *TechTrends*, 64(2), 254–261.

Su, C. Y., & Guo, Y. (2021). Factors impacting university students' online learning experiences during the COVID-19 epidemic. *Journal of Computer Assisted Learning*, 37(6), 1578–1590. 10.1111/jcal.1255534908643

Suldo, S. M., Thalji-Raitano, A., Hasemeyer, M., Gelley, C. D., & Hoy, B. (2013). Understanding middle school students life satisfaction: Does school climate matter? *Applied Research in Quality of Life*, 8(2), 169–182. 10.1007/s11482-012-9185-7

Sultanova, L., Milto, L., & Zheludenko, M. (2021). The impact of the COVID-19 pandemic on the development of higher education. *Acta Paedagogica Vilnensia*, 46, 132–147. 10.15388/ActPaed.46.2021.9

Sun, J. C. Y., & Wu, Y. T. (2016). Analysis of learning achievement and teacher–student interactions in flipped and conventional classrooms. *International Review of Research in Open and Distance Learning*, 17(1), 79–99. 10.19173/irrodl.v17i1.2116

Sydorenko, V., Akhnovska, I., Smirnov, S. V., Verbovskyi, I., & Melnychuk, O. V. (2021). Bridging the digital divide as a basic imperative in higher education. *Estudios de Economía Aplicada*, 39(9). 10.25115/eea.v39i9.5798

Takona, J. P. (2023). Flipping the Script: Post-COVID-19 Opportunities, Challenges, and Threats amidst the Digital Revolution in Higher Education. *International Journal on Social and Education Sciences*, 5(4), 847–863. 10.46328/ijonses.569

Tang, T., Abuhmaid, A. M., Olaimat, M., Oudat, D. M., Aldhaeebi, M., & Bamanger, E. (2020). Efficiency of flipped classroom with online-based teaching under COVID-19. *Interactive Learning Environments*, 31(2), 1077–1088. 10.1080/10494820.2020.1817761

Tanner, J. R., Noser, T. C., & Totaro, M. W. (2009). Business faculty and undergraduate students' perceptions of online learning: A comparative study. *Journal of Information Systems Education*, 20(1), 29–40. https://www.learntechlib.org/p/105718/

Tanner, J., Quintis, L., & Gamboa, T.Jr. (2017). Three perspectives of planning, implementation, and consistency in instructional coaching. *Journal of Educational Research and Practice*, 7(1), 30–44. 10.5590/JERAP.2017.07.1.03

Tatineni, S. (2020). Recommendation Systems for Personalized Learning: A Data-Driven Approach in Education. [JCET]. *Journal of Computer Engineering and Technology*, 4(2).

Tawie, R., Neging, M., & Khan, M. Y. M. A. (2018). Preliminary study on creativity in higher education: Perceptions of engineering instructors. *2017 IEEE 9th International Conference on Engineering Education (ICEED)*. IEEE Xplore. 10.1109/ICEED.2017.8251159

Tayebinik, M., & Puteh, M. (2012). Blended learning or E-learning? *International Magazine on Advances in Computer Science and Telecommunications*, *3*(1), 103-110. https://papers.ssrn.com/sol3/papers.cfm?abstract_id=2282881 Ghimire.

Taylor, J. C. (1995). Distance education technologies: The fourth generation. *Australasian Journal of Educational Technology*, 11(2). Advance online publication. 10.14742/ajet.2072

Tekbiyik, A., & Tepe, M. (2017). Türkiye'de 2001-2017 Yılları arasında yaşanan laboratuvar ve deney kazalarının değerlendirilmesi. [Evaluation of laboratory and experimental accidents that occurred in Turkey between 2001 and 2017]. *International Journal of Innovative Approaches in Education*, 1(1), 11–20. 10.29329/ijiape.2017.84.2

Teo, T. W., Tan, K. C., Yan, Y. K., Teo, Y. C., & Yeo, L. W. (2014). How flip teaching supports undergraduate chemistry laboratory learning. *Chemistry Education Research and Practice*, 15(4), 550–567. 10.1039/C4RP00003J

Thapaliya, M., Adhikari, S., & Rana, L. (2024). Opportunity in COVID-19 crisis: Moving away from chalk and talk to technology-integrated teaching in Nepalese higher education institutions. *E-Learning and Digital Media*, 21(1), 87–105. https://0-doi.org.wam.seals.ac.za/10.1177/20427530231153944. 10.1177/20427530231153944

Tharapos, M., O'Connell, B., Beatson, N., & De Lange, P. (2023). COVID-19 and accounting, accountability and governance. In *Handbook of Accounting, Accountability and Governance* (pp. 448-472). Edward Elgar Publishing.

Thornburg, A. W., Ceglie, R. J., & Abernathy, D. F. (2021). *Handbook of research on lessons learned from transitioning to virtual classrooms during a pandemic*. IGI Global. 10.4018/978-1-7998-6557-5

Thurston, A. (2000). Building online learning communities. *Technology, Pedagogy and Education*, 14(3), 353–369. 10.1080/14759390500200216

Tian, X. (2023). Educational reform and prospects in the post-pandemic era. *Journal of Education. Humanities and Social Sciences*, 19, 262–270. 10.54097/ehss.v19i.11142

Tokatly Latzer, I., Leitner, Y., & Karnieli-Miller, O. (2021). Core experiences of parents of children with autism during the COVID-19 pandemic lockdown. *Autism*, 25(4), 1047–1059. 10.1177/1362361320984317 33435701

Tong, D. H., Uyen, B. P., & Ngan, L. K. (2022). The effectiveness of blended learning on students' academic achievement, self-study skills and learning attitudes: A quasi-experiment study in teaching the conventions for coordinates in the plane. *Heliyon, 8*(12), e12657. ScienceDirect. 10.1016/j.heliyon.2022.e12657

Topping, K. J., Douglas, W., Robertson, D., & Ferguson, N. (2022). Effectiveness of online and blended learning from schools: A systematic review. *Review of Education*, 10(2), e3353. 10.1002/rev3.3353

Torres Martín, C., Acal, C., El Homrani, M., & Mingorance Estrada, Á. C. (2021). Impact on the virtual learning environment due to COVID-19. *Sustainability (Basel)*, 13(2), 582. 10.3390/su13020582

Trullàs, J. C., Blay, C., Sarri, E., & Pujol, R. (2022). Effectiveness of problem-based learning methodology in undergraduate medical education: A scoping review. *BMC Medical Education*, 22(1), 104. 10.1186/s12909-022-03154-835177063

Tsakeni, M., Vandeyar, S., & Potgieter, M. (2019). Inquiry opportunities presented by practical work in school physical sciences. A South African case study. *Gender & Behaviour*, 17(3), 13722–13733. https://hdl.handle.net/10520/EJC-1975177d59

Tsantopoulos, G., Karasmanaki, E., Ioannou, K., & Kapnia, M. (2022). Higher education in a post-pandemic world. *Education Sciences*, 12(12), 856. 10.3390/educsci12120856

Tschannen-Moran, M., Parish, J., & Dipaola, M. (2006). School climate: The interplay between interpersonal relationships and student achievement. *Journal of School Leadership*, 16(4), 386–415. 10.1177/105268460601600402

Tselios, N., Daskalakis, S., & Papadopoulou, M. (2011). Assessing the acceptance of a blended learning university course. *Journal of Educational Technology & Society*, 14(2), 224–235.

Tucker, B. (2012). The flipped classroom. *Education Next*, 12(1), 82–83.

Tülübaş, T., Karakose, T., & Papadakis, S. (2023). A holistic investigation of the relationship between digital addiction and academic achievement among students. *European Journal of Investigation in Health, Psychology and Education*, 13(10), 2006–2034. 10.3390/ejihpe1310014337887144

Tuovinen, J. E. (2000). Multimedia distance education interactions. *Educational Media International*, 37(1), 16–24. 10.1080/095239800361473

Turnbull, D., Chugh, R., & Luck, J. (2021). Transitioning to E-Learning during the COVID-19 pandemic: How have Higher Education Institutions responded to the challenge? *Education and Information Technologies*, 26(5), 6401–6419. 10.1007/s10639-021-10633-w34177349

Turner III, D. W., & Hagstrom-Schmidt, N. (2022). Qualitative interview design. *Howdy or Hello? Technical and professional communication.* 10.46743/2160-3715/2010.1178

U.S. Census Bureau. (2020). *Household Pulse Survey*. U.S. Census Bureau.

U.S. Department of Education [USDOE]. (2017). *Reimagining the role of technology in education: 2017 National Educational Technology Plan update*. U.S. Department of Education, Office of Educational Technology.

UNESCO. (2020). *Education: From Disruption to Recovery*. UNESCO Institute for Statistics. https://en.unesco.org/covid19/educationresponse

UNICEF. (2022). *From Learning Recovery to Education Transformation: Insights and Reflections from the Fourth Survey on National Education Responses to COVID-19 School Closures*. UNICEF. https://hdl.handle.net/10986/38112

United States Department of Education. (2017). *Reimagining the role of technology in education: 2017 national education technology plan update.* Washington, DC: U.S. Department of Education. http://tech.ed.gov

Valencia, K., Rusu, C., Quiñones, D., & Jamet, E. (2019). The Impact of technology on people with autism spectrum disorder: A Systematic Literature Review. *Sensors (Basel),* 19(20), 4485. Advance online publication. 10.3390/s1920448531623200

Vallée, A., Blacher, J., Cariou, A., & Sorbets, E. (2020). Blended learning compared to traditional learning in medical education: Systematic review and meta-analysis. *Journal of Medical Internet Research*, 22(8), e16504. 10.2196/1650432773378

Valverde-Berrocoso, J., Garrido-Arroyo, M. C., Burgos-Videla, C., & Morales-Cevallos, M. B. (2020). Trends in educational research about e-learning: A systematic literature review (2009–2018). *Sustainability (Basel),* 12(12), 5153. 10.3390/su12125153

Van Alten, D. C., Phielix, C., Janssen, J., & Kester, L. (2019). Effects of flipping the classroom on learning outcomes and satisfaction: A meta-analysis. *Educational Research Review*, 28, 100281. 10.1016/j.edurev.2019.05.003

van de Werfhorst, H. G., Kessenich, E., & Geven, S. (2020). The digital divide in online education: Inequality in digital preparedness of students and schools before the start of the COVID-19 pandemic. *Computers and Education Open*, 3, 100100. 10.1016/j.caeo.2022.100100

Van Nuland, S. E., Schmidt, M. C., Engels, N., & van den Berg, J. (2020). Understanding teacher learning in the context of instructional coaching: A systematic review. *Teaching and Teacher Education*, 96, 103158.

Vasilijević, D., Bojović, Ž., Semiz, M., & Sudzilovski, D. (2023). Personal predictors of online teaching - Experiences of the teachers in Serbia in the COVID regime. *International Journal of Cognitive Research in Science. Engineering and Education*, 11(1), 63–75. 10.23947/2334-8496-2023-11-1-63-75

Vassileva, J. (2001). *"Distributed and United".* ICCE'2001, Seoul. https://julita.usask.ca/homepage/Agents.html

Vegas, E., Ziegler, L., & Zerbino, N. (2019). *How ed-tech can help leapfrog progress in education.* Center for Universal Education at The Brookings Institution. https://files.eric.ed.gov/fulltext/ED602936.pdf

Venkatesh, V. (2022). Adoption and use of AI tools: A research agenda grounded in UTAUT. *Annals of Operations Research*, 308(1-2), 1–12. 10.1007/s10479-020-03918-9

Venkatesh, V., Morris, M. G., Davis, G. B., & Davis, F. D. (2003). User acceptance of information technology: Toward a unified view. *Management Information Systems Quarterly*, 27(3), 425–478. 10.2307/30036540

Vermunt, J. D. (1998). The regulation of constructive learning processes. *The British Journal of Educational Psychology*, 68(2), 149–171. 10.1111/j.2044-8279.1998.tb01281.x

Vescio, V., Ross, D., & Adams, A. (2021). A review of research on the impact of professional learning communities on teaching practice and student learning. *Teaching and Teacher Education*, 107, 103423.

Vienlentia, R. (2021). Peran dukungan sosial keluarga terhadap regulasi emosi anak dalam belajar. *Satya Sastraharing: Jurnal Manajemen*, 5(2), 35–46. 10.33363/satya-sastraharing.v5i2.775

Vijayan, R. (2021). Teaching and learning during the COVID-19 pandemic: A topic modeling study. *Education Sciences*, 11(7), 1–15. 10.3390/educsci11070347

Villanueva, O., & Zimmermann, K. (2020). Transitioning an upper-level, integrated laboratory course to remote and online instruction during the COVID-19 pandemic. *Journal of Chemical Education*, 97(9), 3114–3120. 10.1021/acs.jchemed.0c00740

Vlachopoulos, D., & Makri, A. (2017). The effect of games and simulations on higher education: A systematic literature review. *International Journal of Educational Technology in Higher Education*, 14(1), 1–33. 10.1186/s41239-017-0062-1

Vlachopoulos, D., & Makri, A. (2019). Online communication and interaction in distance higher education: A framework study of good practice. *International Review of Education*, 65(4), 605–632. 10.1007/s11159-019-09792-3

Von Prummer, C. (1990). Study motivation of distance students: A report on some results from a survey done at the FernUniversitat in 1897/88. *In Research in Distance. Education*, 2(2), 2–6.

Vygotsky, L. S. (1978). *Mind in society: The development of higher psychological processes.* Harvard University Press.

Wai Yee, S. L., & Cheng Ean, C. L. (2020). Malaysian Private University Students' Perception of Online Discussion Forums: A Qualitative Enquiry. *Sains Humanika*, 12(2), 31–38. 10.11113/sh.v12n2.1610

Walters, A. U., Lawrence, W., & Jalsa, N. K. (2017). Chemical laboratory safety awareness, attitudes and practices of tertiary students. *Safety Science*, 96, 161–171. 10.1016/j.ssci.2017.03.017

Wang, J., Han, M., & Wang, W. (2020). Research on the evolution and classification of digital learning resources. *Proceedings of the International Conference on Education, Economics and Information Management.* Research Gate. 10.2991/assehr.k.200401.025

Wang, X., Wang, Z., Wang, Q., Chen, W., & Pi, Z. (2021). Supporting digitally enhanced learning through measurement in higher education: Development and validation of a university students' digital competence scale. *Journal of Computer Assisted Learning, 37*(4), 1063–1076. Wiley Online Library. 10.1111/jcal.12546

Wang, A. L. (2021). Models of student engagement in music education classroom in higher education. *Frontiers in Psychology*, 12, 668981. 10.3389/fpsyg.2021.73820734484089

Wang, S., Christensen, C., Cui, W., Tong, R., Yarnall, L., Shear, L., & Feng, M. (2023). When adaptive learning is effective learning: Comparison of an adaptive learning system to teacher-led instruction. *Interactive Learning Environments*, 31(2), 793–803. 10.1080/10494820.2020.1808794

Watson, J. B. (1913). Psychology as the behaviorist views it. *Psychological Review*, 20(2), 158–177. 10.1037/h0074428

Weerawardane, D. (2021). Digital transformation of Higher Education: What's next? *New Vistas.*, 7(2), 3–7. 10.36828/newvistas.147

West, S. S., Westerlund, J. F., Stephenson, A. L., Nelson, N. C., & Nyland, C. K. (2003). Safety in science classrooms: What research and best practice say. *The Educational Forum*, 67(2), 174–183. 10.1080/00131720308984555

Whalen, J. (2020). Should teachers be trained in emergency remote teaching? Lessons learned from the COVID-19 pandemic. *Journal of Technology and Teacher Education*, 28(2), 189–199.

Wheeler, S., & Lambert-Heggs, W. (2009). Connectıng distance learners and their mentors using blogs: The MentorBlog Project. *Quarterly Review of Distance Education*, 10(4), 323–331.

White, S., & Downey, J. (2021). International trends and patterns in innovation in rural education. *Rural education across the world: Models of innovative practice and impact*, 3-21. 10.1007/978-981-33-6116-4_1

Wiedmer, Terry L, & Kappan, Phi Delta. (1998). Digital portfolios: capturing and demonstrating skills and levels of performance. *Phi Delta Kappan, 4*, 01.

Williamson, B., Eynon, R., & Potter, J. (2020). Pandemic politics, pedagogies and practices: Digital technologies and distance education during the coronavirus emergency. *Learning, Media and Technology*, 45(2), 107–114. 10.1080/17439884.2020.1761641

Wilson, R. C. (1975). *College professors and their impact on students.*

Windhiyana, E. (2020). Dampak COVID-19 terhadap kegiatan pembelajaran online di sebuah perguruan tinggi kristen di Indonesia. *Perspektif Ilmu Pendidikan*, 34(1), 1–8. 10.21009/PIP.341.1

Win, N. L., & Wynn, S. D. (2015). Introducing blended learning practices in our classrooms. *Journal of Institutional Research South East Asia*, 13(2), 17–27. http://eprints.intimal.edu.my/id/eprint/154

Winnaiseh, L. (2017). *Hubungan regulasi emosi dengan emotional abuse pada remaja akhir yang berpacaran. Doctoral dissertation.* University of Muhammadiyah., http://eprints.umm.ac.id/43797/1/jiptummpp-gdl- leniwinnai- 49754-1-hubungan-n.pdf

Wisneski, J. E., Ozogul, G., & Bichelmeyer, B. A. (2017). Investigating the impact of learning environments on undergraduate students' academic performance in a prerequisite and post-requisite course sequence. *The Internet and Higher Education, 32*, 1–10. ScienceDirect. 10.1016/j.iheduc.2016.08.003

Workman, J. J., & Stenard, R. A. (1996). Student support services for distance learners. *DEOS-NEWS, 6*(3). http://learningdesign.psu.edu/deos/deosnews6_3.pdf

World Health Organization. (2023). *COVID-19 monthly update: April 2023* (No. WHO-EM/CSR/658/E). World Health Organization. Regional Office for the Eastern Mediterranean. 10.1136/bmj.p1246

Wright, P. (2008). *When a school refuses to protect a child with life-threatening allergies*. Print-Friendly. http://www. printfriendly.com/p/g/GYdHrx

Wu, T. T., Lee, H. Y., Wang, W. S., Lin, Ch. J., & Huang, Y. M. (2023). Leveraging computer vision for adaptive learning in STEM education: Effect of engagement and self-efficacy. *International Journal of Educational Technology in Higher Education*, 20(1), 53. 10.1186/s41239-023-00422-5

Wu, T., Fu, C., Gao, Y., & Zhang, P. (2021). Online Flipped Classroom Based on Task-Driven Teaching Practice: Take Introduction to Systems Engineering as an example. *2020 International Conference on Information Science and Education (ICISE-IE), IEEE Xplore*, (pp. 655–658). IEEE. 10.1109/ICISE51755.2020.00147

Xia, L. X., Gao, X., Wang, Q., & Hollon, S. D. (2014). The relations between interpersonal self-support traits and emotion regulation strategies: A longitudinal study. *Journal of Adolescence*, 37(6), 779–786. 10.1016/j.adolescence.2014.05.00725086455

Xia, L. X., Xu, X. Y., Hollon, S. D., & Zhang, J.-F. (2014). The relation of self-supporting personality, big five personality and depression. *Current Psychology (New Brunswick, N.J.)*, 33(4), 630–643. 10.1007/s12144-014-9233-6

Xiaoyu, Z., & Tobias, T. (2023). Exploring the Efficacy of Adaptive Learning Technologies in Online Education: A Longitudinal Analysis of Student Engagement and Performance. [IJSEA]. *International Journal of Software Engineering and Its Applications*, 12(12), 28–31. 10.7753/IJSEA1212.1007

Xue, S., & Crompton, H. (2024). Educational technology research during the COVID-19 pandemic. *Interactive Technology and Smart Education*, 21(1), 83–107. 10.1108/ITSE-05-2022-0067

Yakin, M., & Linden, K. (2021). Adaptive e-learning platforms can improve student performance and engagement in dental education. *Journal of Dental Education*, 85(7), 1309–1315. 10.1002/jdd.1260933825184

Yang, M., & Wen, F. (2023). AI-Powered Personalized Learning Journeys: Revolutionizing Information Management for College Students in Online Platforms. *Journal of Information Systems Engineering & Management*, 8(1), 23196. 10.55267/iadt.07.14079

Yang, Y., Liu, K., Li, M., & Li, S. (2021). Students' affective engagement, parental involvement, and teacher support in emergency remote teaching during the COVID 19 pandemic: Evidence from a cross-sectional survey in China. *Journal of Research on Technology in Education*, 54(sup1, S1), S148–S164. 10.1080/15391523.2021.1922104

Yang, Y., Reniers, G., Chen, G., & Goerlandt, F. (2019). A bibliometric review of laboratory safety in universities. *Safety Science*, 120, 14–24. 10.1016/j.ssci.2019.06.022

Yan, L., Whitelock-Wainwright, A., Guan, Q., Wen, G., Gašević, D., & Chen, G. (2021). Students' experience of online learning during the COVID-19 pandemic: A province-wide survey study. *British Journal of Educational Technology*, 52(5), 2038–2057. 10.1111/bjet.1310234219755

Yau, H. K., & Cheng, A. L. F. (2012). Gender differences of confidence in using technology for learning. *The Journal of Technology Studies*, 38(2), 74–79. https://scholar.lib.vt.edu/ejournals/JOTS/v38/v38n2/yau. 10.21061/jots.v38i2.a.2

Yazgan, Ç. Ü. (2022). Attitudes and interaction practices towards distance education during the pandemic. *Education and Information Technologies*, 27(4), 5349–5364. 10.1007/s10639-021-10843-235079227

Yılmaz, A. (2015). *Laboratuvarda güvenli çalışma* [*Laboratory safety*]. Hacettepe Üniversitesi Yayınları.

Yilmaz, K. (2021). The effectiveness of instructional coaching on teachers' professional development: A qualitative study. *Teaching and Teacher Education*, 100, 103346.

Yin, R. K. (2003). Designing case studies. *Qualitative research methods, 5*(14), 359-386.

Yoon, K. S., Duncan, T., Lee, S. W. Y., Scarloss, B., & Shapley, K. L. (2007). *Reviewing the Evidence on How Teacher Professional Development Affects Student Achievement. Issues & Answers Report, REL 2007-No. 033.* National Center for Education Evaluation and Regional Assistance.

Yuen, S. C., Yaoyuneyong, G., & Johnson, E. (2011). Augmented reality: An overview and five directions for AR in Education [JETDE]. *Journal of Educational Technology Development and Exchange*, 4(1). https://aquila.usm.edu/jetde/vol4/iss1/11. 10.18785/jetde.0401.10

Yükseltürk, E., & Top, E. (2013). Web 2.0 teknolojilerinin öğretmen eğitiminde kullanımı. *In K. Çağıltay ve Y. Göktaş (Eds.), Öğretim teknolojilerinin temelleri: Teoriler, araştırmalar, eğilimler*, 665-680. Pegem Akademi.

Zahara, M., Martina, M., & Alfandi, R. (2022). Hubungan Regulasi emosi dengan stres akademik pada mahasiswa Universitas Syiah Kuala. *Jurnal Ilmiah Mahasiswa Fakultas Keperawatan, 6*(1), 55-63.

Zainuddin, Z., & Attaran, M. (2016). Malaysian students' perceptions of flipped classroom: A case study. *Innovations in Education and Teaching International, 53*(6), 660–670. Taylor & Francis Online. 10.1080/14703297.2015.1102079

Zamani, B. B. E., & Madani, S. A. (2011). Guidelines for increasing the efficiency and effectiveness of teachers in virtual: Education. *Interdisciplinary Journal of Virtual Learning in Medical Sciences*, 2(3), 39–50.

Zamarro, G., Camp, A., Fuchsman, D., & McGee, J. B. (2022). *Understanding how COVID-19 has changed teachers' chances of remaining in the classroom.*

Zappe, S., Leicht, R., Messner, J., Litzinger, T., & Lee, H. W. (2009). *"Flipping" the classroom to explore active learning in a large undergraduate course.* Paper presented at the American Society for Engineering Education Annual Conference & Exhibition, Nashville. 10.18260/1-2--4545

Zawaidy, H. A. (2014). Using Blackboard in Online Learning at Saudi Universities: Faculty Member's Perceptions and Existing Obstacles. *International Interdisciplinary Journal of Education*, 3(7), 45–154. 10.12816/0006902

Zhai, X., Chu, X., Chai, C. S., Jong, M.S., Istenic, A., Spector, M., Liu, J., Yuan, J., & Li, Y. (2021). *A review of artificial intelligence (AI) in education from 2010 to 2020.* Wiley. .10.1155/2021/8812542

Zhai, J. (2023). The Application of Blended Teaching Model in College English Oral Courses in the Post Epidemic Era. *Journal of Theory and Practice of Contemporary Education*, 3(8), 44–50.

Zhang, L., Carter, R., Qian, X., Yang, S., Rujimora, J., & Wen, S.-L. (2022). Academia's responses to crisis: A bibliometric analysis of literature on online learning in higher education during COVID-19. *British Journal of Educational Technology, 53*(6), 1161 1177. 10.1111/bjet.13191

Zhang, L., Basham, J. D., & Yang, S. (2020). *Understanding the implementation of personalized learning: A research synthesis.* Educational Research Review. 10.1016/j.edurev.2020.100339

Zhao, G., & Yuan, S. (2010). Blended learning satisfaction: A study on Peking University students. In *Hybrid Learning* (Vol. 6248, pp. 282–295). LNCS. 10.1007/978-3-642-14657-2_26

Zhooriyati, S. M. (2021). Memahami tekanan perasaan dalam kalangan pelajar. Berita Harian. https://www.bharian.com.my/berita/pendidikan/2021/08/849398/memahami-tekanan-perasaan-dalam-kalangan-pelajar

Zhou, M. (2016). Chinese university students acceptance of MOOCs: A self-determination perspective. *Computers & Education*, 92-93, 194–203. 10.1016/j.compedu.2015.10.012

Zhu, B., Feng, M., Lowe, H., Kesselman, J., Harrison, L., & Dempski, R. E. (2018). Increasing enthusiasm and enhancing learning for biochemistry-laboratory safety with an augmented-reality program. *Journal of Chemical Education*, 95(10), 1747–1754. 10.1021/acs.jchemed.8b00116

Zhu, Q., & Wang, M. (2020). Team-based mobile learning supported by an intelligent system: Case study of STEM students. *Interactive Learning Environments*, 28(5), 543–559. 10.1080/10494820.2019.1696838

Zimet, G. D., Dahlem, N. W., Zimet, S. G., & Farley, G. K. (1988). The multidimensional scale of perceived social support. *Journal of Personality Assessment*, 52(1), 30–41. 10.1207/s15327752jpa5201_22280326

Zizic, M. C., Mladineo, M., Gjeldum, N., & Celent, L. (2022). From industry 4.0 towards industry 5.0: A review and analysis of paradigm shift for the people, organization and technology. *Energies*, 15(14), 5221. 10.3390/en15145221

# About the Contributors

***

**Blessing F. Adeoye's** current research interests focus primarily on the relationship between culture and technology, and the use of research to improve the quality of teaching and learning in schools. He has presented at numerous conferences. Dr. Adeoye has published over 40 peer-reviewed articles and 10 books related to Educational Technology. At Dilla University, he teaches the doctoral capstone and mentors Ph.D. candidates in Educational Technology and Research Methods. Dr. Adeoye has chaired numerous doctoral student dissertation committees.

**Jeehaan Algaraady** is an Assistant Professor at the English Department of Taiz University, Yemen. She received her PhD in Computational Linguistics. Her research interests include Computational Linguistics, Theoretical Linguistics, ELT and e-learning.

**Gökçe BECİT** graduated from Anadolu University, Faculty of Education, Department of Computer Education and Instructional Technology in 2005. Between 2005-2013, she worked as an Information Technologies Teacher in schools affiliated to the Ministry of National Education and worked as an Information Technologies Guidance Teacher within the scope of Fatih Project. In 2012, she completed her doctoral education at Anadolu University Institute of Educational Sciences, Department of Computer Education and Instructional Technology Education and started to work as a faculty member at Nevşehir Hacı Bektaş Veli University in 2013. The author conducts studies on the variables affecting pre-service teachers' intentions towards technology acceptance and use, pre-service teachers' technopedagogical competencies and unintended outcomes of technology; and teaches courses such as Information Technologies, Instructional Technologies, Open and Distance Learning, Web 2.0 Applications in Education.

**Vahid Biglari**, Ph.D. in financial reporting and accounting, has held academic positions at several institutions such as Shepherd University, University of Newcastle, and Henley Business School. He has also gained practical experience in the accounting and audit industries. Dr. Biglari has taught various accounting subjects to undergraduate and graduate students and has supervised numerous dissertations. His research interests include Big Data's impact on accounting and enhancing transparency in financial markets. Recognized for his dedication to education, Dr. Biglari holds the title of Associate Fellow of Higher Education Academy (AFHEA).

**Christine Boring** was born and raised in Pittsburgh, Pennsylvania. She earned her B.S. in Chemistry at Geneva College and her Master's in Teaching at the University of Pittsburgh. She began her career in public education, teaching high school Chemistry for 16 years. In 2016, she transitioned to technical training for the Naval Nuclear Laboratory. After completing her Ph.D. in Instructional Management and Leadership from Robert Morris University, Christine became the Head of Learning and Development for the United States and Canada region at PPG Industries. Her research interests include microlearning, corporate training, accessibility, and DE&I.

## *About the Contributors*

**Caroline Chemosit** is an adjunct professor of mathematics education at the Illinois State University, Mathematics Department. She is also a middle/junior high school mathematics educator. Her research and scholarship interests include mathematics education, skills that enhance learning, lifelong learning, learning strategies, and student achievement. She has published and co-authored several articles both in refereed journals such as the Journal of Personnel Evaluation in Education, and Educational Research Quarterly, book, book chapters and in other professional sources and presented papers at various annual meetings of local (Kabarak & Egerton International Educational Conferences), regional (SERA, MSERA, MWERA, IERC) and national/international professional organizations (AERA, UCEA, WERA, Pacific-RIM, NAAAS).

**Ozan Coşkunserçe** graduated from Middle East Technical University, Department of Computer Education and Instructional Technology in 2004. He received his PhD degree from Anadolu University, Department of Computer Education and Instructional Technology in 2015. Between 2004-2016, he worked as an Information Technologies Teacher in schools affiliated to the Ministry of National Education. In 2016, he started to work at Nevşehir Hacı Bektaş Veli University, Faculty of Education, Department of Computer Education and Instructional Technology and he is still working as a faculty member in this department. His research interests include blended learning, social networks, usability in interactive environment designs, technology-culture interaction and integration, block-based and robot programming. He has been teaching Open and Distance Learning course for undergraduate students for four years.

| **Steven D'Agustino** holds a doctorate from Fordham University's Graduate School of Education and is the Senior Director for Online Programs in the Office of the Provost where his responsibilities include supporting the development of distance learning programs across Fordham University. He has published research in the area of instructional enhancement through the integration of technology and has been awarded a number of grants while at Fordham, the largest of which was a 2.5 million dollar grant to provide access to technology through online learning. Dr. D'Agustino is the editor of two books: Adaptation, Resistance and Access to Instructional Technologies and Immersive Environments, Augmented Realities, and Virtual Worlds: Assessing Future Trends in Education published in 2010 and 2012, respectively. His most recent publications, both in 2013, include "Toward a course conversion model for distance learning: a review of best practices" in Frontiers of Distance Learning in Business Education and "Providing innovative opportunities and options through online credit recovery and afterschool programs" in Expanding Minds and Opportunities.

**G Prasad** is currently working as faculty in the department of Aerospace Engineering Chandigarh University, India. He has 9 years of experience in Teaching and research. He received his Bachelor of Engineering and Master of Engineering degrees with first class and distinction and Doctor of Philosophy in the field of Aeronautical Engineering from the Anna University, Chennai, India. Prof. Prasad G is the author of over 30 technical publications, 1 Patent Published and 1 Book published. His research interests include Unmanned Aerial Vehicles, Aircraft Structures, Computational Fluid Dynamics and Interdisciplinary research. He has completed three funded project sponsored by The Institution of Engineers (India) and Tamilnadu State Council for Science and Technology. Awarded Indian National Science Academy (INSA) Visiting Scientist Programme 2019 and Awarded Science Academies' Summer Research Fellowship Programme (SRPF) 2019. Further he is SPOC of NPTEL- IIT Madras, SPOC of ISRO IIRS outreach coordinator and SPOC for NASA International SpaceApps Challenge. Further key positions such as coordinator of Board of Studies, Outcome Based Education, Project Coordinator, Research Coordinator NBA, NAAC, ABET. He is a Professional Membership of American Institute of Aeronautics and Astronautics, Institution of Engineers, Life Member in Indian Cryogenic Council and Life Member in Shock Wave Society. Reviewer in Aircraft Engineering and Aerospace Technology, International Journal of Engine Research and Journal of Institution of Engineers (India): Series C.

**Rasidat Sade Ganiyu**, a dedicated educator with a B.Ed., M.Ed., and a PhD in Educational Technology, serves as a Lecturer I at Emmanuel Alayande University of Education in Oyo, Nigeria. Specializing in Science and Technology Education, she is a prolific scholar and researcher contributing valuable insights to scholarly journals and book chapters. Driven by a passion for advancing education, she plays a crucial role in shaping the discourse and practices within her field.

**Omer Elsheikh Hago Elmahdi** is a professor of linguistics at the Open University of Sudan and works at Taibah University's Department of Languages & Translation. He is an experienced researcher and team leader in various fields and has authored many papers and books. He also serves as a chef editor and reviewer for many journals. Contact: ohago65@gmail.com, +249 912378698/ +966533584681

**Habibie Ibrahim** received the Bac.Sc. degree in Human Development from the University Putra, Malaysia in 1998, and the MA in Social Work and Social Care and Ph.D. degrees from the University of Bradford, England. Since May 2014, she has been with the Faculty of Psychology & Education, UMS, where she was a Head Program for Social Work Program, 2014 -2018, became a senior lecturer in 2008. Her current research interests include emotion, emotional intelligence, religiosity and child and family social work practice.

**Nagihan Kadıoğlu** received her master's degree in Chemistry Education from Hacettepe University in 2021. She is currently a research assistant at Hacettepe University, Department of Chemistry Education. Nagihan Kadıoğlu has focused on the reflections of today's contemporary education understanding and educational technologies on learning environments since the year she started her doctoral studies and included the flipped learning model, which is becoming increasingly known today, in her research topics. At the same time, Augmented reality, which is one of the new technologies that are becoming increasingly popular and being used in the field of education, and its use in chemistry education is one of her research interests.

**Philip Kaloki** is a Business Administration Professor, trade negotiation expert, highly skilled in the implementation of transformative community projects and programs, an expert in resource mobilization, development/partner relations, a professional with experience in corporate governance, leadership, training, research, and market linkages. Demonstratable knowledge and experience in regional economic and integration development. He has a PhD in Business Administration from University of Nairobi, Kenya, an MBA in Business Administration from Dallas Baptist University, Dallas, Texas and a BBA in Finance/ Economics and Management from University of Mary Hardin-Baylor, Belton, Texas. Has been a Professor of Business Administration for eighteen years where he was awarded an Out Standing Professor of the Year. Dr. Kaloki was appointed by the President of Kenya, to serve as Chairperson, Board of Directors, Kenya Medical Training College for eight years. KMTC is the largest middle – level medical college in Kenya with over 50,000 students and 71 campuses spread across the country. Currently, Dr. Kaloki serves as an Professor of Business at Tarrant County College, Hurst, Texas where he teaches Business Leadership Application, Business Ethics, Marketing and Management courses.

**Chen Kang Lee** is currently an Assistant Professor in the Department of Internet Engineering and Computer Science, Lee Kong Chian Faculty of Engineering and Science, Universiti Tunku Abdul Rahman, Malaysia. He received his BIT.(Hons) degree in Information Technology from the University of Tenaga Nasional, Malaysia in 2004 and Masters in Knowledge Management with Multimedia from Multimedia University in 2007. He completed his Ph.D. in Computing from University of Tenaga Nasional, Malaysia in 2018. His research interests include Human Computer Interactions, User Experience, Educational Technology, Knowledge Management, Multimedia in Education.

**Min Chi Low** is currently a postgraduate student, pursuing Master of Science (Computer Science) in Faculty of Information and Communication Technology, Universiti Tunku Abdul Rahman, Malaysia. She received her Bachelor of Information Technology with Honours from the National University of Malaysia in 2020. Her research interests include Educational Technology and Human Computer Interaction.

**Mohammad Mahyoob** is an Associate Professor of Computational linguistics at the Department of Languages & Translation, College of Arts and Humanities, Taibah University, Madina, Saudi Arabia. He is also an Associate Professor of Computational linguistics at Technical Community College -Taiz, Yemen. He holds his PhD in Computational Linguistics. His research interests include Computational linguistics, Language Disorders, Theoretical and Applied Linguistics, and e-learning.

### *About the Contributors*

**Semiu Olawale Makinde** is a distinguished academic with a Ph.D. in Educational Technology, an MBA in Marketing, and a B.Eng. in Agricultural Engineering. A Senior Lecturer, Science Education Department and Director, Institute of Education, Al-Hikmah University. Dr. Makinde is a dedicated researcher, contributing to reputable journals and book chapters. His multidisciplinary expertise, commitment to education, and innovative contributions to both science education and agricultural mechanization showcase his impact in academia at Al-Hikmah University, Ilorin, Nigeria.

**Nurul Hudani Md Nawi** is a senior lecturer at the Faculty of Psychology and Education at Universiti Malaysia Sabah since 2001. She holds a degree in Humanities (Psychology) at International Islamic University Malaysia (IIUM) and master in Industrial and Organization from Universiti Kebangsaan Malaysia (UKM) in 2001. Then she obtained her PhD in Social Psychology from Universiti Putra Malaysia (UPM). Her current research interests include personality, emotional intelligence, leadership, religiosity and industrial organization psychology.

**Norazah Mohd Suki** is a Professor of Marketing and E-Commerce at Othman Yeop Abdullah Graduate School of Business (OYAGSB), Universiti Utara Malaysia. She has been recognised in the list of the World's Top 2% Scientists by Stanford University since 2019 and has also earned recognition in the 'Career-long World's Top 2% Scientists' list. She is the recipient of the UUM Best Publication Award (Highly Cited Author) 2021, Malaysia's Research Star Award (MRSA) 2018, Highly Commended Paper in Emerald Literati Network Awards for Excellence in 2015 and 2017, and Winners of the IGI Global Seventh Annual Awards Excellence in Research Journal, etc. Her research interests include consumer behaviour, M-commerce, E-commerce, E-marketing, green marketing, Islamic marketing, and areas related to marketing. She has published more than 300 papers in referred journals, book chapters, books, and conference papers detailing her research activities, on top of coordinating and participating in several research projects. She is also the editor of several SCOPUS-indexed books. She has wide-ranging experience as an invited speaker. She can be contacted at azahsuki@yahoo.com.

**Adesoji Oni** a Fulbright scholar is a Senior Lecturer in the Department of Educational Foundations, Faculty of Education, University of Lagos, Nigeria. He specializes in Sociology of Education. His area of research focus includes; Higher Education social problems in education, Social change in education, Teacher Education, social deviances in education with particular focus on students' secret cult in Nigeria. He has published widely in these areas. He has a lot of publication to his credit, which includes; chapters in books; articles that have already appeared in national and international learned journals, His international academic papers appeared in reputable journals based inUSA, India, and South Africa to Uganda, Ghana, Malaysia, UNESCO (France), Japan, Botswana, Switzerland, Cote d'Ivoire, the Philippines, Bulgaria, Turkey, the Netherlands, Senegal, South Korea, Poland, Spain, Tanzania, Canada, Italy, Zambia, Nepal, Kosovo, Kuwait, the United Arab Emirates, Albania and beyond etc, He is serving in the editorial board of so many academic journal globally. Rooney international visiting scholar to Robert Morris University, Moon Township, Fall 2018.

**Özge Özyalçın Oskay** was graduated from Hacettepe University Faculty of Educationin 2001. She received her Msc.Degree in science education from the Hacettepe University in 2003, Ankara, Turkey. Then she received Ph.D degree at Hacettepe University, Faculty of Education, Department of Department of Mathematics and Science Education in 2007. She was appointed as Assistant Professor in Hacettepe University, Faculty of Education, Department of Chemistry Education in 2010. She received her Associate Professor title in 2013. She has been working at the same department as a Professor since 2018. Her main research interests are teaching and learning methods, educational technologies, flipped learning, technological pedagogical content knowledge.

**Harsh Vardhan Pant** is an Assistant Professor at COER University, Roorkee, India and doing PhD. in Computer Science from Graphics Era Hill University, Dehradun.

**Joki Perdani Sawai** is a Senior Lecturer for the Youth and Community Development Program, Faculty of Psychology and Education, Universiti Malaysia Sabah (UMS). She holds a Bachelor of Human Science (Psychology) from the International Islamic University Malaysia (IIUM). She then continued her studies at Master's level and obtained a Master of Arts (Industrial and Organizational Psychology) from Universiti Kebangsaan Malaysia (UKM). She is actively involved in writing journal articles and books in the field of psychology.

**Zahra Pourabedin** is an accomplished Assistant Professor of Business at Shepherd University. She holds a Ph.D. in Marketing from UTM University, and her expertise encompasses digital marketing, social media marketing, and consumer behavior. Dr. Pourabedin's research focuses on the influence of digital and social media on consumer decision-making and brand engagement.

**John Rugutt** is a professor of educational research, applied statistics, measurement, assessment, evaluation and educational technology in the Department of Educational Administration and Foundations at Illinois State University. His research and scholarship focus on teaching and learning environments with special emphasis on using multilevel techniques to understand the contribution of individual and institutional factors on learning. John engagement in scholarly activities has enabled him to publish and co-author book, book chapters, and several articles both in refereed journals such as the Journal of Personnel Evaluation in Education, Planning and Changing, Educational Research Quarterly, Journal of Educational Research and Policy Studies and in other professional sources. He has also presented papers at various annual meetings of regional and national/ professional organizations and has also written research monographs, research grants, book chapters and project reports pertaining to student dropout and youth risk behavior, and on correlates and predictors of Intent to Remain Employed in Family and Children Services.

**Brian Shambare** particular expertise in the 'real-life' constraints and problems faced when technology-based education is implemented. Currently working on a research project examining the complex practices of:TPACK Development,

**Manjit Singh Sidhu** is currently a Professor in the Department of Computing and Informatics, College of Information Technology, Universiti Tenaga Nasional, Malaysia. He received his BSc.(Hons) degree in Computer Science from the University of Wolverhampton 1997 and Masters in Information Technology from Universiti Putra Malaysia in 2000. He completed his Ph.D. in Multimedia Technology from Universiti Malaya, Malaysia in 2006. He is a Fellow, Chartered IT Professional (BCS UK), Fellow, Malaysian Scientific Association, Senior IEEE member and Professional Technologist with the Malaysian Board of Technologies (MBOT). His research interests include Human Computer Interaction, User Experience, Multimedia, Mixed Reality and Metaverse.

**Teresa Torres-Coronas** has a PhD in Business Administration and the recipient of the first prize in the 2000 EADA Management Research Awards. Her research focuses on the application of ICT and on the labour insertion of people with intellectual disabilities. Her notable contributions to educational innovation are evident in her leadership of a project at the Universitat Rovira i Virgili, which garnered the 2016 Jaume Vicens Vives Award from the Autonomous Government of Catalonia. This award recognized the project's innovative analysis, design, and learning processes, utilizing technology as a developmental tool for fostering transversal and professional competencies.Her commitment to inclusivity and skill development was further acknowledged in 2020 when she received the Jaume Vicens Vives Award for her project INSERLAB. This initiative is dedicated to assisting students with intellectual disabilities in acquiring the necessary skills to successfully integrate into the labor market.

**Tuan Norbalkish Tuan Abdullah** is a senior lecturer at the Faculty of Psychology and Education (FPP), University Malaysia Sabah. She earned her bachelor's and master's degrees in counseling, and later completed her Ph.D. in Counseling at Universiti Malaysia Terengganu (UMT). She is a certified and registered counselor recognized by the Malaysian Board of Counselors. Her expertise and commitment to the field are evident through her substantial contributions, particularly in the realm of HIV counseling research, where she conducted comprehensive studies during both her master's and Ph.D. programs.

## *About the Contributors*

**Ayhan Yılmaz** was graduated from Hacettepe University Faculty of Education. She received her Msc.Degree in science education from the Hacettepe University in 1990, Ankara, Turkey. Then she she received Ph.D degree at Ankara University, Faculty of Science, Department of Inorganic Chemistry in 1992. She was appointed as Assistant Professor in Hacettepe University, Faculty of Education, Department of Chemistry Education in 1989. She received her Associate Professor title in 2000. She has been working at the same department as a Professor since 2006. In addition, she has served as Vice Dean of Faculty of Education between 2006 and 2012 and as a Dean between 2016 and 2021. Her main research interests are students' conceptions of science, misconceptions in chemistry and science education, environmental education, active learning methods.

# Index

## A



## B



## C

## D



## E

# F



# G



# H



# I



# K



# L

# M



# O

# P

## U



## V

www.ingramcontent.com/pod-product-compliance
Lightning Source LLC
LaVergne TN
LVHW080353011026
849161LV00009B/2285
* 9 7 9 8 3 6 9 3 7 6 4 5 4 *